D1592080

The Filming of the West

The Filming of the West

JON TUSKA

Doubleday & Company, Inc.
Garden City, New York
1976

Portions of this book originally appeared in Views & Reviews *magazine: Cinematographs 11, 31, 36 copyright © 1970 by Views & Reviews, Inc.; 21 copyright © 1971 by Views & Reviews, Inc.; 2, 3, 7, 16, 17, 37, 40, 46, 53 copyright © 1974 by Views & Reviews, Inc.; 13, 42, 48, 55 copyright © 1975 by Views & Reviews, Inc.*

Library of Congress Cataloging in Publication Data
Tuska, Jon
The filming of the West
Includes index.
1. Western films—History and criticism.
I. Title.
PN1995.9.W4T8   791.43'0909'32
ISBN 0-385-03115-7
Library of Congress Catalog Card Number 75–12830

Book design by Beverley Gallegos

IN MEMORIAM

TOM MIX
(1880–1940)

Acknowledgments

In addition to the many persons cited below, there are several people who deserve special credit for having helped me in the actual preparation of this book. Without this devotion, it would not have been possible to finish it on time. The first of these is Rosemary Ingham, who typed the manuscript, assisted in the selection of the photo illustrations, and helped ameliorate the stresses around me; my secretaries, Linda Barton and Vicki Piekarski, who booked film prints and proofread the manuscript respectively; my wife, Ruth Tuska, who joined me on many of the escapades recounted in the book and who watched most of the films with me; Karl Thiede, who assisted me in the research having to do with motion picture history. I might add that my publisher, Doubleday & Company, deserves my gratitude for having had profound faith in this project, and specifically my editors, Harold Kuebler and James Menick.

Among film companies, I am indebted to Allied Artists Television, Columbia Pictures-Screen Gems, Metro-Goldwyn-Mayer, National Telefilm Associates, Paramount Pictures, RKO General, United Artists Television, MCA-Universal, and Warner Brothers.

Those in the industry and outside of it who have been of assistance to me include:

Joe Abruscato	Cecil B. De Mille
Roy Aitken	George de Normand
Arthur Alexander	Norman Deming
Gene Autry	John English
Trevor Bardette	Dale Evans
Spencer Gordon Bennet	Allen Eyles
Dan Bishop	Bart Farber
Bill F. Blair	Edward Finney
De Witt Bodeen	Nick Fiorentino
Peter Bogdanovich	James Flavin
Walter Brennan	Lucile Browne Flavin
Harry Joe Brown	Henry Fonda
Johnny Mack Brown	Jane Fonda
Olive Carey	John Ford
Texas Jim Cooper	Audrey Foster

Ruth Hall Garmes
Lorraine Gauguin
Maurice Geraghty
Gene F. Giaquinto
Dorothy Gibson
Hoot Gibson
Bill Golden
Ernie Goodman
Jack Gordon
Allen Green
Art Greenfield
Romer Grey
Ken Harris
Henry Hathaway
Howard Hawks
Russell Hayden
George "Gabby" Hayes
Tim Holt
H. Bruce Humberstone
H. Blackmer Johnson
Dell Jones
Tex Jordan
Joe Kane
Harold Kinkade, Jr.
Ernie Kirkpatrick
Miles Kreuger
Jean Larson
D. Ross Lederman
Douglas Lemza
June Gale Levant
Nat Levine
Col. Tim McCoy
Joel McCrea
Bob Malcomson
Frances Marion
Ken Maynard
Kermit Maynard
Ira Michaels

Leonard Maltin
Kemp R. Niver
George O'Brien
David L. Parker
C. M. Parkhurst
Sam Peckinpah
Nancy Ince Probert
Bill G. Rainey
Duncan Renaldo
Tex Ritter
Julian Rivero
Peter S. Rodgers
Sidney Rogell
Roy Rogers
Harry Sanford
Lesley Selander
Lynn Sherman
Teddi Sherman
Glenn Shipley
Robert F. Slatzer
Keith Smith
Barbara Stanwyck
Stanley Stark
Peggy Stewart
Howard Strickling
Ray Swank
King Vidor
William F. Wantz
John Wayne
Michael Wayne
Irving Weiner
Sid Weiner
John Whitesell
William Whitney
Lois Wilson
Jane Wyatt
Adolph Zukor

Among the institutions that have been of assistance to me are the American Film Institute, the Library of Congress, the Motion Picture Academy, the Museum of Modern Art, and the Tex Ritter Memorial Fan Club.

I also wish to express my indebtedness to the following books and authors which have been of immense value to me: *The Autobiography of Cecil B. De Mille* (Prentice-Hall, 1959); *Max Brand: The Big Westerner,* by Robert Easton (University of Oklahoma Press, 1970); *Continued Next Week,* by Kalton C. Lahue (University of Oklahoma Press, 1964); *Directors in Action,* edited by Bob Thomas (Bobbs-Merrill, 1973); *Zane Grey,* by Frank Gruber (World, 1970); *Heroes, Heavies and Sagebrush,* by Arthur F. McClure and Ken D. Jones (Barnes, 1972); *I Blow My Own Horn,* by Jesse L. Lasky (Doubleday, 1957); *La Grande Aventure du Western,* by Jean-Louis Rieupeyrout (Éditions du Cerf, 1971); *The Life and Legend of Tom Mix,* by Paul E. Mix (Barnes, 1972); *The Fabulous Tom Mix,* by Olive Stokes (Prentice-Hall, 1957); *Memo from David O. Selznick,* by Rudy Behlmer (Viking, 1972); *Selznick,* by Bob Thomas (Doubleday, 1970); *Shooting Star,* by Maurice Zolotow (Simon & Schuster, 1974).

Lastly, for his many kindnesses during my long visits in Los Angeles, I want to thank Max Lamb.

J.T.

Contents

The Glittering Twenties

A Time of Darkness and Light

Interlude: The Decline and Fall of the B Western

The Postwar Years

Perpetuation of a Tradition

Contemporary Trends in the Modern Western

Introduction

I have been at work on this book for nearly a decade. In many instances I have had firsthand acquaintance with the principals. I mention this because I wish to tell the truth about my subject as best I can. There are errors in this book—I am sure of that—although I have published much of this material in different form beforehand, permitting corrections to be made or having it perused by those who participated in the making of the films. Many statements or assertions I made on television were modified or altered by the thousands of letters I received from knowledgeable viewers. Much of the accuracy of my enterprise has been the product of correspondence or conversations with participants in these events who wanted me to set the record straight and expect me to finally tell the stories as they actually happened. Perhaps I need not remind the reader of how arduous a task it is to narrate the history of an industry whose primary impetus for existing and whose principal function is the perpetuation of fantasy. Then, too, we are dealing with make-believe heroes and villains, whose roles are sometimes reversed in real life. There are those who would rather not know cinema history this way; they would prefer the comforting illusions which are fostered by publicity departments. But my experience has informed me that among the present generation, they are in the minority. Nostalgia, I feel, is ruinous to film criticism. It has absolutely no place in film history.

When I first published a career study of Ken Maynard some years ago, he had been of assistance to me and I sent him the installments as they appeared in magazine form. Ken and I had become rather close, but when I met him again in February 1970, at the General Service Studio on Las Palmas Avenue in Los Angeles for a screening of his final motion picture appearance in *Bigfoot* (American-Gemini, 1971), he fastened upon me with blazing eyes.

"Drinking!" he rasped. "Drinking, drinking, drinking! That's all you write about. Why do you have to write about that?"

Still, our friendship was not really imperiled. We continued to see one another until he died. The last time I visited him he was a patient at the Motion Picture Home and was not expected to live much longer. I was accompanied by Spencer Gordon Bennet, the director who had frequently worked with Maynard at Columbia, and Max Lamb and Harry Sanford, both Hollywood screenwriters who had long helped me on this book. Ken was emaciated. He had thrown the covers up over his head to close out the world. The cruel and tragic mistreatment to which he had been subjected in his last years I cannot bring myself to retell in this book. Ken looked around at us and then addressed the others, pointing at me.

"He knows my pictures better than I do." His voice was weakened by his terminal illness, but he raised it with an effort. "And he's fair. He tells the truth, but he's fair."

I asked him which of his pictures he would like to see again. For years I had tried to get him to look at one, but he'd refused.

"The Strawberry Roan," he said. "I would like to see *The Strawberry Roan.*"

So it was arranged. The screening took place in the rehabilitation center. There was a sizable audience. Ken was particularly happy that so many of the young nurse's aides were caught up in the film. But one of them had to leave the room in tears. She had to confess that seeing Ken on the screen, so robust, so handsome, and to see him as he looked forty years later was a distressing experience. It is for this reason that I have restrained myself from reproducing any photographs of players from periods long after their prime in public life. Ken didn't sympathize. He perceived my shyness before his physical decay and dismissed it. When I was taking my leave, hurrying down the hallway, he called me back. His voice had the tone of authority in it.

I regarded him searchingly as he did not speak at once. He looked at me with soft eyes, lonely, as he was then, but unafraid.

"Good-by," he said.

He gave me his hand to shake.

Three weeks later, three thousand miles away from him, listening to the dying cello at the conclusion of Strauss's *Don Quixote,* the news was brought to me that Ken Maynard was dead.

I may be faulted by some critics for not making this book more of a survey. A survey of the Western is no longer possible for me. I have seen eight thousand Westerns. I would not recommend that anyone else do it. There has been no appreciable change in my personality or temperament as a consequence. My moral convictions—or utter lack of them—remain unassailed. But you cannot undergo an experience of this kind and not come away with some impressions.

I do not think it is possible to generalize about Westerns as so many have done. I have screened more series Westerns than any other person alive. But I only talk about those that I feel were somehow exceptional or of unusual or possibly comic interest.

The method of operation which I have chosen to pursue in writing this book has been to concentrate on one hundred Western motion pictures from *The Great Train Robbery* (Edison, 1903) to *The Cowboys* (Warner's,

1972). I concentrate on how they were made, who made them, who appeared in them, the lives and times of the people involved in the respective films. This provides my account with a fluidity of time which, ideally, only the motion picture itself has been able to achieve. Originally, it had also been my intention to include complete casts and technical credits for these films, but in practice this proved far too space-consuming and, ultimately, of very limited interest. But by means of emphasizing the plot synopsis and talking generally about the principal personnel which worked on these hundred Westerns, it will become evident that the Western has altered very little, really, and that where it has altered most isn't in what is told so much as in *how* it is told and from what perspective.

Moreover, I am pleased to relate that, with a minimum of inconvenience, it is possible for the reader to see ninety-five of the one hundred titles I have emphasized as representative of their time, their stars, their studios, or of the predominant ideas guiding Western production; as financially successful, exceeding their cost; and in many instances as either confirming a trend or initiating a new one. I have, therefore, included the titles of these films on the contents page and devoted a separate section to providing rental contact information so that at least these particular Westerns can be screened by the reader should he be so inclined.

Perhaps I might remind the reader that when I began this book, not one vintage Western from the years 1903–36 was accessible to contemporary audiences. I am pleased to say that my television work, *Views & Reviews* magazine, this book, and other writing I have done have been influential in changing this state of affairs. And I wish to state unequivocally that this book would never have been possible without the unusual and unprecedented co-operation I have been afforded by the American motion picture industry. Not only has this made research and screenings possible, in some cases the intensive and protracted study of materials, but I have been able to screen myriad Westerns virtually unavailable since the time of their original theatrical release.

Of the thousands of Westerns I have seen, there are a handful I have personally enjoyed to the extent that I have watched them several times. I have liked especially *The Vanishing American* (Paramount, 1925), *Rider of Death Valley* (Universal, 1932), *The Last Outlaw* (RKO, 1936), and *Stagecoach* (United Artists, 1939) from the pre-1945 group; *Cheyenne Autumn* (Warner's, 1964), *The Ballad of Cable Hogue* (Warner's, 1970), and *Pat Garrett and Billy the Kid* (M-G-M, 1973) from the postwar group. The reader may not be able to detect these preferences from what I say about these pictures in the context of this book. It has not been my intention to substitute my opinions for what I have come to believe are the facts. And while the reader may be shocked at the candor that I occasionally show when recounting the life of a player or a director, there are countless untold stories and even a measure of personal torment encountered in the writing of this book that I have deliberately withheld because it could in no wise further my objectives or serve my encompassing design.

One thing I wish to stress. In a very real sense the winning of the West on the screen has been accomplished by some three hundred principals. This is a surprisingly small number. But indigenous to the Western has been the concept of the stock repertory company. It is a familiar terrain we meet in the Western, whether it be the budget films of a bygone era or the super-Westerns which have proliferated since World War II. Beyond this, my narrative, by necessity, has been one of parallel action so that trends in Western production, the rise and fall of a career, are seen against a panorama of simultaneous events.

The truth of film is emotional truth. When you get right down to it, successful pictures, like successful stories, are about individual people. Whatever the location, or the historical setting, or the great events used as a backdrop—and these may be vital to the film as a composite—it's the people in it that matter and the action that centers around them. The traditional Western has reinforced American individualism.

For me the history of the Western motion picture is very much a chronicle of the lives, passions, struggles, and beliefs of the men who made the films. Therefore, this is what I have stressed. They have had an enduring, unshakable love affair with the land and the spirit of the men who pioneered it. I cannot tell you how long the Western will remain popular. I can only say that, today, as I write these words the United States of America is an urban culture enraptured by an agrarian dream of the past, precious to us perhaps because of the hope it once held out.

It is a strange and inexplicable thing that we so often continue to hope when we have no faith left.

HONORÉ DE BALZAC

. . . For history must be past, and yea, the greater its pastness, so one might say, the better for it in terms of its quality as history and for the storyteller, that whispering conjuror of the imperfect.

THOMAS MANN

The Early Years

1 / IN THE BEGINNING

Edwin Stanton Porter, who was born in 1870 at Connellsville, Pennsylvania, happened almost by mistake to enter the foundling motion picture industry. He had disliked school and had worked at numerous odd jobs, from plumbing to house painting. After a stint in the Navy, he became a projectionist, operating the Edison Vitascope for the firm of Raff & Gammon. In the late 1890s, following some experimental efforts on his part to perfect a new projector, Porter became a professional photographer, specializing in news footage and scenic films which he sold to vaudeville houses. The Edison Company was one of his best customers. It was here, at the turn of the century, that he became a full-time employee. His first activities were centered around the development of a lightweight camera, but these gave way at the suggestion of James H. White, production head of the Edison Studio, to the job of cameraman-director, making commercial films.

There has been some controversy about what Porter's contributions to the cinema were, particularly in terms of his direction. But it is safe to credit him with being the first to devise the "story film." He introduced social consciousness into cinema narrative. Among his technical achievements, which outweigh all others, he invented film editing to heighten suspense, he was the first American to use visual effects, he was the first to direct feature films in the United States, and he was one of the first to use creative trick photography.

Porter has written of his early years. "At just about this time," meaning the beginning of the new century, "when 40 or 50 foot lengths were the vogue, I often wondered why it was not possible to produce a dramatic story in motion pictures. . . . I was chief producer of the Edison Company and it seemed peculiarly proper to me for the Edison Company to inaugurate this innovation. Accordingly, I conceived and prepared a story called The Life of an American Fireman, a complete 800 foot story based on a fairly good dramatic element and introducing the fireman's life in the engine house and in his home. The subject became intensely popular and continued to run for a longer time consecutively than any film production previously. Encouraged by the success of this experiment, we devoted all our resources to the production of *stories,* instead of disconnected and unrelated scenes."

Edwin S. Porter.

Photo courtesy of the Museum of Modern Art.

In 1902, the year Porter completed *The Life of an American Fireman,* Gilbert M. Anderson applied at the Edison Studio on Twenty-third Street in Manhattan, having heard that they were looking for models to "pose" before the camera. Anderson was born Max Aronson on March 21, 1882, at Little Rock, Arkansas. He began his adult career as a traveling salesman. Moving about brought him into contact with theatrical people. Enlisting his sister, Leona, the two migrated to New York. Conscious of his Jewish name, he changed it to G. M. Anderson. But work for an inexperienced player was difficult to find. Anderson was reduced to fashion modeling, appearing in a Howard Chandler Christy illustration for *The Saturday Evening Post.* Porter hired him for fifty cents an hour.

Anderson's first complete part was in a short subject entitled *The Messenger Boy's Mistake.* It told succinctly the story of a young beau who quarreled with his sweetheart. In an attempt to make it up to her, he sends flowers and a card. "If you forgive me," the message on the card read, "wear these the next time I call." By error, the messenger delivers a pair of pajamas instead of the bouquet. When Anderson arrives at her house, her brothers meet him and give him a thorough drubbing.

The Great Train Robbery, which in retrospect remains Porter's most memorable film, was inspired by a commercial venture financed by the Delaware, Lackawanna and Western Railroad, titled *A Romance of the Rails.* Porter shot the film in September 1903. Its purpose was to demonstrate to the public that the railroad sponsored immaculate cars and a cinderless right of way. Porter, caught up in the setting, commenced immediately on a new story film built around the subject of a train robbery, always a popular item. The newspapers had made a folk hero of Jesse James. Many could recall with fondness the accounts of his looting, provided they hadn't incurred any personal financial loss.

On hearing that the project was under way, Anderson approached Porter and volunteered his services. Porter demurred, pointing out that the film was set in the West and therefore horsemanship would be required. Anderson never stopped selling as long as he was in the picture business, until his heart had been broken by it and retirement forced upon him. He confided that he could ride any horse as well as a Texas Ranger, that indeed he had been born in a saddle out in Missouri and Porter wouldn't be sorry. It was still two years in the future before Anderson sojourned at a Texas dude ranch and learned how to ride. The initial day of shooting found him falling off his horse at the stable in West Orange, New Jersey, near the Delaware and Lackawanna track outside Dover, where the exteriors were being photographed. He didn't participate in the action until the second day. This time he managed to fall off his horse for the camera during the posse's final cleanup of the gang. Anderson shouldn't be ridiculed in this regard. Many Western players have begun film careers as cowboys without knowing how to ride, although none perhaps equaling Anderson until William Boyd embarked on *Hop-A-Long Cassidy* (Paramount, 1935). Anderson's work in *The Great Train Robbery* influenced the character of all his subsequent years and led to his becoming the first Western star.

The whole feeling of *The Great Train Robbery* is decidedly cinematic. Movement is employed toward and away from the camera, as well as horizontally in front of it. Once or twice the camera is even swung to follow the action. Porter utilized the principle of film editing for this picture and dared introduce parallel action. Without subtitles, he found he was able to handle changes of place and lapses of time, all by means of cutting.

The picture opens to an indoor set of a telegraph office. Bandits tie up the operator and board the train when it arrives. They stop the engine and herd all the passengers out onto the grade. The mail car is robbed. The bandits make away with their loot. The telegraph operator's daughter comes upon him and frees him. He races to alert the townsfolk. A posse is formed. After a chase, the bandits are met by the posse in a field, and a shoot-out ensues. George Barnes as a desperado appears on screen in a close-up and fires his gun repeatedly into the audience. Women screamed or fainted away; men were terrified or fell to marveling.

If the horse chase in *The Great Train Robbery* seems awkward, this must not be blamed totally on Porter. His riders were inexperienced, and it was the first such sequence. It became the most accepted ending to a Western story of any and the one which seems to engender the greatest excitement—followed closely by the shoot-out.

The commercial impact of *The Great Train Robbery* was overwhelming. Nickelodeons were begun all over the country within the next two years, opening to capacity audiences and showing Porter's film as their initial offering. It was easily the most widely exhibited picture of its time and assured many people that the motion picture was here to stay. Adolph Zukor, who came to play such a profound role in Porter's personal fortunes, struck up an association with William A. Brady. Together they formed a series of vaudeville acts called Hale's Tours and road-showed the entertainment group together with the exhibition of *The Great Train Robbery*. It was as a result of this successful venture that Zukor both made the decision to produce films himself and acquired the basic capital to do it.

Porter's costs, all told, did not exceed $150 for the entire production. Consistent with marketing policies of that period, the Edison Company sold prints of the 740-foot film for $11 apiece. Zukor's road-showing, among similar exploitations, eventually led to further restrictions being imposed by producers. As it was, exhibitors ran prints till they fell apart from use or, as was more often the case with the nitrate-based film stock, caught fire from the carbon arcs used in the projection equipment.

The Great Train Robbery wasn't the first Western film; that may have been the vignette *Cripple Creek Barroom* (Edison, 1898). Nor was it Porter's first effort to film a Western, which he did in his *The Life of an American Cowboy* (Edison, 1902), made on Staten Island. But it was the earliest *story* Western and established the classic plot structure the genre has retained: crime, pursuit, retribution. Duke Wayne's *The Train Robbers* (Warner's, 1972), differs only in that it ends before the retribution is quite finished. Whether by luck or instinct, Porter happened upon a formula that tapped the vital source of appeal true of many Western films since. In its way, this was no small accomplishment. Compared with so much of Porter's work at Edison and later, the picture came at just the right time. There was a happy confluence of events that set the course of future production. Porter gave directors and cameramen a new perspective on their art, and he demonstrated once more not only the viability of the story film but the suspense, excitement, and emotional pleasure such films could generate.

Porter himself never truly realized the full significance of *The Great Train Robbery*. He was oblivious to many of its latent themes. This is made rather evident in view of the fact that the only commercial advantage he took of it (other than the fact that its reputation kept him employed for the next ten years) was his disappointing parody *The Little Train Robbery* (Edison, 1905). In this film child bandits rob a toy train and scurry to their hide-out in a forest, only to be captured by children dressed in police uniforms. What Porter neglected, others were quick to perceive. Any number of imitation films sprang up, most of them employing a robbery as the central action.

As a filmmaker, Porter was more concerned with technical aspects than with dramatic or melodramatic overtones. The long-standing box office of *The Great Train Robbery* led, in 1907, to Porter's promotion to a supervisory capacity over nearly all Edison production. He edited a substantial number of the company's films himself. When Lawrence Griffith, an indigent actor with aspirations to be a playwright, presented Porter with a motion picture script based on *Tosca,* Porter was impressed by his looks and hired him as a player. He was first cast as a mountaineer in the forthcoming film *Rescued from an Eagle's Nest* (Edison, 1907). After working in several more Edison films, the young actor adopted the professional name of D. W. Griffith and moved to Biograph, where he became a director. Porter said afterward of Griffith that he always "took direction from me very well."

While Porter busied himself producing novelties for Edison, a young Jewish merchant in Oshkosh, Wisconsin, was learning the rudiments of promotion by giving away free turkeys to large-cash customers of the Continental Clothing Company. For the twenty-year period spanning 1916–36, this man managed to do more for general Western production than anyone else in the industry. Born at Laupheim, Germany, on January 17, 1867, Carl Laemmle arrived in the United States penniless, an untutored immigrant, unable to read or speak English, a member of an unpopular religious persuasion, with more strikes against him than the New York Mets had their first season. A dispute with the Continental's owners over more money prompted him to relocate to Chicago and, investing all of his savings, open a nickelodeon. Laemmle had seen *The Great Train Robbery* and was excited by the financial possibilities of film exhibition. His first nickelodeon in a rented building on Milwaukee Avenue did so much business that before 1909 progressed another two months, he had added a second. Next he started his own film exchange in an endeavor to improve the quality of screen product which he booked. Laemmle became many times a millionaire and then nearly lost it all. But he wasn't in it strictly for the money. He was a curious idealist who liked best about the dozens of cowboys who worked in his pictures over the years precisely that adventurous spirit and carefree willingness to make the best of every opportunity that, after a fashion, explained his own astonishing ascent to prosperity.

The Empire Trust Company had increasingly taken over financial control of the Biograph Studio. In January 1909 Jeremiah J. Kennedy, an officer of Empire, called a special luncheon for the foremost companies in the film industry. Represented were Thomas A. Edison, almost deaf; the powerful trio behind Vitagraph, J. Stuart Blackton, Albert Smith, and William T. "Pop" Rock; the Selig Company; Sigmund Lubin, of Philadelphia; and George K. Spoor, of Essanay. Also present were delegates from the leading French firms, Pathé and Méliès, along with George Kleine, an importer of foreign films. Together they organized the Motion Picture Patents Company, the principal objective of which was to curtail all independent filmmaking and confine manufacture to the participating companies. This necessitated the destruction of all unaffiliated film exchanges. In a typical gesture, Carl Laemmle set himself in opposition to the Trust. He sold a 10 per cent interest in his Chicago exchange to Robert Cochrane for $2,500. The two men formed their own production firm with a studio located at Eleventh Avenue and Fifty-third Street in New York. They called it the Independent Moving Pictures Company of America, IMP for short. With only the daring William Fox pursuing a similarly belligerent course, IMP refused to take its pictures from the Trust's General Film Company. It rejected the Trust's insistence that each proprietary nickelodeon be licensed at a cost of two dollars a week fifty-two times a year. With an aggregate of ten thousand theaters and nickelodeons already in the country (of which Laemmle's were but a small fraction), the Trust became wealthy and powerful on the basis of their licensing practices alone.

Porter grew dissatisfied at Edison as the Patents War began to rage. The Trust opined that they possessed the exclusive patents for the manufacture of motion pictures. Porter did not approve of Edison's attorney, Frank L. Dyer, who organized much of the Trust's strategy, nor was he pleased with the bombings, bribes, and beatings which Laemmle employees faced daily. An attempt was made to strangle IMP with almost three hundred lawsuits, hoping to crush them by the sheer weight of legal fees. Beyond this, Porter was unhappy about the wages at Edison. He couldn't afford to keep promising talent, nor were his own earnings commensurate with the income his films produced. In November 1909 he quit Edison to enter independent production. "I left simply to make money," Porter later said. "All about me I saw men, many with no experience in motion pictures, reaping a fortune overnight. I wanted a share in such rewards."

In partnership with Joseph W. Engel, a nickelodeon operator, Porter founded Defender Pictures Company and opened his studio on the second floor of an old building on Eleventh Avenue and Forty-first Street, a short distance from Laemmle's site. His first employee was Arthur Miller, hired as a combination laboratory assistant and camera technician. He would become one of the most outstanding cinematographers of his time. Porter stuck to one-reel subjects and released them weekly through Laemmle's Motion Picture Distributor and Sales Company.

Porter and Laemmle became close business associates. At Laemmle's suggestion, Porter, disenchanted with Engel, dissolved their partnership after less than eight months. A new firm was organized, called the Rex Film Company. Most of the financing came from Laemmle, who placed William H. Swanson in charge of operations. Legally, Swanson was Porter's partner. Porter deployed himself in production. The company moved to enlarged quarters at Eleventh Avenue and Forty-third Street in the old Cameraphone Studio. Arthur Miller in *One Reel a Week* (UCLA Press, 1968) described Porter's habits at Rex. "He never thought of himself as just a director," Miller commented. "He thought of himself as a manufacturer of motion pictures, capable of handling personally every phase of filmmaking, from turning the crank of the camera to printing and toning the final positive. His life was devoted to the movies, and he did more to create the motion picture business than those who invented the camera."

In 1912, as Laemmle was finally emerging from the mesh of lawyers and legal battles, he introduced Porter to Adolph Zukor. Since touring *The Great Train Robbery,* Zukor had first operated a nickelodeon before associating himself with Marcus Loew in building the Loew theater chain. Zukor, like Laemmle, had been an immigrant. He had come from Hungary and had started in the fur business. Zukor was now in the process of founding his own producing company, to be called Famous Players. He was a year shy of forty; when he became one hundred years of age, he was still chairman of the board. The company would feature top theatrical names in cinema versions of popular plays. Zukor invited Porter to become his production manager. He had previously approached D. W. Griffith at Biograph with the job, offering him $50,000 a year. Griffith declined, heartily urging Zukor to ask Porter. A decade in the future when Zukor did get Griffith, times would so have changed that D.W., like Porter, was only another pioneer that the maturing industry had passed by.

Laemmle, crafty to the end, was anxious to get rid of Porter, although he kept his intentions secret from both Porter and Zukor. He had thought originally that the creator of *The Great Train Robbery* had been stifled at Edison and undercapitalized at Defender. But no more top-notch pictures had been forthcoming. In fact, Porter had spent much of his time developing a new projector together with Frank Cannock, who worked for George Kleine. Kleine instituted a lawsuit claiming their Simplex projector had been devised while Cannock was in his employ and therefore belonged to him. Porter won the suit through default because the patents were registered in his name. Laemmle no longer expected great films from the technically oriented Porter. He quietly, and subtly, recommended Porter to Zukor in an indirect fashion. Zukor snapped up Porter. Porter sold his interest in Rex to Swanson, and the company merged into Laemmle's growing complex. Laemmle issued a clandestine sigh of relief. Zukor had this to say of Porter in *The Public Is Never Wrong* (Putnam, 1953), on the occasion of Porter's becoming director-general and treasurer of Famous Players. "He was distressed by the ups and downs of business . . . and was intrigued by the offer to make pictures and let someone else worry about marketing them and meeting the payroll, while still having a chance at the profits."

It should come as no surprise that Porter's work at Famous Players was undistinguished. He moved to the West Coast Lasky studio. There he made a few pictures with Mary Pickford, including the first *Tess of the Storm Country* (Famous Players, 1914). Mary later remarked that Porter was most interested in what went on *in* the camera and in the darkroom, not in directing the action in front of the camera. He left Famous Players in 1915 and for the remainder of his life tinkered with various technical problems and inventions without notable success.

In his last years, he lived at the Taft Hotel in New York. He told a New York *Times* reporter in 1940 that he seldom went to movies because he had lost "the initiative and excitement" for filmmaking. When he died the next year, almost no one observed his departure from the scene. Yet in *The Great Train Robbery*, despite its primitive crudities, some of the magic and passion which inspired the film can still be said to survive.

2 / THE MAKING OF BRONCHO BILLY

G. M. Anderson was awed at the box-office reception of *The Great Train Robbery*. He was taken aback at the excited comment it prompted. All of which tended to convince him that his future was in the production of moving pictures. Always the entrepreneur, he left the Edison Studio and presented himself to the Vitagraph Company at 116 Morton Street in Manhattan, where he was hired as a director, primarily because of his association with the Porter film. His salary rose to twenty-five dollars a week. Being a director in those days meant something very like what *auteur* theorists imagine it was later with less grounds for the supposition; Anderson worked at everything from property man to scriptwriter to cameraman to actor to executive.

It was during his tenure at Vitagraph that Anderson brought his first literary series character to the screen in the earth-breaking two-reeler *Raffles, the Amateur Cracksman* (Vitagraph, 1904). It was based on the Robin Hood-like thief created by Sir Arthur Conan Doyle's brother-in-law, E. W. Hornung. The picture was a financial success.

The public's demand for new screen product seemed insatiable. The idea of film *rental* had not yet been devised by producing companies, and most prints were sold outright to exhibitors. In order to regularly and frequently change their bills, exhibitors began organizing "exchanges" where they could meet and swap films from various producing companies. The producing companies had no way of policing this activity, and as a result, much of their distribution was by second and third hand. It proved such a trauma, they still haven't recovered. Percentage terms by attendance glimmered in the future. Irked at having to pay producing companies anything, certain affluent exhibitors decided to produce their own films and use them, in turn, to swap for films being manufactured by Edison, Vitagraph, and the others via the exchanges. In 1906 John Harris and Harry Davis, theater owners in the Pittsburgh area, hired G. M. Anderson to produce one- and two-reel subjects for them.

The association was short-lived, but Anderson demonstrated his competence sufficiently to strike out for Chicago in 1907. Several producing

Broncho Billy Anderson in jail. He invented the Western star system.

companies had located there, among them the production arm of William Selig, a spurious colonel who had originally begun in the manufacture of projection equipment. It was Anderson's intention to produce "cowboy" pictures in the tradition, or at least the spirit, of *The Great Train Robbery*. Understandably, he had grown dissatisfied with New Jersey settings as backgrounds. He persuaded Selig to transport a company to Colorado for authentic location shooting. The group departed. Selig, however, was personally apathetic to the idea, and numerous altercations erupted. The upshot was that Anderson returned to Chicago and proceeded at once to negotiate a production partnership with George K. Spoor, born in 1872, a distributor for screen equipment. Once more Anderson's salesmanship was effective. Not until the fantastic popularity of the Anderson Westerns filmed in California became a commonplace did Selig change his mind about location production.

Spoor and Anderson called their newly formed company Essanay, representing their initials. As their trademark, they adopted the Indian head pictured on the United States penny. Anderson was now able to manufacture Westerns according to his own theories. He knew the importance of series characters from his experience at Vitagraph. A Western, he felt, must have an identifiable central character. This was the literary tradition behind popular heroes. He thought it applied equally well to motion pictures. Peter B. Kyne, who would become a prolific writer for the screen, published a story in *The Saturday Evening Post* featuring a character called Broncho Billy. When Anderson read the story, he purchased screen rights to the property for all of fifty dollars. Initially, Anderson's production unit consisted of himself and his cameraman, Rollie Totheroh. When Charlie Chaplin came to Essanay, Totheroh worked with him and stayed with the Chaplin unit for the next thirty years.

The weather conditions in southern California appeared ideally suited to the continuous production of outdoor dramas. The region itself offered an endless number of contrasting natural settings, from deserts to mountain lakes, forests to plains. The troupe left Chicago and set up shop in a downtown Los Angeles hotel. Accompanying them was a vaudeville performer who had begun as a prop man—cross-eyed Ben Turpin. The unit shot several short comedies with him. Meanwhile, Anderson scouted around for a likely prospect to play the Western lead for his proposed series. At long last, sighing, certain the part could not be properly cast, Anderson moved to Niles, California, near San Francisco, and made what remains his most momentous decision—namely, to star in the pictures himself. He knew his own inadequacies. He wasn't handsome but rather rugged, masculine, roughly hewn. The character which first emerged on the screen was that of a "good bad man," a Western variation on the Raffles theme with an even heavier emphasis on melodrama.

Anderson's first Westerns were not Broncho Billy films, a fact sometimes blurred in accounts of his career. In his first starring vehicle, *The Bandit Makes Good* (Essanay, 1908), Anderson played a bank robber, apprehended by the sheriff. On their way back to town, Anderson and the sheriff stop off at a saloon. The sheriff loses the recovered bank money in a crooked card game. Anderson rallies to his rescue, holding the card sharks at bay. He's pardoned by the time of the fade-out, and even made a deputy sheriff. This plot, already hackneyed in 1908, had more life in it than has been generated by the performances of all of the players who have subsequently acted it out till the present day.

Anderson wrote a letter shortly before his death, responding to the query of what the title was to his first Billy film. He opted for *Broncho Billy and the Baby* (Essanay, 1915). The release and copyright dates for this entry make the validity of his recollection doubtful. Most probably the first in the series was *Broncho Billy's Redemption* (Essanay, 1910). Following its release, the Broncho Billy moniker was used on a consistent basis in the titles to the Essanay Westerns, relating each picture to this basic personality—*Broncho Billy's Love* or *Affair* or *Oath* or *Bible* or *Mexican Wife* or *Last Spree*. The plots were sketched briefly before production commenced. Despite the fact that the Billy character might be shot in the picture, or die or marry or what not, he would return again the next time in a new story, starting over at the beginning. The character, not the stories, unified the series. When Essanay later reissued many of the pre-1910 Anderson films, the credits were changed to read "Starring Broncho Billy," as in the rerelease of the two-reeler *Naked Hands* (Essanay, 1909). *Broncho Billy and the Greaser* was another title in the series. It suggests the strong reliance the films had on stock types besides Billy.

Limited to lengths of one reel at first, before long the series expanded to two-reelers. They were produced at the rate of one a week, budgeted at $800 apiece and grossing up to $50,000. The pictures were franchised on what became known as a states' rights basis, where a certain theater chain, or theater amalgam, was licensed to exhibit the films in their region for a specified period of time for a flat fee. When the prints had made their rounds, they were exchanged by Essanay for prints of new titles.

The combination of shrewd marketing plus the creation of a continuously featured personality led to Anderson's phenomenal success. By 1912 he was earning as much as $125,000 a year as a producer, director, and Western star. Anderson counted a total of some 375 short Westerns produced during the years 1908–15. Most have become victims of nitrate decomposition and neglect. In those which do survive, a fair sampling over the years of Billy's productivity, a trend can be seen to more significant production values; the plots become stronger with greater internal logic, careful development, and sharper character delineation; the action sequences mature; the settings, both indoors and out, are increasingly believable; the costuming is credible, which is to say the utter lack of it! Even the sentiment, a necessary ingredient in the decade of the teens, often gives way to irony, disappointment, or tragedy. Billy could not allow the quality of his films to slip. They constituted the staple of Essanay's production. Their continued box office was due to a steady improvement with no more than an occasional inferior entry. Film company hoarding and public indifference, until recently, have created a rather novel situation: Many more examples of Billy's films are to be found in British than in American archives.

In these hundreds of films, Anderson indubitably came upon every conceivable plot variant, borrowing substantially from the pulps and popular Western lore. Billy has since been criticized for this penchant for pulp plots. It is unfair to do so. Many of his contemporaries in the Western literary field, from Zane Grey to Clarence E. Mulford to Max Brand, were Easterners who built up their intimacy with the West from sources other than their direct experience. Over the years Billy actually attempted to incorporate at least a semblance of the atmosphere of the West; after all, the West was very much alive in human memory, and the last roundups occurred as late as 1907. William S. Hart, who is cited for his realism, was as sentimental as Billy. In terms of accuracy in depicting frontier conditions, the Billy films from 1914–15 and 1918–19 rank well with most of the contemporary product from other companies, including the Hart films for Triangle.

If Billy's plots are analyzed as plots, he was justified in remarking near the end of his life that Westerns hadn't altered very much in the interim. The difference is more obvious in the telling. In *Broncho Billy's Redemption,* Anderson again portrays a good bad man, a cattle thief wanted by the law. He risks arrest and conviction when he comes to the aid of a damsel and her father. The father is sick. Billy takes him to town to a doctor. For his heroism, Billy is permitted to go free. As common as this plot was in Billy's pictures, Bill Hart found it inviting enough to vary it several times in his own films. The reader, however, is advised not to believe it very probable in modern America; new concepts of law and order have written a less agreeable ending.

Another plot that retained its appeal, with both Buck Jones and George O'Brien using it in the Thirties, was that of *Naked Hands.* It opened out West but concluded with Anderson coming East to settle his score with the villain. Dressed as an Easterner, Anderson arrives at the villain's house. A terrific battle ensues, the men locked in combat, rolling down a staircase, smashing furniture and glassware. Only the villain's daughter, pleading for her father's life, compels Anderson to stay his hand.

Broncho Billy's contribution to the Western genre is immeasurable. The humor in his Westerns inspired Colonel Selig's imitative Tom Mix vehicles,

Costumes were nothing special in the Billy Westerns. Anderson is to the far left: Harry Todd stands between the men holding ropes.

some of Harry Carey's work at Universal, and nearly all of Hoot Gibson's. Billy's stress on action guided Mix's format at Fox, while humor and action were combined in the Buck Jones Fox Westerns by 1920. The concept of the good bad man was tired formula when Hart abandoned it, but every star after him tried it on and off, right down to *True Grit* (Paramount, 1969). Above all, the sharply defined photography of the Anderson Westerns established a motion picture precedent, providing them later on with a nearly visionary verisimilitude.

Critics and historians do Billy an injustice when they imply that what finally finished him was the competition from Thomas H. Ince and William S. Hart. They had almost nothing to do with it. Most events which have occurred in motion picture history have been grounded in business transactions, not artistic considerations. The Billy Westerns were no exception.

Essanay signed Charlie Chaplin in 1915 for the somewhat unusual salary of $1,250 a week. Chaplin scripted twelve short comedies for Anderson, most of them filmed at the Niles studio. Chaplin has never admitted it, but

G. M. Anderson as he appeared in old age, after he had been rediscovered.
Photo courtesy of *Views & Reviews* magazine.

Anderson assigned Jesse L. Robbins, his own director, to many of the pictures. Rollie Totheroh was deployed in photographing them. Anderson began to involve himself more deeply in the production of other films and so couldn't maintain the schedule of the Billy pictures. Operations were interrupted. The late entries no longer used Billy's name with their titles, only on the credits and promotion. Exhibitors were clamoring for four- and five-reel subjects, not the two-reelers Billy was making. As an experiment, Essanay made a five-reel comedy with Chaplin in Chicago, *Carmen* (Essanay, 1915). Spoor, who supervised it, was satisfied with neither the results nor the financial prospects of feature films. They simply cost too much. You could make a two-reeler and easily recover your investment. But how many features could you make that didn't earn money? Anderson argued with Spoor that in view of the fact that Hart and the others were making feature Westerns, the Billy market could not hope to prosper without revision. Moreover, unless Essanay committed itself to general feature production, the company's future was imperiled. Spoor was obdurate. He had made money on the Billy pictures; Chaplin's shorts were popular. Then the blow fell. Mutual hired Chaplin away at $10,000 a week.

Anderson knew he must make the transition to feature Westerns or he would not survive as a box-office attraction. If Spoor wouldn't concede,

Anderson told him pointedly, then he would be forced to sell out his interest in Essanay. Who knows if it was a bluff? Anderson may have wanted only to bring home the gravity of their plight. Spoor agreed. The buy-sell contract forbade Billy to engage in motion picture production for a period of two years. It prohibited him from using the name "Broncho Billy" in any new pictures he might eventually make. Reluctantly, albeit stubbornly, Billy signed the contract. Spoor went on for the next two years reissuing the Billy short Westerns among other films. When the Trust was broken up, the predominance of feature films and inadequate financing forced him to merge his facilities with other companies into a distribution combine. The road ahead for Spoor was one of decline and oblivion.

Billy busied himself with noncinematic production for the next two years. He achieved some success on the legitimate stage. In 1918, with Essanay about to expire and allowed by contract to resume production, Anderson learned that too much time had elapsed. Audiences didn't remember or had found new favorites. L. Lawrence Weber financed a new series of two-reelers, produced by his Golden West Photoplay Company, released through the Sherry Service. The films were superior to nearly all of the Essanay reissues, but they were still two-reelers. When a feature was made, *The Son-of-a-Gun,* Billy's final film, he was cast as a good bad man. It is beautiful in its way, quite moving as a film document. But it didn't gross anywhere near expectations. It brought down the curtain on Billy's screen career. Anderson persisted as a producer, making new pictures, including a series of Stan Laurel comedies for Metro release. But continual disagreements with both releasing companies and Louis B. Mayer led to his forced retirement.

Until 1948, no one heard from Billy again. Then an enterprising nationwide search located him, living as he had since the early days in Los Angeles. The motion picture industry out of honest if belated regard for his importance awarded him a special Oscar. Even though he was titular head of Progressive Pictures, he hadn't done anything since the twenties. Broncho Billy was one of those resurrected for a cameo in *The Bounty Killer* (Embassy, 1965), a low-budget, shoddy production featuring many old-timers and probably best forgotten. Anderson also appeared on Dave Garroway's "Wide, Wide World" report on the Hollywood Western. When sickness overcame him, Billy spent his final years peacefully at the Motion Picture Country Home in Woodland Hills.

One of his last interviews (and typical of the man) quoted him as saying, "Music doesn't belong in a cowboy picture. I never heard a cowboy who could play a guitar. Those drugstore cowboys—none of them are cowboys, no more than I was." Perhaps he was too harsh with himself. Those examples of his cinematic art available would seem to indicate so.

Shootin' Mad, while prosaic of plot and much akin to his Essanay films, has far improved production values compared to earlier G. M. Anderson releases. It is a well-made Broncho Billy two-reeler, from the Golden West Photoplay comeback series. Anderson had secured rights for reuse of the name from Spoor's crumbling fortunes, but reinvoking the memory was not enough. Harry Todd and his daughter, Mary, want to homestead. They are tricked by the saloon owner, Ace High Cowan. Cowan has Todd shot and makes a play for Mary. Billy, a roustabout, comes to Mary's rescue and by the fade is made sheriff of Bear Gulch, and Cowan's saloon is turned into a church.

The Son-of-a-Gun proved a fitting exit for Billy. It had nowhere near the tension of *Shootin' Mad*. Joy Lewis was back as the girl. Her parents were portrayed by E. A. Whitting and his wife, billed as "Mrs. E. A. Whitting." Paul Willis played Joy's brother, Buddy. Fred Church returned as a crooked foreman named Buck Saunders, and Harry Todd was the sheriff. Billy played a roustabout. He saves Buddy from gambling away money to buy his mother medicine by herding "Double Deck" Harry, played by Frank Whitson, and his cardsharps into a back room. The plot is reminiscent of Anderson's first Essanay Western. Returning the boy to the Bar-O, Buddy's father shoots Billy in the back. He dies. He has given his life to perform a good deed. It is almost as if G. M. Anderson knew this was to be his last film. It ends with a ballad.

> Oh, dyin' was easy, for livin' was hard.
> Ye died for a word or the turn of a card.
> Ye died for a woman. Ye died for a pard.
> Which last, was, I'm thinkin', the best.

Sentiment there was, but it was softer, gentler, less pervasive and offensive than in many of the William S. Hart vehicles. Billy made intense, entertaining, if simplistic, little moral dramas. The Billy Westerns, in terms of costuming or town sets, were as realistic as the more touted Hart pictures; critics who credit Hart with these innovations ignore the fact that filmmakers in the decade of the teens were still too near the real West to know any better. The gaudy displays of the later Autry fantasies, or even the glamour of Ken Maynard's silent Westerns for First National or Tom Mix's Fox thrillers in the twenties, belong to an age separated from the teens by the ugly horrors of a world war and a veneer of newly discovered sophistication. The Billy films were filled with action and a straightforward, unabashed heroism. The best of them may yet claim the modern viewer's attention.

3 / THE WESTERN AT INCEVILLE

It was in the autumn of 1910. Thomas Harper Ince was standing in Times Square. He was eighteen years old. He had a stern, full-moon face, rather white and unhealthy. His tremendous nervous energy may have been due in part to a heart that beat too fast. He could smile, but the corners of his aggressive mouth turned downward toward the pugnacious jut of his chin. He preferred to keep his teeth clenched, as if he suffered from chronic dyspepsia. His full head of brown hair with a slight curl he wore swept back from his temples. But you noticed these things secondarily, if at all. What struck you about him was the austere intensity of his restless gray eyes.

Thomas Ince wasn't a happy man. He may have been brash, ambitious, determined. He could be uniquely charming. Just standing there, he gave the impression of neither ruthlessness nor cunning. During the winter of 1903, he had shared rooms at the Hotel Harrington on Broadway with an aspiring thespian on hard times and an actor-musician no better off. The thespian thought Ince uncommonly selfish. Frank Stammers, the actor-musician, played his cello and kept to himself. The thespian delighted in telling stories of the Old West, particularly of the Sioux Indians whom he had known as a boy in the Dakota Territory.

Ince listened. He hadn't anything better to do. He heard at third hand about the mighty buffalo herds and the massacre at Little Big Horn. Many of the stories were sentimental, centered on the inevitable tragedy of the Indian nations confronted by a superior civilization. The thespian's given name—which he used on stage—was William S. Hart. Ince was rather contemptuous of Hart, and his attitude never really changed. Hart was thirty-three years old, Ince eleven.

At thirteen, Ince had promoted his own stock company. It had failed. It was doubtless his father's aptitude for the boards—he was noted for his Chinese characterizations—that had suggested the theater. Ince's father became a booking agent. That suggested even more to Thomas Ince.

He married Eleanor Kershaw on October 19, 1907, during the two-year run of *For Love's Sweet Sake,* in which he had a featured role. The couple lived in a small flat in Harlem. Standing in the Square, Ince was trying to concoct a scheme to make money. His answer drove up to the curb in a large, shiny automobile, got out, and invited him to lunch. Ince had worked with Joseph Smiley in vaudeville, and now Smiley was well-to-do. He was a moving picture actor for the IMP Company. Ince asked Smiley if there was a chance for him at IMP.

"Why, yes," Smiley responded. "There should be. You're an actor, aren't you? There may be something there this afternoon."

Ince went to Fifty-sixth Street and looked around at the studio. It resembled, he thought to himself, "the dreadful tank-town theaters I had played on tour." An acquaintance Ince had made on stage, Harry Salter, was directing a one-reeler. He gave Ince a small part and paid him five dollars.

Ince got a number of similarly limited roles during the next several weeks. Then he went to Biograph to play a heavy in *His New Lid*. He obtained the part through the film's star, his sister-in-law, Lucille Lee Stewart. The picture was released on November 24, 1910.

It occurred to Ince that he ran a better chance to move up in the industry as a director than as an actor relegated to playing villains. He returned to IMP and talked to the studio manager, Tom Cochrane, brother of Laemmle's business partner, Robert Cochrane.

Tom Cochrane promised him a chance at becoming a director at the nearest opportunity. When one of IMP's regular directors quit, Cochrane made good on it. He handed a fatuous script based on an old poem, "Little Nell's Tobacco," to Ince and told him to get started. Ince completely rewrote the story and produced a one-reeler in an astonishingly short time.

In order for Ince to secure a permanent director's job, Cochrane needed Carl Laemmle's approval. It was arranged for Laemmle to see the picture where it was booked at a nearby nickelodeon. Cochrane told Ince confidentially that he would have his directorship clinched if he'd go along with Laemmle and supervise the Little Champ's reaction. Which is precisely what Ince did. Every positive audience response was underlined by Ince, whispering into Laemmle's ear. It is a commonplace to say that capturing a man's ear is a way to win favor; in Laemmle's case, it was the only way guaranteed to work. Ince got the job.

I wonder what both men would have thought could they, sitting together in the flickering projection light of a darkened theater, have foreseen Thomas Ince's spectacular rise to wealth and fame in the motion picture industry. Perhaps Ince's restless eyes would have gleamed at the vision of the beautiful home Días Dorados he would someday own in Benedict Canyon in Beverly Hills. And Laemmle, would he have been only amused were he able to augur in 1910 that he himself would purchase Días Dorados after Thomas Ince was dead. Laemmle was grinning as the two walked out again into the harsh brightness of the street.

One of the stars Laemmle had attracted to IMP from Biograph was Mary Pickford. IMP gave her top billing and went all out to establish her screen identity with the public. Still fettered by his suits with the Trust, Laemmle wanted to relocate his production facilities to some place where they would be safe from injunctions and persistent interference. He dispatched Ben Turpin on a scouting trip to California. I do not know if Turpin surveyed the idyllic landscape in the cross-eyed fashion typical of him in his comedies. The reader will recall that Turpin had already made some short films in California for Broncho Billy Anderson in 1908. He then left Essanay for IMP. It was an irremediable trait in Laemmle's temperament that when he relied on a person, he relied on him implicitly; moreover, he would sooner rely on a man than not. This policy, as might readily be imagined, was so frequently disastrous that Laemmle did his best to balance it with an omnivorous distrustfulness. Laemmle would erratically sway back and forth, changing his mind a dozen times in the span it took a subordinate to catch on firmly to a single notion and set about executing it. Carl Laemmle's genius was improvisation flexed with Teutonic stubbornness and the blind, but wavering, faith of the Israelites. Turpin informed him that nowhere in California could IMP elude the Trust. Laemmle decided to make movies in Cuba. Turpin quit IMP and, after a time, went to work for Mack Sennett at his Keystone Studio at Edendale, California.

A company of some seventy-two persons under the ubiquitous supervision of C. A. "Doc" Willat departed for Havana. Willat was Laemmle's production manager and Pop Rock's son-in-law. Incredibly, Rock, who was still an officer of the Vitagraph Company and party to the Trust, although he knew of Laemmle's maneuver, said nothing about it. Among those in the troupe were Mary Pickford, Owen Moore, King Baggot, Jack Pickford, Mrs. Charlotte Pickford, Lotte Pickford, and directors Joseph Smiley and Thomas Ince. Smiley had been promoted to director in charge of the King Baggot unit. Ince was unit manager for the Pickford vehicles.

The venture turned out a debacle. Mrs. Pickford threw a fit once she learned that Mary had been secretly married to Owen Moore. The Motion Picture Patents Company made it difficult to get raw film stock. The crew disliked the climate. Ince and Moore clashed violently. Ince's assistant insulted Mary, and Moore jumped him. The police were summoned. Mrs. Pickford arranged for Moore and Mary to return to the mainland.

When Ince arrived back in New York, he had several one-reelers to show for his efforts. He was now an experienced producer-director. Ince continued making short films for IMP while quietly seeking out a better position.

In 1909, when New York Governor Charles Evans Hughes banned horse racing, Adam Kessel, Jr., and Charles O. Bauman were among the countless bookmakers suddenly out of a job. The picture business seemed a

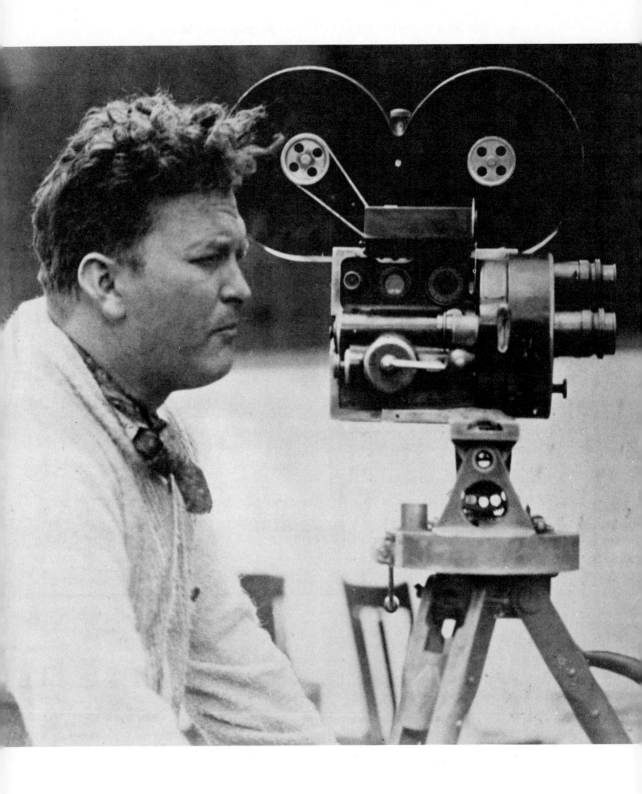

good bet, so the two became partners in a film exchange. Bauman was a pragmatic soul who induced Kessel to invest in a wholly owned production arm while using his personal income to back Laemmle's IMP. Bauman thought Laemmle blithely incompetent. Already in 1910, familiar with Laemmle's chaotic management, he devised a gambit with which he might hope to seize all of the IMP holdings.

By 1911 Kessel and Bauman owned a producing firm in New York called Reliance, had a production unit at Edendale, California, called Bison Life Motion Pictures, which made Westerns; and had agreed to finance Sennett's Keystone comedy unit. Bauman was made privy to Ince's amazing abilities by associates at IMP and let out word that he and Kessel were looking for a production manager to work in Edendale.

"I was entirely ignorant of the fact that Kessel and Bauman were considering me . . . ," Ince later recalled. "I decided to apply for the job feeling I would have greater opportunities in this new field than in New York. A little strategy was necessary, I felt, to impress my prospective employers with my importance, so I allowed a mustache to grow and, on the day of my interview with Bauman, I borrowed a large, sparkling ring from Doc Willat. This, I figured, would give the impression that I was a man of means who did not have to work for the paltry sixty dollars a week which was my munificent salary at IMP."

Ince thought the ruse successful. He hesitated when Bauman offered him $100 a week. Bauman raised it to $150 plus a three-month guarantee and a stock option in the Sennett Keystone unit. Ince was triumphant. But the elaborate strategy was wasted. Ince was a central cog in Bauman's master plan to effect a merger between the Kessel and Bauman holding firm—the New York Motion Picture Company—and Laemmle's IMP. Ince promised Bauman he could take IMP actress Ethel Grandin and several technicians with him when he left. Laemmle had lost Pickford, and his long struggle with the Trust had cost him dearly. Stealing Ince and the others and packing them off to California would force Laemmle's hand. If Bauman made any miscalculation at all, it was his underestimation of the Little Champ.

Ince, his wife, and his small troupe arrived in Los Angeles in October 1911. The Bison Life Motion Picture "studio" had once been a general store that now was refurbished to comprise a cramped office and a film processing laboratory. In the back yard was an unprotected open-air stage without so much as a sunlight diffuser. Props were stored in a shed. A nearby bungalow was rented as a dressing room. "The sets," Ince commented later, "consisted of a few pieces of very bad furniture and one backdrop with a flock of birds supposedly in flight. The furniture was bad enough, but when I thought of stationary birds poised in mid-air as a backdrop for a moving picture, I gave way to a moment of discouragement."

Thomas Ince poised behind the camera in a posed photograph from his Inceville days.

I do not know what impression Ince may have made on the reader at this point. He was still a teen-ager. Ince's accelerated heartbeat created a frantic nervous energy. Ince recorded what constituted an average workday for him when he began at Bison. "I left the house every morning at 7:30 . . . ," he wrote. "I would direct and shoot all day and return home at seven in the evening, eat a hurried dinner and start preparing for the activities of the next day. The results of each day's work had to be carefully inspected. My projection room was the kitchen of my small Hollywood bungalow and, with Mrs. Ince's assistance, I would cut and assemble scenes taken the day before. As she unwound the reel I examined the negative and, as it ran through my fingers, it was caught in a clothes basket on the floor.

"When the film was cut and assembled I would turn my attention to stories and would work until midnight writing scenarios for the following day. With my wife's help I managed to keep my production up to par. . . ." When Ince's guarantee ran out, he was to go on percentage. If he had anything to say about it, that percentage would far exceed the salary with which he started.

Ince turned out acceptable one-reelers. But he knew that he couldn't overcome the dearth of studio facilities forever—or he could only if he confined himself to *outdoor* films. He chose to do the latter. Griffith had been coming to California to produce his Westerns, but they were nowise a Biograph specialty, as were the Anderson films for Essanay. And it is to Ince, rather than to either Anderson or Griffith, that the Western owes its primary production innovations after the initial surge of *The Great Train Robbery*.

Anderson developed a formula that was unique, but he never progressed beyond it. Griffith experimented with the action format and advanced cinematic techniques that sharpened the effectiveness of Western motion pictures. Ince, however, was the first to systematize Western production and put it on solid footing. Most Westerns, as most films, were a haphazard proposition made up on the spur of the moment just prior to, or actually during, shooting. As his company expanded, Ince came increasingly to depend on the scenario as *the* essential ingredient. Action, facial expressions, plot, set design, camera setup, and even dialogue to be mouthed by the actors were incorporated into the shooting script. Ince made filmmaking a collective enterprise. In this sense, I cannot but agree with those French historians who believe that Ince was ultimately more significant in the development of the modern cinema than Griffith. He did not have Griffith's genius—but genius is a *sometime* thing even for those fortunate enough to possess it. Ince organized production methods that would assure him before the film was made what it would most probably look like. If his films included no astonishing bonanzas among them like *The Birth of a*

Nation, they were also spared financial paroxysms like *Intolerance.* Ince was uniquely both pioneer and pace-setter far into the future.

Soon after he had established himself in California, Ince learned that the Miller Brothers' 101 Ranch Wild West Show was wintering at nearby Venice. Business was so bad he found he could hire the entire show on an annual basis for $2,500 a week. Ince made an enthusiastic proposal to Kessel and Bauman to which they agreed and at a stroke had a complete stock company of cowboys, Indians, longhorn cattle, buffalo, tepees, stage-coaches, and wagons—in short, everything needed for continuous large-scale production of Westerns. Ince moved his lot from Edendale to fourteen thousand acres of land north of Santa Monica. It would become known as Inceville. Being near the ocean, the location did present problems of over-cast skies, but the terrain was not without unusual variety.

Ince didn't care two pins about "starring" Westerns in the Broncho Billy vein. He recalled many of the spectacular tales of frontier battles he had heard during those drab nights in New York in 1903. His first 101 Ranch picture was a two-reeler called *War on the Plains* (Bison, 1912). William Eagleshirt, a full-blooded Sioux, was given a major role. Reviews were favorable, and public response was encouraging. Ince proceeded with a series of two-reelers like *Battle of the Red Men* (Bison, 1912), *Indian Massacre* (Bison, 1912), and *The Lieutenant's Last Fight* (Bison, 1912).

What impressed Griffith about these films and obviously prompted him to make *The Battle at Elderbush Gulch* (Biograph, 1914) was the massively scaled action sequences which, of course, the 101 unit made possible. Ince knew the box-office value of such excitement and commercially exploited it. But his view of the Indian wasn't at all what even in Griffith and Anderson might already be called conventional. He retained an essentially sympathetic disposition toward the tragic, doomed plight of the red man. I suspect he acquired at least the outlines of this perspective from his early association with William S. Hart. Unquestionably, Hart himself did have a profound empathy with the Indian. Ince built up an entire retinue of Sioux Indians, still wards of the U. S. Government. He was expected to look after them and work in concert with the local Indian agent. The Indians got drunk, and complaints about them would summon Ince from bed in the middle of the night. They stole brightly colored props; they had an aversion for work-ing. But Ince was proving himself a splendid administrator.

In contrasting Ince with Griffith, I have already commented that Ince was not an ingeniously creative filmmaker but instead a brilliant organizer. He hired Francis Ford away from Vitagraph in 1912. Ford, born Francis O'Fearna thirty years before, was a onetime make-up artist who had played in stock with Amelia Bingham before going to work for the Edison Company. Vitagraph offered him a position as an actor-director much as they had G. M. Anderson before him. Ince intended to use Ford as a second-unit director to expedite production. Ford was of an independent (Ince felt choleric) turn of mind and sought increasing control over the Bison Westerns. This suited Ince, as it freed him from the drudgery of having to do everything himself. But Ince retained what has come to be called the "final cut." He would screen Ford's rushes from the day before, edit them to suit his concept of the story, and prepare the release negative from an assembled work print. Together with his principal scenarist in 1912, Richard V. Spencer; Charles Weston, the property man he had brought along with him from IMP; Ray Smallwood, the former IMP cameraman; and Ford, Ince would regularly conduct production conferences. He not only had the script detailed but now would pencil in fine alterations based on his editing of the rushes.

Ford naturally resented this. He had seen nothing comparable to it at Edison or Vitagraph and heard that Griffith at Biograph got the final cut and all the other cuts in the bargain. When Ince thought well of a Ford picture, he removed Ford's name from the director credits and inserted his own just as he might substitute his name for Spencer's as the scenarist. This convinced Kessel and Bauman and the critics alike that Ince was a superlative filmmaker. Major efforts could conceivably be produced, directed, and written by Thomas H. Ince when in fact all Ince had done was the editing.

Kessel and Bauman hired Grace Cunard, who had been with Lubin, and sent her West to Inceville soon after Ford's arrival. Born Harriet Mildred Jeffries in 1893, she had entered pictures at Biograph in 1910. She had an immediate rapport with Ford and fired his resentment of Ince with further stories about the absolute control she knew from her own experience Griffith had over his pictures. She urged Ford to strike out on his own with another firm.

Ince's most ambitious film as of the summer of 1912 was a three-reeler entitled *Custer's Last Fight,* with the scenario by Spencer based on Ince's own story outline. The picture described the events preceding the cataclysm at Little Big Horn and showed the massacre itself. Francis Ford directed and played Custer. He was supported by Ann Little, an excellent rider from the 101 who would later become one of Bill Hart's favorite leading ladies. Also in the cast were William Eagleshirt, Grace Cunard, and Charles K. French. The film was a fantastic success. It was also a contradictory omen for the merger between IMP and the New York Motion Picture Company. All in all, it had taken Bauman eight months to accomplish his design from the day he hired Ince till the signing of the merger papers in 1912.

I fear I may have somewhat misled the reader by narrating Bauman's schemes while neglecting Laemmle's own motivation. In the first months of 1912, Laemmle was in serious straits. His Cuban adventure had cost him Mary Pickford. Mary returned to Biograph in January 1912, joining

Ince's cowboy and Indian troupe brought out for a group shot during the period when he was making short Westerns.

Griffith's troupe in California right after the Christmas holidays. Griffith had introduced her to the business and she appealed to him as a friend. Moore's drinking had led to much of the trouble with Ince besides producing discord in her own marriage. The IMP situation—constant harassment from the Trust, Cuba, Ince—was impossible. Griffith conceded that he would release her name in connection with the publicity for her pictures but that it would not appear on the credits. It was a temporary compromise at best. Mary had been lured by Laemmle only because Biograph had a strict policy of not crediting their players. Upon her return, one of the pictures Mary made for Biograph was *Lena and the Geese,* filmed in April 1912. Lillian and Dorothy Gish saw the film in a Baltimore theater sometime after its release on June 17, 1912. They had known Mary and even shared an apartment with her and her mother when Mary was still Gladys Smith and both Mrs. Gish and Mary's mother had been desirous of securing careers for their children in vaudeville. The Gish sisters went to Biograph's New York studio at 11 East Fourteenth Street to visit their old friend. Griffith gave the Gish sisters a screen test in a film he was then making, *An Unseen Enemy* (Biograph, 1912), which also featured newcomer Harry Carey.

There wasn't much Laemmle could do about Mary Pickford. He had lost Ince. Edwin S. Porter had turned out a liability. Laemmle was cognizant of how Bauman and Kessel had gotten Mack Sennett, Griffith's apprentice director at Biograph. Sennett owed the two a hundred dollars from losing a bet on a horse from the time when they were still bookmakers. Kessel and Bauman were pretty tough customers who handled their own collections. When they appeared at Sennett's diggings, he confessed he was broke and made a hasty counterproposal. Since they were now in the film business, why not finance him in organizing a comedy company? To Sennett's amazement, they accepted his suggestion and signed him up. His comedies were profitable. So were the Ince Westerns.

Laemmle desperately needed talent for IMP. He wanted the Kessel and Bauman assets and turned a willing ear to Bauman's conniving. No sooner was the deal closed than the Laemmle forces shouted "breach of contract" faster than the Bauman and Kessel forces could. Laemmle's men invaded the Kessel and Bauman facilities, interrupting production. The former book-makers retaliated by raiding the IMP holdings. Ince was nettled by this course of events and strapped on a six-shooter to prevent Laemmle agents from raising havoc at Inceville. He even went so far as to position a prop Civil War cannon at the mouth of the Santa Ynez canyon loaded with scrap iron as a warning to potential Laemmle intruders.

Grace Cunard prompted Ford to make his move. He got word to Laemmle that he—and not Ince—was responsible for the success of the Bison West-erns. An agreement was eventually struck between the warring factions. Laemmle got $17,000 in damages, the exclusive right to use the "Bison 101" trademark, and the services of Francis Ford as actor-director. Grace Cunard went with Ford. Laemmle had a Western unit at last and went about acquiring a California studio location. He settled on purchase of the Nestor Company at the intersection of Sunset and Gower in Hollywood.

Kessel and Bauman, reeling as if from a torrential whirlwind, searched blindly for a new alliance by means of which to recover. They still had Ince and Sennett. And Ince, with the loss of Ford, was busy himself lining up new talent. He was determined to branch out into pictures other than West-erns. It was against this background that *The Invaders* emerged, a beautiful, sensitive film from the height of Ince's collaboration with Francis Ford.

The screenplay for *The Invaders* was written by Richard V. Spencer, with Francis Ford directing and starring. *The Moving Picture World* made reference to an earlier Ford-Ince film when it commented on *Invaders* that Ford gave "a magnificent characterization not unlike that of General Custer." And as in the case of *Custer's Last Fight, The Invaders* was a three-reeler.

Ann Little in red face paint portrayed the Indian maiden, Sky Star. It was during production of *The Invaders* in autumn 1912 that William S. Hart paid his first visit to Inceville. He was touring California in the stage drama *The Trail of the Lonesome Pine*. Ince was apparently pleased to see him and took Hart on the back lot where Ford was shooting the scene of Ann's efforts to warn the post. She was astride the beautiful pinto which she rides in the film. Hart was impressed at her ability to ride bareback over the scrub brush of the Inceville hills. She reined in and, at Ince's signal, rode over to greet the visitor. The pinto reared up, a hoof knocking off Hart's cap. It was Hart's first meeting with the horse he would later make world-famous as Fritz.

Hart spoke earnestly with Ince of his determination to make Westerns himself. Hart had been cast as Cash Hawkins in *The Squaw Man* on stage and had had Westerner roles in the road company productions of *The Virginian* and now *The Trail of the Lonesome Pine.* I will have more to say about Hart's association with *The Virginian* in a later chapter. Ince, learning that Hart would be on tour in *Pine* for nearly two years yet, casually agreed to give the matter of William S. Hart Westerns serious consideration. As indebted as he was to Hart for some of his basic story orientations, including the importation of his tribe of genuine Sioux Indians, he wasn't sold on the forty-two-year-old thespian as a potential motion picture property.

Art Acord also appeared in the film in a small role as a telegrapher. He was born Artemus Ward Acord on April 17, 1890, at Glenwood, Sevier County, Utah, of Mormon parents. Acord grew up at Stillwater, Oklahoma, punched cattle, and became an excellent rider. In 1908 he joined the Dick Stanley-Bud Atkinson Wild West Show, where he was to meet Hoot Gibson when the Hooter later joined the outfit. Wintering in California in 1910, both Gibson and Acord were signed as stunt men by D. W. Griffith, who was making a Western titled *Two Brothers* (Biograph, 1910) at San Juan Capistrano. When Henry B. Walthall, who was in the picture, dropped his hat in the road, Acord rode into the scene, entirely ignorant of Billy Bitzer's grinding camera, swooped down, and retrieved the hat. Griffith paid Acord three dollars for the stunt. Later that day he had Acord take a fall from his horse onto an asphalt road and in one sequence had Acord rear his horse until it fell back upon him.

Acord managed to appear as a stunt man in a few Selig films being photographed in California. Within the first two years of that second decade of the century, Tom Mix, Hoot Gibson, and Art Acord kept crossing each other's paths, working for the Stanley-Atkinson Show, visiting at the 101 Ranch, or working for Colonel Selig. In 1912, after seeing Art Acord perform with the Stanley-Atkinson Show in New Jersey, Adam Kessel, who loved horses, hired him and shipped him out to Inceville. Acord had a letter from the general manager of the Selig Polyscope Company which concluded, somewhat eloquently, "There is no greater rider in the country than Art Acord, champion of the world." Acord showed it to Kessel and again to Ince. Ince responded by assigning most of the Indian falls during battle episodes in *The Invaders* to Acord and had him double Ann Little.

The basic plot of *The Invaders* is a simple one. The Indians sign a treaty with Francis Ford. Ethel Grandin is Ford's daughter. A group of surveyors arrive and violate the terms of the treaty. Sky Star, Chief Eagleshirt's daughter, falls in love with one of them. When Ford refuses to listen to the Indians' complaints, there is an uprising. The surveyors are massacred.

Sky Star makes it to the fort but dies. Ethel begs Ford to shoot her with his last bullet as the Indian storm continues. He is about to do it when reinforcements arrive. Ford pays his last respects to Sky Star.

Francis Ford revealed himself a splendid performer with a natural style of acting that contrasted strikingly to the highly melodramatic approach of William S. Hart two years later. If all or even many of Ince's early Westerns were of the quality of *The Invaders*—and, sadly, they are not known to survive—Jean Cocteau and the other French critics are warranted in their praise of Ince and his accomplishments. *The Invaders,* at the time of its theatrical release through the Mutual exchanges, substituted a KayBee brand name for the Bison trademark. Francis Ford, of course, had already departed for IMP, which was presently to change its name.

I have implied that Ince, in manufacturing these films, employed the studio system, as it was eventually termed. The system may not have been his creation entirely and may, in fact, owe its origin to Pop Rock and J. Stuart Blackton at Vitagraph, who set up a stable of producer-directors and writers prior to 1910. But Ince utilized the system more effectively than his contemporaries, judging by what we have left of the product of that era of the teens. Obviously impressed by Ince's fantastic results, in the picture business where everyone prefers never to be first, the new methodology was hurriedly imitated.

Because we came upon him initially in a cheap hotel room in Manhattan, the reader may be interested in Bill Hart's early life, especially at this juncture when he is about to burst upon the world as a Western hero. He was born on December 6, 1862, at Newburgh, New York. His father, Nicholas Hart, was an itinerant miller and traveled across the country in search of new water sites. The family finally settled in the Dakota Territory, near the Sioux Reservation. A smaller brother died there and was buried near the headwaters of the Mississippi. By the time Hart was fifteen, his mother was in ill health and the family moved back East, where Nicholas became janitor of an apartment house. Hart took an interest in athletics and in singing in the choir at Trinity Church. At nineteen, Bill set a world's record in London for the three-and-one-half-mile walk. While working as postal clerk in New York City's main post office, Hart studied acting, principally under F. F. Markey, an illustrious actor and teacher of the day. "The stage idea just came," he said later, "and always remained, and will be with me when the final curtain is rung down." Hart's first role on the legitimate stage was in *Romeo and Juliet,* which opened in the town of his birth, Newburgh.

For the next twenty years, Hart earned his living as an actor. He had some success and won critical acclaim in the role of Messala in the original *Ben-Hur* company. Hart records in his autobiography, *My Life East and West,* that he saw his first Western in Cleveland and became obsessed with the notion of making Westerns himself. It was this burning passion which prompted his visit to Inceville. When Ince offered him an opportunity to appear in Westerns of his own design after his first visit, Hart was overjoyed with the prospect and vowed to return.

As I have implied, Ince wasn't serious. He was in the flush of new success with his Westerns. By the time Hart did return, the market was glutted with outdoor dramas, and Ince was intent on making different types of pictures. Shortly after his arrival, Ince persuaded Hart to take the role of a heavy in a two-reeler, *His Hour of Manhood* (Mutual, 1914), starring and directed by Tom Chatterton, with Clara Williams as the heroine. Hart was next put into *Jim Cameron's Wife* (Mutual, 1914), a drama with the same principals. Disillusioned and hurt, Hart was too emotional to confront Ince, so he wrote him a letter instead, despite the fact that he was working within a stone's throw of Ince's office. The letter outlined how Ince had promised Hart the chance to make Westerns and how he had come West expressly to achieve that dream. Ince was either touched or disgusted. He sought Hart out and explained to him that Westerns were not doing it at the box office. Hart protested. He claimed that the way he would make Westerns would be entirely different from the solid action format they had universally at that time. He wanted to introduce strong plot ingredients and genuine acting into them.

Ince listened. He responded that he really couldn't afford to waste money on a Western, but he did have a script from an old two-reeler he had done some years before and if Hart could expand it into a suitable story line for a feature, Ince might consider backing the idea. Hart went to work immediately. He came up with a plot that, when he saw it, was praised by scenarist C. Gardner Sullivan. Ince agreed to make the picture and assigned Reginald Barker to direct. It was entitled *On the Night Stage,* with Hart billed third.

Much has been said about William S. Hart's contribution to the Western. In terms of long-range influence, Hart's effect was negligible. He used one of the Miller Brothers' horses in *On the Night Stage,* called Midnight. He gave the horse billing. The same held true for Hart's next Western feature, *The Bargain* (Mutual, 1914), which also credited Midnight. The Millers refused to sell the animal to Hart, and so, henceforth, he used Fritz, purchasing him from the New York Motion Picture Company. This was an innovation. Hart asserted that he wanted to make realistic Westerns, and for many years this was generally believed. However, a great many of his films do survive, and whatever else they may be, they are not any more realistic in terms of dress or setting than Broncho Billy's pictures or Tom Mix's shorts for the Selig Polyscope Company. Where they differ is in their plots. You find the same crudity of attire, dilapidated towns and ranch buildings, dusty streets, and rough interiors in the majority of Westerns from the teens, but seldom will you find elsewhere such keenly romantic, sentimental, melodramatic, occasionally ridiculous plots as are to be found in Hart's Westerns. This was the chief source of their novelty. Action is perpetually secondary to these overstated, fragrant, and idealistic story lines. You do not doubt for a moment the knightly sincerity with which Hart undergoes his religious conversions or emotes in the throes of a throbbing self-recrimination. Not until his last film, *Tumbleweeds* (United Artists, 1925), did Hart alleviate this heavy emotional atmosphere with less oppressive moments of bright comedy. He was entranced by his theological vision of the West and its heroes—gripped by the same frantic thralldom in which Clarence E. Mulford in his home in Fryeburg, Maine, conjured a solitary meal on the prairie or a noisy cattle town or tinkered with the small pieces of wood from his facsimile of the Alamo. History and romance were inseparable, even beautiful, to them, as they sometimes are for essentially lonely people.

Hart got Ince's permission to venture to the Grand Canyon for a few scenes. When *On the Night Stage* was completed, Ince immediately put Hart into another story which C. Gardner Sullivan had just written, called *The Bargain*. Both of these pictures dealt with religious conversions. Hart, of course, was the subject in whom good and evil were at odds. *The Motion Picture News* reviewed *On the Night Stage,* and their critic, Clifford H. Pangburn, commented: "The credit for this must go to many persons who had to do with building the picture, but a large part of it is due to William S. Hart for his nearly perfect acting as Texas. The role of this big-hearted 'road agent' is one of unusual difficulty, but Mr. Hart plays it with naturalness which causes the spectator to forget that he is not watching actual events."

In *On the Night Stage* Hart is a stage robber. He is in love with Belle, a saloon girl. Belle is converted by a parson and she marries him. Hart is so impressed by this that he decides to reform. On a visit to see a friend who is a dance hall queen, Belle is kissed by Handsome Jack and experiences "REVULSION!" Jack tries to pursue the matter, but Hart puts a stop to it. At the fade, the parson and Belle are embracing, and Hart is fondling Midnight, his horse.

Ince wasn't overwhelmed by either *On the Night Stage* or *The Bargain*. He held up release of *On the Night Stage* and sold *The Bargain* to Famous Players. He and Bill Hart parted company, the summer production schedule completed. Hart was pleased to have had his chance. By a fluke, *The Bargain* spurred a positive box-office response. Ince was urged to sign Hart. He contacted him and requested he return to Inceville. He offered Hart a contract at $125 a week to produce, write, and assist in the direction of Westerns for immediate distribution. Hart brought his sister, Mary, with him. The two had always been very close, and he wanted her with him, now that he was convinced that he was in pictures to stay.

The Passing of Two Gun Hicks (Mutual, 1914), a two-reeler, was the first picture Hart starred in under his new agreement. Five months passed and eight two-reelers were made and released before Ince issued *On the Night Stage*. The William S. Hart formula became established. Hart was generally a good bad man who was civilized from his rough ways and converted from godlessness by the office of an innocent, sweet, pure, and generous woman. There is nothing truly Western about this plot. Yet it predominates nearly all of Hart's films. Guns, horses, action of any kind, are a backdrop for this melodrama. Passages from the Bible are frequently quoted, and the story of the film is but a sermon upon them. Possibly the most viable explanation for Hart's popularity in the decade of the teens wasn't the fact that he made Westerns so much as that he invariably located the source of sin in the saloon and dance hall. This matched the popular sentiment of those naïve religionists who were gaining adherents in ever greater numbers in their crusade to make the manufacture and sale of alcohol in the United States a federal crime. Hart was certainly in the vanguard of the movement with films like *Hell's Hinges* (Triangle, 1916), in which the minister is seduced by a dance hall queen and Hart, avenging a woman's honor, burns down all the saloons and dance halls, turning the town into a blazing inferno of outraged retribution.

Ince was cynical about the entire affair, as well he might be. Hart's pictures consistently made money. As Westerns, they were at best anomalies, just as William S. Hart, as a Western player, was a bit of a curiosity. But the money permitted Ince to invest in other motion picture projects more to his personal liking. He kept Hart at his flat salary, but gave him the autonomy he demanded. It was a bizarre exchange, Ince giving Hart his freedom to make the same Western over and over and Hart working his heart out for virtually nothing while the pictures grossed a fortune.

In the spring of 1915, after Hart had made over twenty Westerns, two-reelers and features, the New York Motion Picture Company and Thomas Ince switched into Harry Aitken's growing combine, Triangle Film Corporation doing the releasing. I will have more to say about Aitken in the next cinematograph, but I introduce him into the present narrative because I once had occasion to ask his brother, Roy, who was his business partner, about the kind of man William S. Hart was. The Aitkens got to know Hart rather well while Ince and Hart worked for them.

"What do you remember of him?" I inquired of Roy.

"Bill Hart was an honest man," he responded. "Ince had him under a personal contract. Later on in the game, when Ince was offered a great deal of money to leave Triangle and join Famous Players, we tried to stop the deal from going through. We knew that Zukor wanted Hart because Hart's Westerns made money. Harry and I approached Hart and told him what Zukor and Ince were planning.

" 'You're still only making a hundred twenty-five dollars a week,' Harry told Bill, 'after all this time with Tom Ince. We'll pay you ten thousand a week if you'll break your contract with him and stay with Triangle. What do you say?'

" 'I can't break my contract,' Bill told Harry.

" 'But you can,' Harry said. 'I've read it over and it can be broken.'

" 'Maybe the contract can be broken,' Hart said. 'That's just paper. But I gave Tom Ince my word. And *that* can never be broken.' "

4 / D. W. GRIFFITH AND THE WESTERN

I have already told the reader how D. W. Griffith entered motion pictures via the Edison Company. Edwin S. Porter wasn't so much the fool as not to have recognized Griffith's *La Tosca* as a résumé of Puccini's opera based on Sardou's story. But Porter thought Griffith had the aristocratic mien to make a fine screen actor. Griffith considered himself primarily a playwright, or at the very least a writer. When Porter persisted in wanting him to act, D.W. decided to look elsewhere.

The American Mutascope Company had been founded in 1895, an outgrowth of a friendship between an Edison assistant, William L. Dickson, and Henry M. Marvin, a partner in a machinery firm. Mutascope invented its own camera. When it began film production, the word "Biograph" was added to its name. Finally, in 1909, the American Mutascope and Biograph Company dropped everything except the Biograph.

Abner McKinley, a brother of the presidential candidate, and the New York Security and Trust Company were among Biograph's chief financial backers. Soon the Empire Trust Company joined them as an investor. Serious monetary difficulties in 1908 led to Jeremiah J. Kennedy from Empire being assigned to protect Biograph's outstanding loan of $200,000. He was to examine the books and, if necessary, dissolve the corporation. Kennedy chose instead to become president, retaining Henry Marvin as vice-president.

Kennedy may not have been the first banker involved in the new industry, but the kind of influence he exerted has outlasted any creative or technical contribution over the ensuing years. He was a clever negotiator.

D. W. Griffith during the early twenties.

He prevented the Edison Company from establishing a monopoly only to emerge himself, after a series of discussions, the monopolistic head of the Motion Picture Patents Company, which included Edison. The Trust had an objective beyond curtailment of competition. It wanted to preserve indefinitely the one- and two-reel motion picture production format. A banker's instinct felt anything longer a dangerous risk and, therefore, bad business.

Biograph didn't really have a director in 1908. The cameraman and the actors made the films. A few years previously Marvin had engaged a former stage director of no consequence, George McCutcheon, who tried in producing films to imitate Porter's example of showing a single event without characterization. Even though Kennedy and Marvin were both officers of the Trust, their company still couldn't make successful pictures. McCutcheon had fallen ill with acute mastoiditis and so pushed his son Wallace into his job. But Wallace would direct no more than one picture a week, and the company wanted two or three. There were two cameramen, Arthur Marvin, Henry's brother, and Gottlieb Wilhelm "Billy" Bitzer. Neither wanted to direct. They felt themselves superior to the director, who merely moved actors around in front of the camera.

Griffith took his only published poem—it would be to D.W.'s credit *not* to reproduce it here—and presented himself at Biograph. After Wallace McCutcheon took him on a tour of the studio housed in an old brownstone mansion on Fourteenth Street, Griffith was asked to write some stories for the screen. Poverty further prompted him to avail both himself and his wife, Linda Arvidson, as performers. They appeared in films based on D.W.'s scripts. Lee Dougherty, an ex-newspaperman writing Biograph publicity and generally managing the studio, tried Griffith at directing. He proved satisfactory. Before long, D.W. became *the* director at Biograph.

The reader may recall that when Thomas Ince showed up at IMP in 1910, he got his first acting part from Harry Salter. Griffith introduced Salter to the business in the second film he directed for Biograph, an ambitious little outdoor drama shot in New Jersey and titled *The Redman and the Child* (Biograph, 1908). It was Griffith's first Western.

In the years that immediately followed, Griffith developed what. was a truly extraordinary talent for direction, and his reputation became firmly established. His way of working was invariably to begin with an idea, never a script. The idea would solidify by stages through rehearsals and production. Frequently a notion that caught Griffith's fancy would be used as the basis for a particular picture and then, unhappy with the results, he would employ it again, further perfecting it, producing a second, third, or fourth film. Griffith never really abandoned this methodology. When in 1940 Hal Roach, Sr., hired him to direct a comeback picture, a silent epic *One Million B.C.*, D.W. commenced production with an earthquake scene. He was drinking heavily. He had his principals stand on the set and sway as if the ground beneath them were shaking in a tremor. Prop men were supposed to drop phony apples and *papier-mâché* rocks into the actors' midst. For a week they swayed. The apples weren't falling right. Rocks bonked heads. The actors were swaying synchronously or awkwardly or were jiggling instead of swaying. Roach, angered at these rushes day after day, went down to the set to see what was going on. Griffith was inebriated. And naturally the actors were swaying. Roach exploded, and Griffith ordered him off the set. Roach had no alternative. D.W. was fired. Time had passed him by.

D. W. Griffith began making filming sojourns to California in 1910. Griffith felt that both verisimilitude and ready competition demanded that Biograph do no less than film its Westerns and other outdoor dramas on location. The Biograph troupe arrived in San Juan Capistrano to make *Two Brothers* during a heavy rainstorm. I have already told the reader how Art Acord made his debut in this picture. Hoot Gibson was tagging along with Art at the time and was also put on to handle stock. The troupe checked into the hotel and waited. It rained for three days and three nights. Billy Bitzer was by this time D.W.'s trusted cameraman. As Griffith paced back and forth in the lobby, he would periodically ask Bitzer for a weather report. On the third day, the restless company watched from hotel windows as an Indian funeral procession wound its way through the rain to the semi-ruined mission where services were being held.

The next day the sun was shining. Griffith rushed his troupe into the street and started shooting the first scene. An idea had occurred to him! The film was now to open with a religious parade, several actors marching in borrowed ecclesiastical outfits. Groups of sullen and grumbling townsfolk congregated around the rehearsal. Griffith realized suddenly that they thought the actors were mocking the proceedings from the day before. When the procession neared the mission, the belligerent crowd rushed them. Griffith and his crew sought the security of the hotel. Persuading the Spanish-speaking hotel manager to go out onto the balcony to quiet the crowd, D.W. was able to explain what he was doing. The crowd insisted that some of the cowboys should provide them an entertainment. An unruly bronc was brought forth for one of the stunt men to ride. Art Acord volunteered and quickly broke the animal. Then together with the Hooter, he put on an exhibition of rodeo tricks. When D.W. resumed shooting, several members of the crowd agreed to join in the procession.

There has been some dispute about Griffith's attitude toward the Indians. I don't believe he had an attitude. D.W. was a southern gentleman. His notion of womanhood was one of old-fashioned chivalry. But he did possess that Victorian split between good women who must be worshiped and those creatures of pleasure with whom a man ruts. It has become fashionable now to mildly deplore the one and entirely ignore the other. Lillian Gish is the personification of sainted motherhood, seraphically rocking a cradle in *Intolerance* (Triangle, 1916). Yet D.W. was also not above, at the recommendation of his backers, filming some rather graphic orgy scenes in a real bordello to heighten spectator interest. It wasn't much different with American Indians or blacks. The good ones were incredibly so; the bad ones were heinous beyond description. In view of Griffith's films during the Great War, I would also put the Germans into this category. Given a sentimental story line in a Western like *Ramona,* based on the Helen Hunt Jackson novel and next to the last film of the 1910 California expedition, with Mary Pickford playing the Indian maiden, Griffith went all out to generate sympathy for the Indian. In other films, and certainly *Fighting Blood* (Biograph, 1911) was one of them, the Indians were no more than convenient and faceless villains pressed into service to intensify suspense in a wholly melodramatic plot.

In connection with G. M. Anderson, I mentioned that upon leaving Vitagraph he went briefly to work in production for the Pittsburgh exhibitors Harry Davis and John P. Harris. In 1911 Paul Panzer, who would become famous as the villain in the chapter play *The Perils of Pauline* (Pathé, 1914), with Pearl White, directed an interesting three-reeler for Davis and Harris called *The Life of Buffalo Bill.* It featured the real William Cody and proved popular with exhibitors. The same year, Griffith directed *Enoch Arden* for Biograph, the first two-reeler to be released by any member of the Motion Picture Patents Company. A trend was beginning for longer films which Griffith welcomed enthusiastically. Biograph and other Trust companies did not.

There has been some controversy about whether Lionel Barrymore appeared in D.W.'s *Fighting Blood,* filmed during Griffith's second excursion to California. I have seen the film forty times and I cannot tell you. But far more significant than Barrymore's presence (he had joined Griffith that year) is the plot of the one-reeler. A Civil War veteran and his family settle in the Dakota Territory. Bobby Harron quarrels with his father and leaves home. Riding in the hills, he espies a band of Sioux attacking a homestead. Harron races to his fiancée's farm and warns her family. He takes her to his father's cabin where several settlers congregate. The Indians attack en masse, Griffith positioning his camera on a hill high above the action. If newspapers remarked in 1903 at the gun smoke shown on the screen in *The Great Train Robbery,* Griffith certainly did Porter one better here. It billows and rages like an inferno during the battle. Harron, pursued by whooping savages, rides to bring the cavalry. The Indians set the cabin burning. The children are terrified. The cavalry arrives and disperses the marauders.

Thomas Ince personally liked good stories. His films from the outset tended to have substantial plots. Griffith was more flamboyant. He relied on editing techniques to heighten the effectiveness of his films. This is evident as early as *Fighting Blood.* D.W. is constantly cutting back and forth from the interior of the building to Bobby Harron's ride for the cavalry and, once Harron reaches them, their rapid approach. One setup along a curving road permitted Griffith to scope the cavalry riding in and out of the frame in the distance only to appear suddenly in the foreground. The shot gave the illusion of a great number of riders as it built suspense.

D.W. was impressed with the besieged cabin situation. It not only served as the center of the action in the second reel of *The Battle at Elderbush Gulch* but became the grand climax of *The Birth of a Nation* (Epoch, 1915). Bobby Harron's mad ride was perfected in the exciting close of *America* (Griffith, 1924), where Paul Revere raised a similar alarm. Griffith's custom of elaborate rehearsals did as much to articulate his basic dramatic and cinematic strategies as did his remakes.

Fighting Blood was released on June 29, 1911. A month later, Biograph issued another Griffith Western, *The Last Drop of Water.* It advanced the crosscutting techniques already apparent in *Blood.* I suppose he learned the power of parallel action from Charles Dickens, whose *The Old Curiosity Shop* is an embodiment of it in purest form. *The Last Drop of Water* was the most ambitious film Griffith conceived that year in California. It was also the last picture in which Linda Arvidson was to appear that her husband directed. Their relations had been deteriorating for some time. Linda claimed he was paying more attention to other girls in the troupe than her. It was probably true. But D.W. wasn't a man to fight tenaciously for anything other than his artistic vision. The two separated when they reached New York. Rather than risk a public scandal or attempt to justify himself, D.W. abruptly turned his back on her, but not without promising Linda large support payments and signing a "confession" of his infidelity. This was the only grounds for divorce in New York and so may have little significance. However emotional Linda might have become, she knew what a slave D.W. was to his exaggerated sense of fair play and used it to her advantage.

Linda published a book in 1925 titled *When the Movies Were Young.* Aside from capitalizing on her marriage to D.W. and committing count-less errors of recall, she did provide a description of the making of *Last Drop.* "We set up camp," she wrote, "in the San Fernando desert—two huge tents, one for mess, with cooks and assistants who served chow to the cowboys and extra men. Two rows of tables, planks set on wooden horses, ran the length of the tent—there must have been at least 50 cowboys and riders to be fed hearty meals three times a day. The other tent contained trunks and wardrobe baskets, and here the boys slept and made up."

D.W. collected eight prairie schooners for the picture plus an assemblage of chickens, dogs, horses, and a lone cow to make the wagon train look realistic. Nearly the whole company joined with the uncommon number of extras playing Indians and soldiers, while Blanche Sweet, Charles West, Bobby Harron, Dell Henderson, and Joseph Graybill were among the principals. The plot was elementary. Sweet is in love with Graybill who has a weakness for the bottle. This was Griffith's private joke on the Mary Pickford/Owen Moore alliance. Graybill and Blanche are wed while Charles West, a jilted suitor, stands gallantly aside. West is still a hanger-on a year later when the couple joins a wagon train. En route, the Indians attack. The pioneers are low on water. West goes off to find a water hole. When he doesn't return, Graybill sets out after him. Graybill discovers West dying of thirst. He jeers. Then, overcome by compassion (as Griffith's characters occasionally are—his closest link with Dickens), Graybill gives West the last of his water and succumbs himself. Revived, West can now reach the water hole. He makes it back with water while the cavalry drives off the Indians. A shallow grave is dug for Graybill, positioned in the foreground as the wagon train disappears over the horizon. Henry MacRae found this sentimental touch so appealing that he varied it himself in *The Indians Are Coming* (Universal, 1930).

In July 1911 Griffith went again to Cuddebackville, New York, where he had filmed a number of outdoor dramas. This was the last time. His awe of the spectacular had been whetted by the California landscape in a way the East could not duplicate. Griffith made *The Squaw's Love* on location. It featured a lusty brawl between two Indian maidens portrayed by Mabel Normand and Dorothy West. D.W. wanted Mabel to execute a backward dive into the Neversink River. She agreed. She was willing to do anything once. But *once* was all in this instance. To assure getting the shot, Griffith innovated the simultaneous use of three cameras, something that had not been tried before.

In the years between Griffith's appearance in *Rescued from an Eagle's Nest* and the release of *The Squaw's Love,* the motion picture industry had changed to a staggering degree. That peculiar state of corporate existence which became a way of life during the Depression when Wall Street took over total control of many film companies until today when a production firm can be technically insolvent as an operative principle had its beginning in the teens. For good or ill, Harry Aitken, of Waukesha, Wisconsin, was instrumental in introducing this concept to the business, and D.W., fired by his incredible dreams, did his share to necessitate it.

The film business exerted a fatal charm on Jewish merchants and lawyers. But this group was scarcely synonymous with their investors. The law of the garment industry is fashion. Motion pictures in their production and publicity retained a nearly frantic forward look, always something new, something better. The public came to accept this as natural, financiers less so. The legal philosophy film companies devised in the early teens came chiefly from real estate, where ownership is continual. Quit claims, leases, short-term rentals, and the whole of theatrical contract law for stage players were ingested and promulgated into a surprisingly coherent system. Carl Laemmle stood beaming behind the ticket taker at his nickelodeon on Milwaukee Street and shook his head in amazement as people paid their money and took nothing with them save the experience. The reader will find this a commonplace experience among early founders of production companies.

The United States of America ignored these legal developments and classified the products of manufacture as imaginative in both senses of the word and, therefore, subjected them to the irrational dictates of copyright law, which invention of the printing press had inspired. What copyright law stipulates is that creative works differ from real estate or other personal possessions in that, after a certain specified period of time, the public seizes ownership. Such a position further reinforced the desire to recoup one's investment in a film as soon as possible; long-term gains were not a consideration.

Thomas A. Edison brought an action in the U. S. District Court against Abraham G. Levi, a motion picture manufacturer, seeking to recover damages and prevent the latter from persisting in the duplication, sale, and lease of prints of *The Great Train Robbery*. Edison prevailed. Yet, when Sigmund Lubin remade the film using almost identical sets and the same action as in Porter's original, the argument of unfair competition fell apart. Lubin's film was judged a new physical entity despite its flagrant imitation. The pirating of prints and their duplication for purposes of exhibition under unauthorized circumstances led to an inevitable revision in the existing exchange and distribution system.

The mounting desire for greater control caused certain producing companies to purchase their own exchange networks throughout key cities, staffed with their own sales personnel directly alongside independent exchanges distributing states' rights properties. Others such as Carl Laemmle started in distribution and then, already owning an exchange network, branched out into production. Harry Aitken came to the film business through a series of exchanges which he acquired, beginning in 1905. By 1913 Aitken was the second-largest film buyer in the United States, leasing product and then renting it to exhibitors through his exchanges.

Harry and his brother, Roy, had been Wisconsin farmers. Roy was cautious, protective, sentimental, with a flair for women. Harry was a master builder of airy castles. When the Trust insisted Harry sell his exchanges to them for a pittance, he sought to organize the independents. The Motion Picture Patents Company canceled his purchase agreements.

Harry went to New York. Jules Brulator was the only outlet for non-

Trust product, and Harry worked out his deal with him. It was also while in New York that Harry made his discovery of floating credit. With his exchanges and his exhibitors' sales contracts as collateral, he raised the money to buy the Harsten film exchange on Fourteenth Street from Harsten and his principal investors, Mark Dintenfass and Pat Powers. Harry became acquainted with Tom Cochrane at IMP. With Cochrane's assistance, Harry persuaded Mary Pickford, who had left Biograph to work for David Belasco on stage, to come to work for him. Aitken also contracted Owen Moore. He set up a production firm called Majestic Films. Kessel and Bauman were delighted to meet Harry after their tryst with Laemmle. They sold Aitken their own film exchanges and their production facilities at Reliance studios on Twenty-first Street. Harry integrated his expanded exchange system and called it Mutual. Kessel and Bauman signed exclusive distribution agreements with him for Ince and Sennet product; Harry made them directors on Mutual's board.

Laemmle was somewhat disturbed by this turn of events. He persuaded Jules Brulator to abrogate the agreement with Aitken. Harry responded by starting still another company designed to sell product for a number of small independents.

In the meantime, D. W. Griffith was growing dissatisfied at Biograph. He wanted to make multiple-reel pictures. Biograph didn't. When Kennedy had come to the nearly bankrupt firm in 1908, he was displeased with Biograph's sales volume. Usually up to twenty prints were being sold on each title at the rate of twelve to fourteen cents per foot. In terms of two or three one-reelers a week this didn't allow gross revenues to exceed $5,600 to $8,400. Griffith's popular films accelerated and restored Biograph's solvency. But by 1912 Griffith was weary and frustrated. "The time has come," Kennedy told D.W., "for the production of big fifty-thousand-dollar pictures. You are the man to make them. But Biograph is not ready to go into that line of production. If you stay with Biograph, it will be to make the same kind of short pictures that you have in the past. You will not do that. You've got the hundred-thousand-dollar idea in the back of your head." Through the early part of 1913 Griffith continued to turn out "sausages," as he termed them. Then on September 29, 1913, D.W. announced his separation from Biograph. Among the films Griffith left behind were two of his finest Biograph productions, the two-reel Western *The Battle at Elderbush Gulch* and *Judith of Bethulia,* a four-reeler brought in for $36,000.

At this climactic moment, Adolph Zukor stepped in with his $50,000 proposition. Griffith chose instead to go with Harry Aitken for $300 a week and four hundred shares of Majestic Film Company stock valued at $100 a share. Aitken had offered Griffith what he really wanted—a chance to make two specials a year in addition to directing and supervising the general complement of programmers. Aitken founded another company to handle the Griffith pictures, Fine Arts Productions. Griffith took most of his Biograph troupe with him, including Billy Bitzer, Lillian Gish, Bobby Harron, Henry B. Walthall, and the writer Stanner E. V. Taylor. Griffith commenced production with a potboiler intended to bring in quick money. *The Battle of the Sexes* was shot on a $5,000 budget (Aitken actually expected D.W. to keep within this allowance). Griffith tore through the five reels of *Sexes* in four days, sending Lillian Gish home for a few hours' rest when her eyes were too bloodshot to be photographed. During production, Aitken brought Wall Street financier Crawford Livingston and National Surety's Felix Kahn for a visit. They agreed to invest and were given directorships right beside Kessel and Bauman. Aitken next contracted to finance Ince and Sennett pictures as well as distribute them. Former Milwaukee real estate speculator and now exchange owner, John Freuler, who was making erotic films, also joined Mutual's board. Aitken floated more loans and prepared for further expansion, purchasing the Kinemacolor studio on Sunset Boulevard to house Griffith's production facilities. Aitken then signed loan agreements with the Corn Exchange Bank, the Central Union Trust Company, and the Title Guarantee and Trust, which supplied him with the ready cash necessary to send $20,000 a week each to Griffith, Ince, and Sennett to sponsor new production.

All of this alignment with wealthy bankers and gobbling up of talent, exchanges, studios, and production personnel sent Carl Laemmle into a fit. Aitken decided magnanimously to bury the hatchet and called a peace conference in the bridal suite of the Waldorf Hotel where he welcomed Laemmle and offered him a never-to-be-repeated opportunity to merge IMP into the Aitken conglomerate. Laemmle would have none of it and stalked out. Although still embroiled in his war with the Trust, he came to regard Aitken's enterprises as no less a threat. Laemmle countered by summoning exchange men like Pat Powers and Mark Dintenfass to join in a "stop Aitken" campaign by merging with IMP. At a meeting with the expanded board, it was suggested to Laemmle that he needed a more appropriate name for the enlarged firm. Seeing a Universal Pipe Fittings, Inc., truck in the street below, Laemmle turned to his directors and announced, "Gentlemen, I have it. Universal!" It was a fitting moniker for a company that, as long as Laemmle owned it, strove to be all things to all people. The struggle was on.

Griffith brought South Carolina minister Thomas Dixon, author of the novel *The Clansman,* from which a stage adaptation had been made, to New York to see Harry and Roy Aitken. D.W. wanted to use the story as the basis for his first special. It would require twelve reels to complete it and would cost an estimated $40,000. Dixon wanted $25,000 for the film rights, a far cry from the $100 and $200 fees standard in the industry.

When the time came, the Aitkens characteristically didn't have any money, so Dixon was placed on a percentage instead.

Meanwhile Biograph had just released *The Battle at Elderbush Gulch* in the United States. It proved a popular success while, ironically, marking the advent of Biograph's decline. The firm had lost its essential asset, D. W. Griffith. *Gulch* was the consummation of all D.W.'s efforts at filming a Western and remains his finest achievement in the genre.

In issuing *Gulch* domestically, Biograph changed its mind about using credits before the beginning of the picture. Mae Marsh comes with her sister to live with her uncles in a blockhouse. Lillian Gish and Bobby Harron are married and have a small baby. They come into town in a stagecoach. The district is attacked by Indians. Lillian hides in the block-house. It is stormed by wild Indians. A Mexican is sent for the troops. He returns with them just in time. Mae is saved. Lillian and Bobby are re-united with the baby.

Gulch is an exciting and vivid Western. Griffith builds suspense and maintains it to the end. D.W. declared it his third best picture at the time of the release of *The Birth of a Nation*. I find no reason to disagree with him.

Harry Aitken felt impelled to court Griffith. I think he recognized long before Biograph did that Griffith's loss was their finish. To keep Griffith happy, Harry would have to risk everything on this *Clansman* venture. D.W. impressed most people as being aloof, cold, and inflexible. The women who loved him felt otherwise. Linda Arvidson considered D.W. a superman as an artist, although personally she thought herself his better. Lillian Gish in her memoir *The Movies, Mr. Griffith and Me* (Prentice-Hall, 1969) reveals that she never lost her awe of him. She was convinced that life and the industry treated him badly. Roy Aitken, who used to drive around New York with Griffith in quest of girls to pick up, couldn't help but look upon D.W. as innately fun-loving.

For certain, Griffith was a romantic. He was capable of total, frantic dedication in the decade of the teens to a point where his inspiration carried everything before it. Harry Aitken borrowed $40,000 and instructed Griffith to begin *The Clansman*. The film swelled beneath Griffith's fixation. He asked for more money. Aitken mortgaged what he had left and sent an additional $19,000 to D.W. in California. Harry was caught in a bind. He'd had to form a syndicate to raise such extraordinary funds in which he acted as a guarantor. When the film was completed, he would pay the investors a percentage. If the film didn't gross, he would have to return their money with interest. Aitken hired Johannes Charlemagne Epping, better known as "Little" Epping, from Biograph, where he had been auditor on Griffith's productions and dispatched him to the West Coast to exercise the same function on *The Clansman*. Epping himself paid no attention to Aitken's schemes of empire or Griffith's dreams of grandeur. He invested his money abroad and, finally, in the mid 1920s retired to Switzerland.

Fifty-nine thousand dollars wasn't enough. Griffith began raising money himself and selling shares in the picture, with D.W. the guarantor. When the price of a hundred prints was added to all expenditures, the title altered to *The Birth of a Nation*, the picture came to a negative cost of $110,000. Although Aitken had channeled his money to Griffith through the Majestic Film Company, once the film was finished he settled the copyright and shareholder problems by founding a new company, Epoch Producing. Epoch was to release, rather than the Aitkens' other releasing company, Mutual. This irked the Mutual board members, with the conservative bankers Livingston and Kahn leading the howling pack in which Freuler, Kessel, and Bauman figured prominently. Harry told them flatly that since they had refused to finance *Birth*, they should enjoy none of its proceeds. Mutual responded by removing him as president and electing Freuler in his stead.

I do not think it should surprise the reader when I relate that this new company, Epoch, was short on funds. Being unable to afford nationwide distribution, Epoch determined that it would reserve the major cities and franchise subdistributors to handle the rest of the country. Russian-born Louis B. Mayer, who had relocated to the United States and opened a nickelodeon at Haverhill, Massachusetts, heard about the tremendous audience reaction *Birth* had at its preview at New York's Liberty Theater. Even in 1915 Louie believed in the telephone to conclude business deals. He phoned Aitken at the latter's seven-room apartment in New York.

"Hello, Aitken?" Mayer inquired. "This is Louis B. Mayer, Boston. . . . I've got a couple of theaters here. I've heard the story of *Birth*'s successful matinee opening. How about selling me the New England distribution rights?"

Aitken covered the mouthpiece with his hand. He was grinning. D. W. Griffith was there visiting.

"It's a Louis B. Mayer from Boston," Harry told D.W. "He wants to buy distribution rights."

Griffith's face crinkled into a smile.

"Perhaps," he said, "for a big price. All of us need money."

"Mayer," Harry said into the phone, "how much will you offer?"

"Maybe fifty thousand, with a twenty-five thousand down payment," Mayer responded. "And a fifty-fifty split after I get my investment back."

Harry invited Louie to come to New York and advised him to hurry. Mayer scrambled excitedly to raise the initial $25,000. Louie was shrewd. He wasn't going to risk his own money. He told his secretary, Fanny Mittenthal, that if she had a thousand dollars, he might be willing to put it in the syndicate for her. Fired by his jubilant salesmanship, she gave it to him.

Harry "Pop" Sherman in cap, second from right, Dustin Farnum in the Stetson, from the time when Pop was distributing *The Birth of a Nation*.

Photo courtesy of Teddi Sherman.

Mayer organized a company called Master Photoplays with himself as president; he only owned 25 per cent of the stock. It was for him the beginning of his ultimately disastrous policy of brilliantly running companies in which he did not own a controlling interest.

Birth netted Mayer better than a million dollars, although he'd had to talk Aitken into lowering the down payment to $20,000 on August 2, but following it with $30,000 ten days later. A quarter of the million was Mayer's. Aitken was to get 10 per cent, but Epoch's books indicate that Mayer only paid them $15,000 the first year and $1,500 the second. "Fanny," Mayer confessed to her one day, "I've got bad news. I've got to give you back the thousand dollars you let me have to put in the company. The board of directors objected when they found out you were in. They said they don't want anybody who isn't a stockholder drawing profits from the company. So here is your thousand dollars." She didn't quit, though. Louis B. Mayer was a man on the rise.

Harry Sherman, of Minneapolis, bought rights to *Birth* in sixteen western states for $100,000. When Sherman showed up in New York, Roy Aitken accompanied him to Epoch's bank in Wall Street to deposit his check. Sherman proudly handed the banker the check and commented, "I'll bet you don't see checks this big." The banker smiled, walked over to one of the cages, and returned with a check which he showed to Sherman. It was for a million dollars.

After *Variety* published the grosses from *Gone With the Wind* (M-G-M, 1939), Aitken, hoping to sell remake rights, alleged that *Birth* grossed $50 million. It didn't. The domestic gross for the original issue was approximately $3 million. Of this, Dixon got 25 per cent royalty on net profits, Griffith 37½ per cent plus 180 shares in Epoch valued at $5,000 initially and a half interest in California distribution. Aitken had to pay out profit shares not only to his syndicate investors but to those Griffith had signed up. All told, the Aitkens probably didn't clear more than $800,000, which vanished with the investment Harry made of $200,000 in *Intolerance* and the buy-out of the New York Motion Picture Company.

Freuler and the Mutual board were quite angry with Aitken, especially when *Birth* began its fantastic long-term runs at two dollars a seat. Mutual avenged itself by refusing to distribute program pictures by Ince, Griffith, and Sennett. Harry proceeded to buy the controlling interest from Kessel and Bauman in their holding company. The ex-bookies commenced a comfortable retirement richer by half a million dollars. Aitken then went to La Junta, California, where he put Ince, D.W., and Sennett under personal contract to yet another new corporation. In addition to salary plus profit percentage arrangements, the three directors were given stock options in Aitken's Triangle Film Company. Ince and Sennett, spurred on by these incentives, made their finest films. D. W. Griffith? He went to work on *Intolerance*.

Birth of a Nation influenced all subsequent production, but that of Westerns in particular. Because of its graphic detailing of the Reconstruction period and the carpetbaggers' greedy exploitation of the freed but illiterate slaves, the film has been unduly vilified. Even if such events occurred, minority groups have argued, why remind anyone? Probably the most balanced response came from President Woodrow Wilson when it was screened for him at the White House. "It is," he said sadly, "like writing history with lightning. And my only regret is that it is all so terribly true."

Prior to the New York première, Griffith selected a large orchestra and worked out the synchronized score. D.W. was his life long an avid classical music enthusiast. He incorporated both folk tunes and classical concert pieces into the accompaniment. At the end of the film when the Klan is summoned together for its ride of retribution against poor Gus, the music is the thunderstorm sequence from Beethoven's *Pastoral Symphony*. Griffith had bugles issue the Klan call during the final roundup.

D.W. put everything he was as a man, a Southerner, an American, an artist, a visionary, and a filmmaker into *Birth*. He had Billy Bitzer get down into a shallow pit, placed boards over him and his camera, and had him photograph the Klan riding over him above the lens. It became known as the pit shot and was henceforth used regularly in Westerns. He used his first running inserts, the only suspense innovation he had left out of *The Battle at Elderbush Gulch*. He employed crosscutting to terrific advantage during the last scenes so that the audience was left gasping. He experimented with night photography. He staged hundreds of stunts throughout the film.

Obviously, in view of minority protests, even in its time *Birth* had to be one of a kind. The black versus white panorama of its action couldn't employ Negroes, or actors in blackface, as villains again. Indeed since *Birth,* the screen is notable for the total absence of black villains. Most viewers overlooked D.W.'s intent embodied in the title card, "Viciousness brought forth by war is common to all races." At the beginning of the story we see the inhumanity of the slavers in their treatment of the blacks, the intolerance of the oppressors to the oppressed in all but the few cases where the whites treat the blacks with dignity and sympathy. By the conclusion of the film, this has changed. When the blacks have the upper hand, inspired by the carpetbaggers, they are just as oppressive as their former rulers, raping the whites as the whites raped the blacks, exploiting and humiliating the whites as they had been exploited and humiliated, assuming all the airs and dress and customs of their former masters. Again only a few—this time blacks—demonstrate compassion of soul. What Griffith was saying, it would appear, is that as one would not be a slave, so he must not be a master, that in any event it is the same tyrannical principle. It was Lincoln's sentiment. D.W. wanted *Intolerance* to clarify his views to a public that misunderstood him. In this respect, the minority groups were probably right. *Birth,* I fear, did appeal to audiences for all the wrong reasons. Viewers were not inspired to tolerance or enlightenment. The newly organized KKK made *Birth* its official recruiting film. The violent clash between black and white changed from faces to clothes and was confined to the Western. But Griffith had taught Western filmmakers how to tell their stories more effectively.

When *Intolerance,* costing $750,000, failed miserably, it took something out of D.W. that he was never to reclaim. As the years passed, he took to drinking with increasing vehemence. His brother, Albert, did him one favor. During a rather wild bout, a girl D.W. had taken to his room at the Astor Hotel threatened to sue him for $100,000, claiming he promised to make her a star. Albert got D.W. to invest his money in an annuity from which he could draw no more than $30,000 a year. D.W. was saved the anguish of poverty.

As the twenties advanced, D.W.'s star tarnished, although Zukor wound up with him for a time for $165,000 a year. Griffith became more and more heartbroken. "Writers are the only ones who can express their ego," he

The formation of United Artists Distributing Company on April 17, 1919. Pictured are the four founders, D. W. Griffith, Mary Pickford, Charles Chaplin, and Douglas Fairbanks, Sr. In the background are their attorneys, Albert Banzhaf and Dennis O'Brien.

Photo courtesy of United Artists Corporation.

commented in 1926. "Directors can't, because they have to please the majority. We can't deal with opinions. All we can do is to weave a little romance as pleasantly as we know how." The reader may justifiably wonder how these words came from the same man who in violence conceived and stormed the heavens with *Birth of a Nation* and *Intolerance*. Griffith drank to cloak the bitterness of his disillusionment. When D.W. was high-spirited, enthralled with what he was doing, he was undoubtedly the most singular filmmaker of his time. But his inspiration, alas, was only sporadic; it lacked ultimate discipline.

I think it is an error to believe that he had countless great films in him during the last sixteen years of virtual inactivity. He had said what he'd had to say; he had given his best. No man should be judged on anything but his finest work. But it may be sentimental to postulate that the finest in a man's art is better than the man. A man's art is all of him—some of it good, some of it bad. When Kevin Brownlow, an Englishman curious about American silent films, interviewed Adolph Zukor for his book *The Parade's Gone By* (Bonanza, 1968), he asked Zukor about Griffith. "He didn't fail," Zukor told Brownlow. "No, the procession passed him by. He couldn't keep up the pace. It's age, you know. You can only do certain things up to a certain time." Perhaps Griffith knew better than his admirers. He knew when to quit.

D.W.'s last months were spent at the Hollywood Knickerbocker. He had lived the better part of his professional life in hotel rooms. He was nearly always drunk. He answered neither his mail nor his telephone. Ezra Goodman managed to get a final interview with Griffith through the aid of Seymour Stern, D.W.'s biographer who has never published his biography. A girl who was willing served as a ruse. Griffith pecked at her while Goodman wrote down D.W.'s comments on the back of an envelope.

It took Goodman, who was embittered by Hollywood anyway, a long time to publish the interview. Most editors thought Goodman's portrait of D.W. too sordid. Nor did Griffith really have much to say. He did comment that the movies had forgotten movement. "The moving picture is beautiful; the moving wind in the trees is more beautiful than a painting. . . . In my arrogant opinion, we have lost beauty."

Four months later, D.W. was suddenly stricken with a cerebral hemorrhage. He managed to stumble down the hotel stairs and into the lobby. He was rushed to Temple Hospital where the next day, July 23, 1948, he died. "Unfortunately," said Charles Brackett at the funeral as D.W. passed from life into a troublesome legend, "when he is dead, a man's career has but one tense."

5 / COLONEL SELIG GOES WEST

I have already introduced George Kleine to this narrative. He was a Chicago exchange man and an importer of foreign films, joining forces with Edison and Selig and the others to thwart independent film production. He formed his own producing organization in 1907 with two men experienced in production at Biograph, Samuel Long and Frank Marion, the new firm taking on a synthesis of their initials, Kalem. Their first cinematic venture was a comedy, photographed near Marion's home at Sound Beach, Connecticut. A studio was then leased in New York. Sidney Olcott, who had been touring in a stage version of *Billy the Kid,* had gone to work at Biograph for Frank Marion and now followed him to Kalem, where he became the new company's principal director.

Biograph, even before D. W. Griffith's penchant for filming Westerns and outdoor dramas in an appropriate climate, had established a Los Angeles office in 1906. While Kalem was in the process of filming a one-reel version of *Ben-Hur* in the East, Francis Boggs, chief director for the Selig Polyscope Company, Thomas Persons, head photographer, and a small troupe arrived in California to conclude production on *The Count of Monte Cristo* (Selig, 1908), a picture that had been started in Chicago. Selig was aware of what G. M. Anderson was doing and thought California might be worth a try, especially in view of the fact that Los Angeles was reputed, by the Chamber of Commerce, to have 350 sunny days a year.

When one of Boggs's actors resigned, Boggs replaced him with Hobart Bosworth, a former Broadway actor who had lost his voice when he contracted tuberculosis and was forced to come West for his health. Bosworth was cast as the lead for *In the Sultan's Power* (Selig, 1908), which is still regarded as the first dramatic film made entirely in California. Selig once more got cold feet, as he had when Anderson had gone to Colorado to make Westerns. He wrote Boggs and instructed him to return to Chicago. Bosworth insisted that he couldn't go to Chicago because of his delicate condition. Boggs suggested that Bosworth write the Colonel himself, extolling the virtues of California. Selig had been in California before he had entered the motion picture industry. He determined to take a train to Los Angeles. Shortly after his arrival, he built a small studio at 1845 Alessandro Street. It wasn't long before Kalem followed suit, and then the others. Southern California became the center of outdoor motion picture production.

Selig liked wildlife dramas; many of his pictures were filled with animal action of various kinds. He started his own zoo in an effort to film the adventures of Theodore Roosevelt on his African game hunts. In 1909 the Colonel dispatched Francis Boggs and the outdoor unit to the Cherokee Territory, near Dewey, Oklahoma, to film *Ranch Life in the Great Southwest* (Selig, 1910). It was while making this film that Boggs hired a local deputy sheriff responsible for locking up drunks and keeping gambling honest; this undersheriff was to handle stock and act as safety man. His name was Tom Mix. Tall, lanky, muscular, wild, looking half Indian, Mix asked Boggs for a part in the picture and was assigned a broncbusting sequence during the rodeo section of the film. It was one of the first rodeo episodes ever filmed and was consistent with Selig's desire to present human adventure on the screen. Boggs's unit was exceedingly mobile and was next bound for Flemington, Missouri. Tom was invited along. He made his first starring two-reeler at Flemington, entitled *The Range Rider* (Selig, 1910). In *Ranch Life* Tom was billed as a former U. S. Deputy Marshal on the credits.

Tom Mix as he appeared when a player for the Selig Polyscope Company.

Photo courtesy of *Views & Reviews* magazine.

There is no evidence to substantiate anything of the kind. But it was the beginning of the Tom Mix Legend.

If the Autry Fantasy enjoyed favor in the middle decades of this century, the Tom Mix Legend certainly dominated the silent era. Probably the best way to introduce Tom as a character in this history is to pursue a negative approach. Tom Mix was not born in a log cabin in El Paso. He did not break horses for the British during the Boer War in Africa. He was not involved in the Boxer Rebellion in China, nor did he engage in the battle for the Philippines. He was not a Texas Ranger nor a U. S. Marshal in several territories. He did not insinuate himself into the Mexican Revolution. Mix related all of these tall tales to Francis Boggs, who believed in them implicitly. Buck Jones later undertook to parody Mix's inclination toward fabrication in his picture *The Thrill Hunter* (Columbia, 1933). Boggs couldn't resist the impulse to put Tom's adventures on film. Along the banks of the Des Plaines River, near Chicago, Tom was featured in *Briton and Boer* (Selig, 1910), *Up San Juan Hill* (Selig, 1910), and on the shores of Lake Michigan, Tom made the wholly anticipatory picture *The Millionaire Cowboy* (Selig, 1910). It was after these short films, made in 1909, that Tom was signed to a contract with the Selig Polyscope Company.

The facts of the matter are somewhat less romantic. Tom was born Thomas Edwin Mix on January 6, 1880, in a little hollow in Pennsylvania between the Pennsylvania Railroad line and Bennett's Branch of the Susquehanna River, known as Mix Run, of Ed and Elizabeth Mix. His older brother, Harry, was aged six, his sister, Emma, three. As a child of ten, Tom attended the Buffalo Bill Wild West Show on the Clearfield fairgrounds and was struck with a burning desire to go West and become a lawman. As a child, Tom believed that whatever you may do, you must do it better than anyone else. He attended school at Dubois, Pennsylvania, where his family moved when he was four, and on April 26, 1898, the day after war had been declared on Spain, Tom enlisted in the Army, attached to Battery M, 4th Regiment, United States Artillery. He saw no action. While Tom was stationed in Virginia, he fell in love with Grace Allin, and during a furlough the two were married on July 18, 1902.

Grace didn't want a soldier for a husband. She urged Tom to leave the service. Grace put it to him bluntly that it was either she or the Army. In October 1902 Tom ran off with Grace and by November was listed as a deserter. The military was quite casual in those days when a war was not in progress. Despite Roosevelt's barnstorming, most Americans remained antimilitaristic and retained the Colonial notion of a volunteer army except in time of national emergency. Nothing was done to apprehend Tom Mix, and no charges were ever brought against him even when he became one of the most famous Americans of his generation. Grace's father took the opposite stand. He felt it outrageous that his daughter be married to a deserter. Tom and Grace migrated to Guthrie, Oklahoma, where Grace taught school and Tom held classes in physical fitness. Grace finally left Tom, and her father was successful in having the marriage annulled.

Tom took to odd jobs, including bartending at a saloon on Robinson Avenue in Oklahoma City. The saloon owner had a daughter, Kitty Jewel Perrine, with whom Tom fell in love. Then Tom came to Joe Miller's attention; Joe discussed it with his brothers, George and Zack, and Tom was offered fifteen dollars a week to work with their 101 Ranch Wild West Show which quartered near Bliss, Oklahoma. Tom and Kitty were married in the Perrine Hotel on November 20, 1905. It was a foolish move. Tom tried to conceal his marriage from the Millers. Kitty grew disenchanted with him. They were soon divorced.

Tom Mix was not a Texas Ranger during this period. He did not round up the desperate Shonts brothers; the Ranger archives have no record of even the Shonts, much less Ranger Mix. Zack Miller thought very little of Tom as a cowboy and employed him as a greeter at the ranch, where all Tom had to do was smile and be naturally charming. In December 1908, at Dewey, Tom met and fell in love with Olive Stokes, a girl from a ranch in Montana. Apparently, Tom had a trait in his personality that was reflected to an equal degree in William S. Hart and, somewhat later, John Wayne. He couldn't go to bed with a woman with whom he wasn't at least three-quarters in love. For all that women cost Tom—virtually everything he made during his career—his personal needs were very simple. Other than sexual congress and occasional companionship, he preferred they leave him to his own resources. He very much wanted to become a master of the cowboy's arts, riding, roping, bulldogging, broncbusting, expert rifle and pistol shooting, knife throwing. He loved speed and danger and masculine conversation. For some peculiar reason, he was invariably attracted to women who wanted to possess him, to keep him to themselves, who wanted him to surrender all of the passions in his life other than his love for them. On January 19, 1909, Tom and Olive were married and went to Miles City, Montana, for their honeymoon.

Having completed three seasons with the Miller Brothers, Tom and Olive joined the Widerman Wild West Show out of Amarillo, Texas. Tom put on a thrilling rope exhibition as a special attraction. He next tried his own touring show, but misfortune brought it to an early termination. Tom worked a short stint with Will A. Dickey's Circle D Wild West Show, as did Hoot Gibson. When Tom and Olive settled at Dewey, Tom's friend from the Miller Brothers days, Sid Jordan, introduced him to his father, Sheriff John Jordan, the Cherokee Lawman, as he was known. Tom was hired as a night marshal and, in this capacity, came to the attention of Francis Boggs. Tom and Sid Jordan remained long-time friends, and as soon as he could, Tom got Sid a job with Selig, first doing stunts and then, eventually, featured roles as villains.

On a lark, in 1910, Tom, back in Dewey, borrowed a horse from the Miller Brothers in order to enter a rodeo. He ended up breaking his leg and stabled the horse at the Mulhall ranch. The horse disappeared, and the Millers pressed charges against him. Tom cleared himself by agreeing to appear with the 101 Ranch show while it was wintering in Mexico City. Tom continued on and off to appear with the show over the next several years when he had the time. The little incident of horse stealing would come up again years hence when Zach Miller needed money.

Tom was not strictly a Western player at Selig. He took a number of different roles, some in the lead, others in support. He had a pressing urgency for more money due to his tendency to live slightly above his income. In 1912 Tom left Selig to try the rodeo circuit, where Olive convinced him he could make more money than in films. He went to Calgary, Canada, and aligned himself with Guy Weadick, who was promoting the first Calgary Stampede that year. By 1913, discouraged with rodeo life and having been twice seriously injured, he returned to Chicago and negotiated a new contract with the Colonel. Because of the phenomenal and sustained success of the Broncho Billy Westerns, Selig felt his company needed a star who would appear in a continuing series of one- and two-reelers. Mix was his choice. Tom agreed on the condition that he have his own unit for the manufacture of the films. Selig gave him a contract very similar to that which Broncho Billy had with Essanay, with Mix drawing a portion of his salary as the producer.

Also, in 1913, Selig innovated another novelty by starring contract player Kathlyn Williams in the first legitimate serial, *The Adventures of Kathlyn*. Selig made a deal with the Chicago *Tribune* to run the installments in the newspaper and try to syndicate them all over the country. Readers were invited to see the printed story brought to life on the screen as the Selig Company, every two weeks, released another installment. The first episode, released on December 29, 1913, in three reels, was titled "The Unwelcome Throne." Twelve other installments, each two reels in length, followed. The plot dealt with an American girl who under compulsion assumes a throne in India and battles against numerous intrigues. E. A. McManus, of the Hearst newspaper chain, decided to do Selig one better. He made a deal with Pathé to finance a serial on a grand scale. An actress named Pearl White was engaged to star, and the chapter play was titled *The Perils of Pauline* (Pathé, 1914). Pearl White gained a tremendous popularity during the late teens and early twenties for her fabulous feats of daring, until she was replaced, because of injuries, by Allene Ray in the mid twenties. Kalem began a competing serial series titled *The Hazards of Helen* (Kalem, 1914), starring Helen Holmes, many episodes of which had a railroad background as a setting. Railroads became a commonplace in action and adventure films as a result of the Kalem series, and Mix, in particular, liked to feature them in his later films for the Fox company.

Colonel Selig undertook to bring Rex Beach's adventure novel *The Spoilers* to the screen. The story is of unusual interest in that it was remade four times subsequently. In the original *The Spoilers* (Selig, 1914) the protagonists, who engage in the climactic fight with which the picture concludes, were William Farnum and Tom Santschi. The protagonists in the 1923 version, released by Goldwyn close upon reissue of the Selig film in 1921, were Milton Sills and Noah Beery. Gary Cooper and William Boyd fought it out for the 1930 remake for Paramount; Duke Wayne and Randolph Scott squared off in the Universal version of 1942; and Jeff Chandler and Rory Calhoun sparred in Universal's remake of 1955. The enthusiastic reception accorded the Selig film in 1914 heralded the fact that the feature film had arrived. Selig himself regarded it as a fluke and, like Vitagraph, Biograph, and Spoor at Essanay, persisted in concentrating his production efforts on short films of one, two, or three reels in length. Indeed, in 1915, he formed a distribution combine with Vitagraph, Lubin, Selig, and Essanay known as VLSE. They committed extensive funds to the fight with Laemmle and William Fox, in an effort to maintain their control over new production and to guarantee bookings on their own films regardless of quality or public taste. The Trust was thrown into desperation when it seemed that the U. S. Government was sympathetic to the mavericks.

In terms of the fistfight, probably the 1942 *Spoilers* is the best. But the Selig version in its crudeness, its makeshift sets, its strange and curious passion of composition, has about it an enduring quality. Alex McNamara schemes to swindle the richest mines in Alaska from their rightful owners. He hires a crooked judge to help him do it. The judge's niece falls in love with Roy Glenister, one of the mine owners who has just broken up with Cherry Malotte, a dance hall woman. But the niece becomes estranged to Glenister due to his violence and becomes friendly with McNamara instead. Glenister has it out with McNamara, including the much touted fight, and is finally united with the niece. Cherry falls in love with Wheeler Oakman, the niece's brother. So everyone is happy at the end.

Kathlyn Williams played Cherry Malotte; Bessie Eyton was the judge's niece. They were among the most popular of Colonel Selig's female attractions. A third was dark-haired, sharp-featured Victoria Forde. All three worked opposite Tom Mix in his Western shorts. Lafayette McKee, later known as merely Lafe, joined William Duncan, Wheeler Oakman, and Tom Santschi in frequent character roles. The quality of Tom's pictures varied as the years passed. This was due in large measure to the fact that Tom was in complete charge of the films, from scripting them to directing them. I have already mentioned how William S. Hart began featuring Fritz in his films. Tom did the same with his horse, Old Blue. An insufficient number of Mix's Selig films and Hart's Westerns survive to indicate with absolute certitude who was the very first to feature his horse prominently in the action, but Hart, in all probability, was the first to include his horse's name in the credits of the picture.

Some of the Mix Westerns were romantic and elaborate, as *In the Days of the Thundering Herd* (Selig, 1914). Others, like *Cactus Jim's Shop Girl* (Selig, 1915), were centered on an exceedingly thin story line. In the latter, Mix advertises for a wife. A shop girl responds. Tom travels to Chicago to marry her and bring her with him to the West, whereupon she changes her mind. Tom, ashamed to return empty-handed, uses a mannequin in a woman's dress to fool his friends who are expecting him to show up with a wife. The girl reverses herself again and arrives at his cabin just in time to save Tom the embarrassment of exposure.

The Taming of Grouchy Bill (Selig, 1916) again employed a comic plot. Tom decides to teach some manners to a cowhand who's too rough on his wife. He disguises himself as a woman and pretends to be Grouchy Bill's mother-in-law. In this role, he literally beats and slams the man into humorous submission. By the fade, Tom had produced lasting domestic accord.

Victoria Forde, increasingly, was used in the Mix Westerns. The two were falling in love. In 1917, with the Trust smashed and the members of VSLE unable or unwilling to compete financially in the feature market, Colonel Selig undertook to release all his contract players and disband the Selig Polyscope Company. Tom went to work for William Fox. Victoria Forde was also signed by the Fox Film Corporation. Although Tom had had ambitions of settling down on a ranch which he purchased near Prescott, Arizona, there to live happily with Olive and their small daughter, Ruth Mix, it was not to be. Tom and Olive were divorced that year. Victoria Forde had a good case. What Tom needed most was a woman who could share his greatest interest in life, his motion picture work. The two were married in 1918.

William Fox, born William Fried, of German-Jewish descent, emigrated to the United States in 1880 when he was a year old; his parents occupied a cramped rear tenement on New York's Lower East Side. A dozen more children were born there and six died there before reaching maturity. As a young child, Fox went to work to help support the family. He sold peanuts in the streets and the parks, and he spent a night in jail for causing a litter. When he was eleven, he was fortunate enough to land a job working twelve hours a day for twelve dollars a week in a sweatshop. In his teens, Fox entered into a partnership with Sol Brill in founding a cloth sponging business. It prospered.

One day, Brill told him of a penny arcade for sale at 700 Broadway in Brooklyn. The two of them checked out the location. J. Stuart Blackton, one of the executives with Vitagraph, was the owner. The peep show was teeming with crowds. Fox and Brill purchased it from him, Blackton complaining about the demands of his work in production. The next day the crowds dwindled to nearly nothing; most of the people had been plants used to encourage the sale. Brill became disheartened and quit. Such wasn't the case with William Fox. He refurbished the theater and added vaudeville acts. Fox made the business a paying operation. He began building a chain of nickelodeons. When the Trust confronted him with the proposition that he either sell out his group of theaters for $75,000 or be forced out for much less, Fox retaliated by demanding $750,000 as his sale price. He went further. He founded his own film exchange and, in 1914, began producing his own pictures. Since he could not read English at all well, Fox's wife, Eve, would read story material and narrate plots to her husband. The next day Fox would relate the story as he conceived it to a director who would go about putting it on film.

Fox's first sensation was Theda Bara who played a *femme fatale* in a photoplay based on a stage adaptation of Rudyard Kipling's poem "The Vampire." Bara's line "Kiss me, my fool" became as famous in the teens as Mae West's "Come up and see me sometime!" did in the thirties. Fox exploited sex where he could and brought Betty Blythe to fame in the extravaganza *The Queen of Sheba* (Fox, 1921). Between the Bara pictures and *The Queen,* Fox founded a West Coast studio and endeavored to corner the outdoor market and compete with William S. Hart by developing Tom Mix into a first-rate screen property. Tom's astonishing impact on the public amazed Fox, however, as much as it did anybody. Tom wanted to make feature-length Westerns, and Fox financed them, still permitting Mix to produce the films with his own unit. Tom, who had purchased the original Tony from a friend named Pat Chrisman in 1914, proceeded to make the horse, more than ever, his screen partner. By 1919 Tom was earning $10,-000 a week and was worth every penny of it. In 1920 Tom edged William S. Hart aside as the screen's favorite Western player.

While in the process of liquidating his assets, Colonel Selig undertook to reissue several of his older pictures. In Mix's case, many of his short Westerns were re-edited so as to make two feature films, *Twisted Trails* (Selig, 1917) and *The Heart of Texas Ryan*. What is impressive about these compilations is not that Selig had the gall to do it, but that the results were as successful as they were. Tom did not dress glamorously while at Selig. He did wear gloves, because of his unusually soft hands, and because of his great popularity, set a standard which nearly all the Western players of the twenties and thirties imitated. It wasn't until his Fox period that Mix adopted what might best be called his screen uniform, dress appropriate for the rodeo or public appearances but hardly in the battered mold of his own Selig pictures or the crude clothing worn by Hart, Broncho Billy, and all of the others during the teens. But the twenties were light-years away; the Great War changed the face of the world.

The Heart of Texas Ryan was reissued in 1923 as *Single-shot Parker*. No matter under which title you might happen to see it, the film does have a semblance of cohesion. The story introduced Tom as a puncher on the Ryan ranch. Ryan's daughter, Texas, returns from school in the East and falls in love with Tom. Tom goes after a gang of cattle thieves and, while he captures one of them, is later taken prisoner himself. Texas rushes to his rescue and buys him away from the thieves for $2,000. They embrace.

The Heart of Texas Ryan may not be an especially good Western for Mix, but it is one of the very few of his films from the late teens and early twenties which happen to survive. Contrast with *Just Tony* (Fox, 1922), of which I will have more to say later, does indicate, however, that what may well have made the difference for Mix was simply the polished production values at Fox Film Corporation as opposed to the tight budgets and limited cinematic capabilities of the Selig Polyscope Company. Tom Mix, who had so amused the Miller Brothers because of his ineptitude, through diligence and hard work became the screen's foremost embodiment of wild, daredevil stunting, furious, breakneck riding, coupled with an extraordinary flamboyance of demeanor and natural exuberance. Tom had been brought up in show business through the tradition of entertaining the public. Unlike Bill Hart, he was not an exponent of Western realism any more than he was schooled in heavy, Victorian melodrama. His bright spirit belonged most of all to the flashy decade of the twenties when America's agrarian dream underwent the curious phenomenon of sophisticated urbanization.

6 / THE RISE OF FAMOUS PLAYERS-LASKY

Sam Goldfish was born on August 27, 1884, at Warsaw, Poland. He emigrated to the United States and started as a glove cutter in a glove factory in Gloversville, New York. The factory was owned by Bessie Lasky's uncle. Jesse L. Lasky, who was born on September 13, 1880, at San Francisco, got his start in vaudeville in an act teaming him with his sister, Blanche. He married Bessie Gains at the turn of the century, and the young couple moved into Jesse's home, over which his mother presided. Blanche had had enough of show business. She wanted a straightforward, dependable businessman for an escort. Bessie introduced her to Sam.

I realize this may strike the reader as a complicated family history, but it becomes even more so. Jesse L. Lasky's best friend was a moderately successful playwright named Cecil B. De Mille. De Mille was disenchanted with his state of relative poverty and confessed to Jesse that he wanted to get away from Broadway. When Goldfish would come over to the Lasky ménage for dinner, he would invariably strike up a conversation with Jesse about the possibilities to be found in the motion picture industry. This would tend to turn off Blanche. But there was no keeping Sam down. He had seen a two-reeler with Broncho Billy Anderson and was quite excited by the prospects. Once Sam and Blanche were married, they too moved into the Lasky maternal home. The talk between Sam and Jesse continued.

The barn and stage De Mille rented on the corner of Selma and Vine streets. Dustin Farnum is on stage with his arm raised.

Photo courtesy of the Academy of Motion Picture Arts & Sciences.

Cecil and Jesse met for lunch one day at Manhattan's Claridge Grill, and Cecil told Jesse that his decision to try something new was adamant. "To keep Cecil from doing something foolish alone," Jesse later recalled, "I proposed we do something foolish together." They determined to make movies. Jesse told Cecil that Sam Goldfish and Goldfish's chum, an attorney named Arthur Friend, had discussed the topic seriously and it would require about $20,000 to set up a company. Jesse was willing, if Cecil was. Cecil agreed on the spot. The bottom had fallen out of the glove market and so Goldfish was only too ready to make the plunge himself. Later, when Sam formed his own company with Edgar Selwyn, it was called Goldwyn, and Sam just kept the altered title and used it as his last name. Cecil had trouble raising his $5,000, but he pawned what he could and volunteered his services. On the back of a menu, Jesse had outlined the corporate setup of the new firm, the Jesse L. Lasky Feature Play Company. Jesse was president, Cecil the director-general; Sam was head of sales, Friend the legal counsel.

Meeting at the Lambs' Club on West Forty-fourth Street, Jesse suggested that the company's first film should be a feature. He had been quite impressed by *Queen Elizabeth,* a French four-reeler of 1914 that starred Sarah Bernhardt. It was being released in the United States through a combine that included among its investors Edwin S. Porter, Biograph executives, and Adolph Zukor, treasurer of the Marcus Loew theater chain. They happened to run into Dustin Farnum, who had scored a triumph on Broadway in *The Virginian* and had shared honors with his brother, William, and child actress Mary Miles Minter in *The Littlest Rebel.* Farnum was asked if he would like to star in a feature film.

Sitting at the Lambs' Club that day was Edwin Milton Royle, author of *The Squaw Man.* The play, combining Western settings with London drawing rooms, had made a theatrical sensation with William Faversham as the lead. Farnum may have been passed over for the role. He looked at Lasky and De Mille and said tersely, "You get Royle to sell you *The Squaw Man* and I might agree to join you."

Lasky worked out a deal with Royle and purchased screen rights to the play for $15,000. That left the new firm strapped for money. Farnum acquiesced to sign on for a quarter interest in the company. Jesse and Cecil, after some debate, determined that the picture should be filmed on location. Jesse suggested the troupe go to real Indian country, like Flagstaff, Arizona, where he had been briefly years before while working the boards. De Mille was enthusiastic; Farnum wasn't. If the picture was not to be made in the East, Farnum wanted $250 a week and a four-week guarantee. This threw Jesse into a quandary. He approached his wife Bessie's brother and uncle and persuaded them to buy the fourth quarter block of shares in the new company. Had Farnum taken the stock, by the time of the merger with Adolph Zukor's Famous Players Company it would have been worth $2 million.

A cameraman was hired and Oscar Apfel was signed. Apfel was a film director with experience making one- and two-reel pictures. Cecil and the troupe boarded a train and were at last off to Flagstaff. Sam immediately set about selling states' rights to *The Squaw Man*. Before production began, he had $60,000 in signed contracts for the finished film. It was phenomenal salesmanship when you consider that he was selling a film not yet completed by men who had never made one. But that was part of the optimism of the times.

Arriving at Flagstaff, De Mille could see the climate was all wrong in terms of the screenplay he had worked out. He ordered everyone to reboard. The train was going on to Los Angeles and, De Mille recalled, "I remembered . . . that other picture makers had been working there on and off for some years. The California climate was good, there was a great variety of scenery there, and it was that much farther away, so we thought, from the minions of the Trust, in case any of that inquisitive fraternity decided to take too personal an interest in what we were doing."

When Cecil wired East to Sam and Jesse that he was headed for a place called Hollywood, they grew extremely nervous. Soon after getting there, Cecil rented a barn on the corner of Selma and Vine streets, a shady, rugged area. The players could change in the horse stalls. An outdoor platform was used as a stage. On December 29, 1913, production began on the first feature Western in the history of the motion picture. H. E. Roach, later known as Hal Roach, was a bit player; Art Acord was signed as one of Cash Hawkins' gang.

One day the cameraman, Al Gandolfi, tore a bit of twisted film out of the camera. An extra, standing around smoking a cigarette, picked it up. The strip of film ignited in his hand. Seeing this, De Mille took the precaution of having two negatives made, one stored at the barn, the other at his bungalow some distance away where he lived with a gray she-wolf which he had bought for use in the picture. It turned out to be a wise maneuver. The Trust hired one of the crew to sabotage the production. De Mille arrived one morning—he rode horseback to and from the barn —and found the negative of the first reel crushed and trampled underfoot, lying on the damp floor of the barn. When someone took a pot shot at him on his way home, he started wearing a gun. He began receiving anonymous letters threatening his life if he didn't stop working. "With my revolver and horse," he remarked to Dustin Farnum, "I should be in the picture with you, rather than directing it."

Lasky came to Los Angeles to visit the operation. De Mille, before *The Squaw Man* was in the can, found himself raising additional money from an outside investor, W. W. Hodkinson, who eventually sold his interest in the company for $5 million after the merger with Zukor. De Mille cast himself as a faro dealer to save on costs. When edited, the picture ran six reels. With no previous experience, De Mille brought it in for $15,450. De Mille shared his producer-director credit with Oscar Apfel, and all of the players were credited on the screen and in the publicity, which was still not practiced by most producing companies.

The plot, briefly, is about an Englishman falsely accused of a crime his brother actually committed who goes West to save the family name. He falls in love with an Indian maiden and they have a child. Years later, the brother makes a confession on his deathbed exonerating him. The Indian maiden has murdered a man, and the sheriff wants to arrest her. In a clumsily directed scene, Jim Wynnegate, able now to claim his rightful title in England, accidentally shoots the Indian maiden (in the play, she is a suicide) ; she dies in his arms.

When the final print of the film was screened at a gala affair, it was found to jump about on the screen, frames moving variously up and down. Lasky and De Mille were terrified lest the entire project be doomed. In desperation, they made arrangements to bring the film to Sigmund Lubin in Philadelphia. Lubin was an expert in film processing, but also a party to the Trust.

"Cannily, quizzically, Mr. Lubin listened to our tale of woe," De Mille recalled. Lubin turned the film over to one of his technicians. "I think," De Mille went on, "they were the longest 15 minutes I have ever waited. Then the technician came back." There was nothing wrong with their film. De Mille had purshased a British-made sprocket punch that had punched too many perforations in the film stock to be shown on American projection equipment. *The Squaw Man* was successfully trade-showed in New York and sold in all markets. The Jesse L. Lasky Company was in business. Lasky decided to join Cecil on the West Coast, while Sam co-ordinated sales and promotion in New York. Why did Lubin tell them the truth? It

Dustin Farnum and Red Wing in the foreground, Joseph E. Singleton as
Tabywanna behind them, and Winifred Kingston holding the boy, from *The
Squaw Man.*

Photo courtesy of the Academy of Motion Picture Arts & Sciences.

confused both Lasky and De Mille at the time. It certainly wasn't to
Lubin's advantage. But I would intimate that what prompted Lubin was
the faith the two young men had in him that he would tell them the truth,
that the times were changing and the Trust could not last forever, and that
Jesse and Cecil, by the intensity of their aspirations, belonged to the future.

On April 14, 1914, De Mille commenced production on a solo feature
based on the property *The Virginian.* Dustin Farnum was again the star.
De Mille began experimenting with light intensity. Jesse went to New York
for a visit. He and Sam met with Adolph Zukor at Delmonico's. "Zukor
was small in stature," Jesse recalled, "but I began to think of him as a titan
when he expounded astute theories about the future of the motion picture
business. We found that we had a community of interests, aside from the
fact that we were selling our pictures to the same states' rights men. His
vision and quiet dignity still infused me as I walked with Sam to the offices
we had taken on Fifth Avenue opposite the Public Library.

"'That man is an inspirational force!' I said. 'I want to keep in close
contact with him.'

"Sam agreed, and we never failed to have lunch with Zukor whenever
I came to New York."

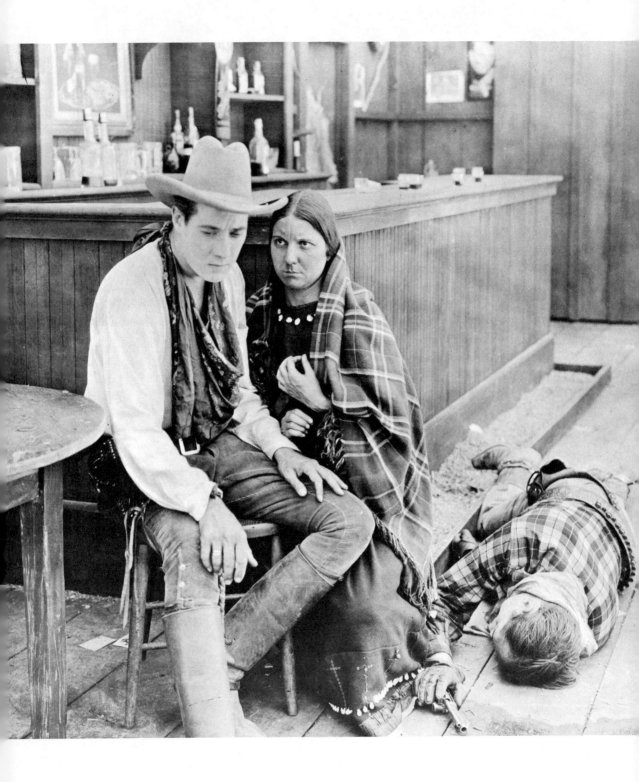

Of course, Zukor is anything but a new character to this narrative. He had come to the New World with forty dollars sewed into the lining of his vest. He was able, in 1907, when the market took a bad turn, to go home to his family and tell them all, in his gentle manner, that it was necessary for them to retrench. A new, more modest apartment had to be found, and one was, above a store. Zukor could then go to his bankers and inform them that it was impossible for him to meet his outstanding notes, but if they would wait, he was economizing in all areas, cutting back on expenses, and planned to pull through the crisis. They backed him.

B. P. Schulberg, who was story editor in Edwin S. Porter's Rex production company, joined the newly formed Famous Players with Porter when Zukor organized the firm in 1912. I will have occasion to reintroduce Schulberg when I come to the sound version of *The Virginian* (Paramount, 1929). The Lasky company went on to produce twenty-two successful feature films while Jesse and Zukor continued to meet socially. Finally, Zukor proposed that the two companies merge. Zukor, by this time, had a great many contract players, including Mary Pickford, and Lasky had the facilities on the West Coast and Cecil B. De Mille as a director. The men struck a bargain, and the two firms were joined to form the Famous Players-Lasky Company, with Zukor as president, Jesse as vice-president, Cecil as director-general and Sam Goldfish as chairman of the board. The merger was a necessary move for Zukor insofar as the idea of bringing stage plays to the screen in the literal sense, with Broadway actors, was not entirely satisfactory.

In 1918, for the Famous Players-Lasky Company, De Mille did a remake of *The Squaw Man*. It starred Elliot Dexter in the Dustin Farnum role and included Noah Beery, Ann Little, Raymond Hatton, and Jack Holt in the cast. De Mille made the picture in a talking version in 1931, produced and released by Metro-Goldwyn-Mayer, this time featuring Warner Baxter as Captain James Wynngate.

Sam Goldfish began running into myriad problems with Zukor. Zukor finally put it to Jesse that he would have to choose between himself and Sam, or the whole company would break apart. Jesse, after much careful thought, chose Zukor, and Sam sold out his interest for $900,000 and set up an independent operation. This was in 1916. The year before, Sam had been divorced from Blanche. He would be involved only peripherally with the Lasky family in the ensuing years. It may amuse the reader to learn that one of the theater owners Sam sold exhibition rights to for the original *Squaw Man* was none other than Louis B. Mayer, who reneged on paying the agreed-upon price. Sam held it against Mayer for a long time.

"What Jesse Lasky and I had was more than friendship," De Mille wrote of their association. "It was an affection warmer and closer than that of many brothers." But of Zukor, De Mille recalled: "The steel and

Dustin Farnum and Red Wing.

iron, the indomitable bravery and driving determination, in that little man. He is little in nothing but physical stature, and even that has still the tough stamina he gave it in his youth as an amateur boxer who could hold his own with professionals of the ring. In his ambitions and dreams, his shrewd judgement, his showmanship, his generalship, he has had no peer in the history of motion pictures. No one in the industry, including a septuagenarian like me, ever calls this man anything but Mr. Zukor."

The first remake of *The Squaw Man* was released as a Paramount Picture. I suppose, indirectly, W. W. Hodkinson, who had assisted De Mille in financing the first *Squaw Man*, brought about the merger of the combined talents of Zukor, Lasky, and De Mille. Hodkinson was in charge of a group of West Coast exchanges. He named his corporation Paramount, taking the name from an apartment house. Hodkinson sketched the mountain trademark on a desk blotter. Pictures released by his company were issued as Paramount features. He signed various distribution agreements, expecting Famous Players to supply fifty-two features a year, the Lasky Company thirty, and so on. The producing company was to receive $35,000 for each picture and 65 per cent of the total receipts. Zukor was dissatisfied with this arrangement because he felt that before long Hodkinson would be dictating the kinds of pictures to be made. After the merger with the Jesse L. Lasky Company, Zukor, through some internal manipulating, ended up assuming control from Hodkinson, and Paramount became one of the principal brand names of Famous Players-Lasky. By insight and rare creative business ingenuity, Zukor had managed to bring together an immense array of human talent and with it built the most enterprising production and distribution firm of the teens.

7 / UNIVERSAL IN THE TEENS

It was on the fifteenth day of the third month of 1915 that one of the really big events in the history of motion pictures took place just north of Hollywood. On horseback, on bicycles, on foot, in wagons, in carriages, in automobiles, ten thousand people poured into an open-air arena. Choked from the dust of the Cahuenga Pass road, sweaty, excited, they pressed through the triumphal arch—made not of stone but plaster and gaily painted stucco, for, after all, this was still Hollywood where nothing has ever been built to last. In the milling crowd were broncbusters, flash riders, nondescript cowboys, Indians in war dress, soldiers, policemen, clowns, hundreds of extras, film dignitaries, local and state officials.

On the back lot, which was purchased in 1914 for $165,000 and measured 230 acres, were barns, sound stages, make-up quarters, storage vaults, prop areas, Western town sets, streets and buildings both modern and old. As the flag of the United States of America was unfurled, the crowd cheered. Thomas A. Edison was the guest of honor, as befitted a moment of great historical impact. The cheering increased to thunderous applause as the beaming, round-faced, five-foot man walked out on the platform 400 feet long by 150 feet wide. The Patents War was over. It was in the past. And all around the little man lay the largest, most far-flung, most ambitious motion picture manufacturing plant in the world. He had been dubbed Uncle Carl because of the many friends and relatives to whom he had given jobs. (Laemmle, it seemed, had been born looking old.) The din quieted enough for him to speak. Restless anticipation shot through the spectators. Then his words came:

"I hope I didn't make a mistake coming out here."

It was entirely characteristic of him. It didn't matter that on this ground Mexican General Andrés Pico and U. S. Army Colonel John C. Frémont had signed the treaty which ceded California to the United States. All Uncle Carl could think of was the tens of thousands of dollars he had spent constructing Universal City. It seemed a bottomless pit. But he smiled seraphically at the crowd and waved a short arm. It was the beginning of an epoch.

Much had happened since Uncle Carl had fought off Kessel and Bauman and rallied against Harry Aitken. Judge Learned Hand had decided an important suit in Laemmle's favor as early as 1912. The U. S. Government then filed suit against the Trust, claiming that the combine was violating the Sherman Act. By October 1915 the Trust was legally compelled to abandon its unlawful practices, and its power of near monopoly was shattered.

It was a Laemmle characteristic to stress ballyhoo. In 1909 he had produced a dozen films commencing with the 988-foot picturization of Longfellow's *Hiawatha*. In 1910 he expanded to more than one hundred films. He added a new studio to the one in New York, this one located at Fort Lee, New Jersey, all the while fighting the Trust. I have already told how he purchased the Nestor lot in California after the scrape with Kessel and Bauman. Now he had taken the giant step of his career in founding Universal City.

In 1912, despite Uncle Carl's rejection of the proposal, a feature-length film was directed by George Loane Tucker with the co-operation of numer-

Harry Carey in character during the teens.

Photo courtesy of *Views & Reviews* magazine.

ous Laemmle employees. Laemmle learned nothing about it until he was asked to view the finished film at his New York office. Laemmle liked the picture, *Traffic in Souls*. Rather than being angered at the deviousness behind its production, he offered to buy it outright for $10,000. The need for funds to fight the Trust, to fight Kessel and Bauman, later to fight Aitken, had induced him to take on several partners and assorted backers. However much he might feel inclined to accept the argument that the public wanted films longer than two reels, he wasn't at all certain he could convince the other principals of it. The picture became a box-office bonanza, grossing in excess of half a million. It only further confirmed in Laemmle's mind his willingness to try anything and the vital importance of promotion.

Perhaps I have given the reader the impression that Laemmle was a rash and even dangerous corporate president. If so, I must correct it. He attracted talent and money to his enterprise precisely because of his free-wheeling, gracious responsiveness. The liberty he held out to creative people in all aspects of his company both made his fortune and led to the endless in-fighting with which he was surrounded throughout his career in the industry.

German was a second language at Universal. Laemmle has since been made an object of ridicule for employing so many Old Country immigrants. But he welcomed everyone; everyone had a place at Universal for as long as he was willing to do a job. Uncle Carl was a munificent and radiant personality. Good ideas and successful pictures came, more often than not, as a result of this openness of heart. To some, Laemmle's expanding empire appeared a medieval fiefdom, filled with intrigue. To Uncle Carl, it embodied the spirit of opportunity, of freedom from undue restraint, of a wildly exuberant democracy of the soul within autocratic bounds, the worst and best from the heady atmosphere of the New World that suited his own mercurial temperament as it fired men to strive toward incredible achievements. In a word, Uncle Carl's management of creative and executive personnel was to put them at liberty and see what they could do. His only way of controlling them was to pit one against the other with only himself as the buffer and ultimate decision-maker.

Having endangered his ownership of the company to win one war in 1912, then triumphing in the struggle against Kessel and Bauman, Uncle Carl next waged craftily a second battle to win ownership back. Mark Dintenfass had begun his business life as a fishmonger. A family quarrel forced him from that occupation as a whim inspired him to buy one of the first motion picture theaters. It failed. As is frequently the case in pioneer activities, incompetence at a lower level urges a man to seek a higher niche. Dintenfass went into distribution and became an investor in the Universal Film Manufacturing Company during the period of Laemmle's united front against Aitken.

Pat Powers, another Laemmle recruit from the same period, decided to wrench the presidency from Laemmle. He needed Dintenfass' stock to do it. Only he was too emotional to proceed prudently. He held many of his weightiest business conferences in washrooms. Dintenfass enlisted a bankrupt jeweler, Lewis J. Selznick, whom he'd known in Pittsburgh, to peddle his stock to the highest bidder. Powers was wary and, not wanting to enrich Dintenfass, refused it. Laemmle bought the stock and regained control. He hired Selznick as an employee, telling him to find some way to be useful.

For the next year or so, the Powers faction rebelled ineffectually against Laemmle, ordering the police to remove stage props during production of a Laemmle film or cornering Laemmle in the Directors' board room so that Uncle Carl had to fling the company books and corporate seal out the window to allies in a cab below. This was child's play for a man with Uncle Carl's experience against the Trust, Kessel and Bauman, and Aitken. He went to Germany to take the waters and allowed the company to run itself. Selznick appointed himself in the interim Universal's general manager and assumed the function of the Purchasing Department. When Laemmle returned to the States, he reacted with dispatch, informing Selznick by letter that his resignation had been received and accepted.

Westerns from this time forth were to remain a Laemmle specialty. He loved his cowboys as perhaps no other producer did and watched their films with as much enthusiasm as any youth in a theater audience. The establishment of Universal City spurred an economic and profligate increase in Universal's Western production. Laemmle set out to develop stars as Thomas Ince had promoted William S. Hart, Colonel Selig Tom Mix, and Essanay Broncho Billy. He utilized Thomas Ince's production methods, some of which Francis Ford brought along. Although Universal sponsored an assembly-line approach to Westerns and employed several units, a corporate story editor was always in evidence to approve each script before shooting began. It remained a steady source of revenue. Francis Ford and Grace Cunard appeared in a twenty-two-chapter serial, *The Broken Coin* (Universal, 1915), and *The Adventures of Peg o' the Ring* (Universal, 1916) in fifteen chapters was released with them the following year. Also in 1916 Jack Holt appeared opposite Marie Walcamp in the first Western serial, *Liberty, a Daughter of the U.S.A.* Pathé competed with *Pearl of the Army,* released in December 1916, with Pearl White cast as the lead in a story dealing with adventures occurring during James Monroe's administration.

Harry Carey was born Henry DeWitt Carey at the Bronx, New York, on January 16, 1878. The son of a New York City judge, Carey studied law at both the Hamilton Institute and New York University. He was stricken by pneumonia in 1899. Some of his biographers have suggested that it was this illness which induced him to give up the bar and try his hand at playwriting. If there is a connection, it is rather dim. More likely, Harry had always wanted to act, and his convalescence, during which he wrote a play called *Montana,* served as a convenient excuse. Friends encouraged him to produce it. Harry himself took the lead. It toured for five years.

Carey wrote *The Heart of Alaska* next, but it proved a bomb. Looking for work, Harry tried motion pictures, joined the Biograph Company in New York in 1909, and, as I have mentioned, worked under the direction of D. W. Griffith. Carey played all manner of parts while at Biograph, from that of a fierce villain in *An Unseen Enemy* (Biograph, 1912) to Westerner roles.

Harry was almost forty when Universal signed him as a contract player in 1915. His rugged, austere visage lent itself to Western heroes better than the few society dramas he made at first, and it was decided to give Harry his own series of Western two-reelers. Francis Ford's first serial for Uncle Carl had been *Lucille Love, Girl of Mystery* (Universal, 1914), a

Hoot Gibson and his first wife, the former Helen Johnson. She is not the same person as Helen Gibson, the stunt woman.

Photo courtesy of *Views & Reviews* magazine.

fifteen-chapter affair. By the time of Ford's next serial, he had hired his younger brother, Sean O'Fearna, as a prop boy. Laemmle at once culled the youth out with that uncanny instinct of his for talent. "Make him a director!" he had said during one of his periodic tours of the back lot, seeing the youngster on the set. "He hollers the loudest." Sean took his brother's surname as his professional name and was credited as Jack Ford. He was a man of impregnable loyalties. Long after Francis Ford had eclipsed, Jack kept him employed as a player in his major studio productions.

Jack searched around Hollywood in 1915 for a buddy with whom he might share the expense of rooms. He came up with a wrangler from among the Universal cowhands, Edmund Richard Gibson, born at Tekamah, Nebraska, on August 6, 1892. I've already introduced him as Hoot Gibson, Hoot being a nickname he'd picked up when, in 1907, he was a bicycle messenger for the Owl Drug Company. His first job was herding cows at fifty cents a head per month from nearby farms to his grandfather's pasture in Tekamah and taking them back to their barns at night. In 1907 he moved to California, where his mother was living for her health. He was employed initially for three months with the postal telegraph and then transferred to Owl.

In 1910 Hoot signed on with the Dick Stanley-Bud Atkinson Wild West Show. It toured the United States, playing small towns. During the off months, Hoot and several others in the company wrangled horses. When the Selig Polyscope Company opened its studio at Edendale, Hoot and Art Acord went to work there stunting and doubling for the principals. It was as a result of this activity that D. W. Griffith hired them during the filming of *Two Brothers* (Biograph, 1910). Hoot recalled that he was paid $5.00 a day for doubling Henry B. Walthall, $2.50 a day for labor and $2.50 a stunt, as needed. The week of shooting *Two Brothers,* Hoot earned $50.00.

Hoot was working as an automobile mechanic in Seattle in 1912 when he read in the newspapers about the Pendleton annual roundup. He went down in the basement of the garage, got out his saddle, and told the owners that he didn't think he'd ever make much of a grease monkey. He went to Oregon, entered the competition, and won a trophy, a silver-plated saddle, and the title All-Around Champion Cowboy. Helen Wenger was one of the congress riders present at Pendleton. Lodgings were difficult to come by, and preference was given to married couples. She and Hoot declared that they were married. Outliving Hoot, Helen insisted years later that she had been Hoot's first wife. This is inaccurate. Hoot did not legally marry until April 20, 1922, and then to Helen Johnson, a vaudeville performer from St. Louis, daughter of Mr. and Mrs. Jerome L. Johnson, of 3953 DeTonty Street, and a graduate of McKinley High School in St. Louis. It was a first marriage for both of them; Hoot's only child, Lois, was born a year later. When Helen Wenger was signed to replace Helen Holmes by Kalem in the mid teens, she adopted the screen name Helen Gibson and occasionally featured Hoot in one of her pictures in the *Hazards of Helen* series. Hoot never objected publicly. I believe they were once in love. In 1915 Hoot was signed by Universal to double Harry Carey.

In *The New York Times Magazine* of September 20, 1959, when John Ford was set to direct and Hoot to play in *The Horse Soldiers* (United Artists, 1959), both recalled their early days. " 'Jack was good from the start,' " Hoot said, " 'a natural. Only 21, and already close to a genius. He'd make up bits off the cuff, shoot them on the wing as he went along, then afterwards scribble them into the script. Anything you hear about run-ins—they were just kid-stuff. Why, he was worse Irish than me. That time he wanted to play "My Wild Irish Rose" on the player piano and I wanted to play something else, I forget what, he picked up the piano stool and broke it on my head. And it was my piano!' "

Ford was asked his response to the Hooter's anecdote. " 'It wasn't "My Wild Irish Rose," ' " he said, " 'and there was no choice. He had exactly one roll for that piano—"Dardanella." He'd sit at that thing playing "Dardanella" morning, noon and night. Even now . . . anytime I have the black luck to hear "Dardanella," I notice my fists are clenched and I'm gritting my teeth. One night I had to get some sleep; I had a tough morning ahead. There he sat and his "Dardanella." Sure I knocked him off the piano stool and smashed it on his head. And then he came at me with a bottle.' "

With the younger Ford directing, Carey starring, and Hoot doubling, the three developed a warm comradeship. *A Knight of the Range* (Universal, 1915), one of Harry's two-reelers, cast Harry opposite eighteen-year-old Olive Fuller Golden; it was also Hoot's debut as a featured player. Harry began courting Ollie, and in 1920 they were married.

Ford promoted the Hooter into parts wherever he could. By 1917 Gibson was playing second lead. The Carey Westerns had done well enough that Uncle Carl agreed to commence feature production. *Straight Shooting* was Jack Ford's first feature; both Harry and Hoot had strong roles. This is one of the very few Ford-Carey Westerns which survive from the teens. *The Moving Picture World* commented that the photography was "clear" and "attractive," "the riding and fighting episodes are enacted with dash and enthusiasm." The film was "so successful" it was ranked with the best Westerns of the period.

Harry Carey as a screen cowboy was quite dissimilar to William S. Hart. His personality was engaging with a comfortable self-sufficiency. He was incapable of Hart's moral intensity and lacked utterly Hart's penchant for sustained melodrama. Carey's natural humor and charm resulted in a characterization that, in some ways, anticipated Will Rogers.

Ford had only been directing some six months when he made *Straight Shooting*. The plot was less than inspired. Ford had been a Klansman in Griffith's *The Birth of a Nation*. Some critics find Ford employing techniques he supposedly learned from watching Griffith. This is folly. Not enough of Ford's early work survives for anyone to determine what, precisely, he may have borrowed from Griffith. Carey did simulate the tortured ambivalence that William S. Hart had made popular with audiences, and his role is definitely that of a good bad man. It would take Tom Mix's astonishing emphasis on personality in his Fox Westerns to break this trend in Western production.

Locations were divided between Universal City's back lot and the old wagon cut at Newhall where innumerable Westerns would be filmed. Hard living, hard drinking, rollicking, and sentiment, more or less Ford trademarks, were already in evidence.

In *Straight Shooting* Thunder Flint is leader of the rancher clan. Flint hires Cheyenne Harry to help him drive the dirt farmers off their land. Hoot Gibson is a ranchman, but he is in love with a dirt farmer's daughter. Harry has a change of heart and decides to throw his lot in with the farmers. There is a terrific fight with the farmers winning, due to Harry's intervention with a band of outlaws who want some excitement. At the end, Harry wins the farmer's daughter, and Hoot has to make the best of it; if the screenplay is to be believed, the lovers will live happily ever after as dirt farmers.

Although the reader may find it difficult to accept on the basis of the foregoing, John Ford was coming into his own directing the Carey Westerns. By 1919, with the making of *The Outcasts of Poker Flat,* based on the Bret Harte short story, critics and public alike were applauding his efforts. Ford perhaps eschewed action for its own sake, but in his choice of remarkable and striking locations and his attention to human characterization—in the folksy vein—he was producing an unusual kind of Western melodrama.

In 1917, following *Straight Shooting,* Hoot volunteered for service and was placed in the U. S. Tank Corps. He attained the rank of sergeant before his discharge in 1919. When he returned to Hollywood, through Jack Ford's recommendation, Universal hired him as a director at $150 a week, "And I grabbed it," Hoot later commented. "I'd always wanted to be a director, and I'd noised it around. By that time I knew my way about, and I had a lot of friends in different studios. I checked into Universal and thought I was off to the races. I helped write a story. In writing the juvenile character, he appealed to me so strongly that I built up the part. The day before we were to start, Breezy Eason, who had turned down the assignment before, decided he wanted to direct the picture after all. The studio straightaway turned it over to him, leaving me high and dry. I crabbed, saying I'd left a good job to accept Universal's. I was told to hang around; they'd take care of me. Breezy was a friend of mine. . . . So I made him a proposition. I asked to play the juvenile lead. He agreed and I got the part. Breezy helped me develop it even more than I had done in the original script. When the picture was finished, my role outshone even the star's."

On the basis of this film, Uncle Carl decided to star Hoot in his own series of two-reelers. *The Man with a Punch* is one of the few surviving pictures from this series. It was based on W. C. Tuttle's pulp short story. Hoot plays an undercover ranger who gets the goods on a crooked sheriff, battles with Ben Corbett, and manages to win the girl by the fade.

The Man with a Punch is no work of art, but in many ways it is far more amusing than the deliberate pacing of *Straight Shooting.*

In 1919 John Ford made a feature with Harry Carey, J. Farrell Mac-Donald, and Joe Harris released as *Marked Men* and based on a story by Peter B. Kyne. It was originally made as *Three Godfathers* (Universal-Blue-bird, 1916), a production with which Ford had nothing to do. But he was so attracted to the story that he kept remaking it. He reused elements from it in the 1921 feature starring J. Farrell MacDonald, Hoot Gibson, and his brother, Francis Ford. The screenplay was based on J. Allen Dunn's "The

Mascotte of the Three Star" from the February 1921 number of *Short Stories*. Harvey Gates was credited on the screen for the scenario. Hoot played a character named Sandy Brooke. It didn't take much variation when, in the thirties, William Colt MacDonald based his prototype of Stony Brooke on Hoot Gibson in his Three Mesquiteers books, a subject I will return to later. "One stunt nearly killed me," Hoot once recalled of the filming of *Action*, the title under which the picture was finally released. "The action called for me to jump my horse off a cliff into Lake Malibu, a height of possibly thirty-five feet or more. . . . In mid-air, the horse turned over, and I barely got out of its way when it landed in the water. I bruised my leg, but the horse was okay."

The property was remade by Universal in 1929 as *Hell's Heroes,* directed by William Wyler. In 1936 Metro-Goldwyn-Mayer purchased rights from Universal and filmed it under the title *Three Godfathers,* directed by Richard Boleslawski and starring Chester Morris, Lewis Stone, and Walter Brennan. Ford did the last make of the film himself for M-G-M in 1948, dedicating the picture to the memory of Harry Carey, and featuring Duke Wayne, Pedro Armendariz, and Dobie Carey, Harry's son, in the title roles.

H. Bruce "Lucky" Humberstone was hired in 1920 at Universal as a prop boy and assistant cameraman. His first assignment was on a Hoot Gibson film directed by Ford in which the unit went out to the Vasquez rocks, north of Hollywood. Ford, Hoot, and the rest of the company had mounts. Humberstone didn't. He carried the raw film stock in cans under his left arm, the camera under his right, and tripod on his back. Reaching the crest of a high plateau, the troupe paused and waited for Humberstone to catch up to them. Puffing, exhausted, he made it at last. Ford snapped his first words at him.

"Humberstone! What do you think of this location?"

"I think," Humberstone responded, wanting to impress Ford with his perspicacity, "that the top of that plateau over there would be better."

"Okay!" Ford shouted. "You heard the kid. Everybody over to the other plateau."

Once he had lugged his gear the great distance while the riders watched him, grinning and joking among themselves, Humberstone had come upon a first principle when working on a Ford picture. If the director asks you a rhetorical question, keep your mouth shut.

The Hooter was wiser in knowing how to deal with Ford's irascibility. "There was this scene," he recalled, "where I come riding round a bend into a river where the water's high as my horse's chest. Jack told us to come at a full run hitting the water head on. I knew any horse did that, he'd explode. Rear up. Chest's his broadest part; it hits a body of water full speed straight across, horse and water go up together like they struck a mine. So just before we reached the water, I slowed my horse and rode him in at an angle.

" 'What's the matter—you yellow?' Jack yelled.

"Every time I'd say to him something couldn't be done the way he wanted, he had to answer back, 'I'll show you!' 'Go ahead, show me!' I said. Jack jumped on my horse and ran him wide open head on into the water. The horse exploded, reared up, fell back on top of him. So then I pulled my horse off of him and dragged him out. He didn't say a word."

Lucile Pinson and Harry Carey at the Carey ranch near Saugus in 1926, a press photo illustrating a party Carey was to give for the American Legion at his ranch.

Photo courtesy of *Views & Reviews* magazine.

Uncle Carl was amazed at Hoot's sudden popularity with the public. It stimulated a characteristic Laemmle gesture. Rather than investing further money and production value into the Carey Westerns, he did not renew Harry's contract, switched the Carey unit to Gibson, and tightened the budgets. Hoot's fantastic ascent to stardom began.

The spirit of the twenties was frolicsome and carefree. Hoot Gibson's penchant for deadpan comedy filled the needs of the day for a nation sufficiently disillusioned by war to turn its back on the righteous moral severity of William S. Hart or the sinewy, tough sentiment true of Harry Carey.

Film Booking Office signed Harry in 1922 to star in a series of Westerns much in the tradition, if not of comparable quality, of those he had been making for Universal. At the time William S. Hart announced his retirement from the screen, Hunt Stromberg contracted Harry for a group of intensely realistic Westerns for Producers Distributing Corporation. Lloyd Ingraham, who had worked under D. W. Griffith, Breezy Eason, and Tom Forman were the directors. Sol Polito was the cinematographer. In brief, no one associated with the technical production of the films approached Carey's experience. The pictures were released on a states' rights basis. Harry went with the fading Pathé, beginning with the 1926 season, and stayed there until early 1928. His career in the twenties had been all in all an arduous one. He did not quite understand what had happened to him. On March 15, 1928, the San Francito Dam burst and wiped out Harry's ranch. His personal fortune was destroyed. He and Ollie got up a vaudeville act and went on tour. There is no telling what might have happened to him had Irving Thalberg not saved the day with the lead role in *Trader Horn* (M-G-M, 1931). Prospects brightened.

No matter what the public's reception to Harry's films during the silent era—and the post-Universal scripts insisted on making the Carey vehicles either resemble a Douglas Fairbanks thriller or a static William S. Hart study in moral affinities—Harry was one of the first Western players to develop a natural screen style. He probably couldn't have altered it, even if he'd wanted to. G. M. Anderson, and to an even greater extent Bill Hart, projected excessive melodrama. Carey changed that. He made it possible for Hoot Gibson and Buck Jones and countless others to make a virtue out of being natural. More taciturn than his close friend Will Rogers, devoid of Tom Mix's cinematic magnificence, Carey nonetheless became a part of the tradition of the twenties. Jack Ford learned as many human values from Harry as Harry learned of acting from Ford, possibly more. Carey's constant, quiet, philosophic personality endeared him to you, but he did not inspire. If his career lacked glamour, it is also reassuring that it escaped the meteoric rise which so often precedes a disastrous fall.

The
Glittering
Twenties

8 / WILLIAM S. HART AT FAMOUS PLAYERS-LASKY

I have already narrated how Adolph Zukor's Famous Players Company merged with the Lasky Feature Play Company. What I did not mention was Harry Aitken's role as a catalytic agent. Aitken was still road-showing *The Birth of a Nation* and pouring a fortune into Griffith's extravagant *Intolerance*. The notion came to him to summon together Adolph Zukor from New York and Jesse L. Lasky, Cecil B. De Mille, and Sam Goldwyn from the West Coast and form a combine with himself as president. Harry was having considerable difficulty getting continuous financing from bankers. The combined assets of the three firms forming a single conglomerate would give them greater borrowing power.

Zukor came West for the meeting. Harry did the honors at the Culver City studio where Ince made his headquarters. During the conferences, Harry showed his fellow picture men—regarding them as partners, now, and not as competitors—the operational records on Triangle's exchange network, the salaries paid to the 250 contract players, the costs and grosses of all the pictures made by Sennett, Ince, and Griffith, the astonishing revenues brought in by the William S. Hart Westerns budgeted at $13,000 to $15,000. The merger did not go through, but Zukor memorized what he saw. When he got back to New York, his company started making counter-offers to Triangle players that substantially increased what the Aitkens could afford to pay them. Douglas Fairbanks defected to Famous Players. Thomas Ince, frustrated by Harry's financial woes, by what he felt to be the gross incompetence of Kessel and Bauman, and by the favoritism he felt was being shown to D. W. Griffith, decided to leave.

Ince owned the deed to the land on which Harry Aitken had built the Culver City studio of the New York Motion Picture Company. He announced that he was leaving the firm and that he intended to put the property up for sale. Aitken, who had known none of this when he bought out Kessel and Bauman and put them on the board of Mutual only to maneuver them out of the newly formed Triangle completely, was dumfounded. But Ince proved to be right, and Aitken had to pay him $250,000 for the land and all the improvements he had paid for once already or lose the lot.

William S. Hart and his beloved Fritz in a candid pose when they worked for Thomas Ince at the Triangle Studio.

Photo courtesy of *Views & Reviews* magazine.

Ince next went to Adolph Zukor with his terms. William S. Hart was under personal contract to Ince. Hart was to make a series of sixteen Westerns for Paramount-Artcraft, the distribution brand name under which Famous Players-Lasky released its product, at an average cost of at least $150,000 a picture. Ince himself agreed to produce two special pictures a year for at least $50,000 each. Charles Ray, Dorothy Dalton, and Enid Bennett, also under personal contract to Ince, would each make a series of films for Famous Players-Lasky, budgeted at $35,000 each. Zukor had a clause inserted into the final contract that all of these agreements would be null and void if William S. Hart were not delivered to Famous Players-Lasky within thirty days of signing. Hart knew very little about his own value to Thomas Ince's career and failed to realize his importance to motion picture producing companies; but he was beside himself with delight when Ince informed him that, finally, he had ten times the budget to work with on every Western he made than he had been accustomed to at Triangle. Hart had unbounded confidence in Tom Ince's business acumen and rejoiced with the prospects now before him.

By the time of his second film, Hart set up operations at the old Mabel Normand studio and leased it. From start to finish, each picture was under Hart's total control. Hart had first met Lambert Hillyer, born in 1893 at South Bend, Indiana, while with Mutual. At Paramount-Artcraft, Hart asked for him to be assigned to his unit, which Jesse L. Lasky was willing to do. Over the next three and a half years, Hillyer directed twenty-five of Hart's Westerns and wrote sixteen of them. The men worked perfectly together.

Ince, for his part, leased the old Biograph West Coast studio lot at Culver City and at once constructed a new studio administration building. He moved in during the fall of 1918. The administration building was given a front to resemble George Washington's home, Mount Vernon. After Ince died, the studio was joined to the FBO holdings, and RKO-Pathé subsequently owned it. David O. Selznick leased it for years, and a photograph of the administration building was generally used to introduce a Selznick International Picture.

Ince had his own production schedule to maintain and began with films such as *The Kaiser's Shadow* (Paramount, 1918) and *False Faces* (Paramount, 1918), with Lon Chaney and Henry B. Walthall. Hart made *The Narrow Trail* (Paramount, 1918) and *Blue Blazes Rawden* (Paramount, 1918). While Ince personally had nothing to do with the manufacture of these or any of Hart's other sixteen Westerns on his first Paramount contract, it was required that Ince be given credit on the titles as producer. Further, Ince and Hart, by contract, had to split fifty-fifty the 35 per cent of the profits they were entitled to from Famous Players-Lasky. Hart went through hell. No one on earth could charm him as could Tom Ince, and he

William S. Hart in costume as he appeared in his series for Paramount-Artcraft.
Photo courtesy of *Views & Reviews* magazine.

genuinely liked the fellow. But he had the increasing suspicion that Ince
was cheating him. He held long discussions out on location with Lambert
Hillyer, telling Hillyer of how he had been offered $10,000 a week to stay
at Triangle; how he had told Ince that he knew for a fact that his pictures
were grossing millions and that after three and a half years of working for
Tom he didn't have $5,000 to his name; how Ince had told him about the
new Paramount deal and how he would at last be making good money.
Most of all, Hart was nettled by Ince's continuing insistence on attaching
his name to everything William S. Hart ever did. To retaliate, Triangle
began reissuing all of the old Hart pictures with new titles. William S. Hart
Productions had to bring a restraining order against Triangle, compelling
the firm to list both the former title and the new title on the screen and on
all publicity.

The Narrow Trail (Paramount, 1918), Hart's first Western on the new
contract, had been filmed for interiors at the Lasky studio. Hart's pinto
pony, Fritz, was featured prominently in the action. Ince, seeing the film
run, complained bitterly about Fritz and told Hart bluntly that he should
use a different horse. Fritz became a symbol of William S. Hart's rebellion.

"You'll never split another dollar with me that Fritz earns by working in my pictures," Hart told Ince heatedly.

Hart announced, first to Jesse and Mr. Zukor and then to the world at large, that Fritz was in temporary retirement due to a personality conflict with Thomas Ince. Thinking Hart a fool, Ince tried in various ways to bring pressure on him to end the altercation and restore Fritz to his rightful place at his side. This Hart refused to do. By the time that Ince's sixteen-picture contract had run its course, he and Hart were no longer talking to one another. Ince's wife represented him at board meetings. As treasurer of William S. Hart Productions, Ince claimed the corporation owed him $125,000. Hart rejected Ince's importunity. It led to a lawsuit.

Douglas Fairbanks now approached Hart and outlined the setup at United Artists. He wanted Hart to join them. Zukor, on the other hand, wanted Hart to stay on at Famous Players-Lasky, only with a new contract having nothing to do with Ince. Zukor was in a perfect position to make such an offer, having succeeded by the middle of 1919 in forcing Thomas Ince out of Paramount-Artcraft completely. Hart decided in Zukor's favor.

Eva Novak, Fritz, and Hart as they appeared in *Sand*.

Photo courtesy of *Views & Reviews* magazine.

The picture Hart was filming when Fairbanks came to visit him was *Wagon Tracks*. It was Tom Mix's custom to kiss or embrace the heroine at the fade. Not so, Hart; he almost invariably rode off, leaving the girl behind, carrying on his lonely life as a frontiersman. The excessive emotion in his films, if anything, intensified after he left Triangle. Hart's theatricalism was different from Mix's. Tom mugged for purposes of comedy; Hart rolled his eyes and looked crestfallen only to describe pathos which, when you think about it, was the one emotion that dominated his screen image. In *My Life East and West,* Hart describes over and over the difficulty he had coming up with plots. I suspect that he is telling the truth, since, from what survives, his films are variations on a theme; he had nowhere Tom Mix's versatility.

Thomas Ince was still credited with supervision on *Wagon Tracks.* Jane Novak played Jane Washburn. She is falsely accused by her brother and his friend of accidentally shooting Hart's brother. Hart stands with tears in his eyes, unbelieving that his brother is dead and that so fine a woman could have done it. The three are part of a wagon train Hart is leading. Hart takes the two men out into the desert and sweats the truth out of them. Jane's brother is the culprit. When the wagon train is visited by friendly Indians, a brave is shot by mistake and the tribe demands a white man's life. Hart volunteers, but Jane's brother is captured by the Indians instead. After guiding the train to Santa Fe, Hart rides off alone into the wastelands.

Without Ince's minimal restraining influence, in his new contract Hart went even further. He organized the William S. Hart Company and insisted on perpetuating his melodramatic vision of a romanticized, sentimentalized, fanciful West of good men and good women pitted against nature and human evil. The religious fervor intensified.

On location at Sonora, Tuolumne County, in order to film the cave scene with which *The Toll Gate* begins, Hart had to cross a deep stream. He rode Fritz across, and the two got caught in a whirlpool. "Twice we went down in this cold, whirling depths and twice we fought our way to the surface again," Hart later recalled. "I knew the next time would be the last. Fritz spoke to me—I know he did. I heard him, and I spoke to him. I said, 'God help us, Fritz.' . . . And God did help us! My little friend could not struggle any more, his eyes were glazed with coming death, and as we were going down for the last time the strong current we had been fighting carried us over the ledge back toward the way we came in, and as we sank we touched bottom and regained our feet."

While working on *The Toll Gate,* Hart was summoned to court through charges of seduction brought against him by a woman who was a nurse. Hart denied having ever seen her before. The judge chose to believe Hart. He described sexual congress in the most fundamental terms and then asked the woman if that is what she had done with Hart. The woman denied physical love; she said they were unified only in the spirit. The case was dismissed. Those were different times, indeed!

As *The Toll Gate* begins, Hart is the leader of an outlaw band. He is betrayed by one of his lieutenants but allowed to escape. The lieutenant starts a saloon and Hart pursues him, setting the saloon on fire. Hart is chased by a posse and hides with Anna Q. Nilsson and her small son, deserted by her husband, who turns out to be Hart's traitorous lieutenant. Hart finally shoots the lieutenant, and the sheriff lets him go, Anna and the child staying behind.

Ince switched distribution from Paramount to Metro, one of the firms eventually merged into M-G-M. By October 1919 he had organized Associated Exhibitors, which consisted of several independent filmmakers such as himself, Mack Sennett, and Maurice Tourneur. Tourneur released an exceptionally fine Western in 1920, *The Last of the Mohicans,* which starred Wallace Beery in the role of Magua. Ince's pictures consistently proved excellent money-makers, but he paused in 1923 to bring Eugene O'Neill's play *Anna Christie* to the screen, with Blanche Sweet in the leading role. Ince commented, "I made that one for the high-brow critics who say Tom Ince can't make anything but box-office pictures."

In late 1924 Thomas Ince held a special conference aboard his yacht with William Randolph Hearst, Marion Davies, Seena Owen, and Dr. Daniel Carson Goodman, the West Coast manager of Hearst's Cosmopolitan Pictures. Ince was negotiating a deal whereby he would take over personal production of the Davies' films which were enjoying an indifferent reception from the public. Ince drank heavily and ate too much. He grew deathly ill. The yacht moored off San Diego, and Ince was taken ashore. According to medical testimony, Ince had been suffering from a series of mild heart attacks. A special car was finally attached to a train, and Ince was transported back to his home in Los Angeles, transferring to an ambulance. He died at five o'clock in the morning on November 19, 1924, at Días Dorados, his home in the Benedict Canyon. His death ended one of the most brilliant and spectacular careers in the history of the motion picture industry. Just before the end, Lambert Hillyer directed a picture for Ince which Ince invited Hart to see at its première. Hart responded warmly, although there had been a definite coolness between them for years. "I am glad Tom wrote to me," he remarked afterward, "and I am glad I wrote to Tom."

9 / THE WESTERN EPIC BEGINS

I

Some of the freshest air in the continental United States was to be found at Pascagoula, Mississippi, when I arrived there in early spring 1970. Pollution hadn't caught up with the city, although an instance of narcotics had; so the city fathers and industrial leaders put together a parade followed by a Boy Scouts rally to promote a positive community spirit. In the great cities of the East, billboards and public transport advertising were mounting a massive campaign to gather support in the war against venereal disease. But here in Pascagoula the whole town was lining the streets for the festivities to culminate that night at the high school auditorium with an appearance of the Tommy Scott Wild West Show, featuring the man who had become the dean of American cowboys: Colonel Tim McCoy.

Tim wasn't in the parade.

"I don't generally appear in parades," Tim remarked as we sat casually in his motel room, sipping highballs.

But a long time ago in Saginaw, Michigan, where on April 10, 1891, the youngest of three sons, he was born to Cathrin Fitzpatrick McCoy and Timothy H. McCoy, and where he grew up, Tim had watched parades.

"You know," Tim said, his blue eyes still very intense, "at the turn of the century children could still dream. There were those who watched the fire wagons and wanted to be firemen; and those who wanted to be policemen. My eldest brother finished college and became a lawyer. He would hurry home at night to bury himself in the great leather chair in the parlor and read the stories in *The Saturday Evening Post*. He wasn't really doing what he most wanted to do."

"And you?" I asked.

"I didn't want to be a fireman," Tim said, smiling, "nor a policeman. And I didn't want to be a lawyer." He paused. "I wanted to be a cowboy."

He told me of his early life and how he came to work on *The Covered Wagon*. He was a sophomore, enrolled at St. Ignatius College in Chicago, when he went to see the Miller Brothers 101 Ranch Wild West Show the

J. Warren Kerrigan and Lois Wilson framed by a prairie schooner in *The Covered Wagon*. Ken Maynard framed a similar shot for his *Wheels of Destiny*.

Photo courtesy of the Academy of Motion Picture Arts & Sciences.

night it opened. Bud Osborne, with whom Tim would fight many times in pictures beginning with the dagger duel in *The Indians Are Coming,* was with the show. Tim attended every performance for the entire week it played Chicago. It was after the show closed that he finally made up his mind to do what, since he had been a small boy, he had most wanted to do. He packed his bag, quit school, chucked everything, and headed West.

The year was 1907, and Tim was aboard a train bound for Omaha, a one-way ticket in his pocket. Only one seat was vacant in the day coach. Tim seated himself beside a tall man wearing a high Stetson. The ride was a long one; they fell into conversation. Tim learned that his companion was heading for Lander, a Wyoming town which served as a center for his activities, rounding up wild horses from the Red Desert and shipping them East. The man suggested Tim come to Wyoming. Tim agreed he would.

When they arrived in Lander late of a Saturday night, a telegram was waiting for the horse trader, summoning him back to Chicago. He left Lander before daylight. Tim would never see him again. In the months that followed, Tim did almost everything imaginable on ranches in the Owl Creek section. Finding a job pitching hay, he soon graduated to wrangling, which is day-herding as opposed to night-hawking. His horsemanship improved along with his ability to use a lariat. Working in the Wind River country, Tim came to know the Arapahoe and Shoshone Indians, tribes which lived in peace on the Wind River Reservation and communicated in the sign language common to Plains Indians. Because of a natural facility for mimicry that permitted him easily to learn gesture and physical expression of emotional meaning, one Arapahoe chief told him, "Long time ago you must have been Indian." Tim developed a profound sympathy for the red men and their simple, tragic view of man's place in nature, of life and death, of hunting and survival. He was amazed at their ignorance of their own history and their rituals of freedom generated by centuries in the wide expanses. In learning their language, Tim could not but learn their traditions and their philosophy, the stark heroism accompanying a fatal consciousness of dwindling numbers in view of a more masterful race of men intent on different ends.

Wyoming crept into Tim's blood. It was there that he took part in the last of the great roundups; had he gone West a year or two later, that would have been impossible. Shortly after arriving in Lander, Tim went to work for Irish Tom. Tom didn't own a ranch as such but leased several range sights from the U. S. Government on which he raised horses. It was with Irish Tom that Tim first learned wrangling. Of a frugal disposition, Tim saved his money and eventually bought a small piece of land in the Owl Creek country, filing a homestead claim. In time, it would grow to encompass 5,200 acres some fifty miles from Thermopolis; it remained his only real home until the late forties when he finally sold it, following his second marriage.

Tim was well established when the Great War came along. Teddy Roosevelt, to whose memory *The Covered Wagon* would later be dedicated, began organizing a special division of volunteers to go to France. Tim wrote the former President and offered to raise a cavalry unit comprised of Wyoming and Montana cowboys. Roosevelt accepted, and Tim recruited the unit only to learn that Roosevelt had been denied permission to go abroad. It was just as well Tim didn't go. It was a different kind of war, and, even so, only thirty had survived T.R.'s charge of San Juan Hill during the Spanish-American War. Tim applied to Officers' Candidate School and emerged a commissioned captain of cavalry. He was again among the last of its kind, for only three divisions of mounted cavalry outlasted the Great War and were finally disbanded, Tim having previously transferred to the artillery.

It was while in the Army that Tim met Major General Hugh Scott, former army chief of staff and last of the great Indian fighters. The general took an immediate liking to the energetic enthusiast from Wyoming with his sincere interest in Indians and the settlement of the West. The general forced McCoy to read extensively and study to the point where he could say, "Tim knows more about the Indians than the Indians know themselves." When hostilities ended, Tim was appointed adjutant general of Wyoming with the rank of brigadier. As an aide to General Scott, McCoy began the pioneer reconstruction work on what actually happened at Little Big Horn, an effort which decided permanently how history was to judge General Custer's massacre.

McCoy accompanied Scott on visits to some of the army's foremost Western posts, including Fort Riley, Fort Snelling, and, in particular, Fort Washakie in Wyoming. When Scott retired from the Army, he was appointed head of the Board of Indian Commissioners, and in this guise, together with stenographers and interpreters, he and McCoy traced Custer's route to the Little Big Horn, talking to Custer's scouts and with Custer's enemies—the Sioux and the Cheyenne. At the Crow's Nest, high point of the mesa which provided cover for men and horses with its basinlike top, Tim and Scott built a rock cairn that is still standing.

I could feel the chill winds of the Wyoming plains as we talked, so many miles and so many years away.

"There was a big Indian celebration in Lander at the time," Tim said. "Arapahoes were camped at one end of town; Shoshones at the other. I am an Arapahoe, an adopted member of the tribe. So I went down to the Arapahoe camp, talked with the elders around the fire.

"Just in conversation—sign talk, you know?—I told of being over the Custer battlefield with General Scott. One old Indian responded with the remark that Water Man, a warrior seated near the fire, had been in the fight.

"I talked to Water Man. Found out that another Arapahoe, Left Hand, was in the camp. There had been five of them. These two were the last survivors of that group."

Tim got an interpreter and a stenographer and interviewed Water Man and Left Hand separately. He turned his findings over to Colonel W. A. Graham, whose books on the subject, primarily *The Custer Myth*, documented Tim's findings that Custer hopelessly divided his forces, intending to bring glory just to himself and his favorites and that, had he survived the battle of June 25, 1876, at Little Big Horn, he would certainly have been court-martialed.

In 1922, stepping on a train bound for the West Coast, Jesse L. Lasky's secretary, Jeane Cohen, who had earlier persuaded him to purchase *The Shiek* and cast Valentino in the lead, slipped Lasky a copy of Emerson

Hough's novel *The Covered Wagon*. He had purchased screen rights to the book on the basis of a synopsis. Now, as the train sped across the flatlands of Kansas and climbed through steep gorges between mountains and rocked relentlessly over the shimmering, silent deserts, Lasky read the novel of migration that described how guts and greed had united East and West by a thin line of white canvas-covered schooners nearly four score years before. It was, for him, almost a mystical experience.

When Lasky arrived, he instructed studio manager B. P. Schulberg to take director George Melford off the picture. *The Covered Wagon* was not going to be another potboiler, budgeted at $110,000, Famous Players' average cost for a Western. Mary Miles Minter was tentatively cast in the role of Molly Wingate. She had been grumbling about the assignment and was ecstatic when Jesse relieved her of the part. He appointed James Cruze to direct and told Schulberg, "It's going to be the greatest show we've ever made. . . ."

While winding through Manhattan skyscrapers in a taxicab with Lois Wilson during the winter of 1973, we talked of *The Covered Wagon*.

"Jimmie was to direct and I wanted the part of Molly," she confided. "If Jesse knew anything about Mary having the role, he never told me. I went to Jimmie and asked for the part. He hesitated because I was so fragile-looking, but I cried. Jimmie couldn't stand to have any woman cry. He gave it to me."

Lois Wilson was born on May 28, 1898, at Pittsburgh. She and her three sisters were raised in Alabama. In 1915, as Miss Alabama, she entered the first Miss America contest, sponsored by Universal Pictures to publicize Uncle Carl's opening of Universal City and to discover young talent. Lois's first film, *The Dumb Girl of Portici* (Universal, 1916), was made in Chicago while she was still one of fifteen finalists. The picture itself was not a success, but Universal went ahead and signed Lois to a short-term contract to play opposite J. Warren Kerrigan in a series of outdoor films to be produced at their new studio. The series proved popular and continued throughout the Great War. Lois brought her family to California to live with her.

In 1919, conscious of her box-office attraction, Jesse L. Lasky invited her to join Famous Players-Lasky. Her first role was in *Love Insurance* (Artcraft, 1919). Her Lasky contract reduced her salary from $125 a week to $75, but Lois and her family thought Paramount had more to offer by way of opportunity. Lois worked opposite Wallace Reid at Famous Players and was directed to very good effect by William De Mille. In 1922 James Cruze first directed her in *Is Matrimony a Failure?* (Paramount, 1922).

Cruze, whose Hollywood reputation would be made by *The Covered Wagon,* was born on March 27, 1884, at Ogden, Utah. As a young man he had trouped with traveling road companies and alternated between playing

Shakespeare and melodrama to touring with medicine shows. Nationwide polls in 1926 and again in 1928 would select him as one of the world's ten greatest directors. He was a naturalist who put people together and let the story grow up around and through them. Although he had directed Westerns before *The Covered Wagon,* he was incapable of creating sustained suspense, and, unlike John Ford and other contemporaries, he wasn't able to stage exciting action sequences effectively. He was no better at this sort of thing when he came in the sound era to direct a major Western like *Sutter's Gold* (Universal, 1936) than he had been in 1923. But with the delicate interplay of human personality, he was more than a match for Ford, as witness *David Harum* (Fox, 1934), which starred Will Rogers.

James Warren Kerrigan was born at Louisville, Kentucky, on July 25, 1880. He worked on the vaudeville stage and even entered the University of Illinois before he began playing in two-reelers for Essanay in Chicago. When Spoor and Anderson split their partnership, Kerrigan became a headliner for Spoor's reorganized American Film Corporation until Universal, offering him starring features, signed him in 1914 and turned him into one of their brightest luminaries. Kerrigan was one of the first players to get his own production unit at Universal, but, as was frequently the case with those who followed him, he was inept at choosing successful vehicles. Universal dropped him in 1919 when Lois left for Famous Players, and he worked for the independents making low-grade films.

Cruze decided he wanted to reteam Kerrigan with Lois Wilson, and Lasky concurred. When *The Covered Wagon* scored at the box office, Film Booking Office purchased reissue rights from Universal to the Kerrigan-Wilson non-Western melodrama *A Man's Man* (Universal-Kerrigan, 1917) and, editing it from seven reels to five, rereleased it theatrically in 1923. Cruze chose by a stroke of genius Ernest Torrence to play Jackson, a tough old trader, and Tully Marshall as the pathfinder, Jim Bridger. Their inveterate comic byplay frequently stole the picture. Alan Hale projected a totally despicable villain.

"A few days after I sent my quarterly budget East," Lasky recalled in his autobiography, *I Blow My Own Horn* (Doubleday, 1957), "Zukor phoned. 'Mr. Lasky,' he said in his quiet way, 'we've gone over your proposed pictures for the next quarter and we all agree the list is very good. But there seems to be a typographical error on your budget for a Western called *The Covered Wagon.* It says $500,000. Isn't the decimal point in the wrong place?'

" 'No,' I said, 'it will cost half a million dollars to make *The Covered Wagon.*'

"There was a ponderous silence. 'But Mr. Lasky,' he protested unemotionally, 'don't you realize Westerns are dead? Even Bill Hart's *Three Word Brand,* which we released three months ago, will hardly break even.

The wagons split for California and Oregon in *The Covered Wagon*.

Photo courtesy of the Academy of Motion Picture Arts & Sciences.

The top boys in distribution think you've lost your mind or that you're out of touch with the changing times for wanting to make another Western at all.'

" 'Mr. Zukor,' I said anxiously, 'they don't understand—but you will. This picture is more than a Western. It's an epic.'

" 'An epic?'

" 'E-P-I-C,' I elucidated, trembling in my boots for the money we'd already spent without authorization, preparing for an elaborate production.

"There was a long pause. Then the still-calm voice came over the wire. 'An epic, eh? Well, that's different. You go ahead and I'll take care of the sales department.' That was all the argument needed to convince the champion of bigger and better pictures. If Adolph Zukor hadn't been in the driver's seat, *The Covered Wagon* would no doubt have stopped dead in its tracks right there. When the carnage was over in the sales department, he wired me: *'Budget approved. Regards and Good Luck.'* "

Cruze combed nine states for suitable locations. He negotiated with Otto Meek, owner of the Baker Ranch, nearly 200,000 acres in the Snake Valley of Nevada, to use it as his principal site. A great lake on the property was banked, an outlet formed, in order to shoot the wagon fording sequences. Thither Cruze went with a company of 127 people and a large staff of carpenters and technical men. Cruze recruited almost a thousand extras from the inhabitants of the district, some coming as far as three hundred miles for ten dollars a day. He enlisted 750 Indians, and Jesse L. Lasky arranged with the Board of Indian Commissioners to be sent a technical adviser on Indian affairs. The man selected was the adjutant of Wyoming, Colonel Tim McCoy, who resigned his commission to work on the picture.

Cruze took a smaller unit to Antelope Island in the Great Salt Lake to photograph the buffalo scenes. A large herd grazed there, owned by the Buffalo Livestock Corporation. Always contrary beasts, it took all of three days merely to get them to run past the camera!

Emerson Hough had originally published *The Covered Wagon* in *The Saturday Evening Post*. It was his most successful novel. Jack Cunningham, who had been born at Ionia, Iowa, and had been a newspaper reporter before pursuing a career as a scenarist, blocked the novel into a tenable photoplay.

"Came winds, blizzards, floods, heat, alkali dust—we had to work through it all," James Cruze later recalled. When the lake dam burst, the camp was flooded. A terrific snow fell and Cruze had it written into the picture. The five hundred wagons used had to be rented, borrowed, or built and formed a caravan three miles long. "Eight trucks a day," Cruze noted, "carried supplies to the two or three thousand people in camp. Indians were transported with bag and baggage. Hundreds of head of stock; all kinds of foodstuffs, lumber—anything and everything to say nothing of fifty carloads of equipment from the Lasky Studio."

Lois Wilson remembered conditions as being very rough. "I got slight frostbite, we ran out of supplies and had to live on apples and baked beans for a while, but I loved every minute of *The Covered Wagon*," she told Kevin Brownlow for his book *The Parade's Gone By* . . . (Knopf, 1968). ". . . The Arapahoe Indians made James Cruze a chief; they called him Standing Bear. James was kind of like a bear. We had one old Indian who had been through the Indian wars, and, I think, the Civil War. Anyway, all he wanted out of life was a Union uniform, which the government had supplied him. He couldn't speak English, but Tim McCoy served as interpreter. The Indians had all been told the story of the film, and they entered into it with great spirit. This Indian was an expert with a bow and arrow, and when he heard that I was to be shot in the film, he volunteered to do it. 'Very good shot,' he said to Cruze, through Tim McCoy. 'Very good. Shoot arrow through lady's shoulder. Not hurt much. Not break bone. Go right through!'"

The company remained on location for a total of eight weeks. Certain routines were established such as feeding the three thousand residents of the five hundred tents in three separate shifts. No one really minded the physical hardships; in many cases, they helped generate verisimilitude on film. Cruze built a facsimile of Fort Bridger, buying barns and houses in the surrounding counties to get lumber. As Cunningham originally projected the story in his screenplay, *The Covered Wagon* ended on the plains. It was felt that continuous scenes of the caravan wending its way cross-country would become monotonous.

"When I saw the completed picture in the projection room, I wasn't satisfied . . . ," Lasky commented. "So I had it rewritten to show both the California and Oregon contingents continue to their goals. . . ." Three months after returning to Hollywood, the company resumed location work at Sonora, California. The wagon train itself, it seems, had become the star, with a personality of its own. The wagons had to be rebuilt, as Cruze observed, "for the old wagons had been discarded, broken up, or sold back in Nevada. This added a big expense, but it gave *The Covered Wagon* its logical culmination. Don't forget that Mr. Lasky deserves his praise for adding this huge item to the final cost—and adding it purely with the thought of bettering a picture which could have been sold as it was." The negative cost on the film, prior to its release, was $782,000.

Public reaction was fantastic. It played to capacity audiences for months. Paramount opined that the returns from just the Criterion in New York and Grauman's in Hollywood would pay for the picture. By 1932 worldwide gross on *The Covered Wagon* was reported at $3.8 million, and as late as 1935 it was still listed among the five top grossing films of all time.

When *The Covered Wagon* was scheduled to open at Grauman's, Lasky asked Tim McCoy to deliver a prologue to the film. McCoy brought fifty Indians with him to Hollywood, braves, squaws, papooses, tepees, dogs, and ceremonial costuming in two special trains. To illustrate the prologue itself, Tim selected Indians who lent some historical import to what he had to say. One of the Indians, Mrs. Broken Horn, was actually a red-haired white woman who had been captured by the Indians when only a child and had herself been part of a wagon train; she was unable to speak English any more. Another of the Indians had fought against General Custer.

I have remarked on Tim's surprise at the indifference of the Indians to their history. I should, therefore, also note that such a prologue to a historical film could not be successful in contemporary America. At the time of *The Covered Wagon,* McCoy knew Indian sign language so well that only Captain Philo Clark and General Hugh Scott were his equals. When we spoke in Pascagoula so many decades later, he stood alone with his knowledge, and no one had ever bothered to record him using the principal means of communication among the Plains tribes.

The prologue proved to be an immense success and played in Hollywood for eight months. It then occurred to Paramount to send McCoy and the Indians overseas to improve the foreign revenues. Bringing the Indians to Hollywood had been one thing; getting them to act properly before cameras had been another; but Tim was truly hard-pressed when convincing them to undertake a trip to Europe, crossing an ocean they had never seen. Tim owed much to one of the ancient chiefs named Goes-in-Lodge who, referring to Tim by his Indian name of High Eagle, spoke encouragement to his friends. "The night is in my eyes," the chief said. "I can't see what's ahead of me, but if my brother High Eagle will take me along, I will follow." Tim and the Indians stayed in Europe for a year.

Nearly everyone associated with *The Covered Wagon* enjoyed subsequent fame and fortune. Cruze had been signed by Famous Players in 1921 at $250 a week. Jesse paid him $400 a week during production of the epic film, but he refused to release him afterward when Cruze received offers up to $1,500 a week. Lois Wilson became a Paramount star. J. Warren Kerrigan experienced a resurgence in his career. Emerson Hough sold rights to several other books to film companies, including *North of '36,* which Paramount scheduled for immediate production. Somewhat ironically, in May 1923, Hough died. Lois and James Cruze commenced at once on a remake of *Ruggles of Red Gap* (Paramount, 1923).

I suppose among the reasons I have spent so much time on the making of *The Covered Wagon* is the fact that it was the first Western epic; it astonished the public by its grandeur; it had a tremendous impact on Western production, an impetus that persisted until 1928; it established the Paramount tradition of a road-show picture a year. And it has been readily disparaged by modern critics. George N. Fenin and William K. Everson in their book *The Western* (Orion, 1962) sum it up: "In actual fact, *The Covered Wagon* was, its photography apart, of negligible creative value."

Technically it is difficult to arrive at an intelligent critical opinion on *The Covered Wagon* because it no longer survives. As first released, it ran 108 minutes, or nearly two hours. All surviving prints today come from the Kodascope Library condensation, reduced to five reels from ten. It is probably only a pale ghost of the total experience audiences had in the twenties. The plot with which I can provide the reader is that of the condensed version, and it is obvious that for the cutters at Kodascope the basic love story, and not the monumental trek through hardship and adversity, was what they chose to preserve. It is senseless to criticize this version if, by doing so, it is confused with the original masterpiece.

A covered-wagon train sets out for Oregon. Alan Hale is in love with Lois Wilson. Lois is in love with Jack Kerrigan. A rivalry mounts that reaches fisticuffs when the train is about to ford a river. Crossing the river, being attacked by Indians, these sequences retain much of their excitement. The train splits up, half going to California, half to Oregon. Lois, estranged from Jack, agrees to marry Alan Hale; but the estrangement ends, and she tells Hale she intends to go to Jack. Hale tries to kill Jack but is shot himself by Tully Marshall. Jack and Lois are united.

Why did *The Covered Wagon* act as such a spur to Western production, and why was it so singularly successful? I don't know, save it may have painted in broader strokes than ever before that readiness of the American people for new and dangerous adventures, long and wild chances at opportunity, and immersion in an enterprise of incredible difficulty in pursuit of the coattail of a dream that was never to be found so much in the realization as in the dreaming.

II

John Ford signed a long-term contract with the Fox Film Corporation in 1921. His reasons for leaving Universal were several. He had agreed in 1920 to direct two pictures for Fox, both of which starred their new screen property, Buck Jones. The first of these, *Just Pals* (Fox, 1920), still survives. Helen Ferguson was the leading lady. The film combined a rural setting with an action plot. The next picture, done consecutively, was *The Big Punch* (Fox, 1921), released shortly after the new year. Barbara Bedford was the girl. Buck Jones was scarcely typecast, this time playing a theological student who, following a misdeed, is sentenced to prison. Once he gets out, Buck is converted by Bedford, who works for the Salvation Army and, in turn, before he marries at the fade, manages to convert his reckless brother.

Neither of these Fox films was a Western in the mode of Ford's output at Universal. It was only natural that he should want to expand into areas other than Western programmers. In April, May, and June 1921 Ford directed three of Harry Carey's last Westerns for Laemmle. He made *Action* (Universal, 1921) in September and *Sure Fire* (Universal, 1921) in November, both with Hoot Gibson. Ford disapproved of Laemmle's decision not to renew Carey's contract. Moreover, Francis Ford wasn't pleased with the Universal management and persuaded Jack to seek his fortune elsewhere.

Ford's initial effort under contract to Fox was a melodrama entitled *Jackie* (Fox, 1921), which starred Shirley Mason as a Russian waif who sought a stage career as a dancer. There was undoubtedly a greater diversity for Ford at Fox. Even work he did with Tom Mix like *North of Hudson Bay* (Fox, 1923) is off-beat. The film has been preserved by the Czech Film Archive. Set in northern Canada, Mix played the brother of a murdered prospector. The starkness of the terrain and the deliberateness of the plot's unfolding permitted Mix scant opportunity for expression of that spontaneous good-natured fun which was so basic to his screen charm. The film, however, does reveal an increasing cognizance on Ford's part of grim savagery and raw emotion, tensed and constricted before the camera. Fred Kohler, Sr., had a supporting role in *North,* and Ford, struck by Kohler's

Francis Powers, George O'Brien, and J. Farrell MacDonald working on the railroad in *The Iron Horse*.

loss of two fingers and a thumb on his right hand, cast him as the featured villain in *The Iron Horse* and incorporated the deformity into the plot.

Kohler was a peculiar man. He was born at Kansas City, Missouri, on April 20, 1889. When fourteen, he ran away from home to work on the stage. Two years in vaudeville, discouraged, ready to return home, Kohler met an actor named William Carleton and, as a result, became a member of a traveling troupe of players. Four years later, in 1910, Kohler signed on as an extra at Selig. Contracted as a featured performer by Paramount in 1920, Kohler appeared occasionally in films for other companies. His exposure in *The Iron Horse* brought him notoriety, if not fame, with the picture-going public, and Paramount promoted him to a principal villain in their Zane Grey series. Having worked with both Tom Mix and George O'Brien at Fox during the twenties, Kohler would be cast opposite them respectively in some of their finest Westerns of the early sound era.

The Iron Horse was intended by William Fox to be his answer to Paramount's epic *The Covered Wagon*. Ford had directed Fox's very popular *Cameo Kirby* (Fox, 1923), which ran seven reels and starred John Gilbert. In the fifties Ford himself claimed that he felt *The Iron Horse* his best picture. It is unquestionably his only epic, with a running time nearly in excess of two hours. The amount of money Fox entrusted to Ford, the scope of the screenplay, the size of the cast in sheer numbers and the dimensions of the total undertaking were enough to permanently imprint the excitement of the moment on Ford's memory.

The production required 5,000 extras and just short of 100 cooks to feed them. Two complete town sets were specially constructed. A train of fifty-six coaches was used for transportation, and the entire company lived under conditions quite similar to those of the original railroad workers, even to the issuing of a daily newspaper. The 5,000 extras were broken down into a complete regiment of U. S. Cavalry, 3,000 railway workers, 1,000 Chinese laborers, and 800 Pawnee, Sioux, and Cheyenne Indians. Among the livestock were numbered 2,800 horses, 1,300 buffalo, and 10,000 head of cattle. Ford eschewed studio sets and, like James Cruze, chose to shoot almost all of the film on actual locations amid great physical hardships.

Those who only knew Ford in his last years, disillusioned and irascible, will perhaps be incapable of imagining what he underwent while making what remains his silent masterpiece. I trust my reader will not discount Ford's pride in *The Iron Horse* as mere vanity. With all those thousands of men and animals and hundreds of thousands of dollars in his charge, he relived the building spirit behind the Western expansion decades after it had passed beyond him. The importance of *The Iron Horse* for John Ford just wasn't the same for him as for those students of the film who now sneer at its content and laud its uses of camera technique. In his own way, by himself, Ford built the railway track that unified a nation, suffered the deprivations, exalted in the achievement of organizing masses of humanity and livestock toward a single, concerted aim. Although he had directed nearly forty Westerns by the time he made *The Iron Horse*, it was that film as no other that taught him the meaning of the pioneer experience.

The Central Pacific Railroad loaned Ford the original transcontinental locomotive Jupiter, and the Union Pacific loaned him Old 119, the twin engine that had played such an important role in the first cross-country railway. Camp Ford, which housed the company, was peopled by natives of more than twenty countries. Ford concentrated his locations in the Nevada desert. Even the interiors of cabins were authentic.

W. E. Teague, an operations manager with the Southern Pacific, was among the railroad officials who visited the camp. His seventeen-year-old daughter, Frances, accompanied him. Benton was historically the town at the end of the track. The women in the cast were preparing to shoot a scene which had actually happened when the female population of Benton

(Cheyenne in the film) rode out on a work train flatcar beside their men to fight off hostile Indians.

"Wouldn't it be wonderful to be in that?" Frances Teague commented to her father while he conversed with Ford.

Teague nodded, smiled, and continued talking. Ford watched the girl and then spoke to Teague in an undertone before turning toward her.

"Would you like to play a part?" the director asked.

She paused first and then laughed.

"Certainly I would. So would I like to slice off some of the rainbow for a dress."

"I can't say anything about the rainbow stunt," Ford returned. "I'd only want the green of it, anyhow. But if you want to play in *The Iron Horse*, I'll give you a part."

So it came that Polka Dot in the picture was Frances Teague, whose great-grandfather furnished teams for the initial grading of the Sacramento lines of the Central Pacific, whose grandfather went to work as an engine fireman, and whose father at eighteen began as a mechanic.

George O'Brien, whom Ford chose for the lead in *The Iron Horse* and whose career as a star can be said to have begun with this film, was born at San Francisco on April 19, 1900. Daniel O'Brien, his father, was chief of police. George O'Brien excelled at all manner of sports, especially boxing, while a student at Polytechnic High School. He joined the Navy during the Great War and won the lightweight boxing championship of the Pacific Fleet before his discharge in 1919. After studying medicine for a time at Santa Clara College, O'Brien participated in school dramatics sufficiently, I presume, to convince him to pursue the course of an actor.

Tom Mix made a personal appearance in San Francisco in 1922. The elder O'Brien served as his escort. Mix took a liking to the chief's son and, as was his wont, helped George in securing a position at the Fox studios as an assistant cameraman. Mix next took O'Brien into his own unit and eventually had him engage in stunt work. Fox put O'Brien into a few featured roles prior to *The Iron Horse*. But it was again Ford who teamed O'Brien with Janet Gaynor and Margaret Livingston just before F. W. Murnau cast the same principals in his silent screen classic *Sunrise* (Fox, 1927).

George's brother Jack O'Brien was given a supporting role in *The Iron Horse,* and Madge Bellamy played the heroine. J. Farrell MacDonald, such a staple for Ford while he was at Universal, was cast as Corporal Casey. Ford liked MacDonald's penchant for Irish brogue and his peculiar background. MacDonald held a B.A. and LL.B. from Yale and an LL.D. from Stewartown University; had some ability apparently as a painter, with eighteen canvases on exhibition then in Los Angeles; was a graduate geologist and mining engineer; had once sung baritone in Lillian Russell's pro-

Madge Bellamy and Gladys Hulette in *The Iron Horse*. Ford saw the West as cutting through social barriers to basic human qualities.

duction of *The Princess Nicotine;* began his film career at Biograph with D. W. Griffith; and was an expert golf player. "Every man has music in his soul," MacDonald was quoted as saying of his brogue. "If it isn't in notes of harmony, it is in the tongue of his motherland. I'd rather hear an Irish brogue than Beethoven or Bach." Perhaps it was this sentiment, more than anything else, which endeared him to that obstinate immigrant element in John Ford's soul that stubbornly kept him a stranger in a strange and wonderful land.

I beg my reader to permit me to recall a reflection made by Robert Louis Stevenson in *Across the Plains,* which he published in 1879. "When I think," he wrote, "how the railroad has been pushed through this unwatered wilderness and haunt of savage tribes; how at each stage of the construction roaring, impromptu cities full of gold and lust and death sprang up and then died away again and are now but wayside stations in the desert . . . and then when I go on to remember that all this epical turmoil was conducted by gentlemen in frock coats and with a view to nothing more extraordinary than a fortune and a subsequent visit to Paris, it seems to me, I own, as if this railway were the one typical achievement of the age in which we live; as if it brought together into one plot all the ends of the world and all the degrees of social rank, and offered the busiest, the most extended and the most varying subject for an enduring literary work."

I must confess to being partial to *The Iron Horse*. Modern film critics have termed it slow. I do not agree. All dramatic or melodramatic films made during the silent era in a greater or lesser measure bear the stamp of that more expansive and leisurely period. Others have criticized it for its seemingly standardized plot. I believe they are wrong. The basic plot against which epic events are set in *The Iron Horse* is essential to grasping in both an individual and a national sense the significance of those events. Ford's intent was to show how men and women, sinful, sentimental, cowardly, raucous, human beings of all different races, nationalities, and backgrounds were brought together and transformed, forced to rise above themselves in service to a cause that in consequence exceeded anything in their personal lives. *The Iron Horse* celebrates the joy of accomplishment that once made America the land of promise.

O'Brien's father is murdered by Fred Kohler. Kohler is a white man running with a band of Indians. Lincoln encourages the dream of the transcontinental railroad. In maturity, O'Brien goes to work for the Union Pacific as a surveyor. Kohler now is a businessman who wants the U.P. to use his right of way. O'Brien meets his childhood sweetheart, but she is engaged to marry a worthless bounder who is in with Kohler. Much is made of Kohler's deformity. Before the two railroads, the Union Pacific and the Central Pacific, are joined on May 10, 1869, Kohler gathers Chief John Big Tree and his Indians for a last concerted raid. The Indians are defeated. O'Brien kills Kohler in hand-to-hand combat. O'Brien and Miriam, momentarily estranged and separated by years, come together at the end.

Although *The Iron Horse* ran for a year at the Lyric in New York, it did not enjoy the critical acclaim of *The Covered Wagon*. Yet I feel it to be a far better film and far more effective cinema. I do not find its typical Ford roughhouse humor unprepossessing. Ford used his camera with extreme care. His cinematographer, George Schneiderman, had worked with him as early at Fox as *Jackie*. Many of his compositions, such as the shadows cast by marauding Indians against boxcars or the pit shot of the rescue train, indicate sensitivity beyond mere ingenuity. But I suppose in the end I am inclined to concur with Ford's own estimate of *The Iron Horse* for another reason. It is symbolized by the small dog that cradles its head on his fallen Indian master's chest; or young Davy at the grave of his father—certainly a

Ford trademark—or J. Farrell MacDonald offering a coolie a chaw of tobacco. *The Iron Horse* is infused with a spirit of human compassion that, in its benign tolerance, not only exceeds the minority of individual relationships and the majority of belonging to an epic event, but affirms a fundamental solidarity at the base of the human enterprise. That solidarity, Ford's later film work would propose, persists long after a man is stripped of every hope and every vision.

10 / UNIVERSAL IN THE TWENTIES

In 1920 Uncle Carl Laemmle and Robert Cochrane succeeded in buying out Pat Powers and became, respectively, president and vice-president of Universal Pictures. The long years of struggle were finally in the past. Uncle Carl entered upon the period of his perpetuation.

His loyalties remained unstinted. He began running a series of paid advertisements in *The Saturday Evening Post*, intimate messages from him to the American people. He was concerned for Germany in her agony, even as he had been firmly committed to the cause of the Allies during the era of conflict. "I am doing everything possible for the starving stricken people of Germany," he said in the *Post*. "Will you help? Will you send money, or clothing, or anything that you can afford? I will distribute it at my own expense. Conditions over there are pitiful in the extreme. Will you forget the war and remember only the call of humanity?"

Uncle Carl collected autographs, signatures of men and women who had shown ability in any field of endeavor, from music to sports to the arts to politics. For this reason, I suspect, he was secretly quite touched when, upon sailing for Europe in 1929, he was given an album signed by virtually every exhibitor in the United States congratulating him on the occasion of his twenty-third anniversary in the motion picture industry. In 1926 William Fox said of him at a gathering in his honor, "You are the man with the greatest courage of all I knew in the picture business . . . and for you I have always had the greatest silent admiration, one I never expressed to you until this time."

The twenties, following the issuance of *The Covered Wagon*, were nearly unprecedented for the promotion of new cowboy personalities. Lester

Cuneo, Bob Custer, Neal Hart, Fred Humes, Leo Maloney, Al Hoxie, Roy Stewart, Wally Wales, and Ted Wells were all featured in Westerns of various grades of low quality, the majority of which do not survive and the available examples of which reveal them not worthy of viewing again, save by those capable of the most acute self-punishment. Universal was probably the leading studio in Western production. On the one hand, Laemmle competed with all the independent producers of cheap Westerns and, on the other, with his Hoot Gibson Specials and other mainliner Westerns matched the quality of the Tom Mix series for Fox and the Zane Grey series at Paramount.

It would be an impossible task for me to recount the lives and films of most of these second-rate players of the twenties. They have been forgotten, or were never really memorable. But Hoot Gibson, Jack Hoxie, Art Acord, and, to a much lesser extent, Pete Morrison, by virtue of being Universal Western stars did leave a definite impact on the time.

George Marshall, who later directed the second *Destry Rides Again* (Universal, 1939), said once of this period and Pete Morrison, "There was no question about good or bad pictures at the time. Universal's several brands released a specified number each year; exhibitors bought them all and cried for more. You could sell anything you could film in those days and the demand for product made leading men of character actors like Pete. There was little question about talent at Universal (and many other lots); it was simply a question of filling the main parts with someone who photographed well and then directing the daylights out of them. Pete was tall, good-looking, and took direction well—what more could you ask?"

Pete was born George D. Morrison at Denver, Colorado, in 1893. While the Selig Polyscope Company was in Colorado making outdoor dramas, Pete got a job as an extra. He went to California and for the next decade

Universal City as it appeared in the twenties.
Photo courtesy of the Academy of Motion Picture Arts & Sciences.

worked on and off for Pathé, Essanay, Triangle, and Universal. His story and that of Jack Hoxie are interesting, I think, because when contrasted with Hoot Gibson's phenomenal popularity, they demonstrate the dual impulses of Uncle Carl's unique approach to Western production. Uncle Carl introduced the assembly-line concept at Universal, where the brand name sold the picture. A Blue Streak Western, for example, was one such brand; during the early twenties, this series featured Jack Hoxie, then Pete Morrison, and, finally, Art Acord. The pictures were sold on the basis of the brand, not who was featured in them.

In 1921 Pete signed with Daniel F. Tattenham, an independent producer who wanted to make a series of Western two-reelers for the states' rights market. Pete then got a job with Cliff Smith to make eight Western features, also for the independent market, signing next with Western Feature Productions in 1923 to make an undetermined number of feature comedy Westerns. Pete returned to Universal in 1923 to work in a serial, titled *Ghost City,* running fifteen chapters, at the same time that George Marshall was directing Ruth Roland in *Haunted Valley* (Pathé, 1923), in fifteen episodes. Pete continued to work in independent Westerns until 1926, when he replaced Jack Hoxie at Universal for one year in the Blue Streak series, after which he became attached to the Hoot Gibson unit as a character actor. By one of those curious ironies, more of Pete's silent Westerns for Universal survive in the national archives than those which starred the Hooter.

Jack Hoxie's career was little different. He was born in a small cabin at Kingfisher, Oklahoma, on January 11, 1885. He knocked around the country and developed some skill as a bronc rider and bulldogger. Like Morrison, Jack was a husky fellow with rough features. He came West to California in 1912 as one of the leading attractions of the Dick Stanley Wild West Show. He had met Hoot Gibson, Art Acord, and Pete Morrison on the rodeo circuits, and he was as taken as they had been with the notion of getting into pictures. He changed his name to Hartford Hoxie and began appearing at casting offices for stunt work or bit parts. Like the Hooter, he got walk-on roles in Kalem's *The Hazards of Helen,* especially after Helen Gibson took over the lead. In 1919 the National Film Corporation, an independent producer of chapter plays, contracted Jack to play the lead in *Lightning Bryce,* which costarred Ann Little. The serial made money, and Jack was signed again the next year to appear in *Thunderbolt Jack* (Arrow, 1920), which costarred him with Marin Sais, a leading lady in cheap Westerns and serials whom he married the following year. Jack's brother Al Hoxie was also in the cast. Francis Ford, on loan from Universal, was the director, assisted by Murdock MacQuarrie, the latter becoming well known to casting departments in the late twenties and early thirties as a character player. Arrow Distributing Company was a syndicate which undertook to market through the independent exchanges much of the product of shoestring producers. Jack continued to star in independent Westerns, his last series in 1922 produced by Anthony J. Xydias' Sunset Productions and directed by Robert N. Bradbury for the most part. Universal negotiated a four-year contract with Jack in late 1923; he became the leading attraction in the Blue Streak series.

No particular care was exercised by Universal in the manufacture of these films, but the assemblage of writers, directors, contract players, the Universal stable of cowhands and stunt men, and the town and ranch sets on the back lot gave an appearance of production value to the Universal Westerns that the independents could not match without spending a great deal more for only comparable results. Some critics have made the claim that Jack Hoxie enjoyed a tremendous popular following during his stint as a Universal Western star. This posture is not borne out by what I have been able to learn through conversations with Universal exchange men who booked the Hoxie Westerns. Jack's films showed a reasonable profit for the middle twenties, but when the Western market slumped in 1926 because of simply too many cheap Westerns, Jack's pictures lost money. Robert N. Bradbury was again his usual director at Universal, and also dreamed up the stories; when he didn't, Al Rogell, a far more astute director of outdoor thrillers, was assigned to them. Rogell did for the Hoxie pictures what Breezy Eason did for Hoot Gibson's programmers: he kept them moving; he injected bright comedy that flowed naturally from the story; and he maintained a visual sensitivity to the locations that resembled John Ford and helped you forget the tired script that was being re-enacted for the penultimate time.

Border Sheriff is one of the few Hoxie Blue Streak Westerns that survive. Directed by Robert Bradbury, it has remarkable story value if compared to the films Pete Morrison was making independently the same year. Based on W. C. Tuttle's short story "Straight Shooting," from *Short Stories* magazine of August 10, 1924, the picture never pauses in its action long enough to permit the viewer to become aware of Jack's total inability to act with conviction. Jack is seen on his horse, Scout, a sheriff patrolling the borderlands. PeeWee Holmes is his side-kick. Jack's foreman has a telegram for him. The foreman is chased by Buck Moulton and his gang. Jack thwarts the attempt and captures Buck. Jack's foreman gives him the telegram. The gang frees Buck and they hightail it. Jack is summoned to Washington. Once there, he is assigned the task of running down a narcotics ring headed up by Carter Brace, played by ex-train robber Al Jennings. Henry Belden and his daughter, Joan, are on the train West. They are to meet Carter Brace in San Francisco.

Joan's father wants her to like Brace. Jack and PeeWee run after the same train and leap aboard. Joan is smitten by Jack. Jack suspects Joan

The inimitable Hoxie and his faithful horse, Scout, from their days as
Universal players.

Photo courtesy of *Views & Reviews* magazine.

and her father of being in with Brace. Cut to Chinatown in San Francisco.
That night at Foo Chow's, Jack frustrates an attack on Belden led by
Buck Moulton and his gang. Frank Rice plays a crooked lawyer in with
Brace. They intend to swindle Belden out of his ranch so they can run
narcotics across the border, using his property.

It was a long-standing policy of John Ford's that in making a Western
the action sequences were supposed to be unrehearsed so as to have a
natural spontaneity. This became a principle of direction at Universal, out
of genuine respect for Ford's results, and a necessity on Poverty Row, where
the camera recorded everything only once. In trying to rope a steer, Jack's

Jack Hoxie in rather uncharacteristic make-up as an Indian brave, from his golden period in the twenties.

Photo courtesy of the Academy of Motion Picture Arts & Sciences.

horse takes a terrific fall, Jack smashing to the ground. The episode was left in the picture. After some misunderstandings, Jack gives chase to Brace and Frank Rice, who have kidnapped Joan, and the entire gang is rounded up, Jack and Joan handcuffed together.

Pete Morrison worked in the Blue Streak Western series for the 1926–27 season, as did Art Acord. By the 1927–28 season, Morrison was dropped, but Acord stayed on until the beginning of the 1928–29 season. Jack Hoxie did very little in pictures after leaving Universal. He continued for the remainder of his life to tour with Wild West shows and, near the end, managed a dude ranch. Art Acord was a wholly different personality. I have already introduced him in connection with the Westerns in the teens being filmed by Selig, Thomas Ince, and D. W. Griffith. For all that, Art was a saturnine, profoundly moody, violent, kindly, hopelessly mercurial creature. He won a world's championship for steer-throwing in twenty-four seconds at Pendleton, Oregon, in 1912. In 1916 he duplicated the feat, beating out the Hooter at the New York Stampede. He entered the Great War and was sent to France in the American 4th Division. He was awarded the Croix de Guerre at Verdun.

Returning to Hollywood sometime after the Hooter, Art was signed to a three-year contract with Universal to make short Westerns and serials. Universal put him at once into *The Moon Raiders* (Universal, 1920), an eighteen-chapter serial. Directed by Breezy Eason, it proved to be a box-office sensation. Universal was caught off guard. They had no follow-up script. Ford Beebe was put to work on a new serial at once, while Art, in the meantime, made five two-reelers on an independent deal with Dominant Pictures which costarred Pete Morrison. *The White Horseman* (Universal, 1921), in eighteen chapters, was next, which pitted Art, dressed as a white phantom, against the White Spiders gang for possession of a secret Indian treasure. Also the same year, Art appeared in *Winners of the West* (Universal, 1921), in eighteen installments, a historical drama with Art cast as Arthur Standish in quest of a lost gold mine. *The Oregon Trail* (Universal, 1923), eighteen chapters directed by Edward Laemmle, costarred Art with Louise Lorraine, another historical drama set in the period of the Louisiana Purchase. The troupe went on location to Big Bear Valley, some fifty men and three women. "The exiles of art from Universal City are living in log cabins built in a circle around a clearing," it was noted in the *Universal Weekly* for January 13, 1923. "There is little thought of rank. Art Acord sleeps in what has been definitely established as the most draughty cabin and his horse and dog share the single room with him. Louise Lorraine, the pretty little leading lady of many Universal productions, has another cabin and builds her own fire at five o'clock each morning, although there are a dozen strapping big cowboys who would freeze their fingers cheerfully to do it for her. Edward Laemmle, the director, his assistants and two men of the cast occupy a larger cabin on Pneumonia Point, a strip of clearing that runs to the shore of the frozen lake. Filming begins with the breaking of dawn, for the days are short."

The reader may recall the story H. Bruce Humberstone related to me of his beginning as a prop boy working with Jack Ford and Hoot Gibson. He told me this story in his apartment shortly after we had arrived there from a screening at Warner Brothers' Burbank studios. We had viewed *The Dragon Murder Case* (First National, 1934), another in the popular Philo Vance photoplay series and the first of a two-picture deal Humberstone had had with Jack L. Warner in the thirties. Humberstone went on to become an important director under Darryl F. Zanuck at 20th Century-Fox Film Corporation in the late thirties and forties. His first solo effort was a two-reeler, *Universal in 1925,* which is still in existence. It was an exploitation film, released by Universal to promote tours of the Universal City studios and new Universal films then in production. Humberstone is known as Lucky to his friends. He is a short, compact man with a blazing personality and a concentrated, nervous energy.

"You know, Jon," he remarked offhandedly to me, "you're responsible for getting me to smoke again. I thought I'd kicked the habit until you started me on all this stuff."

I relaxed in the large chair he had offered to me.

"This is the apartment where Edmund Goulding was living when he committed suicide," Lucky went on.

"That's a morbid thought to have to live with," I returned. "You damn prima donna, why won't you let me tape-record you so we've got some sort of record. I can never figure that about directors. They're so used to telling everyone what to think and feel, but they can't stand to be tape-recorded."

"I've got no use for those contraptions," Lucky replied. "Besides, I don't want you quoting the wrong things."

"What's an example of a wrong thing?" I shot back.

He shrugged his shoulders. He grabbed another cigarette and I leaned forward to light it for him.

"Hummph!" he grunted, expelling smoke. "Hoot Gibson was indirectly the reason for me getting my nickname."

"How so?" I asked.

"Breezy Eason one day on the set—I was his assistant director for a while at Universal—Breezy invites me to a party Gibson was throwing that night. I was just a kid. 'It'll be a lot of fun,' Breezy tells me. So that night I get into Breezy's sports car and we drive out to Gibson's house in the hills. It was one of those nude affairs, you understand, with everyone smashed."

"The Hooter loved parties," I interjected.

"You're telling me," Lucky quipped. "Well, it was near dawn when Breezy and I pull out. Breezy was lit up. He speeds along Mulholland Drive like he was fleeing from the devil. Coming up the road, as we round a curve, is a large truck. Breezy doesn't see it until it's too late. He turns the wheel and we plunge over the side. The driver pulled us out. He helped me up the steep incline and sat me down in the back of his truck. 'What's this?' he asks me, picking up my nose from where it was hanging by a thread on my chest. He stuck it back on my face. 'I'd better get you to a hospital,' he says. Breezy was out cold. When Breezy could get around, he came to my room, saw my nose, calls me Lucky. The name stuck, especially when Gibson and the others found out about it."

Art Acord when he was a Universal star.

"Now, I'll tell you a story," I put in, lighting a cigarette myself. We were sipping coffee. "Rex Lease told me he was once working on a Hoot Gibson picture. Art Acord came out to location to watch the doings. Art was also working for Universal at the time. Art goes up to the Hooter and says, 'Gibson, I can whip your ass!' Hoot stops everything and on the spot fights a long, hard bout with Acord."

"You're telling me," Lucky said. "Breezy was always being a referee. I remember one time he tried to break Acord and Gibson up, and when he couldn't, he belted both of them. That did it. Art and Hoot went after Breezy and beat hell out of him for twenty minutes."

"I remember," I said, "the Hooter once saying that his best fight with Art was one which took place in the Universal City stables. Art took a swing at him, hit a post instead, and broke his hand. The Hooter yelled, 'Good! You son of a bitch!' and really let him have it, Art all the time trying to protect his broken hand."

"They were crazy," Lucky said, shaking his head. "But everything was

This lobby card inspired Uncle Carl Laemmle to want to make a picture
entitled *The Indians Are Coming.*

Photo courtesy of A. J. Brokop.

crazy in those days. That short of mine you mentioned. That was made to
promote *The Phantom of the Opera* [Universal, 1925], among other pictures. Old man Laemmle had hired Irving Thalberg in New York. Thalberg
was just a kid. Laemmle made him his secretary, brought him out here, and
put him in charge of Universal City. The first intelligent thing Thalberg
did was to fire Erich von Stroheim. Von Stroheim talked German and so
Laemmle had hired him. But he was costing hundreds of thousands of
dollars making pictures that no one wanted to see. Thalberg put together
The Hunchback of Notre Dame [Universal, 1923], with Lon Chaney, and
then *Phantom of the Opera.* Those pictures brought Universal prestige as
well as money. Westerns always made money. But it took Thalberg on the
lot to show what could be done with the Universal facilities."

"And then Louis B. Mayer spirited him away," I said.

"If you want to put it that way," Lucky said, and laughed. "But with
Mayer, Thalberg could make his kind of pictures all the time, whereas with
Universal they were possible only once in a while."

Art Acord's first Blue Streak Western was *The Call of Courage* (Universal, 1925), which cast Olive Hasbrouck, the girl in Jack Hoxie's *Border Sheriff*, as the girl, Duke Lee, Frank Rice—in short, the Universal stock Western company. Art was a good player, of striking features, if not handsome, an excellent rider, a loyal friend. But he was deeply troubled. His despair led to marijuana, then serious drug addiction; he married four times; he was almost always drunk; he fought with everyone. Uncle Carl finally let him go. In the very late twenties, Art made a few Westerns for cheap, independent outfits like Exhibitors Film Corporation and J. Charles Davis, and then vanished from sight.

"Do you know what happened to him?" Lucky asked me.

"No," I replied. "He died in Mexico, in Chihuahua. I put the same question to the Hooter. 'You tell me,' he said. 'The Mexican Government insisted it was suicide, but I heard different. I heard he was in bed with another man's wife and got caught and it was hushed up. All I can tell you, Jon, is this: Art was found in bed, in a hotel room, disemboweled. It warn't no suicide!' It was reported in the American newspapers as having occurred January 6, 1931. I've got this notation from *Photoplay* magazine, by Kirtley Baskette. 'Wild Art Acord,' it says, 'who used to fight all comers

Dustin Farnum as Custer and the Hooter as his scout in *The Flaming Frontier*.
Photo courtesy of *Views & Reviews* magazine.

in the old corrals at Universal City, just for the fun of it, was killed in a knife scrape in Mexico.' That's all I know."

Lucky sighed.

"Come on," he said then. "Let me make you a sandwich."

Hoot Gibson was the most popular star at Universal in the twenties. His fan mail from all over the world required four vans a week to transport it. His salary rose to $14,500 a week, and his 1924 contract called for a million dollars to be paid to him over a three-year period. The Gibson Westerns varied from ordinary sagebrush dramas to elaborate specials, like *The Calgary Stampede* (Universal, 1925) and *The Flaming Frontier*. Hoot's appeal to audiences was his lack of artifice, his natural spontaneity, and the way in which he seemed to be constantly in trouble not of his own devising. He had a rare gift of pantomime, and he adamantly refused to take himself seriously. He was a fun-loving, charming, readily likable fellow.

The Flaming Frontier is unquestionably his best film from the twenties, judged in terms of what survives and what the trades of the day reported. Since Thomas Ince's time, General Custer's fall at Little Big Horn had intrigued filmmakers. It was the center of *Flaming Frontier*. The picture opens with scenes of the Indians growing restless and jealous of the merciless trek and advance of the white man. On the plains, settlers and soldiers blaze away at the red men, while in Washington politicians and profiteers bargain to sell whiskey and arms to the Indian. Hoot plays Bob Langdon, a pony express rider and friend of General Custer's, portrayed by Dustin Farnum. Through the agency of Senator Stanwood, Hoot gets an appointment to West Point. There he meets Lawrence Stanwood, the Senator's son, and his sister, Betty. It is love at first sight between Betty and the Hooter. U. S. Grant is President. Custer is seeking to bring about peace in the West, but his efforts clash with the profiteers and they manage to disgrace Custer in Grant's eyes.

In order to get at Senator Stanwood, the plotters involve his son with Lucretia Belden at West Point. There is a scandal, and Hoot, to shield the Senator, takes the blame and is expelled. He returns to Custer's command. The Indians, prodded by renegade whites, unite under Sitting Bull to mount an attack on the white men. Custer, misled as to their numbers, campaigns against them on the Little Big Horn. He has four hundred men; the Indians number in the thousands. Custer sends Hoot through enemy lines with a message to Major Reno to come to the rescue. Reno fails. Custer and his command are slaughtered. The profiteers are joyous, but it is short-lived. The settlers, learning of Sam Belden's chicanery as a crooked Indian agent, set upon him and burn the whole town to the ground, handled in sweeping panorama shots, smoke billowing from the buildings; Edward Sedgwick, the director, even used a few aerial setups. Just before the fade, Lawrence Stanwood, dying during the raid, writes his sister, Betty, a letter exonerating the Hooter, which allows them to marry happily at the fade.

The footage of the Indians coming together, the apparently thousands of extras, the spectacular fights between the cavalry and the Indians, and the burning of the town provided stock scenes for Universal Westerns for decades to come.

"In those days, everything was different," the Hooter once remarked.

"How?" I responded.

"I never wore a gun belt, for one thing," he said. "I usually wore my gun tucked into my trouser belt or in my boot. I was no fancy pants, like Tom Mix. I didn't even have a horse . . . or rather, I had a half dozen of them."

"I remember Mutt and Starlight from the sound era."

"Yeah, well I had a lot of horses, a whole stable of them when I was at Universal. I left that to everybody else, to have a horse in their pictures with 'em. I played just an ordinary cowpoke. Sometimes the heavies laughed at me. But my Westerns were the same as everyone else's. People like Westerns because they always know who's gonna win."

He shook his head. This was 1959.

"But it ain't that way in life," he said. He smiled.

11 / THE FADING OF WILLIAM S. HART

Following *Three Word Brand* (Paramount, 1921), William S. Hart's personal producing contract with Paramount expired and he retired from motion pictures. The reader may recall that in connection with the box-office potential of *The Covered Wagon*, the Paramount Sales Department specifically cited this picture as a loser and an indication of a declining interest in Westerns. The stirring success of *The Covered Wagon* inspired the Paramount executives, and in particular Adolph Zukor and Jesse L. Lasky, to request William S. Hart return to the screen for a new series of Paramount features. In early summer 1923 Hart signed a new contract which called for a total of nine more pictures but with a new clause declaring that either side could unilaterally terminate the contract after one feature. Hart's desire to have this rider included had nothing to do with general business considerations. He had been made victim of a terrible scandal.

Getting set on the back lot at Universal City to film the greatest land rush in history, from *Tumbleweeds.*

Photo courtesy of *Views & Reviews* magazine.

It had all begun in December of 1916. Hart's sister, Mary, who customarily went through his mail, told him that an eastern woman of substantial education who had been a fan of many years' standing was presently in town and wanted to meet him. Hart told Mary to invite the woman to dinner. The three of them met at the Hoffmann Café and spent a casual evening together. The woman's name was Elizabeth MacCulley. Hart did not hear from her again until November 1918. She telephoned him to say she was in town again and that she had brought their baby with her. Hart accused her of joking. She was insistent.

" 'Well, if you're not joking,' " Hart responded, " 'it's tough on you, lady, for you're crazy.' "

Within two weeks, Hart was informed by the district attorney that the woman had filed a claim for support against him for the fifteen-month-old child. Hart was in a dilemma. He was innocent, and he knew it. But he did not know how he could prove it.

One of Hart's temperamental peculiarities was his ability to convince himself that he was profoundly in love with his leading ladies. Katherine

MacDonald declined marriage proposals from him on several occasions. Anna Q. Nilsson accepted him as her affianced briefly, but it was broken off before the wedding. Eva Novak refused him. Hart became engaged to Eva's sister, Jane, but it was called off. Winifred Westover, who played opposite Hart in *John Petticoats* (Paramount, 1919), apparently surprised even him when she said yes, and surprised him even more when she went through with it on December 7, 1921. Hart was fifty-one years old when their son, William S. Hart, Jr., was born on September 6, 1922.

The marriage itself lasted only a few months, however, before Hart moved out on his wife and returned to living with his sister. Winifred Hart, who was twenty years Hart's junior, was awarded a divorce on the grounds of desertion on February 11, 1927. These were the final grounds. Already by 1923, Winifred Hart was contesting the marriage on the basis of cruelty. Hart fought her with everything he had at his disposal. With Elizabeth MacCulley suing him simultaneously for support for the child she insisted he had sired, Hart told the press he suspected the MacCulley woman had been put up to it by Winifred.

Hart's case was compromised by the independent action of the Famous Players-Lasky Legal Department which, in a premature effort to hush the matter up, had clandestinely agreed in 1919 to pay the woman fifty dollars a month in support payments. In 1923 she demanded that this be increased to a hundred dollars. Hart's protest that he had known nothing of the earlier payments and, had he known, would not have condoned them, fell on deaf ears. The MacCulley woman won her case without any proof of paternity whatsoever. (The final outcome to the case will be found in Chapter 20.) Winifred altered her grounds and demanded half of Hart's estate for abuses supposedly incurred while being married to him.

In this atmosphere Hart made *Wild Bill Hickok* (Paramount, 1923). The picture was felt to be inferior to the Tom Mix Fox Westerns by the Famous Players-Lasky Sales Department, and Jesse L. Lasky was instructed by New York to bring pressure on Hart to revise the basic formulas to his Westerns. Zukor had a warm, personal friendship with Hart, but he was quite enchanted with Tom Mix's screen style. He suggested to Lasky that Hart, who was responsible for introducing solid story value into Western motion pictures, now stress comedy and action and horsemanship in the fashion of the Mix films. Hart took all of these comments as an attack on his integrity as a filmmaker and grew exceedingly recalcitrant. His next film, *Singer Jim McKee* (Paramount, 1923), was, if anything, to be even more deeply entrenched in the William S. Hart tradition.

Hart was filming his pictures at the Lasky West Coast Studio, and at first the Paramount executives attempted to exert some control over him. But he shook them all off, reminding them of the artistic freedom guaranteed by his contract. Here is the plot to *Singer Jim*. Singer and his chum Buck

Holden rob a stagecoach to obtain money to support Buck's motherless daughter. Buck is killed by the sheriff, but Singer Jim and Mary Holden make good their escape. Some fifteen years later, McKee again dons the mask in order to provide new clothes for the seventeen-year-old Mary, who is weary of her old-fashioned riggings. Singer Jim is caught and sent to prison for his crime. Once he is released from prison, McKee returns to the hills only to find that Mary has always loved him and now they will live happily ever after.

The Paramount Sales Department did not think it could sell this kind of picture. Hart was too old to be playing such a part, and the story was somewhat more sentimental than that made popular by audiences who preferred Tom Mix, Buck Jones, Hoot Gibson, and John Ford. Zukor served Hart notice that if he intended Paramount to finance any more of his Westerns, he would have to submit to story approval or the whole deal was off. Hart would hear none of it, and retired from the screen a second time. The film was attended by viewers curious as to what caused all the furor, but William S. Hart was finished at the box office as a Western player.

Hart was an unusual man, "one of the originals," according to Adolph Zukor. He lived quietly and drank like a gentleman. He loved a game of stud poker, never becoming impassioned whether he was winning or losing. He went night clubbing when on location, but was seldom to be seen socially in Los Angeles. He reacted unpredictably to misfortune. When a substantial investment in the Dakota Land Banks was wiped out, he simply shrugged his shoulders. When on location shooting *John Petticoats* (Paramount, 1919), he was informed that Thomas Ince had stolen the Hart company books, he only paused long enough to say, "I'll be damned." But when a female driver bumped into his new car and dented a fender, he was unfit to work with for two days. He divided all men into friends or enemies, with nothing in between, and all women were automatically ladies.

With some fanfare, United Artists announced in 1925 that Bill Hart was returning to the screen in an epic Western about the Cherokee land rush. Problems between the founding partners, Mary Pickford, Charlie Chaplin, D. W. Griffith, and Douglas Fairbanks had led to Joseph M. Schenck being appointed head of production. Schenck was brother to Nicholas Schenck, president of Loew's, Inc. Hart was to have a financial interest in the picture, and the budget was set at $312,000. Most of the exteriors were shot at Universal City. Barbara Bedford was signed as the leading lady. The final negative cost of the picture proved to be somewhat under budget at $302,000.

Tumbleweeds did not compromise Hart's formula for the Western, as one may have reasonably expected—with so much riding on it. C. Gardner Sullivan, who had been scenarist on Hart's most melodramatic Triangle releases, did the adaptation of a story by Hal G. Evarts which appeared initially in *The Saturday Evening Post*. The plot has to do with the play of

Barbara Bedford and Bill Hart in a dramatic clinch from *Tumbleweeds.*

fundamental human emotions—love and greed—set against the opening of the Cherokee strip. The full impact of the plot, however, does not emerge on the first viewing, for, beyond the epic qualities of the great land rush of supposedly a hundred thousand settlers and the romance between Don Carver and Molly Lassiter, is the archetypal drama, the passing of an age and an entire way of life. The viewer feels this again and again, first with the termination of government leases which have permitted mighty ranches to prosper, or the vacating of the strip, long, endless herds of cattle moving as giant serpents. Hart and a group of punchers look on at their last trail drive with sadness, Hart pulling off his Stetson and commenting, "Boys, it's the last of the West." It is felt again as the hordes of people and wagons and animals make their way to Caldwell, Kansas, in preparation for the mighty rush into twelve hundred square miles of Indian land across a two-hundred-mile front.

No land rush sequence in the history of the Western is as visually dramatic and compelling as that in *Tumbleweeds*, although Wesley Ruggles

Hart, Gertrude Claire, and George Marion in a scene from *Tumbleweeds*.

Photo courtesy of *Views & Reviews* magazine.

comes close to it in *Cimarron* (RKO Radio, 1931). Hart's intense dislike for stunting detracts somewhat from the total effect, and only one wagon is seen to crash, and that rather ineptly handled. But even with such a considerable drawback, the massing of men, women, and children in wagons, buckboards, and carriages, on horses, mules, and bicycles, is still electric. At one time, the bottom of the cutting frame is just slightly above the incline on which Hart is riding, and the horse atop which he is sitting appears to be galloping across the sky, the light diffusing evenly around him and silhouetting the set of his jaw and the determination of his posture. By means of skillful editing, there are exactly 684 frames between the title "Ready for the signal for the maddest stampede in American history" and the beginning of the rush; these are divided into twenty-five separate shots, the shortest of which runs for only five frames (a fraction less than one fifth of a second), all of the shots ranging between the anxious, intense homesteaders, the indifferent cavalrymen, and images of clocks, watches, and the shadow of the cannon and the cannon rope. Directly the hour is noon; the cannon is fired; and a quick shot of Hart's horse is given, frightened by the noise, breaking away from its tether to a tree; and then a magnificent pan shot of the mighty front of wagons and humans as the rush begins. By composition there seems to be simply hundreds of wagons, thousands of humans, beginning as an avalanche the desperate, exciting stampede for free land.

Tumbleweeds opens to the vacating of the strip of livestock. Hart, for the first time, has a side-kick, played by Lucien Littlefield as Kentucky Rose. The Box K for which they work is the choicest spread. Hart and Kentucky ride into Caldwell. Kentucky meets a widow woman with three children and a pig; he is attracted to her. Hart stops a heavy from beating up a boy and his dog.

The heavy is the boy's half brother, Noll. He plots with Bill Freel to invade the strip as "Sooners," entering before the signal. Freel wants as his price for partnership the half brother's support in his suit for Molly's hand. Molly is Noll's half sister. Hart falls in love with Molly, and she with him.

At his old boss's request, Hart rides into the strip to check on strays. Since he is registered for the rush, he is arrested as a Sooner when Freel turns him in. Molly is heartbroken when she sees Hart in custody.

Kentucky, in the meantime, trails Noll and Freel into the strip and witnesses them shooting a soldier. Hart is kept in a pen with the other Sooners. Kentucky tells the major about Noll and Freel. Hart has Fritz nearby when the land rush begins. He jumps from the pen by means of a pole vault, mounts Fritz, and races for the Box K. Molly and her little brother enter the race in a buggy.

Arriving at the Box K, Hart drives Noll and Freel off the place. Freel discredits Hart to Molly. Molly rides up and tells Hart what she thinks of him. Noll and Freel make an effort to jump a claim held by an elderly couple. Hart saves the day and takes the two of them in. When Molly learns the truth, all is forgiven, and she and Hart are united by the fade.

Despite good reviews and a successful New York engagement, the United Artists executives were not entirely pleased with the results. Joe Schenck insisted that Hart agree to have the film edited for seven reels to five. This Hart refused to do. In retaliation, United Artists deliberately booked the film into minor theaters and second-run houses. Hart took the case to court. His contract with United Artists stipulated that they were to make every effort to realize a commercial profit from the distribution of *Tumbleweeds;* this they had obviously failed to do. Hart estimated his personal loss at nearly half a million dollars in potential revenues.

The case was settled in Hart's favor, and he was awarded $190,480. United Artists appealed the suit. The case dragged on in the courts until 1950, when at last, plus interest, the firm was compelled to pay a total of $278,209. But it went to the William S. Hart estate, since Hart was, by then, dead.

In his autobiography Hart noted of his financial relations with Famous Players-Lasky that "an organization that can make financial mistakes over a period of years can have the capacity for making mistakes which involve human beings and their careers. Only in the latter case there are no books kept—and unfortunately there can be no accounting. . . . Of the 27 pictures I *produced* and turned over to Famous Players for *distribution*, the last two, which they claim failed, are, at this writing, fifth and tenth, respectively, in *gross receipts.*" The year he wrote the above lines was 1929.

By then, the memory of William S. Hart may not have diminished, but any influence he may have exerted on the Western in its germinative period of the teens had vanished as surely as if it had never existed. In terms of William S. Hart the man, this was tragic; because he was a noble, sensitive, honest human being; his love of animals led him to fire anyone working for him who would ever dare abuse them. He lived by a rigorous code that demanded fair play at all times; he dealt in life as he expected to be dealt to; his character and his simplicity of feeling made him a shining example of the best of the men the Western summoned to the screen. But in terms of the unhappy, unrealistic, even neurotic plots he insisted on imposing on the genre, the brevity of his career—actually some eight years during the decade 1914–25—both had its effect and let the Western form prosper in more capable, more cosmopolitan, more worldly, yes, even more cynically wise hands than his. I trust the reader will not think me too harsh when I look with disinterest on the plots of Hart's films, or am merely amused by them; for, of the man, I have only the highest praise. Perhaps William S. Hart is best remembered for being the man he was, and not for the films he made; for, I suspect, it was the man that theatergoers loved, and not the hapless vehicles in which he so frequently cast himself.

12 / THE SILENT ZANE GREY WESTERNS

Zane Grey was the most popular American writer of his time. Of the eighty-nine books he published during his life, fifty-six were novels set in the West. As a writer, he knew little of brevity, and most of his novels averaged 100,-000 words in length. His books enjoyed millions upon millions of readers. Some of them are classics of literature, like *Riders of the Purple Sage* (Harper's, 1912), *Man of the Forest* (Harper's, 1920), and *The Thundering Herd* (Harper's, 1925). His best books, however, did not inspire the best motion pictures; and several of the finest pictures based on his books were filmed around inferior novels. This was undoubtedly the case with *The Vanishing American* (Famous Players-Lasky, 1925).

Zane Grey was born Pearl Gray of Lewis M. Gray and Josephine Zane at Zanesville, Ohio. His father was a preacher turned dentist. Zane began his career in dentistry; but as soon as he could afford it, he turned to writing as his occupation. Born in 1872, it wasn't until 1903 that he published his first novel, *Betty Zane,* with the Charles Francis Press. In 1910 he published *The Heritage of the Desert* with Harper & Brothers. The firm also took a few juveniles from him, but they were unenthusiastic about *Riders of the Purple Sage.* It took much pressure from Grey and finally a personal visit to a senior editor to get them to consider it. After that, the story is the old one of another phenomenon of the publishing industry.

Grey was an aggressive fellow. When *The U.P. Trail* (Harper's, 1918) became the best-selling book of the year, William Fox bought motion picture rights for three of Grey's novels: *Riders of the Purple Sage, The Rainbow Trail* (Harper's, 1915), and *The Border Legion* (Harper's, 1916). Grey felt he could reap a fortune from his books if, rather than selling photoplay rights, he produced the motion pictures himself. Zane Grey Productions was formed in 1919 with Ben H. Hampton as Grey's partner. Hampton was in charge of production. Grey confined his activities to occasional visits to the office or location; most of the time, he was off writing books or on hunting or fishing trips.

The idea of having his own film company proved a bust. After three or four abortive efforts, Grey paid off his partner and sold the company, stock, fixtures, and good will, to one of the few genuine Western enthusiasts in Hollywood making movies, Jesse L. Lasky, at Famous Players-Lasky. William S. Hart had just retired from the screen for the first time, and Jesse thought it a good idea to obtain the use of Grey's name as a selling tool in promoting the Paramount Western photoplays. For the years 1921 through 1928, Paramount made at least two Zane Grey Westerns a year— usually several more. Other than the Tom Mix series at Fox and the Hoot Gibson Westerns at Universal, the Zane Grey Paramount films were the best made, most consistently popular Western features produced during the decade of the twenties.

The silent Zane Grey series brought two Western players to the forefront, Jack Holt and Richard Dix. Holt made his screen debut in 1913 when he rode a horse over a thirty-foot cliff, doubling for House Peters, Sr. He was born Charles John Holt at New York City on May 31, 1888, the son of an Episcopal minister. He was enrolled at the Virginia Military Institute but was expelled in the spring of 1906 for painting a campus statue of George Washington with his class colors. He became a sand hog on the Hudson River Tunnel before venturing to Alaska, where he hauled mail and trapped. In 1913, as part of a surveying crew, he wound up in Los Angeles and did the stunt I have mentioned above in *Salomy Jane* (Universal, 1913). He played a villain in *The Broken Coin* (Universal, 1915), a twenty-two-chapter serial, and was a Texas Ranger in *Liberty, a Daughter of the U.S.A.* (Universal, 1916). After being trained for Zeppelin duty, Jack was released from the service after the Armistice and was signed as a contract player by Famous Players-Lasky in the early twenties. He had married a girl named Margaret Woods, and they had a son, John Charles Holt, and a daughter, Jennifer. Both were to appear in Westerns.

In 1925 Jack appeared in two of the finest Grey Westerns of the decade, *The Thundering Herd* (Paramount, 1925), released in March, and *Wild Horse Mesa*. Noah Beery was frequently the principal heavy in this series and proved himself a splendid actor. Beery portrayed Randall Jett in *Thundering Herd,* Jack was Tom Doan, and Lois Wilson was Milly Fayre. Colonel Tim McCoy played Burn Hudnall; Fred Kohler was Follansbee. William K. Howard was the director and Lucien Hubbard was the scenarist.

There was domestic tension between the Holts. After completing *Herd,* Jack arranged dinner at his home for Louella Parsons, with Lois Wilson as a guest. During table conversation, Tim, as the young boy was called by the family, captivated by Lois, turned to Louella and announced, "Look what Daddy brought home with him from Texas! Isn't she pretty?" Holt gave his son a cold stare. The marriage would soon end in divorce, Jennifer going with the mother, Tim staying with Jack.

Wild Horse Mesa, as most of the Grey Westerns, was filmed in an exotic location, this time in Colorado. Panguitch, a wild stallion, is the leader of an outlaw herd. The film gave rise to a series of Westerns, produced by Pathé and suggested by George B. Seitz, starring Rex, King of the Wild Horses. Seitz was the director on *Wild Horse Mesa*.

George Irving, in a desperate move to raise money, decides to try to trap wild horses and sell them. George Magrill convinces Irving to use barbed wire. Jack Holt and his friend Bernard Siegel, playing a Navajo chieftain, are already at the mesa. They are preyed upon by Noah Beery and his gang. Jack, in wretched condition, is taken in by Irving's outfit. He falls in love with Billie Dove and persuades Irving not to use his barbed-wire trap. Beery returns to the scene and wants to use the trap, but is dispatched by a shot from the Navajo's rifle. After capturing the wild stallion, Jack and Billie free Panguitch to once again roam the mesa.

If production values and $125,000 were not enough to make the Zane Grey Westerns produced by Paramount superior products of their kind, certainly the very cogent story lines would have been. Other studios, including Fox, occasionally undertook to film Grey's novels, but Paramount exercised greater care, it would seem, and built a special unit around production of the series that minimized variance in quality.

In fact, the stiffest competition from the Fox Film Corporation came in

Jack Holt and Raymond Hatton on a lobby card from *Born to the West*.

Photo courtesy of *Views & Reviews* magazine.

Building a set for *The Vanishing American* on the Navajo Indian Reservation on the Utah-Arizona border.

1925, the year Tom Mix was cast in the remake of *Riders of the Purple Sage,* released in March, with Tom playing Jim Lassiter. The plot finds Tom as a Texas Ranger swearing vengeance on a lawyer named Lew Walters, who abducts Tom's sister and her daughter. In the course of his search for Walters, Tom becomes ramrod for Jane Withersteen's spread. Walters is played by Warner Oland, famous already for his oriental roles in Pathé chapter plays. Tom shoots down Oland without mercy. A posse is organized. Tom and Jane are chased to Paradise Valley. The only approach to their hiding place is a set of stone stairs cut into the face of the cliff. The posse starts up the stairs. Jane cries to Tom: "I love you Lassiter —*roll that stone!*" A gigantic boulder, if hurled down the stairs, will cut off the posse, but also any chance of the two being rescued from the valley. Tom rolls the stone.

Two months later, in May, Fox issued *The Rainbow Trail,* again with Tom Mix in the lead. This was the sequel to *Riders,* and so, quixotically,

Tom is recast as John Shefford, nephew to Jim Lassiter. Doc Roberts plays Lassiter in this film and Carol Halloway plays Jane. As Shefford, Tom prevents Jane's adopted daughter, abandoned of necessity when Lassiter sealed off Paradise Valley, from marrying George Bancroft and succeeds in freeing his uncle and Jane from their imprisonment. Bancroft was the leader of the evil element that had originally sought to falsely blame Lassiter for having dispatched Lew Walters. The story ends now with the nephew and ward in love and the love between Lassiter and Jane finally legitimatized.

The previous year Fox had remade *The Last of the Duanes* (Fox, 1924), with Tom Mix in the role of Buck Duane. The combination of Tom Mix and Zane Grey put the Fox entries at the zenith of box-office popularity. Many of the supporting players were interchangeable between studios, so George Bancroft or Fred Kohler might menace Mix in a Fox-Grey picture, next moving over to the Lasky studio and menacing Jack Holt. After the surge of Mix remakes, Fox left the field more or less to Paramount until 1930, at which time Fox decided it was time to remake the Zane Grey properties the firm owned for a third time with George O'Brien as the star.

I had best introduce Ernest Carlton Brimmer at this juncture. He was born at St. Paul, Minnesota, on July 18, 1895, and completed his college education at Northwestern. Brimmer attempted a career on the stage. His first important motion picture appearance was in *Not Guilty* (First National, 1921), in which he adopted the screen name of Richard Dix. He played twin brothers. He was cast as John Storm in *The Christian* (Goldwyn, 1923), directed by Maurice Tourneur. At the recommendation of Cecil B. De Mille, he was signed as a Paramount contract player in 1923. Dix played John McTavish in Part Two of De Mille's *The Ten Commandments* (Famous Players-Lasky, 1923) and that same autumn appeared in two of the studio's Zane Grey entries, *To the Last Man* (Paramount, 1923) and *Call of the Canyon* (Paramount, 1923).

Richard Dix's costar in both of these features was Lois Wilson. They fell in love while making *To the Last Man*. The picture was directed by Victor Fleming, and Doris Schroeder, of the Famous Players-Lasky Writing Department, did the adaptation. Harry Sherman later had her perform a similar function when he brought Clarence E. Mulford's Bar 20 novels to the screen. The plot dealt with two families sworn to enmity until one or another is totally wiped out. Dix and Lois, of the respective clans, are the only survivors; naturally, they marry.

"Why didn't I marry him in real life?" Lois asked me, her eyes gazing at me gently as we sat across from each other, a coffee table between us. "Maybe, ultimately, because I was so very close to my family. But I didn't think so at the time. I remember while we were shooting *To the Last Man,* Vic Fleming wanted to go to the Grand Canyon for some scenic locations. We were camped on the floor and had to ride these small but wiry little mountain ponies up a steep path carved out of the side of the canyon wall. There was scarcely enough room for one horse; one slip, and rider and horse would plunge over the side.

"Well," Lois continued, leaning back and smiling, "I was a good rider. I went up that narrow trail with the others and I enjoyed it. After a couple of days, I figured, I could do it without holding my breath. Dick didn't want me to make the ride. But I went anyway. Then, when we got to the top, he came over to where I was sitting on my horse and he asked me if I had been afraid.

" 'Not at all,' I told him bravely.

" 'I don't think I could love a woman who wasn't afraid of a thing like that ride,' he said then.

" 'You can't love me,' I returned, 'because I wasn't afraid.'

"By the time we made our next picture, he was right; the romance had cooled."

Victor Fleming again directed and Doris Schroeder did the screenplay for *The Call of the Canyon*. Lois and Richard Dix did not appear together in another film until *The Vanishing American,* unquestionably one of the finest entries in the whole Paramount series and a picture which, in its touching sympathies for the Indian nations, would seem to be far more effective with audiences today than upon its initial release, if the trade papers of the time are to be believed.

Nothing that George B. Seitz had done before while working for Pathé directing Pearl White serials with Spencer Gordon Bennet as his assistant director, nor any of his Famous Players pictures other than *The Vanishing American,* including *Wild Horse Mesa,* nor any of his pictures subsequently, Westerns such as *The Thrill Hunter* (Columbia, 1933), with Buck Jones, or the Andy Hardy series for Metro-Goldwyn-Mayer in the thirties, combined technical brilliance, grandeur of conception, and poetic lyricism as did this film. *The Vanishing American* is Seitz's magnum opus as a director. I confess that I first saw the film with an audience in a downtown theater in Detroit in 1971 with organ accompaniment using a Wurlitzer which reverberated throughout the movie palace. This is the way in which the film should be seen, and not screened in silence or in a screening room.

I cannot hope to engage in a critical examination of the ideas about successive human races indulged in by the scenario. An article on this picture in *The American Film Heritage* (Acropolis, 1972) indicts it for being fascist in its orientation by opening with a prologue that shows one race succeeding the next, each basing its supremacy on some new invention. It is very fashionable among young American intellectuals in the 1970s to question the usual standards of measurement applied to judging one civilization superior to another and to champion the cause of primitive soci-

A shot of a set from *The Vanishing American,* with Lois Wilson and Richard Dix flanking director George B. Seitz.

Richard Dix in costume for *The Vanishing American.*

eties. Such passions appear to me to be fleeting in their effects and trivial in their supposed discoveries. *The Vanishing American* is not a political tour de force, but rather a kindly, occasionally sentimental portrayal of the red man as he adjusts to the white man's civilization. It does nothing to advance our notions about the origins of the Indian wars because it dwells on the humanity, the loves, experiences, sorrows, of individuals. It was the abiding vision of articulate filmmakers in the first half of this century to depict America, lacerated and bleeding from its factional wounds, healing together as a cohesive society without classes and without prejudices. It never occurred to these filmmakers that America might never heal, or that the social cohesion they proposed might result in hopeless national apathy.

The Vanishing American opens to a quotation from Herbert Spencer's *First Principles* on the survival of the fittest, then a shot of Monument Valley. The saga of the Indian nations in North America is told. Cut to modern reservation life with Noah Beery as the crooked assistant of a dim-witted Indian agent. Richard Dix as Nophaie falls in love with Lois Wilson, the schoolteacher. Beery frames Nophaie so he can have a clear hand with Lois. The Great War marches through the world, and the Indians volunteer to go overseas. When they return, after having fought valiantly, they find that Beery is now agent and that he has moved the tribe into a desert. They go to battle against him, and both Beery and Nophaie lose their lives in the holocaust before justice is done to red and white man alike.

Famous Players-Lasky continued to produce on an average four Zane Grey entries a year, released as Paramount films. This was cut back to two a year, beginning in 1929, because of the deleterious effect sound was thought to exert on the commercial viability of outdoor dramas. Lois Wilson went East in 1927 to film *New York* (Paramount, 1927). While in production, she received a telegram from B. P. Schulberg, who had recently rejoined Famous Players-Lasky as head of production at the Lasky studio. He wanted Lois to return to California at once to appear opposite his new cowboy discovery, Gary Cooper. Lois had only nine months to go on her contract; she had better offers, including one at triple her present salary from Irving Thalberg. She declined Schulberg's summons, and Famous Players placed her on suspension for the remainder of her contract time. Schulberg went about trying to build Cooper into a major Western property, starring him in series Westerns with a horse called Flash and in Zane Grey entries such as *Nevada* (Paramount, 1927). Richard Dix signed with RKO and won a nomination for an Oscar for his performance with Irene Dunn in *Cimarron* (RKO Radio, 1931).

Grey's deal with Paramount called for a fifty-fifty split of the profits his pictures made. The firm had to agree that, at least in part, each of his novels adapted for the screen had to be filmed on the actual locations featured in the books. There was more than authenticity at stake in this prerequisite. Grey, as a novelist, tied his characters to the land and the land to the course and substance of the plot; they were integral, one to the other. The character of the land was what unified narrative events, wild, barren, or free—the land more than anything else was the prime mover, and so in the Grey-Paramount films, as in the novels, it was the most distinctive personality on the screen.

13 / INDIAN SUMMER—THE SAGA OF FRED THOMSON

Fred Thomson is now little more than a memory. Very few of his twenty-five Westerns survive, and in his time he appeared in only thirty films. He was by all accounts a likable, charming man, two inches over six feet, weight at nearly fifteen stone, with rich, wavy chestnut hair and steel-blue eyes. All of his life he was blithefully naïve, artless, and a hopeless enthusiast.

He was born Frederick Clifton Thomson at Pasadena, California, on February 26, 1890, the son of a Presbyterian minister. He earned a bachelor's degree at Occidental College in Los Angeles and went on to attend Princeton Theological Seminary in 1910. He was ordained a Presbyterian minister in 1913.

Thomson was of an athletic bent. While at Occidental College, he participated in football, baseball, and track, taking first place in the National Track and Field competition of 1910 with a total of 7,009 points. The next year he repeated his victory, scoring 6,709 points. At Princeton, Thomson beat Jim Thorpe's world record in 1913 by winning 7,499 points. Curiously perhaps, this new record was shattered in 1921 by Fred's brother, S. Harrison Thomson, who later became a professor of ancient history.

Toward the end of 1913, Fred assumed the pastorship of Hope Chapel in Los Angeles and married Gail Dubois Jepson. In 1915 the Thomsons relocated to Goldfield, Nevada, where Fred served as pastor to the Presbyterian Church and was appointed state commissioner of the Boy Scouts.

If I have given my reader the notion that there was nothing spectacular about Fred Thomson as a minister of God and that he might have been better advised to pursue a career of a professional sportsman, I have to counter it by saying that Thomson was in no way a self-seeker. He was an extremely handsome fellow who blundered, or was subtly persuaded, into almost everything that ever happened to him. Restless more than disconsolate when his wife succumbed after a short illness in 1916, Thomson entered the U. S. Army and was made chaplain of the 143rd Field Artillery Regiment stationed at Camp Kearney, San Diego. During an interservice exhibition football game, Thomson broke a leg and was consigned to the field hospital.

Mary Pickford, dressed in the uniform of an honorary colonel, had ridden horseback down San Francisco streets with the 143rd. She was scheduled to pay a visit to the regiment's camp at Santa Ana and asked screenwriter Frances Marion to accompany her. Frances had been previously married and was a cynic about "love at first sight." But the idea became lyrical upon seeing Thomson in his hospital bed. Within a fortnight, the two had already made plans to marry right after the war. "Fred and I were much in love," Frances Marion once recalled. "But he was the son of a Presbyterian minister, was himself ordained, and planned to follow in his father's footsteps. If he married me, a twice-divorced woman, as he wanted to, it would mean the end of his very promising career in his church."

Thomson was sent overseas to France. Shortly after the Armistice, he took part together with his brother in the Inter-Allied Games held in Paris and won the decathlon event and France's gold medal for grenade throwing. Returning to the States, Thomson renewed his suit with Frances Marion, who was working for William Randolph Hearst's Cosmopolitan studios in New York. They married in late 1919 and set out on a European honeymoon. Despite her professed reservations, Frances' long-time friend Hedda Hopper asked her why she had married Thomson and received by way of a reply: "I couldn't get him any other way."

Fred Thomson when he was at the height of his popularity in the twenties.

Photo courtesy of Bill Rainey.

A month following their marriage, the couple was joined in Europe by Mary Pickford, who had just married Douglas Fairbanks. Thomson was suddenly possessed of an impulse that soon became an obsession. He wanted to make Westerns in the vein of the Fairbanks adventure thrillers, but starring a horse. It was an incredible scheme on the face of it.

When the Thomsons returned to New York, they went to New England to see a magnificent gray outlaw stallion. Fred experienced his own "love at first sight." He determined to buy it and named the stallion Silver King.

Frances had written a story for Mary Pickford called *The Love Light* (United Artists, 1921). Mary was so enamored of it that she insisted Frances direct her in it. The tale concerned an Italian peasant girl who saves a man from the sea, falls in love with him, and marries him only to learn that he is a German spy. She exposes him, after much emoting, and he is shot. "The picture was ready to go into production," Frances Marion recollected, "but we hadn't yet been able to find the right actor for the German. An actor named Raymond Bloomer, who had been selected to play the real heroic lead, one day turned to Fred and said, 'Why don't you play the German?' Fred treated it as a big joke, but Bloomer persisted, and when Mary and I took up the idea, Fred gave up and played the part." Fred also took a part in Frances' story *Just Around the Corner* (Paramount, 1921), which was released in December.

The couple migrated to the West Coast, taking Silver King with them. On an old farm outside New York, Fred had taught the animal to kneel, bow his head in prayer, dance by swinging his rump, play dead, and grin menacingly. Once in California, Fred got to know several of the reigning cowboy stars, and Hoot Gibson offered him a rent-free stall in his stable for Silver King. Fred appeared in *Penrod* (First National, 1922), and then Maurice B. "Lefty" Flynn, who had played football with Fred at Princeton and who had remained friends, urged him to portray a villainous rum runner opposite Dustin Farnum in *Oath-bound* (Fox, 1922); Fred agreed when Farnum seconded Flynn. At Fox, Fred met Tom Mix, and the cowboy star spent hours telling Thomson about the importance of daredevil stunts and stunt men. Mix found Thomson amusing, whereas Hoot Gibson thought him a little simple-minded. "Man," Hoot remarked one day to Fred outside Silver King's stall, "you going to make cowboy pictures with *that* horse?"

"Try to," Fred replied.

"Wish you luck."

"I'll need it."

"You sure will, brother. Nobody ever saw a horse like that on a range. Kids might laugh at you." Then Hoot reflected for a moment. "Screwy idea, but you never know in this game what's going to hit the bull's-eye."

Film Booking Office (FBO) was a small producing and distributing company that had been an outgrowth of the Mutual Film Corporation which had had Harry E. Aitken as its first president. After the series of disasters that forced Aitken from the company, Mutual became known as Exhibitors Mutual Film Corporation. It then became part of the Robertson-Cole company. Pat Powers, having settled with Laemmle and Cochrane for a reputed $2 million, took over the firm and changed its name to Film Booking Office. Joseph P. Kennedy, of Boston, whose financial dealings had involved him in everything from whiskey to Wall Street, was hired on as an economic adviser. Kennedy liked athletes and cowboys, and in the wake of *The Covered Wagon,* he suggested the company specialize in the release of Westerns. Ben Wilson, a Poverty Row producer of low-grade Westerns starring eventual stunt expert Yakima Canutt, was the first to switch to FBO distribution. It would be a mistake, I believe, to conclude that Kennedy ever took a profound interest in filmmaking. He saw his association rather as an opportunity for stock manipulations in New York, which in a matter of a mere thirty-two months would net him personally in excess of $5 million. During his brief stay in Hollywood, in addition to a great many other things, he promoted first Fred Thomson as a Western star, then Tom Tyler and Bob Steele, the last a son of director Robert N. Bradbury. Finally, when Thomson had left FBO for Paramount and just prior to the astute Pathé merger he masterminded, Kennedy lured the great Tom Mix to FBO. Years hence, when he sought illustrious political careers for his sons, he hadn't forgotten what he had learned of popular image-making in Hollywood.

Fred Thomson and Frances Marion knew nothing of all this as they, desperate and near despair, met with Kennedy in an effort to convince him to make Westerns starring Silver King. Kennedy played his role with uncommon shrewdness. Once Fred had explained his idea, Kennedy began a series of crafty arguments. He wondered who would be able to handle Silver King. "If you choose some well-known actor," he commented in a cordial tone, "he'll insist on being starred ahead of the horse. And I'm sure you wouldn't want to trust any ordinary actor or even a cowboy to show off the unusual tricks you've taught that magnificent animal." Before the conference had ended, Kennedy had not only talked Thomson into starring in the Westerns himself but also into accepting the lead in a fifteen-chapter serial, *The Eagle's Talon* (Universal, 1923), opposite Ann Little, William S. Hart's former leading lady who had, the reader may recall, started with Tom Ince and was now a matinee queen. "A brilliant man, Joe," Fred said as he left the interview.

Fred commenced production on his Westerns at once so that the new series would receive the maximum exposure from Universal's publicity for him in the serial and in an isolated feature he made for them, *A Chapter in Her Life* (Universal, 1923). Fred's first FBO Western was released in

January 1924, entitled *The Mask of Lopez,* although his March 1924 release *Galloping Gallagher* was copyrighted November 23, 1923, as *The Sheriff of Tombstone.* The early Thomson entries were kept at budgets of $10,000. Harry Joe Brown, who was born at Pittsburgh on September 22, 1892, and graduated from Syracuse University as a lawyer, was production manager and director for the initial films, and Marion Jackson was the scenarist with ample assistance from Frances Marion, whose name did not appear on the credits. In 1926 Brown and Jackson left the Thomson unit to make Ken Maynard Westerns for First National. Al Rogell, who had directed Jack Hoxie at Universal and who with his brother, Sid, also worked on the Thomson Westerns of 1924–25, departed with Brown and Jackson. Thomson himself had an enduring interest in photography and created many of his most imaginative setups. Kennedy did not finance the Thomson Westerns but acted as a guarantor while Monogram and Robertson-Cole put up the money. By the tail end of the FBO series in 1927, Fred had assembled a more or less permanent company with Lloyd Ingraham, who had worked with D. W. Griffith, directing and William Courtright in support.

Thundering Hoofs dates from the first full year of Thomson-FBO production. Directed by Albert Rogell, it was financed by Robertson-Cole money. Marion Jackson is credited with the continuity. Fred takes Silver King from Luke Severn, an obvious snake. Severn is a bandit and a rustler. But he is engaged to Carmelita, with whom Fred falls in love. The film climaxes during a bullfight sequence with Fred wrestling a bull. Severn is exposed and the story concludes happily.

I do not think by any stretch of the imagination you could call Hoot Gibson or Jack Hoxie beautiful men; Tom Mix and Buck Jones were more flamboyant than Broncho Billy or William S. Hart, but their faces were distinctive of character rather than of the softer contours of the Greek god. Joseph P. Kennedy introduced the specter of the romantic idol into the Western in the person of Fred Thomson. Exaggerated goodness and purity of soul went hand in hand with being good-looking.

Kennedy rapidly acclimated to Hollywood methods. It was meet and just that he should do so since his saintly cowboy was being constantly urged to demand more money through the example set by Tom Mix, through his wife's promptings, and through his own Calvinist sense of pecuniary reward. At the recommendation of FBO's general studio manager, Kennedy agreed to star Tom Tyler in a series of Western two-reelers as a backup to Thomson.

Tyler was born Vincent Markowski at Port Henry, New York, on August 9, 1903. He was raised in Detroit. His visions of an acting career met with severe parental disapproval, but he remained intent and at an early age ran away from home. He showed up as a miner in the Pennsylvania coal fields, a seaman aboard a tramp steamer, a lumberjack, a prize fighter, and, finally, displaying his altogether splendid physique, a sculptor's model. He arrived in Hollywood in 1924 and under the name of Bill Burns sought extra work. He landed a small part in *Ben-Hur* (M-G-M, 1925) and was tested at FBO along with seventy-five other hopefuls. He was signed at $75 a week for the first three months, $100 a week for the next three months, and $125 a week for the balance of his first year.

The Tyler two-reelers proved popular and were soon expanded to feature proportions. While the Thomson films continued to cost from $35,000 to $45,000 each, the Tyler Westerns were kept at the initial budgets of $10,000. By 1927, through persistent importunity, Thomson was earning an estimated $6,000 a week, which included a percentage on his films and a base salary. Tyler was raised to $200 a week, and FBO announced to the trades that he was being groomed as Thomson's replacement.

I have termed Thomson an enthusiast. He was also extravagant. When Silver King had six doubles, Thomson set about bringing the number to nine. When Fred wanted to build, he ignored soaring land prices and bought twenty acres at $4,500 an acre in San Fernando Valley. He began designing a home large enough to house an increased staff to attend the elaborate stable he projected. "Pine trees studded every tier," Frances Marion recalled, "while on top rose a huge house with a drawing room two stories and a half high, rare tapestries on the walls, an Aeolian pipe organ, and windows overlooking five acres of lawn. Beautifully laid out on the terrace were a tiled barbecue, an aviary, and a hundred-foot swimming pool. Fred and his horses and I had gone Hollywood!" They called it the Enchanted Hill and it cost almost $650,000. When in the tenebrous winter of 1929 Frances had to sell it, with Hedda Hopper's help, William Barnes was found, who paid $450,000 in cash for it. After the many debts were retired, Frances invested what was left in annuities, which protected her through the rest of her days.

Fred's contract with FBO expired in March 1927. He demanded $100,-000 per film at four films per year and a production budget per picture of $225,000. Kennedy stalled. FBO and Kennedy's interest at Pathé had flooded the market with cheap Westerns. Kennedy was aware that what Thomson needed was what Thomson was insisting on: first-run bookings in first-run houses. FBO couldn't do it. The company simply didn't have the distribution. Fred opened negotiations with Famous Players-Lasky. Kennedy, meeting with Zukor in New York, suggested the possibility that he might finance the Thomson Westerns for Paramount release. Paramount could get Fred first-run bookings and saturate the small towns where his greatest strength was.

Zukor made the decision to go ahead with Thomson independently of Kennedy. In April 1927 Fred was signed by Famous Players with a drawing account for production purposes. Fred was to turn the finished Westerns over to Famous Players for distribution. Thomson's salary of $100,000 a picture at four pictures a year was to be taken from the drawing account. The contract was to run for one year and four pictures.

Thomson went into production on his first Paramount film, entitled *Jesse James* (Paramount, 1927), just as the Western market hit a sudden slump. As reports began to roll in, only Tom Mix films were maintaining a high gross. While in 1926 the average Western could be expected to gross domestically at least $100,000, this declined to $75,000. Most bookings were at a flat $10 for seven days. The Paramount sales executives estimated the gross of Fred's *Jesse James* to be $1.5 million. Joseph P. Kennedy, returning to Hollywood, began making overtures to Tom Mix to come to FBO.

Jesse James was released in October 1927. It proved a disaster. Thomson's plot line completely whitewashed the bandit while the public and the censors wildly disapproved. The picture elaborated the usual Thomson stunts, and in one scene Fred and Silver King led thirty men in boarding through open windows a passenger train moving at thirty-five miles per hour. Action couldn't save it. Fred's FBO side-kick, William Courtright, played Parson Bill. In Missouri, where there was still strong reason to re-

Fred Thomson as frontier scout Kit Carson with Dorothy Janis as an Indian princess in *Kit Carson*.

Photo courtesy of A. J. Brokop.

member the wanton evil of the James brothers, the state censor ruled that Paramount had to delete the title from the film in which Courtright was quoted as saying, "If this is justice, durned if I'll be a preacher any longer."

Fred selected the story and its screen treatment. Very little of his Presbyterianism appears to have survived his Hollywood experience. Included was a scene in which he as Jesse together with former Tarzan James Pierce, who was cast as Frank James, and Harry Woods as Bob Ford, whom the James brothers save from destruction, go swimming naked in a creek and catch sight of Nora Lane, clad to her ankles in a bathing suit from the turn of the century. They flee. The James boys were presented as loyal Confederates, fighting on the side of righteousness, and even Quantrell is portrayed as a hero.

"That a bad man can be a good man only when he's a dead man," *Variety* reported on October 19, 1927, "may be Paramount's excuse to turn out *Jesse James* as the reason to charge more for Fred Thomson as a Western actor than FBO did when Fred Thomson made Westerns without disguise. . . . He was probably the first gangster in America following the Civil War, having aptly graduated from a band of cutthroats. . . . The James brothers were known 30 or 40 years ago, with but little difference between the two in their evilness, although Jesse was looked upon as the leader of his brother and of their band of robbers and murderers."

Jesse James finished Fred Thomson in pictures. Even with three more films to go on his contract, *Variety* reported on December 14, 1927, the "making of *Jesse James* sounded the exit march of Fred Thomson on the Paramount releasing program after the completion of his three remaining contracted films. . . . Sales executives feel it's their fault for permitting the film. During the past few months *Jesse James* has been the toughest nut to crack, due to prices that they asked for [it]. First run dates have been practically limited to the Publix group, which is allied to Paramount."

The Pioneer Scout (Paramount, 1928) and *The Sunset Legion* (Paramount, 1928) followed. The films died at the box office. No one in Hollywood would touch Fred Thomson. In a desperate effort to recapture his fame, Fred made *Kit Carson* (Paramount, 1928) as his last Western for Famous Players, this time invoking a legitimate folk hero. Fred's FBO production unit had made the transition with him: Lloyd Ingraham directing, William Courtright as Fred's side-kick, and young, attractive Nora Lane most often as the feminine lead. Silver King remained prominent in most of the action and in *The Sunset Legion* even played a dual role, appearing in a tailormade suit of black cloth when Thomson's part required he ride a charcoal stallion.

Fred's dashed hopes and his despair were kept from the public. On October 31, 1928, *Variety* mentioned that Frances Marion was named the object of a $200,000 alienation of affection suit over an M. C. Ross who had worked on the Fred Thomson pictures and had managed an apartment building for Frances before that. The suit was filed by Genevieve Ross and was termed "ridiculous" by Frances Marion. Thomson devoted himself to tending his horses.

"It was a warm evening," Frances Marion later recollected, "and we stood for a long while, silenced by the beauty that lay before us: the twinkling lights of myriads of outdoor Christmas trees in Beverly Hills. In the far distance Catalina Island brooded in somber, stark outline, while the sea continued its age-old process of lashing at the base of the cliffs. Sound carried upward and we could hear laughter, voices calling to voices, and Christmas carols played on Victrolas. Our minds met, our hands touched, our hearts were one. 'This will be our ninth happy Christmas together,' he said. As he put his arm around me and we walked into the house, I noticed that he limped a little. A year before, doing one of his stunts, Fred had broken his leg, and I asked if it was troubling him. 'No, I stepped on a rusty nail and it bothers me a little. Nothing to worry about.' "

On the day before Christmas 1928, Fred Thomson entered Queen of Angels Hospital. The doctors felt at first that he was suffering from gallstones and operated, but he did not rally. When it was learned that he had stepped on a rusty nail ten days previously, immediate blood transfusions began. It was too late. Shortly before midnight Christmas Day, Fred Thomson was dead of tetanus.

"Blessed are little children," Frances Marion said afterward, "for they are spared the agonizing grief of parting from those we love." Only it wasn't quite so. Children especially mourned the loss throughout the United States. His financial estate, exclusive of the house and its furnishings, amounted to somewhat more than $25,000, divided between Fred's mother, Mrs. Clara Thomson, of Princeton, New Jersey, and three-year-old Fred, Jr. Frances, who was separately provided for in the deed to the property, and their two-year-old adopted son, Richard, were excluded.

The reader may be disconcerted at this point. How much of the story idea and screen treatment to *Jesse James* did Frances Marion contribute? How could Fred Thomson be around horses for so many years and not know the dangers of tetanus? Why did Fred agree to adopt Richard as an infant and then disinherit him? Were the Thomsons as happily married at the end as at the beginning? I suppose the more significant question remains, what does it matter at this late date? Fred Thomson's films, had they survived, might today inspire ridicule where once they inspired awe. His charm and his magic—and his magical horse—belong to a period of innocence that, even at his passing, even as Ken Maynard's *The Red Raiders* and Al Jolson's *The Jazz Singer* were opening in the same week, was dropping away as the nation that had borne him began to adopt the unmistakably gaunt, haunting, starved look of the Great Depression. The harsh, brittle realities of the next decade would so deny historical truth in the Western that Roy Rogers and Gabby Hayes could make *Days of Jesse James* (Republic, 1939) with a musical setting and have the matter accepted with nonchalance, even indifference.

14 / FOX FILM CORPORATION IN THE TWENTIES

I have already bandied Buck Jones's name around. He was born Charles Frederick Gebhard at Vincennes, Indiana, on December 12, 1891. He was only a few months old when his father purchased a three-thousand-acre spread at Red Rock, Oklahoma, and moved there with his family. It was while learning to ride as a small boy that the ranch hands dubbed him "Buckaroo," and it was later shortened to Buck.

By fifteen, Buck Gebhard wanted to see the country. He persuaded his mother to help lie for him so he could join the Army. On January 8, 1907, Buck was enlisted in G Troop, U. S. Cavalry, giving his date of birth as December 12, 1888, and was stationed at Columbus Barracks, Ohio.

It was rather exciting. Buck saw action along the Mexican border and, on September 7, 1907, G Troop set sail for the Philippines, where for the next two years they were deployed fighting Moro bandits. Buck was severely wounded in the right leg just above his knee and carried a six-and-a-half-inch scar for the remainder of his life. He was mustered out of the service on December 20, 1909. Buck returned to his father's ranch for a time and then went to Indianapolis, where he became a mechanic at the Speedway. By October 14, 1910, Buck was again in G Troop. He was promoted to sergeant during this hitch. He wanted to become a pilot and was transferred to the Signal Corps, Aviation Squad. They made him a mechanic instead, and so Buck let his enlistment expire on October 23, 1913.

Buck knocked around for a while, finally trying out with the Miller 101 Ranch Wild West Show. "I put resin on my chaps to help me hold the saddle," Buck later recalled, "and drove horseshoe nails into the heels of my boots to keep my spurs on. Then I went over and asked for a tryout." He landed the job, and soon Zack Miller moved him up to the position of top rider and roper. When the show played Madison Square Garden early in 1914, Buck was a headliner. It was here that he met Odille Osborne. Or, perhaps better said, it was the other way around. Dell, as she was better known, came across Buck sleeping off a drunk, stretched out on a bale of hay. Dell was one of the congress riders, and Buck gave her lessons in horsemanship. They fell in love. When the 101 announced plans to tour England, Buck and Dell quit the show and joined the Julia Allen outfit. They were married in the ring at Lima, Ohio, on August 11, 1915, amid great fanfare.

When the Great War broke out, Buck and Dell relocated to Chicago, where Buck got a job as a horsebreaker for the British and French armies at the stockyards. When the United States entered the conflict, he stayed on, doing the same thing. Once the war was over, he and Dell joined the Ringling Brothers' Circus at fifty dollars a week. At the end of the season, in 1918, Dell now pregnant, the two set out for Los Angeles in a car Buck bought for twenty dollars. They set up housekeeping in a small place near the Edendale lots. Buck looked for extra work and even landed an occasional part as second lead in a series of two-reelers with Franklyn Farnum, no relation to the other two Farnums in films. Dell listed herself as available for work as a double.

One morning, William S. Hart stopped by their place and asked her to come and double May McAvoy, who was currently making a Western with him for Famous Players. Dell was of slight build and her pregnancy scarcely showed. She agreed. The jerking and jarring of her day in the field produced Maxine, their only child, rather suddenly. Buck was irked at Dell's recklessness.

The Fox Film Corporation put Buck on as a wrangler, first to watch livestock and then to perform stunts in Westerns. Buck met Scott R. Dunlap, who worked for Fox at the time, and the two became friends. Dunlap brought Buck to Sol Wurtzel's attention. Wurtzel was production manager. A screen test proved successful, and Buck was signed as a contract player. Winfield Sheehan, born on September 24, 1883, had organized Fox's Hollywood studio in 1914 and then set to work building up the firm's foreign exchange network. He was now the general manager in New York. He wrote Buck a letter on October 9, 1919, giving him various instructions. "Please bear in mind that you will give personal, painstaking attention to the following," he wrote.

"1. Your hair in pictures must always be neatly combed unless you are in a fight. You should arrange to have your hair cut and washed and oiled once a week to give it proper appearance and gloss.

"2. Your teeth require proper attention with polishing and cleaning by a dentist once every two months and very careful attention several times daily. It should be a practice of yours to open your mouth a little wider when you smile so that your teeth are seen more.

Buck Jones before he had his teeth capped.

Photo courtesy of *Views & Reviews* magazine.

"3. The new suits of clothes, shirts and collars you are having made should be worn by you so that you will get in practice of wearing these kind of clothes and collars so you will not appear strange in them before the camera. I have noticed that several actors seem uneasy in other than Western clothes. A little practice on your part will help you appear at ease before the camera.

"4. You should give attention to your fingernails so that they are clipped not too close and that they are always in clean order."

None of these considerations would have been thinkable were it not for the terrific impact Tom Mix had made upon the Western. Hart's rugged sentimentality and Harry Carey's glamourless characterizations were giving way, daily, to the magical aura which invariably surrounded Tom Mix. Buck's first film, *The Last Straw* (Fox, 1920), was not a Western. Nor did he appear anything like what he had looked in Canyon Pictures' two-reelers with Farnum. His teeth were capped, and, as his series Westerns began, his outfits became more elaborate, showing a Mexican influence toward gaudiness.

William Fox's intentions were, of course, obvious. He cared very little about Buck Jones. Tom Mix was drawing $10,000 a week and was insisting on a raise. Fox thought he would teach Mix a lesson. He let it be known in

A portrait of Tony, Tom Mix's costar at Fox and throughout his later career.

Photo courtesy of *Views & Reviews* magazine.

the trades that Buck was a potential Mix replacement. The $150 a week he was paying Buck was a sound investment. Mix would hear nothing of it. He got nasty. Once, when Buck was shooting a picture on the back lot, he needed an extra gun. He asked around and a grip suggested he ride over to where the Mix unit was filming and borrow one from Tom. Buck thought it a good idea and rode over. Mix told Buck where he could go and, henceforth, snubbed him.

Hart's popularity took a sharp decline, already in 1920, as I have said. His sermonizing was alien to the times. Mix readily surpassed him at the box office. Tom threatened to quit Fox altogether if he didn't get his raise,

Buck Jones or anyone else notwithstanding. William Fox yielded. Tom was increased to $17,500 a week. Tom's career attained its height by 1922. It was in that year that their daughter Thomasina was born to Tom and Vicky Forde; his $250,000 Hollywood mansion was finished; his seven-car garage was filled with fancy imports; his Arizona land holdings were increased; and the TM brand was placed on virtually everything, including William Fox's fortune. Tom built his own permanent sets at Mixville, located on sixty acres of land in the Fox Hills. Off screen, Tom began the fantastic sartorial displays for which he was much talked about; an electric sign flashed his initials into the Hollywood night outside his home.

I now have to tell Tony's story. Hart's publicity about Fritz and Tom's promotion of Old Blue while he was still at Selig had begun a tradition. Buck Jones—Jones being the name Buck chose for the screen—bought his own gray in 1922 and named him Silver. It was a necessity. Tom Mix had made *Just Tony* (Fox, 1922), and everyone was astonished by the sorrel who was so talented that he even handled Mix's second unit direction. It was a typical Mix novelty.

Tony was born in Los Angeles in 1910. His mother, range-bred in Arizona, had been shipped into California. There was no record of Tony's father. An Italian vegetable peddler bought Tony's mother to pull his cart. He gave the colt to his young son. The boy was ten years old and named the horse Tony. One day, as Tony was trotting along after the vegetable wagon drawn by his mother, he was observed by Tom Mix and Tom's ranch foreman, Pat Chrisman. Mix offered at once to purchase the animal. The Italian refused. They would have to negotiate with the boy. That night Tom and Pat went to work on the kid and dislodged the horse for $17.50, when the boy's mother suggested he would need the money for law school.

When Old Blue died in 1917, Tony succeeded him. Tony was sent to the Mix ranch on the Hassayampa in Arizona and taught to be a cutting pony. Pat's twelve-year-old daughter, Babe, was gentle with the two-year-old and became Tony's first rider. Tony was especially fond of Babe Chrisman, as among leading ladies he liked particularly Patsy Ruth Miller, Marion Nixon, and Clara Bow. Tom debuted Tony as a four-year-old in *Cupid's Round-up* (Fox, 1918).

Just Tony required that Tony be the leader of a wild horse herd. Tom's cameraman at Fox was Daniel B. Clark. Whoever was scheduled to direct the picture, Mix and Clark handled most of the production between themselves. Tom gave Tony instructions as to what he wanted, much of which was accomplished by the animal a half mile from the camera setup. The literary source for the film was Max Brand's *Alcatraz* (Putnam's, 1923), published in book form after the release of the film.

Despite his evident wealth, Tom remained close to his old friends and would visit with childhood acquaintances on his return to see his family in Dubois. Tom was generous with his money and would invest in wild schemes merely out of the kindness of his heart. In 1924, when his Fox contract was up, Tom renegotiated and came up with a new three-year deal. Through a confusion in his shooting schedule, he thought he might have several months free in 1924 and agreed by contract to appear with the Miller 101 Ranch Show. Fox altered the shooting, moving it up, and the Millers sued Tom for breach of contract. Finally, Mix worked out an agreement with them to appear in major cities, both helping the show and promoting his new Fox films.

In 1925 Tom and Tony embarked for Europe. They made personal appearances in England, France, Belgium, Holland, and Germany. Tony was reputedly the first horse to climb the circular staircase at the Opera House in Paris. Never before had a screen cowboy been so popular, mobbed, saluted, greeted by royalty, worshiped the world over.

Tom tried a costume drama in 1925, *Dick Turpin*. Along with *Sky High* (Fox, 1921), *Riders of the Purple Sage* (Fox, 1925), *The Last Trail* (Fox, 1927), *The Great K & A Train Robbery*, and, naturally, *Just Tony,* it is one of the very few surviving pictures from Tom's Fox period. It was a bust

Tom costumed in the guise of a Mountie in *Ace High,* one of his first adventure films after leaving Colonel Selig.

Photo courtesy of A. J. Brokop.

at the box office. But it does feature an interesting cameo appearance of Buck Jones. Buck got dressed up as an extra and challenged Tom to a sword fight as an on-the-set spoof during production of the film. It marked the beginning of friendly relations between the two of them, following Tom's renewal of his contract at $17,500 a week; Buck was only being paid an eighth as much.

The Buck Jones unit was consistently making programmer Westerns of comic or lighthearted story lines, involving nothing like the $150,000 average budgets on the Mix Westerns. Buck was extremely fond of Carole Lombard, a Fox contract player, and had her featured where he could in his films. W. S. Van Dyke was usually Buck's director. Once out on location, Buck and Woody concocted a practical joke to play on Carole. Woody was wearing a gun as a protection against snakes. He loaded it with blanks. When Carole emerged from the make-up truck, Van Dyke and Buck fell to violent quarreling as to how the scene should be shot. Van Dyke, in his rage, pulled out his gun and plugged Buck squarely in the chest. Buck, palming catsup, slapped his chest in a hopeless gesture, red oozing over his shirt front, and collapsed. Carole ran to him, holding him to her and weeping. Van Dyke leered, turned on his heel, and arrogantly walked away. Carole was beside herself, shouting for someone to get an ambulance. Then Buck opened his eyes, smiled at her, began laughing. Realizing what had happened, Carole dropped his head smartly on the ground and indignantly told both Van Dyke and Jones what they could do with themselves. Clark Gable, who later married Lombard, liked her especially for her ability to speak her mind directly and bluntly, an admirable thing in a woman in those days.

The Gentle Cyclone may not be the best Western Buck Jones made for the Fox Film Corporation, but it is probably typical of the comic photoplay he was accustomed to appearing in. Based on the story "Peg Leg and the Kidnapper," by Frank R. Buckley, which appeared originally in *Western Story Magazine,* the plot cast Buck as Absolem Wales, a peaceful man who tends to be good with his fists. When June Prowitt inherits a strip of land desired by both of her uncles, it tends to intensify the feud between them. Will Walling tries to hire Buck to fight on the side of the Marshalls; Stanton Heck wants to hire Buck to defend the interests of the Wilkeses against the Marshalls. Grant Withers was cast as the younger Wilkes. Oliver Hardy, before he was teamed with Stan Laurel by Hal Roach, appeared as the sheriff. Each side thinks Buck is working in its behalf; every time any of the warring factions happen to meet, a fistfight is the result. Before he is finished, Buck has to fight virtually everyone in the picture, including the sheriff. Buck finally resolves the feud by adopting June and taking over the strip of land for himself.

"Buck Jones in the role of a stalwart who loves peace so much that he is ready to fight like a fury for it," *The Motion Picture News* reported, "keeps busy in the five reels of action which make up his latest contribution to the screen's vast store of Western plays, and if the sum total of the entire proceedings seems pointless and thoroughly bla-a, the responsibility for this condition cannot be charged up to him." *The Moving Picture World* commented that "Buck Jones gives a pleasing characterization of the title role which is somewhat suggestive of his role in *Lazybones* [Fox, 1925], while Stanton Heck and Will Walling capably portray the two uncles. Rose Blossom is attractive as the girl and the other roles are all in good hands. There is a lot of action, but much of it seems inconsistent and lacking in punch and spontaneity."

The Western market began tightening in late 1927, and the coming of sound boded ill for the future of outdoor dramas. Tom Mix's contract with Fox had a year to run. Buck had not been on vacation for several years. He asked Sol Wurtzel for his permission to take a trip to Europe. Sol told Buck that he could go with his blessing and that the studio would continue to pay his salary during the four weeks Buck was gone. Buck was regarded as primarily a second-string Western player, and the Fox management was distrustful of the future. When Buck returned to the lot, he tried to pick up his vacation pay. It was refused. Buck went to Sol to complain. Sol merely shrugged his shoulders. Buck flew into a rage and told Sol that if he was not going to be a man of his word then he would quit, and he did. After having worked for Fox Film Corporation for nearly nine years, Buck Jones suddenly found himself out of a job. The studio concentrated on filming Mix Westerns for the new season.

I once had occasion to ask Duke Wayne about his association with Tom Mix.

"You worked at Fox during the time when Mix was their leading attraction, didn't you?"

He nodded.

"How well did you know him?"

"I worked with him on *The Great K & A Train Robbery*," he responded. "Or maybe I should tell you that I went to Colorado with the Mix unit for the filming of *The Great K & A Train Robbery*. I was a prop boy. We were standing around talking one day and Tom comes walking near us. 'Hello, fellas,' he says. That was the closest I came to working with Mr. Tom Mix."

He said the name, I thought, with some bitterness. Maurice Zolotow, Duke's long-time friend, has written a biography of John Wayne titled *Shooting Star* (Simon & Schuster, 1974), which tells Duke's life story the way Duke wants it to be told and the way he remembers it as having happened. Zolotow relates how Wayne first met Mix as a youth and how hurt and disappointed he was when Mix didn't give him a chance in pictures, something apparently Mix had promised to do for him. But Mix was prob-

Buck and Dell Jones on their way to Europe. The trip cost him his job at Fox.

Photo courtesy of Dell Jones.

ably not to blame. He had been subject to the importunity of countless people for many years, persons who wanted favors of him for no other reason than that he was successful and they wanted to be. Nor, with the advancing years, has Duke Wayne been any more willing to promote new, untried talent in his films, harking back constantly instead to the loyalties of years' standing, keeping old friends employed, not really desiring the acquaintance of new personalities. In Duke's case, it may be old age, or perhaps an impatience with people which has increased with the passage of time. The young John Wayne may have irritated Tom Mix as much as he did Tim McCoy when Duke worked with McCoy.

From what remains of Tom's features from the twenties and what was written about them at the time they were made, they were apparently unique among series Westerns. For one thing, the pacing of the action is breath-taking; this may not be true of *Riders of the Purple Sage*—in fact, it is a weak film on just this account—but Mix's other surviving pictures

Tom, dressed all in white as was his custom, fixing himself a meal in his completely electrified kitchen during his golden period.

Photo courtesy of *Views & Reviews* magazine.

are flushed with the exhilarating hectic of their unrelenting and thrilling motion. Like many of the Mix Westerns for Fox, *The Great K & A* was filmed at the site of a national wonder, the Royal Gorge in Colorado, for the railroad footage, with scenic exteriors a short distance away in virgin country. Daniel B. Clark, who later, recalling Tom's penchant for using trains in his films, commented that he had mounted his camera at every conceivable location, incorporating some of his most visually exciting photography into the cinematic narration of a story of propelling action.

The picture opens to spectacular footage of a train passing through the gorge. Tom is an undercover detective hired by the president of the railroad to get to the bottom of a series of train robberies. There is breath-taking stunting all the way through the film. Tom learns that the president's secretary is an informer to the gang. In the process of bringing the robbers to justice, he happens to fall in love with the president's daughter, and the two are united by the last reel.

Tom Mix was a legendary character, even in his own time; he not only knew it, but did what he could to perpetuate the legend. But beneath it was a man of conviction; behind the storytelling and the obvious fabrication was a man who believed in the idealized life he was responsible for depicting on the screen. His refusal to smoke, drink, or swear in his films removed the Western somewhat from reality; his emphasis on cavalier derring-do detached it more. Tom's Westerns, however, were life-affirming, totally devoid of the almost perverse moral fervor of William S. Hart's zealous prose-lytizing. Tom Mix was a man of extraordinary personal flamboyance. Hoot Gibson, and to an even lesser extent Buck Jones, joined Mix in being light-hearted. It was a bright and cheerful world they lived in; one could not imagine that it would ever come to an end. William Fox offered to buy out Adolph Zukor and take over Paramount, just as he laid the groundwork for seizing the vast empire of Loew's, Inc., and Metro-Goldwyn-Mayer. And over it all, Tom Mix's star of good fortune shone, undimmed and, seemingly, impregnable.

A photograph of Tom Mix's plush Hollywood home during the twenties.

Photo courtesy of *Views & Reviews* magazine.

15 / TIM McCOY AT METRO-GOLDWYN-MAYER

Shortly after the greatest merger in motion picture history brought Marcus Loew, Nicholas Schenck, Louis B. Mayer, and Irving Thalberg together, and the emergent company assumed the name Metro-Goldwyn-Mayer, Thalberg proposed the formation of an outdoor unit. Thalberg's experience with Carl Laemmle had taught him the commercial importance of series Westerns. Mayer, who was in charge of the studio, gave a green light to the project.

Thalberg chose the key people for the unit with sensitivity and insight. To direct the Metro Westerns, he selected W. S. "Woody" Van Dyke, who had had many years in the industry working on serials and series Westerns, the latter, as mentioned earlier, chiefly with Buck Jones at Fox. Van Dyke was capable of fast, economic shooting; he had a way of getting things done on time; and he was resourceful—when Thalberg hired him he was as yet awaiting an opportunity to fully utilize his talents. Louise Lorraine, one of Universal's most durable serial players, was put under an option at $400 a week. Colonel Tim McCoy, despite his work at Famous Players-Lasky, had been passed over there as a Western lead. Thalberg perceived in him a dashing, romantic hero, ideal for action vehicles, a man of poise, frontier learning, military achievement, and good looks.

The first entry, *War Paint* (M-G-M, 1926), called upon McCoy's experience with the Plains Indians, both as a wrangler before the Great War and as an Indian agent afterward. The writers had been stumped for weeks, trying to think up a suitable first plot to get the new series off to an exciting start. Van Dyke finally broke the paralysis himself by inviting McCoy to his home, sitting him down, and insisting that he talk for two hours about Indians, everything he knew about them. The finished plot told of Iron Eyes, played by Chief Yowlachie, who becomes disgruntled with reservation life and is placed under arrest by the Army and imprisoned for anarchy. He escapes, however, and the commanding officer of the post orders his men to enforce his threat against the Indians, that unless Iron Eyes is given up within twenty-four hours the tribe will suffer the consequences and be uprooted from their reservation. A detachment is sent from

Tim McCoy locked in a dagger duel with Chief Yowlachie in *War Paint*.

the post to make good the threat, thus leaving the settlement unguarded. Iron Eyes, in the meantime, returns with a group of renegade braves and lays siege to the post. Tim, after penetrating enemy lines to get help, engages Iron Eyes in a knife battle and defeats him. Having made it to the Arapahoe camp, Tim convinces the chiefs that war is a tragic solution to the red man's ills and can only result in his extinction; he does this by means of sign language, as fascinating as any pantomime to be found on the silent screen. Tim returns with the rest of the tribe to the post, where the siege is lifted and Indian and cavalry make peace. Tim, who has fallen in love with the commandant's daughter, played by Pauline Starke, wins her in the end and the story concludes happily.

War Paint opened on Broadway to mildly enthusiastic reviews and did well at the box office. Much of its success Van Dyke attributed to the authenticity of its setting. The second entry, *Winners of the Wilderness,* furthered the dependence on historical accuracy, but moved back in time from the era of the Plains to the French and Indian War. The outdoor elements of stunting and action were foremost, but to them were added the glamour and aura of Colonial pageantry. The major event of the pic-

Joan Crawford and Colonel Tim McCoy in *Winners of the Wilderness*. She was also a blonde in the picture.

Photo copyright by Metro-Goldwyn-Mayer.

ture was Braddock's tragic defeat by a handful of French regulars and Pontiac's Indians. John Thomas Neville wrote the visually powerful screenplay, basing his account in large measure on historical sources, above all George Washington's own description of the battle. Neville also managed, with Van Dyke's assistance, to present at once the savage tortures of the Hurons and the peculiar sense of loyalty true of the red man. No motion picture would ever again detail the defeat so accurately or so directly.

M-G-M initiated a major publicity campaign for McCoy, headed by Howard Strickling (who remained a good friend of Tim's over the years), hoping to quickly gain a reputation for Metro as a manufacturer of the best outdoor dramas just as it was the corporate objective to be the best with all other kinds of pictures. Joan Crawford, a versatile actress who had been signed by M-G-M in 1925, was cast opposite Tim in *Winners,* with Louise Lorraine playing the part of her petite maid and doubling her in the action. Edward Hearn, one of Woody's best friends and an actor he consistently found work for when neglected by other studios, was given the role of Washington. Van Dyke confessed honestly to Tim that he preferred seeing the colonel in costume dramas rather than the dust-caked thrillers he'd been used to making with Buck Jones.

Braddock in *Winners* is not quite the fool history books picture. It was customary throughout the course of the British Empire for the British to consider their own theories and methods superior in a particular situation to those derived by hard-won experience by the persons native to the locale. Only upon an irrefutable empirical demonstration, such as that which was presented to Braddock, would the British alter their thinking and adopt a somewhat more practical course of action. Washington, who was an aide to Braddock, thought him to be a "man whose good and bad qualities were intimately blended. He was brave even to a fault and in regular service would have done honor to his profession. His attachments were warm—his enmities were strong—and having no disguise about him, both appeared in full force. He was generous and disinterested—but plain and blunt in his manner even to rudeness." This is the impression one gets on the screen.

Tim plays an Irish officer attached to Washington's bluecoats under the generalship of Edward Braddock and is charged to spy on the French and give an account of their plans to conquer the Ohio Valley. He meets Renée, Contrecoeur's daughter, and they fall in love. In the forest Tim encounters Pontiac, and, following a fight, he spares Pontiac's life. Tim is captured after Braddock's fateful defeat and is sentenced to be shot. Renée pleads for his life, but Roy D'Arcy is delighted getting rid of a rival so easily. Pontiac, however, remembers Tim's kindness, spares his life, and Tim is able to escape with Renée, the two of them marrying once they are safely behind British lines.

Louis B. Mayer was a man of singular qualities. Friendship wasn't one of them, so history has tended to deal harshly with him, unjustifiably so. With one exception—that he didn't like Westerns—he had an unerring instinct for a good picture: he could identify potential box-office talent as well as the best and better than most; he was an expert showman who instinctively understood the masterful art of exploitation; he was a brilliant businessman who could correctly and effectively solve the many complexities between production and distribution. But withal he had two very great—and because of his immense power, almost tragically human—shortcomings: he shied off from total responsibility, depending instead on teamwork and committees; and he couldn't *put together* a great motion picture. Thalberg knew best how to mount a successful film, and this is precisely what brought him so close to Mayer and what made for his nearly mystical reputation.

Harry Rapf at M-G-M wanted Westerns, not period pieces. After all, hadn't McCoy been signed as a cowboy player for M-G-M? His first two pictures cast him as a military officer, chiefly because W. S. Van Dyke felt he best looked the part. But friction was developing that would lead to the diverse character of Tim's vehicles for M-G-M. Rapf wanted a Western star in the mold of Fred Thomson at FBO. *California* (M-G-M, 1927) was somewhat of a compromise, changing the locale at least to the Southwest and the conflict to that between the United States and Mexico, but Tim was still a military man. Van Dyke again managed to include some truly awesome battle sequences, particularly in the ambush of General Kearney's command by the Mexican Army. *The Frontiersman* (M-G-M, 1927) was another period piece, with Chief Big Tree back as Grey Eagle.

Tim played Captain John Dale, a member of Andrew Jackson's Tennessee militia, attempting to make a peace treaty with the Creek Indians. Louise Lorraine was one of the feminine leads. Reginald Barker was the director, and it was from Barker and Van Dyke that Tim learned the art of acting for the camera. McCoy had always felt that William S. Hart had expressed too unrestrainedly the emotions he was called upon to display. Van Dyke and Barker both stressed the matter of control when playing a difficult scene. Beyond this, they tended to leave Tim to his own resources. But Tim was already adept at personifying that quality of uncanny self-possession true of most of his screen portrayals and which, inevitably perhaps, led him to create the "man of destiny" image in his later sound films.

I am not certain that Tim's next two films for Metro could really be termed Westerns except in the loosest sense. *The Adventurer* (M-G-M, 1928) had him cast as a mining engineer involved in a Latin American revolution and was directed, in part at least, by Viachetslav Tourjansky, although Van Dyke finished it. *Foreign Devils* (M-G-M, 1927) found Tim as Captain Robert Kelly attached to the American embassy in China during the Boxer Rebellion. *The Adventurer* was actually begun in sequence but, due to its incomplete state, missed the scheduled October 1927 release date and wasn't issued until the next year.

McCoy's pictures with the aid of the production unit Thalberg had assembled and the guaranteed distribution that Mayer's business genius had created were doing well at the box office. But they were less and less Westerns, Rapf argued with Mayer, for whom he had worked since 1921. Moreover, they were costing considerably more than Westerns made by other companies. Thalberg's budgets started at $125,000, where those of other companies stopped at their most extravagant. *Spoilers of the West* (M-G-M, 1927) and *Wyoming* (M-G-M, 1928), seventh and eighth respectively in the series, were to be shot on location in Lander where Tim had spent many years of his life and still owned a ranch. David O. Selznick, soon to become Mayer's son-in-law, was made production supervisor for these pictures on the basis of postulating a novel suggestion to Mayer. Selznick proposed to shoot both pictures simultaneously, thus saving on costs. Harry Joe Brown had just tried something on this order with the Ken Maynard Westerns for First National, but I do not think David was aware of it. Mayer agreed and the unit was dispatched. As a result of this economy move, David brought in both films, budgeted at $90,000 apiece according to Thalberg's minimal estimates, at about $60,000 each. This encouraged Mayer's budget contentions concerning Metro Westerns, and Rapf was put in charge of the pictures thenceforth, Van Dyke being assigned to other Thalberg enterprises.

Some of the footage of *Spoilers of the West* was later used by Columbia in producing *End of the Trail* (Columbia, 1932). John Thomas Neville was credited with the screenplay, with Marjorie Daw cast as the heroine.

Again the story called upon the close relationship between the red man and the cavalry, with Tim cast as a cavalry officer. By general decree the reservation lands are to be cleared of all white men, which is charged to Tim, playing Lieutenant Lang, and which is accomplished save for Benton's Settlement. The Indians serve notice on the cavalry that, unless Benton's Settlement is moved, war will result. As in *War Paint,* Tim manages to engage in some stunting, in this instance riding atop two horses. One interesting, and rather comic, episode occurs when Tim meets several of the settlers from Benton's, ropes one of them who turns out to be Marjorie Daw, and she steals his horse through a ruse and makes a getaway, leaving Tim stranded and somewhat foolish in front of his men. It resolves happily, however, after Tim defeats Marjorie's brother in a long and exciting fist-fight at the settlement, with Marjorie being placed into Tim's custody by the commanding officer of the post, once the recalcitrant settlers have surrendered. General Custer is among the military detachment, suggesting by his presence more than by any overt action in the screenplay that the enforcement of the treaty is at best temporary and that a more tragic ending to the story is yet to be written.

The Law of the Range (M-G-M, 1928) is an excellent film to use in contrast with Tim's earlier pictures because it was the first of the new order under Rapf. Directed by William Nigh, the more conventional settings were very much in evidence. Tim, who never really looked the part of the saddle-weary, begrimed, dust-ridden, rough-and-tumble cowpuncher, carried his military bearing over, his straightness in the saddle, the immaculate clothes, the neat, careful appearance of the man accustomed to being responsible when it comes to grooming. He wore a black shirt and a white hat and rode a white horse. Another point of contrast with the earlier films is the performance of Joan Crawford in the role of Betty Dallas, rather pale alongside the enduring image of Renée. Rex Lease, who was to play opposite Tim frequently in sound films, was cast as his brother, from whom he was separated when a child during an Indian raid on their parents' wagon train. The Indians take Billy, only a baby at the time, while the Texas Rangers rescue Jim Lockhardt, played in maturity by Tim. The unifying mark identifying the two as brothers is the tattoo which they share, imprinted uniformly on each child's breast. I don't think this was a specially new plot in 1928; it certainly got reworked during the thirties, most notably perhaps in Ken Maynard's *Western Frontier* (Columbia, 1935), in which the brother became a sister played by Nora Lane in maturity, and in *Cavalcade of the West* (Grand National, 1936), with Hoot Gibson and Rex Lease, again, as the outlaw brother, a little older maybe but as weak as ever. The weak brother routine, in fact, was as commonplace to the Western as the good bad man.

When Betty Dallas, on the way to her ranch by stagecoach, is held up by the Solitaire Kid, played by Lease, she notices the tattoo. Later, when she meets Tim, who is now a Texas Ranger himself, she is horrified upon discovering his tattoo and suspects him of being the Kid. Unwittingly, she employs the real Kid on her ranch. Tim, having fallen in love with her but troubled by her suspicions, believes Lease to be the bandit. One unusual scene shows Joan Crawford, silhouetted by kerosene light, combing her hair, late at night, whereupon the Kid, torn between his attraction to Betty Dallas and his life of crime, resolves to pursue crime. In the end he is caught by Tim, amid a gigantic grass fire, and is brought to die in their mother's house, where Tim, too, learns the truth, with Joan lending him moral support. When Joan later pooh-poohed her Metro Westerns, I imagine she had this picture in mind as opposed to *Winners of the Wilderness*.

The plot of *Law of the Range* was still complex enough to be consistently entertaining, but the concept of Tim's Westerns from this point on remained firmly in the programmer category. The films which followed were scarcely experimental vehicles, and much of the publicity effort to build Tim into a major star, rather than a strictly Western player, was abandoned. *Beyond the Sierras* (M-G-M, 1928), typical of the new conventional approach, opens with Tim overhearing the plottings of Roy D'Arcy and his cronies in a gold mine which they want to steal from a Spanish don and which Tim, by assuming a Zorro-like costume and engaging in some spectacular sword fights with D'Arcy and his gang, prevents and thus wins the don's daughter. *The Desert Rider* (M-G-M, 1929), last in the series, was a product surprisingly similar to the kind of Westerns Tim would soon be making for Columbia. Playing Jed Tyler, an express rider, Tim is waylaid and robbed, left to wander aimlessly through the desert until finally he is rescued by a Spanish padre. Special effects were well used in the mirage sequences, and inevitably even the most conventional plots, as in this case the exposure of veteran villain Harry Woods as the leader of the mail robbers, were highlighted and pleasantly accentuated by action and the extraordinary stock company of M-G-M repertory players.

In a sense Rapf was vindicated by the circumstance that the McCoy Westerns continued to earn money even with the reduced budgets, standardized stories, and mundane production values. The Metro gloss permitted the pictures to look like more than was being put out by the competition. McCoy, whose long career in the sound era sadly never called upon his real acting talent (talent both Thalberg and Van Dyke had clearly perceived and strove to exploit), recognized the immense financial return his pictures had domestically, outgrossing on an individual basis any of the films with Garbo or Navarro. But M-G-M stars were paid a flat salary with an annual bonus which was unrelated to specific gross, only corporate profits. Tim went to Mayer to ask for a raise, as it turned out only shortly before his option was up for renewal.

In February 1929 Metro had announced that they planned to go into production on the McCoy films for the 1929–30 season. The sound engineers remained doubtful as to the viability of making talking pictures out-of-doors. Mayer's natural antagonism toward sound had kept the Westerns silent, without even music or synchronized effects. But he was becoming keenly aware that studios producing series Westerns were curtailing production or discontinuing it altogether, cognizant that the silent Western was finished and the sound Western reputedly impossible. Only Rin-Tin-Tin was working at Warner Brothers. Fox had abandoned Westerns. Tom Mix was still working, but Buck Jones wasn't. Ken Maynard and Hoot Gibson were fighting with Carl Laemmle about sound.

Mayer peered across his polished desk at Tim, wrung his hands, breathed a deep sigh, began complaining that he was losing money on Westerns, how the future looked very dark, tears welling up in his eyes. These physiological phenomena need not be directly attributable to tab sheet reports on the McCoy pictures because the films were still doing well; rather, they were simply the typical Mayer response to requests for pay increases. McCoy didn't get his raise, and his option wasn't renewed. Metro-Goldwyn-Mayer never again made series Westerns.

16 / KEN MAYNARD AT FIRST NATIONAL

Ken Maynard was born on July 21, 1895, at Vevay, Indiana. Later, studio biographers would feel impelled to change his birthplace to Mission, Texas. In addition to Ken, William H. Maynard and his wife, Emma May Stewart, had three daughters, Trixie, Willa, and Bessie and, on September 20, 1897, a second son whom they named Kermit. When he was twelve, Ken ran away from home to join a traveling Wild West show. His father, who was a building contractor by trade, caught up with the boy and compelled him to return home. But Ken remained obsessed with the idea of becoming a circus performer. At sixteen he asked for and received permission to join a touring carnival. His formal education ended there, although studio biographers, again, attributed to him, as to Tom Mix, attendance at the Virginia Military Institute. Ken was doing what he wanted to do.

In 1914 Ken was the leading attraction with the Kit Carson Show. Hav-

Ken Maynard in a typical action shot, riding Tarzan.

Photo courtesy of the late Ken Maynard.

ing moved from show to show and from job to job, Ken had perfected his horsemanship, learned to rope (largely from the famed Mexican roper Oro Peso, with whom Maynard once traveled), to stunt, and to perform numerous riding tricks. One day a new female rider from the Ringling Brothers congress came to the Carson show and asked Ken to demonstrate some of his tricks. Her name was Odille Osborne. Later that year at Madison Square Garden, Odille met Zach Miller's top rider with the 101 Ranch Wild West Show, Charles "Buck" Gebhard. The reader will recall how the two were married with great fanfare in the center ring of a circus. Maynard, unaware of the marriage, sent Dell a large portrait of himself. Buck was outraged when he saw it and tore it up.

Maynard moved on to the Hagenbeck and Wallace outfit in 1915. When the Great War came, he enlisted in the U. S. Army, was stationed at Camp Knox, Kentucky, as an engineer, and married a mountain girl. When he was discharged, he left both the girl and Kentucky and rejoined the Hagenbeck-Wallace show. In 1920 Ken became a member of Pawnee Bill's troupe and, dressed as Buffalo Bill, rode in the Rose Bowl parade. At the insistence of friends, Ken entered the Pendleton Rodeo that year and won a trophy as the All-Around Champion Cowboy of the World. Ringling Brothers signed him as a center attraction in 1921. Meeting Dell and Buck Jones in Hollywood, Ken was impressed with the success Jones was having at Fox Film Corporation. Maynard set his mind to getting into pictures himself.

Ken got to know Tom Mix, and the latter helped him get a walk-on in *The Man Who Won* (Fox, 1923), but it didn't lead to anything. On February 14, 1923, Maynard married Jeanne Knudsen in Los Angeles. The marriage was short-lived. In 1924 Ken finally got his break from William Randolph Hearst whose Cosmopolitan Pictures company was making a new Marion Davies film entitled *Janice Meredith,* shot in and around New York at Hearst's International Studios. Maynard's role was that of Paul Revere, which he won on the basis of his superior riding ability. Hearst paid him $1,000 a week. If it had been for a year instead of four weeks, Maynard figured it would far outstrip the $40,000 a year he was making with the Ringling show.

When the Davis Distribution Division, a small, independent producing company, approached him to make a series of eight Westerns, Ken jumped at the opportunity. Although fewer than eight may have been made before the firm went defunct, beginning with *$50,000 Reward,* these Westerns helped establish Maynard as a screen personality. The Davis pictures were entertaining, if cheaply made, filled with plenty of horse action and stunting from Ken and in *The Grey Vulture* (Davis, 1926) even some bathing beauties in relative distress. A massive publicity campaign was launched to promote the new player. The only objection the make-up people at Davis had was the way Ken parted his hair; they felt he looked like a barber and wanted to give him a permanent wave. Maynard flatly refused.

While still with Ringling Brothers, newspapers had carried stories of the death of Mazie, one of the performing horses Maynard had used; photographs had been published of him with Brownie, a mare with which he had traveled twenty thousand miles. But it was at Newhall, California, that Ken bought a golden three-year-old palomino for fifty dollars. He named him Tarzan, after Edgar Rice Burroughs' jungle hero. Tarzan began appearing with Ken in his Davis Westerns. In 1926 Ken was signed to do a non-Western called *North Star,* with Strongheart, a German shepherd and perhaps the most able competitor of the great Rin-Tin-Tin. He got his name in the papers when he married Mary Leeper on the set, a girl from South Bend, Indiana. It was her first, Ken's third. Ken never had any children, either from this marriage or from any of the others.

Charles R. Rogers then proposed to Maynard that he star in a high-budget series of Westerns intended for First National release. The contract represented that First National would undertake to build Maynard into a strong screen property and that Tarzan, like Tony and Silver, would receive billing. First National hoped that Ken Maynard would be as successful for them as Hoot Gibson was at Universal or Tom Mix and Buck Jones were at Fox.

In mid 1926 First National was definitely a studio on the rise. A group grew up around Maynard at First National, one member or another of which would be associated with him for all of his most bountiful years in the industry. Had he not later abandoned the last of them, Sidney Rogell, his career would not have nose-dived. Foremost was Charles R. Rogers, producer of the Ken Maynard series. He was a Ken Maynard fan personally and resolved to fully exploit the young circus rider. Sid Rogell was primarily a businessman who knew how to manage money. He was placed in charge of business matters on the First National Westerns and many times proved his worth. When Maynard signed again with Universal in 1933–34, Sid was the man he called upon to act as his financial and production adviser.

Harry Joe Brown, who was given credit on the eighteen Westerns Maynard made for First National as the production supervisor, was actually the associate producer for the series and worked closely with Charles Rogers. I have already told of Brown's affiliation with the Fred Thomson FBO Westerns; he brought the same expertise to the Maynard vehicles. He assigned Marion Jackson to the unit to write the screenplays, handled Maynard's screen image himself, and even, upon occasion, took over direction of the pictures. Albert S. Rogell, the unit's principal director, brought with him the wealth of silent Western action technique which he gained working with Jack Hoxie at Universal and then Fred Thomson at FBO. When sound retarded Western production in 1930, it was Al Rogell personally who engineered Maynard's contract with Tiffany Pictures. It was also Rogell who directed the finest surviving Western with Tom Mix, *Rider of Death Valley* (Universal, 1932). It was to this group and their astonishing genius for motion picture production that we owe one of the best series of programmer Westerns ever manufactured, the Ken Maynard productions for First National and the Universal first and second series. Maynard's only really notable Westerns separate from them are *Dynamite Ranch* (World-Wide, 1932), and, perhaps, *In Old Santa Fe* (Mascot, 1934). That others such as Buck Jones were successful for a longer period of time rests upon the fact that he retained skillful management, whereas Hart, Maynard, and, especially, Fred Thomson, when they eschewed it, could only blame this for their fall. Tom Mix, of course, was the exception, but there could only have been one Tom Mix.

Senior Daredevil, the initial entry, was budgeted at $75,000 and emphasized Maynard's fabulous horsemanship. The pacing in the Maynard vehicles was brisk, just as was the case with the best Fox Westerns with Tom Mix, but to this was added the romance and good-natured humor true of the Fred Thomson pictures at FBO. Ken played Don Luis O'Flagherty who comes in the nick of time to save his father's wagon hauling business from J. P. McGowan's chicanery. The film was well received by the public, and even the critics admired Maynard's dexterity and his good looks. *Photoplay,* however, was anything but enamored of the plot. *The Unknown Cavalier* (First National, 1926) was second with a story that stressed comedy and suspense. It was remade as *Ride Him Cowboy* (Warner's, 1932) in the thirties with John Wayne. The fifth entry in the series was titled *Land Beyond the Law* (First National, 1927) and costarred Ken with Dorothy Dwan as a victim of her evil guardian, played by Tom Santschi. It was remade under this title in 1937 with Dick Foran. I will have something to say about these remakes later. As the series progressed, increasingly wild and complex stunts were worked out for both Ken and Tarzan, all of which the two performed in close-up for the camera. As many precautions as Maynard would take, at times things went wrong.

When the troupe went to Montana to film both *The Red Raiders* and *Gun Gospel,* a typical incident occurred during production of the latter. The action called for a leap from a sixty-foot cliff into a lake and a swim to the opposite shore. Technicians rigged up a wooden runway at the top of the cliff, arguing that this would help Tarzan to clear the edge and run no risk of striking shallow water. Tarzan, with Ken on his back, galloped at full speed to the runway; at the very edge, he slipped on the newly planed boards, turned over in mid-air, and landed in the water with Ken beneath him. They went down about thirty feet. When they came separately to the surface, Tarzan was so terrified that he tried to climb on top of Ken, who evaded him and swam to shore. As Ken reached the nearer bank, he looked

Harry Joe Brown, Ken Maynard holding his inevitable cigar, and Sid Rogell from their days at First National.

Ken standing on the running board of his new Packard showing off Tarzan, nearest the car radiator, and Tarzan's doubles at the stables on the Tiffany California studios back lot.

Photo courtesy of the late Ken Maynard.

back over his shoulder to see Tarzan carrying out his picture instructions and swimming for the farther one. Arrived there, the animal spied Ken and immediately swam back, attaining the shallow water near Ken, who had waded out to meet him, dropping to his knees, and nestling his head in Ken's arms. The shot, as it was supposed to be, was still so impressive to Warner's cutters as late as the forties that it was frequently included in two-reelers devoted to picture stunt work, such as *Spills and Thrills*.

Tarzan may have been the most exceptional horse in pictures. Unlike Trigger, billed as "the smartest," and Champion, billed as a world wonder, Tarzan was not the creation of studio publicity. His only rival would be Tom Mix's Tony. But Tony's supremacy is confined to his ability to direct horse action, and in this, Tarzan equaled him in Ken's sound film *Come on, Tarzan* (WorldWide, 1932). Readily trained by means of one-syllable instructions, Tarzan was Ken's costar in virtually every film. Scenes were constantly written into Maynard's pictures calling for the horse to dance, to bow down, to roll over and play dead, to nod his head in response to questions, to ring a fire bell, to pull Ken from a turbulent river, to chase desperadoes by himself, to untie Ken, to jump from great heights or great distances, to plunge into burning buildings, to drag Ken hanging onto his tail on land or in the water, and, of course, to give the reticent hero a push into the heroine's arms. Ken's reliance on Tarzan and the variety and breakneck pacing of their performances together were a most obvious emulation of Mix. While at First National, Maynard assembled an entire string of palomino horses to support Tarzan, one of which would buck or rear, one of which would run up to a certain point and stop cold, one for pulling and tugging at objects like jail bars. Horse action became a hallmark of the Maynard Westerns to an even greater extent than was the case with almost any other player. Ken kept the retinue until Tarzan's death in 1940. I trust the reader will not take me amiss when I say that in a far different way than Thomson with Silver King or Mix with Tony, Ken loved Tarzan deeply, in a manner that he never loved a human being. Tarzan reciprocated.

The budgets on the First National series rarely exceeded $80,000 and were usually less. It is to Harry Joe Brown, rather than to either David O. Selznick at M-G-M in connection with the Tim McCoy vehicles or Harry Sherman who produced the later Bar 20 pictures in this fashion, that the innovation of shooting series Westerns two at a time to save on costs is owed. Brown stressed the pit shot which D. W. Griffith used in production of *The Birth of a Nation.* In *The Red Raiders,* when a band of wild Indians is chasing a stagecoach, Brown had the camera positioned beneath the turf, covered by boards with just enough light falling on the lens for a clear picture. The players were then instructed to ride across the boards. The chase was photographed seemingly from beneath the ground.

Rogell also went out of his way to effect unusual camera shots and angles. William S. Hart's notion of having himself and his mount photographed while galloping along a rise, making it appear in *Tumbleweeds* as if he were riding through thin air, was varied by Rogell in *The Red Raiders* so that Maynard, riding furiously on Tarzan, with dust swirling about the steed's legs, looks to be riding atop a whirlwind cloud. Rogell next positioned his camera on a truck in such a way as to enable him to get a shot of Maynard, riding fast, bending over Tarzan's left side, reaching down to Ben Corbett being dragged by a running horse, recording Maynard's face muscles contracting from the physical strain at extreme close-up. Corbett was a good man to be used in stunting sequences. He had been a rodeo rider prior to being hired by Thomas Ince at the time of the Bison Westerns in the teens for trick riding and doubling. He spent the rest of his career as a character actor in Westerns.

At the opening of the picture, Indians attack the stage carrying both Ken and Ann Drew to the fort. The driver and guard are killed. Maynard leaps astride a horse, catches up to the runaway team. He jumps across, taking hold of the harness, and then, racing alongside one of the horses Indian-fashion, he grabs hold of another rein. He leaps atop the horse, falls onto the tongue of the wagon, rescuing two more reins from beneath the thundering hoofs; he is able then to climb into the driver's seat. Rogell managed to capture all of this harrowing action with facial close-ups of Maynard to leave no doubt in the spectator's mind as to who, precisely, was performing the stunts.

Seventh in Maynard's First National series, *The Red Raiders* may be Ken's finest silent Western and in terms of the action footage with Maynard himself as the principal participant, he was never to duplicate it in the sound era. Since only five of six reels of *Somewhere in Sonora* (First National, 1927) and *The Red Raiders* survive in anything like complete form, I cannot be more definite than I have been in assessing the quality of Maynard's work before the time of his part-talking features at Universal in 1929. Only *$50,000 Reward* and *The Grey Vulture* remain from his Davis period. But based on only these four films, very few of the extraordinary feats done by Yakima Canutt and stunt men of the thirties and forties were not already anticipated by Maynard in his early silent Westerns. *The Red Raiders* was especially close to Maynard himself, and he frequently borrowed footage from it to use in pictures made subsequently for different companies. The scene of the Indian camp of the Sioux, announced by a title card in the second reel, and a war dance from the original negative are still missing because he reused that footage in 1934 without replacing it for *Wheels of Destiny;* Sid Rogell supervised the later deletion. The Indians galloping toward the camera during the opening credit crawl of the Tim McCoy serial *The Indians Are Coming* (Universal, 1930) was borrowed from this picture, as well as Maynard using the identical footage again in *Wheels.* The shots of Maynard leading a group of racing wagons across a flat, employed in *Wheels of Destiny* briefly and more substantially in *Western Frontier* (Columbia, 1935), was taken from *The Red Raiders.* Above all, the shots of the Sioux rallying for war in *The Red Raiders,* whipped into a frenzy by Chief Yowlachie, were used over and over by Hollywood studios in the thirties.

I have told the reader that Tom Mix had a penchant for tall tales. I have related how it was his custom, whenever he knew people at all well, to tell them some fantastic story about his early years before pictures. He confided to Dell Jones, for example, that his real name was Whitzelschmidt and that his first job was tending bar. He mixed drinks so well, he became known as Tom "Mix." One of his favorites, which he told the Stokes family when he married Olive Stokes, was that his real name was Tom Lowenthal, that his father had died when he was very young and his mother remarried a Greek named Mixopoulos. Tom simply dropped the *-opoulos.* He would point to his nose and say, "Jewish, not Cherokee."

An inside joke on *The Red Raiders* was Marion Jackson's making a reference to this story in the screenplay. Paul Hurst, cast as Ken's troop sergeant (he had personally directed Maynard in several of the Davis entries), objects to Izzy Epstein played by Harry Shutan using his hands when he talks. Later, Izzy and Ben Corbett see some Indians visiting the fort, dressed in fancy regalia. Izzy notes that they are talking with their hands. He surmises that they must be his people, the lost tribes of Israel. The camera does a close-up of an Indian's nose. Izzy points to his own nose to prove they are "brudders." He takes the two Indians aside, talking what he thinks is sign language, and trades all their clothes and jewelry for a lot of junk he carries in his pockets. When he walks back toward Corbett, now joined by Hurst, he shakes his head sadly and remarks, "They're not my people." The implication is that Izzy's people would never have been so easily *schmoosed*. It is one of the few Jewish sequences I can recall in a Western from any period.

The plot of *The Red Raiders* is quite similar to *War Paint,* made the previous year by Metro with Tim McCoy, even down to Chief Yowlachie being the principal troublemaker. Washington is about to grant the Sioux nation a permanent reservation. Yowlachie stirs the braves up into a war-like spirit, and they determine to raid the fort. Ken and Ann Drew fall in love. Warning all the ranchers, Ken's detail instructs them to head their wagons for the fort and make fast against the uprising. The Indians are subdued and peace comes, Ken and Ann together at the fade.

In making the picture, Harry Joe Brown had most of the local boys dress up as a cavalry detachment and used the Crow Indians as the braves. They were given blank cartridges for their guns. When the fort was attacked for the camera, an old brave was apparently shot from his horse. He was carried to his tepee, whereupon he announced that he was dying. No one believed him. Ken insisted to both Al Rogell and Brown that when an Indian says he's going to die, he does. The Indian died. When I related this to Harry Joe Brown, he agreed that it had happened that way. But what he had not told Ken at the time was that some of the local boys had put nails in the wax heads of their blank cartridges.

"What Ken didn't know," he commented to me, "was that the bullet that hit the old Indian was real enough to kill him. First National settled the matter with the tribe out of court."

In 1928 First National was bought by the Warner brothers, and the companies combined their facilities at the First National Burbank studio. Jack L. Warner took over as the head of production. Warner did not care much for series Westerns, and so the studio, under his management, produced very few of them. Ken finished his series. *The Royal Rider* (First National, 1929) was released in a synchronized effects version. The Vitaphone recording engineers informed Warner that talking Westerns would be a preciously expensive undertaking. Ken's First National contract was not renewed. Charles R. Rogers and Sid Rogell associated themselves with the newly organized RKO-Pathé. Harry Joe Brown and Maynard endeavored to find financing for a new series of Westerns elsewhere. In retrospect, I think it can be said of *The Red Raiders* that it possesses all of the excitement, thrills, and production value which characterized the silent action Western at its best and, among surviving materials from the twenties, ranks well with *The Great K & A Train Robbery* and the finest of the McCoy Westerns.

A Time
of Darkness
and Light

17 / UNIVERSAL IN 1930

The impact of sound films had affected all aspects of production by 1929, especially that of outdoor dramas. It changed the fortunes of nearly all the Western players and exerted a profound influence on how Westerns were henceforth manufactured. Industry leaders at the time attributed the slump in attendance to the talking picture innovation and realigned their schedules. There was some truth in this. But most of them overlooked the major cause and so it has been minimized by historians—the fact that the nation was plunged into the midst of its worst economic panic. Rather than combat something intangible, and probably insoluble, motion picture producers sought instead to blame the source of their problems on the kinds of films they were making and so instituted drastic changes.

I have already told of how Jack L. Warner decided not to renew Ken Maynard's contract on the basis of projected cost estimates of producing sound Westerns and how Louis B. Mayer shied away from the M-G-M series with Tim McCoy for the same reason; certainly they both used this as their principal excuse. Harry Joe Brown approached Carl Laemmle at Universal and negotiated a contract with him to film a series of Ken Maynard Westerns on the Universal lot. Universal agreed to finance the pictures with Brown as production and business manager. Based on the First National budget sheets, Brown insisted on and received a production allowance of $75,000 each for the films, which was to cover all costs including salaries. Unquestionably, Uncle Carl was sticking out his neck, but his faith in the integrity of the Western was unshaken.

In 1930 Hoot Gibson embarked on the final year of his second million-dollar three-year contract with Universal. He did not suspect that it was the beginning of the end for him. He was distracted completely from his work at the lot. Hoot was madly in love with Sally Eilers.

Helen Johnson Gibson was outraged by Hoot's flagrant public infidelity. Fights and stress quickly mounted. Hoot walked out on her. She sued for divorce, and it was awarded to her on February 7, 1930. Hoot, by court order, was compelled to settle upon her half his real estate holdings, one of his cars, and a minimum cash outlay of $150 a week until a total of $30,000

Mauser Street as it looked during the thirties.

Photo courtesy of *Views & Reviews* magazine.

had been paid. He also was committed to carry $100,000 in life insurance for his daughter, Lois. On February 10, 1930, Hoot presented Sally Eilers with an engagement ring.

Although in his forties, Hoot could perceive no possible wane in his popularity. Earning as much money as he had in the twenties, the sumptuous home he deeded Helen, his Newhall ranch, and his place in the mountains had nonetheless been purchased under mortgages that could permit no hiatus in his income. He flew a great deal in his private airplane and in 1931 managed to win the National Air Races in Los Angeles. He had a motorcycle that did 100 mph. Most of his ready money was spent on women, high living, expensive parties. Middle age did nothing to dim his attraction for Hollywood starlets, and he remained one of the foremost off-screen Don Juans.

Confident that his desperate financial straits, precipitated by his divorce, would soon be resolved, Hoot made what under the circumstances was a tragically foolish blunder. His 1928–30 contract with Universal called for him to have his own production company. Beyond the $330,000 a year he collected in salary, of which even then taxes claimed better than half, his unit was to participate in the profits made from his Universal Jewel Westerns once negative costs were recouped. Hoot reckoned that were he able to cut back on the production expense of his films, there would be more money for him and just as much profit to split. His obligations were by now so overextended that it seemed the only way. Most of his salary went to pay off the second mortgages which had resulted, in a single action, from paying up the quarter-million-dollar mortgage on Helen's home.

Hoot cast Sally in his pictures. The exposure on the screen is what she wanted most. It was as a consequence of her work in *Roaring Ranch* (Universal, 1930), *Trigger Tricks* (Universal, 1930), and *Clearing the Range* (Allied, 1931), all with Hoot, that Sally got the part in *Bad Girl* (Fox, 1931) that made her for a time one of the screen's hottest properties. On June 27, 1930, Hoot and Sally were married before a preacher amid 150 assorted cowboys at Hoot's ranch. From that point on it was downhill. It may be ironical to anticipate, but Sally's next husband was none other than Harry Joe Brown, who, after parting company with Maynard, became an increasingly important executive, again with Charles R. Rogers and then at Fox.

Carl Laemmle was in attendance at the Hollywood première at the Criterion Theater of *In Old Arizona* (Fox, 1929). Ken Maynard and Harry Joe Brown were also in the audience. The Fox Film Corporation had done very little in the way of Westerns since Buck Jones quit and Tom Mix was released. *In Old Arizona* was an experiment in an all-talking outdoor drama, a feat Laemmle's sound engineers said was impossible. It was the first sound picture featuring the Cisco Kid, and so I will have more to say about it later. "My Tonia" was the principal song, and the musical setting was charming.

When he got back to his studio, Laemmle called an emergency conference with Hoot Gibson and persuaded him that his six Universal Jewels for 1930 would have to be all-talking, not partially so as *The Long, Long Trail* and *Courtin' Wildcats,* the final entries for 1929, had been. Hoot had neither agent nor business manager; he felt that his friendship with Uncle Carl was all that he needed. Hoot expressed his willingness to absorb these costs into

The Hooter and Uncle Carl greet Local 1267 of the American Legion to a tour of Universal City.

Photo courtesy of Dorothy Dunstan Gibson.

his production budget. It required of Universal nearly a half million dollars a year, considering all expenditures, to make six Hoot Gibson Westerns. It is an interesting figure to contrast with Trem Carr's total negative cost of little over $75,000 for six all-talking Westerns with former FBO star Bob Steele for Tiffany release in 1930. Fox, at the success of *In Old Arizona,* signed a distribution agreement with Educational Film Corporation to distribute Educational product through the Fox exchanges, guaranteeing films like the Tiffany Westerns as many play-offs in Fox theaters and second-run houses as Universal generally secured without a theater chain. Tiffany Westerns were less expensive to book than Hoot Gibson Jewels and far more cheaply made and, therefore, more profitable. Fox began their own Western series with George O'Brien.

Laemmle met next with Ken Maynard. As shrewd as the old man was, he couldn't convince Brown and Maynard that to make their Westerns all-talking would not appreciably increase their costs over the allotted $75,000 budgets. Laemmle could have them all-talking if he wanted it that way, but Universal must pay all additional costs for sound recording. The haggling went on for some time, but Laemmle finally had a rider to the contract drawn to indicate that Universal would absorb the extra expense.

The initial four Maynard Westerns, *Wagon Master* and *Senior* ["*Señor*"] *Americano,* released in 1929, and *Lucky Larkin* and *Parade of the West,* in 1930, were quite similar to Ken's First National series with elaborate plots, plenty of action and stunts, and a solid romantic interest. Marion Jackson, who had scripted some of the best pictures at First National, came to Universal with the Maynard unit and worked on the early entries. Maynard was intrigued by the songs and the musical content of *In Old Arizona.* He wanted to incorporate these elements into his films. On April 1, 1930, Tiffany released one of their *Voice of Hollywood* filler shorts. In it, Maynard was introduced. He brought Tarzan on stage with him, then took up a fiddle and sang "The Drunken Hiccoughs." That same month, Universal released *The Fighting Legion,* still, as the first four, only part-talking in one version and completely silent in the other, but in the sound version featuring a male trio, the Hook brothers, played by Les Bates, Bill Nestel, and Slim Whitaker, performing a saloon ditty.

The Fighting Legion is a transition picture that had a special significance for Maynard. Frank Rice played his side-kick, Cloudy, in the film and remained Ken's preference in the role, appearing with him later in *Sunset Trail* (Tiffany, 1931) and, extensively, in his second Universal series of 1933–34. Bowden, the tough city Ken enters impersonating a Texas Ranger, is the town set Paramount built for use in *The Virginian.* Dorothy Dwan is the girl, and Ken kissed her at the fade. For all of the fight sequences and the hard riding episodes, *Fighting* ended with straight drama. Ernie Adams is responsible for having shot the real Ranger. Ken has served notice that he will be coming to the Empire Saloon at midnight to get the man who committed the murder. While Stanley Blystone and Jack Fowler are the leaders behind all the trouble, Adams is one of their hired killers. For almost two reels, the suspense in the saloon intensifies. Outside, it is raining, the wind blowing; inside, the town's good faction and its evil faction alike wait for the moment of reckoning. Ernie's deterioration is quite effective. When, at last, Ken does arrive, Ernie empties his gun, is captured, and confesses that Fowler and Blystone put him up to it. Brown had Ken reuse the footage of his jump with Tarzan from *Gun Gospel* at one point in the picture, shooting around it. But it was the psychological emphasis that was the most unusual characteristic of the film. Ken liked the plot so well he used the deterioration sequence, even to the rainstorm, although completely restaged with Alan Bridge in the Ernie Adams role for his later *The Lone Avenger* (WorldWide, 1933).

From the outset the Maynard films had been billed and sold as all-talking. The complaining from exhibitors grew bitter. Universal decided to put up sufficient funds to do the job right. *Mountain Justice,* also known as *Kettle Creek* and released next at the end of May, was a legitimate sound film with several songs. Ken performed some brilliant stunts for this film, and cinematographer Ted McCord gave him a reel of several of the takes that weren't used in the final work print that Ken kept for the rest of his life. Ken had to race around a curve driving a buckboard. The buckboard spills, throwing Ken to the ground. Ken jumps back on the front wheels, still attached to the horses, and races off. The wheels are lost and Ken mounts the horses' backs, riding with a leg on each mount. In this fashion, he gallops alongside a moving train, sees Les Bates on a flatcar, transfers to the car, and fights with him. Ken suggested the story himself, recalling his earlier experiences in Kentucky, where he was stationed during the Great War.

Song of the Caballero and *Sons of the Saddle,* which finished Maynard's 1930 schedule, increased their song content, and even Maynard, who always claimed that he sang loudly rather than well, performed several numbers, accompanying himself on the fiddle or banjo. In fact, somewhat surprisingly under the circumstances, Maynard cut a test record with Columbia Records and actually issued an album of six songs, a few of them having been featured prominently in his films. Frank Rice was Ken's sidekick again in *Song.* In *Sons of the Saddle* Ken was pitted against villain Francis Ford while the picture stressed the song "Down the Home Trail with You." Singing and musical backgrounds were a novelty that very much appealed to Maynard, and he planned to develop the notion more extensively, but, with the completion of *Sons* in July 1930, Laemmle informed Brown that Universal would not be renewing the Maynard contract for the 1930–31 season. Grosses weren't off so much as expenses were up, both with sound recording and with having to distribute the films in several different formats to service theaters variously wired for sound or not wired at all. With the exception of its summer serials in 1930 and 1931, respectively *The Indians Are Coming* and *Battling with Buffalo Bill,* Universal would not resume regular series Western production again until signing Tom Mix in early 1932. Laemmle bought from Maynard and Brown all residual rights to their pictures, and the two went their separate ways. The parting was by mutual agreement. For Maynard, who was strong-headed and overly self-indulgent, this separation would prove to be the first decisive miscalculation among many which needlessly shortened his career. Ken and his wife, Mary, set out for Indiana, stopping on the way at the Grand Canyon. Harry Joe Brown went to work for RKO-Pathé.

Hoot Gibson's six all-talking Westerns for 1930 began with release of *The Mounted Stranger* on February 8 of that year. Hoot felt impelled to persist in his screen image of an unglamorous cowpoke. I have read certain critics who have termed Hoot's concept of filmmaking an effort at streamlining. This would be true only if he were contrasted with William S. Hart in the early twenties. By 1930 Hoot's pictures definitely looked old-fashioned compared to the furious daredevil stunting and slick polish of the Maynard ranch romances. At their best, Hoot's Westerns were populated by interesting and bizarre characters whose multitude of unlikely adventures would have been fascinating no matter what the setting. In *Mounted Stranger* Hoot's objectives are to avenge his father's murder, perpetrated by lanky Fred Burns, and both rescue and marry lovely Louise Lorraine, the latter having taken to free-lancing when her Metro contract expired. Arthur Rosson's screenplay was based on the pulp story "Ridin' Kid from Powder River," by H. H. Knibbs, and was actually a remake of the Hoot Gibson Jewel of 1924 which bore the same title as the story. Hoot took all the melodrama in blitheful nonchalance, adding a humorous commentary on what he thought of cowboy music-making in the Maynard pictures when he, PeeWee Holmes, and the rest of Francis Ford's wranglers join in a little raucous campfire singing.

Consciously attempting to imitate himself, never thinking that repetition might grow wearisome and audiences become jaded, Hoot's next picture, *Trailin' Trouble,* was a return to the zany and incongruous plots which he seemed to prefer. These same basic plot ingredients would be used again and again in his post-Universal films. As later in *Hard Hombre* (Allied, 1931), Hoot in *Trailin'* is a devoted son to his mother who wants him to stay peaceable and out of trouble. Pete Morrison was cast as Buck Saunders, Hoot's rival for Margaret Quimby's hand. Hoot is charged by Margaret's father with selling his cattle in Kansas City, due to Hoot's reputation for honesty. During most of the picture, Hoot is dressed in a stylish business suit. He is robbed of the money while trying to save Ming Toy, a Chinese girl, from a gang of ruffians. He escapes, gets back to the ranch in an airplane, where Margaret's father accuses him of theft. Ming Toy returns the money. Hoot captures Buck, and Arthur Rosson's story ends happily.

Sally Eilers first appeared with Hoot in *Roaring Ranch,* released on April 27, 1930. Wheeler Oakman as a villainous geologist discovers oil on Hoot's property and tries to gyp him out of his ranch. Hoot and Wheeler are vying with each other for Sally's affection. The precocious and garrulous Bobby Nelson and a small infant are Hoot's wards, narrowly escaping death when two of Oakman's henchmen set fire to Hoot's house. Hoot learns of the hidden wealth just in time to save his land, turning Oakman over to the sheriff. Breezy Eason was the director. Nate Gatzert borrowed the plot of this picture for Ken Maynard's *Heir to Trouble* (Columbia, 1935), after seeing a print of it run in a Universal screening room.

The fan magazines were busy making copy of Hoot's new flame. Three weeks before the gala wedding, Universal issued *Trigger Tricks.* Eason directed and was responsible for the story. Hoot sets out to avenge his brother's death. His brother was Sally's foreman on her sheep ranch. It amused Hoot no end to make the arrogant Sally a shepherdess; she never suspected the joke. Sally enlists Hoot's aid in her battle against evil cattle king Robert Homans, who was responsible for the murder. Stressing comedy, Homans' gang is held at bay by a Victrola recording while Hoot brings Homans in.

The Hooter tying a diaper from *Roaring Ranch.*

Photo courtesy of MCA-Universal.

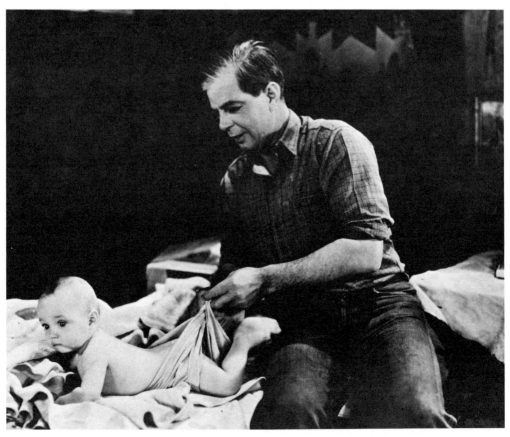

PeeWee Holmes, Buddy Hunter, Helen Wright, and the Hooter, with Hoot's palomino horse, Mutt, in the background, on location for *Spurs*.

Photo courtesy of MCA-Universal.

For his next production Hoot featured, as he had in *King of the Rodeo* (Universal, 1929), some of the thrills and spectacular horsemanship of the Hoot Gibson Round-Up, now an annual Hollywood event. Sally served as cohost with Hoot in 1930. The rodeo was a unique entertainment of its kind. Almost all of the stock footage of hog tyin', steer wrasslin', bronc and Brahma bull bustin', used in Westerns throughout the thirties and forties was provided from scenes originating at the roundup. By September 1930 rumors were circulating that all was not well between the Gibsons, back from their Canadian honeymoon, Sally living with friends. Hoot drank and caroused. *Spurs* emerged against this background.

Hoot, among the reigning Western stars, proved one of the most natural and adaptable to the sound medium. In 1929, reviewing the Gibson pictures, *Photoplay* complained about the repeated use of identical sets, giving the films an unpleasant sameness. Hoot relied more heavily on location shooting in 1930, and *Spurs* was filmed at Lone Pine, with Harry Neumann's breath-taking photography of the mountains, deserts, and cloud formations. Pete Morrison outdid himself as a nasty rustler. Buddy Hunter, who played Buddy Hazlet, had a short-lived career, appearing the next year in *Sunset Trail* with Ken Maynard, and he would have a walk-on in *King of the Arena* (Universal, 1933), another Maynard Western. Helen Wright and Philo McCullough had the greatest problems emoting effectively before the microphones.

In *Spurs* Philo McCullough is secretly in with Pecos and his gang. Hoot and his side-kick, Shorty, make it inside Pecos' stronghold and learn that Indian Joe killed Buddy Hazlet's brother, but that McCullough put him up to it. A rodeo is held and Hoot emerges the champion. Afterward, he beats McCullough into submission and then, with a posse at his rear, rides hard for Pecos' hide-out, where Shorty and Buddy are held prisoner. The gang is rounded up, and Hoot wins Helen Wright, $1,000, and a pair of silver spurs.

Hoot's final Universal film was *The Concentratin' Kid,* released on October 26, 1930. Arthur Rosson was the director. The story opened out West with Hoot, as Concentratin', in love with Kathryn Crawford, a singer on the radio. Hoot boasts that he'll marry Crawford, and the wranglers bet him a radio he won't. Duke Lee, foreman of the Bar Q where Hoot works, is in league with Jim Mason and his band of rustlers. Robert Homans as Stile brings Kathryn Crawford and a group of show girls to town. The comedy reaches its high point when Hoot, attending the show, tries his courtship, and Crawford, learning of the wager, rejects his suit. Hoot returns to the ranch, where he finds that Mason's gang has rustled the cattle. Hoot sets out to get the herd back. He battles triumphantly against Mason, who has kidnapped Crawford, runs off his gang, and by the fade wins his bet.

Uncle Carl's parting with Hoot was sad. For Hoot, it was a shock from which he would never recover, mentally or financially. Hoot had worked for Universal since the opening of the North Hollywood lot. Uncle Carl told Hooter frankly that the studio was near bankruptcy and that no more series Westerns were to be manufactured. The Western, with sound, despite a fluke here and there, might have no future at all. Uncle Carl himself was thinking of retiring and turning over the burden of management to his son, who would bring younger ideas to bear. Ken Maynard had signed with E. W. Hammons at Educational Pictures to make a series of Westerns to be released as Tiffany productions. Hoot should attempt to find work in the independent market. If prospects improved, Uncle Carl promised to draw up a new contract at once. Uncle Carl liked to fire people as much as he liked to hire them. But firing Hoot Gibson was one of the hardest things he had ever had to do. Hoot spoke fondly of the old man, even to the last years of his life.

By April 1931 Hoot had signed an agreement to make six Hoot Gibson Specials a year for Allied Pictures, financed by Max H. Hoffman and produced by his son, Max, Jr. Only they weren't really specials, never approaching the standards or budgets of even the Universal Jewels. In the *Film Daily Yearbook,* Carl Laemmle commented in his forecast for 1932: "However bitter the experience of the past year has been, it certainly taught us a lesson. It has given us an insight into the real and fictitious values in the moving picture business which have been a tremendous revelation. Very few businesses have been as successful as we have been in realizing the nonessentials and in ridding ourselves of them. The moving picture business has an elasticity which has more than once proved its salvation."

Sally Eilers appeared with Hoot in his first Allied picture, released in May 1931 through the Capitol exchanges on a states' right basis. Capitol was primarily a distributor for foreign films. *Clearing the Range* must be considered on its merits when I come to Hoot's misfortunes in the thirties, but the contrast of Sally's aloofness toward him and his own broken spirit, as the screenplay casts him for a time as a weakling and coward until it develops that it is all just a ruse, is painfully illuminating.

Bad Girl was released through the Fox exchanges on August 13, 1931, with James Dunn as Sally's costar. It was rated fourth in *Film Daily's* Ten Best Pictures of 1931 and was second in the National Board of Review's Supplementary Ten. Caroline Somers Hoyt summed it up in *Modern Screen:* "In other words, when Sally and Hoot walked to the altar Hoot was the big shot, the celebrity, the star of the family. Sally was Hoot Gibson's wife. Today the situation is reversed—Sally is the important member of the family. And Hoot is Sally Eilers' husband." On May 9, 1932, Sally and Hoot separated, Sally going home to her mother. *Movie Mirror* commented wryly, "Hoot issues a new manifesto declaring that since Sally clicked in *Bad Girl* she's had the worst case of enlarged hat in history, and no dame is going to get that way and get away with it, as far as he is,concerned."

Trigger Tricks is Hoot's best Western with Sally, if in the Gibson vs. Eilers match you happen to be for Hoot; *Clearing the Range* is the best if you're for Sally. Their marriage and its ups and downs became a subject of national interest. People attended their films. Despite all that, Hoot's best all-talking Western for Universal is probably *Spurs*. It is nowhere as entertaining as most of his films from the mid twenties, judged by those which survive, and both *Cowboy Counsellor* and *The Fighting Parson* among the Allied features are better Hoot Gibson Westerns, if not as expensively mounted nor as carefully made. Above all, *Spurs* reveals Hoot Gibson as he never was to be again after 1930—on top of the world, carefree, nonchalant, in love with life, confident, and vivacious. In the boisterous enthusiasm of those years, you could imagine Hoot and Art Acord beating each other half to death in the periodic fights they would stage during their drinking bouts, laughing and enjoying it. But by 1930 it was all over; Art Acord was dead, and Hoot had fallen on hard times.

18 / THE WESTERN SERIAL IN TRANSITION—PART ONE

When M-G-M refused to renew Tim McCoy's contract in 1929, the Outdoor Company was disbanded. The firm concentrated on musicals and very talky playlike features. Tim had no place in that world. He made a one-reel musical short, directed by Nick Grindé and released by the Fox exchanges, in which he and a group of cowpunchers sang around a campfire. It did not lead to a series.

Tim, unhappy, feeling that his career in pictures might well be at an end, took a six-month vacation in Europe, staying longest in France, and then returned to his ranch in Wyoming. He was married to the former Agnes Miller, and they had two sons and a daughter. He thought seriously of settling down once more to become a rancher as he had been before *The Covered Wagon* had altered the course of his life.

It was in this mood that he received a telegram from his good friend Edward Small, a talent agent, later a producer, summoning him back to Hollywood. It was fifty miles from his ranch to the train depot and a lot farther than that to Hollywood, but Tim loved making pictures; he undertook the trip. At this point a strange quirk in Carl Laemmle's personality and the desire to prove something to Uncle Carl on the part of Henry Mac-Rae, production head of Universal serials, converged with Tim's fallen fortunes. Ever since the publicity had been prepared for *The Flaming Frontier,* Uncle Carl had been saying that *The Indians Are Coming* was a great title for a picture. Edward Sedgwick, or one of the other producers or directors working on the Universal lot, would approach Uncle Carl from his blind side and outline to him in vivid and bright hues the perfect re-creation of his idea for a film based on this theme. The Little Champ would readily agree, tear off a check for $10,000, and production would begin on a picture that would probably be based in New York City and dwell on the antics of a Follies girl or perhaps life on a southern cotton plantation.

"Ve shouldt make a serial—whether it's a serial or a feature, I don't care—but it's gotta be called *The Indians Are Coming!*" Uncle Carl had said. The idea for a real serial about the Indian wars struck Henry MacRae as exactly the right vehicle to prove old Mr. Laemmle's pessimistic sound engineers wrong. An outdoor drama could be made with sound equipment. Previously, Uncle Carl had always said no to a sound Western serial, knowing what the Ken Maynard Westerns were costing him and chuckling at what sound was costing Hoot Gibson. MacRae argued and cajoled. Colonel Tim McCoy would star, assuring its authenticity. Uncle Carl rose from his desk and shook his finger menacingly, "Ja, budt dis time the Indians gotta come!" Tim didn't know it, on the way to Hollywood, but he was about to get the Story Department and more than one director off the hook at Universal Pictures. He was going to star in their last silent serial and, simultaneously, their first sound Western serial. He was to make his own first serial, and his career would advance further than it ever had during the silent era.

Universal City in 1930 remained that incredible collection of incongruities it had always been, reflecting the impulsive and contradictory personality of its owner. Uncle Carl, in keeping with his concept of the depressed economy, entertained the notion for a time of dumping the lot altogether, grown to encompass 410 acres. The Western town set on Mauser Street currently being used by Ken Maynard and Hoot Gibson was now

Uncle Carl Laemmle in the middle between Jim Thorpe, one of Uncle Carl's favorite Indians, and Lucile Browne, prior to filming *Battling with Buffalo Bill*.
Photo courtesy of Lucile Browne Flavin.

just down the road from the medieval European sets used in *The Man Who Laughs* (Universal, 1928). Whatever might be absent in terms of glamour, Uncle Carl compensated for with a *gemütlich* radiance. Filmmaking had come to mean for him an expression of his own sense of gratitude for all the New World had given him. He reckoned, and justifiably so, that he had taken momentous part in the most important artistic and technical development of the twentieth century; and that Universal Pictures had reached out to become an integral element in the lives of millions of people the world over.

The Indians Are Coming proved to be as much a compromise as Ken Maynard's first Westerns on his contract—part sound, part silent, with recorded dialogue and extensive dubbing of sound effects with music. Exhibitors in many cases did not want the sound version, so as a result the serial went into distribution in a silent version, a silent version with disc accompaniment and a movie-tone (or recorded sound track) version. The chapter play commenced production in July 1930, just as Maynard was finishing up his last film. It cost $160,000 to manufacture. By the time it finished with its play-offs, it grossed over a million dollars.

Henry MacRae, associate producer of *Indians,* had been and would continue to be head of the Serial Department for many years; soon after his retirement in the forties, the unit was discontinued. When Uncle Carl first opened Universal City, MacRae was already an employee. His motion picture experience went all the way back to the early days in Chicago when he joined Colonel Selig and Laemmle was but beginning his struggle against the Trust. Those films in which he took a special interest, such as *Indians,* could not help being in the best showmanship tradition, an inclination he shared with Laemmle. If MacRae made any miscalculation with regard to *Indians,* it was in electing to direct it himself. Here his weakness due to intensive training in the direction of silent melodrama interfered with his ability to put over dramatic dialogue sequences, although the action in the serial compares well with the best that Universal ever did. MacRae was apparently cognizant of this shortcoming in that he confined most of his future efforts to supervision.

Indians was based in part on Buffalo Bill's book *The Great West That Was,* which property Universal initially acquired for the filming of the silent serial *Fighting with Buffalo Bill* (Universal, 1926), but even more so on Bill's Wild West show. George H. Plympton and Ford Beebe worked on the continuity. Beebe would eventually leave Universal's Story Department to work at Mascot, winding up at Columbia, where he directed one of Tim McCoy's best sound Westerns, *The Law Beyond the Range* (Columbia, 1935). When Universal made *Battling with Buffalo Bill* (Universal, 1931) the next year, MacRae added Yakima Canutt, about whom I will have more to say later, thus streamlining the second-unit work; but William

Desmond and Francis Ford, experienced serial performers at Universal, carried the later chapter play. *Battling,* in fact, stands up better than *Indians,* but it certainly had nowhere the commercial impact of the earlier title.

Allene Ray was Tim's costar in *Indians.* She was born Allene Burch on January 2, 1901, and had worked in two-reel Westerns in the teens and early twenties until Pathé signed her in 1923. She proved a sensation in *Way of a Man* (Pathé, 1924), a Western chapter play based on an Emerson Hough story. Her director was George B. Seitz, who knew well how to handle her very reticent and introverted nature before the camera. Pathé began an immediate publicity campaign to build her into a property the equal of Pearl White and, toward the end of the silent era when she was teamed with Walter Miller, very nearly succeeded. Allene's peculiar puritanism made rough language, natural to technicians, impossible on the set. But she was an enterprising woman who won everyone's respect by her utter unwillingness to ever employ a double, no matter how harrowing the stunt.

Allene was incapable of registering any emotion other than acute embarrassment. I know this sounds like an unlikely personality for a serial queen, but Seitz was painstaking and gentle in his approach and managed, by various devious methods, to get from her what he wanted. Seitz's assistant director was Spencer Gordon Bennet. Bennet at the age of nineteen entered the industry by agreeing to jump off a cliff at the Edison Studio for $124. He joined Pathé in 1914, two year later, as a stunt man and worked in the early Pearl White serials. Bennet codirected *Sunken Silver* (Pathé, 1925) with Seitz on location in Florida; it teamed Allene with Walter Miller for the first time. From then on, Seitz left it to Bennet to see that Allene reacted as the script called for. In order to have her appear properly tense or frightened, Bennet was compelled to resort to all manner of tactics including having grips fire hand arms behind the set, which invariably set Allene's teeth on edge. The curious thing about this stratagem is that it always worked.

Probably Allene's finest Western serial for Pathé was *Hawk of the Hills* (Pathé, 1927), with Walter Miller, opposed by the usual villain in her chapter plays, Frank Lackteen. Spencer directed it himself. MacRae screened a print of it at Universal and from it and *Fighting with Buffalo Bill* drew his basic concepts for *Indians,* the writers depending on the book primarily for atmosphere and setting. Allene was free-lancing by 1930, Pathé having quit the serial field. MacRae felt that her name value coupled with that of McCoy, a Metro star, was an excellent combination. But what he hadn't reckoned on was Allene's peculiar inability to demonstrate emotion. The problems which she had at Pathé were amplified now by the fact that MacRae, as the director, must himself keep absolutely quiet through the course of most of her key scenes, shot on interior sets with even

Tim McCoy and costar Allene Ray in a posed scene from *The Indians Are Coming.*

the camera housed in a soundproof box so that the humming of its gears would not be picked up by the recording equipment. Moreover, her voice proved unpleasantly pitched for the role of a heroine, no matter how invitingly her blue eyes and bright blond hair photographed. During static scenes totally dependent on dialogue, not only could she not register any strong emotion but her exaggerated sense of gesture, developed under strain to compensate for her inhibitions, only made the situation unnerving.

Edmund Cobb, who had been a silent star of low-budget, independent silent Westerns, was cast as Tim's pal, Bill Williams, with Francis Ford— by now a fifteen-year veteran of Universal chapter plays—given a dual role as George and Tom Woods. Wilbur McGaugh, an inept actor before the microphone although sardonically photogenic for the silent version, played the villain, Rance Carter. McGaugh became associated with the Hoot Gibson unit while it was still on the Universal lot and left the studio with

Spencer Gordon Bennet in the director's chair in a trick photograph from an outdoor location used in *Hawk of the Hills* as well as countless other Westerns.

Photo courtesy of Spencer Gordon Bennet.

Hoot to work as an assistant director on his Allied films for M. H. Hoffman, Jr. He ended up working with Tim again in this capacity when Tim made *The Whirlwind* (Columbia, 1933), *A Man's Game* (Columbia, 1934), and *The Westerner* (Columbia, 1934) some years later. Bud Osborne was cast as Bull McGee, Rance's henchman, and Charles Royal handed in only a tolerably comic performance as Uncle Amos. Tim was given a dog named Pal. The picture was shot in its entirety at Universal City, with the use of substantial stock footage from earlier silent Universal Westerns.

Whatever its artistic failings, *Indians* advanced the Western technically. Because of its closeness to the silent film with musical accompaniment on the track, it was one of the first major Westerns to use background music during action sequences. The practice would die out for the next several years in the belief that audiences would be confused as to where the music came from, only to be reinstituted with *The Red Rider* (Universal, 1934), Buck Jones's second Universal chapter play, and soon in Westerns generally.

The Indians Are Coming was the embodiment of everything Uncle Carl had hoped it would be. The very phrase itself suggests the slightly ludicrous, and the film combined two well-established American institutions: the Wild West show and the melodrama, which had formed the basis of Buffalo Bill's popularity. Each chapter was introduced by an old prospector who narrated (actually he read the title cards for the sound version) the action of preceding episodes, much as Buffalo Bill introduced the various acts in his show. The story itself was the same as that comprising the countless melodramas which played mining camps and settlements throughout the close of the last century and the beginning of the twentieth. With such a format and such a broad popular base, little wonder Universal was able to book the serial into the exclusive Roxy Theater on Broadway for its New York opening.

The plot of *The Indians Are Coming* is almost completely described by its title. For the first few episodes, Tim leads a wagon train West through Indian territory, and the train is attacked. Rance Carter and his gang are with the train. The remainder of the serial is spent depicting Carter's attempts to force Allene Ray to marry him and to get possession of Francis

Colonel Tim McCoy battling Indians in *The Indians Are Coming*.

Photo courtesy of MCA-Universal.

Ford's gold mine, while everyone is generally beset by Indians and Carter even enlists their assistance. But this last proves a mistake for Carter, and his men meet their end at the hands of the Indians.

Occasionally critics will make the claim that *The Indians Are Coming* was such a solid financial success because it was a talking serial, but it wasn't the first talking serial nor was it the first talking Western. In terms of outdoor production standards, it was surpassed technically by Hoot Gibson's Westerns and by Ken Maynard's *Sons of the Saddle,* filmed concurrently. Despite the presence of Tim McCoy, no special empathy is created for the Indians, who appear to be unmotivated and rather capricious savages, variously on the warpath or suddenly friendly, depending on script demands. Much of the exhilarating footage of the last two chapters is but a reflection of the silent epic *The Flaming Frontier,* even to close-ups of Dustin Farnum leading the troops. The popularity of *The Indians Are Coming,* I suspect, was a fluke. The notion of a grand trek westward of a wagon train preoccupied *The Big Trail,* (Fox, 1930) and it failed at the box office. If pressed, I would have to admit that it was most probably the one hundred Indian headdresses given away to early arrivals at the theater and the zany attraction of Uncle Carl's title for the picture that sold it.

Historically, *Indians* is an important film. It marked the moment of transition. As the thirties moved into full swing, the melodrama of the teens and the action of the twenties would be played down for an emphasis on the *glory* of the Old West. The longing for purity and the sheen of frontier knights amid the gloom of that anxious time created a new image. When Tim McCoy began his series of feature Westerns for Columbia Pictures, he made the alteration easily and never again wore buckskins.

19 / CLASSICS OF THE EARLY SOUND ERA

Owen Wister's *The Virginian* is generally regarded as a classic. It may be that. It was certainly the first significant Western novel of this century. Yet, while it may be an unhappy confession to make, I did not enjoy the book when I read it years ago, and I found it tedious upon making its reacquaintance in order to write about it now. To my way of thinking, there is no excuse for a writer to bore his reader, and Wister tends to have that effect on me. Moreover, I find eastern values superimposed on the West, as they are in this novel, inappropriate, and Wister seems to falter in his understanding of basic human relationships.

Whatever my reservations, however, *The Virginian* had a tremendous national impact when it appeared in 1902. Wister himself was a curious, neurotic man who was born in Philadelphia in 1860 and died at North Kingston, Rhode Island, in 1938. He studied at Harvard and in Paris to be a musician. Ill health led him to desert that career for banking in New York, and a nervous breakdown prompted him to quit banking and venture to Wyoming to recuperate. Wister wrote a couple of novels other than *The Virginian;* they are not remembered. After the Great War, he wrote very little.

It didn't greatly matter. *The Virginian* was a best seller for years. It was made into a stage play in which Dustin Farnum starred, and Farnum was the lead in the photoplay version of 1918, produced by the Jesse L. Lasky company and directed by Cecil B. De Mille. When Wister returned East from his sojourn in Wyoming, he studied law at Harvard and was a Philadelphia lawyer at the time *The Virginian* was published. The book remains a romantic fantasy, a view of the cowboy such as the cowboy would scarcely understand.

William S. Hart, who played in the stage version of 1907–8, liked the role but made the mistake of pointing out to Wister his inadequate grasp of Western life which, perhaps unavoidably, Wister held against him. "In the first place, the foreman," Hart wrote about the Virginian, "would have refused flat-footed to trail his friend, and the ranchers would have respected him for so refusing. In the next place, if he had led the posse he would have led them the wrong direction and the ranchers would have expected him to do so, and again, respected him for it. And if he had led them to his friend and found his friend, he would have done it for a reason. He would have stepped to his friend's side and said: 'Well, gentlemen, I have done my duty and brought you here, but if you hang him, you've got to hang me, too! And we ain't neither of us strong for being hung while we've got our guns on.' "

Hart objected to the Virginian's lack of loyalty. On the frontier, loyalty counted for much more than some murky vision of abstract justice which seems to preoccupy Wister's hero. The blood lust for capital punishment obsessed Wister, who was its staunch advocate, to the same extent that it repelled Walter Van Tilberg Clark when he wrote his own rather well known Western narrative, *The Ox-bow Incident.* Dashiell Hammett, writing detective stories, described the orientation of Wister's ranchers in *Red Harvest* (Knopf, 1929); they have become "blood simple."

B. P. Schulberg, born at Bridgeport, Connecticut, on January 19, 1892, decided to film *The Virginian* in 1925, during the interim period between his early association with Jesse L. Lasky and his rejoining Adolph Zukor's Paramount, when he was engaged in independent film production. His scenario was based on the stage adaptation by Owen Wister and Kirk La Shelle. The plot from the novel was simplified to presenting the Virginian falling in love with Molly Woods, a schoolteacher from the East. She rejects him when he leads a posse after some cattle rustlers, participating in the hanging of Steve, his friend since childhood. When the Virginian is wounded later, trailing Trampas, leader of the rustlers, Molly nurses him back to health, rejecting him again when the Virginian goes up against Trampas in a street gunfight. The two lovers are brought together by the end, once Trampas is dead. With the exception of outdoor photography, apparently even less alteration was made in the stage version for the Schulberg film than in the 1918 photoplay.

Gary Cooper and the technical crew on location for the filming of *The Virginian*.

Preparing for the hanging. Gary Cooper and Eugene Pallette with the three rustlers in the foreground, James Mason, Richard Arlen, and Charles Stevens.

Photo courtesy of the Museum of Modern Art.

By 1929 Schulberg had rejoined the Paramount group and was head of production for the West Coast studio. He determined to film *The Virginian* again, this time as an all-talking Western, undoubtedly a daring, experimental gesture. The third version had, by far, a stronger cast. Whereas Kenneth Harlan, later a character actor during the thirties and forties, had been the Virginian in the 1925 picture, Gary Cooper, recently made a Paramount contract player, got the role for the sound film. Richard Arlen played his long-time friend, Steve; Mary Brian was Molly Wood; and Walter Huston was Trampas. Victor Fleming, who had directed some of the stronger entries in Paramount's silent Zane Grey series, was the director.

The story opens to a trail herd being driven through a town set on the Paramount lot. Steve is the Virginian's best friend. The Virginian meets Trampas, a bad hombre, at the saloon, and the two have an immediate dislike for one another. Steve begins trailing with Trampas and is finally caught rustling cattle. The Virginian has led the search party and watches as his friend is hanged. The Virginian trails Trampas and is wounded in the process. When he recovers, the schoolmarm in love with him, he meets Trampas for a gun duel in the street and wins. There is one comic episode in the early part of the picture which was reused frequently in other Westerns. Steve, as a prank, exchanges clothes of several babies brought to a christening so that there is hopeless confusion. Mary Brian's scene trying to dissuade the Virginian from confronting Trampas in the street is fully in anticipation of Grace Kelly's similar effort with Coop in *High Noon* (United Artists, 1952).

The Virginian was an exceedingly lethargic picture, verbose and painstakingly slow in its development. But it played to an encouraging box office, and Paramount decided to continue to produce at least two entries a year in their Zane Grey series, these to be filmed as all-talking films. Gary Cooper became a leading player in the sound era and would give a fine account of himself in several Westerns, including *Fighting Caravans* (Paramount, 1931) and, of course, as Bill Hickok in De Mille's *The Plainsman* (Paramount, 1937). Walter Huston was signed by Universal in late 1931 to play a major role in *Law and Order,* their first serious all-talking Western feature since Uncle Carl had suspended the Gibson and Maynard units.

The orientation of *Law and Order* was no different from that of *The Virginian.* The film centered around a pathetic hanging. John Huston worked on the screenplay. He had his father say repeatedly that the West really doesn't want law enforcement. Walter Huston was supported by Harry Carey, Raymond Hatton, and Russell Hopton. They were all apparently related, very much like the Earp brothers, and the film was one of the first cinematic treatments of the taming of Tombstone and the shoot-out at the O.K. corral. Huston played Frame Johnson, better known as "Saint" Johnson because of his reputation as a lawman. The four of them are virtually the only ones who have any strength of character in the film.

Based on W. R. Burnett's novel *Saint Johnson,* the picture opens to stock footage from Universal Westerns like *The Indians Are Coming* accompanied by the usual serial chase music. Huston is made sheriff of Tombstone and sets about subduing the lawless element headed up by Ralph Ince, Harry Woods, and Dick Alexander. Andy Devine plays an unfortunate who has the distinction of being the first man legally hanged in Tombstone. There is a confrontation at the livery stable on Mauser Street, and Huston is the only one left standing after the shoot-out.

The savage, predatory world view of W. R. Burnett's *Little Caesar* is very much a part of *Law and Order.* If I were asked to determine the beginning of the post-World War II trend toward Westerns which reach out of their historical context to comment on the current scene, I would suggest that it began with this film at the dawn of the sound era. The taming of the land, the agrarian vision of the Western, dropped away utterly for a concentrated glimpse of human brutality, the violent nature of men. The despair of the Warner Brothers' gangster films of the early thirties crept into this picture and altered the very cast and content of the Western.

Paramount remade *The Virginian* in 1946 and cast Joel McCrea in the lead role. Of all the Virginians—Dustin Farnum, Kenneth Harlan, Gary Cooper—McCrea seemed the most natural in hanging his best friend. Universal remade *Law and Order* in 1953 with Ronald Reagan. The original had no women to speak of; the remake had two, of which Dorothy Malone had the more substantial role. Neither film had anything much to offer. The psychological context had vanished. Apparently the predominant social atmosphere was no longer that of being overwhelmed by the prospect of lawlessness and the necessary harshness of frontier justice. But both films marked the advent in the thirties of a fabulous proliferation of Westerns, both major productions and series films.

There is a loss of innocence in the very passion with which *The Virginian* and *Law and Order* were produced that, henceforth, invaded the genre, an element of doubt, an unsureness, a caution about the myth of the westward expansion that did not come fully to fruition—and then brazenly, hopelessly so—until the sixties.

20 / FRONTIER LEGENDS—PART ONE

"One of the grips saw it first," Johnny Mack Brown recalled. "A small cloud of swirling dust far off in the distance. It kept coming closer. We could make out that it was a rider. We were on location filming the cave scene on the desert where Billy gets starved out. The rider was nearer now. We could finally recognize him. It was William S. Hart."

"He acted as the technical adviser on that picture, didn't he?" I asked.

"Yes," Johnny Mack assented, "and I'm proud to say that we became friends afterward. You know, he wrote books and would give me autographed copies. He taught me a great many things. How to crouch, for instance, and to turn your left side away, to protect your heart. 'Diminish your target,' he told me. 'Diminish your target and keep your heart as far away as you can from an enemy's bullet.' I followed his advice when I had a gun battle in the picture. He even gave me one of Billy the Kid's guns. I still have it."

It was in 1930 that Laurence Stallings and King Vidor wrote a script about the life of Billy the Kid. Vidor was born at Galveston, Texas, on February 8, 1894. He was a contract director at M-G-M. He took the story idea to Irving Thalberg. Together with Laurence Stallings, Vidor held a story conference in the tonneau of Thalberg's limousine as Irving and his assistant, Eddie Mannix, went to pay respects at Mabel Normand's funeral.

"Too many murders," was Thalberg's whispered comment as they sat dutifully before the flower-draped casket.

Vidor had begun the conference by saying that Billy shot his first victim because of an insult to his mother. "This bit of historical half-truth was emphasized in the hope of convincing Thalberg that all of the Kid's murders were understandable, if not entirely excusable," King Vidor later asserted. "Then I took Billy through scenes of murder in self-defense, and murders on the side of justice if not on the side of law."

On the way back to the Culver City studio, Thalberg broke in with a question.

"Was Sheriff Pat Garrett his friend during the time of the last five murders?" he asked.

Thalberg promised Vidor he would think the idea over and get back to him. Both Vidor and Stallings were convinced that the screen was ready for a more truthful presentation of violence. They were right, of course. Warner Brothers was about to begin its cycle of gangster movies with the brutal realism of William Wellman's *The Public Enemy* (Warner's, 1931).

I doubt if violence was the major source of reservation for Thalberg, especially once it was minimized in the revised screenplay. Metro got New Mexico Governor R. C. Dillon to endorse the film in an open letter to the public reproduced on the screen after the credit crawl. William S. Hart, amid strong publicity from Howard Strickling at M-G-M, was added to give the film the ring of authenticity. All of this was done for a scenario that represented Billy as the victim of repeated injustice, that minimized the terror attached to his person by casting warm, extremely likable Johnny Mack Brown in the role, that completely distorted his finish to meet with M-G-M's typical happy ending, a concession that Cecil B. De Mille refused to make later in his presentation of Bill Hickok's demise in *The Plainsman* (Paramount, 1937). The Kid and his girl ride off into the sunset while Pat Garrett smiles after them.

Although the studio in the person of Louis B. Mayer, seconded by Harry Rapf, had opined outdoor Westerns with sound recording impossible, here was Thalberg's chance to once more prove them wrong and he took it. Vidor went on location to the Grand Canyon to shoot exteriors. The Fox

Johnny Mack Brown as Billy in *Billy the Kid*.

Film Corporation had devised a new, wide-screen process and filmed *The Big Trail* (Fox, 1930) to reveal its full capabilities. *Billy the Kid* was photographed simultaneously in 65mm. and standard 35mm.

"In running off each day's work," Vidor remarked subsequently, "I had the opportunity of comparing the two films. There was no doubt to any of us working on this picture that the large-screen process was a tremendous advantage over the conventional screen, particularly for outdoor shots." *Billy the Kid* was released in two versions, some dozen theaters across the country actually projecting the picture against what Metro called the Grandeur Screen. However, the idea was scrapped as unfeasible when most exhibitors complained that they were still paying for the installation of sound equipment and didn't appreciate any more innovations.

Vidor's film opens to a trail herd led by two Englishmen, Tunston and McSween. They have come to settle in Lincoln County, which is dominated by James Marcus. Wallace Beery as Pat Garrett is Marcus' right hand. The Englishmen hire Billy and his side-kick, Santiago, to protect them from Marcus. They are both killed. Billy is captured by Pat and taken back to Lincoln, where he is imprisoned. He escapes and runs to Kay, Tunston's former fiancée. Pat smiles after the happy couple as they ride away into the sunset.

Wallace Beery is a grand old rogue. His role as Pat Garrett led to a whole group of pictures in which he played lovable villains, the best, and maybe the worst, being *Bad Bascomb* (M-G-M, 1940), in which in very sentimental fashion Beery is made to give himself up, a wholly reformed man, because of the devotion of a small child played by Margaret O'Brien. I do not know what Bill Hart thought about this variation of his own screen efforts at playing a bad man reformed by noble women. Nor do I know what, if anything, Hart honestly felt about the highly fanciful screen treatment of William Bonney's life. Obviously, he didn't object to the romantic conclusion as he willingly lent his name to the project.

The reader may find it curious that Fred Thomson's career should have been dashed only a few years before for whitewashing a frontier gangster and yet that, in the thirties, this tendency became increasingly powerful as a trend in both major and minor Westerns. I am no philosopher. I cannot say for certain why this was so. But I might suggest that at least part of the reason lay in the widespread distrust of government which came about with the Crash of 1929 and the onset of the Depression. What Franklin D. Roosevelt proffered to the people, in effect, was the glib security that things were not as bad as they appeared. Resentment at social injustice led audiences to endorse the revaluation of bad men and the transposition of lawmen into the real villains. Sam Peckinpah when he came to make his version, *Pat Garrett and Billy the Kid* (M-G-M, 1973), about which I will have more to comment presently, advanced the premise that things, far from being

Wallace Beery as the lovable villain.

better than they appeared, were indeed worse than anyone could have suspected and that even living itself in such a world of savage injustice isn't worthwhile. The frontier is a perpetual battlefield, and murder is the only therapy against despair.

The thirties, after *Billy the Kid,* were relatively quiet for Hart. He published his autobiography, *My Life East and West,* in 1929. Shortly after the Metro feature was issued, Hal Roach approached him with a proposal that they make a picture patterned after *Wagon Tracks.* The deal fell through just as did negotiations with RKO to make a Peter B. Kyne story with Hart starring and Lambert Hillyer directing. Hart insisted on making these films his way, and his obdurate attitude kept the plans from materializing. Hart rode out to the Columbia ranch to visit with Hillyer while the latter was directing *The Fightin' Fool* (Columbia, 1932). Hillyer introduced Bill to the film's star, Colonel Tim McCoy. *Screen Snapshots* (Columbia, 1932) released a segment in their series for that year showing Hart and Tim together, shot at Hoot Gibson's May Round Up, Hoot and Sally co-hosts, with Tom Mix, William Powell, Ginger Rogers, and Mary Pickford also present among the guest celebrities.

In 1935 Sol Lesser bought remake rights from Hart to *O'Malley of the Mounted* (Paramount, 1921). The film of the same title released in 1936 by Fox with George O'Brien bore virtually no resemblance to Hart's original. Hart was sufficiently irked with the results not to sell any more of his properties for remakes.

Astor Pictures agreed with Hart in 1939 to reissue *Tumbleweeds.* He filmed an eight-minute prologue to precede the showing of the picture. It was photographed and recorded at his Horseshoe Ranch at Newhall. Dressed as of old, but looking very much like an old Westerner rather than merely a silent-movie cowboy, Hart in his resonant voice told graphically of the opening of the Cherokee Strip. Then, becoming more confidential, his voice occasionally breaking with the intensity of his emotion, Hart told the audience what making Westerns had meant for him and how age and injuries precluded his again engaging in such perilous feats of horsemanship. "It was as the very breath of life to me," Hart lamented. The reissue helped him recover some of his initial investment in the film. The scoring of the music and effects track was stunningly appropriate and transformed a visual epic into a lyrical symphony on the magnificent passing of the West.

With his sister Mary's help with style, Hart pursued his writing, publishing *Hoofbeats* in 1933, *The Law on Horseback* in 1935, and *All Points West* in 1940. Finally, in 1939, Hart appeared in Los Angeles Superior Court before Judge Thomas Gould and received, in the judge's words, a "belated vindication" in the paternity suit first brought against him in 1919. For nearly twenty years, the boy's support was paid out of the trust fund Hart had been forced to set up for him. The court ordered the funds re-

William S. Hart as he appeared in Superior Court on August 18, 1939, for the final denouement on his paternity suit.

Photo courtesy of *Views & Reviews* magazine.

turned to Hart on the basis of testimony indicating that the woman had lied to the extent that the child had not even been conceived by her.

Republic vitalized interest in Billy the Kid in their series Western units, beginning with *Billy the Kid Returns* (Republic, 1938), with Roy Rogers and Smiley Burnette, directed by Joe Kane. The picture proved a success, and so an entire series was started with Bob Steele, by then under direct contract to Republic, appearing as Billy. When Bob was promoted into the role of Tucson Smith in the Three Mesquiteers series at Republic and after the impact of Metro's new version of *Billy the Kid* with Robert Taylor, Producers Releasing Corporation began a series of $12,000 Westerns featuring Buster Crabbe as Billy and Al St. John as his side-kick, Fuzzy. In almost all of these films, Billy was a Robin Hood figure working on the side of the law, bringing outlaw gangs to their doom. Billy joined the B ranks of Hopalong Cassidy, the Lone Ranger, and other more recent commercial creations as a mythical and legendary character in whom young people were asked to believe and whose extremely stylized life they might even be expected to imitate.

Warner Brothers was having a solid box-office response featuring their top players like James Cagney and Errol Flynn in high-budget Western productions. Metro decided to follow suit in 1940 by trying Robert Taylor out in a Western. What better property to resurrect for the occasion than *Billy the Kid?* Howard Strickling contacted William S. Hart and arranged for Taylor and a studio photographer to pay a visit to the Horseshoe Ranch. Ostensibly Hart, who was never known as a fast draw, showed Taylor how to jerk a gun with the best of the frontier gun-slingers.

Irving Thalberg was dead. Louis B. Mayer was firmly in charge. M-G-M films, for the most part, conformed to his values and his outlook. Mayer liked beautiful pictures, pictures that stressed the importance of motherhood (and mothers were always good cooks), that showed the stability of the family, that glamorously and sentimentally depicted the essential good nature of nearly all men. *Billy the Kid* (M-G-M, 1941) was made to fit this formula.

The picture was filmed at Monument Valley. It was given the benefit of Technicolor. When nature fell short, the Metro artists took over and painted in mesas and picturesque cloud formations. Billy is left-handed, one historical accuracy. Pat Garrett isn't even in the picture. Billy is hired by Gene Lockhardt to help his gang eliminate Ian Hunter, an English cattle rancher, from the district. Billy's boyhood chum, Brian Donlevy, works for Hunter. They meet during a cattle stampede, and Donlevy recalls for Billy how Billy loved Donlevy's mother's pies and had been wont to take them without asking. This was the beginning of Billy's life of crime. Billy's meeting with Ian Hunter is just as touching. Hunter plays the piano for him, tells him little parables about why it is better to be good than bad, and causes him no little consternation by his refusal to wear a gun. Billy can't understand why a man wouldn't wear a gun. Hunter announces that he is protected by Billy's code never to shoot an unarmed man. It is a code upheld by all Western bad men.

After a build-up like this, all that's left is for Ian Hunter to get shot down by Gene Lockhardt's men. Billy takes vengeance on them. As due punishment for this foul deed, he comes to confront Brian Donlevy in a gun duel having reversed his draw to the right side so that, naturally, he is killed.

In view of the fact that this is rather typical of the kind of story line of Metro Westerns during the Mayer era, I think we who happen to enjoy Westerns are fortunate the studio chose not to make more of them. Billy the Kid deserved a more adequate screen treatment. By comparison, King Vidor's version was a powerfully realistic document. Howard Hughes was next to attempt a Kid picture. Hughes went into preproduction phases about the time of the second Metro version's release. Jane Russell, the dentist's receptionist Hughes intended to build into a screen property, was the star. She played Rio. Jack Beutel was the Kid; Walter Huston was Doc Holliday; Thomas Mitchell was cast as Pat Garrett.

According to Jane Russell, Hughes had two versions of this film manufactured, one for commercial release and one for private viewing by himself and his close circle. The latter featured Jane without any support garment at all, naked from the waist up. The commercial version showed Jane's ample bosom piled into a "heaving" brassiere of Hughes's own design. It was Jane's erotic contribution to the film that was displayed on the publicity and which had the censors up in arms. Hughes released the picture initially through United Artists in 1943, was forced to withdraw it, and, finally, reissued it through RKO in 1946.

Hughes dealt with everything in his customarily exotic fashion. Jane was openly regarded as a means of gratifying sexual congestion but was scarcely as valuable as a horse. Billy had several fast and chilling gun duels, so well staged that it didn't matter greatly that Beutel was no actor. For the reissue, Hughes had a line dubbed in near the fade concerning the probability that Billy and Jane were to be married, but as originally released the two merely ride off into the sunset, to lives of killing and fornicating, while Garrett conspires in the fraud by burying another body in the grave marked for William Bonney.

While Hughes was tinkering with his Billy the Kid picture, titled *The Outlaw,* Hart's sister, Mary, died on October 1, 1943, and Hart made one of his increasingly rare public appearances in probate court to hear a reading of her will on January 14, 1944. Hart's eyesight began failing him. He wrote to G. W. Dunston, a long-time friend and admirer, "At times I can scarcely see at all." Death came to him in a Los Angeles hospital on June 23, 1946. He was buried in Greenwood Cemetery in Brooklyn. His estate was valued at $1.17 million the bulk of which went to Los Angeles County for the express purpose of turning his ranch into a public park. "The truth of the West," he wrote in *My Life East and West,* "meant more to me than a job, and always will."

The Billy the Kid saga continued to inspire motion pictures over the years. I cannot hope to mention all of them in the course of this chapter, for that would mean spending time on such obvious idiocy as *Billy the Kid vs. Dracula* (Embassy, 1966). But in the seventies the saga returned with great intensity, and through it contradictory notions of the meaning of the Western clashed. I am not certain Sam Peckinpah's *Pat Garrett and Billy the Kid* can be fully grasped as to its total implications without reference to Duke Wayne's *Chisum* (Warner's, 1970). In *Chisum* Duke is cast as the land baron of Lincoln County, Geoffrey Deuey is the Kid, and Glenn Corbett is Pat Garrett. *Chisum* is not a particularly strong picture for Duke, but it was made to advance certain of his views on men and society.

At the outset, Duke and Ben Johnson, as Chisum's close friend and employee, Mr. Pepper, are talking about the West, their beginnings, and how the times are changing. Change, Duke asserts, is usually for the better. Three years later, the same idea would open Peckinpah's picture, when Garrett tells Billy that the times have changed. "The times, maybe," says Peckinpah's Billy, "not me."

William Bonney goes to work for a mild-mannered Englishman named Tunstall. He helps Duke shoot up some horse thieves. Forrest Tucker plays a bad capitalist, taking over Lincoln by means of unfair advantage and political conniving. Duke's Chisum is a friend of the Indian. He believes they had a good way of life, but that it couldn't last. Billy falls in love with Duke's niece and she reciprocates. But Garrett points out that there is a difference between infatuation and love and instructs the niece that the difference between Duke and the Kid is that the Kid wants revenge, Duke wants justice. Tunstall is kind to Billy and has him reading the Bible. In one overstated scene, Billy even balances the Bible in one hand and his gun in the other. But Tucker plots to have Tunstall murdered. This act sends the Kid on the path of outlawry again. On one occasion, Duke manages to give the Kid a paternal lecture.

Chisum recognizes that political structures are inadequate and frequently crooked. It affirms that, in many cases, the only way to see justice done is to invoke the law of the .45. But not wantonly, as Billy does. When Tucker and his crooked sheriff and his gang have the Kid cornered in Duke's store, Duke and his men ride to town for a showdown. Stampeding a herd of cattle through a barricade, Duke's wranglers rout Tucker's men, Duke crashing through a window atop his horse, tackling Tucker and fighting with him to the death. Billy rides off at the end, while Duke has Garrett appointed sheriff. When Ben Johnson comments to Duke's screen niece that there is no law west of Dodge and no God west of the Pecos, the line rings all the way back to a wry comment made by Gary Cooper as Hickok in *The Plainsman* (Paramount, 1937). Duke has an answer different from Cooper's. "Wherever there are people who come together," he says, "the Law is not far behind and they'll find, if they look around, that God has already been there."

Chisum stresses a love of the land. It represents that men have many options before them and that the West is the embodiment of hope for a better world. Peckinpah chose to reverse these tendencies. His version of the Billy legend advanced the notion that all options are closing for the individual, that political favoritism and downright dishonesty rule the day, that American capitalism as symbolized by Chisum and the big ranchers or Wall Street investors has choked off the individual's right to be free. The times are changing, yes, but for the worse, and the light of hope is fading, perhaps never to return.

The Left-handed Gun (Warner's, 1958), in my opinion, is one of the most incongruous screen treatments of Billy the Kid, but it is probably the one that most influenced Peckinpah, even down to his borrowing events and sequences from it. Arthur Penn was the director of this moody, almost allegorical, darkly shadowed production in which all of the characters, and chiefly Billy, are nearly psychotic and appear to have escaped from the world of Ingmar Bergman. Paul Newman was cast as Billy, an excellent actor to bring off the role in the heavily symbolic atmosphere in which he was compelled to function; John Dehner was Pat Garrett. The Christ-identifications are suffocating, even to Billy drawing from an empty holster and pitching forward at the fade in a tortured martyrdom.

It is the Christmas season 1972, and we have come to Durango, Mexico. It is here that Duke Wayne's Batjac company filmed *Chisum,* and it is here that now two motion picture units have come. Duke is back, making *Cahill, U. S. Marshal,* a Batjac picture for Warner Brothers release. Sam Peckinpah is directing *Pat Garrett and Billy the Kid* for Metro-Goldwyn-Mayer. It is Peckinpah who concerns us. It is Sunday evening. He is seated quietly in one corner of the El Dorado café, the only decent eating place in town, playing poker with Jack Elam, some stuntmen, and Kris Kristofferson, who plays Billy. The poker game has been going on since the previous night.

Peckinpah is dressed as always in worn-out, beat-up clothes, a dirty bandanna twisted into a headband, his gray hair sticking out from every direction. He plays the game in deadly earnest. Nearby sits Emilio Fernández, at his own table, a powerfully built man with an enormous leonine head who played the Mexican general in Peckinpah's *The Wild Bunch* (Warner's, 1969). Once Mexico's top film director, he turned to acting after he shot the producer on his last picture years ago. He is dressed in a black *charro* suit, scarlet hand-tooled boots, and wide black sombrero, a Colt .45 strapped to his hip. This is no costume but his usual attire. He terrifies some of the Peckinpah people, but not Sam. Everybody knows that he has in fact shot several men dead and they try to avoid him. He plays the role of Paco in Sam's picture. Arriving with Fernández at the customary Mexican dinner hour of ten o'clock was a stunningly attractive Indian girl with raven

Sam in his sunglasses.

hair hanging loosely to her hips. She wears a long Indian dress and an intricate Mexican pelisse of bright colors. She listens stoically as Fernández condemns Hollywood. He is drunk and sways about on his heels, everyone keeping out of his way. The indifference is genuine. The girl understands no English and is only nine years old anyway, which is not strange when it is recalled that Fernández' last wife was fourteen.

The next morning Dub Taylor, a character actor in the Wayne picture, squints and says, "I'll tell you this. After Sam gets through nobody will ever make a pitchur about Billy the Kid again. *This is it!* They'll never touch Billy again."

Peckinpah has made over Pancho Villa's fort, called Chupaderos, into a facsimile of Fort Sumner, New Mexico, the locale of *Pat Garrett and Billy The Kid*. M-G-M has paid the bills. Villa heralded from Durango. In the center of the town set is a scaffold and a group of extras, costumed as pioneers, standing around getting instructions from Peckinpah. The blond women and children are the wives and kids of the crew, which is common practice when on location shooting Westerns. Most of Peckinpah's crew are either British or Mexican. He employs very few Americans.

Jim Coburn, Sam's Garrett, all in black, puffs on a cigar, spits, and says he feels better. Like almost everybody else, he has been suffering from what is euphemistically called *el charro*. He ambles up a narrow stairway entering a small room which overlooks the street. Up there, in the room over the jail, R. G. Armstrong and Kris Kristofferson are playing a card game. The crew is squeezed tightly inside and nobody else can get in, although the finished scene will have the sense of desolate, spacious emptiness.

Peckinpah, identically attired from the previous night, stands next to producer Gordon Carroll, a tall, lanky, retiring man who is explaining to the group that Billy the Kid has been made into a contemporary figure. Carroll introduces Rudy Wurlitzer, the screenwriter. Wurlitzer wears jeans and a straw hat, his face covered by a long red beard. Wurlitzer is remarking to Katie, Peckinpah's secretary, that he hopes Bob Dylan, the folk singer, who is in the picture, will write the musical score and Kris sing it.

"Jesus," Katie responds. "Everybody in the world will buy it."

"Everybody in the world will come to see the picture," says Carroll.

"You can always tell when you have a winner," Katie says. "There is a feel to it and this one is a winner. I just know it."

What no one does know is that *Pat Garrett and Billy the Kid* will not earn back one half of its cost upon theatrical release, that Metro-Goldwyn-Mayer itself will close its exchanges before the film has finished making the theatrical rounds.

"This is the definitive work on Billy the Kid," Sam Peckinpah remarks. These are the only words he utters.

A female reporter poses a question for Sam.

"Isn't this a rewrite of *One-eyed Jacks* which you wrote for Marlon Brando in 1957 and which you said in *Playboy* magazine was the definitive work on Billy the Kid?"

Peckinpah doesn't appreciate the question. He glowers at the reporter, turns on his heel, and disappears.

Gary Combs rides up atop a strawberry roan. He is Kris's stunt man, and yesterday he was thrown and knocked unconscious, but he's been X-rayed and is uninjured. He is worried about his wife's reaction when he gets home. He lost an eye in *Little Big Man* (National General, 1971) when he got shot by an arrow. In his first picture following that accident, Ralph Nelson's *Soldier Blue* (Avco-Embassy, 1971), he was nearly burned alive in an asbestos suit he was wearing. His wife suggested the possibility of some other occupation.

He is a shy man. He comments to a reporter how Peckinpah brought three Los Angeles hookers down to play tarts in the picture.

"They had the room beneath me at the Durango Hotel," he recalls, "and, man, the noise down there kept me awake. There was traffic in there all night."

One scene, deleted from the release print but visible in publicity stills, shows James Coburn being bathed by four or five naked women. Other shots show them all in bed, and in their very midst is Sam Peckinpah, the beat-up clothes, the headband, the wrap-around sunglasses.

Sam's cinematic life of Billy is intense, deeply troubling, told in almost parable form, at times inarticulate, filled with brooding, twilit, apocalyptic landscapes. The motivations of some of the characters are so complex that the film has to be seen several times before they begin to unravel and make sense.

There is no spirit of the land here, no new frontier, only barren wastes, a desert punctuated by silvery, surrealistic lakes and streams. Much of the film is photographed in shadow, dusk, hazy light, or nightfall. The overwhelming effect of the picture is one of despondency, or perhaps even despair. There is a hopelessness in the terrain, an agonized loneliness in the principals, a frustrated quest for identity, a bitter confrontation with futility, and, moving through it all, desperately erupting, a sustaining violence, a lewd intimacy with death.

The date given is 1881, Old Fort Sumner, New Mexico. Pat Garrett comes to visit with Billy. Pat tells Billy that he will soon be the sheriff of Lincoln County. They were once outlaws who rode together. The law is the protection sought by politicians, by investors in the New Mexico territory, by Chisum and the big cattle ranchers. Pat leaves.

"Why don't you kill him?" one of Billy's henchmen asks.

"Why?" returns Billy. "He is my friend."

Cut to Billy and two men surrounded by Pat and a flock of deputies. Billy is to be arrested for the killing of Buckshot Roberts. The other two are shot to pieces. Billy surrenders, holding out his arms sacrificially, a Christ figure, a symbol of martyrdom.

Billy is sentenced to hang. He plays poker in the room above the jail with Garrett and Matt Clark while a scaffold is being erected outside. Pat leaves to collect some taxes. Billy finds a gun in the outhouse, but one suspects, after a time, that perhaps Garrett put it there. He shoots his way out and rides off.

Pat goes to visit the military governor, played by Jason Robards, Jr. He tells the politicians that he intends to bring the Kid in.

Pat takes an old sheriff and his wife on the manhunt. The sheriff, like a crazed Noah, is building a boat with which to escape in the middle of the desert. The sheriff is shot to death. Billy's pals are gunned in the fracas. Pat is joined by a special deputy, reporting only to the governor.

"This country is gettin' old," Garrett tells the deputy, "an' I want to get old with it. The Kid don't want it that way, an' maybe he's a better man for it."

This is Pat's chanting refrain. The coming of the law does not indicate the coming of order or civilization, as those terms have been traditionally interpreted in Westerns or even in previous versions of the Billy the Kid legend. The coming of the law means legalized banditry, the sheltering of the greed, lust, and criminality of the wealthy and the powerful.

Pat encounters Bob Dylan and two of Billy's cronies. He attacks the cronies, but spares Dylan. He is to warn the Kid to get out. Pat rides to a cat house and sleeps with Billy's whore. She tells him where Billy is hiding. Garrett with two deputies goes to Paul Fix's place at Fort Sumner. Garrett sits outside the window as Billy makes love. When Billy goes to get something to eat, Pat slips into the kitchen. He waits for Billy to enter. When he does, Billy, gun in hand, is frozen; Garrett shoots him in the heart and then shoots at his own image in a faded mirror. The governor's deputy would cut off Billy's trigger finger and nail it to a post. Garrett hits him in the face and breaks his arm. The next morning, at dawn, Garrett rides off, a child throwing stones after him. Billy's partly naked body is laid out on a table. The girl, still with his smell about her, mourns his passing.

Sam Peckinpah's version of Billy the Kid is a dark study in spiritual bankruptcy. The West, in its promise, if it ever even existed for Peckinpah,

Matt Clark, Kris Kristofferson, R. G. Armstrong, and James Coburn in the card-playing sequence from *Pat Garrett and Billy the Kid*.

is rapidly fading; the legend, by its pastness, its starkness, and its fragility becomes a somber lament. Like Peckinpah's *Major Dundee* (Columbia 1964), *Pat Garrett and Billy the Kid* was the victim of studio tampering. A total of fifteen minutes was cut from the completed film, material that, according to Peckinpah, more fully explained the motivation of the characters. Garrett is first supposed to be seen in a prologue depicting the year 1908. He is riding in a buggy. One of the Santa Fe ring, who originally rode with him in pursuit of the Kid, is now herding sheep on the strip of land given Garrett by Chisum for subduing the Kid. Garrett wants the sheep cleared off. He is ambushed and shot several times. Interspersed with the bullets tearing his aged body apart are cuts of chicken heads being shot off by Billy and his gang. The entire film was thus intended to be a flashback of events running through Garrett's mind as he pitches from the buggy into the dirt road. Also deleted were scenes between Garrett and his wife describing the dismal state which their marriage had reached and a bargaining session with Chisum, played by Barry Sullivan. The picture ends with Garrett dead, murdered by the very forces he had once allied himself with and which have finally turned on him as he had turned on the Kid. Had Garrett's demise been shown the way Peckinpah filmed it, it would have been easier for the viewer to discern that, in betraying Billy, Garrett put to death his own reason for living, that in betraying Billy's way of life Garrett only survived the Kid physically but, spiritually, he was plunged into a state of hopelessness.

Metro further insisted on stressing Bob Dylan's music track with the notion of creating a best-selling album to spur attendance. It didn't work. But whether by oversight or intention, nevertheless it is Dylan as Alias who is left behind, a skulking, forlorn witness whose shifty glances betoken a silent misery, a decay of the personality that would have bewildered more than dismayed that former generation that once smiled when Wallace Beery smiled in letting the Kid retain the last vestige of his humanity—his liberty.

21 / THE WESTERN SERIAL IN TRANSITION—PART TWO

The serial underwent significant changes during the late twenties, especially with the competition provided Universal by Pathé. The Pathé chapter plays emphasized action over melodrama, stunting and harrowing escapes in contrast to strong plots. Infused into their serial product was a consistent sense of excitement brought to fullest fruition in those films directed by George B. Seitz and Spencer Gordon Bennet. John Ford would inquire of Bennet, when upon occasion he would meet him in the steam room of the Hollywood Athletic Club, when Bennet would let him direct the second unit on one of his serials. It wasn't a facetious comment. Bennet had an intimate and intuitive knowledge of pacing and movement before the camera.

Mascot Pictures, an independent company owned by Nat Levine, entered the serial field in late 1927, and for the next several years limited its activity to the production of serials. The early entries of the silent era were cheap, with shoddy production values, but made with an almost hysterical velocity that seemed to overwhelm as it pleased exhibitors and public alike. During the early thirties, with Pathé out of the running due to mergers, Universal and Mascot competed directly, Levine matching his uncanny skill at casting and organizing talent against Universal's distribution network and financial power. Stars in decline as well as young hopefuls got a chance at Mascot.

In 1931, with all the major studios stressing "talking" films, Westerns and action serials, or serials of any kind, were somewhat in eclipse. Levine, ignoring sound as a gimmick, retained an action format in his talking serials and, above all, the exhilarated pacing. Because of the rapidity with which all of the Mascot serials were produced, averaging twenty-one days, and the work scheduling which customarily had technical crews and cameramen, director and sound engineers, players and extras outside, ready to go, waiting for the first rays of brittle sunlight to appear over the Hollywood hills, on location until dark, at times shooting a scene by flickering torchlight, this pacing may well have been just another extension of Levine's acute budgetary consciousness.

As a producer, Nat Levine sought neither prestige nor profundity. He loved the serial as a very special medium and assembled on his rented sets and leased lots a dedicated group of professionals that, very often, made the budgets of his pictures a secondary consideration. Mascot story lines were invariably fantastic, highly original, but visually powerful, even unforgettable. The serials were mostly intended for youngsters and so stressed images and settings and situations that appealed instinctively and indelibly to youthful imaginations. In fact, one of the strongest and most notable aspects of the Mascot serials is this importance of make-believe. It served not only Levine, but many filmmakers in the late twenties and early thirties, creating pictures often compromised by the test of time and the increased cynicism of modern audiences.

Rin-Tin-Tin was certainly one of the most successful actors of the silent era, although his drawing power and popular following might be almost unthinkable today. The animal—that is, the real Rin-Tin-Tin and not his many doubles—had an intuitive responsiveness before the camera, a striking perceptiveness, and a nearly human range of emotions, able to depict by physical posture and facial expressions very subtle feelings and sudden shifts in mood. And then there were his eyes, deeply sensitive, variously bright, fierce, sad, a mirror to moods seemingly beyond the ken of his comprehension. That he was also an action star may be less consequential in forming a judgment of him than acknowledgment of the fact that his success stemmed most precisely from the touching, tragic, and tender moments he portrayed on the screen.

After sound, dog pictures never inspired the fascination they once had during the silent era, perchance because there was ultimately only one Rin-Tin-Tin, and none of his offspring, and decidedly none of his many imitators, could equal him as a serious performer. In the twenties studios were generally not to be outdone by Warner's and so had at least one canine star under contract, such as Klondike, Strongheart, Nat Levine's own imitations Tornado and Silver Streak, Kazan, others, all with the same bag of tricks, but none of which could breathe human meaning into what they did as could Rin-Tin-Tin. In *The Lighthouse by the Sea* (Warner's, 1924), Caleb Gale, keeper of the light, played by Charles Hill Mailes, has gone blind. This fact is hidden from his superiors by his daughter. A storm rages, and Rinty and his master, William Collier, are shipwrecked only to be rescued by the keeper's daughter, played by Louise Fazenda. Collier and Fazenda fall in love. But it is Rinty who comes to the old man's aid when rumrunners overpower him, and it is Rinty who once more ignites the light. Darryl F. Zanuck did the screen adaptation. In *The Night Cry* (Warner's, 1926), Rinty is accused of turning criminal when a herd of sheep is preyed upon by a giant condor. He is sentenced to die. John Harron is his owner, June Marlowe, Harron's screen wife. Harron hides the dog. When the condor steals their child, Rin-Tin-Tin races after him, rescues the child, and kills the bird after a terrible fight. No man has ever stood accused at the bar of justice and been innocent, yet borne up under his torment as Rinty did in this picture.

Rin-Tin-Tin was responsible for supporting Warner's long enough, despite their penchant for expensive, money-losing pictures with Broadway actors like John Barrymore, for the studio to take advantage of the Vitaphone process. One of the reasons behind Rinty's box office may have been his ability to win enduring favor, most of all with juvenile audiences, because he was able, at least in part, to project a nobility and degree of loyalty that would not be credible in a human being. A dog doesn't have such a highly developed ego which must go before all else in his life, and so his behavior may actually be altruistic at times.

Competition hurt Rinty, but not the coming of sound. He made *Frozen River* (Warner's, 1929), a part-barking, part-talking film; and *The Million Dollar Collar* (Warner's, 1929) was part-barking. D. Ross Lederman directed the latter. In *Man Hunter* (Warner's, 1930), Rinty helps save Nora Lane's West Africa Ivory and Rubber Company, with full recorded sound. *Rough Waters* (Warner's, 1930), released in June, was Rinty's last picture for the firm, in which he plays a police dog who helps capture two payroll robbers.

Nat Levine took the plunge into sound with Rin-Tin-Tin. He signed him for $5,000 in 1930 to appear in Mascot's first all-talking serial *The Lone Defender.* Buzz Barton, a Pathé child star of Westerns, and June Marlowe were also signed for the picture, with Walter Miller, star of Pathé serials, as the mature male lead. *King of the Kongo* (Mascot, 1929), featuring Boris Karloff, had been part sound, part silent. The serial with Rinty was a tremendous success.

D. Ross Lederman, who had frequently directed Rinty at Warner's, was in need of a break. Nat Levine gave it to him in his next serial for 1930, *Phantom of the West,* a ten-chapter affair starring Tom Tyler, the former FBO backup player to Fred Thomson, in his first sound enterprise. Lederman, as a director, was certainly an oddity. His businesslike attitude toward making pictures somehow had not ingratiated him to the major studios. His principal concerns would remain budget-cutting, getting actors to do their jobs themselves with only minimal interference, and most of all he was interested in personal income. He took no particular pride in the pictures with which he was charged. The Mascot serial was responsible for landing him a job at Columbia Pictures, directing the Tim McCoy Westerns. He worked for Harry Cohn for most of his active years. Yet he respected no man, least of all Cohn.

"I gave them the idea about the dog's collar," he remarked to me. "They wanted a story idea for Rinty's next picture—"

"The Lightning Warrior," I interjected.

The principals of *The Lightning Warrior,* left to right, George Brent, Lafe McKee, Georgia Hale, Frank Brownlee, Rinty, Pat O'Malley, and Frankie Darro.

Photo courtesy of *Views & Reviews* magazine.

"Yes," he went on, *"The Lightning Warrior.* I gave them the idea about the dog's collar. I had directed Rinty in *The Million Dollar Collar* for Warner Brothers. They never thanked me for it, and they certainly didn't pay me."

"What was it like to direct Rin-Tin-Tin?"

"You probably think his trainer, Lee Duncan, always told him what to do. He may have in the beginning. I don't know. But when I worked with him we needed very few retakes and almost no extensive rehearsing. That dog knew just what was expected of him. He would watch Duncan for a signal, if movement was required. He couldn't tell time. But as for emoting, or playing a scene right, he didn't need any coaching. That's the unusual thing about that dog. He actually seemed to understand the story line well enough to bring off his role better than most of the other actors in the picture. I had more trouble with McCoy and Jones later at Columbia than

I ever had with Rinty. He was one of the few truly professional actors we had in Hollywood at that time. He just went about his business."

Nat Levine paid Lee Duncan another $5,000 for Rinty's participation in *The Lightning Warrior*. Rinty was already quite old, upward of thirteen, and so had to be used chiefly for close-ups and emoting. There was little enough of such fare, though, with the dog firmly integrated into the fast-paced action formula; a thespian no longer, at Mascot Rinty was constantly leaping, fighting, and, rarely, asked to make an intelligent deduction. Rinty bore it all with equanimity, however, and perhaps even a shrug of the shoulders. He well knew the irrational ways of men.

Of course, most of the stunting was handled by doubles, including a stuffed wolf dog for startling sequences in chapters 2 and 4. In the former, the animal was required to leap through the air into a moving ore car hundreds of yards above the ground, while in the latter he took a plunging fall into a treetop, then dropped to the ground. Rinty was particularly adept at limping and playing wounded. His right foreleg had been broken during a personal appearance in New York, and Lee Duncan set it himself. The dog would trust no one else. It didn't heal properly, and Rinty was left with a permanent disability.

Richard Talmadge straddling a rope over the Kern River lagoon in *The Lightning Warrior*.

Photo courtesy of *Views & Reviews* magazine.

The Lightning Warrior was filmed variously at the Prudential studio, Universal City, and in North Hollywood in the autumn of 1931. Costing $45,000, it was Rin-Tin-Tin's last film and one of Mascot's best, a pace-setter for the industry. No Mascot serial after it was made with such passion, offering the same high degree of breath-taking stunts, thrilling cinematic techniques, competent acting in all departments, and, a stamp peculiar to the Mascot product as it was uncommon in any of the others, intense archetypal imagery. *The Lightning Warrior* persists to this day as a fond tribute to the screen's greatest canine star. Rin-Tin-Tin died, upon jumping into his owner's arms, on August 10, 1932, thus ending a relationship which had begun with his discovery among a litter in a trench in France during the Great War and had reached the dizzying heights of stardom, the dog even being driven to work in his own limousine. Nat Levine, who liked featuring dogs in his serials, replaced the original with one of the sire's many offspring, Rin-Tin-Tin, Jr., debuting in *The Wolf Dog* (Mascot, 1933), but his black-faced father, supposedly named by the Indians (according to the script) the "lightning warrior," has to his credit a series of Westerns and melodramas that has impressed lastingly all who have happened to see them.

Rinty's final picture was one of George Brent's first. Having worked on the stage in New York, Brent came to Hollywood with the intention of getting a job in pictures, not so unlikely a prospect in that he had a fine bari-

Frankie Darro performing one of his own stunts in *The Lightning Warrior*.

tone voice and excellent elocution. Mascot signed him for the serial. Brent performed his part with admirable aplomb, easily appearing to be the most experienced player in the company other than Rinty, despite the presence of Georgia Hale, who had been Charlie Chaplin's leading lady in *The Gold Rush* (United Artists, 1925), and the many veteran character actors.

It was about this time that Yakima Canutt, who had played Western leads for the independents in the middle and late twenties, now turned decisively to stunt work and raised it to the level of an art. Levine put him under contract, simultaneously giving him a small part in *The Lightning Warrior* and permitting him to devise, or realize, some of the most hair-raising antics ever recorded on celluloid. Canutt engaged Helen Gibson, still claiming to have once been married to the Hooter, to double for Georgia, and Kermit Maynard was hired as Yak's assistant. Yak had proven to everybody's satisfaction, I believe, but especially to Levine that, primarily because of the addition of his second-unit stunting, the Universal summer serial for 1931, *Battling with Buffalo Bill,* was far superior to the earlier *The Indians Are Coming.* Born on November 29, 1895, at Colfax, Washington, Canutt was paid $125 a week, year round. This meant that when Mascot wasn't in actual production, Yak could still free-lance for additional money. From this point forward, it was Canutt's fabulous second-unit work which raised the Mascot serials to pre-eminence in the field, a pre-eminence which was only enhanced when Mascot merged to form Republic.

Benjamin Kline, henceforth for years a chief cameraman at Columbia Pictures, was given the action segment of the outdoor direction. As an economy measure, Levine usually divided the directorial task on a serial between two directors, one for exteriors and action footage, the other for interiors and dramatic interplay (what little there was of it). The same procedure had been initiated by George B. Seitz at Pathé. Armand Schaefer was adroit at watching the rushes from the previous day's shooting and taking up an interior sequence where, the day before, the exterior unit had left off. Since almost no exterior shooting in *The Lightning Warrior* involved anything other than hectic action, the fact that Kline was more a cameraman than a director didn't matter greatly. Only a most talented cinematographer could have positioned his cameras so as to capture all of the dangers and excitement of Canutt's daredevil stunting.

Last in the line of players I wish to speak about, and first on the credits, was acrobatic thirteen-year-old Frankie Darro, a child star of the front rank whom Levine would use repeatedly in subsequent serials. Darro was a willing performer, at times challenging Canutt himself in his enthusiasm for dangling from ore cars, hanging on ropes across deep chasms, or jumping about on roof tops. He was an excellent rider.

No doubt many of the stunts performed in *The Lightning Warrior* will never be duplicated, which is to say they were *really done,* not process shots

and not special effects. What Levine's magnetism was for people is hard to say, but they gave their hearts and souls and risked their lives for next to nothing to make his serials as compelling and memorable as they were. Maybe his secret, in the end, consisted in this: He let his players, technical crews, and stunt men alone, and, possessing unbounded freedom, working as hard as they could and as devotedly as they were able, he got from them what no amount of simple supervision and front office insistence possibly could.

Ollie Carey and I were once sitting in the front room of her cozy, tree-encompassed home at the end of a dirt road near Santa Barbara. She lit another cigarette. She was in her eighties.

"Harry always said I smoked like a chimney," she chuckled delightedly, "but I'm still here."

Harry Carey, following his success in *Trader Horn* (M-G-M, 1931), had appeared in three chapter plays for Mascot, two of them with his *Trader* costar, Edwina Booth.

"How does it come that you know so much about what happened on Harry's pictures and even on his Mascot serials?" I asked.

"Because I was there on the set with him almost every day," she responded with animation.

"Wasn't that a little unusual?"

"Not at all! Harry couldn't drive. I had to drive him to work and pick him up at night."

"Didn't he ever learn how?"

"Never!"

"But, Ollie, I saw him driving a car in *The Vanishing Legion* (Mascot, 1931)."

"You did not. You saw him steering a car they were tugging with ropes. Oh, he tried to learn once, but he ground the gears and the transmission collapsed. He swore he'd never try to drive again and he was a man of his word."

I paused to light a cigarette myself and fixed myself more comfortably in the wicker chair.

"Ollie," I began, "I've asked this question of a lot of people, including Nat Levine. What made for his astonishing success?"

"That's an easy one," Ollie returned. "And you can tell Nat Levine I said so. As long as he ran his office out of his vest pocket, he was a good businessman. When he started hiring others and moved into an office himself, he wasn't so good. He was the kind of man who worked best when he was right there, while they were shooting, making the picture. Once when Harry was doing *The Vanishing Legion*, one of the actors needed a business suit. He'd forgotten to bring one with him. The scene had to be shot. Nat jumped into a rain barrel, took off his own pin stripe, and gave it to the actor."

George Brent about to be ambushed by a Hollywood Indian in the bluffs near Kernville.

The Wolf Man giving instructions to Bob Kortman and Dick Dickson at the caves at Bronson Canyon.

Photo courtesy of *Views & Reviews* magazine.

I was laughing.

"You can't be serious, Ollie."

"You can laugh, if you want to," Ollie said, "but it was that kind of spirit that made Nat Levine everything he ever became!"

The Lightning Warrior begins when the Wolf Man leads a band of Indians in a war against the settlers of a mining district in the hope of scaring them off their claims so he might possess the rich vein which runs through all the surrounding mines. Pitted against him are George Brent, Frankie Darro, and Rinty. Georgia Hale and Brent fall in love. Suspicion travels from one character to another in the quest as to who the Wolf Man is. The Wolf Man uses the caves at Bronson Canyon for his hide-out, the caves being remnants of the quarry used to supply bricks for the Los Angeles streetcar system. In the last chapter, Frank Brownlee, foreman of

Frankie Darro's mine, is revealed as being at the bottom of the trouble, and even the Indians turn out to be white men in disguise, finally vanquished when Indian George brings the real Indians from their secret valley to restore peace to the district.

For all of their furious action, Mascot serials had more story packed into each chapter than any of the Universal serials or any of the later Columbia chapter plays. No amount of elaboration could demonstrate the thrill of the serial as a whole, the pace of its stunting with at least three unusually daring feats in every chapter, or the charm of Frankie Darro and Rinty pitted against the powerful forces of a hostile world. The viewer believes because the characters themselves believe, so caught up in the basic premises of the far-fetched and imaginative plot that, for the moment at any rate, all critical faculties are suspended before the somewhat awesome spectacle. The overwhelming visual impact of Levine's images—and they must be attributed to him, and not to others, because they appear in all his early serials to a greater or lesser extent—have an existence of their own and generate a psychic excitement rarely to be found in waking life, a dream-like quality which is vivid and unassailable.

22 / BUCK JONES AT COLUMBIA

Jack Cohn was born in the city of New York October 27, 1889. In 1902 he went to work for the Hampton Advertising Agency and, while in its employ, met a man named Joe Brandt, with whom he became fast friends. Jack grew dissatisfied and by 1908 found himself a new job working for Carl Laemmle's IMP, starting in the laboratory.

Joe Brandt, born July 20, 1882, in Troy, New York, was thinner than Jack Cohn and quieter. Unlike Jack, he hadn't been brought up in the rough-and-tumble of New York City street life. While working at Hampton's, he was studying law at New York University. Joe tried private practice, worked for a short time for *Billboard* and then as advertising manager of the New York *Mirror*.

There was such a great fluidity in Laemmle's company that Jack Cohn found it relatively easy to move from one position to another. He approached Uncle Carl with an idea that the old man accepted at once. Jack had taken over as editor and producer of the *Universal Weekly,* Laemmle's house organ which was distributed throughout the industry, telling exhibitors and exchange managers alike what was happening at Universal, who had been hired, who fired, and who was making what picture. Jack proposed that the company start newsreel production by placing camera crews in key cities to cover major events. The footage submitted each week was edited into a comprehensive short subject and sold to theaters as filler. The innovation was a success.

When describing Uncle Carl's battle for supremacy within the Universal organization, I had occasion to mention how the feature *Traffic in Souls* was made without anyone's knowledge and how it proved a stunning success, grossing $450,000. George Loane Tucker directed it, but Jack Cohn had been his mainstay and had personally cut and titled the finished film. Laemmle approved beamingly of Jack Cohn's courage in having persisted in the project. Jack suggested to Uncle Carl that he hire Joe Brandt. The old man did, making him his private secretary. Joe found it only a matter of time before he was general manager of the Universal Film Manufacturing Company.

Jack's brother, Harry Cohn, was born on July 23, 1891, in New York City. He pursued a career as a song plugger. He had started as a streetcar conductor. What got him ahead was his notion that moving pictures could illustrate songs. It was a custom of exhibitors at the time to project slides with lyrics on them, while the piano player in the pit provided an accompaniment. Harry wanted songs that moved and that, as the lyrics progressed, could be sung by patrons. Jack got his brother a job with Laemmle producing a series of song shorts featuring Universal players. This so impressed Uncle Carl that Laemmle promoted Harry to the capacity of his personal secretary for the West Coast studio and shipped him off to California. Harry was to keep Laemmle posted as to what was happening.

In 1919 Jack Cohn decided to leave Universal to start his own film production company. Jack conceived an idea of a motion picture fan magazine, a series of *Screen Snapshots* of the stars and other film personalities at work and at play. The series was a success, and soon Jack was able to invite Joe Brandt to join him. The two put their heads together and felt they needed a third with actual production knowledge. They approached Edward Small, the agent, but Small declined. Finally, Jack recommended Harry, and Joe acquiesced. The firm was incorporated as Cohn-Brandt-Cohn and known as CBC. A. P. Giannini, an enterprising officer in the Bank of Italy with a flair for speculation, gave loans to newly formed motion picture firms, and CBC borrowed $100,000 from him. The partners hit upon the notion of bringing a comic strip to life via motion pictures—namely, H. A. McGill's strip for the New York *Telegram* called the "Hall Room Boys." A crew was hired long-distance from New York and set to work. Before long, the money borrowed from Giannini was completely gone, and the finished product was found to be unmarketable. Harry was dispatched at once back to California to do what he could to save the day.

Harry set up an alliance with Morris Schlank, who operated a tiny studio housed in a collection of clapboard buildings resembling a chicken coop. Cohn, with this as the base of his operations, located off Sunset Boulevard between Gower Street and Beachwood Drive, hired Alfred Santell to produce the first *Hall Room Boys* short. It was well done and sold readily. The firm was in business. But beyond their obvious genius for producing marketable pictures, the CBC management came up with a practice that literally permitted them corporate survival. All salaries, expenditures, rentals in California, after maximum delays, were paid out of the CBC account in New York; similarly, all checks to be issued for payments in New York were drawn against the CBC account in California. Transit alone was four or five days. Harry Cohn later remarked that had there been airmail in those days, there would have been no Columbia Pictures.

A "Sunshine Comedy" series was soon started starring Billy West. These comedies were imitations of Charlie Chaplin, with West's portrayal probably being the best of many. In 1922 the firm produced its first feature, *More to Be Pitied than Scorned,* at a negative cost of $20,000. It was sold via states' rights for $130,000.

On January 10, 1924, CBC became incorporated as Columbia Pictures Corporation. By 1926 the firm started to franchise exchanges, permitting them to receive a portion of the profits made by the local distributor. Soon all of the then existing ten principal exchange centers were covered by a Columbia outlet. Next, Columbia began buying up the franchises rather than renewing them. By 1929 Columbia had a complete domestic exchange network.

Columbia's first big commercial success was *Submarine* (Columbia, 1928), directed by Frank Capra and starring Jack Holt, who was simultaneously appearing for Paramount in the last entries of the silent Zane Grey series. Capra prospered at Columbia by avoiding Cohn's merciless rule, and Columbia prospered by leaving Capra alone. Capra had virtual autonomy because he stood up to Cohn, and Harry was such that he refused to respect a man unless he did stand up for what he believed in.

Buck Jones Productions was organized in 1928 with the intention, on Buck's part, of producing his own pictures. His salary at Fox at the time he quit was $2,500 a week. He had accumulated a small fortune and decided to strike out on his own. His first effort was *The Big Hop,* a silent film with titles. Synchronized music and sound effects were added as a novelty, employing the Cortella Phone disc system. The picture was distributed on a states' rights basis. Neither the distribution nor the story line, which cast Buck as a ranch hand who becomes an aviator, did much for the enterprise, and Jones, reportedly, lost $50,000.

Suddenly in need of money and with no motion picture offers, Buck next tried a Wild West show. Fox, in its promotion of Jones, had come up with the idea of a youth club called the Buck Jones Rangers. By 1929 the club had some 4 million members. Buck sought out Scott Dunlap and retained him as his business manager. He brought together a group of acts and set off on a touring circuit. The Rangers were instructed to spread publicity information prior to the show's arrival in those cities where membership was most highly concentrated. The Rangers weren't very skillful promoters. The American Circus Corporation felt Buck to be unfair competition and saw to it, where possible, that his posters were covered up by their own announcing rival play dates for their own organization. Buck made the mistake of hiring a man of questionable character as his wagon master and show manager. The man was in charge of accounting. Since the shows played to capacity audiences, Buck and his wife, Dell, who accompanied him, naïvely thought the venture a success. Meanwhile, the show manager called the principal acts and cowboys to one side and told them privately that Buck was in severe personal financial trouble and asked if they would willingly wait a few weeks for their money. Everyone agreed and, out of sympathy for Buck and Dell, kept their sacrifice secret.

When the show closed in Danville, Illinois, Buck, Dell, and the whole company retired to their Pullman cars to sleep and, come morning, wake up in the next city. Dell was first to waken. Looking out her window, she was astonished to find that the train hadn't moved. She woke Buck, who immediately set about investigating what was wrong. He learned that the show had been stopped with several attachments which had been following them from previous towns they had played. The show manager was nowhere to be found. Buck loaded his .45 and went to the hotel where the manager was staying. When he discovered that he was out, he sat in the lobby waiting for him to return, still carrying the gun. The manager never came back.

To his chagrin, Buck was made aware of the extent of his losses in terms of salaries owed and expenses incurred. It wiped out his life savings of $250,-000 and amounted to still more. Buck confronted his creditors squarely and assured them that, if he were not forced into bankruptcy, he would make good on every dollar of it. They consented to give him the opportunity. Buck made his way back to Hollywood, looking for a job. Dell sold her diamonds for train fare.

Sol Lesser, born at Spokane, Washington, on February 17, 1890, had entered the industry through distribution and theater ownership, finally journeying to the West Coast to involve himself in production. Harry Cohn was anxiously looking for product to fill up his release schedule. He signed an agreement with Walt Disney to distribute the latter's cartoons. He contracted with Lesser to release Sol's projected series Westerns. Scott Dunlap, Buck's business manager, heard about the deal, found Lesser was without a firm contract for a star, and introduced him to Buck Jones. Buck signed with Sol's Beverly Productions to make eight Westerns during a one-year period at the reduced salary of $300 a week.

Buck was a proud man. He felt the burden of his debts keenly. Dell had not wanted him to go into the circus venture; he asked her to tap their savings to get the project started. Now they were reduced to living in very humble circumstances. Buck gritted his teeth and set to work rebuilding his lost fortune.

The Lone Rider (Columbia, 1930), with which the series began, was Buck's first all-talking Western, and his voice came across effectively. Silver joined him, although the gray never achieved the importance in Buck's films that Tom Mix's Tony or Ken Maynard's Tarzan enjoyed. In *The Lone Rider* Buck played an outlaw who thwarts Harry Woods's efforts to abduct Vera Reynolds during a stage robbery. Vera asks Buck to be her protector. Bringing her to safety, Buck is made head of the local Vigilance Committee.

Harry Woods, one of the most familiar heavies of the thirties and forties, confronting Buck Jones.

Photo courtesy of Dell Jones.

Buck helps Carmelita Geraghty escape from three toughs. Carmelita's brothers were screenwriters, Gerald and Maurice Geraghty, the latter becoming a noted director and producer at RKO.

Woods decides to capitalize on the fact that Buck was once a member of his gang. The plan goes haywire, and Buck ends up being pursued by both the vigilantes and Woods's gang. He squares himself when he brings Woods to the bar of justice. This plot was remade as *Texas Gun-Fighter* by Tiffany in 1932, starring Ken Maynard, with Harry Woods again in the role of the outlaw chief.

It was an auspicious beginning, and Buck's unquestionable acting ability stood him in good stead. His next film was *Shadow Ranch* (Columbia, 1930). Frank Rice plays Buck's side-kick. The picture was shot at the Tiffany California studio lot. When Rice is killed helping Marguerite de la Motte save her ranch from Al Smith's scheming, Buck takes over and in a terrific fight at the end beats Smith into submission and confession. This plot was also remade at Tiffany as *Sunset Trail* (Tiffany, 1931), again starring Ken Maynard, and featuring Frank Rice in the same role.

Men Without Law was third in Buck's series for Sol Lesser. Harry Woods was back as the villain, and Carmelita Geraghty, sister to both Gerald and Maurice Geraghty well known in the middle and late thirties for their literary contributions to Western production, played a Spanish don's imperiled and imperious daughter. Carmelita would play a dance hall queen in Ken Maynard's *Fightin' Thru* (Tiffany, 1930) and had been featured in Myrna Loy's first talking picture, *Rogue of the Rio Grande* (SonoArt-WorldWide, 1930). Maynard, of course, wasn't alone in his tendency to borrow. Buck had been impressed with the musical formats of Maynard's films for Universal. In *Men* one of the desperadoes sings "I'm an Old Cowhand," and the Mexican setting for the Del Rey hacienda occasions both a dance sequence with musical background and a Mexican love song. Later, however, when the singing in Westerns reached an absurd emphasis, Buck was foremost in violently denouncing the practice.

Lesser's budgets rarely exceeded $12,000, and the resulting starkness gave the pictures an austere tone reminiscent of William S. Hart's rather expensive vehicles for Paramount, by necessity rather than intention. In common with Hoot Gibson, Buck continued to inject humor into his sound Westerns. One hilarious scene in *Men Without Law* takes place when Buck is locked up in jail with Fred Kelsey, who worked with Laurel and Hardy, as his keeper. Buck gives Kelsey a Chinese puzzle to solve. Kelsey takes it away with him, Buck whistling the "Cuckoo Song," which was the Laurel and Hardy theme, Kelsey marching in time to the beat until he pulls himself up short, irked by his own behavior. Another amusing moment occurs when Buck, escaping from Harry Woods's hide-out, lassoes one of the outlaws, stringing the rope over a beam jutting out from the peak of a gable. Lowering himself on the other end, he ties the rope to the door, the outlaws clamoring to get outside. Ben Corbett makes his way to the second floor, cuts the rope loose, the bound outlaw falling, only to land on the others piling out the door. No sooner do they pick themselves up than Corbett falls the two stories, sending everyone sprawling again.

Men Without Law opens to action at the front, in No Man's Land. Buck gets to know Manuel, Carmelita's brother. Manuel dies at the front. Buck returns to the States and finds his own brother a member of Harry Woods's gang. Buck saves Carmelita and her father from losing everything to Woods's schemings, Buck winning Carmelita in the end.

It has always been a curiosity to me how the nation readily assimilated the Great War into folk culture. It was a somewhat less serious affair. Those were robust and optimistic times, at least in the rural areas, with the men returning. World War II was another matter entirely. The character of human existence forever changed, producing a tense, bitter, uncertain disillusionment.

The Dawn Trail (Columbia, 1930) came next. Buck played a sheriff. It was one of the few Westerns in which he wore two guns. The film stressed realism. Buck drank and smoked. An interesting camera setup had Buck, riding up to a burning shack, photographed from inside the shack, the flames roaring before the lens. The tension between the nesters, who have plenty of water for their sheep during a drought, and the cattlemen made desperate by watching their herds thirst to death is quite compelling.

Barbara Bedford, Hart's leading lady in *Tumbleweeds,* played opposite Buck in *Desert Vengeance* (Columbia, 1931). For some reason, in the early sound era, Barbara was usually cast as an adventuress. In this picture she attempts to deceive Buck, who plays an outlaw leader, and, upon discovery, is taken to Buck's hide-out and put to hard labor. A rival gang attacks his stronghold. Barbara and Buck are the only survivors, who, in the desolation of the aftermath, decide to try to build a new life together. There was apparently more to it than the screenplay, and, for a while, Buck and Barbara were rather strongly attracted to each other.

Dorothy Revier was the girl in Buck's next film, *The Avenger* (Columbia, 1931). She was an exquisite woman. Buck played a Mexican, Joaquín Murietta. Roy William Neill, who later did the Sherlock Holmes pictures in the forties for Universal, was the director. It is his camera setups and imaginative direction, along with the unusual lighting on the part of cinematographer Charles Stumar, that make the picture memorable. The film opens to Buck serenading La Revier in a lurching stagecoach, his voice obviously dubbed. It was generally axiomatic in Hollywood that Mexicans could sing; certainly in the Columbia Westerns of this period, no Mexican dared appear on the screen without a guitar or mandolin. When Buck enters the saloon looking for his younger brother, Juan, played by Paul Fix, the recording equipment adroitly mixes his queries of the bartender with the schemings of three rough prospectors who are plotting to steal the Murietta gold mine. Buck is seized when he arrives at the mine. He is tied to a tree and forced to watch his brother being hanged as a horse thief. Neill managed one stunning shot when Buck, a black silhouette against a clouded horizon behind which the setting sun blazes, rides off into a diffused haze.

Buck's Westerns for Sol Lesser were a substantial box-office success. Harry Cohn acted with dispatch. Columbia had just signed Colonel Tim McCoy for his own series of starring features. Cohn negotiated with Lesser and bought Buck's contract from him. For the 1931–32 season, Columbia would produce the Buck Jones Westerns directly, with Harry Cohn as the nominal producer. Buck was raised to $500 a week, $100 more a week than Tim McCoy was receiving. While the two players had almost nothing to do with one another while at Columbia, in 1941 Scott Dunlap would re-enter the scene and put both stars under contract for a new series of Westerns to be distributed by Monogram.

I would like to say that Harry Cohn's takeover improved the Buck Jones

Syd Saylor shaking hands with Buck Jones, Silver in the background, from *Men Without Law*.

Photo courtesy of Columbia Pictures.

series. The budgets were increased from $20,000 to $25,000. The shooting schedules were between two and three weeks. The directors, however, had none of the variety as had been the case under Lesser, confined generally to Lambert Hillyer or D. Ross Lederman. Cohn hoped to do again with Buck what Columbia had been able to do with Jack Holt. As Buck's Columbia series progressed, with greater frequency he was given non-Western roles to play, more in the adventure category of the Jack Holt films. Columbia tried to do the same thing with Tim McCoy, and, for the 1933–34 season at least, it was Columbia's intention to keep Tim out of Westerns, which would have happened had Buck not signed with Universal.

Louis King directed Buck's second entry under Cohn's management, *Border Law* (Columbia, 1931). Buck played a Texas Ranger; Frank Rice was his side-kick. When Buck's brother is shot by Jim Mason and his gang in an attempt to rob the express office, Buck gets a leave of absence and goes after the gang for retribution. Buck becomes friendly with Mason, who believes him to be an outlaw. Stuart Anthony did the screenplay. This story was subsequently used by Ken Maynard as the basis for his *Whistlin' Dan* (Tiffany, 1932). Then Buck remade it as *The Fighting Ranger* (Columbia,

1934). Buck, I think, got more mileage out of it, since a variation of it was again used in his *Law of the Texan* (Columbia, 1938). The plot invariably ends that the undercover Ranger gets the crooked gang to pull a phony job across the border; everyone except the leader is captured; the hero races after the leader to his hide-out below the border; the two clash in a fistfight which finally culminates in a shoot-out, the hero victorious. Tim McCoy in his series for Puritan had one intriguing alteration to this plot in *The Lion's Den* (Puritan, 1936) when, at the end of the picture, in order to meet a note at the bank he cashes Frank Glendon, Dick Curtis, and the rest of the gang in for the reward money, matching each man with the Wanted poster Glendon used as a hold over them.

Range Feud (Columbia, 1931), directed by D. Ross Lederman, with a story by George Plympton, costarred Duke Wayne. Buck is a sheriff. Two ranches are warring with one another, stirred up by Harry Woods, who is using the opportunity profitably to rustle cattle from each and blame it on the other. Duke is Edward LeSaint's son. Buck was raised by LeSaint. When the head of the other faction is murdered by Harry Woods, Duke is blamed. Buck is forced to arrest Duke, and does so after a thrilling chase in and around the Tiffany California studio lot. Duke got a better chance to act in this picture than in either of the films he made with Tim McCoy while at Columbia and came away with an admiration for Buck. This plot was varied in Buck's later serial, *The Red Rider* (Universal, 1934), with Grant Withers in Duke's role, while being itself a variation on the earlier *The Dawn Trail*.

Possibly Buck's best picture for Columbia was *Deadline* (Columbia, 1931). It was directed by Lambert Hillyer. Loretta Sayers was the girl. She had appeared opposite Buck in his last picture for Sol Lesser, *The Fighting Sheriff* (Columbia, 1931). Buck is placed on probation and released from prison. Robert Ellis framed Buck on a manslaughter charge, killing a man who was trailing him for cattle rustling. Buck does not know who framed him, but intends to find out. The townsfolk ostracize Buck. He is not permitted to fight. The tension of his probation, the social opprobrium, and the near scrapes Buck gets into are gripping. Conversely, Buck's relationship with Loretta's younger brother, Jimmy, is rather touching, set against the barrenness of the emotional climate. Edward LeSaint is Loretta's screen father and, in the course of the picture, one of the few commendable bankers to be seen in series Westerns at any time, but especially during the thirties.

Loretta was back for *High Speed* (Columbia, 1932), second to last in Buck's second series of eight Westerns for Columbia. It was not a Western and cast Buck as a race car driver, something of course he had done years before at the Indianapolis speedway. *South of the Rio Grande* (Columbia, 1932) finished out the season. Lambert Hillyer directed. Although this picture was made nearly a year after *The Avenger*, Paul Fix was back, identically attired, playing Buck's weak brother, only doing himself in rather than being victimized. Buck is again a Mexican, named Carlos, a captain in the border Rurales. George Lewis was cast as Buck's protégé; Philo McCullough, who had better adjusted to sound since *Spurs,* was the principal villain. Scenes of dancing and singing from *Men Without Law* were interpolated during the early part of Buck's visit to George Lewis's home, but it was done with such precision that unless you were familiar with the footage it couldn't be detected.

Hello, Trouble (Columbia, 1932) opened the 1932–33 season. The most memorable thing about it may well have been its cast of characters. Ward Bond was a ranch hand in love with Frank Rice's daughter, Ruth Warren. Lafe McKee was the sheriff. Lina Basquette was the girl, her false eyelashes frequently getting in her way. Al Roscoe, one of Frank Capra's chums, played the chief heavy, with Wallace MacDonald as his henchman. Lambert Hillyer directed and was credited for the story. Lina got married while the company was shooting on location at Bronson Canyon, and Buck threw a party for her on the set. Lina was soundly spanked with a pair of chaps, Western style. With the cast having all this fun, it is unfortunate that they couldn't have done better with the plot which made Lina and Buck co-owners of a ranch with silver ore deposits on it that Al Roscoe hopes to snatch away from them.

It was the season for Buck to try various experiments. In his next picture, as is obvious from the title, *McKenna of the Mounted* (Columbia, 1932), he was a Mountie, and in his third, *White Eagle* (Columbia, 1932), he was an Indian. The best programmer he made for that period was probably *Sundown Rider* (Columbia, 1932). Buck plays a cowhand who happens on Wheeler Oakman changing some brands. Oakman leaves him to tend the fire, and Buck is surrounded by a posse hunting the rustlers. Rather than hanging him, in a horrifying sequence they brand him with the running iron Oakman had been using. The viewer is conscious of the brand in a queer, psychological way throughout the film, although it is never shown, attention being called to it in other ways. Its being kept from sight, indeed, intensifies the suspense. Glenn Strange, that familiar Western heavy, sings a range song, while Niles Welch plays a crooked banker. The story was a good one by John Thomas Neville, who wrote Tim McCoy's *Winners of the Wilderness,* Buck's *The Dawn Trail,* and who, at Universal, would do one of Buck's very best screenplays, *The Ivory-handled Guns* (Universal, 1935). That same season Buck was billed sixth in a straight dramatic, high-budget picture, *Child of Manhattan* (Columbia, 1933).

Buck was signed on a special deal by Henry MacRae to appear in Universal's summer serial for 1933, a Western in twelve chapters titled *Gordon of Ghost City.* Buck played Buck Gordon. He is hired by William Desmond to hunt down a gang of cattle rustlers preying on Desmond's herd. Madge

Bellamy lives with her grandfather in Ghost City, Mauser Street made over to simulate a deserted town. Madge's grandfather has discovered a rich vein of gold under his store. A mystery man, revealed at last to be Francis Ford, his onetime partner, tries to prevent him from mining the gold. Walter Miller was cast as Desmond's foreman and the secret leader of the cattle rustlers. Battling against one villain or the other, Buck was kept busy. Uncle Carl took an immediate liking to him. It would prove to be helpful to Buck in the future. In the meantime, he returned to Columbia to finish his four contract pictures for the season.

23 / TOM MIX RIDES AGAIN

All Quiet on the Western Front, Universal's great antiwar film of 1930, brought the studio prestige and critical acclaim, and it seemed, above all, to justify Junior Laemmle's policies. Uncle Carl listened and gave him his head. Now, Junior reasoned (or at any rate argued), Universal could promptly move to the forefront and apparently challenge M-G-M, Paramount, and the rapidly expanding Warner Brothers on equal footing. Junior was a dreamer. The big studios were big, with galaxies of stars, producers, and directors, because they had mighty financing behind them, massive theater chains which guaranteed their pictures play-offs. Uncle Carl persisted in charming exhibitors because Universal pictures still had to be *sold* to get the requisite bookings. The old man continued to publish the *Universal Weekly,* filled with folksy chatter for theater owners and managers. His advertisements in *Photoplay* and other trade publications were cozy, personal letters to exhibitors and public alike. The sales organization preoccupied the Little Champ more than production. But now, *All Quiet* won the gamut of awards, beginning with an Oscar, the *Film Daily* poll, the gold medal of the Faculty of Arts of London, the *Photoplay* gold medal.

Junior, who had frequently been indulged by his generous father even to the old man stuffing $1,500 cash in his hand during a poker game and telling him to go amuse himself, was educated in New York. On his twenty-first birthday, as a gift, Uncle Carl made him studio manager. The year 1931 marked Uncle Carl's silver jubilee in the motion picture industry. It was wholly natural he should want to retire, and succession became a major consideration. Lewis Milestone, Maxwell Anderson, and George Cukor had worked together on *All Quiet,* but Junior took the credit. He'd preceded the picture with *King of Jazz,* a Paul Whiteman vehicle that had failed, and filmed talking versions of *Frankenstein* and *Dracula.* Universal wasn't going to be making Westerns and programmers any more. It was a major studio, as far as Junior had any say in things.

No one in Hollywood, least of all Junior, really comprehended that the country was in the throes of a massive Depression. Junior spent money wildly. But the sales force, the image of family entertainment, the commercial significance of the Universal logo which Uncle Carl had given a lifetime to make synonymous with a certain kind of picture, were ill-prepared for these mad forays.

Sol Lesser, between the time he sold out Buck Jones's option to Harry Cohn and acquired George O'Brien's contract at Fox Film Corporation, joined the Universal management in response to a generous offer from Uncle Carl. The old man was disturbed about sagging sales. It had not occurred to him that a few expensive, albeit successful, films could not hope to substitute for the staple of pictures Universal had been accustomed to producing over the years and which had safeguarded its economic viability. Uncle Carl's daughter, Rosabelle, married Stanley Bergerman, an agent, and true to custom Laemmle hired him, telling him simply to find something with which to occupy himself.

One day Uncle Carl summoned Lesser to his office.

"I want you to go to New York," Laemmle said, "and fire Phil Reisner."

Lesser had at first thought he was being hired to produce pictures and then had adjusted to the idea of working in sales. But this was too much.

"How can I do that?" he asked Laemmle. "He's one of my best friends."

"Good," said Uncle Carl. "That'll make it easier."

Lesser agreed to go to New York and find out what was the matter. Upon arrival at the Park Avenue offices, he interviewed everyone connected with general sales, from Reisner on down. The problem was expensive pictures. Exhibitors wanted the cheaper, old-time programmers and Westerns. The sales people agreed; the high-budget market was too small, the competition too stiff.

"Cannot sell expensive features," Lesser wired Uncle Carl. "Change policy."

"Junior will not change policy," Laemmle wired back.

Lesser wired again that it was imperative that Junior be persuaded to alter his policy.

"Do not persist," Uncle Carl responded. "You will give Junior a breakdown."

"Junior will break down Universal if policy is not changed," Lesser cabled him bluntly.

Stanley Bergerman, Uncle Carl Laemmle, and Junior.
Photo courtesy of the Academy of Motion Picture Arts & Sciences.

Reisner was fired, going to RKO to become foreign sales manager. Uncle Carl, to escape the pressure of the situation, took another of his long cures in Germany. The news that continued to reach him was all bad. The studio was in desperate condition. He reluctantly relieved Junior and replaced him with his son-in-law, Stanley Bergerman. But the blade had fallen. Junior, no matter what the realities, was absolutely determined that Universal, under his guidance, could match and outdo anything Thalberg had done when he was there and could now successfully compete with M-G-M. The final irony was still in the future when Uncle Carl, in his humiliation, would be compelled to approach Irving and Norma Thalberg for a substantial loan to prevent bankruptcy.

Both James Flavin and his wife, Lucile Browne, were Universal contract players at the time, appearing in Henry MacRae's serials. Sitting in their comfortable sunroom many years later, I asked Jimmy about Universal under Junior's management.

"It was the craziest lot out here," Jimmy commented. "Laemmle hired all those relatives from Germany and had them making Westerns when they'd never even seen a horse. But he'd turned the lot over to Junior who was just a kid."

"What did you think of Junior?" I asked.

"He was a jerk!"

"Jim!" Lucy put in. "There's more you can say about him than that. Jon wants to be able to write down what you tell him."

"No. He was a jerk. I was an actor just out here from Broadway. I did a screen test. After they'd screened it, I was asked to go to the Make-up Department. I sat down and the hairdresser said he was going to pluck out all my eyebrows and pencil them in. I said, 'Nothing doing.' 'But you have to do it,' he insisted. 'Who says I have to?' 'Junior.' 'Well, you tell Junior I'm not going to do it.'

"Next, I got a summons to Junior's office. Here was this little guy sitting behind this big desk in a big office.

" 'Nobody does that to one of my directives,' he shouted at me.

" 'Does what?'

" 'Refuses to obey them!'

" 'You mean about the eyebrows?'

" 'That's just what I mean.'

" 'I'm not going to have my eyebrows plucked so I look like a goddamned fag for you or anybody else. If that's the way it's going to be, you can rip up my contract and I'll go back to New York.'

"Junior was on his feet like a shot. He thrust out his arm toward the ceiling and pointed his index finger straight into the air.

" 'No one dares to talk to me like that. Get out of my office.'

"So I went. I met Sylvia Fox on a studio street.

" 'Jim,' she said, 'you've got to teach me how to talk with a Brooklyn accent for my next picture.'

" 'What d'y' mean, Sylvia? You're a Hebe. You grew up in Brooklyn. You don't need me to tell you how to talk!'

" 'I don't want anybody to know about that out here,' she told me. 'Come on to my dressing room.'

"And so I went and we sat around having a drink when Junior walked in.

" 'So! This is how it is!' he shouted and stormed out of the room.

" 'What's that all about?' I asked Sylvia.

" 'Junior and I are keeping company,' she said, 'and now he's jealous.'

"As if I wasn't in enough trouble over the eyebrows, she had to do this to me. I collected my checks, but I never worked on the lot except for *The*

Airmail Mystery [Universal, 1932]. I wouldn't have worked in that serial, but they couldn't find a leading man. In the middle of production, they dropped my option."

Bergerman returned to programmer production but was infused with Junior's extravagance. Harry Cohn was producing Tim McCoy Westerns for $12,000 to $15,000. The Buck Jones films seldom cost more than $25,-000. At Universal, the budgets for Westerns would be first-class. Following the experimental Western *Law and Order* (Universal, 1932), the studio made the decision to get the world's greatest cowboy, Tom Mix.

I do not think it was ever any consolation to Tom Mix that the Fox management which he and Buck Jones had been responsible for putting on the map did not survive their departure by eight years. Those same years held too many surprises, reversals, and indirections for him to think about much of anything except perhaps his own situation.

For the 1928–29 season, Joseph P. Kennedy persuaded Tom to sign with Film Booking Office to make a series of Westerns. Kennedy regarded the ploy an excellent comeback to his problems with Fred Thomson. Tom's price worked out to $15,000 a week, which was a substantial investment for the small studio. Kennedy thought his name value worth the price and that alone it might be able to overcome the distribution problems that continued to plague FBO. On the other hand, Kennedy needed some FBO films that would rack up impressive grosses if he hoped to proceed with his merger plans to unite Film Booking Office, Pathé studios, and the Keith-Orpheum theater circuit with General Sarnoff's Radio Photophone sound recording process company to form what became RKO Radio Pictures and RKO General. The deal came off with Kennedy profiting somewhat over $5 million for putting it together. By 1931 he was in a financial position to back Governor Franklin D. Roosevelt from New York for the presidency in exchange for a break on liquor taxes and an ambassadorship to Great Britain. Inadvertently, Tom Mix helped him do it.

Kennedy chose to cut corners on production values in the Mix pictures which, in terms of Tom's career, was a folly. Daniel B. Clark was unable to break his Fox contract and so could not work with Mix. William Fox only chuckled and went ahead with his personal merger plans while Louis B. Mayer struggled frantically to stop his own company from falling into Fox's hands, bringing pressure through Herbert Hoover, whom he had helped elect, to bust up the Fox trust and force the man into ruin. Mayer, who had once sold scrap iron and who had come from humble origins, found himself sleeping in the White House. Both he and Kennedy agreed on one principle: Money's greatest power was the political favor it could buy in a democracy.

Norman Devol was Mix's cinematographer on the films. Without Clark, the Mix magic seemed strangely minimized. In *King Cowboy* (FBO, 1928), the screenplay was by S. E. V. Taylor, who, the reader will recall, had scripted D. W. Griffith's Westerns. It found Tom in North Africa battling an Abdul only to win the girl and become Emir of El Kubra. The picture did no more for him than *Dick Turpin* (Fox, 1925) had done. For *The Drifter* (FBO, 1929), his last picture in the series of six, the screenplay was by Oliver Drake and Robert De Lacy. The plot involved Tom as a deputy marshal on the trail of narcotics smugglers going to work on Dorothy Dwan's ranch, discovering both the whereabouts of the smugglers and a hidden gold mine. *"The Drifter* is his cinema swan song," *Photoplay* summed it up, "his last picture on his last contract. Unfortunately, it won't emblazon the famous Mix initials in film history. Just another Western, but send the kids anyway, just to see the aeroplane."

Tom had bought Tony, Jr., from a New York florist and had him trained to be a circus horse. He began in 1929 to make appearances with the Sells-Floto Circus, owned by John Ringling. His name as a headliner brought in the crowds, and by means of a percentage agreement, his earnings climbed as high as $20,000 a week. Tom certainly needed the money. The crash wiped out a million dollars in paper assets. Tom was forced to sell first his Beverly Hills home and then, finally, his magnificent Arizona ranch.

The 101 Ranch Wild West Show was going bankrupt, and, with his two brothers dead, Zack Miller decided to reopen the old lawsuit against Tom in the state of Pennsylvania. It was settled by Tom agreeing to pay off $20,000 in notes held against Miller. The shortage of money permitted Tom to settle the disputed accounts for $.10 on the dollar, or about $2,000.

Tom was the principal attraction of Sells-Floto from 1929 through 1931. The circus averaged over one hundred performers and eighteen to twenty-four band members. It was rough work. In October 1929 Tom fell from his horse while performing in Dallas and shattered his shoulder. It was wired together. Several weeks later, the shoulder bothered him to the point where it had to be rewired. By November 1930 Tom was hospitalized complaining of back trouble. Dr. R. Nicholas Smith removed the wire from Tom's shoulder completely, because it was found to have caused arthritis of the back.

In March of that year, Tom had appeared in tax court and was fined $1,000 on each of three counts of accidental tax evasion, as well as paying $175,000 in back taxes. His income tax expert, Marjorie Berger, who prepared his tax forms, was sentenced to a prison term. In June, Tom tried to stop his daughter, Ruth, from marrying Douglas Gilmore at Yuma, Arizona. When he failed, he cut off her allowance of $225 a month which he had been paying her since 1917. Ruth brought suit against him. The case was settled in Tom's favor on July 5, 1930, and, ironically, on July 9, 1930, Ruth's marriage ended in an annulment.

Tom's fourth wife, who had shared the munificent years with him as a

Fox star, decided she had had enough of it and obtained a legal separation from him on November 26, 1930. She was awarded a divorce on December 25, 1930. Vicky told the court that Tom frightened her by frequently twirling a loaded .45 on his finger. Tom was in despair. "When a man's been married half a dozen times," he once remarked, "any sentiment about anniversaries is as cold as the ashes of last year's campfire. Payin' all them alimonies sorta drowns out the romance."

The Sells-Floto Circus traveled 14,891 miles in 1931, on tour 177 days. Late in the year, Tom was struck down by peritonitis, apparently the result of a ruptured appendix, but rumor had it he had been shot by one of his former wives. On November 25, 1931, a special serum was flown by plane that saved his life. In February 1932 in Mexico, Tom was married for the fifth time, to Mabel Ward, an aerial performer with the Sells-Floto Circus.

"You're asking me if I'll go back to the pictures again?" Tom responded in an interview for *Shadowplay Magazine*. "I figger it this way. A fella can't live on buttons. And that's all we were gettin' paid in at the studios a while back. So I figgered anyhow that if I left the studios, I had enough buttons on my breeches and enough silver on Tony to let me and Mrs. Mix eat for a while yet. . . . But I may go back. Anyway, it isn't for lack of offers." Presently, it was announced that Tom Mix would be returning to the screen as a Universal star.

Tom was fifty. He was terrified of the sound equipment. He would have to make it as a dramatic actor, which he was not. He had always taken pride in doing his own stunts, and he didn't think that the years he was carrying were conducive to making action films. But had he not once said that it was easier for a cowboy to become an actor than for an actor to become a cowboy? Universal's offer was really too generous to refuse.

The studio agreed that Mix could have his old cameraman, Daniel B. Clark. I honestly believe Mix was correct in his conviction that Clark alone among cameramen knew how to photograph him to advantage; more, that Clark in his own right was one of the uniquely talented cinematographers of the time. Universal gave Mix nearly total control over the pictures; they would be made his way. The budgets were to have a spread of $100,000 to $150,000, with Mix drawing a weekly salary of $10,000, scheduled at the rate of six features a season to be shot over three to five weeks apiece. Mix could pick his own stories, provided they were approved by Stanley Bergerman before production began. Tom was given casting privileges. How could he possibly demur?

Tom's first Universal film was *Destry Rides Again* (Universal, 1932), about which I will have more than a little to say when I get to the chapter devoted to it and the 1939 remake by Universal. Uncle Carl Laemmle himself presented Tom Mix in *Destry Rides Again,* produced by Carl Laemmle, Jr., with Stanley Bergerman as associate producer. This satisfied everyone in the family, and Mix, too. His second Universal series Western was *Rider of Death Valley,* which originally had the working title of *Destry of Death Valley.* But it was felt that the identification with the first picture, released more quietly than one would have expected, was no longer necessary as box office began to mushroom. *Rider* is the finest Tom Mix film which survives. Although this is strictly my personal opinion, I do not think there was a series of Westerns made in the thirties or forties that surpassed the Mix Universal films, nor was there a B Western during the entire sound era that has come close to this picture.

Lois Wilson was the heroine in *Rider.* I was surprised, when I wrote to her in 1972, that she hadn't ever seen the film in its entirety. I promised her that the next time I was in New York I would arrange for her to see it. "I remember quite a few things in connection with the picture," she wrote to me in the meantime. "Most of the interiors were taken at the Universal studio. The rest of the picture was shot on the desert surrounding Yuma, Arizona. I had never met Mr. Mix until the day we started shooting. During the following week or two, I did not like him. I don't remember why. Then we went on location and I became acquainted with an entirely different man. His wife, Mabel Ward, of the famous 'Flying Ward' family, went on location with us. She was charming and I liked her very much. Then one day I was allowed to ride one of Tom's horses. He complimented my riding ability and we started talking horses. I love them and I was rather proud of my ability to ride. Then, when we had our box lunches, his wife would join us, and she and Tom would entertain us with circus stories. I found Tom a fascinating storyteller and our friendship grew from then on. He saved me from a bite from a Gila monster which he saw crawling under one of my voluminous skirts as I sat on the sand. Without blinking, he pulled his revolver and shot said little monster. I was startled but grateful when I found out why. Even though his gun was filled with blanks, a blank can do quite a bit of damage, shot at close range. He deserved his fame as a crack shot. And I remember that he went right on telling me the story he had started without any further comment than, 'Lois, you'd better sit in a chair.' "

During the Christmas holidays of 1973, I arranged for Lois to see the film. Miles Kreuger, probably the greatest living authority on the American musical, was kind enough to invite both of us to his spacious New York apartment. I called for Lois at her apartment house, and as we were heading across town, she told me of her recent experience.

"I was mugged," she said. "Right outside my apartment house. The thief stole my purse with all my charge cards in it. He started charging things to me at various stores. The police caught him, but they decided not to press charges because it would take too long to get him to trial and the court would only let him off anyway."

Lois leaned back against the car seat.

"You don't talk, Jon, about the operations you've had any more," she sighed. "Not if you live in New York. Everyone talks about his mugging."

I could not help laughing.

Miles was a brilliant host. He had just assembled a group showing of George Gershwin pictures at the New York City Cultural Center. He had seen every surviving musical film made, but, curiously, he had never seen a Tom Mix Western.

"If you could see any film he made," I told him, as we sat in his comfortable living room on the Upper West Side, "I'm pleased that it's *Rider of Death Valley.*"

I turned to Lois as Miles was threading the projector. She retained the petite, fine features she'd had when she worked in Hollywood, and the years had been most gentle to her.

"There's been a lot of nonsense written about Tom's supposed voice problems," I remarked. "He only made ten sound films, nine features for Universal and a fifteen-chapter serial for Mascot. I have seen them all. Apparently, this observation is based upon seeing him in the chapter play *The Miracle Rider.* It was produced under harried conditions. Universal took care with his features. Tom was unsure of himself before a microphone, had difficulty adjusting to it in his first film, *Destry Rides Again.* But by the time he made *Rider,* he was becoming accustomed to the equipment."

"Al Rogell directed this picture," Lois returned. "I know when he gave me the screenplay, I was surprised at how much of it was really like a silent film. We all had our dialogue. But most of the film depended for its effectiveness on visual drama and facial expression, with dialogue as a supplement."

The room darkened, and *Rider of Death Valley* began. Forrest Stanley and Fred Kohler are covetous of Willard Robertson's gold mine, and Kohler does Robertson in. Tom happens on the scene and has the map to the mine torn into three parts. When Lois Wilson arrives from the East, Tom proposes they set out into Death Valley to locate the mine. By the time they make it to the mine, they're nearly out of water, and there is no water at the mine. Tom sends Tony back for help. Kohler and Stanley both lose their lives through greed, and Lois comes to know the truth. At one point in the dialogue, she anticipates this when she says: "Death Valley fills you with terrors, doesn't it?"

"It's all in how you look at it, I guess," Tom replies slowly. "I kinda like it myself. It doesn't pretend to be anything it isn't."

On March 20, 1932, Tom and Mabel Ward were remarried at Yuma, Arizona, in front of the courthouse. Lois was the bridesmaid and Dan Clark was Tom's best man. Mabel feared that her Mexican marriage certificate wouldn't be valid in the United States.

Mix's annual release schedule in the twenties at Fox called for seven pic-

Tom and little Edith Fellows on location for a scene from *Rider of Death Valley*.

Photo courtesy of MCA-Universal.

tures a year. His talking Westerns were so popular with exhibitors that the Universal management pushed ahead in order to have seven completed features for 1932, which meant working through the summer. Tom Mix again reigned supreme. In every aspect, his productions were superior. Virtually every other major Western star was compelled to work on very tight budgets for small independent companies, including at this time Harry Cohn's Columbia Pictures.

Tom's next picture, *Texas Bad Man* (Universal, 1932), with a screenplay by Jack Cunningham, was directed by Edward Laemmle. Fred Kohler was back as a villain. Laemmle, incidentally, was not related to Uncle Carl. When the Laemmle studio fortunes fell, he changed his name to Edward Lawrence. In *My Pal, the King* (Universal, 1932), Tom's fourth entry, Mickey Rooney was cast as the boy monarch of Ruritania, while Tom and Tony took great delight in educating him in the ways of a true Westerner.

The Fourth Horseman (Universal, 1932), Tom's fifth picture, was one of his very best, with Margaret Lindsey, like Lucile Browne another Universal ingenue, as the female lead. Fred Kohler and his gang take over a township which Margaret Lindsey owns but which has become valuable only because of a new dam project. Tom undertakes to put Kohler and his men out of business, and succeeds in winning Margaret's love as well.

During production of Tom's next picture, *Hidden Gold* (Universal, 1932), Tony took a terrific spill and seriously injured his hip. The working title of the film was *Oh Promise Me*. In the closing sequence, when Tom and Tony were to ride abreast the villain and fight, the horses keeping astride, until Tom toppled him, Tony stepped into a gopher hole and the two slammed to the ground. Tom broke three ribs and suffered internal injuries. For a while, doctors feared for his life.

A reporter from *Hollywood* magazine visited Tom shortly after his recovery at his bungalow on the Universal lot. "One room of the bungalow, approximately 40 feet square, is outfitted for a gymnasium," he wrote. "In the center is a regulation ring such as you will see in any fight club. Around the walls are punching bags, parallel bars, weight devices and a complete assortment of Indian clubs, dumb-bells, etc. And Tom, at 50-plus years of age, still devotes several hours a day to 'keeping fit.' Universal's trainers report that his endurance and agility are almost miraculous. Not long ago, he boxed three fast rounds with one of the leading light-heavyweights of the Pacific Coast. And they weren't courtesy rounds, either."

At twenty-three, Tony was retired. He was turned out to pasture at Mixville, Tom's newly acquired ranch some miles from Hollywood. Tony, Jr., was to be his official replacement. Tony related his story to Jack Hill

Tom and Lois Wilson interacting in *Rider of Death Valley*.

Photo courtesy of MCA-Universal.

Tom and Lois's double escaping just in the nick of time before the explosion.

Photo courtesy of MCA-Universal.

for an article in *Movie Classic*, published in January 1933. "If I were to circulate a petition for reinstatement," Tony was supposed to have commented, "there would be plenty of signers—people I've met, prominent ones, too. There would be ex-President Coolidge—I've been photographed with him; likewise President Hoover. I also knew Presidents Taft, Wilson and Harding. Four times I visited the White House, once inside to meet Mrs. Harding. Forty-eight governors, including Alfred E. Smith and Franklin D. Roosevelt, and mayors by the hundreds are my personal friends. Furthermore, royalty and foreign notables would come to my rescue. The Prince of Wales chatted with me in Tetterhalls, London. I met President von Hindenburg in Berlin, and the late President Gaston Doumergue in France. Sir Arthur Harris, Lord Mayor of London, looked me over and said I was a

Tom and Mabel Ward Mix being remarried at Yuma, Arizona, on March 20, 1932. Lois Wilson is standing right behind Mabel. Dan Clark, with his hand on the young girl's arm, was the best man.

Photo courtesy of *Views & Reviews* magazine.

fine horse, and der Herr Sehr Hoch-geboren Heinrich von Kleinberg, Burgermeister of Berlin, had the same idea only in German. On the same trip, I was presented to Prince Henry, of Prussia; Queen Marie, of Roumania; the Prince and Princess of Belgium; the Duke of Veraga, in Spain; Cardinal Merry del Val in Brussels and the Burgermeister of Amsterdam. . . ."

Tony went on. But he hastened, also, to stress what he and his long-time caretaker, Stumpy Simms, thought of the decision. "At first, Stumpy and I thought my retirement came, perhaps on account of the 'talkies'—you see, we started in the 'silents.' Stumpy knows a lot—he's a colored boy, only 63 and my groom for years, who sleeps in the same stall with me—but Stumpy pointed out that the 'talkies' hadn't retired Chaplin. He doesn't say any more in the new pictures than I do—and he is a good actor, too." At last, Tony recalled how he had always been on the side of law and order. "Say," he commented, "I've helped run down, outwit and arrest more bandits, cattle rustlers, stagecoach and bank robbers than are in jail right now. One thing I could never understand, though—after we caught 'em, they always got out and came back and robbed again. There were Duke Lee, Fred Kohler and even George Bancroft—we caught 'em robbing trains again and again, kidnapping, rustling cattle. But they never stayed in jail, at least not for long, they'd be back in the next picture—still bad."

Duke Lee was the villain in *Flaming Guns* (Universal, 1932), a comic, sophisticated Western with a modern setting which featured Ruth Hall as Tom's leading lady, screen daughter of William Farnum. The picture concludes with a wild chase on the part of Farnum, Fred Burns as the sheriff and the sheriff's men in one car, Tom and Ruth in another, racing for the border so they can be married. Tom switches to Tony, Jr., midway, and the two make it across and to the church.

Tom's next film was *Terror Trail* (Universal, 1933), which pitted him against John St. Polis and his paint horse gang, called that because all his riders have pinto mounts. Humor was effectively interjected into this picture: in one scene where Raymond Hatton's promiscuous shooting arouses Tom from his bed and brings him downstairs to the saloon on the run, having stopped to strap on his guns but having forgotten his pants; and in the last reel, where Tom exchanges the gang's usual mounts by saddling a bunch of unbroken mustangs that throws the outlaws every which way in their attempt to effect an escape.

It was an excellent series. In fact, I have said that the budget Westerns of the thirties would never include another series like it. And it came to an end with *Rustlers' Round-up* (Universal, 1933). Tom took another fall. His rib cage was heavily bandaged to the point where he had trouble speaking. But it was an excellent film. Tom went on location to Hoot Gibson's Round-Up and employed some unusual footage of himself leading a congress of riders and then the main events themselves. Halfway through the picture, Tom had a stagecoach race with Douglas Dumbrille. Dumbrille, together with Roy Stewart, a star of cheaply made independent Westerns in the twenties, plots to take Diane Sinclair's ranch away from her. Her screen brother, Pidge Beery, Noah's son, believes in Tom, Diane in Dumbrille. During the race, Dumbrille keeps hitting Tom in the face with his whip. Finally, fed up with it, Tom, in close range of the camera, jumps from his coach onto Dumbrille's, takes the whip away, jumps back, breaks the whip, and throws the pieces across at Dumbrille. Tom insisted on doing all of his own fights and, in one sequence, had Frank Lackteen, Bud Osborne, and a third heavy hanging on his neck. Henry MacRae directed the picture. The film also contained stock shots from *The Devil Horse* (Pathé, 1926) and a memorable meeting between Tom and William Desmond as a sheriff, which was written into the picture at Tom's request and which served little purpose except to demonstrate Desmond's ability at shooting a .45.

Tom's body was shattered. He felt tired and too old to keep the pace of producing a picture every seven weeks. He went to Uncle Carl and asked to be released from his contract. He suggested Hoot Gibson as a good substitute. Tom and Hoot may have fought their share in the twenties, but Tom respected the cowpoke and honestly thought he was more up to making Westerns than Tom was. Tom projected a world-wide tour with Tony, Jr., as less taxing to his metabolism. Both Bergerman and Uncle Carl were acutely disappointed. Tom's films were leading the Western field. Mix was obdurate.

"I've nearly died twice making these films," he told the old man. "The risks aren't worth it any more."

The Mix pictures were costing the studio a million dollars a year, but they were grossing three times that much at the box office. Uncle Carl argued with Tom, but to no avail. The Ralston Purina Company had approached him with a generous radio contract for the use of his name in a network program to be devoted to the exploits of Tom Mix. The nice part of the package was that Tom wouldn't have to do anything other than let them use his name.

Tom limped through his last scenes in *Rustlers' Round-up* and, on Christmas Day 1932, having crammed nine pictures into the schedule allotted for six, he rode off at the fade for what he thought was the last time. He even kissed Diane Sinclair firmly on the mouth.

24 / TIM McCOY AT COLUMBIA

Tim McCoy's second serial for Universal was *Heroes of the Flame* (Universal, 1931). George Morgan, Basil Dickey, and George H. Plympton were assigned to the continuity. Dickey and Plympton would be responsible over the years for generating some of the most exciting Universal serials, including the studio's *Flash Gordon*. Plympton, moreover, followed McCoy after *Heroes* to Columbia where he scripted Tim's first talking feature, *One Way Trail* (Columbia, 1931). And Plympton would have the distinction of scripting the last serial ever made for theatrical release in the United States, *Blazing the Overland Trail* (Columbia, 1956). *Heroes* was Tim's first non-Western, having a contemporary setting with Tim cast as a fire fighter.

Tim was scheduled for a third serial, to be based, as was *The Indians Are Coming,* on William F. Cody's memoirs. It was titled *Fighting with Buffalo Bill,* and Tim was to be cast as Cody. Good fortune smiled on Tim in the form of Samuel J. Briskin, who was associated at the time with the production of budget features at Columbia Pictures. Briskin had been with Columbia's president, Harry Cohn, since the founding of the company in the early twenties. Columbia was making money distributing the Sol Lesser/Buck Jones Westerns and was interested in expanding Western production. Tim was fully cognizant that the major studios had stopped making Westerns altogether, and the independents continued to dominate the field. Tim signed on as a contract player with Columbia in 1931 and was destined to remain with that studio longer than for any other. Tom Tyler, who had been appearing in a series of cheap Westerns for Syndicate, was picked up by Universal and cast as Buffalo Bill in *Fighting*. Although he would make several series Westerns in the thirties and early forties, his popularity in the sound era would never equal what it had been in the closing years of the twenties.

McCoy fared somewhat better. In all, he would make thirty-two features for Columbia, twenty-four of them Westerns. A first series of sixteen Westerns was followed by eight dramatic and adventure films that were distinctly in the programmer category, a precedent for which had been set by Tim's earlier period pieces at Metro and especially his second Universal serial. These were followed, in turn, by a second series of eight Westerns. While quality varied, at times drastically, these Westerns on the whole set a standard seldom maintained by any Western player of the thirties.

Tim McCoy sitting in his study at his home in Thermopolis, Wyoming, in the late twenties.

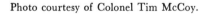

Photo courtesy of Colonel Tim McCoy.

The budgets for the first series averaged between $15,000 for pictures like *Silent Men* (Columbia, 1933) and $20,000 for some of the others. The general exploitation of McCoy at Columbia imitated Harry Rapf's program for him at M-G-M. Music was occasionally, and tastefully, included in several of the films, and Tim even found himself singing in *Daring Danger* (Columbia, 1932), although a decidedly non-Western song. He played his Westerner roles at Columbia with the same legitimacy and intensity that he had at Metro. The attempt to give McCoy matinee idol status led to naming a white lead horse from the Columbia stable "Pal," a moniker Tim kept whenever he called his horse anything. His costume was standardized with the assistance of Trem Carr, of Monogram, who would later work on the Three Mesquiteers wardrobe for Republic. Usually, it consisted of a dark blue shirt—cavalry blue to match his strikingly blue eyes—and an orange neckerchief, topped with a high-crown beaver Stetson.

The most distinctive aspect of McCoy's apparel was the hand-tooled leather trouser belt and gun belt with buckles of intricately designed Mexican silver. The ensemble was created for him by Ed Bohlin, a Swedish cowpuncher from Wyoming who ran a saddle shop in Hollywood. Generally, Tim would wear only one gun, a silver-plated, pearl-handled .45, although upon occasion, as in *The Law Beyond the Range* (Columbia, 1935), he might use two guns, utilizing the second holster slot on the gun belt.

Tim's image of the restrained, self-possessed Westerner really dates from this period. At Columbia he perfected the fastest draw of any cowboy on the screen. Otto Meyer, the film editor who worked on most of Tim's early Westerns, once told him how fast his draw actually was. At the rate of twenty-four frames per second, it took Tim exactly six frames from the blur of his hand to the smoke issuing from the end of his gun. This was part of Tim's reputation as a cowboy star during the talking picture era; the other part, the "man of destiny" image, was also born at Columbia.

If the "man of destiny" had a prototype, it was Tom Mix. In Mix's case, it was a psychological necessity, given his overwhelming fear of sound recording equipment and, therefore, minimal dialogue. Tim's first Columbia film was *One Way Trail* (Columbia, 1931), which, in plot, was quite similar to his earlier M-G-M features, above all *The Law of the Range* (M-G-M, 1928), particularly one scene where Tim was present at the death of his brother. Ray Taylor was the director on *One Way Trail*. Tim, recognizing the similarity of the scene with that in *Law,* studied his role sedulously, throwing himself into the part. The first take, swearing to avenge his brother, saw him wring emotion from his soul. The scene was played so powerfully that the technicians on the set were weeping; even Taylor was. But when it was finished, Taylor called Tim to one side, tears still in his eyes.

"You can't feel that much, Tim," he said. "If *you* do, your audience won't. You've got to play down the way you feel, so the audience can respond, feel it for you."

Tim went back and did the scene again, this time exercising control. He underplayed the part, forcing the viewer to guess by the merest suggestion as to the intensity of his emotion. It was effective. This became indigenous to his style when playing a complex scene.

Initially, at Columbia, Tim wore all-black outfits. William Boyd copied these when he came to play Hopalong Cassidy. Tim switched to a white Stetson with his third picture, *The Fighting Marshal* (Columbia, 1931). But like Ken Maynard, Tim alternated between white and black Stetsons throughout the thirties. There was no true identification of hats with hero and villain roles, at least not consciously; although many people, thinking back to the gloom that hung palpably outside darkened movie palaces, prefer to remember Tim—as I confess even I do—as he appeared in one scene in *Bulldog Courage* (Puritan, 1935). He is standing in intense sunlight, reflectors playing the glare off the brightness of his Stetson, shining in his cold, clear eyes, his face gleaming, the orange neckerchief flapping in the breeze, sharply contrasted with the blackness of his other attire.

William Colt MacDonald, who had achieved some success as a writer of Western fiction for the pulps, was hired by the Columbia Story Department in early 1932. Sometimes alone, but more commonly in collaboration with Wallace MacDonald, actor, writer, and eventually a producer in his own right, his stories were used as the basis for the McCoy features. The plot lines varied in quality from the very conventional *Daring Danger* (Columbia, 1932) to the totally confused *Cornered* (Columbia, 1932) to the genuinely suspenseful and engaging *Man of Action* (Columbia, 1933). Wallace MacDonald, in addition to scripting parts for himself in the McCoy films, had had a long association with motion pictures in general and, in Westerns like Ken Maynard's *Fightin' Thru* (Tiffany, 1930), gave a fine account of himself on the screen, typically playing drunks or tramps. Together the two MacDonalds helped make the McCoy series both remarkable and, at times, disappointing. They were, however, among the best writers Tim would have during the sound era, although no Westerns he ever made after leaving M-G-M could compare in terms of production value with the final entries in the Columbia series of 1934–35.

While Tim's life as a screen player was again becoming secure, his personal life was undergoing severe changes. On July 20, 1931, Agnes McCoy sued and won a divorce from him in Denver, Colorado. The decision gave her control of the ranch in Wyoming and possession of their three children, a daughter having been born a short time before. The grounds were cruelty, but Agnes summed it up more casually in an interview, saying Tim had "gone Hollywood." Agnes was awarded $200 a month alimony until the children became of age; Tim was still granted visiting privileges at his wont. The ranch at Thermopolis would remain Agnes' home for many years. Tim became an increasingly prominent figure in movie society. His long-time friendship with Ronald Colman dated from this period, as did close relationships with Warner Baxter and Richard Barthelmess. Since he was a youth, Tim had been self-sufficient; his enthusiasm for the entertainment industry was balanced by a perpetual curiosity about history and an interest in new surroundings. He did not really mind the disruption of his married life, became an extremely flashy dresser, and did not remarry for more than a decade.

John Wayne, having been dropped as a contract player by Fox, came to Columbia in 1932. Among other things, he managed to make an appearance in two of the McCoy series Westerns, *Texas Cyclone* and *Two Fisted Law*. In both he played a character sympathetic to Tim, although his morose attitude at having so few speaking lines estranged him from Tim, and his personal reaction to McCoy was that the Irish cowboy was cold and distant and he didn't like him. In *Texas Cyclone* (Columbia, 1932), the first team project with the two MacDonalds, Tim, cast as Pecos Grant, rides into the Arizona town of Stampede only to be greeted by everyone as Jim Rawlings, who is thought to be dead. Confiding in Vernon Dent, the silent comedian cast frequently in the McCoy films as a bartender, that he really isn't Rawlings, a knife flung at him, being drawn down upon, and

Tim in a poker game from *Riding Tornado* with Lafe McKee, Wheeler Oakman, and an unidentified extra. Vernon Dent looks on.

Rawlings' beautiful wife, played by Shirley Grey, all persuade him to stay. Although not exactly a dual role as he would play in *Riding Wild* (Columbia, 1935), the incredibility of a hero's look-alike quality to another character in the story was completely ignored and became a popular cliché in Westerns of the thirties, Ken Maynard probably using it more often than most.

In *Riding Tornado* (Columbia, 1932) the drama and tensions of a poker game were featured with facial studies of the players, Tim telling Wheeler Oakman that he plays cards to read a man's character and thinks it worthwhile to lose a thousand dollars just to see Oakman haunted by fear. This kind of sequence was popular with Tim and recurred regularly in subsequent years, most notably in *Aces and Eights* (Puritan, 1936), in which Tim was a professional cardsharp, *Six-gun Trail* (Victory, 1939) and *Trigger Fingers* (Victory, 1939), in which Tim played series character Lightning Bill Carson, and *Arizona Bound* (Monogram, 1941), the first in the Rough Rider series.

Two Fisted Law (Columbia, 1932), directed by D. Ross Lederman, as were most of the Columbia films with McCoy, credited William Colt MacDonald for the story and cast Wallace MacDonald and John Wayne playing Duke as Tim's loyal ranch hands. Tim has lost his ranch to Wheeler Oakman (on which fact *Photoplay* chuckled, "Heh! heh!"), who once loaned him money and then rustled his cattle so he would be unable to make good on it. Wally MacDonald and Duke were present for only part of the action, but it does indicate the direction in which William Colt MacDonald was heading and is, I suppose, among his first experiments with the trio Western idea he would develop in his forthcoming pulp novels about the Three Mesquiteers which, in its evolution at Republic, would include Duke Wayne as one of the heroes. As a scenarist, William Colt MacDonald's strongest suit, already apparent at Columbia, was his ability to draw sharply dramatic scenes and create a rugged, austere backdrop. This was, after all, the basic tradition of the pulps, and some writers, like Ernest Haycox, perfected it to an art. But, as was also true of the pulps, MacDonald's stories did not always enjoy consistent plot development, his narratives suffering from bad pacing, at times too much action, time lapse, and story transition packed into six reels. The impression of the pulp story is overwhelming when viewing many of Tim's features, but practices acceptable in literary fiction were not capable of effective cinematic treatment. When, as in *Man of Action* (Columbia, 1933), the story was suitable for the screen in every regard, a small masterpiece was the result. *Man of Action* is perhaps significant for another reason. It cast Julian Rivero as Tim's side-kick. It was from Julian that Tim learned the exaggerated Mexican accent which he used frequently in his later films for the small independent companies as the thirties came to a close, the screenplay generally calling for him to disguise himself as a Mexican or gypsy.

In autumn 1932 Tim made his masterpiece of the sound era for Columbia. McCoy persuaded Irving Briskin, Sam's brother, who was head of Western production, to appropriate nearly three times the money and take the entire company to Lander, Wyoming, to film a Western using the Arapahoe tribes which resided there on the Wind River Reservation. The screenplay was by Stuart Anthony. Anthony was a free-lance scenarist who was often assigned by Columbia to the Buck Jones Westerns. His plots, while commercial, were nothing extraordinary. But Tim talked with him, and together they worked out Tim's impassioned monologues in which Tim set down in the strongest possible terms the staggering injustices the red man had suffered in the wake of the white man's greed and insensitivity toward an alien race.

End of the Trail is in every way exceptional. It is acted, directed, and photographed with such intensity of feeling, with such passion and dedication, that it stands out among not only McCoy's Westerns of the thirties but among any series Western Columbia was ever to make. Benjamin Kline was the cinematographer, and the stock Indian footage from the film became a staple in subsequent Westerns both at Columbia and at other studios. As originally conceived, the plot was carefully and beautifully structured, filled with an impending sense of the total futility of the Indian, the tragedy of a crushed, dying race of men, driven literally to extinction. This historical conception of the red man was not only in contradiction to the typical Hollywood approach of *The Indians Are Coming,* but more, it deserves contrast with John Ford's agrarian dream, Chief John Big Tree saluting the flag of the thirteen colonies at the end of *Drums Along the Mohawk* (20th-Fox, 1939). It is simultaneously a repudiation of the glib fantasy of the one and the idealistic notions of the other.

Cast as Captain Tim Travers, McCoy is assigned to escort a small covered-wagon train through the Indian lands with a complement of twenty men. The Indians beset the train, and only Tim and two others escape. An envious fellow officer, Major Jenkins, played by Wheeler Oakman, who himself has been secretly supplying the Indians with rifles, throws suspicion on Tim in the eyes of Fort Raine's commanding officer, Colonel Burke, ably portrayed by Lafe McKee. When Oakman plants a letter in Tim's handwriting on a dead gunrunner, Tim is court-martialed and dishonorably discharged from the service.

Colonel Burke, in passing sentence, faults Tim for his sympathy with the red man.

"For reasons that you very well know," Tim responds in the first of his soliloquies, delivered with amazing effectiveness, "from the time that this government began dealing with the Indians, they have not kept a single one of their treaties. The Harney-Sanborn treaty ceded this country to the Sioux, the Arapahoe, and the Cheyenne. This treaty specified that all

One of the most familiar stock shots of the black and white era, the race across the Powder River in *End of the Trail*.

Photo courtesy of Columbia Pictures.

the land north of the North Platte River to the Yellowstone, from the Black Hills west to the Little Big Horn belonged to the Indians—ceded to them in a sacred treaty. When the white men made that treaty, they were very, very glad to get the rest of the country and leave the Indians this one little plot of ground. The Indians, on the other hand, realized that sooner or later the white men were going to smother them under and—if they could only protect their hunting grounds where the elk, the deer, the antelope, and the buffalo were, the country in which was buried the bones of their fathers—they were pretty well satisfied, too. If the white man would only live up to that treaty—and they expected him to do it. Now, some white fool has discovered gold in Montana. White settlers are pouring into that territory and pleading with the government to send troops out to protect them so they can take a short cut across the Indian country to the gold fields. And that's what we are here for: *to protect white men seeking gold!*"

The way *End of the Trail* was intended to conclude. Lafe McKee, Luana Walters, and Chief White Eagle gathered at Tim's grave. It didn't end this way and the footage long ago vanished.

Tim recalls Red Cloud's parley at Fort Laramie where the chief swore, " 'before I surrender that land, I'll fight and die fighting for the place where my fathers are buried.' We've never kept a single treaty with them. That's why I'm for the Indians, because in every instance the white man has been to blame. And—if these Indians take the warpath now, which they're surely going to do—I want to say to you, sir, the bloodshed that results will not be the fault of the Indians. The responsibility must rest entirely on the white man." Stripped of his rank, bitter and humiliated, Tim leaves the post with Sonny, an orphan whose parents were killed by Indians and whom Tim has adopted.

Three times during the course of the picture Lederman has the camera take a close-up of a soldier playing assembly on the bugle. Seated beside the swift current of the Powder River, where they have paused to rest, Sonny wants his stepfather to put him through his paces. In his boyish soprano, he imitates reveille, and would imitate taps, but they are overtaken by Wade Boteler who has deserted the post to join them. Before leaving, Boteler broke a man's arm and Major Jenkins is hot in pursuit. Sonny mounting behind Tim, the three make a break for it.

Sonny is mortally wounded in the chase. He dies before they can obtain medical assistance and is buried in a simple grave. A bluff, cutting off the dying sun, casts a shadow into the valley as Tim and Boteler make their way, smoke signals rising white, and then black against the sky. The Indians swoop down and surround them, Boteler remarking, "What difference does it make? We might as well be killed comin' as goin'."

They are taken to the Indian camp, tepees set along a mighty rock canyon wall, across an expanse of icy, silvery water. Tim greets Chief White Eagle, playing Red Cloud, as a friend. Luana Walters plays Luana, an Indian maiden who falls in love with Tim. Tim sits in consultation with the chiefs.

"I came to your council today to talk for peace," Tim tells them. "There must be *no* war. I know, I know all that, I know all that. . . . The Arapahoes have many grievances. I, too, have my grievances. My little boy, my son, was killed by my own people. Still, I talk for peace. Not because of what might happen to the white man, but thinking of you, my red brothers. The white men are as thick as the grass on the prairie. Their lodges and villages extend clear to the rising sun. When one white man is killed, a hundred others will come here to take his place. When an Arapahoe warrior is killed, there is an empty place in the lodge. Who is going to fill his place? That is why I talk for peace."

Burke, convinced that Tim is "a menace to the whites and a bad influence on the Indians," wants him returned to the fort. Tim is arrested and taken prisoner to face charges of treason. The Indians, enraged, circle the post and begin a siege, firing, outnumbering the men inside by five to one. Most of the soldiers are dead before Colonel Burke, having heard Major Jenkins' dying confession that he had framed Tim and was himself responsible for the crimes imputed to the other, pleads with Tim to stop the slaughter. Tim agrees to do so only when he reflects that it is the Indian who will suffer most from a victory. When the Indians win, it is called a massacre; when the cavalry takes its vengeance, it is called campaigning, until there isn't a single Indian left.

Appearing outside the post doors with a white neckerchief on his sword blade, he stops the fighting, only to be shot in the back by a crazed soldier. He dies in Lafe McKee's arms, having brought peace again between the

Indian and the cavalry. The film was intended to conclude with the solemn playing of taps over his grave, Luana, Chief White Eagle, and Lafe McKee in the foreground, the soldiers and Indians circled in the background.

The stills were prepared; the advance publicity was ready, the continuity and press books telling the story, the tragic enactment of the battle for a continent. But the Columbia executives felt the public would be offended by such an ending. What would the many children say to see their hero die before them on the screen? It might jeopardize McCoy's value as a property. And so fear pervaded. A work of art, direct, moving in its appeal, expired on the cutting-room floor. A new concluding sequence was shot when the troupe returned from Wyoming, with Tim, his arm in a sling, receiving his commission as Indian agent for the Powder River Res-

Si Jenks and Walter Brennan when playing old-timers at Columbia Pictures in the Tim McCoy series.

Photo courtesy of Columbia Pictures.

ervation. This is the picture as we have it today. But not even the compromise of its ending can spoil its dark and tragic counterpoint, its unforgettable poetry, force, and majesty.

George Melford, who was originally slated to direct *The Covered Wagon* before Jesse L. Lasky assigned James Cruze to the picture, directed Tim's next film, *Man of Action*. Several more Westerns and Columbia put Tim into a series of non-Western adventure pictures for the 1933–34 season. The policy decision was based on Columbia's appraisal of Tim as an actor and the feeling that he could be developed into another Jack Holt, also under contract to the studio at that time. Harry Cohn, tempestuous production chief, was incessantly and heatedly battling with Holt and hoped to use McCoy as a backup. Probably *Speedwings* (Columbia, 1934) was the best of them, although *Police Car 17* (Columbia, 1933) had elements to recommend it, as did the last film in the series, *A Man's Game* (Columbia, 1934).

Uncle Carl Laemmle, however, entered again upon Tim's fortunes. McCoy might have consolidated his career as a dramatic and action player had Laemmle not lured Buck Jones away from Columbia. Uncle Carl, having fired Ken Maynard after a dispute, replaced him with Jones. This left Columbia without a Western star. Tim was put back into Westerns for the 1934–35 release schedule. This second series of Columbia-McCoy Westerns represents the finest work Tim did in a group of films during the sound era, with only one weak release in the lot, *The Westerner* (Columbia, 1934), and among many good pictures two excellent entries, *The Law Beyond the Range* (Columbia, 1935) and *Justice of the Range* (Columbia, 1935).

Because in a final sense Tim McCoy was more an actor than anything else, action or melodrama in his films meant less than they would have in similar vehicles by Ken Maynard or Buck Jones. He had, therefore, in order to give a memorable performance, to depend for success precisely on what was the weakest element of the assembly-line Western in the thirties: the story, dialogue, and screenplay. In any Western, new or old, it is never the story itself that is so important, but how the story is told, how the events are shown to evolve, the characters to develop, the plot to unfold. As in classical tragedy or historical pageant, the basic outlines of the story are already well known to the audience before even the drama begins; this is part of its charm. Columbia, more often than not, provided Tim with intriguing scripts.

In 1935, after *Riding Wild,* Tim's five-year contract with Columbia Pictures was up for renewal. He had already been approached by Puritan Pictures, an independent company, to do a series of ten Westerns which, ostensibly, would give him greater opportunity to concentrate on serious acting. He wasn't totally committed to the idea, but Sigmund Neufeld and

Leslie Simmonds, producers for the series, kept pressing him. Columbia on the other hand wasn't certain whether or not they wanted to pick up McCoy's option. Their hesitation was reasonable. Larry Darmour, who had been independently making films on a states' rights basis under the Majestic banner, was negotiating with Columbia to release his series of Ken Maynard Westerns. Columbia thought Maynard might have a greater box-office draw. Bob Allen, who had played second lead to Tim in several of his second series entries, also wanted his own series, and Irving Briskin felt he might have potential. The budgets on the McCoy films in 1935 were nearly what they were in 1931 for both the Jones and the McCoy series Westerns combined. Columbia's delay was decisive for Neufeld and Simmonds. They got Tim to sign just hours before Columbia communicated its desire to renew Tim's contract.

Working now for Puritan meant Tim was entering a new phase in his career. He had worked for M-G-M, Universal, and then Columbia, always established film companies with strong distribution systems and a network of exchanges. Tim hadn't been happy, in the latter days, with the prevailing atmosphere at Columbia. But signing with a small independent using a states' rights system of distribution was a daring risk. Tim was guaranteed $4,000 a picture and one week shooting time for each of the ten projected films. He would never again work for a major studio as a contract player, nor, with the exception of *Bulldog Courage* (Puritan, 1935) and *The Gunman from Bodie* (Monogram, 1941), would he ever again make Westerns on a par with both Columbia series. Although the Columbia films were produced in blocks, they had about them an individuality and integrity that most of his later films lacked. Once more he was passing though an important transition in his life, keeping faith in Eddie Small's advice to never be out of work, no matter what else happened.

25 / HOOT GIBSON ON HARD TIMES

I have narrated how, upon leaving Universal, Hoot Gibson went to work for M. H. Hoffman. He signed a three-year contract, agreeing to make six specials a year. The films were initially budgeted at $60,000 with Hoot being paid $16,000 a picture. They were released on a states' rights basis.

Clearing the Range (Allied, 1931) was the first feature to be marketed. It was consistently amusing. I had occasion once, when Hoot was an old man, to ask him what his favorite sound film was, and he claimed it was *Wild Horse* (Allied, 1931), which followed *Clearing the Range*. Step'n Fetchit was cast as a humorous distraction, and the action centered around Hoot's beautiful palomino horse, Mutt, and the attempt to capture him. *Hard Hombre* (Allied, 1931) came next, which portrayed Hoot as a look-alike to a notorious bandit.

Local Bad Man (Allied, 1932) was fifth in the series. It was based on the Peter B. Kyne story "All for Love," which had appeared in *Cosmopolitan*. Sally Blane, Loretta Young's older sister, was the girl. *Spirit of the West* (Allied, 1932) was the last entry in the first set, with Hoot pretending to be a dumb cowpoke and getting the goods on Hooper Atchley and Al Bridge.

The pictures met with very poor distribution despite the many virtues of the screenplays and Hoot's performance in them. Hoot's marriage to Sally Eilers still preoccupied the fan magazines. *Movie Mirror* reported in the June 1933 issue that Sally went home to her mother on May 9, 1932. By May 10 attorneys for both sides issued a manifesto that the two were only having a marital vacation. Ben Lyon and his wife, Bebe Daniels, then made an effort to bring the couple back together, which apparently worked, and by the end of the month of May, Hoot had purchased a new home with his Allied money and he and Sally appeared to be happy again. On March 12, 1933, the press discovered that Hoot and Sally were no longer living with each other. By April 11, 1933, Sally commented to reporters, "Hoot is wooing me all over again. He is the perfect lover. We are working our lives out on a new, fresh basis. There is nothing like receiving real attention from the man you love. Life is just one perpetual courtship. It's a true love match. We are the happiest couple in Hollywood!" Hoot's reaction was to be quite depressed when he read this in the papers. On September 20, 1933, at Chihuahua, Hoot and Sally were divorced. "I hope Sally is very happy now," Hoot was quoted as remarking.

The Dude Bandit (Allied, 1932) began Hoot's 1932–33 season of Allied releases for Hoffman. It was a remake of *Clearing the Range;* even much of the dialogue was the same. *A Man's Land* (Allied, 1932) was the slowest and dullest picture in the series to that point, with Marion Shilling as the girl who inherits a spread with Hoot and wants to turn it into a dude ranch against Hoot's wishes.

Cowboy Counsellor (Allied, 1932) proved to be a far stronger entry, coming closest in comic content to the best of his Universal Jewel Westerns in the mid twenties. Fred Gilman, who physically resembled Hoot and was used frequently as his double, is framed by Jack Rutherford for a stage robbery. Sheila Mannors was cast as Gilman's sister and loquacious Bobby Nelson as his young brother. Hoot is a law book salesman whom Skeeter Bill Robbins recognizes as the same man who some years before was around selling medical books. Skeeter is Sheriff Al Bridge's deputy. Sheila goes to Hoot for help.

There are a number of comic interchanges between Hoot and various other characters in the film. Hoot suspects Rutherford and decides to search Rutherford's ranch. Without having any evidence, Hoot manufactures some by dressing up in the bandanna which the bandit wore and robbing the stage a second time, with the territorial judge on board. To keep Rutherford out of the courtroom to give testimony, Hoot plots with Sheila to promise to run away with him. Hoot is exposed during the trial, and the sheriff and his posse chase him out of town. On the way, Hoot encounters Rutherford, pursues him, the two finally plunging over a steep grade in the buckboard. The loot is found on Rutherford. Hoot is exonerated. He and Sheila are free to marry at the fade.

Hoffman did not have any better luck marketing the new Hoot Gibson Specials than he had had previously, since the bottom was falling out of the Western market. He had Hoot under contract but informed him that unless he received additional financing, there would be no more new production. Hoot entered the National Air Races once more that third of July, 1933. Ken Maynard was also entered in the race. Ken and the Hooter set out to lambaste each other, tried daredevil stunts, racing closer and closer to the guide poles. Forty thousand spectators saw Hoot's plane crash to the ground. Hoot was rushed to the emergency tent on the field, although he insisted on walking to the operating table. June Gale, one of the four Gale sisters in Hollywood seeking work in pictures, had been going with him since Hoot broke up with Sally, and she stayed at his side.

"As for June Gale and I getting married," Hoot told the press when he

Hoot Gibson and Kathryn Crawford in a comic sequence from *The Concentratin' Kid*. It was repeated exactly in *Trailin' Trouble* with Ken Maynard and Lola Andre.

Photo courtesy of Harold Kinkade, Jr.

could talk, "that is not going to happen. She wants a screen career and we both feel that marriage at this time would not help her. She is a very lovely person, though, and we both expect to continue our friendship and companionship." The newspapers carried stories of how Ken Maynard risked his life to aid Hoot after the smashup.

Hoot was off the screen for the 1933–34 season due to Hoffman. When Maynard had his falling out with Universal, Uncle Carl immediately approached the Hooter with an offer to return to the lot and resume Western production. Hoffman refused to release Hoot from the Allied contract. Finally, after some negotiation, Hoffman sold Hoot's contract to First Division pictures, and Hoot appeared in *Sunset Range* (First Division, 1935) and *Rainbow's End* (First Division, 1935), both of which had Hoot battling in a contemporary West setting with automobiles and big city gangsters.

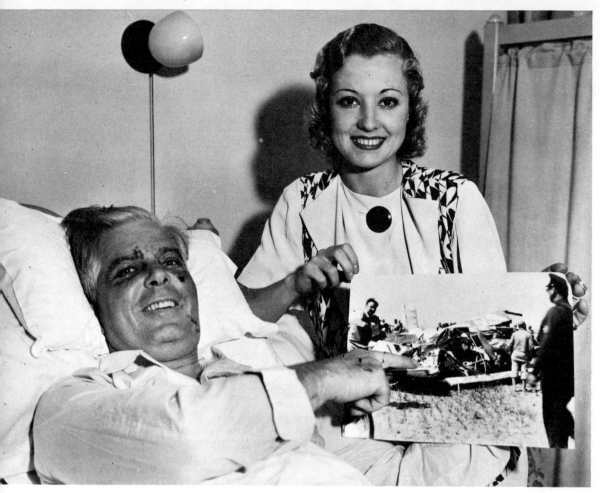

The Hooter pointing to the wreck of his plane after the National Air Races of 1933, with June Gale at his bedside.

Photo courtesy of Dorothy Dunstan Gibson.

With the exception of *Cowboy Counsellor* and *The Fighting Parson* (Allied, 1933), none of the films Hoot made for the independents in the thirties showed any sensitivity for his amazing capacity for pantomime, the fact that he was a first-rate cinema comedian, capable of provoking uproarious laughter by means of subtle facial and bodily gestures and expressions, low-keyed humor and clever antics, combined with his expert horsemanship. The independents instead kept trying to make Gibson into a matinee idol and in this they failed.

Hoot made two special appearances for RKO Radio, *Powdersmoke Range* (RKO, 1935) and *The Last Outlaw* (RKO, 1936), about which I will have more to say later. Meanwhile, he signed a contract for six independent Westerns to be produced by Walter Futter's Diversion Pictures and released through the Grand National exchanges. The entries were uneven in quality, due in large measure to F. W. Futter, Walter's younger brother, who was in charge of production. He had a penchant for semi-classical and sentimentally romantic music, which led to Otto Nicolai's Overture to *The Merry Wives of Windsor* being played under the credits at the beginning and end of several of the films, and in *Swifty* (Grand National, 1935), *Riding Avenger* (Grand National, 1936), both with June Gale as Hoot's leading lady, and *Cavalcade of the West* (Grand National, 1936) the addition of hopelessly inappropriate and emotionally discordant music being played now and then throughout the course of the action. This sickly musical accompaniment is constant in *Cavalcade of the West,* to such an annoying extent that the film simply cannot be enjoyed. The music does not follow the story line or the action, but rather is a symphonic composition pursuing an existence of its own.

Frontier Justice (Grand National, 1935) had a little well-synchronized background music; *Feud of the West* (Grand National, 1935) and *Lucky Terror* (Grand National, 1936) were notable in having none at all. Moreover, *Frontier Justice* and *Lucky Terror* were favored by entertaining screenplays that made some use of Hoot's aptitude for comedy and should therefore probably be ranked among his more memorable sound Westerns. Charles King's best role, utilizing him as a comedian and not as a villain, came with *Lucky Terror,* in which he played a derelict lawyer.

Candid photos of June Gale and Hoot together in Hollywood night clubs appeared frequently, even in *Photoplay* where it was rumored that Hoot was to make *A Cowboy in London* for British-Warner's, the film to be followed by an around-the-world tour, shooting a Western in exotic corners of the globe. It was a tragically difficult time for Hoot. None of these projects came to be. He swore he would never remarry, and he didn't until the forties. His film career as a star was at an end.

June Gale eventually married Oscar Levant. Shortly after Oscar died, I called June at her Hollywood home.

"Oscar was a wonderful man," she told me over the telephone. "I would be glad to tell you anything you want to know about him."

"It wasn't Oscar I called about," I said.

"No?" she asked slowly, suspicion in her voice.

"No," I said. "I wanted to ask you about Hoot Gibson."

"I don't remember a thing," she said sharply. "That was when I was a very young girl and a very long time ago."

It was nearly four years before he died of abdominal cancer at the Motion Picture Home that Hoot talked to me about the impact marriage had on his career. He had been a front man for Aristo-Blue Chinchillas, a firm that sold both chinchillas and franchises, a get-rich-quick scheme where breeding chinchillas in your basement or back yard was like having a gold mine.

"The demand got too great," Hoot said, laughing. "All these people would come out to see me and would get sold chinchillas. I was getting three hundred dollars a week and expenses to travel around the country. To come up with more chinchillas, the Aristo-Blue people started crossing them with rats and rabbits. The strain became so impure that you would have long ears or a ratlike tail. I got out of it as soon as I learned what they were doing."

"If you were to look back over your career in motion pictures, what would you say was most memorable about it?" I asked him.

"Never marry, Jon," he responded sagely. "Not when you're in the big money. The same thing happened to Tom Mix. Tom and I kept getting married, and the California divorce laws kept halving our holdings every time we got divorced. I lost four million dollars on marriages. I think Tom Mix lost a lot more." He sat back and regarded me for a moment. "I'm just a dumb cowpoke, I guess," he said then. "Because it was so much fun, I know I'd do it all over again."

He smiled and his eyes were clear.

26 / KEN MAYNARD AT UNIVERSAL

When he left Universal in 1930, Ken Maynard signed a contract for an undetermined number of pictures with Tiffany Productions. Samuel Bischoff was the production manager. Bischoff, who was born at Hartford, Connecticut, on August 11, 1890, first entered motion pictures in the mid twenties. He was appointed production supervisor at Columbia by Harry Cohn in 1928 and in 1931 took over at Tiffany. Bischoff's earliest directorial efforts were short comedies for E. W. Hammons' Educational Pictures. Educational was organized in 1920. Tiffany, which first emerged in 1929, had become an Educational subsidiary by the time Bischoff joined it.

Trem Carr, the independent producer associated with Tiffany who was sponsoring six Bob Steele pictures a year, was only another of a group of low-budget filmmakers who released through Educational. None of Maynard's Tiffany Westerns had any musical content save for his humming in his first feature, *Fightin' Thru* (Tiffany, 1930). Oddly enough, the influence of the musical content of Ken's Universal productions of 1929–30 could be seen reflected in Trem Carr's Westerns such as *Headin' North*

A landscape shot of the Warner ranch, a frequent location for outdoor pictures in the twenties and thirties.

Photo courtesy of *Views & Reviews* magazine.

(Tiffany, 1930), in which Bob Steele and Perry Murdock disguise themselves as an English dance hall team, singing and dancing through several arrangements.

Hammons had his own Educational exchange network supplying second- and third-run houses with a steady flow of cheap features and shorts. Educational maintained several distribution agreements with independent producers so as to provide a full release schedule. Most of the filming for these productions was done at the Tiffany California studio and, for interiors, at the Tec-Art studio. Space and equipment were also leased to other small production units to get maximum usage from existing facilities.

Neither Trem Carr nor Samuel Bischoff were really satisfied with the Educational setup. In 1932 Bischoff organized KBS Productions, the initials standing for the three partners, Burt Kelly, Samuel Bischoff, and William Saal. Trem Carr agreed to have KBS physically handle his second series of Bob Steele pictures and so they bore the KBS WorldWide logo.

Hammons and Educational's board of directors signed an exclusive contract with the Fox Film Corporation to release their films through the Fox exchanges for the next five years. W. Ray Johnston and Trem Carr joined together and founded Monogram Pictures Corporation, buying up the Educational exchanges for distribution purposes.

Johnston was born at Bristow, Iowa, on January 2, 1892. After an early career in newspaper reporting, real estate, and banking, he met the Shallenberger brothers who, when they purchased the old Thanhouser Film Corporation, hired Johnston and inducted him into the film business. While associated with the Shallenbergers, Johnston was responsible for introducing former train robber Al Jennings to the screen in a series of Western films. During the early twenties, Johnston had been vice-president under W. E. Shallenberger of Arrow Film Corporation, probably the major supplier for those years of low-low-grade Westerns. In 1924 Johnston organized his own company, Rayart Pictures, and, among other things, featured Kermit Maynard, Ken's younger brother, under the name of Tex Maynard in a series of starring Westerns. The Monogram distribution network in 1931 included twenty franchise holders and nineteen wholly owned exchanges. This was more or less the distribution system Monogram brought with it when, in 1935, it merged with Mascot and Consolidated to form Republic.

In 1932 Sid Rogell approached Jack L. Warner with an intriguing idea. He proposed to remake some of the Ken Maynard silent Westerns with John Wayne in a sound series, reusing all of the action footage and with Wayne dressed identically to Maynard to optimally match shots. Warner agreed to try the idea for six pictures in 1932–33. John Wayne was to get $125 a week; the pictures were to be filmed around stock. The first of the series, and the weakest, was *Ride Him Cowboy* (Warner's, 1932), based on Maynard's *The Unknown Cavalier* (First National, 1926). Leon Schlesinger, the cartoonist, was the nominal producer, Rogell his associate. The picture did have a good cast with Henry B. Walthall as the grandfather of young, attractive Ruth Hall. Wayne was give a palomino horse called Duke, which was readily translatable into adjoined sequences featuring action with Ken's Tarzan. Frank Hagney played the Hawk, a notorious bandit, who tries to frame Wayne and succeeds to the point where a mock trial is held before Otis Harlan as an incompetent judge. Rogell included a musical interlude at Walthall's ranch during a party in Ruth's honor.

By the time of the last film in the series, Duke was already working in Mascot serials. *The Man from Monterey* (Warner's, 1933) was based on Maynard's *The Canyon of Adventure* (First National, 1928) and depended very little on stock sequences. Ruth Hall played Lafe McKee's daughter, set in California in 1848 during the transition from Mexico to the United States. Duke was an army officer who prevents Ruth from being swindled out of her hacienda by Francis Ford.

Although the pictures were a moderate success, Ken hired Sid Rogell away to become, once again, his business manager at Universal for his new contract. Warner himself was apathetic. Duke signed with Trem Carr at Monogram for a series of Westerns to be produced by Paul Malvern. These Lone Star Westerns were intended to replace the Bob Steele series and were shot in as few as three days on $5,000 budgets. I will have more to say about these films later, but all of Duke's subsequent work for Republic for the next two decades was as a result of continuations, extensions, and revisions of this original Monogram contract.

Maynard's Tiffany pictures, on the whole, were nothing to write home about. Produced on minimum budgets of $12,000 to $15,000, with nearly identical casts, the action content was considerably reduced from what it had been in Ken's series for First National and Universal. Thanks to Bischoff's reorganization and independence from Tiffany's monetary limitations, his subsequent series for KBS was a substantial improvement. Ken's final Tiffany release, *Hell-Fire Austin* (Tiffany, 1932), was separately financed by a group of independent investors called Quadrangle Productions and, undoubtedly, holds up the best of the entire group. Maynard did a lot of trick riding; Nat Pendleton was an engaging side-kick; and the film ended with an exciting horse race.

Dynamite Ranch (WorldWide, 1932) was Ken's initial entry for KBS and, like the Duke Wayne Warner features, was filmed on the Warner ranch. Ken had been so impressed with Ruth Hall that he insisted Bischoff engage her for the picture and that the screenplay have a stronger love interest than was customary in programmer Westerns. It is a lyrical, poetic film due in large measure to the magic between Ken and Ruth on screen and Ted McCord's sympathetic photography. McCord had been Maynard's cameraman at Universal, and Sid Rogell had hired him for the Duke Wayne series. "Ted McCord . . . ," Ruth responded enthusiastically, as we sat together at the dining room table in her Hollywood apartment in 1970, "gave me every break he could with camera angles and lighting. I was referred to as 'the girl.' The girl had to hit her marks, which were chalk marks on the floor or the dirt, in order to receive the best light. Ted took the effort to give me the best light he could. . . . The girl had to play her scene right because there were no second takes and, horrors, of course no retakes. The main stars were coached but not the girls. Here Ted taught me how to use the light to my best advantage." When the Academy recognized Ted McCord's work with an Oscar for *The Sound of Music* (20th-Fox, 1965), it was acclaim he well deserved. Only Daniel B. Clark was his equal in series Westerns in the late twenties and early thirties. McCord photographed Maynard's finest sound Westerns, and it was one of the most intelligent things Ken ever did when he took McCord along with him for his second Universal contract.

Come on, Tarzan (WorldWide, 1932) followed *Dynamite Ranch* and was probably the most ambitious film Ken did while with Bischoff. Tarzan was cast as the leader of a herd of wild horses endangered by the schemings of Niles Welch, an agent for a dog food company. The horse footage was truly exceptional and was clipped as stock into numerous Westerns over the next twenty years. I commented in an earlier cinematograph how Tarzan rivaled Tony in directing horse action in *Just Tony* (Fox, 1922) in working with the wild herd in this picture. Edgar Rice Burroughs wasn't impressed, however. He brought suit against Maynard for using the name of his jungle hero in the title, terming it unfair competition. Ken answered Burroughs' allegation by pointing to the fact that he had been giving Tarzan billing since his First National days. The case was settled in 1935. Burroughs lost.

Ken cast Ruth Hall again for *Between Fighting Men* (WorldWide, 1932), his next picture after *Come on, Tarzan*. A scene was included which required Maynard and Wallace MacDonald to lasso Ruth, pull her to the ground in her boy's clothing, and, still thinking she's a boy, try to pull her pants off. Ruth had already met cinematographer Lee Garmes, who had begun in the industry with Thomas Ince at Culver City. Garmes would call for her every night in a limousine. On September 10, 1933, Lee and Ruth were married. However pugnacious Ken may have been to work with, he was always gallant and respectful toward his leading ladies. He confided to me years later that Ruth Hall was the loveliest person ever to play opposite him.

Some of the KBS pictures were blatantly absurd like *Tombstone Canyon* (WorldWide, 1932), in which Sheldon Lewis played the Phantom, a madman and murderer whose face has been disfigured by Frank Brownlee's heel. Lewis in a wild getup reminiscent of the Wolf Man in *The Lightning Warrior* keeps Brownlee and his gang terrified. At the conclusion of the film, in a rather improbable scene, Maynard discovers that Lewis is really his long-lost father. The picture is perhaps notable in that it marked the first time Cecilia Parker worked with Maynard.

In 1933 KBS changed its name to Admiral Productions, and Bischoff sold out, departing to join Warner Brothers, where he was to stay. Maynard's contract expired. But he had assembled quite an entourage for making Westerns: Alan James, who began directing him in *Come on, Tarzan;* Ruth Hall, Cecilia Parker, and Dorothy Dix as his leading ladies; Frank Rice as his off-and-on side-kick; and, naturally, Ted McCord.

I have already narrated to the reader how Uncle Carl tried to replace Tom Mix with Hoot Gibson. When Laemmle began making overtures to Maynard, Ken had Sid Rogell negotiate the contract. In the interim, Max and Arthur Alexander, two Poverty Row producers, got in touch with Maynard and proposed to sign him to a series of six Westerns. Ken informed them that a deal with Universal was imminent and that he would only accept their offer if the deal fell through. The Alexander brothers ignored this and began preparing stories, casting and arranging for crews and equipment. On the day they were set to commence shooting, Ken telephoned them at their office in Gower Gulch and said that the contract with Universal had been signed.

Max Alexander was in a quandary. He had a director, cast, and crew standing on location expecting Maynard to show up momentarily. He ran out of his office and searched the gulch for a cowboy suitable to star. He found one having his boots shined. After a brief conversation, he brought him back to his office and signed him up. It was none other than Jack Hoxie. Since Universal had dropped him, his career had completely eclipsed. He had made a serial for Mascot in 1927 and then tried touring with circuses.

"It seemed like such a good idea," Arthur Alexander recalled for me, "and, as Max pointed out, we were getting him so cheap. Just imagine how we felt when we rushed him out to location in a touring car, screeched to a halt, handed him a copy of the script, only to find out that Jack couldn't read!"

Ken had been receiving $8,000 a picture from Bischoff on the Tiffany productions. The KBS Westerns had $75,000 budgets, with Maynard raised to $10,000. At Universal he was to get $10,000 a week for each week shooting, $10,000 for the story, and a percentage of the profits the pictures made. He was to have his own unit. The pictures were to be Ken Maynard Productions. Henry Henigson, Universal story editor, was to have script approval, but after that Ken could make the films as he pleased. Ken would eventually go to work for the Alexander brothers in 1938 and make six pictures for them, being paid $2,500 for each; by that time, it was the best offer in town.

Universal needed a picture at once. Tom Mix's last Western had been released on March 16, 1933. Ken commenced production with a film tentatively titled *King of the Range*. Upon issue, it was altered to *King of the Arena*. He built a substantial part of the Wild West show sequences from stock footage of both himself and Jackie Hanlon doing numerous stunts and tricks from Ken's earlier Universal film *Parade of the West* (Universal, 1930). The Coleman Bros. circus was playing in North Hollywood, and he arranged for the show to be included in *King* as it had been in *Parade of the West,* so he could best match shots. Sid Rogell taught him how to do this as an economy move. Lucile Browne was cast as the girl.

Whatever else, by having his own unit and his freedom, Ken Maynard left his mark as a Western filmmaker. Kermit had found it difficult getting steady employment since his series for Rayart, and Ken gave him a job as his double while at KBS. Kermit was abstemious, and the brothers fought violently about Ken's drinking. Frank Rice appeared in nearly all the entries as Ken's side-kick, although he only played a small part as a policeman for *King of the Arena*. Ken appointed Alan James the unit director.

Ken further indulged his tendency for wild and outlandish plot ingredients. In *King* he featured his airplane and added some unusual flying interludes involving the crash of an adroitly constructed model. Michael Visoroff, who had played a friendly if not very convincing Mexican bandit in *Arizona Terror* (Tiffany, 1931) with Ken, was back for *King* as a cruel border outlaw in possession of a chemical pellet that, upon discharge, would char a man's face and was known as the black death. In *Fiddlin' Buckaroo* (Universal, 1933), next in the series, Ken is a ventriloquist. Ken pretends that Tarzan is capable of human speech, which so disconcerts jailer Bob McKenzie that Ken and Frank Rice are able to make good their escape. Although Ken had never been formally trained to read music, he did so by ear and could play the fiddle, guitar, banjo, and piano. In *Fiddlin'* he opened the picture at the depot on Mauser Street performing a few numbers while the townsfolk danced and Fred Kohler and his gang robbed the bank and the express office.

Ken's third film for Universal was *The Trail Drive* (Universal, 1933). It was one of his best, and I should like to narrate how it was conceived. If the reader has come to assume that sound altered the improvisational character of film production, the impression should be corrected at once. Improvisation was still the consort of creativity.

On a warm Friday afternoon in late June 1933, Ken called Nate Gatzert to his office in his bungalow on the Universal lot. Nate was the writer attached to Ken's unit and Ken's art director. Ken told Nate that he planned to take his wife, Mary, on a long-promised weekend to San Diego. While the Maynards were gone, Nate should put his mind to the story they would next film. Details could be worked out the following Monday. Above all, Ken stressed, he needed the money.

When the two met at Ken's bungalow on Monday, Gatzert was chagrined. He hadn't come up with a story.

"Neither have I," Ken said, laughing.

"I'm afraid you'll have to fire me," Nate said, "because I don't even know where to start."

Ken suggested they go to see Henigson anyway. They needed his approval before they could get money. They walked casually into his office and sat down. Henigson pretended to be slightly deaf.

"Have you got a story?" Henigson asked.

Ken nodded. "It opens," he said, "with ten thousand cattle stampeding. We're going to run the credits over the stampede."

Henigson now leaned forward so he might better hear.

"I'm the trail boss," Ken added.

"The girl?" Henigson inquired peremptorily. "How does the girl get in it?"

"Her father is killed and she is forced to go on the drive," Gatzert interjected.

"To protect her interests," Ken clarified. "Her father's already dead when the picture begins."

They spun out the story, making it up as they went along. They knew their business. A Western had to have action, villains, and a girl. When they finished, they had a check for $10,000 with which to commence production.

Ken found a herd large enough to give the illusion of ten thousand cows at the Miller and Lux ranch where he and Sig Rogell had previously gone to film *Land Beyond the Law* (First National, 1927). In exchange for a two-reel film about life on the ranch, shot by Maynard's unit, the owners permitted Ken to run thousands of dollars of beef off the cows before the picture was done, provoking a stampede and compelling the cattle to swim the Kern River. Ken composed the words and music of the theme song for the picture, titling it "The Trail Herd." It was played over the credits at the beginning (without the stampede!) and at the end, as well as Ken singing it himself near the campfire just before the final reel.

The leading lady was Cecilia Parker. The film contains the most exhilarating action footage in any of Ken's Westerns since *Kettle Creek* (Universal, 1930). It also has one totally incredible episode. Ken is trussed up to a wooden towel rack on a door opening onto the second-floor balcony of William Gould's saloon. Ken works the hinges of the door loose with his spurs and, still dragging the door, ostensibly falls backward onto the rumps of four horses hitched below. The horses bolt, and Ken is carried to the edge of town, where he is knocked to the ground, the door smashing in the process, Maynard uninjured. The stunt was managed by means of some clever dummy work.

Ken decided for his next picture to build the entire story around a song. He purchased screen rights to Curley Fletcher's ballad "The Strawberry Roan," had music added, and worked out his own fiddle accompaniment. Fletcher, in a few years, would portray Tom Mix on radio.

Exteriors for *The Strawberry Roan* were shot at the Prudential lot in Newhall and on the Universal back lot. Ken did not have unlimited access to a herd of wild horses and had to transport one to the Newhall location. He also obtained footage from *The Devil Horse* (Pathé, 1926), produced by Hal Roach and starring Rex, King of the Wild Horses, and Yakima Canutt. *The Devil Horse* contained a terrific battle for leadership of the herd between Rex and a paint billed on the credits as simply "The Killer." Ken chose to stage his spectacular sequences for *Roan* in the same dry ravine Roach had used in filming the earlier picture.

Ken Maynard, Frank Yaconelli, and Charles King singing the theme song to
The Strawberry Roan.

Ruth Hall had been signed as a contract player by Universal and had
appeared with Tom Mix in *Flaming Guns* (Universal, 1932). Ken chose
her to play opposite him for a third time. In the continuity, Ruth is thrown
from her horse and threatened by the onrush of a stampede. "As I recall,"
Ruth said, "the cameras were on a hill, so I do not think they really photographed what we saw. . . . Kermit and I were in a deep ravine behind
what appeared to me to be a board-and-bat structure in the middle of the
ravine. The thundering herd of wild horses came down upon us and some
of the horses were even breaking down the structure. It was a frightening
experience."

There was a compromise when it came to the scene where the roan was
to break into the bunkhouse. Superimposition shots of the roan in the room
were matched with actual shots of him smashing the door to enter and

jumping out through the window to escape. Ken wanted his waddies to stay in the bunkhouse through the entire sequence, but the roan he used was both mean and dangerous, and none of the wranglers would chance it.

Cliff Lyons stunted for Ken, especially in the horse action, while Kermit doubled him at other times. When Kermit later left the Maynard unit, Cliff remained Ken's principal double for the remainder of Ken's career in pictures. "Kermit was a pillar of strength and encouragement to me," Ruth Hall remarked, "and I will never cease to be grateful to him for his understanding and kindness. He seemed to have more control over Ken than anyone else. If he had to be spoken to, it was Kermit who approached him."

Ken sang twice in *The Strawberry Roan,* and the ballad completely dominated the film. If Maynard is to be cited as having created the format of the musical Western, this film is probably the first full-fledged realization of it. Frank Yaconelli and Charles King were Ken's saddle pals and, oddly enough, musical support. Charlie had been rather a brutal heavy in Ken's films for Tiffany, but his role in *Roan* is one of the very few that fully appreciated his latent talent for comic and humorous byplay. Typecasting, unfortunately, defeated what hopes Charlie may have had in pursuing this direction. He was born on February 21, 1895, at Hillsboro, Texas, and had entered the industry by being an extra in *The Birth of a Nation.* In the late twenties he had appeared in comic two-reelers for Universal. But in the sound era he was almost invariably a villain. Charlie constantly overspent the $125 a week he was paid and was always negotiating small loans from Ken, Alan James, Ted McCord, or Nate Gatzert. Charlie's untrusting wife would march up to the pay window on Fridays and collect Charlie's wages. But Charlie was a free spirit who bore his wife's watchful eye with a shrug of the shoulders.

As *The Strawberry Roan* opens, Ken rides up to a campfire where Charlie as Curley and Frank Yaconelli as Shanty are performing the theme song, which, in a splendid rendition, is also played under the beginning and end credits. Ken tells the story of how the song came to be written. Ken and his side-kicks are involved in the group roundup of the roan and the competition to break him. In the process, Ken exposes Harold Goodwin, James Marcus's foreman, of rustling horses and blaming it on the roan; and he and Ruth Hall fall in love. Together with Ruth, Ken sets the roan free, the theme coming up as they embrace at the fade.

Ruth's display of emotion was nowhere as passionate as her kissing John Wayne at the end of *The Man from Monterey* (Warner's, 1933). She had made the decision to leave the screen. Lee Garmes had presently signed with Sir Alexander Korda and was preparing to resettle in England.

It may well be that Ken Maynard's inner vision was of a world and a life-style none of us have ever known. But he wasn't commercially exploiting the dreams and hopes of theatrical patrons; he really believed in the possibility of what he projected on the screen. His personal life might contradict his cinematic fantasies, but the fantasies were what mattered most to him.

Cecilia Parker was back as Ken's leading lady for his next film, *Gun Justice* (Universal, 1933), which went into production in October and was released in December. It was a tightly plotted Western, if a trifle dull, with Walter Miller and Hooper Atchley as heavies vying with each other to steal Ken's uncle's ranch. Ken liked Hooper and had worked with him frequently in his Bischoff films, because Hooper was "such a little guy." The romantic interludes between Ken and Cecilia increased in their quaint charm.

When Maynard had completed *Gun Justice,* he left at once for Europe. His wife, Mary, accompanied him. His initial stop was London. Ken was pleased to learn that Universal was advertising British release of *The Strawberry Roan* on the sides of trams. He was amazed by the crowds that thronged everywhere about him. Many Londoners were curious as to just what a strawberry roan was. It sounded more like a flavor of ice cream than a horse. Ken hadn't screened the finished film at the studio. He saw it for the first time in Paris, dubbed into French.

Maynard was ebullient upon his return. In the drawing room of his new, spacious home on Las Palmas Avenue in Los Angeles, he sat at the piano and set to music the words he had written while traveling abroad.

> We're on our way to California
> On the wheels of destiny, roll on,
> Roll on you wheels through time and space
> Through all eternity.
>
> The red sun sets in our path in the West
> And our staggering wagons must come to a rest,
> With glory on high, we'll do or die
> We're children of destiny.
>
> CHORUS: Yo-ho, yo-ho, roll on, roll on,
> Our spirit never dies
> Through trackless sand to our promised land
> On wheels of destiny.

Ken later copyrighted the words and music, as he did the lyrics for the theme from *The Trail Drive,* and published both in his *Songs of the Trails,* which M. M. Cole brought out in piano/guitar format in 1935.

In a brief afterword which Maynard wrote for the novelization of *Wheels of Destiny,* published in 1934 by the Engel-van Wiseman Five Star Library, Ken commented, "the romance, the excitement and the villainy of the early

Ken, Frank Rice, Dorothy Dix, and little Freddy Sale, Jr., held up by Philo McCullough, out of camera range, in *Wheels of Destiny*.

West provide the material for your entertainment. Most of it is from real life. Men and women and even children lived dangerous lives in those pioneering years. When the frontier moved still further West there came the great ranches for cattle raising. The cowboys are the people who created the romance and the adventure that the Wild West has given you. Theirs is the story I like best to tell. . . ."

Wheels was Ken's first picture for the 1934 season, and he made it especially to please Uncle Carl. He budgeted it at $125,000, and Laemmle approved the expenditure when Maynard told him the picture would concern the Indian wars and would consist of the long, arduous, but ultimately successful quest for the promised land. Henigson could not authorize such an expensive outlay; and the picture ran over budget at that. But Uncle Carl didn't mind. He felt the subject matter particularly important.

Had Maynard not relied on stock footage as much as he did, including all the great Universal Indian films of the twenties from *The Flaming Frontier* to *The Indians Are Coming, Wheels* might easily have cost as much as a Cecil B. De Mille spectacular. Location shooting was done at Lone Pine at the base of Mount Whitney where salt flats, prairie lands, and mountain landscapes could be found within a few miles of each other. Maynard additionally made full use of both the Log Town and Mauser Street Western sets. He simulated a rainstorm and engineered a crossing of a river replete with lightning flashes on the Miller and Lux ranch. Among the Indians under contract to Universal, Ken made a wise choice in selecting John Big Tree to play Chief War Eagle. Big Tree's performance in *Wheels* makes an interesting contrast with his prior role in *Winners of the Wilderness* (M-G-M, 1927) and his later role in *She Wore a Yellow Ribbon* (RKO, 1949). Nate Gatzert based much of his screenplay on the major events depicted in *The Covered Wagon* and Raoul Walsh's *The Big Trail* (Fox, 1930). Ken's theme music, when fully orchestrated, so dominated the film and so aptly embodied the pioneer spirit that James Rolph, governor of California, recommended that it be adopted as the official state anthem.

For his leading lady, Ken picked Dorothy Dix, with whom he had worked in *Drum Taps* (WorldWide, 1933). She had a wide-eyed, innocent countenance that appealed to Ken. Whenever a film meant a lot to him, or the plot was close to his inveterate romantic streak, he named his heroines Mary. He did so here.

The film opens to the sparkling letters *GOLD,* a magic cry, it is said, that throughout the ages has tempted men to follow its glittering promise. Ken joins a wagon train to California, mostly because he is in love with Mary, Jay Wilsey's sister. Wilsey was still recognizable from his silent-film days as Buffalo Bill, Jr. Ken and Frank Rice interfere with Philo McCullough and his gang in their attempt to rob the map to Jay's gold mine. Ken embraces Mary as the wagons circle in full view of Mount Whitney, shining in the sun.

Ken: Well, honey, there's the end of our trail.

Mary: The promised land.

Ken's next picture was *Honor of the Range* (Universal, 1934). He had seen *She Done Him Wrong* (Paramount, 1933) and was quite taken with Mae West and her Gay Nineties setting. He tried to incorporate as many of these elements as possible into *Honor*. Nate Gatzert did the screenplay; Alan James directed. The picture begins with six heavy-hoofed dance hall girls doing a number. A drunk in the audience claims he knew one of them back in Indiana. In *The Pocatello Kid* (Tiffany, 1931) Maynard had played a dual role as the Kid and a crooked sheriff. The sheriff is killed off early in the action. In *Honor* Maynard revived a variation on this notion, playing Ken, an honest sheriff, and Clem, his twin brother, a crooked store-keeper. A high budget permitted a number of split-screen confrontations between the twins.

I cannot help but think that by virtue of the frequency with which he used this plot, perhaps it expressed some deep psychological impulse. While to the public the Maynards appeared happily married, the opposite was true. Ken brought back a large door from Venice which he hung on the entrance to his new home. He had a weather vane cut in the image of a horse and rider, marked with the initials KM, mounted on the peak of his Spanish-style roof. Mary began extensive socializing and often gave bridge parties. Maynard was resentful. He was keeping Mix's pace of a picture every seven weeks, returning from the lot late at night, studying his lines for the next day with the overhead light on in his limousine. His drinking intensified. Mary grew ashamed of Ken before her friends. This only made Ken worse. Purely for shock effect, he carried one of Mary's girl friends up the hall stairs to a bedroom, the terrified woman swooning. Ken bought a forty-foot yawl, hired a chauffeur (who would later work for Gene Autry), and took to living it up at his bungalow on the Universal lot.

Cecilia Parker was Ken's leading lady in *Honor*. If Ken wasn't in love with her, he certainly was in love with the innocence she projected. When Cecilia remarked to him that she had been raised in a convent, Ken attributed a similar background to Mary and delighted in telling friends of how he had kidnapped her by abduction one night when the nuns weren't looking. In *Honor of the Range* Ken's evil and weak brother spirits off Cecilia who is Ken's betrothed, taking her to Fred Kohler's hide-out in Bronson Canyon. I believe, in his frustration and unhappiness, Ken felt at times much in common with Clem. When it came to the most fundamental emotions, Ken Maynard was wholly inarticulate.

The plot of *Honor* called for Ken to disguise himself as Eddie Barnes, a song-and-dance man, performing a choreographic number, "She's Only a Bird in a Gilded Cage." There is a fabulous chase across the roof tops on Mauser Street. The film concludes with a long fistfight between Ken and Fred Kohler at the hide-out. The traditional song, "Buffalo Gal," dominates the picture.

Uncle Carl liked Ken's romanticism and the films he was making; he didn't care much for Maynard's irascible temperament. The Westerns were proving popular with exhibitors. But they were costing too much. Out of seven features, Maynard had not brought in a single film for less than $90,000, most of them costing more. Uncle Carl suggested to Junior that both he and story editor Henry Henigson keep a closer rein on Maynard. The Ken Maynard Westerns were getting bookings, but not anywhere near as many as the Tom Mix vehicles had. One of Ken's pictures would average ten thousand play-offs on a flat $30 one-to-seven-day contract. This figure should be contrasted with the Columbia Westerns with Buck Jones. The Jones pictures similarly averaged ten thousand play-offs at $25 flat rental, grossing $250,000 but costing no more than $25,000 to $35,000 to make. When Tom Mix made his last screen appearance in *The Miracle Rider* (Mascot 1935), the firm which was accustomed to eight or nine thousand bookings for their serials suddenly had bookings leap to better than twelve thousand. Uncle Carl thought that, frankly, the studio might be better off with Buck Jones. When Buck came on the lot again for his summer serial *The Red Rider* (Universal, 1934), Uncle Carl made it a point to meet and visit with him.

Ken knew that his budgets were excessive, but he closed his ears. Junior would prance onto his set twirling his long gold watch chain. He would order Maynard to exercise caution. Maynard would fly into a rage. He'd yell aloud to anyone within earshot that his films were all Ken Maynard Productions and that he knew very well what he was doing. The clashes between Junior and Maynard grew more bitter. Even Sid Rogell had to confess that he had problems controlling Maynard.

In May 1934, irked at all the pressure, Ken began work on *Doomed to Die*. It was his custom at the time to fly to Yucatán or South America in his airplane and take home movies during his crocodile hunts. Ken told Nate Gatzert to somehow get crocodiles into the screenplay and he'd charge his next trip off to the budget, getting miscellaneous shots. Gatzert had his difficulties, so Ken spun it out for him. No one was going to tell him how to make a Western. The final story, credited to Maynard, incorporated diffuse elements. Two Negroes were prominently in the cast, Martin Turner as Cinders and Hattie McDaniels as Clementine. Gloria Shea, who had been Ken's heroine in *Fiddlin' Buckaroo,* was once more cast opposite him.

After a semi-classical theme, the picture begins in the middle of a conversation with a blond-haired Maynard telling William Gould that he knows what Gould did to his father. They fight, and Harold Goodwin, back as Gould's son, murders Gould and blames it on Maynard. Cut to a dense jungle, Ken in heavy beard. Walter Miller as Dick Evans in one of Ken's familiar outfits is searching for Ken. Miller is a Texas Ranger. While they are not in the States, he arrests Maynard anyway, Maynard claiming that from the first he was "doomed to die." Attacked by crocodiles via the footage Ken shot with his own camera, the two splash around in the back lot lagoon. An obviously fake croc is stopped when Maynard props its mouth open with a stick. Miller is badly mauled. Later, in a shack, Maynard announces that he learned from the Indians how to amputate a leg with a white-hot iron. While Ken is heating the iron, Miller, justifiably skeptical, shoots himself. Regarding the corpse, Maynard is no less amazed than the viewer to discover that he and Miller beneath their beards are exact lookalikes.

This is scarcely an acceptable development. But it gets worse when Maynard returns to the town where Gould was killed, and both he and Walter Miller presumably lived only to have everyone save Gloria Shea recognize him as Ranger Evans rather than renegade Ken Masters. This is more than two reels into the picture. It turns out that Harold Goodwin is holding Bob Masters, Ken's father, prisoner at the deserted Masters' mansion because gold has been found beneath it. Insane for years, the elder Masters' reason is restored when Wally Wales hits him on the head with a gun barrel. Both Gloria Shea's father, who is a Ranger captain, and Cinders, Gloria's butler, although they have known Dick Evans since infancy, do not see through Ken's deception despite acknowledging the elder Masters at once. It is evident that they have known Ken and his father for years.

Maynard, according to his chaotic wont, intended the film as a parody. He thought it funny and entirely in keeping with the spirit of frontier hyperbole. Junior felt differently. He thought the picture ridiculous and complained vehemently about it to his father. Uncle Carl definitely wanted to replace Ken with Buck Jones, so he responded promptly. Ken was in Havana on a personal appearance. Uncle Carl summoned him back to the studio.

When Maynard entered the president's office, Uncle Carl jumped up from his desk, shaking a rebuking forefinger.

"You have made me a very bad picture, Ken," he said. "Why didn't you spend two or three thousand dollars more and make it a good picture?"

Maynard became irate. He referred to both his first Universal series and the present one.

"Mr. Laemmle," he stormed, "I have made sixteen very bad pictures."

"Change the picture, Ken," Laemmle insisted.

"This is Junior's doing," Maynard protested. "I'll quit first."

And he did.

I asked Ken years later if he harbored any animosity toward Uncle Carl.

"No, no," he responded passionately. "I loved the old man. Junior was the one I couldn't stand. My fight was with Junior."

I doubt if *Smoking Guns*, as the picture was called upon release, would have been an issue if the Laemmles hadn't desperately needed money and had Ken not made his Westerns such an expensive proposition. Like all series Westerns, Universal sold the Maynard Westerns as units, and the story line of *Smoking Guns* was no more nor less absurd than those of a good many such films, including several of Buck Jones's subsequent entries for Universal. Junior wanted Maynard out, and Uncle Carl liked Buck and wanted to cut costs.

Ken's cantankerousness and perversity may have finished him as an independent filmmaker, but his product at its best set the tone and character of the sound Westerns henceforth during the thirties and the early forties. They moved, with action and music. This basic formula, indeed, would produce such a state of cinematic lunacy in the decade ahead that no one prior to that time, not even Maynard, would have thought it feasible.

27 / BUCK JONES AT UNIVERSAL

Almost coincidentally with Tom Mix's retirement from the screen, the Western market hit an unprecedented slump. On April 1, 1933, *The Motion Picture Herald* reported: "A rapidly declining market for Westerns is cutting down production of this type of feature 50 to 75 per cent in Hollywood, threatening to eliminate them completely from the releasing schedules of motion picture distributors. Large and small distributors on both coasts currently agree that the market for Westerns is narrowing daily. Several companies will abandon such production completely, while others plan curtailment."

There were many factors and circumstances in the lives of Western players and financial situations behind the scenes with producers that led to many of the shifts and contractual agreements during the thirties and the fluidity of Western stars in their trek from studio to studio. This had not been the case in the twenties. Tom Mix and Buck Jones were with Fox for most of that decade. Hoot Gibson was at Universal for all of it. Tim McCoy and Ken Maynard, who came upon the scene in the middle of the decade, were only unseated by the advent of sound.

But undoubtedly the single largest cause of instability during the thirties was the Depression, which, as I have pointed out, everyone succeeded in ignoring. At any rate, the reasons for the slump in 1933 were variously cited as the move among exhibitors against double features, the money limitations of the independent producers, the restriction of action in sound films, and the proliferation of cheap Westerns. Trem Carr at Monogram was apparently the only one who recognized the money shortage as a contributing factor. "In other days," the *Herald* quoted Carr as saying, "a producer of Westerns could take from the South, alone, two-thirds or more

Buck and Uncle Carl Laemmle in 1935 at Universal City, entertaining boys from the East Side of Los Angeles composing the Buck Jones Rangers' Band.

Photo courtesy of Dell Jones.

of his production cost. If a picture cost $5,000, the producer was assured of getting $3,000 of it from that one territory. But the South has been the most seriously hit by the Depression. . . ."

I have told how Columbia made an effort to star Tim McCoy in non-Westerns. In part, this was generated by the slump in the Western market. The *Herald* commented, "Irving Briskin, in charge of Columbia Western production in Hollywood, said no agreement had been reached with Buck Jones on financial phases of a new contract. . . . From Columbia's headquarters in New York, Vice-President Jack Cohn attributed the decline to over-production of Westerns. 'There are far too many made,' he said. Columbia is handling 16 in the current season and the same number probably will prevail during 1933–34. . . . For the first time in his long cowboy career, Columbia's Buck Jones appears currently in a role far removed from the corral and wide open spaces, in a setting of skyscrapers and night clubs, in *Child of Manhattan*. In this, he plays an adventurer on Broadway, and later, in a Mexican border resort."

In reaction to the slump, RKO abandoned their Tom Keene series and did not resume series Westerns until much later with the coming of George O'Brien. Jack L. Warner used the slump as an excuse to discontinue the John Wayne series and didn't begin again until the late thirties with Dick Foran. Allied Pictures employed the slump as an explanation for their problems with Hoot Gibson and the discontinuance of his series of specials. The Freuler Film Associates stopped production on their Tom Tyler series of low-low-budget features. Educational-WorldWide, with the departure of Samuel Bischoff from KBS and the termination of Ken Maynard's contract, pointed to the slump as their rationale for no longer distributing Westerns. Fox Film Corporation sold out George O'Brien's contract to Sol Lesser, who agreed to independently produce the O'Brien Westerns for Fox release. Paramount once more slowed down production on their Zane Grey series.

Universal and Mascot were the exceptions to this trend. In Universal's case, Uncle Carl liked Westerns and continued to believe in them. While all of this cutting back was taking place, Universal contracted Maynard to make Westerns on what, by comparison, were excessively lavish budgets. "Mascot Pictures," the *Herald* noted, "has struck upon a unique solution. They are injecting into their Western features and serials a bit of modern life and action, using airplanes instead of horses, in a chase of villains, and other such phases, in which they have met some success. J. L. Wickland, production manager for Mascot, believes there will always be a demand for some Westerns. 'Perhaps some of the producers are suffering from overproduction of Westerns,' he said. 'We are modernizing them.' "

It was in this atmosphere that Buck finished out his contract with Columbia. His last four features following the hiatus to make *Gordon of Ghost City* for Universal were among the weakest pictures of his career. The *Herald* was wrong in its contention that he had never made a non-Western, but Buck's principal motivation as a man and as a filmmaker was his deep-seated desire to make Westerns. *The Thrill Hunter* (Columbia, 1933), best of the four, directed by George B. Seitz, cast Buck as a cow-puncher who negotiates himself a Hollywood contract on the basis that he is a world champion racing driver and stunt pilot. He concludes the picture saving Dorothy Revier by commandeering a plane in which to overtake the villains. Tim McCoy had a similar plot for his *Speedwings* (Columbia 1934) in which McCoy chases by airplane the villains who have kidnapped Evalyn Knapp and are holding her prisoner on a rushing train. I have already told the reader how Ken Maynard included his plane in making *King of the Arena* (Universal, 1933).

The Fighting Code (Columbia, 1933) was a straight Western combining plot ingredients from Tim McCoy's *Texas Cyclone* (Columbia, 1932) and Ken Maynard's *The Lone Avenger* (WorldWide, 1933). *The Fighting Ranger* (Columbia, 1934) was, as I have noted, a remake of *Border Law* (Columbia, 1931). The only thing that can really be said in its favor is that Dorothy Revier made a far more attractive Tonita than Lupita Tovar had in the earlier film. Buck's final Columbia entry was *The Man Trailer* (Columbia, 1934), which was a remake of *The Lone Rider,* (Columbia, 1930), his first film for Columbia release.

Buck's Columbia contract was not renewed. He was still negotiating with Irving Briskin when he went to Universal in June to make another summer serial, *The Red Rider*. While in production on it, Ken Maynard had his blowup with the Laemmles. Buck was immediately summoned to Uncle Carl's office and an offer made to him to become a Universal contract player. Buck jumped at the opportunity. He had been very depressed at Columbia and not at all happy with his latest vehicles. Universal proposed to increase his weekly earnings from $500 to $1,000, the total to be charged off against the $65,000 budgets allotted to each of his Westerns. Buck, like Maynard, was to be responsible for making six Westerns a season; like Maynard, he was to have his own production unit; but unlike Maynard, he was to have no participation nor anything like either the salary Maynard had been commanding or the budgets Maynard had insisted on and received. Buck was, needless to say, ecstatic, and the Laemmles were pleased to have cut their costs by one-half for an identical number of pictures with a Western player nearly comparable to Maynard in popularity.

There was, however, one stipulation. By a separate contract, Buck had to agree to make two more summer serials for Henry MacRae. He would be paid for these on a per serial basis and would have to film them in June of each year. Since the shooting schedules on Buck's features were a month or less, this gave him a regular salary plus a substantial payment for the chapter plays in return for seven months' work a year. But it also gave him maximum theatrical exposure. The serials were to run fifteen chapters each, which, when combined with six features, gave him a potential twenty-one-week playing time in thousands of theaters across the country. Production for the 1934–35 season was set to commence in August.

The Red Rider was based on a novel by W. C. Tuttle entitled *The Redhead from Sun Dog*. Buck liked the novel when he originally read it and bought motion picture rights to it from Tuttle. Jones proposed to MacRae that the story would be a good one for a serial and suggested MacRae read it. Universal ended up buying the screen rights from Buck for $25,000. When Tuttle learned from Buck what had happened, he sent

Buck an additional copy, inscribed with his hope that the *Redhead* would be the best picture of the year.

As an adaptation, *The Red Rider* followed rather closely the outlines of the plot in the book. Buck changed the lead character's name from Brick Davidson to Red Davidson, but most of the principal events were transposed from the novel to the screen. There was humor in Tuttle's story, and this element was emphasized for the chapter play. Walter Miller was cast as Jim Breen, the leader of a gang of rustlers and border bandits. Charles K. French, the star of so many early short Westerns in the teens, was Marion Shilling's screen father. Grant Withers played Buck's long-time chum, Silent Slade. But the most splendid casting of all was that of Richard Cramer as Joe Portos, with Jim Thorpe and Monte Montague as his slow-witted cousins.

Virtually all the heavies in *The Red Rider,* beginning with Jim Corey, Richard Cramer, Walter Miller, Monte Montague, Art Ortega, Bud Osborne, Jim Thorpe, and Al Fergusson.

Photo courtesy of MCA-Universal.

Having seen virtually all of the sound Western serials and a good many of the silent entries, I can say of *The Red Rider* that, while it may not have had much action or a powerfully dramatic story line, it did possess exceedingly human characterizations. There are many scenes of ranch life with Buck and Edmund Cobb as his pal Johnny Snow, or romantic scheming among the women, Marion Shilling for Buck, Margaret La Marr for Grant Withers, or Cobb's crush on Marion, or the informal scenes of life at Breen's hide-out and the detailed relationships between Breen and his gringo bad men and Joe Portos and his Mexican cousins—all of which remain utterly unique among the series Westerns produced during the thirties or forties, and above all among the Western serials from the sound era. The comedy grows out of situation and human nature in its eccentricity. Assessed in these terms, *The Red Rider* might very well be Buck Jones's finest talking Western.

After Buck allows Silent Slade to escape from his jail, Silent heads south and joins the gang led by Walter Miller, the man guilty of the crime of which Silent was accused. Buck follows. Miller is partners with Joe Portos in trying to get possession of the Rancho del Rosa. Buck frustrates their plans, and Silent is cleared by the end of the final episode.

Buck's first feature for Universal was *Rocky Rhodes* (Universal, 1934). For his initial entries, Buck kept Ted McCord as his cinematographer. Al Raboch, best known at the time for the art direction on *Ben-Hur* (M-G-M, 1925), was the nominal director, but just as much as Maynard, Buck intended to make films *his* way. Like *The Red Rider, Rocky* was based on a story by W. C. Tuttle and even featured Walter Miller again as the principal villain. Because of Buck's penchant for using his books as the basis for his screenplays, Tuttle began sending him every new novel he wrote, inscribing them typically, "To Buck, who makes 'em in celluloid." Sheila Terry, who had appeared opposite John Wayne in *Haunted Gold* (Warner's, 1932), was the girl. Stanley Fields played Buck's side-kick and made an obvious effort to imitate Wallace Beery in his characterization. The story opens in Chicago but swiftly changes to Arizona, where Buck and Fields venture after hearing about Walter Miller's land-grabbing activities.

When a Man Sees Red (Universal, 1934) came next. It was directed by Alan James and photographed by Ted McCord. It was Buck's first production to stress situation over action, with Peggy Campbell playing the girl, actually Buck's ward, whom he brings West and attempts to guide in the ways of the world. Syd Saylor, who had appeared with Buck in *Men Without Law* (Columbia, 1930), was back, and Dorothy Revier, following the format laid down by *The Red Rider,* was the second feminine lead. Dorothy and Buck apparently became rather close. She appeared with him several times, of course, at Columbia, and worked with him frequently at

Universal. Buck got Bill Boyd to have her cast in *The Eagle's Brood* (Paramount, 1935), the second Hopalong Cassidy film Boyd made for Harry Sherman.

Buck incorporated his production unit under the name Buck Jones Productions and appointed Irene Schreck as his business manager. He took an active interest in the continuation of the Buck Jones Rangers and had a group of boys, all from poor families in Los Angeles, outfitted in uniforms and bought them musical instruments. The band gave a special performance on the Universal lot for Uncle Carl, who was delighted with the whole thing. Although Buck had completely recovered from the financial catastrophe of his circus venture, it left its stamp on him. He was more often serious, even grave. His pictures, now that they were wholly his personal vehicles, were not without humor, but they never approached the totally comic, free-wheeling atmosphere that his silent Fox films had had.

Buck was an insatiable reader of pulp literature, not only Westerns but science fiction. In his own way, he had as great a proclivity as Maynard had for zany and bizarre plot ingredients. *The Crimson Trail* (Universal, 1935), Buck's third feature, cast John Bleifer in the role of Loco. Bleifer, if he is remembered at all, probably enjoyed his moment of glory in this film, followed by his portrayal of Boris Karloff's keeper in *Charlie Chan at the Opera* (20th-Fox, 1937). He overdid it. His cackling and weird chuckling, with Buck bound to a chair hand and foot, his counting off on his fingers the four men he has pushed over a cliff to their doom, Buck making five, grasping his thumb and grinning crazily at Buck, it would be difficult to be sincerely terrified. Polly Ann Young, Loretta's eldest sister, was Buck's leading lady, proving herself to be a surprisingly capable actress. Ward Bond was the principal heavy. Unquestionably, Ward was unhappy with his lot. He had battled unsuccessfully against Buck in the early days at Columbia and was presently menacing Ken Maynard in Ken's series of features for Larry Darmour. Ward couldn't see any reason why he shouldn't be a hero. He bought one of Maynard's fancy gun belts for his role in *The Crimson Trail*. John Ford later indulged his sense of perverse fun considerably at Ward's expense once he realized the passion which inspired the man's ambition. Cliff Lyons became Buck's customary double. This entry made up for in action whatever it may have lacked in logic, with nearly three reels devoted to an extended chase sequence implemented by running inserts and truck shots.

Stone of Silver Creek (Universal, 1935) slowed everything down again, with virtually no action of any kind. But the film remains one of Buck's best, a combination light comedy and delicate social drama. The plot is actually a reversal of the Hart formula. Instead of being reformed by Niles Welch's sermonizing, Buck manages to win the parson around to solving criminal problems by means of Western justice rather than Bible-thumping.

After completion of *Border Brigands* (Universal, 1935), which featured Fred Kohler as the chief villain, Buck went into production on his third Universal chapter play, *The Roaring West* (Universal, 1935). It is probably Buck's most disappointing serial, Universal's competitive offering against Mascot's *The Miracle Rider,* with Tom Mix. Entire episodes were built out of stock footage. Chapter 6 was shot around lengthy sequences from Ken Maynard's *The Wagon Master* (Universal, 1929), with Maynard and Tarzan, looking nothing at all like Buck and Silver, plainly visible in medium and long shots. Music was introduced into natural settings, such as the performance of "The Strawberry Roan" when Charlie King, this time a villain, enters a saloon in Chapter 9.

The Ivory-handled Guns was Buck's second entry of six for the 1935–36 season. Ray Taylor, who had directed *The Roaring West* (Universal, 1935) and before that *Gordon of Ghost City* (Universal, 1933) was a good man at both action and drama. Buck chose to use him increasingly in his films until Taylor signed with Republic in late 1936. Taylor directed *Ivory-handled Guns.* The film was shot at Universal City and the Monogram

John Bleifer menacing Buck Jones in *The Crimson Trail*.

ranch. It opens to tension over a poker game. Buck is challenged by Joseph Girard, but he refuses to draw against him. Walter Miller, back this time as the Wolverine Kid, calls Buck yellow and is knocked cold. Buck walks out of the saloon. Frank Rice is his side-kick.

Buck genuinely liked Walter Miller and, I think, preferred to cross swords with him. He was perhaps more aptly cast as a villain than he had been as a serial hero at Pathé. Ken Maynard, Buck, and George O'Brien, with all of whom he worked, treated him with professional respect. When, subsequently, Miller worked at Republic, this wasn't the case. He died on March 28, 1940, two days after appearing in a fight sequence for a Gene Autry Western where no punches were pulled. He was felled by a heart attack, the result of undue strain.

Buck's father, played by Carl Stockdale, is crippled and in a wheel chair. Walter Miller as the Wolverine Kid is sworn to kill Buck. Both the Kid and Buck have an ivory-handled gun. Buck's father tells Buck that peace will not reign until only one man has possession of both guns. Buck gives chase of the Kid in the last reel to the agitato theme from *Mystery Mountain* (Mascot, 1934). In the ensuing fight, the Kid's gun goes off, apparently killing the Kid and possibly crippling Buck, as Buck's father had been crippled fighting with the Kid's father.

The Ivory-handled Guns is unquestionably a mature Western, although it may have a bit too much story to be adequately told in only an hour. Indeed, Buck's Westerns generally from this point on introduced definite elements of maturity not at all common to matinee features. In part this came about as a result of Buck's extensive reading of Western fiction, and, in part, because of Harry Sherman's series for Paramount release based on Clarence E. Mulford's novels.

William Boyd and Buck had long been friends when Boyd was signed to play Hopalong Cassidy. They both thought it immensely funny and that it could never last. Between marriages, Boyd, in his carousing, would make it to Buck's back door in the wee hours, and the two would sit in the kitchen talking until the sun was warm against the windows. Once Bill became identified with the role of Hopalong, he was sadly irritated when children, whom he hated with a passion, would accost him in public for his autograph. At a football game with Buck, the two were mobbed, Boyd breaking out into scathing invective, demanding the "little bastards" stay away from them. "Careful of those little bastards, Bill," Buck remonstrated him. "They're your public. Without 'em, you haven't anything."

Sunset of Power (Universal, 1935), Buck's next feature after *The Ivory-handled Guns,* owes much of its composition to Boyd. Buck had seen *Hop-A-Long Cassidy* (Paramount, 1935) and decided to duplicate certain elements. Charles Middleton, who had played Buck Peters of the Bar 20, was cast in *Sunset* as a crafty and fusty ranch owner. Ben Corbett

Silver untying Charlotte Wynters in *The Ivory-handled Guns.*

Photo courtesy of MCA-Universal.

and Charlie King were Buck's side-kicks, forming a trio. Dorothy Dix was the girl.

Pell Mitchell, production manager of the Darmour studio, currently producing a Ken Maynard series, was widely quoted in the trades as saying, "Westerns must have a more romantic atmosphere. The people are satiated with the old-time, stereotyped, rubber-stamped 'horse operas.'" Harry Sherman was emphasizing situation over action, and so was Maynard, with the usual Maynard stress on romance. Buck revised his story lines in keeping with what he felt were the new trends.

Unfortunately, he got carried away and, disarmingly, began writing his own stories, which in many cases combined totally contradictory elements. *The Cowboy and the Kid* (Universal, 1936) closed out the season. Buck sent Dell on a round-the-world tour, and Dorothy Revier was back as his costar. La Revier, who had been specializing by this time in playing screen tarts and trollops in films like *Sin's Pay Day* (Mayfair, 1932), *Widow in Scarlet* (Mayfair, 1932), and, as I have mentioned, the Mae Westian strumpet in *The Eagle's Brood,* felt really out of character as a school marm. Buck milked the situation for more than it had, playing father to a boy orphaned by villainy at the beginning of the picture.

The Phantom Rider (Universal, 1936), Buck's fourth serial, was a pleasant interruption to all this. Suggested by *Sunset of Power,* Buck played both an undercover ranger and, when cloaked in a white cape and white sheath for his Stetson, a Phantom frustrating the efforts of Harry Woods, Charlie King, and the gang to seize possession of the Hidden Valley ranch. A special song featuring a reference to Hidden Valley was composed for the serial and sung in several episodes, as well as an excellent rendition of "The Old Chisholm Trail." The chapter play had surprisingly fine production values when compared to *The Roaring West.*

Between the release of Buck's third Universal serial and his fourth, the studio passed into the hands of new ownership. Despite Stanley Bergerman's attempt to restore some of the former guidelines to the kind of film fare Universal produced, Junior was never silent in his ambition to make big pictures. Junior got his father's approval to produce a Western epic, to be directed by Sergei Eisenstein and to star British actor Francis L. Sullivan. The Universal financial condition was such that no extraordinary expenditures of any sort should have been made. Junior argued that it was worth a risk and, besides, it would be a Western and an epic, and the combination never failed at the box office.

The production, however, appeared to be jinxed. The subject was to be the life of John Augustus Sutter, who in 1849 discovered gold in California. The role eventually went to Edward Arnold, who seemed perfectly cast as the German-born immigrant who dreamed and speculated, found gold, and finally lost everything. Howard Hawks took over the direction for a few sequences and then James Cruze was assigned to the picture. Cruze intended to make *Sutter's Gold* (Universal, 1936) an epic successor to his silent masterpiece *The Covered Wagon* and his grand *Pony Express* (Paramount, 1925). Cruze spent thousands upon thousands of dollars Universal didn't have filming widespread location scenes, a spectacular gold rush, battle and mob scenes. Uncle Carl, who apparently believed in the project, went to A. P. Giannini, now with the Bank of America, and requested a substantial loan. Giannini, after consulting his board, informed the Little Champ that Myron Selznick, the agent and one of the bank's shareholders, rejected the proposed loan, ostensibly out of resentment of Laemmle's firing Lewis J. Selznick from IMP years before in New York. Laemmle next went to Irving and Norma Thalberg, as I had occasion to mention previously, and received a personal loan sufficient to finish the picture. But it was already too late for the Laemmles. Under acute pressure, Uncle Carl sold out his interest in Universal and retired from the industry, the transfer of stock taking place on April 2, 1936, *Sutter's Gold* being released to very little business on April 13, 1936, lacking as it did a name star and constituting, at best, a loose, episodic story that defied coherence.

J. Cheever Cowdin was elected chairman of the board. Charles R. Rogers, who had produced the Ken Maynard First National Westerns, became the new vice-president in charge of production at Universal City studios. Uncle Carl, reputedly, received $5 million for his stock. He immediately set about investing some of this in annuities for his children, Junior and Rosabelle Bergerman. Concurrently, Sid Rogell became studio manager for RKO Radio Pictures and RKO-Pathé. Rogers at Universal established a new policy of developing star values and, with the tremendous success of James Whale's *Show Boat* (Universal, 1936), began stressing musicals with Deanna Durbin.

None of this really affected the Buck Jones unit. The 1936–37 season began with *Ride 'Em Cowboy* (Universal, 1936), with the original story by Buck Jones. Buck got an additional $10,000 when he wrote his own stories. He and Dell had considerably improved their standard of living during mid decade. Buck now owned a stately Hollywood home and a ranch back in the hills. He bought an eighty-six-foot yacht in 1937, naming it the *Sartartia*.

George Cooper, who had played Buck's side-kick, Spooky, in *The Phantom Rider,* was back for *Ride 'Em Cowboy.* The plot involved a race car which Buck has to drive to win in order to save the ranch belonging to J. P. McGowan and his screen daughter, Luana Walters. The film was directed by Lesley Selander. Selander had first directed Buck in *For the Service* (Universal, 1936) from the previous season. Selander, who had been an assistant director under Lucky Humberstone at Fox, had come recommended to Buck by W. S. Van Dyke, who had directed Buck at Fox during the silent era. Buck signed Selander as the unit director for the new season. With Frances Guihan to write the screenplays, the camera team of Allen Thompson and John Hickson and now the addition of Selander, Buck was at last able to bring to full expression whatever his intentions and desires as a Western filmmaker. *Ride 'Em Cowboy,* no matter how incongruous its plot, demonstrated more logic and continuity and more intelligent action than any of the subsequent Buck Jones Westerns on Buck's Universal contract.

Buck on his own was rather unpredictable as a filmmaker. His screen stories, whether based on pulp novels or his own devising, became increasingly moody and even, at times, neurotic. Perhaps the most satisfying film that season was *Left-handed Law* (Universal, 1937), which cast Noel Francis as the girl. Buck liked her as much as he had liked Carole Lombard at Fox and tried to do many of the same things with her on the screen. He introduced Silver, Jr., this season, a gray speckle.

The strangeness of the Jones films became really obvious during the

1937–38 season. In *Boss of Lonely Valley* (Universal, 1937), with virtually no action in the film, much low comedy, and some romance, the finish takes place at the Prudential studio town set. The outlaws are barricaded in the saloon ready for a shoot-out. Buck arranges for a hymn to be played on the church organ. The effect, psychologically, is so devastating that the outlaws turn tail and flee. *Sudden Bill Dorn* (Universal, 1937) was, if anything, worse.

Buck had been negotiating with the new Universal for nearly a year concerning his next three-year contract. Charles R. Rogers did not feel the company in sufficiently sound financial shape to offer Buck a pay increase. If he was to sign for a new three-year term, it would have to be at $1,000 a week, plus $10,000 for any stories he might write and total budgets of $75,000 for his six annual Westerns. Buck talked the matter over with Bill Boyd. Boyd told Buck, frankly, that he thought Buck a fool if he went along with that kind of a proposition. Why, he himself was going to ask Pop Sherman for a raise to $25,000 a picture for the Hoppy pictures, and he knew damned well that Pop would have to pay it.

Buck was approached by Monroe Shaff, who offered him $16,000 a picture for an initial contract of six pictures to be financed independently but to be released by Columbia Pictures. Buck was naturally irked that Boyd, who cared nothing about being a cowboy and still had trouble riding horseback, should be asking that kind of money and that he should be expected to work for less. The exhibitor polls indicated that Buck was the most popular screen cowboy. Buck determined to leave Universal. It was, in retrospect, a folly no less whimsical than his leaving Fox over vacation pay or his circus investment. *Sudden Bill Dorn*, released in December 1937, was Buck's last starring feature for Universal.

28 / THE AUTRY PHENOMENON—PART ONE

I

Continuing success prompted Mascot Pictures to expand in 1933 by assuming the lease for the vacant Mack Sennett studio. Nat Levine did not wish to commit the capital he needed for new production to an outright purchase, so he rented the facilities instead with an option to buy. The trustees were asking $190,000 for everything, including equipment. In the end, Levine would have made more on the real estate, had he bought it, than he made as a result of his eventual merger into Republic Productions. He also expanded serial production to five entries in 1933 and began seriously to enter the independent feature market. By 1935 feature production alone was covering his basic operating expenses, and what he made on chapter plays was profit.

Nat put young John Wayne under contract in 1932 for three serials, the last of which, *The Three Musketeers,* was released in 1933. Duke was billed fourth on the credits after the three principals, Jack Mulhall, Raymond Hatton, and Francis X. Bushman, Jr. Ruth Hall was the feminine lead. The Mascot Publicity Department contradicted the screen on both lobby cards and posters. John Wayne and Ruth Hall were played up in an effort to cash in on Warner Brothers' promotion of the two of them in a pair of Duke's six remakes of silent Ken Maynard vehicles—*Ride Him Cowboy* and *The Man from Monterey*—in which Ruth was Duke's costar.

Levine personally was quite taken with two novelties in the early thirties that would have an enduring impact on Western production and earn several fortunes. The first was the notion of trio pictures with three distinct heroes. Wallace MacDonald, when he left the Columbia Story Department, went to work for Mascot. William Colt MacDonald had conceived of the idea of the Three Mesquiteers and started writing pulp stories featuring them while Wallace MacDonald was still at Columbia working with him on the Tim McCoy pictures. The idea wasn't exactly new. In his frontier saga in the teens Clarence E. Mulford had created the Bar 20 trio, William "Hopalong" Cassidy, Red Conners, and Johnny Nelson. Nat Levine was taken with Alexandre Dumas's literary invention of *Les Trois Mousquetaires* and translated them into modern counterparts in the French Foreign Legion for Duke's final chapter play.

The second notion was Levine's exploitation of the musical Western. Nat was visibly impressed with what Ken Maynard had been doing at Universal. When Junior Laemmle ousted Maynard from his contract, Ken took Mary with him on a second European voyage. Nat reached Ken via long-distance telephone in London. It was Nat's intention to produce a series of musical Westerns in both serial and feature form. He commented that he agreed with Maynard that action by itself was no longer sufficient to keep audiences interested. The proposed Mascot contract would provide Ken with $10,000 a week for each week that he worked, and Nat wanted Ken for an undetermined number of pictures. Since both feature and serial production at Mascot were on four-week shooting schedules by this time, Ken would be getting about the same as he had at Universal. "When I signed Ken Maynard for a serial at forty thousand dollars," Nat Levine remarked to me, "his name value justified this investment." No other screen cowboy was making as much in 1933–34.

But the signing of Maynard wasn't the significant thing. The truly significant decision Nat made was to bring Gene Autry to Hollywood. Perhaps no personality in the history of the Western cinema presents a greater

Ken and Mary Maynard outside their Spanish-style home on Las Palmas Avenue in Los Angeles in 1934. The house is still there.

Photo courtesy of the late Ken Maynard.

paradox to critic, historian, or modern viewer alike than Gene Autry. There would be no profound contradiction between his screen image and his private life, as was the case with William Boyd. Barring Tom Mix, no cowboy player in series Westerns made as much money for as long a time as Gene Autry did during his active career; Maynard couldn't maintain his stability nor his earnings; and no Western player was less a cowboy and more a businessman than Gene Autry in enterprises outside and exclusive of the motion picture industry. One quality about Autry must be kept in mind above all: He divorced himself utterly from reality. No one before him developed quite the thoroughgoing and consistent fantasy world he did, as no one for better than a decade and a half was the same again in Western programmers. I am not speaking here so much of the musical content of the later Autry films as I am of the prospect of Gene Autry as a Western hero.

There is a fable which, I believe, adequately parallels the Autry Phenomenon. It is the tale of the little tailor. The little tailor was seated in his pantry one day, eating a jelly sandwich. Flies were attracted by the jelly, and the tailor, in a fit of temper, swatted several of them. Proud of his accomplishment, he immediately sewed a championship belt for himself, imprinted with the words "Seven at One Blow." Unwittingly, folk from all over the country attributed to the tailor the reputation of being a giant killer. One of his adventures brought him face to face with two particularly horrible and very powerful ogres. They had fallen into a deep sleep. The tailor, keeping his presence a secret, manages to invoke a violent fight between them, the upshot of which is that they kill each other and he emerges the victor, winning not only a kingdom but the fair princess in the bargain.

Prior to Autry's appearance on the screen, Western heroes were customarily strong, capable, occasionally austere men, true frontier types who might believably undertake many of the escapades attributed to them in the scenarios. In Autry's case, this wasn't so. But he was surrounded nonetheless with an almost magical aura. He lived, it seemed, a charmed life whereby, battling against frequently incredible odds, he invariably triumphed.

Gene was born on September 29, 1907, at Tioga, Texas, to Delbert and Nora Autry. After attending high school in Tioga, he went to work on the San Francisco railroad as a night telegrapher. It was as a boxcar dispatcher at the depot in Chelsea, Oklahoma, that he met Will Rogers one evening, Autry strumming on his guitar and singing a modern range song. The comedian told him he should be on the radio. Whatever Rogers may have meant by that comment, the fact remains he might have said something similar to a hundred such and have had it come to nothing. But not so with Autry. Gene took it seriously and decided to give it a try, working for various Oklahoma stations before finally, in 1930, going to work for the

NBC affiliate in Chicago, where he stayed for the next four years. WLS, the affiliate owned by Sears (its call letters standing for World's Largest Store), broadcast the National Barn Dance, and Autry's appearances on the show led to an American Record recording contract. American Record was owned by Herbert J. Yates, who was also involved in the film processing business. Yates processed all the Mascot film at Consolidated Film Industries and knew Nat Levine well enough to loan him money.

Nat had a reputation for giving young, inexperienced talent a chance with his company. "I received a dozen letters from Autry during 1933," he wrote to me, "asking for an opportunity to work for me in anything I would suggest in pictures. Autry's name value at the time was limited to a . . . radio station in Chicago, practically an unknown with questionable ability. On one of my trips East, I stopped off in Chicago, not to meet Autry, but for business I had with my distributor. But I did get to meet Autry and he virtually begged me for an opportunity to come to Hollywood and work in pictures. While he was nice looking, it seemed to me he lacked the commodity necessary to become a Western star: virility! I wasn't impressed and tried to give him a nice brush-off, telling him I would think about it. For a period of six months he wrote to me continually, conveying that he would do anything for the opportunity."

Yates was enlisted by Autry to put in a good word with Levine. Yates told Nat that Gene was selling a lot of records. When Ken Maynard signed with Mascot, Levine went ahead and put Autry on salary with a five-year option. He also signed Lester "Smiley" Burnette, who had worked two years with Autry, and Frank Marvin, one of Gene's backup men. Autry was hired at a hundred dollars a week, Burnette and Marvin at somewhat less. It was Levine's notion to use Autry, who could sing, to support Maynard, who really could not. "Gene was completely raw material," Levine continued "knew nothing about acting, lacked poise, and was awkward. A couple of days after his arrival I had him at my home and invited my production staff to meet him. The next day all of my associates questioned my judgment in putting him under contract. They thought I was slipping. But I persisted, and for the first four months he went through a learning period. We had at that time, in our employ, a professional dramatic and voice teacher, and Autry became one of her pupils. He wasn't much of a horseman either, so I had Tracy Layne and Yakima Canutt teach him how to ride."

"I don't believe he ever acknowledged my contribution to his career," Nat added, "nor did I ever receive thanks." Lucile Browne told me of how Gene loved going to baseball games even then, for she worked with him in his initial Republic feature, *Tumbling Tumbleweeds* (Republic, 1935), made as the first of a series of eight features after Gene scored a success in *The Phantom Empire* (Mascot, 1935). I asked Gene about his work at

George Hayes, Tarzan, Ken, Evalyn Knapp, Kenneth Thompson, and
Wheeler Oakman posing for a lobby card for the picture *In Old Santa Fe*.

Photo courtesy of *Views & Reviews* magazine.

Mascot in the early days. He suddenly became very vague. "Well, I sang
a few songs in *In Old Santa Fe* and then I made a serial for them." For
whatever the reason, Nat Levine was right: Autry had forgotten.

Levine went the whole route. Production was set to begin in September
on Maynard's first musical Western feature, tentatively titled *Down in Old
Santa Fe*. Wallace MacDonald contributed to the screenplay. Nat had purchased a song and named the picture after it. He projected a musical interlude at a dude ranch in which Gene Autry, Smiley Burnette, and Frank
Marvin would provide suitable entertainment. Levine also had a serial
script in preparation with a strictly action format titled *Mystery Mountain*.
The serial after that, *The Phantom Empire*, was again to surround Maynard with a musical setting.

Sid Rogell had attempted at length to persuade Ken to reshoot *Smoking
Guns*, if necessary financing the new sequences out of his own pocket. Ken

would never get a better deal than he had with Universal, Rogell argued. Maynard was deaf to all importunities. He reveled in his belligerence. Ken was a strong-willed man who would have everything his own way, or have nothing at all. Once Maynard joined Mascot, their hurried production methods caused him to halt shooting for hours on end, flying into long tirades. Ken's drinking intensified. His marriage to Mary was crumbling. Ken and Kermit had a terrible brawl in a bar while Ken was still at Universal, and Kermit cut off personal relations. The fight was ostensibly about Ken's drinking, but the truth of the matter was that Maurice Conn, head of a small, independent producing company called Ambassador Pictures, had quietly approached Kermit and asked him to star in a series of very low-budget features. Kermit agreed. Conn sold the series on the basis of publicity billing K. Maynard as the star and with Kermit dressed in outfits identical to those Ken wore on screen. Kermit lacked completely Ken's magical personality and his free-wheeling love of life, his romanticism, his childlike enthusiasm. Ken instituted an action against Ambassador and Kermit to desist. The format of the films was altered, but, ultimately, Kermit proved temperamentally unsuited for hero roles and by 1937 was again reduced to character parts, stunt work, and walk-ons. When Ken's father died, Ken's mother chose to come and live with Kermit and his wife, Edith, neither liking nor approving of Mary Maynard. The brothers had little use for one another throughout the remainder of their lives. Maynard resembled no one so much as King Lear, betrayed, violent, desperately inconsolable. At the height of his financial success, his personal fortunes languished in a despair that would never desert him even when he had lost everything and everyone he cared about in the world.

David Howard was set to direct *In Old Santa Fe,* as the film was titled on release. Born David Paget Davis III in Philadelphia, Howard had become an assistant director under D. W. Griffith in the teens and then was an assistant to King Vidor at M-G-M during the mid twenties. In 1930 Howard signed with the Fox Film Corporation to direct their Spanish language versions of feature films for distribution overseas. Fox loaned him out occasionally, which is how Mascot got him for a limited engagement. Howard's short-term contract expired before the conclusion of *In Old Santa Fe,* although he still received full credit on the screen.

Levine was in a quandary. He did not wish to renew Howard's contract, nor was he willing to pay Howard extra to finish the picture. So he assigned one of his film editors, Joe Kane, to finish the film. One sequence had Maynard in an exterior shot wearing a double-breasted suit coat over his Western outfit. The shot with which it had to be matched was an interior with Maynard simply in his dark blue outfit, without the suit coat. Kane shot a short interlinking scene in which Maynard, silhouetted against a curtained window, stripped off his suit coat before climbing inside through the window.

Ken's part in the musical interlude also had to be reworked. "I made the mistake of trying to kid with Ken," Joe Kane recalled. ". . . When I handed Ken the revised portion of the script, I said I understood he needed a few minutes to memorize that much. I started away but suddenly found myself whirled around, facing a furious man holding a six-gun aimed at my middle. Ken decided I was being sarcastic. He had a violent temper and a low boiling point. At first I thought he must be putting on an act, but he wasn't. His eyes told me that. He invited me to take the other gun from his belt. I guess they were really loaded."

Gene Autry intervened. He got the fuming Maynard to one side. Kane would work subsequently with Autry on several pictures, but this was to be his last association with Maynard. Autry for his own part idolized Ken Maynard and sought to model himself after him. Even after Ken had left Mascot and was working for Larry Darmour in a series for Columbia release, whenever Gene wasn't working in one of his own pictures he would visit the Maynard set and quietly sit on the sidelines watching Ken. He would say nothing.

Evalyn Knapp, who played the heroine, was a vivacious flapper. Like Ruth Hall, she had been elected a Wampus Baby in 1932. She had appeared in the remake of *The Perils of Pauline* (Universal, 1933) and another serial effort, *Law of the Wild* (Mascot, 1934), in addition to a series of non-Western adventure films for Columbia opposite Tim McCoy, of which *Speedwings* (Columbia, 1934) was her best. She had done much light comedy work on stage in both New York and Hollywood. No matter what the degree of her professionalism, she was, according to Ken, either very bold or very naïve. One day on the set, when Ken was scheduled for a noon call, due to her penchant for dispensing entirely with underclothing and wearing thin, clinging gowns, the crew had Evalyn backed up against a fireplace in which a fire was roaring. She was being photographed, the transparency of her clothing beneath the brilliant lighting fore and aft leaving nothing of her flapper figure to the imagination. Maynard arrived unexpectedly and stormed onto the set, morally outraged.

George Hayes was cast as Ken's side-kick, Cactus. Hayes had been slowly transforming his screen image from parental roles to a sensitive combination of humor and pathos. He was born at Wellsville, New York, on May 7, 1885. While he had played both side-kicks and villains opposite Duke Wayne in Duke's low-budget series of Lone Star Westerns produced by Paul Malvern for Monogram release, it was on the basis of his performance in *In Old Santa Fe* that Harry Sherman put Hayes under personal contract for support in his Bar 20 series. H. B. Warner, who had been Cecil B. De Mille's Christ at Pathé in the silent era, portrayed Evalyn's father.

The basic plot of *In Old Santa Fe* featured a mixture of romance and charm with action and music. The script invoked a conglomeration of anachronisms that were typical of Mascot and were readily incorporated into the subsequent Republic Westerns of ensuing years: automobiles and horses, an old-fashioned stage robbery by modern city mobsters, Park Avenue styles, and Western outfits. These incongruities were made palatable only by the superabundant dreamlike quality invested in all Mascot products, be it a serial like *The Lightning Warrior* or a musical Western. The fantasy content was predominant at Mascot, as it was at Disney's, and during the dark Depression period accounted for much of Nat Levine's extraordinary success. Without this phantasmagoric orientation, I doubt seriously if the studio would even have considered Autry a screen possibility.

As the film opens, Ken and Cactus are riding along a desert road, Ken singing, Cactus scowling. They meet Evalyn Knapp and are headed for her father's dude ranch where Ken will enter Tarzan in the horse race. Kenneth Thompson and Wheeler Oakman arrive at the ranch and try to muscle into H. B. Warner's holdings, Thompson even wanting to marry Evalyn. Ken interferes with their plans and, after a few suspenseful moments, manages to bring the two confidence men to justice.

Levine next went into production on the serial *Mystery Mountain* (Mascot, 1934). It was based somewhat on the story ideas of the earlier *Hurricane Express* (Mascot, 1932), with John Wayne. A railroad was under siege from a phantom outlaw leader who, by means of a series of rubber masks, could assume the identity of anyone in the cast. To further confuse the viewer, Edmund Cobb was cast as the Rattler in his phantom disguise, while Edward Earle was unmasked in the final episode. When the Rattler spoke, it was Cobb's voice. Autry still wasn't very good on a horse, so he was given a small nonsinging role, as was Burnette. There was no musical content other than the rousing theme, composed by Lee Zahler, played under the credits.

Maynard insisted that the picture be shot on the Universal lot. His agreement with Levine called for him to be paid $10,000 a week for each week that he worked. The schedule was four weeks. But Maynard back on the Universal lot spelled disaster. Ken insisted on changing the story to suit himself. As the shooting script had it, the first chapter was to conclude with Maynard being pursued by three of the Rattler's men and falling to his doom over a high grade. It doesn't end that way. The Rattler was supposed to be seen in the episode; he isn't. Maynard had his own ideas. In the first reel, when the Corwin Transportation Company was introduced, Maynard used stock footage from *The Wagon Master* (Universal, 1929), showing a wagon train. Next he interpolated the exciting race between three stages from *The California Mail* (First National, 1929), which was the highlight of that picture. The original script was further altered, inserting scenes intended for the second installment; namely, bringing the heavy, Bob Kortman, to town only to have him escape through the office of the Corwin Transportation Company and leaving a gap of five minutes' shooting time for Chapter 2. Syd Saylor, who Levine thought had an appeal for children, had appeared previously in *The Lost Jungle* (Mascot, 1933) with Clyde Beatty. He was back for *Mystery Mountain,* but his comedy hadn't improved. Maynard had him fill up this slot with a static, slow, labored, unfunny battle to get the reins of a team of stage horses organized. Maynard then shot additional background footage for the stage race which involved a coach in which Saylor was riding, followed by one in which the Rattler was supposed to be, with Maynard and Jane Corwin, played by Verna Hillie, in the third coach.

When the exposed stock was edited into a coherent chapter, the results were unpleasant. Maynard, who had his guns on when the chase between himself and the Rattler's men began, lost them in the fracas, had them again when he brought Bob Kortman into town, and suddenly lost them for a second time when he disarmed Jane Corwin's coach by means of holding up her men with a stick. Moreover, the absence of the Rattler physically in the beginning episode made his appearance on the title cards of Chapter 2 somewhat of a shock.

Breezy Eason, having been twice fired by Levine, wanted to come back to Mascot to work. He promised no more drinking, no more late to the set, no more days off, and his very best efforts. Levine tried him out again in *Law of the Wild* (Mascot, 1934) and kept him on. Eason stayed right through the merger to form Republic. He was assigned to *Mystery Mountain* together with Otto Brower. Levine had groomed Armand Schaefer, about whom I will have more to say presently, for supervision, and Eason replaced him as a regular serial director. After codirecting *Law of the Wild* with Eason, Schaefer did not direct a serial again until *The Miracle Rider* (Mascot, 1935), with Tom Mix, and this only because of its immense importance.

Mystery Mountain was intended to cost $65,000 but ended up costing $80,000, with Maynard getting an extra $10,000 for an additional week's work. The added time was due directly to Maynard's emendations and his truculence. Schaefer, not Levine, was supervising the production, so Nat only came to know the problems secondhand and from screening rushes. If Schaefer or one of the directors didn't like one of Maynard's changes, or crossed him, Ken would fly into an abusive rage. When they were on location, Maynard's drinking led him to develop an even more surly disposition. One of Maynard's more colorful sessions was recorded by the sound engineers and played back for Levine. Nat summoned Maynard to him and told him he would be finished at Mascot if it continued. Further, he counseled, the scenario was to be shot as written and Maynard had better do as he was told. Ken admired Levine's forthrightness, but he was finished at Mascot anyway. Levine had already made the decision to chuck him after *Mystery Mountain,* but he wanted a finished picture first. Autry was about to get his break. The publicity for *The Phantom Empire,* up for production next, which pictured Maynard as the star, was junked. Levine never regretted his decision, even though *Mystery Mountain* was the second highest money-maker during the entire history of his company, second only to Tom Mix in *The Miracle Rider,* which grossed $1 million and cost $80,000.

II

"We constantly strove to be pathfinders," Nat Levine reminisced for me. "*The Phantom Empire* was one of the innumerable productions which proved it. Here was science fiction that would be readily acceptable today, and not considered old-fashioned." One cannot but agree with him. Had there been no *Phantom Empire,* it is doubtful if there would have been a *Flash Gordon* from Universal in 1936, budgeted at $360,000, or a *Buck Rogers* (Universal, 1939) or two more Flash Gordon serials. There perhaps would have been no *Undersea Kingdom* (Republic, 1936), nor would science fiction have become so much a staple of serial production for the next ten years. Yet there is nothing more patently absurd than an empire 25,000 feet below the earth's surface and a singing cowboy for whom the cliff-hanger usually meant whether or not he would make it back to Radio Ranch for his daily two o'clock broadcast. Nor can I think of any more appropriate vehicle to launch the Autry Fantasy onto a jaded and, certainly, unsuspecting public.

Part of the plot of *The Phantom Empire,* we owe to James Churchward, who wrote a series of books in the early thirties devoted to his scientific and mystical discovery of a strange civilization which vanished from the face of the earth more than twelve thousand years before. The first book in the series, published in 1931, was entitled *The Lost Continent of Mu.* Churchward was anything but an empiricist, and a totally tenable hypothesis is made to appear all the more incredible due to the weird quirks and pet beliefs of its propounder. The remains of the Muranian rock quarries are on Easter Island, and the statues of their gods still survive. Mu was located in the Pacific Ocean where today only the mountaintops remain as numerous islands. Churchward, basing his record on ancient writings in the Orient, claimed the continent sank suddenly. Perhaps certain of the American Indian tribes are descended from the Muranians. The Mascot writers concocted another theory.

Wallace MacDonald, Gerald Geraghty, and Hy Freedman were employed on the screenplay. MacDonald claimed at the time that the plot came to him while he was in a dentist's chair, under the influence of anesthesia. Maybe so. Here's the plot. When Mu sank beneath the earth's surface, not all of its inhabitants were destroyed. Some survived and created a city within the interior. Basing his conception of this world on a combination of Jules Verne's *Journey to the Center of the Earth* and Edgar Rice Burroughs' adventures inside the earth's core, MacDonald conceived of a wholly advanced, miraculous world, calling the citizens, aptly, Muranians. Undisturbed by the continual wars and conflicts of the surface people, the Muranians have lived for centuries in peace. Even the credit crawl to each episode with the theme from *Mystery Mountain* played beneath it showed three different views of the scientific city of Murania. They have developed a great many scientific wonders which, by surface standards, are nearly magical. Among medical triumphs, they can resuscitate the dead. Almost all physical labor is performed by robots (if you knew MacDonald, this was highly typical of the man). Their work in the area of television permits them to record and perceive events at tremendous distances while a series of special facial masks, covering the olfactory organs, permits them to breathe the much drier air on the surface. Without these masks, they are reduced to gasping inactivity. Surface men do not seem conversely inhibited by Muranian air, however, and do not need any protection when they descend to the depths. At one point in the story, for this reason, I suppose, as much as because he is always singing, the Muranians want to dissect Autry's lungs. Because of the great radium deposits, the Muranians have devised very powerful ray-projecting machines, one of which brings about the final destruction of the kingdom.

No Mascot serial went so far in stressing fantasy elements as *The Phantom Empire*. The Muranians have their own social order, but the viewer cannot help but think, as their society is wiped out, that the dissent among certain elements, led by Wheeler Oakman as the Lord High Chancellor Argo, came only as a result of undue contact with the disorganized, perpetually warring world of the surface men. This is the one serial in which Mascot stepped beyond the confines of pure adventure and firmly into the realm of what sober critics call social relevance. There is both wistful sadness and aristocratic pride in the voice of Queen Tika, portrayed by Dorothy Christie, as she watches the behavior of the surface people, rushing about their business, obsessed with their machines, fighting and killing so that one man may gain control over another. The closer the contact with the surface men, the stronger these latent impulses appear among the Muranians, eventually bringing about the dissolution of their mighty, tranquil, enlightened civilization.

Levine budgeted the serial at $70,000. The cast wasn't very expensive. Frankie Darro, who was already smoking and driving fast cars, returned to play a teen-ager for $5,000. Betsy King Ross, teamed as Frankie's sister, had come to Hollywood to appear in George O'Brien's *Smoke Lightning*

(Fox, 1933). Levine had used her for his serial *Fighting with Kit Carson* (Mascot, 1933), with Johnny Mack Brown. After being signed for *The Phantom Empire,* she suddenly grew two inches and so had to stoop over slightly so as to avoid revealing her height; Levine was quite irked about it. Autry and Burnette were contract players. This left a lot of money to be spent on production and, fortunately for once, Levine did it. His special effects for *The Phantom Empire* are superior to anything in *Flash Gordon,* even though the latter cost five times as much. Wyndham Gittens, Mascot's story editor at this time, was so taken with the fascinating theme of science fiction in a Western setting that he sold an original story to Puritan Pictures for use in their Tim McCoy series, emerging as *Ghost Patrol* (Puritan, 1936), in which Lloyd Ingraham, as a scientist, invents a super ray capable of forcing internal combustion engines to malfunction, thus aiding a gang of mail robbers headed by Walter Miller to bring down government and commercial airplanes. Screenplays like this would not have been possible had Mascot not pioneered the format with *The Phantom Empire* and demonstrated that audiences would accept such an incongruity of ingredients. I would go so far as to assert that no Mascot picture so influenced other studios in the programmer field as this one did.

To compensate for Autry's lack of public exposure, Levine had Gene use his real name so that the character he played in *The Phantom Empire* and henceforth was always Gene Autry. It was an intelligent gimmick in that the twelve-chapter serial gave Autry continuous publicity in better than ten thousand theaters, on the promotional literature, the press releases, the advertising, the screen credits, and throughout the course of the installments. If Autry had made twelve features playing differently named characters, he could not have become as effectively known by his own name. Subsequently the practice became widespread among Western players, newcomers and old-timers alike.

While humor had been in the Western almost from the beginning and side-kicks had been around since the early twenties, the Autry films introduced the "stooge" as a stock character. Smiley Burnette and William Moore provided the comic relief for *The Phantom Empire,* but the comedy was singularly confined to slapstick antics and simply incompetent and stupid behavior. In the early years at Republic, Burnette, who was born at Summum, Illinois, in 1911, moved right along with Autry as his stooge. Credit probably goes to Burnette as much as to Autry for making a stooge a regular feature of Western melodramas for the next two decades. Countless imitators stepped forth, and nearly every cowboy in the forties had at least one stooge, some of them two or more.

Gene Autry was totally incapable of convincing emotion. He was the blandest of screen personalities. For this reason, he was invariably surrounded with singing and a stock company of competent performers;

others were expected to play on the sympathies of the audience. In *The Phantom Empire* every sentence he utters is spoken with painstaking care, Gene's mind obviously on enunciation and diction, not meaning. Maurice Geraghty, who began his career as a writer at this time and who later became a very successful producer and director, commented to me, "The first Mascot picture I worked on was the feature version of *The Phantom Empire*. My brother Gerald had worked on the serial version and together we figured out what transitional scenes were necessary to tie it all together as a feature. This was Gene Autry's first picture and we worked under the supervision of Armand Schaefer, who worked for many years with Autry, on and off. . . . Gene was chosen because his records were selling sensationally and Nat Levine was canny enough to capitalize on that. Nobody, not even Levine, expected Gene to make another picture, although he had a hold on Gene, just in case. As you know, the picture hit big and opened up a whole new era in Westerns, the singing, musical Western."

Nat Levine afterward claimed credit for creating the musical Western. He does deserve credit for discovering Gene Autry, but the first Autry films added nothing that wasn't already present in Ken Maynard's *The Strawberry Roan*, save that the emphasis was shifted. Ken was primarily an action player who occasionally sang and who built a few of his films around hit songs. Autry was primarily a singer who consistently tried to build his films around hit songs and, almost begrudgingly, incorporated action sequences. Indeed, Autry at Republic made not so much musical Westerns as Western musicals. He appealed to parents, extolling the virtues of his clean films (implying, thereby, that others weren't clean); he encouraged the public to believe that Westerns were intended strictly as family pictures. He borrowed and imitated, revolutionizing the form before leaving it an exhausted husk, himself a wealthy man. As his phonograph recordings became increasingly popular, he did come to have his own network radio show. His performances were quite the same here as in his films, with all the stooges and heavies clustered around one microphone, Autry at the opposite end of the stage, alone before his silver microphone, gaudily dressed, singing his non-Western ditties.

In order for me to explain the fabulous success of the Autry films, I may have to anticipate somewhat, giving at least moderate indications as to what exactly the Autry Fantasy was and what it became. The Autry Fantasy sold Gene's pictures, not the fact that he sang. All of his imitators came to nothing by comparison; neither Tex Ritter nor Roy Rogers, foremost among his competitors, could ever match his volume sales. What Gene Autry alone had was the Fantasy. Without it, his films would never have dominated the field in the way they did, nor could a producer duplicate the phenomenon with another singing cowboy.

The Autry Fantasy was the mutual invention of Nat Levine, Armand

Schaefer, and Gene Autry. It is difficult for me to say who contributed what, but together they created it. Armand Schaefer, whom I have already introduced to the reader, was born at Tavistock, Ontario, on August 5, 1898, starting out as a prop man at the Mack Sennett studio and then a director for the Action Pictures division of Pathé, producing Westerns and serials. He joined Mascot and by 1933 was into supervision. In 1935 he was extremely concerned as to how the public would react to a steady diet of singing Westerns and, more importantly, to Autry's rather fragile physical appearance. Occasionally in the early entries, the screenplay poked fun at Gene's guitar strumming, the heavies heaping ridicule on him. These hostilities were resolved by Autry in exciting chase footage and lusty fistfights, as incredible as that may seem considering Autry as the principal. Tracy Layne and Yakima Canutt had done their work well, and already in *The Phantom Empire* running inserts were included of Gene riding furiously. Cliff Lyons stunted for him in *Tumbling Tumbleweeds*, and the first Republic films stressed action as much as or more than singing, as later the Autry pictures for Columbia in 1949–53 would.

But by 1936 the Autry films began to evolve their unique identity. Gene was increasingly presented as a dandified hero, the presentation itself accounting for much of his personal charm. Even if partially unconscious, the results were exceedingly tangible. A constant ingredient was Gene's fablelike quality, his singing nonchalantly through forests of villains, walking confidently amid giants, overcoming every sort of danger by submerging it into the dulcet melodies of some sweet song. He gave the underdog, the man of slight physical attainments, a hero that could be idolized. Another aspect of the Autry Fantasy was the image of Gene as the Pied Piper. In *Red River Valley* he softens the sentiments of an assemblage of disgruntled dam workers impatiently awaiting their long-overdue pay by having them join together singing the theme song, using his silver-plated .45 as a conducting baton, George Chesebro the lead tenor, the others a supporting chorus. Afterward, when the men finish and cluster around him, Gene remarks quietly: "Now, don't you feel better? There's nothing like a song." This is not an isolated instance but a characteristic of many of the Autry pictures.

In *Mexicali Rose* (Republic, 1939) Gene persuades Noah Beery, Sr., quite obviously and painfully down on his luck playing a Mexican bandido, not only to release him from bondage but even to sacrifice his life on the side of the law by singing to him about Robin Hood. Tied up at the campfire, Autry and Burnette discover that Beery's principal recreation is collecting Gene Autry records. When Beery's recording of the title song is broken, Gene takes over and continues the song, a full orchestra accompanying him right out there on the prairie, the bandidos forming a male chorus. There is no attempt at even suggesting reality or realistic motivation; that is the point of the Autry Fantasy. It is a wholly consistent substitute for reality.

In *South of the Border* (Republic, 1939) Gene convinces all of the terrified caballeros to participate in a cattle drive by singing to them. Perceiving their love of music reflected in the number of instruments they are packing up perforce to leave for safer parts, he transforms the expression on the face of every man, woman, and child to a beaming smile merely by performing a short ditty with Smiley Burnette accompanying him. Whatever might be the response to such a depiction of human emotion, from laughter to shocked incredulity, nonetheless the Fantasy inspiring the screenplays and, above all, Autry himself is so fervent that it seems instead to be a demonstration of an immutable law governing human behavior. I do not doubt for an instant that Autry believed totally in the Fantasy; I think for a time that audiences believed in it, too.

I sincerely feel that Autry's massive appeal as a modest cowboy troubadour leading a uniquely charmed life, a musical magician who could turn darkness into light, sorrow into happiness, tarnish into splendor, a Pied Piper able to control men and alter the course of world events by means of a song, is the most tremendous single occurrence in the history of the American Western cinema. Gene Autry in his magnificent outfits, yodeling a pop tune, is an image so remote from the actual man of the frontier as to rival any fairy tale. If you compare Autry to Tom Mix, or even William S. Hart, of the previous generation, he appears hopelessly inept. But once you accept him on his own terms and find yourself enthralled by the Autry Fantasy, the others begin to look clumsy, plebeian, vulgar. Whereas screen cowboys once flaunted their fast draw, Autry customarily carried his gloves between his gun butt and his holster. If Mix's soft hands led to cowboy players even wearing gloves, Autry's indifference to firearms created a new plethora of imitators, from Tex Ritter to Tim Holt, who similarly deported themselves. Gene boasted that in his films he seldom threw the first punch, and he certainly never fought vigorously from 1936 to 1948. He insisted on never killing anyone, and I cannot remember that he did, save indirectly.

Gene Autry on screen met every reversal of fortune, every threat of villainy, with the honest reassurance of a song. Critics of the film mock Autry or dismiss him; they try to ignore him, term him an anomaly, discredit him as a temporary lapse into lunacy, reject him bitterly, sneer at him, or are silent; but Gene Autry made more money and was more consistently popular during his time in the movies than any of his Western peers. His career was without the rise and fall of nearly every other cowboy player. The Autry Fantasy like the Mix Legend only reinforces the fact that the Western is basically an imaginative myth. Yet Autry ruined the programmer Western at the same time because, as he moved further and further into the golden reaches of the Autry Fantasy, he only intensified the grand lie about the true nature of man which World War II began to shatter with its agony of genocide, concentration camps, and total destruction. Gene Autry, although he outlived it by a few years, belongs very much to that generation of Depression-weary gentlefolk who tried to hide from the truth until it mushroomed before their startled eyes at Hiroshima.

If in terms of artistic or critical assessment, I have appeared to deal harshly with Autry, I must hastily point out that this has nothing to do with his popularity, particularly in rural areas, where Saturday night at the local theater would see farmers and their families forsaking the traditional barn dance to attend the latest Autry opus. Gene's Westerns for Republic, bearing titles like *The Old Barn Dance* (Republic, 1938), *Western Jamboree* (Republic, 1938), *Gaucho Serenade* (Republic, 1940), *Melody Ranch* (Republic, 1940), and *The Singing Hills* (Republic, 1941), reveal their intention and attracted much the same kind of audience that Lawrence Welk has had in many successful years on television. The Autry films expanded the Radio Ranch format of *The Phantom Empire,* as Republic Westerns incorporated the blend of new and old from *In Old Santa Fe* and the Mascot serials as their trademark. In time, action was only incidental to the singing and music-making, and beyond it all the perpetuation of a viable alternate to real life.

III

Herbert J. Yates, born in 1880, got his start in the tobacco industry, first with American and then with Liggett & Myers. In 1916 Yates joined Hedwig Film Laboratories. He was thoroughly convinced by 1918 that the film processing business would undergo tremendous expansion with the continued growth of motion pictures. Yates bought Republic Laboratories. In 1919 he formed Allied Laboratories Association, and by 1927, after more mergers, he finally organized Consolidated Film Industries. Yates had learned from the tobacco industry that in the course of intelligent mergers, the controlling company could readily remove the former managements and the take-over become complete with the executives of the controlling company emerging in ascendancy. His son, Herbert, Jr., went to work in accounting for what was left of the Biograph interests, still marketing the old D. W. Griffith pictures during the silent era and renting space to new production units at the Biograph studio in the Bronx. Herbert, Sr., gained a majority interest in the firm, and in 1928 Junior came to work for his father at Consolidated. Herbert J. Yates wanted his own motion picture producing and releasing company.

It would be useless speculation to conjecture what would have happened to Mascot had it not merged in 1935. The company was both reputable and profitable, which is why Yates wanted it. Consolidated, as I have said, did all of Mascot's lab work. Production costs began rising sharply in the mid thirties, and the days of the independent producing company without substantial financing and dependent on states' rights distribution seemed limited. Mascot's total production, even when it attained four serials and eight features in one year, was insufficient to dominate any of the independent exchanges which handled their pictures; the films were inevitably blocked into more comprehensive packages. Nor could Levine make maximum use of his new facilities at the Sennett lot, in turn renting space to other independent firms like Majestic and Chesterfield.

Yates also did most of the lab work for Monogram Pictures. What Yates proposed came to this. Monogram, Mascot, and Consolidated Film Industries should combine their assets. Monogram would bring the John Wayne Westerns and their distribution network to the merger. Mascot would contribute their serial production, the projected singing Westerns with Gene Autry and the Sennett lot. Yates would provide additional capital and a total laboratory service. Since the new firm would still have a limited release schedule, he recommended that the three jointly purchase the total film packages set for release from Liberty Pictures, a small company founded by M. H. Hoffman, Sr., together with his son, following their ill-fated Allied Pictures venture, and Majestic Pictures, the sale to include all contracts and players as well. The parties involved thought the merger a good idea, and by March 1935 Republic Productions was born. Mascot completed its serial production for that year under its own logo, but its last chapter play, *The Fighting Marines,* was distributed via the Republic exchanges. Gene Autry's first feature, *Tumbling Tumbleweeds,* was a Republic release, referred to in the publicity as a "Mascot brand name." John Wayne's first Western for the new company was *Westward Ho!* (Republic, 1935).

Tumbling Tumbleweeds is an important picture historically for a number of reasons. Prior to firing Maynard, Nat Levine showed him the basic story for his next projected feature, which became *Tumbling* on release. Nat had gambled on Autry in *The Phantom Empire,* but when it nearly equaled *Mystery Mountain* at the box office, he willingly launched into the Gene Autry singing Westerns which were originally to star Maynard with Autry as musical support. Maynard on the other hand had been negotiating with Larry Darmour ever since leaving Mascot to make a series of Westerns. Darmour intended for the films to have Majestic release but switched to Columbia after the Republic merger. This took time, and Maynard was off the screen for several months. The first Maynard Western for Darmour was *Western Frontier* (Columbia, 1935).

Maynard knew from reading the plot of *Tumbling* that it involved a medicine show as an excuse for a musical setting. Nat had Lucile Browne slated to play the heroine. So it came about that Maynard, credited for the story of *Western Frontier,* incorporated a medicine show setting into the plot with Frank Yaconelli as musical backup. Lucile Browne was the heroine. The film was released through the Columbia exchanges on August 25, 1935. No sooner had she finished *Western Frontier* than Lucile Browne went at once to Mascot/Republic to make *Tumbling Tumbleweeds* with Gene Autry with a medicine show setting, Smiley Burnette and Frank Marvin as musical backup. *Tumbling* was released through the Monogram/Republic exchanges on September 9, 1935. The "Doc" was played by Otis Harlan in *Western Frontier* and by George Hayes in *Tumbling.* Cliff Lyons stunted for Maynard one week and for Autry the next. I do not suppose that the strong similarities between the two pictures, issued almost simultaneously, mattered to anyone. But they symbolized the passing of Maynard's mantle as the screen's singing cowboy to Gene Autry. Mascot had paid Ken $10,000 a week with a guarantee of $40,000 per picture. Darmour was only paying him $8,000 a picture with a guarantee of eight pictures. Autry was getting his contract salary of $100 a week. *Western Frontier* also marked the end of big salaries for Western players at Columbia and Republic. Buck Jones and George O'Brien were the only stars commanding considerable money in 1935. This was undoubtedly another reason producers chose to alter their product, promoting a whole new group of singing troubadors: they were less expensive personally and their films were cheaper to make.

That Republic was ultimately successful is very much the consequence of the Gene Autry Westerns, the Mascot/Republic serials which include the first *Dick Tracy* (Republic, 1937), produced by Nat Levine, and the John Wayne Westerns, in about that order. Because of Autry's importunity for more money as early as 1936, Levine began competing Western series at Republic, principally the Three Mesquiteers. But there was no denying Autry his popularity. Trade papers found his box office inexplicable; the public compared him to Will Rogers; reviewers praised his "natural" screen style.

One of the fundamental reasons that Autry and Nat Levine didn't get along was Nat's rather low opinion of Autry as a performer. The first Republic biographies of Autry stressed the Fantasy elements, quite the equivalent of the Mix Legend, that Autry had supposedly learned how to ride before he could walk; that, like Ken Maynard, Autry had run away from home at fourteen to join a traveling show; that, like Maynard, Autry had been a rodeo champion. When Tom Mix went to work on the Mascot lot, Gene fell in love with a white-tailed sorrel Mix used in hard riding sequences to double for Tony, Jr. He offered to buy the horse from Mix, and

Tom sold it to him. The sorrel had been foaled the day Lindbergh flew the Atlantic and was called Lindy. Gene changed the name to Champion. It was the first of three movie Champions that he used. Autry was costumed originally in outfits designed by Trem Carr which closely resembled Maynard's.

Yates himself never understood the Autry Fantasy and was only amused at Gene's popularity. He quickly went about edging Trem Carr and W. Ray Johnston out of the company, persuading Nat to join him in buying their stock. Republic kept the John Wayne contract. Next Yates moved against Levine, buying him out in late 1937. At last he owned it all, the Autry pictures, the serials, the John Wayne features, and the other Western and action picture series.

While road-showing with the National Barn Dance in 1932, Gene had married Ina Mae Spivey and the marriage lasted; they never had children. "I know that I owe about all I have to the devotion and support of the kids," Autry later commented. ". . . To youngsters, Gene Autry is not simply a human being, but a kind of superman. They accept anything he does or says as the right thing. That's why Gene Autry has to be so careful about the way he handles himself." Gene was always a businessman first and knew fully what would hurt his career and avoided it.

Whereas William Boyd hated children, beginning with *The Phantom Empire* Gene liked to have them in his films, the way Mix did at Universal. Frankie Darro and Betsy King Ross formed sort of a vocal fan club, urging Gene on to daring feats in the serial, and Gene capitalized on it. He spent several thousand dollars on the silver and leather riggings for Champion. When Levine left, Gene started his sartorial displays which surpassed anything Mix had done off screen. While in the first few films, Gene wound up with the girl, the Autry Fantasy dispensed with this cliché. After all, if he was Gene Autry in every film, he couldn't possibly marry every girl he met! Romance, a vital ingredient in the best Maynard films, was thus easily done away with, and the heroine's role was confined to smiling when Gene sang and being, upon occasion, victim to the villains' evil designs.

IV

Red River Valley was fifth in Gene's first series of Republic Westerns. It is strictly a transitional film and scarcely what by 1938 could be called a typical Autry entry. His films, after this first series, became uncommonly alike until he left Republic; they had a specific and defined audience and seldom varied their successful format. The Autry Fantasy was emerging, and while its contours were roughly shaped, it had not as yet been shaded into its final form. There is almost continuous action in *Red River Valley*.

"Sing your way out of this one, ditch rider!" with George Chesebro punishing
Gene Autry in *Red River Valley*.

Photo courtesy of National Telefilm Associates.

The singing interludes occur only at agreeable moments, rather than domi-
nating the whole as was true later. Following the example of Harry Sherman, background music is employed generously through, the "Dance of the
Furies" by Christoph Gluck twice, the "Ride of the Valkyries" by Richard
Wagner once, the "Murania music" by Lee Zahler from *The Phantom Empire* once. George Chesebro, when he first meets Gene, who is volunteering
for the position of ditch rider, comments, "That's a *man-sized* job, Autry."
Later, when Chesebro gets a hammer lock on Gene, doubtless resentful from
having been forced to lead the chorus, he remarks, "Sing yourself out of

this one, ditch rider." Gene proceeds to give him a thorough beating, harking back to the traditional scope of the Western the Fantasy was presently to overcome.

The film was budgeted at $75,000 and earned better than three times that much upon release. It was shot at several locations: Monogram City (which Gene would later purchase and rent out) for the town sequence, the Sepulveda Dam site on the Kern River (now completely submerged by the increased irrigation system to keep Los Angeles supplied with water), the old fort in the Arizona desert near Yuma used in the serial *The Three Musketeers* (Mascot, 1933) and, again, as late as *Sahara* (Columbia, 1943), with Humphrey Bogart, and interiors at the Sennett studio.

Opening after the title to that charming custom of the thirties of reviewing the leading players by means of short clips of them as they appear in scenes from the film, there is a comment via overlay about the importance of water to fight drought. Gene comes to the rescue, thwarting the efforts of the banker, George Chesebro, and Charlie King from destroying the construction on the dam. During the course of his adventures, he is dunked four times in the Kern River, a circumstance that must have prompted Nat Levine to chuckle. It was an integral part of the Autry Fantasy that the stooge placed more impediments in the hero's path than the villains could. This is about the extent of Smiley Burnette's contribution to the film, plus singing a number.

The Autry Fantasy, as I have described it in connection with *Red River Valley,* was still too much under the influence of Nat Levine for mature development. Unfortunately, most of Levine's additions to the Fantasy were openly satirical of Gene. With the departure of Levine from Republic, Armand Schaefer and Gene refined the Fantasy and were at last in a position to exploit it without hindrance to its full magnitude.

Clarence E. Mulford was born on February 3, 1883, at Streator, Illinois. He was his lifelong a quiet, reclusive man. As a youth, he was strongly taken by the then newly emerging genre of the literary Western. The Mulfords relocated to Brooklyn in 1889. Clarence entered the civil service rather than college. He was as much under the spell of Theodore Roosevelt as Owen Wister was, and with avid interest he read and studied Wister's *The Virginian*.

Mulford was essentially a lonely man. He lived to a great extent in his own imagination, and he began assembling a library on the development of the American frontier. He thought he might try writing about the West. He entered a Western short story in a contest sponsored by *Metropolitan Magazine* and shared in the first prize. He followed this with a series of connected stories featured in Caspar Whitney's *Outing Magazine*. The series was published as a picaresque novel titled *Bar 20* (Outing, 1907). Mulford next wrote his first legitimate novel, *The Orphan*, very much an imitation of the spirit and style of *The Virginian*. It was published in 1908.

Over the next two years, Mulford conceived of his notion of a saga of novels with Western settings and a group of basic characters that would use as a background the major historical events in the settling of the Southwest, the great cattle ranches, the trail drives, the coming of the railroad and barbed wire, the war with Mexico, the mining camps, the shift from the Southwest to the Northwest with the discovery of gold in Montana. One of the central characters in the saga was a red-haired, swearing, smoking, drinking, rough but grimly ethical galoot named Hopalong Cassidy, who had first appeared in *Bar 20*. Mulford switched his publishing affiliation to A. C. McClurg, of Chicago, which house he stayed with until he became a Doubleday writer in the middle twenties. What helped put him over with Doubleday was the decision of the Fox Film Corporation to bring *The Orphan* to the screen, starring none other than Tom Mix as the wronged Gordon boy who sets out after Tex Wilson, played by George Bancroft, finally bringing him to justice and finding love at the same time. The film was released as *The Deadwood Coach* (Fox, 1924) and didn't remain com-

Bill Boyd in what Harry Sherman considered his "monkey suit" from *Hop-A-Long Cassidy Enters*.

pletely faithful to the events described in the novel. Mix took his unit to the Badlands to film the picture, and it was given a solid promotion.

Mulford was a man not much given to love or romance. His books were painstakingly accurate as to detail, his style careful but without distinction. His sentiment was Athenian, as it were, and his stories from the school for character. *Hopalong Cassidy* appeared in 1910. It told of Hoppy's love affair with Mary Meeker and ended in their marriage. *Bar 20 Days* in 1911 was another picaresque collection of related stories set in a different time and narrating various adventures of the Bar 20 punchers working for Buck Peters: Hoppy, Red Connors, and youthful Johnny Nelson. It also featured Tex Ewalt, a fast gunman and cardsharp who had been introduced in *Bar 20*. The next book in 1912, *Buck Peters, Ranchman,* found Peters leaving the Bar 20 to found his own spread in the Montana Territory. It wasn't until *The Coming of Cassidy* in 1913 that Mulford narrated the gun battle Bill Cassidy had been in which created a permanent limp in his right leg and led to his moniker as Hopalong.

Johnny Nelson was featured as the main character in *The Man from Bar 20* (McClurg, 1918), and the next book, *Johnny Nelson* (McClurg, 1920), told of Johnny's marriage. *The Bar 20 Three* in 1921 found Hoppy and Red Connors helping Johnny out of some difficulties in a strange cattle town, and *Tex,* published the next year, described Tex's marriage and settling down. At this point, Mulford had written ten books, and only three of them had the appeal to romantic sentiment which, so obviously, accounted in large measure for Zane Grey's tremendous popularity with feminine readers. Mulford wouldn't compromise. He wasn't very good at drawing women; they held no special interest for him as characters. *Bring Me His Ears* in 1923, *Black Buttes* of the same year, and *Rustlers' Valley* of 1924 were books written about different characters not included in the Bar 20 outfit, but set against equally divergent locales and dealing with separate events. *Hopalong Cassidy Returns* in 1924 described the loss of Hoppy's wife and child and his encounter, together with his side-kick of old, Red Connors, with Mesquite Jenkins, a hard, lean, wild youngster. Time out for a novel of the mining camps, *Cottonwood Gulch* in 1925, Hoppy and Mesquite returned for *Hopalong Cassidy's Protégé* in 1926. *Corson of the JC* introduced still another assortment of characters, followed the next year by *Mesquite Jenkins,* which narrated Mesquite's adventures alone on the trail. Finally, in 1931, Mulford undertook to bring several sets of these characters together in *Hopalong Cassidy and the Eagle's Brood*. This novel featured Hoppy, Johnny, and Tex Ewalt joined by Matt Skinner from *Rustlers' Valley,* Dave Saunders from *Cottonwood Gulch,* Wyatt Duncan from *Black Buttes,* and Corson from *Corson of the JC*.

In 1924, with the money he received from Fox, after writing Western stories for seventeen years, Mulford took his first trip West. He had married at thirty-seven years of age to Eva Emily Wilkinson in 1920 and in 1926 settled permanently in Fryeburg, Maine. It may strike the reader as somewhat curious that Mulford should choose to write about the deep Southwest while living at almost the farthest point East within the continental United States. Mulford customarily vacationed at Bridgeport, Connecticut, during the summer months. He indexed his library of Americana on some seventeen thousand file cards covering every activity of the West. He was still writing furiously and had published two novels in 1934, the year after his wife succumbed to a tragic illness, when, in early 1935, he received Harry Sherman's letter proposing a series of motion pictures to be based on his Bar 20 saga.

Sherman had remained in various aspects of distribution after his franchise for *Birth of a Nation* expired, finally coming to Hollywood. He sought production work and was hired by Paramount to do the all-talking remake of *The Light of Western Stars* (Paramount, 1930) in their Zane Grey series. Known by his friends as Pop Sherman, Harry rented office space at the Paramount Marathon Street studio. He was convinced that he could do as much, or more, with Mulford's saga than had already been done with Zane Grey's novels, both at Fox and at Paramount. Mulford was enthusiastic about the project and suggested the two of them get together. He proposed New York.

It must have been rather a shock for Sherman, meeting Mulford. Nothing in the man's novels had prepared him for the total Easterner, in puttees, plus fours, and a cap worn at a rakish angle. The two negotiated a contract in a Brooklyn saloon. Harry didn't have any money, he told Mulford, so would Mulford settle for a flat 5 per cent of the gross? Mulford cannily agreed. Harry didn't have any paper on him, and so, in a bind, the two, not quite sober, drew up the contract on a piece of toilet paper and signed it. When Pop returned to the West Coast, his two daughters, Lynn and Teddi, met him at once and asked if his trip had been successful. Sherman said it was a deal but he had lost the piece of toilet paper.

"I don't know," he said, "I looked in my pockets, everywhere, but I couldn't find it . . . I probably blew my nose in it."

Sherman next approached Paramount for financing. The studio agreed to release the pictures, but declined putting any money into them. The Western market seemed too unsure, and there were more than enough Westerns being made as it was. Sherman had proposed to James Gleason that he star in the film as Hopalong. When Gleason learned that Paramount was to release the picture, he increased his asking price. Sherman dumped him and approached David Niven. Niven refused.

Harry secured financing from William Fisk and Nicholas Luddington, who were in the tire business. They agreed to finance the initial entry at $85,000. Paramount distribution should bring them a return of at least

The cast and technical crew assembled from *The Bar 20 Rides Again*. Boyd in casual clothes is sitting next to Muriel Evans, who is next to Pop Sherman. George Hayes is on the balcony, Jimmy Ellison fourth from the right.

Photo courtesy of Teddi Sherman.

$250,000. But Sherman was still without a leading man. He asked around the Paramount lot, and William Boyd's name was brought up. Boyd was born on June 5, 1898, at Cambridge, Ohio, and had come to Hollywood in 1919 convinced that his handsome countenance, blue eyes, and blondish hair would land him in pictures. He was right. He was hired as an extra by Cecil B. De Mille for *Why Change Your Wife?* (Paramount, 1920) and went on, in the twenties, to work in several high-budget features, including De Mille's *The Volga Boatman* (PDC, 1926) and Howard Hughes's *Two Arabian Knights* (United Artists, 1927). In 1929 Boyd made an exceptionally fine Western for Pathé, *The Painted Desert,* which featured William Farnum and J. Farrell MacDonald as the two old prospectors that find him as a child and Clark Gable as the villain who battles with him in his maturity. A shoot-out at the end between Farnum and MacDonald finds Boyd standing in the middle only to be winged. "I don't know which one of you did this," he comments, "but you're both bad shots."

Sherman thought Boyd worth a try. Bill's career had plunged into obscurity in 1931, in part because of bad nationwide publicity concerning another actor, William "Stage" Boyd. Producers felt his name might hurt box office even though he was wholly innocent. Boyd took to drinking heavily and had married beautiful Dorothy Sebastian, whose career was flourishing and who was well able to support both of them. It was Boyd's third marriage, Dorothy's second. "Dorothy made a picture with Bill only a little while after her engagement to director Clarence Brown took a complete nose dive," Katherine Albert reported in *Photoplay* in October 1932. "One day she started to tell Bill all about it. He didn't say much—he never does, but he was intuitive enough to know that the hard look in Dorothy's eyes and her set grim mouth were indications of unhappiness and so, because he was lonely too, there sprang up a very real friendship."

Sherman rang up Boyd at Dorothy's beach house. When he couldn't get him, he made an appointment with Dorothy's twelve-year-old daughter to come out and see her stepfather about a part in a picture. The girl went out onto the beach where Boyd was sleeping off a two-day drunk and sobered him up with Dorothy's assistance and two pots of black coffee. Sherman arrived. Pop had been prepared as to what to expect from De Mille. He told Bill that if he would quit his excessive drinking, he'd give him $5,000 to play Hopalong and a chance at a whole series of pictures. Boyd gave Pop his word. The man who became Hopalong Cassidy became a teetotaler for the duration of his Hoppy career.

I have already commented that, impressed by George Hayes's performance in *In Old Santa Fe,* Sherman engaged him for the first Bar 20 picture with an option for a three-year contract as a player. As Johnny Nelson, Sherman needed a youthfully boyish actor, filled with energy and native charm, handsome enough in a peculiar way so he could appeal to men and women alike. He found him in Jimmy Ellison. Jimmy boarded at the Los Angeles YMCA with Pate Lucid, a film cutter at Paramount whom Pop chose to act as his production manager. Charles Middleton, who as a Fox player had worked opposite both Will Rogers and George O'Brien and who was currently menacing Tom Mix in *The Miracle Rider* for Mascot, was signed as Buck Peters. Frank McGlynn, Jr., was cast as Red Connors.

The first picture was titled *Hop-A-Long Cassidy* and was based on Mulford's 1910 novel. Exteriors were shot at the Prudential studio lot on the Kern River with interiors kept to an absolute minimum in order to economize. Although *The Painted Desert* had been a Western, Boyd had been extensively doubled and was afraid of horses. During the first week of production, he fell from the white stallion Pop had rented from Fat Jones and broke his leg. Pop told director Howard Bretherton to shoot around Boyd as much as possible. Bill's leg was put into a cast, but he couldn't help limping. Sherman came up with the idea of using the accident to advantage and had a scene written in for Bill to be shot in the leg, to be out of the picture for a time, and to be named "Hopalong" as a result of the limp. By the time of the second film, *The Eagle's Brood* (Paramount, 1935), the leg had healed and so the limp was dropped without any explanation. Nor was any other reference ever made to why the character was called Hopalong in the fifty-two features Pop made subsequently.

Bill had been impressed with Tim McCoy's Western uniform as it appeared in his early Columbia films *One Way Trail* (Columbia, 1931) and *Shotgun Pass* (Columbia, 1931) and modeled himself after it. Like Tom Mix, Bill insisted on wearing gloves. Pop and Bill had their first big fight about what Pop considered Bill's "monkey suit," but Bill was stubborn and held out. It was probably no more preposterous for Bill to dress all in black than for Tim McCoy, that same year, in making his Westerns for Puritan Pictures, to contrast the blackness of his clothes with his shining white sombrero and light-colored neckerchief, appearing on the trail, confronting the outlaws, bathed in brilliant sunlight, silver gleaming, eyes blazing, the reflections bounding from his silver-plated gun, an archangel in all his majesty, an avenger from the heavens. Pop wanted realistic Westerns, fully in keeping with the tone of Mulford's novels. His hopes were dashed from the outset.

Sherman had been deeply impressed at the frenetic tension aroused by the ride of the Klan in *Birth of a Nation*. He resolved that just such a finish would be ideal for *Hop-A-Long Cassidy*. Griffith had a profound interest in classical music and had chosen his own themes, in fact had filmed sequences with the rhythm and melody of the score in mind. Pop so conceived the screenplay that it built to a high point of outrage, followed by a tempestuous gathering of the forces of retribution. He chose for his musical accompaniment the "Dance of the Furies" from Gluck's *Orfeo ed Euridice*. The exciting exhilaration of the score guided the composition and cutting of the sequences preceding the confrontation of the rustlers atop Thunder Mesa. It was the only music used in the film and, consequently, starkly effective in its violent contrast with the silence after George Hayes, as Uncle Ben, expires.

The film opens to a visual commentary setting the story in the days before the barbed-wire fences. Hoppy returns to the Bar 20 only to find rustler trouble. Jim Meeker, of the H2, and Buck Peters, of the Bar 20, are kept at each other's throats by Kenneth Thompson as Pecos Jack, Meeker's foreman. Eventually the truth comes out, and the two spreads join forces against the outlaws, taking them atop Thunder Mesa after a violent gun battle.

Hop-A-Long Cassidy was a success. Out of the returns, Pop began production on the next entry, *The Eagle's Brood* (Paramount, 1935). A good many events from the novel were altered for the screenplay, but Sherman

The accelerated windup with which Harry Sherman Westerns ideally ended, William Duncan and the Bar 20 punchers racing to save Hoppy, Lucky, and Windy in *Hopalong Rides Again*.

Photo courtesy of Paramount Pictures.

wanted to stress story values and drama over action in this film. His transpositions and changes served to further this end. The emphasis was clearly on character studies and situation. William Farnum was cast as a Mexican bandit, El Toro, whose son and daughter-in-law were cruelly murdered by Big Henry and his gang, leaving his grandson to wander as an orphan. George Hayes was cast as the bartender, Spike. Lois January played a Spanish dancer in Big Henry's saloon located at Hell's Center. When El Toro saves Hoppy's life, Hoppy pledges to save his grandson. Johnny tags along. Dorothy Revier was cast as a saloon tart named Dolly. Bill, strolling up to the bar, turns to look at her, murmuring, "Hmmm, not bad." It was typical of Boyd, perhaps, but as unthinkable for the character in the book as Boyd's drinking sarsaparilla would have been.

Pop chose stunningly beautiful scenic locations in the Sierra mountains for the exteriors, plus using the Monogram town set and interiors at the Paramount lot. The music within the cantina was totally appropriate and quite atmospheric, although the lack of any kind of action finish precluded an agitato for chase sequences. In terms of character development and story line, *The Eagle's Brood* was superior to *Hop-A-Long Cassidy;* moreover, it began the shift of the Bar 20 films generally away from a simple action format to one of complex human interrelationships. It was this shift, above all, that distinguished Pop Sherman as a Western filmmaker and rendered such an enduring quality to nearly all of his early Bar 20 films and almost all of his non-Hopalong Westerns.

Gerald Geraghty joined Pop Sherman's staff in preparing *The Bar 20 Rides Again* (Paramount, 1935) for the screen, assisting Doris Schroeder. Howard Bretherton continued as the director for all the early entries, and Archie Stout was the cinematographer. J. P. McGowan played Buck Peters in this entry, and the exteriors used by Buck Jones in filming *The Crimson Trail* (Universal, 1935), including the corral where Buck tamed a horse, were used again, this time with Bill Boyd taming the horse. Ethel Wales was cast as Buck's sister, and Harry Worth turned in a splendid performance as the outlaw leader struck with Napoleon's career. Hoppy in a bit of dialogue with George Hayes—Boyd dressed as a gambler, Hayes as a prospector—anticipated the scenario to *Three on a Trail* (Paramount, 1936), in which the Bar 20 burns down Pecos Kane's saloon via some poor model work

Bill Boyd and Nora Lane, who played Hoppy's sweetheart in *Cassidy of the Bar 20* and *Hopalong Rides Again*. She later committed suicide in despondency over her off-screen marriage.

Photo courtesy of Paramount Pictures.

with Onslow Stevens as Kane. George Hayes kept changing his status in the films, from an outlaw father in *Call of the Prairie* (Paramount, 1936), whose girl is in love with Johnny, to one of the Bar 20 crew in *Three,* to an old retainer of the Jordans in *Heart of the West* (Paramount, 1936).

De Mille was starring Jimmy Ellison in *The Plainsman* (Paramount, 1937) and so Pop couldn't use him at the same time for the seventh film in the series, *Hopalong Cassidy Returns* (Paramount, 1936). Rather inept casting led to William Janney being featured as Hoppy's younger brother, Buddy, and one of the best of Mulford's novels became the basis for the weakest Bar 20 picture until that time. Evelyn Brent, however, handed in a superb performance as a saloon keeper and leader of an outlaw band. Ellison was back for the next two entries, *Trail Dust* (Paramount, 1936) and *Borderland* (Paramount, 1937), then he dropped out permanently to appear first in Sherman's new series of films based on Rex Beach's Alaskan stories before signing as a contract player with RKO Radio.

Paramount took over direct financing with the 1936 schedule, and Pop received the usual 17½ per cent as a producer's percentage. The budgets were increased to $125,000 a picture. Boyd's salary was raised to $10,000 a picture. Pop told Pate Lucid, who was still his production manager, that he had come to a decision about a replacement for Ellison, namely Pate. Russell Harlan, who photographed nearly all of Harry Sherman's later pictures, was an understudy to Archie Stout at the time. Pate took for his screen name Russell Hayden, a variation on Harlan's name. George Hayes was now given regular casting as Windy Halliday, one of the Bar 20 punchers. Through a brilliant bit of casting, Pop had selected silent-film star William Duncan to play Buck Peters in *Three on a Trail* (Paramount, 1936). Duncan was ideal for the role, and, indeed, it was this group—Boyd, Russ Hayden, Hayes, William Duncan—that appeared in the finest Bar 20 films. Russ's first picture was *Hills of Old Wyoming* (Paramount, 1937).

Some of the entries were pedestrian, like *Rustlers' Valley* (Paramount, 1937), which had very little action. Others, like *Hopalong Rides Again,* which was Lesley Selander's first picture for Sherman after he joined the unit when he left off directing Buck Jones at Universal, were uncommonly strong. *Hopalong Rides Again* was based on *Black Buttes* (Doubleday, 1923) and cast Harry Worth again as the principal villain, a phony professor of paleontology. The film also introduced Nora Lane as Hoppy's love interest, a role she would continue in the thirties, returning to it once more in *Cassidy of Bar 20* (Paramount, 1938), an otherwise unremarkable and yet entertaining film. *Hopalong Rides Again* was the first Hoppy picture to feature youngsters, a tendency which persisted till the end of the series.

The quality kept varying in 1938. *Bar 20 Justice* (Paramount, 1938) was one-half interior sets inside a gold mine; *The Frontiersman* (Paramount, 1938) was rather pedantic with a story about schoolchildren and featuring Dick Jones as a small, recalcitrant pupil and Buck and Hoppy praising the virtues of education. For *Sunset Trail* (Paramount, 1938), Bill borrowed Buck Jones's sheepskin chaps and disguised himself as a dude at a dude ranch in order to bring the villains to justice. *Silver on the Sage* (Paramount, 1939) started the new season with a plot of double indentity. *Range War* (Paramount, 1939), which introduced Brett Wood to the series, replacing George Hayes, who signed with Republic, was filmed on the existing sets from Cecil B. De Mille's *Union Pacific* (Paramount, 1939), particularly scenes of the end of track.

In 1940 Pop started shooting the pictures two up, doing the exteriors for two films at one location with shifting casts, and then all the interiors. He cut his budgets, raised Boyd's salary, and made even more himself. *Doomed Caravan* (Paramount, 1941) was an interesting film with Hoppy battling to save the life of a freight line threatened by Morris Ankrum, who had become a regular villain in the series with *Hopalong Cassidy Returns* (Paramount, 1936). *Wide Open Town* (Paramount, 1941) was the most

Director Lesley Selander, actress Jean Parker, and Bill Boyd clowning on the set of a Bar 20 picture.

Photo courtesy of Lesley Selander.

ambitious in the series, running eighty-eight minutes and actually being a remake of *Hopalong Cassidy Returns,* with Evelyn Brent again as the female outlaw leader, Victor Jory as her right hand. It was Russell Hayden's last entry before he joined Columbia Pictures for more money and a chance for a starring series of his own. His parting with Pop was difficult for both of them.

Outlaws of the Desert (Paramount, 1941) replaced Russell with Brad King and was set in the Arabian desert with Duncan Renaldo cast as a sheik seeking Hoppy's assistance during a horse-buying trip. *Stick to Your Guns* (Paramount, 1941) started a decline in the films, introducing both inertia and the Jimmy Wakely Trio. Gerald Geraghty was joined by his brother Maurice Geraghty, and both Lynn and Teddi Sherman, Pop's daughters, worked on the screenplays. Mulford would constantly complain that none of the pictures ever followed his novels; Pop would respond by sending him another box of cigars. The pictures were consistently making money.

There was a certain distance between Pop and Bill, especially over Bill's increasingly mild interpretation of the role. Sherman thought of himself as Hopalong Cassidy and wasn't at all enamored of Boyd's portrayal; but it was popular at the box office. Boyd confined his drinking to a little white wine and, finally, in 1939 married Grace Bradley, his fifth and last wife. With Pop taking over the Paramount Zane Grey series in addition and Bill being paid $25,000 a picture, it seemed that prosperity had come to stay.

George Hayes looked at it differently. He was resentful of Pop Sherman for prohibiting him from using the screen name of Windy at Republic and was compelled to change it to Gabby Hayes. Andy Clyde, who replaced both George Hayes and Brett Wood as the series side-kick in 1940, harbored some bitterness toward William Boyd in the way he was treated. According to Clyde, when Boyd began television production, Clyde was upset to learn that, after waiting at Bill's request for several months and turning down jobs in the interim, he had been passed over for Edgar Buchanan, a fact which he learned by reading *Variety* and which Bill never told him. Yet, for all that, the Hoppy group worked closely for many years and developed a considerable rapport among themselves.

The reader may recall that *Heritage of the Desert* (Harper's, 1910) was Zane Grey's first Western novel. Famous Players-Lasky brought it to the screen in 1924. It was directed by Irvin Willat and starred Bebe Daniels in the role of Mescal, a Spanish-Indian ward of August Naab. Naab was played by Ernest Torrence, with Noah Beery as the heavy. In the very early thirties, Paramount decided to remake several of the silent Zane Grey Westerns in sound. B. P. Schulberg, who was still in charge of studio operations, thought this a better notion than Harry Joe Brown's proposal that the studio commence production on a series of programmer Westerns. Sam Jaffe came up with the idea that the films should be so constructed that each entry could call upon much of the footage from the silent Grey Westerns, so as to give the finished picture the appearance of much higher production value than it actually had.

Jaffe selected Henry Hathaway from among the Paramount contract directors to direct the films. Hathaway had worked on *The Virginian* (Paramount, 1929) and was enthusiastic about the project and about getting a chance to direct his own pictures. Jaffe dispatched Hathaway and a writer to go on location and prepare a script shooting around the 1924 version. When Hathaway returned, he learned to his dismay that Jaffe had been fired as a result of an altercation with Josef von Sternberg.

David O. Selznick had just joined Paramount as Schulberg's assistant. Selznick's assistant was Harold Hurley, a man who had worked in publicity on several of the films with which Hathaway had been associated. Hathaway approached him with the idea, and after a two-hour discussion, Hurley responded, "We've got a job, I'm going to produce and you're going to direct." The series was successful, and Hurley was promoted to producing twenty pictures a year for Paramount release. Paramount paid its associate producers $17 \frac{1}{2}$ per cent of the profits; Hurley made out quite well. "But— the son of a bitch—I was an assistant director," Hathaway recalled many years later. "I was making a hundred fifty a week (I was a high-priced assistant), and when I got my first job as a director the check was for a hundred bucks! He said, 'That's all I can afford to pay you. You wanna make

Jack Holt confronting Tom Kennedy and Warner Oland in the first make of
Heritage of the Desert.

Photo courtesy of *Views & Reviews* magazine.

the picture for a hundred?' I directed two pictures for a hundred a week and
then they had the big depression and they cut everyone's salary and they
cut mine to sixty-five a week. I directed two pictures for sixty-five bucks a
week! I was making less money than the prop man and all the crew because
they were working by the hour on union rates."

The Depression permanently altered the composition of Paramount. Sam
Goldwyn had long ago been eased from the company by Adolph Zukor.
During the late twenties, Cecil B. De Mille had been quietly removed as a
director-producer, although he was later to return at Zukor's urging, and
once returned, stayed for the remainder of his career. Sam Katz, who
managed the expanding theater chain, the subsidiary known as Publix
Theaters, was locked in a power struggle with Sid Kent, who headed the
Paramount Sales Department. At a board meeting in New York, Jesse L.
Lasky volunteered to have his name removed from the parent company
corporate title, and Zukor proposed that the new firm name be Paramount
Publix. Katz, who had begun his association with motion pictures as a
piano player in one of Uncle Carl Laemmle's nickelodeons in Chicago, introduced some of his wealthy Chicago friends to Zukor. John Hertz, the
Yellow Cab magnate, and Albert Lasker, a millionaire advertising executive, brought new money into the company, averting a move to sell out the
Publix chain as office space and dispose of the studio facilities to M-G-M.
Before it was over, Lasky was compelled to leave the company and enter
independent production; Schulberg was fired and Selznick left; Mae West
came to Hollywood, and her flashy sex comedies restored vitality to the

failing fortunes of the Paramount empire. Despite all the corporate manipulations, Adolph Zukor managed to adroitly skirt danger and retain his position.

Randolph Scott was born Randolph Crane at Orange City, Virginia, on January 23, 1903, and was educated in engineering. Advised by a physician to go West after a bout with ill health, Scott began his acting career at the Pasadena Community Playhouse. He made his screen debut in *The Far Call* (Fox, 1929) and was signed by Paramount as a contract player in 1931. It was Scott that Hathaway chose to play the part of Jack Hare in the talking remake of *Heritage of the Desert* (Paramount, 1932). David Landau was bad man Holderness; J. Farrell MacDonald played Naab. Big Boy Williams was cast as Holderness' right hand. Sally Blane was the girl. The scenic locations were well photographed, and Hathaway drew a rather touching portrait of the developing, hesitant love between Randy Scott and Sally. The town set used in *The Virginian* was employed for Holderness' hide-out.

It was, in fact, this note of delicacy which Hathaway invested into the Zane Grey Westerns of 1932–33 and which made them so utterly unique for the time. *Wild Horse Mesa* (Paramount, 1932) followed, again with

Gary Cooper as he appeared in *Fighting Caravans,* one of the early entries in the sound Zane Grey series.

"How do you know so much about it Murdock?"

An action sequence, also from *Fighting Caravans,* featuring an Indian attack.
Both Gary Cooper and Randolph Scott had important roles in the sound Zane
Grey series for Paramount.

Photo courtesy of *Views & Reviews* magazine.

Scott in the lead, assuming the Chane Weymer role Jack Holt had played in
the silent version. Sally Blane was the girl, and Fred Kohler took the old
Noah Beery part. By filming on the identical locations, Hathaway was able
to match shots so well with the older footage that it was virtually beyond
detection; nor did it matter, since Hathaway stressed the human interplay
between the principals and not the spectacle.

In 1933 Hathaway directed some of the best entries ever made in the
Zane Grey series since Paramount had begun producing the pictures and,
certainly, pictures which rank among the best Westerns of the period and
in Hathaway's career. One after the other, he made *Sunset Pass, Under
the Tonto Rim, To the Last Man, The Thundering Herd,* and *Man of
the Forest.* Noah Beery was restored as the chief heavy, and, if anything,
his villainy had intensified over what it had been in the twenties. *To the
Last Man* featured Esther Ralston as the heroine, who marries Randy
Scott by the final reel. In addition to fighting viciously against the heavies
to save Randy's life, Hathaway inserted a gentle counterpoint, a nude swimming scene with Esther appearing as some primitive Eve in a distant
paradise. Harry Carey joined the cast for *The Thundering Herd* and *Man
of the Forest.* As fine as Victor Fleming's direction had been in the silent

entries, or George B. Seitz's work in the series in the late twenties, I cannot help thinking that perhaps Hathaway came closest to the romantic spirit of the Grey novels. To the rugged beauty and endurance of the land was added the idyllic experience of first love. Whether the heroine was Sally Blane, Esther Ralston, or Verna Hillie, Hathaway chose them for their innocence, their pluck, their gameness. They were sensuous without ever being overtly carnal, vibrant without being vulgar. His $90,000 budgets did not permit Hathaway to encompass grandeur, other than use of stock footage; but intense working with his players allowed him to sustain a poetic lyricism that glowed quietly on the silver screen.

For *Man of the Forest,* Hathaway revised the screenplay from the 1926 version. *Man* was first filmed in 1921 by Zane Grey Productions, with Benjamin Hampton producing. It was one of Grey's finest novels, and the scenario followed the story in most details. Al Auchincloss, played by Harry Lorraine, sends for his two nieces to take over his land empire; Claire Adams and Charlotte Pierce played the nieces. Carl Gantvoort was Milt Dale, the man of the forest who hides the girls from Lem Beasley's schemings. The 1926 remake featured Jack Holt in the role of Milt Dale. The nieces were trimmed to a single heroine, portrayed by Georgia Hale. When Georgia is sent for by her dying uncle, Jack frustrates Clint Beasley's plans of murdering her by abducting the girl and hiding her in his forest retreat. Warner Oland played Beasley. Georgia suspects Milt's intentions and has him jailed. Milt escapes with the assistance of his pet cougar, confronts Beasley, and settles the score, Georgia coming to realize that Beasley was behind her uncle's death.

The reader may have remarked himself about the peculiarity of Grey's names for his characters. The names would undergo slight modifications from film to remake that, in many cases, the character would not; the plots, on the other hand, made cause for wonder, for so altered did they become by the late thirties that the only thing they had in common with the novel was its title.

In Hathaway's version of *Man of the Forest,* Randy Scott is Brett Dale. He hides Verna Hillie, who plays Harry Carey's daughter, from Noah Beery's schemings. Beery murders Carey and has Brett arrested for the crime. Brett's pet lion helps him escape. Big Boy Williams provides some comedy by wrestling with a sitting mule used for similar purposes in *Wild Horse* (Allied, 1931), *Ride 'Em Cowboy* (Warner's, 1932) and *The Painted Stallion* (Republic, 1937). Beery is finally done in by his housekeeper, jealous of the attentions he has shown Verna.

Hathaway, who met Zane Grey while working on the Paramount features, once commented, "He didn't talk much, but he listened a lot, and he was always working on a new story. His books were marvelous. There was always something fresh and different about them." Hathaway introduced

Shirley Temple to the screen in *To the Last Man* (Paramount, 1933); he gave Randolph Scott a hold on playing in action and adventure films which lasted for nearly three decades; he won stirring performances from veterans like Harry Carey, Noah Beery, Fred Kohler, Raymond Hatton, Big Boy Williams; above all, he made his own films—oftcn remakes of remakes—as fresh and different as he himself found the novels.

In 1934 the Zane Grey series was cut back to only two entries a year, due to the slump in the Western market, and Hathaway was otherwise employed. The pictures made through the middle thirties were entertaining but fundamentally lacking in the magic and broad conception which had previously characterized them. By the end of the decade, Paramount suggested to Harry Sherman, who was already doing the Mulford stories, that he take over production on the Zane Grey series. Pop agreed and at least with *The Mysterious Rider* (Paramount, 1938) and *Heritage of the Desert* (Paramount, 1939) made two notable Grey Westerns before Paramount abandoned their production entirely, shortly after Grey's death in 1939.

I have always found Sherman's production of *The Mysterious Rider* engaging, with Douglas Dumbrille teamed with Sidney Toler and pitted against Robert Barrat. Maurice Geraghty, who did the screenplay originally, did not agree with me. "I wrote the script with George Bancroft in mind," he commented to me, "but as I recall Harry had a salary dispute with George and wouldn't pay his salary, so to my dismay and horror Douglas Dumbrille, who was a nasty heavy and had no warmth at all, suddenly was signed to star. I called Harry and pleaded with him to switch back, but it was too late. I was sunk and, to my mind, so was the picture."

Pop used his Bar 20 unit to manufacture his Zane Grey entries and featured Russell Hayden in nearly all of them. Geraghty, who worked on *Mysterious Rider,* and Norman Houston, who did the screenplay for *Heritage of the Desert,* were entirely unaware that Paramount or any other studio had done these novels before; the approach was to be based only on a reading of the novels, and no matching of stock footage or use of former scenarios. For this reason, Pop's *Heritage* stands by itself when contrasted with the two earlier Paramount productions. Pop used his basic Western formula in bringing it to the screen: open big, forget the middle, and come to an exciting finish. The only mention of the horse Silvermane, so prominently featured in the novel, is confined to a passing sequence; but this is more mention than this plot ingredient got in the previous versions.

Donald Woods is in his attorney's office as the film begins. He decides to go West to look over his land holdings. C. Henry Gordon is Woods's manager. He tries to put Woods out of the way. Robert Barrat is the senior Naab, Russell Hayden the last of his sons not killed by Gordon. Russell is eventually murdered, and Naab, together with Woods, Sidney Toler, and a posse of ranchers, have a terrific shoot-out with Gordon and his gang.

Pop Sherman and Sidney Toler out on location for *Heritage of the Desert*. Pop liked Sidney and continued to cast him in his Westerns even though Sidney was under contract to 20th Century-Fox to play Charlie Chan.

Photo courtesy of Teddi Sherman.

Westerns based on Zane Grey's novels did not end with the conclusion of the Paramount series produced by Harry Sherman, but Paramount's intimate association with Grey's literary properties did come to an end with these last entries. It is unfortunate that literary rights caused the negatives to most of the Paramount features to change hands so many times that many of them are lost forever due to decomposition. But those which still do survive, or surviving prints, indicate what a vigorous and energetic inspiration the Grey novels were in Western production during Grey's lifetime.

31 / THE THREE MESQUITEERS

I

William Colt MacDonald, the reader may recall, had worked in the Columbia Pictures Story Department in the early thirties. He published the first of the Three Mesquiteers books in 1933, *Law of the .45's*. He followed it with several more: *The Singing Scorpion* (Outlet, 1934), *Powdersmoke Range* (Outlet, 1934), and *Riders of the Whistling Skull* (Crown, 1934). They were formula stories, but steeped with action and rather complexly plotted, if ultimately weak in character delineation.

A small, independent producing company bought screen rights to *Law of the .45's* and prepared it for release through Grand National under the same title. MacDonald's characters were a *Western* transposition of *Les Trois Mousquetaires,* by Alexandre Dumas. Tucson Smith was the leader of the group, Stony Brooke his confederate, and, in *Law,* they were joined by Lullaby Joslin. The film version, directed by John McCarthy, starred Big Boy Williams as Tucson and Al St. John as Stony. Lullaby did not appear. Nor was the trio concept of the stories consolidated in *Too Much Beef* (Grand National, 1936), in which Rex Bell played a trouble shooter named Jack Argyle who adopted the name of Tucson Smith while investigating some cattle rustling. The screenplay by Rock Hawkey, however, was based on a story by William Colt MacDonald.

The first true Mesquiteers film was produced by RKO Radio Pictures in 1935 with Harry Carey in the role of Tucson, Hoot Gibson cast as Stony, and Big Boy Williams playing Lullaby. The casting was quite consistent with the descriptions MacDonald provided in the novels. "Tucson Smith," he wrote, ". . . was a rangy, raw-boned individual with brick-red hair and humorous gray eyes from the corners of which ran crow-footed tiny laugh wrinkles." Of Stony, he said "he was solidly compactly built, and was, considering the wide shoulders and barrel-like torso, surprisingly fast on his feet. He [had] a snub nose and a wide mouth that tilted upwards at the corners giving his face an expression similar to that of some medieval gargoyle."

RKO billed the picture as the "Barnum and Bailey of Westerns" and cast a great many Western players in it, beginning with Tom Tyler and Bob Steele and even calling on old hands like William Farnum, Buddy Roosevelt, and William Desmond. Bringing the picture up, however, gives me the opportunity to tell the reader what these principals were doing at the time. In addition to the three Mascot serials Harry Carey agreed to appear in after the success of *Trader Horn* (M-G-M, 1931), he was signed by Louis Weiss to make an undetermined number of Westerns to be released as Artclass Pictures in the independent market. Harry was to be paid $5,000 a picture. He probably should not have made them; they were awful. *The Night Rider* (Artclass, 1932) was typical. It had no production value, primitive recording, and a plot which joined George Hayes and Julian Rivero with Harry in rounding up a mysterious hooded figure. Weiss ran into financial difficulties and sold out Harry's contract to Maurice Conn, of Commodore Pictures, who continued making them until 1937. Harry wasn't paid and had to sue Weiss for his salary. Weiss sold off his scripts to A. W. Haeckle, of Supreme Pictures, and so it came that *The Night Rider* was remade as *The Desert Phantom* (Supreme, 1936), with Johnny Mack Brown. In the later films, Carey returned to the character of Cheyenne Harry from his Universal days. The quality didn't improve. *Ghost Town* (Commodore, 1936), for example, was interesting in that it cast Jane Novak, William S. Hart's leading lady from the twenties, as a blond gang moll, but she couldn't act any better than the rest of the cast and Harry seemed to be the only professional.

Hoot Gibson was simultaneously working off his contract with Walter Futter, and Bob Steele had just signed with A. W. Haeckle to make a series of low-budget films to be directed for the most part by his father, Robert N. Bradbury. Based on the success of *Powdersmoke Range,* Bob made *Sundown Saunders* (Supreme, 1936), in which he played the gunman portrayed by Tom Tyler in the Mesquiteers feature. Some of these films were enjoyable, like *Smokey Smith* (Supreme, 1936), which did run to violence when Warner Richmond had to shoot off Bob's father's finger in order to steal his ring; and some were terrible, such as *Trail of Terror* (Supreme, 1936), in which Richard Cramer and several of the gang are in one prison cell in a penitentiary, Bob in the other working undercover to get back an express shipment—there is only one cot in the Cramer cell and no lavatory facilities, while the express shipment has been casually buried in a cave used by the remaining gang members as a hide-out.

Tom Tyler was contracted for an independent series of six pictures a year under the Reliable logo. He was paid more to appear as a villain in *Powdersmoke Range* than he received as a star. He went on in 1937 to make a series of eight Westerns for Sam Katzman's Victory Pictures. They were even cheaper and more shoddily made than the Tim McCoy group made the next year. Buddy Roosevelt had appeared in a series for Superior Talking Pictures that reached the height of ineptitude in *Boss Cowboy* (Superior, 1934), which had only the skin-tight dresses of the heroine to recommend it, although her figure left something to be desired. This was more or less the Western environment at the time that trio pictures were introduced. Just as the novelty of the singing Western, they were made necessary by the depths to which routine Western production had fallen.

II

Powdersmoke Range followed the novel more closely than any of the Mac-Donald books subsequently filmed. The Guadalupe Kid, who was introduced in the novels in *Law of the .45's,* has promised the Mesquiteers that he will go straight. The Mesquiteers thwart a stage holdup by Ethan Laidlaw. They take Laidlaw into Los Portos only to discover that the town is run by Sam Hardy and that Adrian Morris is a crooked deputy. The Kid,

Bob Steele, an undercover lawman, is letting Charlie King out of jail in *Trail of Terror.*

Photo courtesy of *Views & Reviews* magazine.

A reproduction of the original art work used for the one-sheets in promoting
Powdersmoke Range.

Photo courtesy of *Views & Reviews* magazine.

played by Bob Steele, is being held prisoner by Ogden. The Mesquiteers free
him and they ride off together to the Tresboro ranch. The Kid is in love
with Boots Mallory, daughter of the deceased ranch owner. The Mesquiteers
set to making the ranch pay.

Hardy hires Sundown Saunders, a notorious gunman, played by Tom
Tyler, to put Tucson out of the way because of the interference to his plans.
Tucson buys himself a pair of 32.20's to the consternation of all his friends.
During the street confrontation, Tucson pulls down on Saunders from nearly
a hundred yards away, wounding him, Saunders being inaccurate at that
distance. Next, Tucson gets himself appointed a special deputy and stages a
showdown between Hardy's men and the Tresboro punchers. He finally
shoots it out with Hardy in the office above Hardy's saloon.

Powdersmoke was one of the few early talking Westerns which contained
indoor/outdoor sets, so that the camera recedes in tracking fashion as
Tucson buys his guns and walks from the interior into the street, or as the
Mesquiteers walk through the bank onto the boardwalk without any cutting
or change in camera position. It proved a popular Western, but RKO did

not follow it with a series. Nat Levine at Republic Pictures, who had already brought a similar format to the screen in his serial *The Three Musketeers* (Mascot, 1933), seized upon the idea, purchasing screen rights not merely to a novel but to the characters themselves. He began his own series with a different cast.

Powdersmoke Range did not prove an important picture for either Carey or the Hooter, but it did lead to their appearing together the next year in *The Last Outlaw* (RKO, 1936). It was an uncommonly fine Western based on John Ford's original screenplay from a 1919 two-reeler he made for Universal. Carey played an aged outlaw released from prison into modern civilization, only to learn how much times have changed. Hoot Gibson played a cowpoke who falls in love with Carey's daughter, and Fred Scott appeared as a singing cowboy much in the Autry tradition. Henry B. Walthall was magnificent as a frontier sheriff, demoted by progress, while Tom Tyler played a big-city mobster. The picture was filled with comedy and action, and none of the rapport Carey and Hoot had had in the early days was lost when they were reunited for this film.

Ford had every intention of remaking *The Last Outlaw* himself and urged Harry to buy the rights from RKO in 1942. Harry did so, but Ford went into the service. He told Harry to wait until after the war. RKO was required to destroy the original camera negative and so the picture went out of circulation. However, Carey became seriously ill in 1946, retiring from the screen, and died in August 1947. It was never remade. A few scattered prints survive, which is unfortunate, since *The Last Outlaw* was the best sound Western Carey made.

III

The Republic Three Mesquiteers Westerns were made on very much smaller budgets. First in the series, *The Three Mesquiteers* (Republic, 1936) featured Ray Corrigan in the role of Tucson Smith, Robert Livingston as Stony Brooke, and Syd Saylor as Lullaby Joslin. It was a contemporary story of veterans returning after the Great War and settling in the West only to be confronted by J. P. McGowan and his gang of cattle thieves. Saylor proved inappropriate for the part and was replaced in the next film with ventriloquist Max Terhune as Lullaby. Terhune was popular, although his appearances with his dummy, Elmer, were a far cry from the image of the capable gun-slinger MacDonald projected of Lullaby in the novels.

Bob Livingston was born Robert Randall at Quincy, Illinois, on December 9, 1908. His parents were newspaper people, and his first job was as a reporter for the Los Angeles *Daily News*. He started acting at the Pasadena Community Playhouse and entered motion pictures at Universal in 1929. He became a contract player at M-G-M in 1933 but secured a release from them when Levine contacted him to join Republic and star in the serial *The Vigilantes Are Coming* (Republic, 1936). In it, Livingston portrayed a masked figure reminiscent of Rudolph Valentino's The Eagle, battling against Fred Kohler's efforts to secretly mine gold on Bob's ranch. Ray Corrigan appeared briefly in the first and final two episodes as a character named Captain Fremont. Kohler hires a band of Russian Cossacks, living in California, to assist him.

The serial proved such a success that Levine decided to revive the Zorro property, which Douglas Fairbanks had brought to the screen in the twenties, with Livingston in the lead role. The film was titled *The Bold Caballero* (Republic, 1936) and was photographed in the new two-color process. As the picture opens, Sig Ruman is seen as a tyrannical commandant who mercilessly exploits the peasants and levies taxes so high as to keep them impoverished. Don Deago Vega is a roaming minstrel, exceedingly handsome but generally regarded a coward. He and the commandant became friends, particularly when the commandant seeks the Don's aid in his suit for Heather Angel's hand. Secretly, at night, the Don is the masked figure, Zorro, who with sword and pistol robs from the commandant and turns his gains over to the suffering poor. After some thrilling chase sequences, Zorro is captured and unmasked by the commandant. He is sentenced to be hanged. Heather is in love with him. While the Don is led to the gallows, his supporters surround the commandant's military outpost and spring a surprise attack. There is a terrific fight with Zorro finally triumphing over Ruman and winning Heather in the bargain. The picture inspired several subsequent Republic serials, the best of which was probably *Zorro's Fighting Legion* (Republic, 1939), which, apparently by sheerest accident, featured character actor Reed Hadley in the role of Zorro.

The Mesquiteers were far more popular in terms of the trio concept than Harry Sherman's Bar 20 pictures. *Ghost Town Gold* (Republic, 1936), second in the series, already emphasized in the screenplay the very real competitiveness which existed between Corrigan and Livingston. The credits began billing Stony Brooke first, although the story line invariably presented him as headstrong, easily infatuated, or drawn into crazy schemes. *The Riders of the Whistling Skull* was fourth in the Republic series and actually the first to be based on a novel, although the plot had nothing to do with the novel of that title and was instead an adaptation of *The Singing Scorpion* (Outlet, 1934), whereas *The Purple Vigilantes* (Republic, 1938) was based on MacDonald's plot to *Riders*. The film opens to a group of archaeologists in quest of a lost and hidden tribe of Indians who are supposed to dwell beneath a rock formation shaped like a skull through which the wind whistles eerily. The Mesquiteers act as their guide into the hinterland. The picture was filmed on location at St. George, Utah. Levine

Producer Harry Grey with a later trio of Mesquiteers; Bob Steele, Bob
Livingston, and Rufe Davis.

Photo courtesy of *Views & Reviews* magazine.

suggested that the screenwriters employ many of the identical images that
had been used to such good effect in *The Lightning Warrior*. The same
lonely tom-tom music is used, and the early appearances of members of the
lost tribe are presented in terms of shadows moving against rocks and along
canyon walls. Roger Williams and his gang have been secretly stealing the
Indians' treasure. Once the Mesquiteers arrive at the Valley of the Skull,
Williams tries to turn the Indians against the invading party, but the attempt is fruitless. The Mesquiteers release Professor Marsh, who has been
held prisoner in a cave, and shoot it out with Williams and his gang.

The early entries had rather strong plot lines. *Hit the Saddle* (Republic,
1937) dealt with the roundup of wild horses and incorporated the painted
stallion fight from *The Devil Horse* (Pathé, 1926); *Gunsmoke Ranch*
(Republic, 1937), directed by Joe Kane, told of flood victims swindled by
an unscrupulous politician; *Come on, Cowboys* (Republic, 1937) featured
the falling out of the owners of a circus; *Range Defenders* (Republic,
1937) cast Tom Carr, later a director at Republic, as Stony's brother,
falsely accused of murder; *Heart of the Rockies* (Republic, 1937) concerned the illegal killing of animals in a game preserve.

Just before *Trigger Trio* (Republic, 1937) was scheduled to be made,
Bob Livingston suffered a fractured skull in an accident. He was replaced
in this picture by Ralph Byrd, star of the Dick Tracy serials at Republic,

who played Tucson's brother. Livingston returned to the series and made six more films, beginning with *Wild Horse Rodeo* (Republic, 1937), which featured Roy Rogers in a bit as a café singer.

In 1938 Republic signed John Wayne again after a hiatus at Universal. The tension between Livingston and Corrigan had reached such a point that the studio determined to star Bob in other vehicles. Duke was cast as Stony Brooke, with Corrigan staying on as Tucson and, in the initial entries, Max Terhune as Lullaby. Republic upped the budgets proportionately with what they felt the increased star value which Duke Wayne's addition brought to the series. *Pals of the Saddle* (Republic, 1938) was the first film with Duke and was directed by George Sherman, who, in 1937, had taken over as principal director for the Mesquiteers pictures. The next entry, *Overland Stage Raiders* (Republic, 1938), featured Louise Brooks, who had gained a substantial reputation in the late twenties.

After his appearance in John Ford's *Stagecoach* (United Artists, 1939), Duke still made four more Mesquiteers films, the best of which may well have been *Three Texas Steers* (Republic, 1939), which, again, had a circus setting and even managed to include Ray Corrigan doubling as a gorilla. When he wasn't acting in pictures in future years, Corrigan would occasionally agree to play apes and gorillas. *Wyoming Outlaw* (Republic, 1939), Duke's seventh Mesquiteers, was based on a true incident whereby a small-town waiter did in a notorious bandit. Donald Barry played the bandit, and David Sharpe, later a stunt man and double, portrayed the waiter.

When Republic began to build Duke into a major property, Bob Livingston returned to the series as Stony Brooke. Max Terhune's contract had expired after the sixth Wayne film, *Three Texas Steers,* and was not renewed. Raymond Hatton replaced him. Corrigan, confronted with this change in personnel, opened negotiations with Monogram Pictures to make a new series of trio Westerns. Monogram signed both Corrigan, who was to star, and Terhune and added John King to form a threesome known as the Range Busters. The films were open imitations of the Mesquiteers series, but with shoddier production values, weaker stories, and rather routine action. David Sharpe soon replaced John King.

Herbert J. Yates then suggested to Duncan Renaldo, who was a Republic contract player, that he join Livingston and Hatton. Duncan played an entirely new character named Rico, and Hatton played Rusty, so that the Mesquiteers were no longer even based on MacDonald's fictional heroes. Harry Grey, who had begun with the series as musical supervisor, took over as associate producer. *Oklahoma Renegades* (Republic, 1940) was based in part at least on the script to the very first Mesquiteers entry, this time the trio defending the property rights of veterans returning from the Spanish-American War. Production values were cut again, with a heavier reliance on stock footage, even to a wagon crash which had been used in *The Lightning Warrior* (Mascot, 1931). Gerald Geraghty did the screenplay for *Pioneers of the West* (Republic, 1939), in which Noah Beery was cast as a crooked judge, the period being removed to 1876. Indeed, the time and location of the Mesquiteers films varied as much as the scenarists, so that the three could battle very modern Germans, in keeping with the spirit of the times, or old-fashioned cattle rustlers and land-grabbing bankers.

Under Texas Skies (Republic, 1940) saw Duncan leaving the series and Bob Steele taking his place. Rufe Davis also began in this picture, playing the role of Lullaby, replacing Ray Hatton. Livingston's last Mesquiteers film was *Gangs of Sonora* (Republic, 1941), directed by John English. Bob Steele was promoted to first position, and Tom Tyler was cast as Stony, which was more or less the balance maintained in the novels.

The trio concept of Westerns ran its course and ended shortly after World War II. It symbolized in its way the collectivism and group spirit of the period and managed, incidentally, to elevate the status of the side-kick— in the instances of Terhune and Hatton, at least—to more than a buffoon.

32 / THE GOLDEN AGE OF THE WESTERN SERIAL

I have told how Republic used contract player Bob Livingston in starring features and serials while he was Stony Brooke in the Three Mesquiteers series. The studio did the same with Ray Corrigan. The locations at St. George, Utah, employed in filming *The Riders of the Whistling Skull* so impressed Nat Levine that he decided to shoot an entire serial there. Ray Corrigan, who had starred in the chapter play *Undersea Kingdom* (Republic, 1936) the previous year, was given the lead as Clark Stuart. Ray was a very aggressive horseman, yet he would occasionally fall from the saddle of his horse when trying a quick mount or a precarious maneuver. George de Normand doubled for Ray and started calling him "Crash" Corrigan. Ray ignored the humor and kept "Crash" as a nickname.

The story idea utilized the basic notion of *Trader Horn* (M-G-M, 1931). Julia Thayer, later known as Jean Carmen, played the mysterious Rider, a blond-haired white girl, raised by the Comanches after she was rescued from a massacred settlement. Because of her hair, she is worshiped by the Indians as a goddess. She has grown up with one thought in mind, to preserve peace and prevent bloodshed. Thelma "Babe" De Freest was Julia's double during the demanding riding sequences.

William Witney, who had been hired and trained as a film cutter by Mascot Pictures in the early thirties, went along with the troupe, headed by directors Alan James and Ray Taylor. Bad weather plagued the company, and Taylor was usually under it. Taylor was finally taken off the picture and Witney promoted to replace him. It began Witney's career as a director. He went on to direct or codirect twenty-four out of the sixty-six serials produced by Republic Pictures between 1936 and 1955. "We had a lot of things going on," Witney recalled. "Locations up in Utah and some money to spend. But much of the credit should go to Bill Nobles, the cameraman." The budget was $300,000 and the serial exceeded it.

Hoot Gibson was signed for the role of Walter Jamison, wagon master for the first wagon train of merchandise dispatched to Santa Fe. It was Hoot's last screen appearance until he returned in the Trail Blazer series for Monogram in 1943. Jack Perrin, a hero for the independents during the twenties and generally a heavy during the early thirties, was cast as Davy Crockett. Wally Wales, having changed his name to Hal Taliaferro, which was his real name, appeared as Jim Bowie. Sammy McKim played the young Kit Carson.

The Painted Stallion is exceptional due to the production standards, the very stirring musical score, and the heroic theme of a wagon trek West. But what makes the serial most intriguing is the Rider of the Painted Stallion. Her presentation in the first several episodes is as a protector, one whose nature is essentially peaceful. She is surrounded by an aura of kindliness. It is only in Chapter 6, when the odds against the wagon train are incredible, that she places her whistling arrows in the service of destruction and then, one after the other, from high above the ambushers, she shoots them down. The addition of the comedy team of Oscar and Elmer served as an unpleasant distraction, but a minimal complaint in terms of the chapter play's over-all excellence.

Hoot Gibson as wagon master and Ray Corrigan as special U.S. envoy to Mexico set out on a wagon train to open trade agreements with the new governor of Santa Fe, which is still under Mexican rule. The deposed lieutenant governor is LeRoy Mason, Duncan Renaldo his right hand. The wagon train is prey to constant raids inspired by Renaldo and his men. When the train finally reaches Santa Fe, Mason is compelled to flee into hiding. He carries on the fight from outside the city. The Americans are protected at every turn by the Rider of the Painted Stallion. Mason is finally dispatched and Corrigan and the Rider are together at the fade.

The Painted Stallion had the fast-paced action typical of the Mascot serials, but the story line was somewhat thinned to permit a smooth-flowing sequence of events. The Rider herself was nearly archetypal, stressing again the arrow theme which had been so strong in *The Lightning Warrior*. There were many Western serials made after it, by Universal, by Republic itself, and by Columbia Pictures, which entered the chapter-play field the year *The Painted Stallion* was released. Perhaps only one ever came close to it, *Overland with Kit Carson*, which Columbia issued in 1939.

Gordon Elliott, who was born Gordon Nance on a farm in Pattonsburg, Missouri, in 1904, studied acting at the Pasadena Playhouse and made his motion picture debut in the early thirties. He became a contract player for Warner Brothers in 1934 and played all manner of roles. Warner's began a series of singing Westerns in 1935 with Dick Foran. Many of the screenplays were based on the old Ken Maynard First National series, although, unlike Sid Rogell's series with Duke Wayne, there was little or no reliance on stock footage from the silent films. Gordon Elliott was a heavy opposing Foran in *Moonlight on the Prairie* (Warner's, 1935).

Columbia Pictures selected Elliott to appear in the lead for their serial *The Great Adventures of Wild Bill Hickok* (Columbia, 1938) on the basis of his appearance in the Foran Westerns. The chapter play cast Sammy McKim, who had been Kit Carson in *The Painted Stallion*, and Frankie Darro, who had been a frequent child hero in Mascot serials. Kermit Maynard had a substantial role. Elliott played Hickok, consciously basing his

Ray Corrigan and Julia Thayer in a scene from *The Painted Stallion*.

Bill Elliott, Jack Rockwell, and James Craig from an early sequence in
Overland with Kit Carson.

Photo courtesy of Columbia Pictures.

interpretation of the role on Gary Cooper in *The Plainsman.* Hickok is
marshal of Abilene. He is opposed to the Phantom Raiders, a gang preying
upon a gigantic cattle drive from Texas to Kansas. Hickok organizes the
boys in Abilene, including Dickie Jones as well as McKim and Darro, into
an organization known as the Flaming Arrows. The effect of using youngsters in this way was quite the same as Autry's use of them in *The Phantom
Empire;* the serial was an astonishing success.

Columbia had been making a series of third-string Westerns with Jack
Luden to balance their Charles Starrett units. With Elliott's success in
The Great Adventures, they signed him as a contract player, dropped the
Luden series, and started a new one with Elliott as the star. *In Early Ari-
zona* (Columbia, 1938) cast Bill Elliott, as he was now publicized, as
Whit Gordon, summoned to Tombstone by Wyatt Earp to assist Earp in
cleaning up the town. This was a relatively high budget Western. Inter-
spersed between $100,000 productions like this one and those like *Frontiers*

of '49 (Columbia, 1939), which were specials, Elliott appeared in more standard fare in the $60,000 Wild Bill Saunders series for Columbia in the 1938–39 season.

Bill's second chapter play for Columbia, and Columbia's eighth serial, was *Overland with Kit Carson*. It was a lavishly mounted production with a $340,000 budget and a thirty-six-day shooting schedule accomplished in six weeks. It remains, in my opinion, the best Western serial Columbia ever made. Stock footage and interpolations from previous Columbia productions were at a minimum. A few shots from Tim McCoy's *End of the Trail* were included, particularly in Chapters 3 and 4, but the lighting, blending, and costuming were such, and the shots themselves of a brevity, that to the untrained eye the source would be unidentifiable.

Two production units were assigned to the picture, one under Sam Nelson, the other under Norman Deming. Deming had been directing action pictures since working with Hoot Gibson at Universal in the twenties. The assignment was a matter of economy, but, unlike Nat Levine who had pursued this practice at Mascot and then Republic, the script, which was the size of the New York telephone directory, was not divided up according to interiors and exteriors, with a director deployed exclusively on one or the other. Norman Deming recalled that no extraneous footage was shot and that each of the two units attacked the script an episode at a time, one with Bill Elliott and the leading man group, one with Trevor Bardette and the heavy group.

While the idea of a white renegade leading a band of Indians had long been a standard prop of the serial, it wasn't until *The Lightning Warrior* that the variation was used of having the renegade leader simultaneously masquerade as a prominent citizen of the besieged community. Pegleg in *Overland* summons his forces by means of a wolf call, as did the Wolf Man, and, as in *The Lightning Warrior,* in *Overland* the chapter synopses are delivered by an invisible narrator. Benjamin Kline, who had codirected *The Lightning Warrior,* was by now chief photographer of Columbia action productions and was charged with the photography on *Overland.* The concept of a legion of riders dressed in black was inspired by the Don Cossacks.

The most novel, dramatic, compelling character of all in *Overland* was Pegleg, played by Trevor Bardette. Bardette had to play both Arthur Mitchell, a fur trader at Stewart's Post, and the peg-legged, deformed leader of the Black Raiders. Bardette really did play both roles, not, as in so many cases, letting an actor not otherwise included in the film be cast as the disguised mystery man and then unmasking one of the credited characters in the last chapter. Bardette was scrupulous about his characterization. To his portrayal of Pegleg he added an archetypal suggestiveness by conjuring the strange dreams of power and the crazed fanaticism of Captain Ahab in *Moby-Dick.* "I did not consciously copy Ahab," Bardette wrote to me some time ago from his ranch in Arizona, "but I had read *Moby-Dick* and an actor is inclined to organize his *total experience* when preparing a role."

Bardette's make-up as Pegleg was complex. The scars on his left cheek attributed in the script to a birth defect (another link with Ahab which was in turn a reference to the mark placed upon Cain in Genesis) were made of latex, applied often twice a day, depending on the necessary shifts in characterization. The leg was a very complicated harness, consisting of a special boot with a long strap built into its top which was attached to a broad, heavy leather belt at the waist, pulling the right foot upward and forward. Onto this contraption the pegleg was strapped, fitted to the knee and around the thigh and calf. It was painful, and Bardette could stand it for little more than an hour before his leg would go to sleep. The rest was camera angle. Bardette's double in all this was Earl Bund, a remarkable stunt man who really had only one leg and who also doubled several others in the cast, although John Dahdin stood in for Bill Elliott.

The Pegleg disguise.

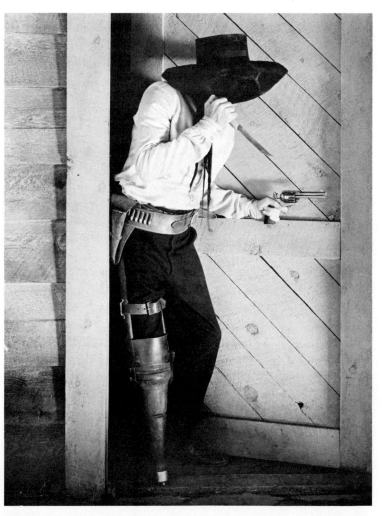

Bill Elliott instructing the Indians in the traditional view of red men as uneducated children.

When Pegleg evokes his men to his dream of empire in the first episode, or when he is seen seated atop his black stallion with a throne-shaped rock behind him in later chapters, or looking down from a high precipice as he frequently does to the action below, or as in chapters 14 and 15 when he is silhouetted against the flares and fires of the camp and iron smelter, the drama and tragedy of his insane ambition are portrayed in such a manner by Bardette as to raise the story line above the mere mundane fare of a matinee serial. Deming, who directed Bardette, was awed by his portrayal.

Viewed in sequence and at one sitting, as serials were never intended to be, *Overland with Kit Carson* may appear to be one long series of fights, clashes, gun battles, brawls, raids, chases, and pitched attacks. This is because Columbia always insisted on a set formula in its productions. After the three-reel first chapter, every succeeding episode has at least one breath-taking escape; we see Pegleg once, usually at his camp; and the Indians or the Black Raiders spring a surprise ambush. Only when viewed individually and a week apart do these episodes carry their full impact.

Overland was shot in large part at Kanab, Utah, in the natural caves and on the plain. Pegleg's killer stallion, Midnight, was a horse belonging to Ralph McCutcheon, named Blackie, brilliantly photographed. The musical score by Lee Zahler consisted, as Wagnerian musical drama, of themes or leitmotivs identified with certain characters or groups, increasing the tension and even, at times, anticipating the action. The thundering and demonic musical motif used for Pegleg was deepened in its effectiveness by the choice of camera angles and lighting surrounding the one-legged figure in white satin shirt, atop his black charger, with a wide-brimmed sombrero, the crown of which shadowed the right side of his face, the left side heightened and accentuating the scars. The scars were hidden, supposedly, by a false beard when Bardette was playing the trapper, Mitchell.

Bill Elliott and Richard Fiske join forces fighting against Pegleg and his Black Raiders and their Indian allies. Bill, as Kit Carson, organizes a group of vigilantes. A series of pitched battles ensues until Pegleg is reduced to making a last stand. His men are defeated and he races to escape, Kit after him. Pegleg's killer stallion, Midnight, stamps him to death. Bill and Iris Meredith are united.

When Columbia came to make their last chapter play in 1956, *Blazing the Overland Trail,* it was built largely out of footage from *Overland with Kit Carson* with a minimum of new material. Dennis Moore was costumed identically to Bill Elliott, and Lee Roberts was dressed as Richard Fiske to facilitate matching shots. At best, it was a sad farewell to the chapter play. Spencer Gordon Bennet directed it, marking his forty-second year in serial production. Universal closed down its unit in 1945 when Henry MacRae died. Republic disbanded their serial unit in 1955. However timebound the formula, it did have its bright moments, and *The Painted Stallion* and *Overland with Kit Carson* are certainly among them.

33 / GEORGE O'BRIEN IN THE THIRTIES

George O'Brien once described himself as "a man of a few thousand words." During the silent era following *The Iron Horse,* as a foremost contract player for Fox studios, he appeared in more dramas than Westerns and was known primarily as an action star. He had been the fifty-ninth actor Ford had tested for the epic. He and Mervyn LeRoy had been renting a room in a little house that took on boarders; Gary Cooper was among them.

To the time of this writing, O'Brien continues to think of *The Iron Horse* as his favorite film "because it was a success, and it could have been an awful flop, and Ford and I would still be trying to make a living someplace. So it did two things: it gave me my opportunity and it gave Ford his opportunity, because up until that time he'd been making Harry Careys." A friendship was struck up between Ford and O'Brien that terminated only upon Ford's death. O'Brien once described Ford as a coach. "You see," he said, "I was young enough to want to go all out—'Let me do it, coach.' Impressionable, if you want. People like Duke . . . John Wayne, and Maureen O'Hara, claim he has eyes in the back of his head. Because you'll be working out some business for a scene, you'd get in the scene, and he'd say, 'Here's what I'd like you to do—not what you were trying over there.' And you'd say, 'How did he know that?' Then he'd come over and put his arm around you like a coach, and say, 'Nice going.' That's all you need sometimes. Also, I think Ford, myself, John Wayne, we started from humble beginnings, and when we realized we were up against it we went to work. And work in those days meant practically living in the studio. I slept in my dressing room many times."

In 1926 Ford made another exceptional Western for Fox, *Three Bad Men.* It was initially intended to star Fox's three leading Western players, Tom Mix, Buck Jones, and George O'Brien. O'Brien was the only one who ultimately appeared in the film as its nominal hero while character actors Tom Santschi, Frank Campeau, and J. Farrell MacDonald were the three bad men of the title. The film was a Ford Western made in the spirit of William S. Hart, austere, sentimental, and mounted on a grand scale with

George O'Brien from the period when he was under contract to Sol Lesser.

Photo courtesy of *Views & Reviews* magazine.

its own version of the Cherokee Strip land rush harking back to Hart's *Tumbleweeds* of the previous year.

O'Brien in 1927 appeared in F. W. Murnau's silent classic *Sunrise* together with Janet Gaynor and Margaret Livingston. In 1929 he made *Noah's Ark* for Warner's, directed by Michael Curtiz, which was part talking. Ford starred O'Brien in *Salute* (Fox, 1929), with sequences shot on location at West Point using University of Southern California football players John Wayne and Ward Bond in walk-ons. O'Brien made *The Sea Beneath* (Fox, 1931) for Ford and, after filming it, took a six-month trip with Ford to the Orient, most of the time Fox executives having no idea where they were. William Fox was in the midst of his empire-building which, briefly, brought him into control of Loew's, Inc., and, in effect, of Metro-Goldwyn-Mayer before, as a house of cards, his stock manipulations collapsed.

It was production manager Sol Wurtzel's idea to get back into Western series films. Sol Lesser had proven with his Beverly Productions that Buck Jones was still box office. Since O'Brien's contract had been renewed and he was on salary, Wurtzel decided to mount a series of sound Westerns with O'Brien as the star. Several of these, such as *Riders of the Purple Sage* (Fox, 1931) and its sequel, *The Rainbow Trail* (Fox, 1931), were remakes of the Tom Mix films of the twenties, which had been themselves remakes of Fox's Zane Grey entries of 1918. *Fair Warning* (Fox, 1930) was a remake of Mix's *The Untamed* (Fox, 1920), and *Last of the Duanes* (Fox, 1931) was a remake of Tom Mix's 1924 version of the Zane Grey story, which was again in turn a remake of the earlier 1919 film. *Mystery Ranch* (Fox, 1932) featured heavy Charles Middleton, who schemed to compel Cecilia Parker to marry him in order to legally control her land. David Howard directed it. Ingredients from this picture were used later in the composition of the screenplay for *Lawless Valley*. Middleton had Noble Johnson, a mute with his tongue cut out, and Charles Stevens strangle or hang anyone who interfered with his plans. While O'Brien appeared in non-Westerns during this same period, his talking Fox Westerns were in every way exceptional vehicles. When Sol Lesser sold his Buck Jones contract to Harry Cohn for the 1931–32 season and following his short stint with Universal, Wurtzel contacted him and had him join Fox as associate producer on the O'Brien Westerns.

By 1933 Fox was facing the severest crisis in its financial history. Lesser set up offices on the RKO-Pathé lot and called his firm Atherton Productions. In 1934 Fox stopped financing the O'Brien pictures, so Lesser secured money elsewhere while Fox continued to distribute the films. The budgets on these Westerns were generous on the whole, with shooting schedules in excess of a month and excellent locations in Utah, Monument Valley, Montana, and Colorado. On July 15, 1933, O'Brien married Fox contract player Marguerite Churchill. The marriage resulted in two children. They were divorced in 1948.

In 1935 the Fox Film Corporation merged with the Twentieth Century company. Twentieth Century had been founded by Joseph M. Schenck, former head of production at United Artists and brother of Nicholas Schenck, president of Loew's, Inc. It was financed by Louis B. Mayer. Darryl F. Zanuck, previously from the Warner's Writing Department, was made executive in charge of production, and one of Mayer's sons-in-law, William Goetz, became Zanuck's assistant. Sol Wurtzel was retained by the newly titled 20th Century-Fox Film Corporation as head of B production until personal misfortune led to his replacement in 1939 by Harry Joe Brown. O'Brien's last Lesser film for Fox release was *The Border Patrolman* (20th-Fox, 1936), whereupon O'Brien's second contract ran out.

George A. Hirliman was born on September 8, 1901, at Fort Lee, New Jersey. From 1916 until 1927 he was involved in various aspects of the film laboratory business. When he sold out his laboratory complex to Herbert J. Yates in 1927, he founded Exhibitor's Screen Service, which he sold out to

National Screen Service in 1933. From 1933 to 1935, he worked as production executive for Yates at Consolidated Film Industries, overseeing features and shorts under the subsidiary name of Select Pictures. In 1935, with Yates masterminding the Republic merger, Hirliman formed his own production company. He signed George O'Brien in 1936 and secured an RKO release agreement. Lesser, in the meantime, went to work as an associate producer at RKO, specializing in drama and action pictures.

Hirliman set up a company for Western production, Condor Pictures, and associated himself with Max Hoffman, Jr., who produced the first of a series of projected Condor Westerns with Ken Maynard for Grand National release. I describe elsewhere how the Hoffman-Maynard pictures fared. Hirliman's personal financial involvement in the fading fortunes of Grand National led him to dissolve Condor Pictures in late 1937. He sold O'Brien's contract to RKO, which agreed to finance and produce the O'Brien Westerns directly. O'Brien's contract called for him to receive $21,000 a picture, which made him for a period the highest paid player in the Western market. In March 1938 William Boyd's new contract with Pop Sherman raised his price to $25,000 a picture, placing him on top, with Buck Jones third, getting $16,000 apiece for his Coronet releases.

At RKO, Bert Gilroy was made associate producer on the O'Brien Westerns in 1938 until the end of the series. David Howard, who had directed O'Brien as early as *The Rainbow Trail* (Fox, 1931), had directed many of the Lesser entries and did nearly all those for RKO, beginning with *Daniel Boone* (RKO, 1936), the first O'Brien picture under the Hirliman contract.

Judging from the Fox O'Brien films, *In Old Santa Fe,* and the RKO O'Brien series, David Howard may well have been the best B Western director in Hollywood in the thirties. Unequivocally, the George O'Brien Westerns were among the finest series produced in that decade. Even at RKO, where shooting schedules were tightened to three weeks and locations were generally no farther removed than Foxborough or Sedona Valley, the pictures were almost always characterized by A-budget elements, fine production techniques, and strong supporting players. O'Brien's many years of working with Ford taught him more than a little of the importance of secondary roles. With some regularity, O'Brien would sit down with the writers and work out bits of business for various characters in the story, stressing genuine humor and human interest.

O'Brien remade *The Painted Desert* (RKO, 1938), although the later picture owes virtually nothing to the original version except substantial action footage literally snipped out of the earlier negative. The story was by Jack Cunningham, with the screenplay by John Rathmell and Oliver Drake. I might mention that Rathmell worked on both *In Old Santa Fe* and *The Riders of the Whistling Skull.* Fred Kohler, Sr., is cast as a

Kay Sutton and George O'Brien, who starred together in *Lawless Valley*.
Photo courtesy of *Views & Reviews* magazine.

mining agent. He cheats Laraine Day's father and then has him murdered. It was probably because of their association in *The Iron Horse* that O'Brien liked having Kohler around as the lead heavy. Laraine and George become partners in a tungsten mine on O'Brien's property. William V. Mong is cast as a banker who loans O'Brien money to start operations. "I know how you bankers are," O'Brien tells Mong. "If I don't meet these notes, you move in and I move out." Mong joins with Kohler in an attempt to jump the claim. The footage of the racing ore wagons and the mine explosion, both from the original, is spectacular. Only by watching the two pictures together can one appreciate what a fine film *The Painted Desert* (RKO-Pathé, 1929) was, which, of course, is not meant to detract from the O'Brien film, which stands on its own merits.

Lawless Valley was next. It was again directed by David Howard, with a screenplay by principal unit writer Oliver Drake. The original story was based on a novel by W. C. Tuttle. Fred Kohler, Sr., liked the picture because it once more gave him a chance to play father on screen to Fred, Jr., this time with both of them heavies, unlike *Toll of the Desert* (Commodore, 1935), in which Junior, as an honest sheriff, hangs Senior for the savage outlaw he is without recognizing Senior's paternity.

As the picture begins, O'Brien is released from prison. He meets Walter Miller on the way back to Valley Junction. Miller is really a secret investigator assigned to the case. O'Brien manages to expose Earle Hodgins and Chill Wills, the sheriff and deputy respectively, as being in league with the

Kohlers to frame him. O'Brien forces their hand and captures them and the missing express money which prompted his being sent to prison. At one point, Fred Kohler, Jr., says to his father, "If you do that, you're a fool." Senior's reply is "Careful, you're talking to your dad, you know."

Marshal of Mesa City (RKO, 1939), one of the last entries in the O'Brien series, was another instance of truly effective cinema. Produced by Bert Gilroy and directed by David Howard, the story with some very subtle alterations was substantially that of *Powdersmoke Range*. Leon Ames played a suave but ruthlessly crooked sheriff who was romantically interested in Virginia Vale. Mary Gordon, perhaps more familiar for her portrayal of Mrs. Hudson in the Basil Rathbone/Sherlock Holmes films, played an engaging Irishwoman, owner of a boardinghouse. Howard utilized some novel miking setups, such as recording O'Brien and Vale while riding along a trail without subsequent dubbing, or while they were walking down the boardwalk of the RKO town set. O'Brien got the writers to insert some poignantly comic lines in his dialogue. When he interrupts a stage holdup and asks one of the bandits to unmask, he remarks ironically upon seeing his face: "I don't blame you for wanting to hide it." When Slim Whitaker takes to his heels after an unsuccessful ambush attempt, O'Brien tracks his fleeing form with his gun but does not fire, commenting, "I never could shoot a man in the back."

In 1939 Tim Holt entered the series as second lead. When O'Brien's contract ran out after *Triple Justice* (RKO, 1940), RKO decided not to renew but immediately put Tim in the series as a replacement, beginning with *Wagon Train* (RKO, 1940). Tim was at a lower salary figure, and budgets could be trimmed by nearly a third. O'Brien was cheerful. He had invested his money wisely. With the outbreak of the war, he enlisted for service in the Navy. John Ford brought him out of retirement later for his RKO Westerns in the late forties. Nothing RKO did subsequently, however, nor as fine as the later Tim Holt films became, indeed no budget Westerns of the forties, ever captured quite the same combination of enchantment and polish as the O'Brien series. It is unfortunate that television syndication never undertook to make them as familiar a property as most of the budget Westerns of the era, so that a later generation might be in a better position to assess what a fine product a medium-budgeted Western could be when given a rare combination of creativity, inspiration, and care.

34 / CECIL B. DE MILLE AND WESTERN SPECTACLE

It has long been my regret that out of the many thousands of Westerns I have seen, I have been unable to screen William S. Hart's *Wild Bill Hickok* (Paramount, 1923). What I have learned of his portrayal, I have acquired from secondary sources. Hart's suspicion that Hickok may have been going blind added to the pathos of his characterization. It permitted him to inject a note of tragedy into the stark, somber story of the gunman's death, to more or less expose himself to violence while he still had all his faculties than to be hunted down and killed later when he was less able to defend himself. That isn't the way Gary Cooper enacted the historical personality in *The Plainsman* and, certainly, not the way De Mille wanted it conceived.

The role allowed Cooper to project the image of a saturnine, melancholy man, fierce in his independence, who lived by his own code of what he felt to be right and who was truly a lonely wanderer in the world. De Mille's screenplay got bogged down with all the romantic fuss about the supposed civilizing influence of woman. No matter, we owe to Cooper's personation the viability of the Hickok mythos, the reverse draw of a brace of pistols, the austere, silent, controlled persona which Gordon Elliott went on to perpetuate for years at Columbia beginning with his first starring vehicle, *The Great Adventures of Wild Bill Hickok* (Columbia, 1938).

De Mille prefaced *The Plainsman* with a short explanation, stating "the story that follows compresses many years, many lives and widely separated events into one narrative." His intention was to invoke the lives of Hickok, Calamity Jane, and Buffalo Bill. He borrowed James Ellison from Harry Sherman and cast him as Buffalo Bill. A diminutive beard helped overcome Ellison's excessive boyishness. While his acting was competent and quite the best he had done to that point, his personality lacked the deep, tragic quietism Cooper invested into his role as Hickok. Although it was no one's intention—and certainly not De Mille's—Cooper's characterization dominated the film.

The casting of Jean Arthur as Calamity was questionable. De Mille insisted on authenticity and had her practice on his wrist with her bullwhip, but even he had to admit to Jean's "piquant loveliness" as one of his reasons

Jean Arthur and Helen Burgess as they appeared in *The Plainsman*.

for selecting her. Jean's vivacious enthusiasm only added to the fantasy quality of the whole enterprise. De Mille cast his son-in-law, Anthony Quinn, as an Indian brave. For his group fight sequences, he relied heavily on process screen effects. The story was set in the days after the Civil War, but Charles Bickford and Fred Kohler, the gunrunners, were selling repeating rifles to the Indians a few years before they should have been. As any fantasy *The Plainsman* can be entertaining—General Custer is a hero. But all of this merry historical nonsense is swept away before Gary Cooper's sad, troubling depiction of Hickok which constitutes a brooding, sustained image. Adolph Zukor, who always championed De Mille, argued with him about the advisability of killing Hickok rather than letting him marry Calamity at the fade. De Mille stuck to history. Zukor countered that a more manly villain than the snively Jack McCall should do him in. De Mille wouldn't listen. He had more than fact on his side. Cooper played the role in the manner of classical tragedy, and from Hickok's first appearance on the screen his violent, hopeless end stalked him palpably. It did much to establish Cooper as a mute symbol of private agony, a sensitive, bleeding, uncomplaining contradiction to the superficial optimism in which Americans generally prefer to perceive themselves and their national destiny.

The Plainsman opens to Lincoln making plans for the postwar world. He wants to develop the West. Working against this are the financial interests in Washington which hire Charles Bickford and his gang to sell guns to the Indians. Calamity Jane is in love with Bill Hickok. Hickok and Bill Cody are enlisted by Custer in the battle against the Indians. Hickok is shot in the back by Jack McCall while he plays poker, drawing two pair, aces and eights. *The Plainsman* marked De Mille's return to Western production, but in a way it only served as preparation for De Mille's best Western, *Union Pacific*.

In the course of her long career, Barbara Stanwyck has made a number of exceptional Westerns, from *The Great Man's Lady* (Paramount, 1942), with Joel McCrea, to *Cattle Queen of Montana* (RKO, 1955), directed by Allan Dwan, to *The Maverick Queen* (Republic, 1956), directed by Joseph Kane. Yet in terms of her total output, even including her television se-

Gary Cooper and Victor Varconi in a scene from *The Plainsman*. William Boyd was originally considered for the Cooper role.

Photo courtesy of MCA-Universal.

ries, she could scarcely be considered primarily a Western player. When Joel McCrea, president of the National Cowboy Hall of Fame, brought her to the Oklahoma City headquarters in 1973 to be admitted along with Buck Jones, elected posthumously, the event was a bit of a curiosity.

De Mille, who cast her in *Union Pacific,* commented in his *Autobiography* (Prentice-Hall, 1959): ". . . I would have to say I have never worked with an actress who was more co-operative, less temperamental, and a better workman, to use my term of highest compliment, than Barbara Stanwyck. I have directed, and enjoyed working with, many fine actresses, some of whom are also good workmen; but when I count over those of whom my memories are unmarred by any unpleasant recollection of friction on the set or unwillingness to do whatever the role required or squalls of temperament or temper, Barbara's name is the first that comes to mind, as one on whom a director can always count to do her work with all her heart."

When Ella Smith published her uncritical and laudatory book *Starring Miss Barbara Stanwyck* (Crown, 1974), she ended it by quoting Barbara's impression of receiving her Wrangler award and the reaction of the audience at the Hall of Fame to a group of clips from her Western films and her television series, "The Big Valley." "Whoever edited this did a sensational job," Barbara is reputed to have said, "because, when they started showing the stunts, it looked as if I was breaking my ass and my neck. The people oohed and aahed. It was quite stirring."

Barbara possessed more of the fine qualities that one might expect in a frontier woman than most who have appeared in Westerns. She preferred to do her own stunting and ran her own risks. For years, while she projected tough-minded, strong-willed females on the screen, she lived in the most desolate loneliness. She was capable of intense personal suffering, but it was never allowed to shadow the rigid haughtiness of her cinematic portrayals. In her later Westerns, her screen characterizations altered the usual conception of a Western heroine, and she was more than a match for the weak and sometimes evil men with whom she was surrounded. I do not know why she never won an Academy Award. She was the most respected actress among innumerable producers and directors in Hollywood who could only admire her constant professionalism and her dedication. It is unfortunate that she wasn't cast at one time or another as Calamity Jane; she had more than a little in common with the woman.

I was an invited guest at the Hall of Fame that year. I was given to understand that Barbara had recently undergone surgery on her liver; that she was not supposed to drink and had done very little else, alone in her room, since her arrival three days before in Oklahoma City. I had been conversing with Joel McCrea and his wife, Frances Dee, and then had wandered to a secluded part of the Western Heritage museum. The awards dinner was

Joel McCrea, Barbara Stanwyck, and Robert Preston as they appeared in
Union Pacific.

about to begin. There, standing before a showcase filled with Western
leatherwork, quite by herself, was Barbara Stanwyck. I approached and introduced myself. Her eyes were soft, tearful, filled with ineffable remorse.
She held out her hand in supplication.

"That saddle," she remarked unsteadily. "I used one just like that in several of my pictures. Just like that."

We talked for a time. Joel McCrea joined us finally and escorted Barbara into the awards. When her moment on stage came, her back was
proudly arched, her step assured. She commanded her audience. She knew
exactly what to say and do. Her career had been her art. She had refused to
suffer publicly. She avoided roles, whether as heroine or villain, in which
she was unable to show strong character, nerves of steel, self-possession, and
nearly invincible fortitude. She was a cliché-breaker, and none but the public, perhaps, knew how to accept her. But acceptance was reserved. The
public demands that its heroes and heroines upon occasion should appear

deeply flawed, imperfect, even miserable, whereas Stanwyck was all determination: even if you've had a lot of bad breaks, you don't crab about it but go on giving your best with your heart and sinew.

De Mille was rather taken with his subject matter when he came to make *Union Pacific*. Like John Ford, he wisely chose to tell epic events as a backdrop to the ironies and passions and humor of his characters. He cast Lynne Overman and Akim Tamaroff as roughs in support of Joel McCrea, much as Ford had done with Tully Marshall and J. Farrell MacDonald in *The Iron Horse*. They were so successful he used them again in his next picture, *North West Mounted Police* (Paramount, 1940), with Gary Cooper.

Joel McCrea was born on November 5, 1905, at Los Angeles. He attended Pomona College and, upon graduation, acted in theatricals at the Pasadena Community Playhouse. He was given a feature role in *The Jazz Age* (FBO, 1929) and continued in a number of melodramas through the thirties. He appeared in Frank Lloyd's *Wells Fargo* (Paramount, 1937) opposite Frances Dee, whom he had married on October 20, 1933. It was one of Paramount's large-scale Westerns of the period. McCrea consciously based his screen style on William S. Hart's austerity and Tim McCoy's reserved bearing. There was little enough action in *Wells Fargo,* but *Union Pacific* two years hence established McCrea as a leading Western player. In

Indian marauders attacking a train in *Union Pacific*.

Photo courtesy of MCA-Universal.

the forties Harry Sherman starred McCrea in a number of his more ambitious Westerns, including *Buffalo Bill* (Fox, 1944), with Maureen O'Hara, *Ramrod* (United Artists, 1947), with Veronica Lake, and *Four Faces West* (United Artists, 1948), which again teamed McCrea with Frances Dee. McCrea also appeared in the fourth make of *The Virginian* (Paramount, 1946). Like Randolph Scott, McCrea continued to star in high-budget Westerns through the fifties for various studios.

McCrea's quiet confidence and, seemingly, introverted self-sufficiency, which so pleased audiences, were not mere posturing. But through it all ran an ornery streak. He wisely invested his income in California real estate. When oil was discovered on his land, obstinacy as well as craftiness prompted him to hold off selling drilling rights until he was offered $13 million with the stipulation that no drilling be done within sight of his home. M-G-M made him wealthy all over again when it purchased land from him for a new back lot site as virtually its last act before the studio was dissolved.

On screen, McCrea was a man of fierce loyalties, not particularly easy to know, convinced of his own importance, willful, superficially pleasant but basically inflexible. De Mille perceived these qualities and balanced them aptly with Robert Preston's charming irresponsibility, "more weak than wicked," to use De Mille's description of the Preston character. Preston was Brian Donlevy's partner in crime, joined by Harry Woods, one of De Mille's favorite character actors, and Anthony Quinn.

Union Pacific marked the forty-first time Joseph Crehan donned whiskers and smoked a cigar to portray Ulysses S. Grant. Eight weeks later he played Grant the President in *Geronimo* (Paramount, 1939). Crehan made almost a career out of playing Grant, to whom he bore a striking resemblance, although he was reputed to dislike cigars, which, to make his characterization accurate, the role invariably demanded he smoke.

De Mille was unflagging in his research. William M. Jeffers, president of the Union Pacific, opened his files, and De Mille's assistants even found letters of complaint from prostitutes concerning services that had gone unpaid. Jeffers loaned De Mille his fastest track-laying crew, and the footage showing their skill and precision was later reused in government training films. De Mille surpassed himself with the miniature work he employed in this film. His train crashes are every bit as effective as that which David O. Selznick subsequently staged full-scale in his *Duel in the Sun*. Where De Mille falls short is that very sense of spectacle which was so much a part of the man throughout his career. You do not have the impression, as you do in *The Iron Horse,* of men building a railroad, of common men welded into a great enterprise. The awe is there, but being a part of it slipped through De Mille's fingers; you are a passive witness; the link with the gameness of the frontier has receded. De Mille shows his characters and events from the outside; you never got within them sufficiently to understand in some intrinsic way their humanity and their collective grandeur.

It was a good year for Ernest Haycox with one of his Western stories the basis of John Ford's *Stagecoach,* and *Trouble Shooter* (Sundale Press, 1937) the narrative fabric for *Union Pacific.* I must confess, as much as I enjoy Haycox's ability as a storyteller, he had little feel for the contradictoriness and complexity of human personality. John Ford did. That's why Ford's characters in *Stagecoach* remain in the memory. De Mille did not. Barbara's rich Irish brogue, Donlevy's curious habit of dipping his cigar end in a whiskey glass—they are surface affectations. Only in Barbara Stanwyck's eyes can you detect her defiance of all dependency, but De Mille overlooks it, and his characters are only partial creations.

Union Pacific took nearly four months to produce. Robert Preston and Brian Donlevy are hired by an eastern capitalist to retard progress on construction of the transcontinental railroad. Joel McCrea is hired by General Dodge to smash the causes for delay. Barbara Stanwyck falls in love, first with Preston, and then, after Preston is killed, she is free to love McCrea. Donlevy establishes a saloon at the end of track and tries to keep the men from working. McCrea succeeds in driving him out and then seeing the railroad completed on time.

During production, De Mille collapsed at the studio from apparent overwork. He directed part of the picture from a stretcher, fixing it to a camera boom so that he could swing up into the air or down. The Union Pacific aided the Paramount Publicity Department in promoting the picture. A special train making stops along the way traversed the distance from Los Angeles to Omaha. De Mille and Stanwyck and several others were on board. Both the theme and the spectacle helped the film open to good business and rank as De Mille's most successful Western.

35 / FRONTIER LEGENDS—PART TWO

The trend in the thirties which found the causes for criminal behavior to reside in existing social conditions came to full maturity in Warner Brothers films near the end of the decade, from *Angels with Dirty Faces* (Warner's, 1938) to *Angels Wash Their Faces* (Warner's, 1939) to *They Made Me a Criminal* (Warner's, 1939). In all three of these films were the Dead End Kids, a gang of New York Lower East Side toughs that had appeared on stage in *Dead End* and then in the Samuel Goldwyn film based on the play directed by William Wyler and released in 1937, before they went under contract to Warner Brothers.

Audiences were acclimated to the notion of society being the ultimate villain when *Jesse James* was again brought to the screen with Tyrone Power portraying Jesse and Henry Fonda cast as Frank James. The attempt to exonerate Jesse somewhat for his life of banditry which had once incited such a fierce public reaction proved so popular by this time that a sequel to *Jesse* was made, *The Return of Frank James*. *Jesse* indicted big business, especially the St. Louis Midland Railroad embodied in the character of Donald Meek. *Frank James* went further and showed how big business corrupted law enforcement but not the courts; here justice could still be found.

This trend persists forward into the future so that by the time of *The Wild Bunch* (Warner's, 1969), Sam Peckinpah is well within his rights to indict the railroad, the military, government, and the vested interests of businessmen generally for having diminished all of the options open to free men and to depict a life of crime as a heroic alternate in a world where all men of character are more or less criminals. The legends of the frontier, as in the case of Billy the Kid, were increasingly pressed into service to depict an alternative to industrialization. Americans, it would seem, were not at all certain that they had chosen the best course in terms of national development. They fell to self-doubts during the Depression that would never subside in the decades ahead, an unsureness that could only become more intense and searching. The James boys, the Daltons, Billy of course, the Hole in the Wall gang, all became part of this self-examination. The same thing was true for the depiction of the life of General George Armstrong Custer

The James Gang robbing the Northfield Bank in *Jesse James*.

Photo courtesy of 20th Century-Fox Film Corporation.

on the screen, from the heroic images of Cecil B. De Mille in *The Plainsman* (Paramount, 1937) to Errol Flynn in the role in *They Died with Their Boots On* to *Sitting Bull* (United Artists, 1954) to *Little Big Man*.

Henry King directed *Jesse James*. The plot told how Brian Donlevy and his gang originally forced the James brothers into being outlaws fighting against the crooked scheming of Donald Meek and the St. Louis Midland Railroad. Randy Scott is a law officer sympathetic to Jesse. John Carradine shoots Jesse in the back for the reward money. "I don't think even America dislikes Jesse," Henry Hull says over his grave. "His times produced him."

Fritz Lang, the German director then under contract to Fox, was charged with directing the sequel once it was found how tremendously popular *Jesse James* was at the box office. Lang made three Westerns of dubious quality generally praised by critics; *The Return of Frank James*, *Western Union* (20th-Fox, 1941), based on the novel Zane Grey was signing copies of two days before he died (and not a story erroneously attributed to Grey, as some have said), and *Rancho Notorious* (RKO, 1952), with Marlene Dietrich as an outlaw gang leader. The contrast between *Jesse James* and *The Return of Frank James* is quite profound; whereas the former was romantic, the latter is sentimental; while the former was symphonic and lyrical in its progression, the latter was at times crude and dull. Lang's heavy-handed approach to Westerns was of little credit to him or the pictures he directed. *Western Union* was an improvement over *Frank James* only insofar as Harry Joe Brown was the executive producer and mapped out for Lang what he expected of him. Brown was quite impressed with Randy Scott's ability as a Western player, and much would later come of this association at Fox in the early forties.

Frank James opens with the scene of Jesse's death. It carries on Frank's story, his settling the score with the Ford brothers for Jesse's murder and his finally being granted a full pardon. Gene Tierney plays the love interest, trying to get Frank to go straight.

The Maverick Queen (Republic, 1956) was one of Herbert J. Yates's last Westerns, shot in color on location near the Royal Gorge in Colorado. The supposition is that the Younger brothers, who rode with the James boys, have gone to join the Wild Bunch led by Butch Cassidy and the Sundance Kid. Barbara Stanwyck is Kit Banion, a secret leader of the gang and their principal informer. This was made, however, in the fifties and the shift in emphasis is quite clear. Scott Brady, who plays Sundance, is a rat even if it is implied that he is sleeping with Stanwyck, although he never so much as kisses her. Stanwyck is the bad woman of the forties who, by the new decade, is now an object of pathos. Her criminal involvements are excusable to an extent because she is a beautiful woman with a woman's gentler promptings, but the sense of justice implicit in the screenplay demands that she die at the end of the picture. Barry Sullivan plays a Pinkerton detective who pretends to be Jeff Younger so he can work his way in with the gang. Jim Davis is the real Jeff Younger. When Davis shows up, Stanwyck risks her life to save Barry Sullivan from exposure and loses it in the effort.

Curiously enough, the top grossing Western of all time as of this writing is *Butch Cassidy and the Sundance Kid* (20th-Fox, 1969), directed by George Roy Hill and starring Paul Newman as Butch and Robert Redford as the Kid. None of the romantic pathos of *The Maverick Queen* has survived. Butch and Sundance are clearly bandits, and the viewer joins them taking part in several train robberies and holdups. "I've got vision," says Butch, "and the rest of the world wears bifocals." The tension and suspense of the film are embodied in the pursuit of the two by a persistent posse. "Who are those guys?" Butch keeps asking Sundance. They flee to Bolivia where they begin a new series of robberies. By a deliberate stroke, the viewer does not see Butch and Sundance shot down in the street in Bolivia. The film concludes with a freeze frame of the two running into the face of certain death. There is no psychological or sociological theorizing as to the possible justification of their lives of crime; there are few mediating circumstances for their actions; and while they are both bandits, they are likable in and for themselves, and what sympathy the viewer may feel for them is on the basis of their personalities. The neurotic need to whitewash frontier bad men, by the late sixties, vanished and was replaced by a rather exciting chronicle of their escapades.

I have already commented on Warner Brothers' featuring Errol Flynn in top-grade Westerns in the late thirties and early forties. *Dodge City* (Warner's, 1939) was the first of them and one of the best. Directed by Michael Curtiz, Flynn was costarred with Olivia de Havilland. Colonel Dodge sums up the railroad as "a symbol of America's progress—iron horses and iron men." For Colonel Dodge, as he is portrayed in this picture, "the West stands for honesty, courage and morality." Errol Flynn is the embodiment of these qualities. Flynn is flanked by Alan Hale and Big Boy Williams confronting the crooked machinations of Bruce Cabot and Victor Jory. The sequence of Flynn as a wagon master is impressive, and Curtiz staged a fabulous saloon brawl. The film ends with Colonel Dodge enlisting Flynn to help clean up another town, *Virginia City* (Warner's, 1940), which again would join Curtiz and Flynn.

After several pictures in this romantic and optative mood, Warner Brothers decided to cast Flynn as General George Armstrong Custer in *They Died with Their Boots On*. While Custer's massacre had inspired numerous photoplays, *They Died* undertook to narrate his biography from the time he joined West Point until he valiantly gave up his life in the service of his country, of honesty and morality at the Little Big Horn. However fanciful historically, Flynn in the role made Custer a hero of the first rank. Produced by Hal B. Wallis and directed by Raoul Walsh, Flynn was once more costarred with Olivia de Havilland, with Anthony Quinn cast as Chief Crazy Horse, the Indian leader who finally does Custer in—according to the screenplay.

Any real problems between the cavalry and the red men were minimized here, and the sources of friction were more or less confined to dishonest businessmen, profiting from trading guns to the Indians, and evil political appointees in Washington. The screen treatment of Custer does provide, however, an interesting contrast to the depiction of the lives of frontier bad men. Custer symbolizes the military. In 1942 *They Died* was well within the spirit of the war effort against fascism; *Sitting Bull,* from the fifties, could afford to be more realistic in its appraisal of both sides in the conflict; in *Little Big Man,* from 1971, in its protest against genocide and produced amid the national agony of the Vietnam War, Custer had to be caricatured. To be truthful, I cannot tell you why gangsters were once compelled to serve as legitimate heroes with traits and actions they would never have been capable of in the course of their lives; nor why, later, it was possible to view their crimes with equanimity and without the impulse to mitigate their banditry. The ambivalence toward Custer, the guilt at the solution of the Indian problem in the New World, the clash between cultures, also has about it this same sort of frank distortion.

They Died with Their Boots On opens with Custer riding into West Point in 1857 in a cavalier's uniform. It traces his military career from his heroism during the Civil War through his marriage to Olivia de Havilland to the Indian campaigns. Custer is somewhat on the side of the Indians, and there is genuine rapport between him and Chief Crazy Horse. Arthur Kennedy and his father, running whiskey and guns, are behind all the unrest. Custer sacrifices himself and his men to prove the validity of his cause against the evil white men.

Sitting Bull (United Artists, 1954) isn't a very good film, I will frankly confess. Yet its presentation of Custer is probably the most accurate to reach the screen. Iron Eyes Cody, interestingly, is credited with being the Indian adviser. J. Carrol Naish, who began playing Indians as early as Colonel Tim McCoy's *The Whirlwind* (Columbia, 1933), was cast as Sitting Bull. Dale Robertson was the nominal star, a soldier both idealistic and a champion of

A promotional trip to encourage attendance at Errol Flynn's first Western, *Dodge City*. Included among the celebrities are June Gale, Gilbert Roland, Matt McHugh, Maxie Rosenbloom, Errol Flynn, John Garfield, Wayne Morris, John Payne, Alan Hale, Sr., Hoot Gibson, Buck Jones, Big Boy Williams, Humphrey Bogart, and Ann Sheridan.

Photo courtesy of Dell Jones.

the Indians. John Litel was a commanding officer. Custer was played by Douglas Kennedy.

Sitting Bull opens the picture by presenting the Indian point of view. The Indian agent is a rabid Indian hater; Custer is little better. Robertson becomes a friend of the Indians after defeating Iron Eyes Cody, as Crazy Horse, in a dagger duel. Sitting Bull demands that President Grant come for a parley or there will be an uprising of all the nations. Grant comes, but it is too late. Custer distrusts the Indians and orders his regiment to attack them as a warning not to continue their war preparations. The Indian warriors ride with saddles under their blankets, but the massacre is well staged. Sitting Bull comments that they will not scalp brave men. A great plain of dead stretches across the battlefield. This is historically accurate, unlike the later *Little Big Man*. The 7th Cavalry was not scalped, and Custer's body was washed and laid out solemnly in death. The Indians paid him tribute as a heroic foe. This dignity would never have been shown to the madman we see in *Little Big Man*.

Sitting Bull comes to a maudlin ending. Robertson is court-martialed and sentenced to be shot. Only Sitting Bull, riding up to the fort and talking personally with President Grant, gains him a stay of execution.

The anguish of the late sixties was Vietnam. Its repeated shocks tore apart the American sensibility; it split the nation almost as deeply, I suspect, as had the Civil War. The idealism which had for so long inspired American history books cut sharply against the political realities of living in the twentieth century. Extravagance, wherever you find it, reduces the market price, and overpopulation reduced the value of human life, cheapened it, stripped it of that marvelous preciousness with which it had been endowed by the Enlightenment philosophers of the eighteenth century. Wyatt Earp, as I will have occasion to remark later, summed it up in *Doc* (United Artists, 1971): "You'd be surprised what problems you can solve with a bullet."

Soldier Blue (Avco-Embassy, 1971) was not the first protest film against American military intervention, but it was the most articulate and the most horrible. It dealt with the Sand Creek campaign of November 29, 1864. Candice Bergen played Cresta, a white captive of the Indians who is restored to her race. Peter Strauss was Honus, the soldier boy who falls in love with her. Donald Pleasence, the most singularly despicable villain—on the screen!—to come to prominence in recent years, played a vicious, lecherous gunrunner. The viewer, nearly sick with despair, watches as the cavalry ravages a peaceful Cheyenne village, lopping off heads, shooting down children, raping women. The mothers and babes hide in a shallow arroyo; they are butchered, the soldiers yelping amid the wild slaughter. Critics said it was the historical prototype of the My Lai massacre.

I cannot tell the reader if, as a result of the small-scale wars since 1945, Americans have finally resigned themselves to the fact that exertion of great

Errol Flynn as Custer leading a gallant charge during the Civil War.

Photo courtesy of United Artists Corporation.

political power backed by military might means, of necessity, that innocent women and children must be shot down, that tanks must be used against men with only stones, that gas and all manner of fiendish war machines must be loosed upon civilian populations, that when those populations will not submit they must be exterminated. The protest films would indicate the converse. But all of this notwithstanding, I must admit to the reader that I am too cynical to think it can ever be otherwise, at least in my lifetime, no matter how cogent or eloquent the protest. For all of their fear of loneliness, men have always had tremendous difficulty living with each other, and civilizations, like the great religions which have torn humanity asunder in holy bloodshed, have a curious way of ignoring the rights of others to be contrary.

In this mood, then, I come to *Little Big Man,* directed by Arthur Penn, whom the reader may remember as the director of the neurotic treatment of Billy the Kid in *The Left-handed Gun* (Warner's, 1958). The indictment is not satisfied with criticism of the solution to the Indian problem; white civilization is held up as hopelessly corrupt, hypocritical, depraved. I am not sympathetic with this type of extremism any more than with the glorification of Custer in *They Died with Their Boots On*. The treatment of the Indian nations engenders a guilt borne by the whole of society. This is simplistic thinking, to be sure; and the black and white contrast of Western melodrama persists with only a total rotation of roles, the Indians as the tragic heroes, the cavalry as the dark savages.

It is an involved plot and a long picture; the entire film is ironic and satirical in tone. Dustin Hoffman is made up to be a man 121 years old who relates to a researcher his experiences being captured by the Indians as a youth, being raised as a Cheyenne. During the course of his life, he passes back and forth between the Cheyenne and the white man's civilization. He is a witness to Hickok's death, and he is present at Little Big Horn to see Custer go mad and wander aimlessly around the battlefield.

Richard Mulligan as General Custer, going quite mad during the battle at Little Big Horn, as historically inaccurate as the Errol Flynn account from the other direction. The scene is in *Little Big Man*.

Photo reproduced by permission of Swank Motion Pictures.

The warp of legend is such that it must mean different things to men of different generations. If making heroes out of frontier gangsters represents one kind of alienation, the changing image of George Armstrong Custer represents another. And I trust I have made that tendency in the Western transparent without being overly portentous; the Western, in one respect, is an alienated view of the present, an attempt at an alternate perspective. In the restless dissatisfaction Americans sometimes feel with themselves, the Western is a fantasy in which values are re-evaluated, viewpoints altered, history distorted to pursue, if only in the imagination, a different course from the one it did follow.

36 / THE DUKE WITH SPURS

John Wayne has been moving in and out of this narrative for some time now, but his proper entry belongs here. He was born Marion Michael Morrison on May 26, 1907, in Winterset, Iowa. As a child, he was unhappy, lonely, and neurotic. He enjoyed the movies, and Harry Carey was his favorite Western player. His father, who was a druggist, decided to try farming in California, and eventually the whole family relocated West. Marion grew up at Glendale, California, and Bob Bradbury, later Bob Steele in pictures, was his closest friend.

As a youth, Marion had an Airedale named Duke. At one point the Morrisons occupied a house near a fire station, and the firemen started calling the boy Duke after his dog. The name stuck, and he was known as Duke Morrison through his college years.

There was a serious side to Duke's nature which prompted him to be a voracious reader; even in old age, he reads a book a night. From his early youth, he enjoyed pretending and would assume different roles in fantasy. But there was also that side of him which was tough, hard-bitten, and a fighter. Once he had begun college and excelled at football for the University of Southern California and Tom Mix got him a job as a prop boy at Fox in exchange for some tickets to a game, Duke met John Ford, who was then a contract director on the Fox lot. Ford loved to goad people until they exploded; it told him what they were really like. Ford liked Duke, and the two, after a fashion, became friends; Ford gave him a small part in *Hangman's House* (Fox, 1928).

During his summers, Duke worked at Fox. Finally, disenchanted at school, and desperately and hopelessly in love with Josephine Saenz, a proper and charming girl from an aristocratic family whose parents felt her relationship to Duke Morrison highly undesirable, Duke quit school to work in the Property Department. When Duke was to appear as a football player in Ford's *Salute* (Fox, 1929), which starred George O'Brien, another USC player who bullied his way into a part in the picture was Ward Bond. Years later, when Bond would simmer exasperatedly at Hollywood, Duke would tell him, "I did my damnedest to keep you the hell out of the picture business. But you had to shove your fat butt into the bus, so you got only yourself to blame."

"Mr. Ford called me over," Duke once told me of the filming of *Salute,* "and told me how he wanted me to stand in the line-up with the other players. It was a game sequence. He kept pushing me to do it his way. When I was in a squatting position, he would reach over with his foot and kick me so hard I would fall flat on my face. I got mad. I told him to show me what he wanted himself. He took position. The field was muddy nearby. I reached across and kicked him right into the mud. He was covered with it when he got up." Duke laughed.

Duke got his chance to be a star in 1930. Raoul Walsh saw him walking down a studio street. He asked his assistant director, Edmund Goulding, who that prop man was. Goulding identified him, and Walsh sent him over to talk to Duke. Goulding advised Duke not to get his hair cut.

The picture Walsh wanted Duke for was *The Big Trail* (Fox, 1930), which costarred him with Marguerite Churchill and which was to be *The Covered Wagon* of the sound era. Walsh sat down with Sol Wurtzel, after viewing Duke's screen test, and debated as to what he should be called. Winfield Sheehan was also present. Walsh suggested Anthony Wayne. Sheehan thought that too Italian. Walsh tried Tony Wayne. Wurtzel felt that sounded like a girl's name. Sheehan came up with it. "What's the matter with just plain John?" he asked. "John Wayne."

The Big Trail was made in what was then called the Fox Grandeur process, similar to the wide-screen process, used by King Vidor in filming *Billy the Kid* (M-G-M, 1930). The action was splendid; the Indian attack on the wagon train and the fording of the Colorado River were many times more impressive in this picture than the previous efforts in Cruze's *The Covered Wagon.* Yet *The Big Trail* did not gross. Perhaps its optative mood came at the wrong time, surrounded by the swirling despair of Depression; perhaps John Wayne's name as a box-office attraction had been inadequately exploited. Duke was sent around in buckskins to hold press conferences and was always being asked if he came from Texas and wore such clothing as his usual attire. Perhaps it was the lack of acceptance of the new medium of projection. Whatever the explanation, John Wayne was finished before he had begun; he was relegated to secondary roles in a few Fox films, and his option was not picked up.

Duke was signed, after some aggravation, as a bit player by Harry Cohn's Columbia Pictures. The first film in which he appeared was *Men Are Like That* (Columbia, 1931). Cohn, wretchedly disconsolate in his marriage to Rose, was playing the field; he had a crush on one of the starlets on the lot. A prop man told him that Duke Wayne was making a play for the same girl. Cohn became enraged. He sought to humiliate the Duke. He saw to it that Duke was confined to juvenile supporting roles in Tim McCoy and Buck Jones Westerns. In *Maker of Men* (Columbia, 1931) Duke was cast as a football player of weak character who sells out his college to a gambling ring.

Buck Jones made *Sundown Rider* (Columbia, 1932) about this time. There is a line in it that Harry Cohn might have taken to heart. When Buck is dishonestly framed on a charge of cattle rustling by Wheeler Oakman, Buck catches up with him. He tells Oakman that he is a man who always pays his debts, both kinds. This has certainly been true of Duke Wayne. When Mascot signed him for three serials to be done collectively for $2,000, Duke was at least the star. When his agreement with Columbia ran out and he was contracted to appear in the Warner Brothers remakes of the silent Ken Maynard pictures, Harry Cohn telephoned Sid Rogell and told him that Duke Wayne was a worthless drunk who was totally unreliable. Rogell and Duke had it out. Duke carried a grudge against Cohn for the remainder of his career and never again would work in any film for Columbia, no matter what the property or the money.

Duke met Enos Canutt while working for Mascot. I have already introduced him as Yakima Canutt, Yakima being the name Canutt assumed while working the rodeo circuit because it sounded more Indian. They became good friends with a bottle around the campfire on location during the cold desert nights. Canutt stunted for Duke, and Duke openly admired his horsemanship, his physical dexterity, and the fact that Yak made more money than the star. Duke never liked horses, and doesn't down to this day; but Canutt taught him how to sit in a saddle and how to guide a horse with expertise.

On June 24, 1933, Duke Morrison and Josephine Saenz were married in the patio and gardens of Loretta Young's Bel-Air home. Loretta was Josie's best friend. The marriage was doomed. Josie immediately set about trying to rebuild Duke's character and, above all, to get him to stop drinking, playing cards with his friends, and being gone so much of the time on Jack Ford's boat or hunting and fishing with Ward Bond, Grant Withers, Paul Fix, and the growing circle of Duke's picture business friends.

Duke was introduced to Trem Carr, who had just organized Monogram Pictures. Carr needed a star to work in his low-budget Westerns. Duke was suggested to him by Al Kingston on the basis of the Warner features. Carr's idea was to budget the pictures at $5,000 to $8,000 and shoot them in as few as three days. Duke was contracted and given $2,500 a picture. Carr gave Duke a thousand-dollar advance because he and Josie needed the money.

Yak was Duke's double at Monogram. Paul Malvern was placed in charge of production. Robert N. Bradbury, Bob Steele's father, directed most of the entries and even wrote many of the original stories. There was some novelty in this series, although Trem Carr wasn't beneath reusing a script that had first been used in the earlier series of Bob Steele Westerns for Tiffany release. George Hayes was a regular, either as an outlaw or as the girl's father, although increasingly he was working his way into the role of a side-kick. Hayes added much to the comic effect of a chase involving a Model T, a railroad handcar, and horses in *The Lucky Texan* (Monogram, 1934); in *West of the Divide* (Monogram, 1934) his support of Duke was sympathetic.

Bradbury borrowed as much as Trem Carr did. He had directed his son in *The Mojave Kid* (FBO, 1929), with a screenplay by Oliver Drake. Bradbury resurrected many of these plots for the Monogram series. Moreover, Bradbury had directed Trem Carr's series of Tom Tyler Westerns for Monogram in 1931; Duke had replaced Tyler as the lead. So *Partners of the Trail* (Monogram, 1931) was remade again as early as 1934 in *West of the Divide*. What recommended the pictures was Canutt's daredevil stunting. Canutt himself generally figured prominently in the cast as a villain. But he came up with interesting ideas such as an underwater sequence in *Sagebrush Trail* (Monogram, 1933), in which Duke, doubled by Canutt, hides from his pursuers by submerging himself in a stream and breathing through a reed. Verna Hillie, after her appearance opposite Randolph Scott in *Man of the Forest* (Paramount, 1933), was signed to appear in *The Star Packer* (Monogram, 1934) and *The Trail Beyond* (Monogram, 1934). This latter title also featured Noah Beery, Sr., and his son, Pidge. Senior and Paul Malvern did not hit it off. Beery became outspoken. Malvern asked Canutt, as a favor, to beat the hell out of Beery when doubling Duke for the fight scene. Canutt responded, "I'd be glad to, if you'll make him say to me the things he said to you."

Randy Rides Alone (Monogram, 1934) had Smith Ballew's singing dubbed in for Duke in a primitive musical sequence. Ballew went on in the middle thirties to star in a short-lived series of his own. The picture schedule only demanded eight weeks a year from Duke; it was an easy load. He was being paid moderately well. But he wasn't happy—not with his career, not with budget Westerns, and not in his marriage.

When Monogram merged with Mascot to form Republic, Duke made his Westerns for Republic release, beginning with *Westward Ho!* (Republic, 1935), with Bradbury directing.

As the series progressed, the production values were improved. Duke's salary was raised to $4,000 a picture and then raised again. The second entry for Republic was *The New Frontier* (Republic, 1935). Paul Malvern was still production supervisor; Robert Emmett (Tansey) did the screenplay; Carl Pierson, the film editor on the Monogram features, was the director. The picture opens to stock footage from the Cherokee Strip land rush and Ken Maynard's *The Red Raiders*. Cut to Monogram City, the location where nearly all of the Duke Wayne Westerns were filmed. Warner Richmond shoots Duke's father. Duke is a wagon master. He takes over as town marshal upon hearing the news. Together with Al Bridge and his gang, Duke sets fire to the town in a final reckoning reminiscent of William S. Hart's *Hell's Hinges*. It was a strong picture in its category.

"I made up my mind," Duke Wayne once recalled, "that I was going to play a real man to the best of my ability. I felt many of the Western stars of the twenties and thirties were too goddamn perfect. They never drank nor smoked. They never wanted to go to bed with a beautiful girl. They never had a fight. A heavy might throw a chair at them, and they just looked surprised and didn't fight in this spirit. They were too goddamn sweet and pure to be dirty fighters. Well, I wanted to be a dirty fighter if that was the only way to fight back. If somebody throws a chair at you, hell, you pick up a chair and belt him right back. I was trying to play a man who gets dirty, who sweats sometimes, who enjoys really kissing a gal he likes, who gets angry, who fights clean whenever possible but will fight dirty if he has to. You could say, I made the Western hero a roughneck."

The kind of suspense that is to be found in *Haunted Gold* (Warner's, 1932), one of Duke's remakes, is absent from the Monogram-Republic series; the story values are different. Duke wanted his hero to be human and, therefore, flawed. I doubt that Ford knew anything of this as he bellyached about Duke's low-grade career and the cheap, lousy pictures he was making year after year. Ford's constant ragging probably made Duke think they were cheap and lousy. But some years ago when I clipped a few of these pictures in "They Went Thataway," National Telefilm Associates followed it up by releasing all of the John Wayne pictures from Monogram and Republic to television. They did a bonanza business and were soon playing in every market, despite their antiquity. Duke Wayne was not alone in being a Western player who emerged during the thirties, but he was the only major performer to spend such a long time on Poverty Row.

"I might be there still," he once remarked to me, "but for John Ford." Then he smiled. "And after Ford got me out of B pictures, everyone said, 'Yeah, John Wayne, he's only good in Ford pictures.' Sometimes I thought there was no winning."

Duke and Josie had four children, but the parents were not compatible. Duke once sat on one of her fragile French chairs and smashed it. He had a den furnished for himself with heavy furniture. Josie objected violently to

Duke's drinking, which reached a quart of whiskey a day and stayed there for forty years. She tried to convert him to the Catholic religion. She wanted him to give up his friends and even his career in pictures. At the hearing leading to their divorce, the question arose concerning Josie's coldness. She pointed to their four children in response.

"Yeah," Duke muttered to Beverly Barnett, his close friend and press agent, "four times in ten years."

When Trem Carr broke with Herbert J. Yates and reorganized Monogram, to assist in gathering revenue he went to work as a producer at Universal. He invited Duke to follow him. Beginning with *The Sea Spoilers* (Universal, 1936), Duke started appearing in a series of non-Westerns. The films were cheaply made and, for their kind, far worse products than Duke's Republic Westerns. When his contract ran out, Duke quit pictures and tried to find other kinds of work. It was a last effort to hold his marriage together. Before leaving for Universal, Yates had offered him $24,000 a picture. When Duke's job as a stockbroker went bust and he went back to Yates, the price had fallen to $16,000 a picture and not solo Westerns, either. Duke was to replace Bob Livingston as Stony Brooke. Duke lowered his head and resigned himself to his fate.

Ford had read a two-page short story in *Collier's* magazine by Ernest Haycox, titled "Stage to Lordsburg." Ford at the time commented that it was really a revision of Guy de Maupassant's *"Boule-de-Suif."* In fact, Jean-Louis Rieupeyrout in his excellent book *La Grande Aventure du Western* (Éditions du Cerf, 1971) goes so far as to remark: *"L'on étudie, ligne par ligne, 'Boule-de-Suif'; la Dallas de Ford n'était-elle pas conforme en tout point à la Élisabeth Rousset, fille légère chez Maupassant? La situation ne présentait-elle pas une analogie frappante avec celle de la patache française offerte sans défense aux périls de la guerre de 1870 proche de Paris? Les Prussiens ne se conduisaient-ils pas comme de vrais Apaches et l'esprit de sacrifice n'animait-il pas la seule et tendre Élisabeth face à la pleutrerie et à la couardise des autres occupants de la carriole?"* *

"Boule-de-Suif" is one of the finest short stories in the French literature of the last century, and I have read it many times. But I cannot find this correspondence. It would seem to me that Rieupeyrout had a far more valid insight into the origins of *Stagecoach* when he drew a parallel between the characters Ford and Dudley Nichols added to the screenplay that were not

---

* "Line for line, it reads like 'Tub of Lard'; doesn't Ford's Dallas conform in every way with Elizabeth Rousset, Maupassant's wanton maiden? Is not the situation a striking analogy with that of the French coach exposed without defense near Paris during the perils of the Franco-Prussian War? Don't the Prussians conduct themselves like real Apaches and doesn't the spirit of sacrifice animate the singular and tender Elizabeth confronted with the whining and cowardice of the other occupants of the carriage?" Author's translation.

in the Haycox story and Ford's early picture *The Outcasts of Poker Flat* (Universal, 1919), based on the short story by Bret Harte. He finds Dallas to be a synthesis of the Henriette of Haycox's story and the Duchess of Harte's story; Doc Boone to be based on Harte's Uncle Billy; and the gambler, Hatfield, to be based on John Oakhurst.

Nowhere, not in Maupassant nor Harte nor Haycox, do you find, however, what makes *Stagecoach* such an exceptional Western: the perpetual motion of the stage as it proceeds on its journey. It is truly symphonic. The journey, interrupted by a pause in which we get to know the passengers better; the journey, and another pause in which they are revealed again in a new light; the journey, and then the danger presses in upon them in which the outlaw and the whore and the drunken physician show the greatest valor and the gambler gives his life for a romantic notion, whereas the whiskey salesman and the banker show themselves to be cowardly and, in the latter's case, wholly corrupt. Ford's *The Grapes of Wrath* (20th-Fox, 1940), from the next year, would employ the same sort of cinematic punctuation.

The character of Malpais Bill was reworked into the Ringo Kid for the screenplay. It ran 123 pages and was finished when Ford invited Duke to come sailing with him on the *Araner*. Duke expected Ward Bond, Grant Withers, Paul Fix, and the others to be there; they weren't. He was alone with Ford. Jack gave him the short story by Haycox and the screenplay to read. They set sail. Duke was to pass his opinion on what he read.

That night, in the galley, the stench of Ford's cigars gave Duke a headache. Reading the screenplay, Duke knew he was perfect for the part of the Ringo Kid, but he was certain Ford had no intention of casting him in it. They played gin rummy until late.

"I need some help from you," Ford said, puffing a cloud of cigar smoke in Duke's face.

"Sure, Pappy," Duke said.

"You are acquainted with some of the new young actors. I was wondering if you knew one that could play the Ringo Kid."

Duke came up with the name Lloyd Nolan. Ford was disgusted and went to bed. Duke retired with a bottle of cognac and drank until he passed out. He was late to arise the next morning. His hangover was colossal. For the remainder of the voyage, Ford kept chaffing him about the Republic quickies and his inability to find an actor suitable for the part of Ringo. When they docked at San Pedro, Ford turned to Wayne.

"Duke," he said, "I want to tell you something. I have made up my mind. I want you to play the Ringo Kid."

It hadn't been altogether easy for Ford. He had tried to interest several studios in the property, and even tried RKO, but with no luck. Walter Wanger had a picture left on his contract with United Artists, and Ford

John Ford as he looked at the time of *Stagecoach*.

Photo courtesy of *Views & Reviews* magazine.

intrigued him with the idea for the picture because it was likely to be cheap. Wanger had already been paid for his lot of pictures, so an inexpensive film was to his advantage. *Stagecoach* was to be John Ford's first sound era Western.

Wanger wanted Gary Cooper and Marlene Dietrich to star in the film. Ford didn't. He wanted Claire Trevor, whom he had wanted to work in one of his Fox pictures but who had had an unfortunate bout with cold sores at the time, and Duke Wayne. Wanger told Ford to start testing people. Ford tested.

"He even tried Bruce Cabot," Duke related to me. "It was kind of comical. There was this dummy stage and Pappy wanted Cabot, as the final part of the test, to jump off of it while it was in motion. 'Just jump onto the ground,' he told Cabot. 'I'll be damned if I'll do that,' Cabot told him. 'Well, it doesn't matter anyway,' Ford said, 'because Duke Wayne is getting the role.'"

Ford claimed that he discovered Monument Valley when he was driving through Arizona in the early thirties and thought it would make a fine location for a Western. Duke Wayne insists that it was he who showed the valley to Ford, having first found it when a prop man on a George O'Brien Western. However it was, Ford filmed many of the exteriors at Monument Valley, and it became associated with his vision of the West.

"There was a dry lake that was perfect for the Indian attack," Ford later recalled. "We didn't have any camera cars in those days; we just put the camera on an automobile and shot on the run. It was fast. I asked the driver how fast we had gone, and he said forty to forty-two miles per hour. You wouldn't think that horses could go that fast, but they did. The chase took two days to shoot. That chase—every half-assed critic says, 'Why did it go on so long? Why didn't the Indians just shoot the horses?'

"I tell them, 'If the Indians had done that, they would have stopped the picture.'

"The real truth is that the Indians were more interested in the horses than in the white men. They fought on foot most of the time, and they needed horses. Besides, they were notoriously bad shots on horseback."

Ford assembled a splendid cast, Thomas Mitchell, John Carradine, Andy Devine, Berton Churchill, George Bancroft, and Louise Platt, who was under contract with Wanger. Ford predicted the picture would cost $220,000; it actually cost $531,374.13.

Duke was an upstart from low-budget films. Ford won his acceptance from the rest of the cast by treating him unmercifully. The cast pulled together and supported Duke.

"I said hold your position before you turn," Ford told Duke on the set. "Chrissakes, can't you even walk? Not skip, just walk. Goddamn fairy. Put your feet down like you were a man."

"I remember once in the beginning of the picture I had a scene where I was supposed to splash my face with water," Duke Wayne once recalled. "I turned around and wiped my face with a towel, but it didn't seem to satisfy Ford. He made me do it over and over again, until my face was almost raw from rubbing it with the towel. Finally, Jack Holt's son, Tim, said to him, 'Jack, why don't you lay off the poor guy?'"

Claire Trevor also had memories. "I did a test with Duke Wayne, whom I had never met before. *He* was testing, not me. Ford had us do the scene after the birth of the baby, about the only real scene we had together. The idea was that he was very respectful of me. He didn't know I was a hooker. Ford had us play the scene standing against a fence. At one point, Ford took Duke and shook him.

"'What are you doing with your mouth?' Ford demanded. 'Why are you moving your mouth so much? Don't you know that you don't act with your mouth in pictures? You act with your eyes!'

The stage heading into Monument Valley in *Stagecoach*.

Photo courtesy of TV Cinema Sales Corporation.

"It was tough for Duke to take, but he took it. And he learned eight volumes about acting in this picture."

Ford improvised, as he always did, which is why actors would stand around even on days when they were not on call—in the hope that he would invent something on the cuff. While on location in Arizona, it snowed. Ford was overjoyed. He put snow into the picture and had Andy Devine later explain it on the basis of taking the high road through the snow country because the Apaches hated snow.

"One day," Andy Devine said, "he got sore at me and said, 'You big tub of lard. I don't know why the hell I'm using you in this picture.'

"I answered him right back: 'Because Ward Bond can't drive six horses.'

"Ford didn't talk to me for six years. But I worked for him again, of course. Every time I did, he saw to it that I had a Mexican wife and nine kids."

Duke tells the story of how Ford invited him one day to screen the rushes and evaluate Andy Devine's performance.

"I thought," Duke commented, "that Andy held the reins too loosely and told Ford I thought so. Ford said to me that it was an important point and he wanted everyone to hear it. Well, he called everybody to him, the cast, the technical crew, the wardrobe workers, the grips, even the electricians. 'I want you all to know,' he told them, 'that Duke thinks this is a great picture and that we're all doing one helluva job—but he can't stand Devine's performance.'"

Ford felt, even then, that Duke all too often took a director's point of view, and not that of an actor. Ford wanted to develop Wayne as an actor. At Duke's recommendation, he had hired Yak to head up the second unit. At night, in their hotel room, Duke would rehearse his lines with Yak as his critic. He didn't like Ford keeping after him the way he did.

Probably in no picture John Ford ever made was music so important as it was in *Stagecoach*. The composers who won Academy Awards for their contribution certainly deserved them. And Thomas Mitchell won a Best Supporting Player Award for his role as Doc Boone.

Many critics have subsequently cited *Stagecoach* as the finest Western ever made. The remake in 1966 is beneath comment. All I will say is that *Stagecoach* cannot be appreciated on television. It must be viewed without interruption. It demands that sort of hypnotic continuity to achieve its effects. Ford patched the film together out of fragments. His locations ranged from the crossing of the Kern River to the old wagon cut at Newhall through which the stage passes just before the Indian attack filmed at

Most of the principals assembled at a way station. From left to right, Donald Meek, John Wayne, Andy Devine, Claire Trevor, George Bancroft, Louise Platt, Tim Holt, John Carradine, Berton Churchill, Francis Ford, and Thomas Mitchell.

Victorville; he used the Republic town set and did the interiors at the Sam Goldwyn studios.

The picture opens to an army encampment in Monument Valley. Geronimo and his braves are on the warpath. A stagecoach filled with assorted passengers heads into the danger area. Duke is picked up along the way. Louise Platt has a baby at a way station. The stage is attacked, but the cavalry comes to the rescue. At Lordsburg, Duke is permitted to shoot it out with the Plummer gang, and finishes them with three bullets, all he has in his Winchester. He and Claire Trevor are united at the fade.

Stagecoach was previewed at the Village Theater at Westwood. Duke saw to it that the Republic brass had tickets. Duke spotted them sneaking out of the theater afterward, so he knew they had come. And why not? Duke was the best Western player Republic had and now he was suddenly in a major Western. No one said anything to Duke the next day, nor again on the next. At last, Duke broke down and asked Sol Siegel what he thought of the picture.

"If it's a Western they want to make," he returned succinctly, "let them come to Republic to learn how to make it."

Duke had four more Three Mesquiteers Westerns to make before concluding the 1939–40 commitment. They were good pictures—superior to those which had preceded *Stagecoach*—but the formula was circumscribed and the plots necessarily routine. Wayne's Republic contract had four more

Roy Rogers, Duke Wayne, and Gabby Hayes together for *The Dark Command*.
Photo courtesy of National Telefilm Associates.

years to run. Through the intercession of Walter Wanger, Charles K. Feldman took over representation of John Wayne. Feldman and Wayne bargained with Yates and got him to agree to Wayne making pictures for other companies, provided Duke continued to make pictures for Republic at the same salary. Duke altered this somewhat in 1941 by adding a one-page rider to his contract with Yates that he was to receive 10 per cent of the gross profits of his films in addition to the salary. Yates, by that time, was pleased to concur with this stipulation.

In late fall 1939 Duke made *Allegheny Uprising* for RKO, which again costarred him with Claire Trevor. Yates felt the time was right for Republic to take the plunge and make a major motion picture. The property he selected was *The Dark Command,* based on a novel by W. R. Burnett. The budget was set at $750,000, and Raoul Walsh was contracted to direct. After a decade, this reunited Duke with the director who had worked with him on his first bid for stardom. Claire Trevor was also signed and by contract received top billing; Duke was second; Walter Pidgeon was third.

Republic insured the production with Lloyd's of London for $670,000. A delay caused by Claire Trevor falling ill brought about a suspension of production on December 23, 1939, after a month of shooting. Republic had paid $30,000 for the insurance and was paid $250,000 by Lloyd's as a settlement for the delay. Production was resumed on February 1, 1940, and completed in sixteen days at a total cost in excess of $1,000,000, or twice as much as *Stagecoach* had cost. During suspension, Walter Pidgeon took time out to make *It's a Date* (Universal, 1940).

Canutt headed up the second unit and in both the sequence when a buckboard hurls off a cliff with four men on board into a ravine below and in the re-creation of the burning of Lawrence, Kansas, surpassed himself. George Hayes was cast as Duke's side-kick, and his own development as a player since the Monogram days was impressive. Roy Rogers was included in the cast as Claire's younger brother.

The Dark Command is set in Kansas in 1859 as political tensions between the states continue to mount. Duke and Gabby go up against Walter Pidgeon as Will Cantrell, a schoolteacher who makes a bid for power. Claire Trevor is the romantic interest. Roy Rogers is her brother. Roy joins Cantrell during the Civil War. Duke and Claire, estranged when Duke is forced to arrest Roy on a manslaughter charge, are brought together by the finish, with Cantrell and his men raiding Lawrence, Kansas, and being finally subdued.

In terms of slick production values, brilliant action sequences and expert stunting, excitement, cogent story line, and vital musical support, *The Dark Command* ranks as probably the best film Republic made in its first five years of corporate existence.

As a result of *Stagecoach, Allegheny Uprising,* and *The Dark Command,*

Duke Wayne became a central box-office attraction, a position he would maintain for the next thirty-five years. Ford cast him in *The Long Voyage Home* (United Artists, 1940), again with Thomas Mitchell; Henry Hathaway put Wayne in his idyllic and lyrical *The Shepherd of the Hills* (Paramount, 1941) with Harry Carey; and Cecil B. De Mille, after no end of resistance from Duke because of an old grudge, got him to star in *Reap the Wild Wind* (Paramount, 1942), which proved exceedingly popular. I have already mentioned that Universal cast Duke opposite Randolph Scott and Marlene Dietrich for the 1942 remake of *The Spoilers*. After twelve years of trying, John Wayne had arrived.

On May 2, 1943, Josephine Saenz was granted a legal separation from her husband. His marriage was ended just as his future as an international star and world personality had begun. Duke's work became the most important thing in his life.

37 / REBIRTH AND DEATH

I

There is an oil on canvas by Albert Bierstadt that is part of the Jasper D. Ackerman Collection. Bierstadt, born in 1830, completed the canvas in his thirty-seventh year. He called it "Sunset on the Oregon Trail."

The subject of the painting is the journey of a wagon train of emigrants en route to the promised land. The left side of this gigantic canvas is bathed in hues of lustrous gold, burnished reds, rich yellows, glowing browns—an explosion of intense colors which the medieval painters reserved to depict the divine. The lumbering wagons, the straining animals, the hardy pioneers, stretch forward from the tenuous shadows of dusk into this glorious effusion. There is nothing overwhelming in Bierstadt's draftsmanship or his palette, but somehow from the two of them and from somewhere deeply within himself, his emotions transmitted via this confluence of oils the rapture of a timeless vision. That rapture in other men was sufficient to prompt them to travel thousands of miles to live in a one-room hut of sod, log, or adobe furnished with little more than a table, chairs, stove, kerosene lamps, and perhaps an iron-frame bed draped with animal hides.

Uncle Carl Laemmle had first heard of the quest for the promised land as a child in his synagogue at Laupheim. The youth might have seen in his mind's eye the Israelites begin their long trek, crossing a mighty sea in their carts and wagons, waging war against the elements, terrific rains and howling winds, wandering aimlessly about in a barren desert, starving, fighting the strange, mounted Hyksos, provided a Law unto themselves, reaching the summit of a fertile valley, their mighty leader dying in the progress before the journey's end. The fragrances from summer-blooming flowers diffused magically into the cool night air of his garden in Beverly Hills, heavily laden with the damp smell of dew. As he strolled about overlooking the sixty acres of his Golden Days estate, he may have reflected upon it all again.

The early years during which he had hired Edwin S. Porter on the basis of *The Great Train Robbery;* how he had given Thomas Ince a job as a director; how he had hired Francis Ford away from Ince to head up his West Coast Western unit; the Cheyenne Harry Westerns with Harry Carey that had brought John Ford into direction; the rise of Hoot Gibson during the twenties; Ted Wells, Art Acord, Jack Holt, Jack Hoxie, William Desmond, Pete Morrison, Roy Stewart, the many cowboys who had worked on his lot in the silent era—he could perhaps call it all readily to mind. Or Tim McCoy, who had made the first Universal talking Western serial; Tom Mix, who made his first sound Westerns and some of his best films at Universal; Ken Maynard and Buck Jones, to whom he had given their own units to make Westerns as they saw fit; Johnny Mack Brown, who began making serials on his lot in the thirties—nearly every important Western player and most of the minor players worked for him during the first four decades of the century. Uncle Carl Laemmle loved Westerns, and so he made more of them over a longer period of time than any of his contemporaries.

He had guided his company through numerous eleventh-hour rallies. When he was unable to carry on, he had chosen to live in quiet retirement. In late September 1939, at his home, at seventy-two death crept upon the man who had rebuilt a cathedral for the people of Laupheim and who had found work for myriad friends and relatives who followed him to what Uncle Carl firmly believed *was* the promised land. At 12:30 the day of the funeral at the Wilshire Temple, all the studios in Hollywood and all the personnel in the Universal exchanges around the world stood silent for five minutes in memoriam of the man who had, against fantastic odds, created an empire out of shadows, who had fought the Trust and defended the individual's right to free enterprise. He had arrived in the New World penniless. The estate he left behind was valued at $4 million with annuities amounting to $500,000 reverting to his two children. "He had courage and vision and he kept his honor bright," the *Motion Picture*

Herald said of him. "He fought for what he believed to be right and kept his plighted word. He gave more than he asked. His friendship braved the storm. Carl Laemmle had and deserved the deep personal affection of all who knew him."

II

Max Brand was the pseudonym under which Frederick Faust wrote his popular series of Western novels. He was born in Seattle, attended the University of California, married Dorothy Schillig in 1917, lived in New York, and published *The Untamed* in 1918. Tom Mix starred in the motion picture version. Later, when he moved to Italy, Faust could regularly produce a book every three weeks. Dodd, Mead published *Destry Rides Again* in 1930. It went through two editions before A. L. Burt Company brought out an economy volume that easily went through six printings. Universal bought screen rights to the novel in 1931, and Tom Mix agreed to make it the basis for his first film under his new Universal contract.

Changes had to be made. As Brand had originally written it, the story involved a man unjustly sent to prison by his townspeople, twelve of whom had served on the convicting jury. When Destry gets out, he systematically takes vengeance on each jury member. It was the enduring avenger theme, symbolizing frontier justice in its most ruthless and effective form. There was no way that Universal, which had held up release of *Frankenstein* (Universal, 1931) due to worries about religious objections to the artificial creation of life, was going to authentically demonstrate on the screen that justice was sometimes ill served by due process. This was considered a bit too heretical for young people. Mix agreed. Richard Schayer, the scenarist, who had worked for M-G-M on *Dance Fools, Dance* and *Trader Horn* in 1931, was assigned the task of making the story acceptable. He did this by transposing responsibility from the jury for a false verdict to a group of crooked witnesses who, by perjury, forced an otherwise noble, honest, and forthright body of men to participate in a gross injustice. The system was never questioned. Dishonesty, working outside the system to undermine it, was blamed.

Ben Stoloff was the director. Claudia Dell, who was obviously wild about working with Mix, was cast as Sally Dangerfield, changed from the Charlotte (unfeminine "Charley" for short) of the novel, and Harrison Destry became Tom Destry. Zasu Pitts was added for comedy purposes during an early sequence. After that, what little comedy there was confined itself to interchanges between Tom and Young Willie, played by George Ernest, for the remainder of the picture was preoccupied with Tom's determined, cold-blooded pursuit of his false accusers.

Tom Mix atop Tony when the two of them became Universal stars in 1932.

Four major episodes were carried over from the novel, although their relationship to plot development was altered. The saloon scene with the Ogden brothers (less Destry's shooting them) was kept; the courtroom scene with the warning (to the witnesses, instead of the jurors); the breakfast table sequence at the Dangerfield's interrupted by Jerry Wendell (sheriff, according to the screenplay); and the dialogue between Destry and the boy at the hostelry. Dan Clark did his best to convey that electrifying magnetism of Tom's personality, his way of carrying himself that was in itself inspiring, through his adroit, intelligently planned camera setups.

Destry Rides Again opens with Tom riding down a steep incline atop Tony, jumping a fence, and talking to the schoolchildren. He is framed by his partner in a stage-line business and sent to prison. He swears vengeance against the calumnious witnesses. When he gets out, he goes about it relentlessly, adding his ex-partner to the group. Claudia Dell was the love interest, and Tom wins her by the end of the picture.

III

After leaving Universal, for the 1933–34 season, Tom Mix signed on as an attraction with the Sam B. Dill Circus, which traveled some 14,000 miles in its motorized units. In 1935 Tom bought the enterprise, renaming it the Tom Mix Circus. He paid $400,000 for it. Under his ownership, the show traveled 13,275 miles in 1935.

Tom was on the road when Nat Levine, of Mascot Pictures, got in touch with him. Nat was clever in his approach. He learned of Tom's right-wing inclinations and sought to entice him by means of them. He knew that money meant nothing to Mix, much less the idea of returning to pictures. Universal still had the Mix features in release. The effectiveness of Levine's strategy became manifest in a press conference Mix gave in which he described the reasons for his undertaking the serial. "I was mad at conditions I saw and read about each day," he remarked. "Criminals on the loose. Boys and girls learning Communist propaganda in schools. Crime news filling the papers. So I figured I could help by returning to the screen in a picture which would set an example for kids to follow—one with good old-fashioned virtues and Western justice. When Mascot Pictures Corporation showed me the story *The Miracle Rider,* I knew I had the kind of rip-snortin', he-man chapter play which would thrill every kid in town."

Tom was paid $10,000 a week for four weeks' work. *The Miracle Rider* (Mascot, 1935) was Levine's first fifteen-chapter serial. Tom felt that the fifteen units would give him renewed exposure he needed to keep interest in his circus venture. The story revealed Mix to be the champion of the Indian against modern, organized gangsters. Because of Mascot's produc-

Tom with Claudia Dell, his leading lady, in the courtroom scene from *Destry Rides Again.*

Photo courtesy of MCA-Universal.

tion methods, each scene was done rapidly with no particular attention paid to Tom's performance; Cliff Lyons stunted for him with the second unit, and, in fact, three units were employed on filming the serial. The cast was not especially notable. Joan Gale, one of the lesser known of the Gale sisters, was cast as the love interest. She had played an Indian maiden in the earlier *Last of the Mohicans* (Mascot, 1932), with Harry Carey. Charles Middleton joined Jason Robards, Sr., heading up the group of standard heavies.

One of the most impressive aspects of the whole enterprise was the publicity. Mascot released a massive press book, countless press articles, news stories, and so on. M. M. Cole Company in Chicago issued *Tom Mix's Song Book* with a song to which Tom wrote the lyrics, several that he had nothing to do with, and a centerfold filled with production shots from *The Miracle Rider*. Armand Schaefer was assigned to direct Mix, and Breezy Eason handled all of the exteriors. Maurice and Gerald Geraghty assisted on the screenplay.

Many have since claimed that Tom should not have made the serial; that it is tedious, slow, flimsily plotted; and that his dramatic portrayal does not show him at his best. All of this is true. But it grossed over a million dollars upon its theatrical release and remains the one Tom Mix picture most people have seen. It was the only Mascot serial since *Mystery Mountain* (Mascot, 1934) and the last Mascot effort that would avoid a collectivity. Tom Mix had always been his own show, and he was so here. Dan Clark was not Tom's cameraman and Mix may be slightly less superhuman, but his presence is more than a match for all the heavies. *The Miracle Rider* also demonstrated a sympathy for the Indian nations.

In 1936 Tom traveled 12,236 miles with his circus, making 217 stands, and 10,521 miles in 1937, making 195 stands. Tom's fortunes fell. His troupe was reduced to a mere fifty performers and eleven band members by 1937. In 1938, as happened to almost everyone else, the circus was forced to close early due to financial difficulties induced by lack of attendance. Tom had broken his leg on October 4, 1935, when his horse fell during a performance at Alva, Oklahoma, and he was injured again when the tent was flattened by a storm on May 20, 1936. Tom turned increasingly to drink as his frustration and despondency mounted. Upon occasion, he failed to appear when his call came. His fifth marriage was not working out as well as he had hoped. His daughter Ruth joined him and stayed on tour with him. Many of Tom's closest friends worried about him when he would leave of a night and drive for hours in his high-powered sports car in an effort to get away from his depression. Tom got in a fistfight with a spectator outside of his circus tent and was taken to court for aggravated assault.

On April 11, 1938, Tom's 1933 contract with the Ralston Purina Company was renewed, and the Tom Mix radio programs were continued, with

Tom lending himself as an endorsement to the firm's products. In May 1938, with a huge white stallion Tom called Tony II, Mix embarked on a second European tour. When he arrived in England, he was relieved of eight pistols and five rifles, the press commenting that Tom represented "the largest armed force that has tried to land on British soil since the last attempt by the Stuarts, almost 200 years ago." Tom and Tony II were a big hit at the Birmingham Hippodrome in September 1938. Having regained his firearms, Tom amazed the British public with his marksmanship. He could shoot a .45 slug at a butcher knife and put out burning candles situated on both sides with only one shot. Welcomed again by royalty, Tom's spirits improved. He returned to the United States with plans to resume his motion picture activities.

Jimmy Stewart as Tom Destry, Jr., with La Dietrich in *Destry Rides Again*.

Photo courtesy of MCA-Universal.

IV

Joe Pasternack was born at Szilagysomlyo, Hungary, on September 17, 1901. He had been an assistant director at Paramount in the early twenties and went to work for Uncle Carl Laemmle at Universal as an assistant director in 1926 and rose to the position of production manager. He went back to Europe, where he produced several pictures for the German and Hungarian cinema before returning to Hollywood in 1937. It was Pasternack who made all of the popular Deanna Durbin pictures for Universal and who, in 1939, thought to try his hand at filming a Western with a musical comedy setting. He resurrected the title *Destry Rides Again,* but with a wholly new screenplay. James Stewart, cast as Tom Destry, Jr., and Marlene Dietrich's barroom character which had made her famous as early as *Der Blaue Engel,* produced in Germany in 1929 and directed by Josef von Sternberg, were combined in the plot. As early as 1935, Mae West had introduced musical comedy sequences into the traditional Western setting in *Goin' to Town,* released by Paramount.

Mischa Auer, James Stewart, Samuel S. Hinds, Brian Donlevy, and Waren Hymer in a confrontation from *Destry Rides Again*.

Destry was Universal's answer to the large-scale Westerns which many of the major studios had undertaken in the late thirties. It was primarily an elaborate put-on and resulted, the next year, in the production of *My Little Chickadee* (Universal, 1940), which united Mae West and W. C. Fields in a Western. Dietrich's vocalism and her ability to play the cabaret tramp were the essential novelty items of the second *Destry*, and the film awakened renewed interest in Dietrich as a box-office property.

The second *Destry Rides Again* featured the mild-mannered hero which the Autry Fantasy had made commonplace, a strikingly absurd contrast with the power and energy of the original version with Tom Mix. To all concerned, Tom Destry's son appeared a laughingstock and an incorrigible buffoon. But by the end of the film, he reduced Brian Donlevy and his evil horde to total capitulation through a raid on the saloon by several irate women. George Marshall was the director.

Una Merkel was cast as a good woman. She recalled the making of *Destry* for an interview with cinema historian Leonard Maltin and the filming of her great fight scene with Dietrich. "I had never met Miss Dietrich until that day," she recalled, "and they outlined exactly what places they'd like us to hit on the set. We were not supposed to do anything but a few feet, and they had the stunt girls there to take over. But Mr. Marshall said, 'Once you get started on this, just keep going as long as you can; don't worry, the camera will follow you.' We did the whole thing, and we turned our checks over to the stunt girls! We did the whole battle, and then at the end Jimmy Stewart came over and dumped a pail of water over our heads. Then we had to do it again for close-ups, and do it for *Life* magazine. . . . I went to the hospital after that picture. I finished it, but I was a mess of bruises, because I had little flat heels on, and Marlene had high spiked heels. All through the fight scene we were whispering to each other, 'Are you all right?' 'Can you finish it?' 'Are you O.K.?' We did it in one continuous take; I thought they'd never call 'Cut.' "

Tom Destry, Jr., is the mild-mannered son of the old frontier fighter. He comes to Bottle Neck and subdues Brian Donlevy, the saloon owner, and his gang, with the help of the women of the town. Marlene Dietrich was cast as Frenchy, a dance hall girl who helps Donlevy cheat at cards by spilling coffee or whiskey on unsuspecting players so their hole cards can be palmed. She is shot at the end of the picture and dies in Destry's arms.

I would not say that *Destry Rides Again* established a lunatic trend as encompassing as the Autry Fantasy, but a number of Western spoofs followed in its wake. In 1955 George Marshall directed a remake entitled *Destry* for Universal, starring Audie Murphy. It was virtually the same screenplay without Dietrich and her magic; and without them, the film had nothing at all.

V

The Tom Mix Circus had folded for good, and Tom had moved his live-stock to a little ranch about twenty miles from Hollywood. The personal appearance tour of England had been completed, and Tom was making a series of appearances in the southwestern states. The last one was at Tucson, Arizona. He was headed for Phoenix next.

Tom visited with Sheriff Ed Echols, an old friend whom he had once asked to prevent his daughter Ruth from marrying Douglas Gilmore at Yuma, and Walt Coburn, the Western writer. A fortuneteller stopped to read Tom's palm. She looked into his sad, stricken face. She shook her head slowly and refused to tell him anything.

It was Tom's hope to attempt a motion picture comeback. He may have been thinking of that as his custom-built Cord roadster sped along a lonely Arizona highway that Saturday afternoon. He was wearing fancy boots, a diamond-studded belt buckle, and a white ten-gallon Stetson. In his pockets, he had stuffed $6,000 in cash and $1,500 in traveler's checks. Tom loved speed. I do not know what he might have thought of *Destry Rides Again* had he seen the musical version. "I ride into a place owning my own horse, saddle, and bridle," he had summed up his concept of Western filmmak-ing. "It isn't my quarrel, but I get into trouble doing the right thing for somebody else. When it's all ironed out, I never get any money reward."

Tom came upon a crew of highway workers. He swerved the car into a detour. The Cord went down a dry wash and up the other side, where it overturned, pinning him beneath the wreckage. Tom probably knew no pain. A metal suitcase, on the back ledge of the car, broke his neck upon impact. When the highway workers finally freed his crushed body, Tom Mix was dead. His white suit was nearly unwrinkled.

John Ford personally interceded with the War Department so that Tom could be buried wrapped in the flag of the United States of America, which, as a screen hero, he had served so well. The quartermaster general of the United Spanish War Veterans responded to Ford's letter, "Confidentially, I wish to advise that Tom Mix evidently, in the days of his youth, was a soldier of fortune and just seemed to want to be in everybody's war. He had an honorable discharge from the war service and was mustered out in 1901 as a First Sergeant. He enlisted again a few days later and then, as you remember, the Boer War was starting and Tom left without saying 'Good-bye' to Uncle Sam."

Tom left behind only a modest estate of $115,000, after having earned better than $6 million in his lifetime. Tom's fifth wife and Tom's daughter, Thomasina, inherited what there was. "He was wonderful," William S.

Hart said of him. The Arizona Highway Commission erected a memorial to Tom Mix, a monument mounted with a riderless horse at the place where he met his death. "In memory of Tom Mix," the inscription read, "whose spirit left his body on this spot and whose characterizations and portrayals in life served to better fix memories of the old west in the minds of living men."

Even as he died, the Western had changed, perhaps irretrievably, from what he had once made it. Gene Autry paid tribute to him in Madison Square Garden as one of the leading promoters of cowboy sports. And what of William Fox, who alone had joined Carl Laemmle in fighting the Trust, who had promoted Tom Mix into unexcelled stardom? The thirties saw his empire topple, his assets liquidated, and Fox himself sentenced to prison for stock manipulations. A different time had found different heroes.

Interlude:
The Decline and Fall
of the B Western

The reader may recall how Columbia Pictures reacted when Tim McCoy left in 1935 to make ten independent Westerns for Puritan release: they contracted with Larry Darmour to supply an undetermined number of Ken Maynard features, of which *Western Frontier* (Columbia, 1935) was the first. The picture went way over budget, and Darmour took precautions on the second entry, *Heir to Trouble* (Columbia, 1935). Joan Perry, whom Harry Cohn would eventually marry, was cast as the female lead. Darmour then engaged Spencer Gordon Bennet to direct. Bennet was known for his speed, and that was precisely what Darmour needed since he wanted the picture finished in a maximum of six days.

Shooting customarily began early in the morning at the Darmour studio on Santa Monica Boulevard or on location at either Kernville or Lone Pine for exteriors. *Heir to Trouble* was the last Maynard vehicle for Darmour that utilized Mauser Street at Universal City. I think Ken hoped, till the last possible moment, that Uncle Carl would change his mind and invite him back. From the time of *Western Courage* (Columbia, 1935) on, the Darmour unit used Monogram City as their town set.

In the beginning Maynard became involved in long, heated arguments with Darmour as to how the picture should be made. He would show up late on the set and take out his frustrations by beating his horses. Darmour was so shocked by this behavior that he asked Bennet to have the sound engineers record it. Maynard was drinking heavily; he was disconsolate. He had been forced to sell his home on Las Palmas Avenue in order to invest in a circus venture, the Diamond K Ranch Wild West Show. Before he was finished, he had some four hundred people on his payroll including the clown Emmett Kelly, but the show was not a financial success. Ken fell in love with one of his high-wire performers, Bertha Rowland Denham. Mary became extremely suspicious, so Ken had a secret panel built into his dressing room at the Darmour studio which would allow either Bertha or Maynard himself to slip away unnoticed.

Unlike Alan James, who always strove to get a consistent performance from Ken, which, quite frequently, required concentrating more on May-

Charles Starrett actually took his role as a cowboy player for youthful audiences rather seriously. Here he is autographing a broncho doll for two admirers.

Photo courtesy of *Views & Reviews* magazine.

nard than on the rest of the picture, Bennet addressed himself to the whole production. Bennet's direction was never inspired in any of the seven pictures he did with Ken, but it was surprisingly competent in view of the budget allowed him and the quality of the scenario. One sad example of corner-cutting was the scene in *Avenging Waters* (Columbia, 1936) where Ken, supposedly being dragged to his death by a runaway horse, is saved by Tarzan coming up alongside and permitting him to catch hold of the stirrup and then gain the saddle. The shot was managed by means of rear screen projection, and the attempt on Ken's part to grab hold of an obviously celluloid horse is farcical. Yet Bennet had little choice. Maynard's irregularities compelled him to constantly shoot around him with Cliff Lyons acting as his stand-in.

Ken's leading lady in the final entries for the 1936 season was Beth Marion. Beth had an attractive face and a rather shapely figure, having worked previously with both Johnny Mack Brown and Bob Steele in their A. W. Haeckle Westerns. Cliff was engaged to marry her. He nearly came to blows with Maynard when Ken insisted on trying to make more of the screen romance than was indicated in the script.

In a way, I suppose, Ken was justified in his irritation with Darmour. As the series progressed, it became increasingly apparent that Larry wanted Ken to imitate the Autry Fantasy. Gene's presence on the set didn't help. In *Heroes of the Range* (Columbia, 1936), there is a scene where Maynard has to prove his identity as Lightnin' Smith to Harry Woods and Bob Kortman by accompanying himself on the fiddle rather than with a six-gun.

After *The Fugitive Sheriff* (Columbia, 1936), Darmour dropped Maynard and signed Bob Allen to six Westerns, retaining Spencer as the director. Allen had appeared in several of the later McCoy Westerns of 1935 as second lead. His ambition, even then, to have his own starring series had seriously nettled McCoy and was one of the dissatisfactions Tim felt at Columbia. For all his ingenuous charm and native good looks, Bob Allen lacked the screen magnetism of a Western hero, and neither his series nor Darmour's contract was renewed.

At this juncture, Max Hoffman, Jr., returned to the scene. I have already described how his Allied Hoot Gibson Specials dissipated Hoot's career when the Hooter left Universal. Well, it so happened that Max had several scripts lying around, and he thought the moment ripe to produce Westerns again, this time with Ken Maynard. Max worked out a financing deal with Grand National and then signed Ken for eight films. Ken was to be paid only $2,400 a picture, which looked good against his failing circus enterprise. But Ken was stubborn. Cutting back on personnel, he went out year after year and lost money. This continued well into the forties. Maynard would be jailed for shooting up small towns or leave ill will in his wake for slapping around small children. When Roy Rogers began following him on the rodeo circuit, his reception was always reserved, until he reassured the townsfolk. Gene Autry drank quite a lot on his tours—one-night stands are a hard grind—but he managed, as ever, to remain a blithe spirit. And Autry only *appeared;* shrewd businessman that he was, he never insisted on owning his own circus the way his predecessors had, and so only made money, never lost it.

Ken's first picture for Max was *Boots of Destiny* (Grand National, 1937), a script originally scheduled for Hoot Gibson but never filmed. Maynard had broken his foot and had to wear a special boot so enlarged that it would accommodate even his plaster cast! It was an indifferent picture, featuring an aged and unhappy Claudia Dell, but the next one was even worse. *Trailin' Trouble* (Grand National, 1937) was what I would call a "composite" remake. The basic screenplay was Hoot Gibson's *Hard Hombre* (Allied, 1931). Instead of being a timid man mistaken for a notorious killer, as Hoot had been, Ken played a dual role. Probably the most amusing scene in the picture was that in which Ken dupes Lona Andre into tracing glasses, mustache, and beard on her face in charcoal, unaware of what she is doing. This sequence was borrowed in toto from Hoot's *Courtin' Wildcats* (Universal, 1929). Moreover, Tex Ritter's backup men accompanied Ken in a musical number. Ken's singing had been off key when he worked for Darmour; in fact, he had exploded when Darmour dubbed him. At Grand National, Maynard's brand of music-making was—to put it charitably—grotesque.

Hoffman fell sick. Although under somewhat different conditions than in the Hooter's case, he put Ken's contract up for sale. The Alexander brothers, who had tried to get Ken for six pictures in the early thirties and wound up with Jack Hoxie, got him for six pictures at last in 1938. The first two were also released by Grand National, *Whirlwind Horseman* and *Six Shootin' Sheriff,* Maynard suffering from a bad head cold, the most notable observation to be made about either picture. The final four Maynard Westerns were released independently—no singing, no comedy, and almost no action.

Immediately after McCoy's departure, Irving Brisken at Columbia undertook to test several contract players in an effort to find a suitable replacement. He came up with Charles Starrett. The Darmour contract supplied only half of the necessary Western units in Columbia's annual release schedule. Starrett would make up the rest. On the whole, Starrett was a wise choice, especially when you consider his record, 132 Westerns for a single studio, from *Gallant Defender* (Columbia, 1935) to his last feature, *The Kid from Broken Gun* (Columbia, 1952).

Starrett was born the youngest of nine children on March 28, 1904, to Leroy S. Starrett, founder of the Starrett Precision Tool Company. Royalties on the elder Starrett's inventions and patents kept the family wealthy.

Charles Starrett attended the best schools, beginning with the Bellerica Military School, the Worcester Academy, and, finally, Dartmouth College. Always of an athletic bent, Starrett excelled at varsity football. His first motion picture appearance was a bit part in *The Quarterback* (Paramount, 1924), which starred Richard Dix and which was filmed, in part, on the Dartmouth campus.

Upon graduation, Starrett decided to try acting, went to New York, and landed a small role in a play that closed in a week. Undeterred, he took a job at Wanamaker's department store playing in short skits. He was invited to join the Stewart Warker stock company and toured New England for three years, returning to Broadway to appear in a play entitled *Claire Adams*. He was seen by a talent scout and in 1930 went to Hollywood under contract to Paramount. He was cast in collegiate roles until he was loaned out to M-G-M for their glossy *The Mask of Fu Manchu* (M-G-M, 1932), in which Boris Karloff played the devil doctor and Myrna Loy was cast as his wayward daughter, Fah Lo Suee, who was sexually intoxicated by Starrett and was quite intent on forcing him into a love match. The role was of advantage to him when Paramount deigned not to renew his option and he signed with Columbia to work in a series of mysteries and society dramas.

Starrett's first three Columbia Westerns were directed by David Selman, D. Ross Lederman's assistant who had directed Tim McCoy's entries for the 1934–35 season. This intensified the link with McCoy, as did Starrett's costume, dark clothes with a light-colored bandanna and a blindingly white beaver Stetson. Joan Perry was the girl. C. C. Coleman, Frank Capra's assistant director on films like *Lost Horizon* (Columbia, 1937), directed the next several entries. The plots were engaging, and the musical support from the Sons of the Pioneers was a regular feature.

The Sons of the Pioneers was a musical group founded by Roy Rogers (under the name Dick Weston) and Bob Nolan in 1934, "the bottom of the Depression" as Roy once put it to me. Tim Spencer and Hugh Farr rounded out the quartet. They first came to prominence over station KFWB in Los Angeles. Their motion picture debut was in *The Old Homestead* (Liberty, 1935), with Roy billed under his real name, Len Slye. They next appeared in *Tumbling Tumbleweeds* (Republic, 1935) as musical support for Gene Autry and, as a result of the film, produced a hit song. Irving Briskin at Columbia signed the Sons to supply a musical setting for the projected Starrett Westerns, commencing with the initial film, *Gallant Defender*. There was some friction between Roy and Bob Nolan during this period, and Roy attempted, where he could, to free-lance or try out for leading parts. Roy appeared on and off in the Starrett films until early 1938.

The studio came increasingly to depend on formula patterns as the series progressed. In 1938 Columbia filled out its release schedule with a short-lived series of Buck Jones Westerns produced by Coronet Pictures. When Bill Elliott began his "Wild Bill Saunders" series the next season, all the Columbia Westerns were again studio product. Iris Meredith, Elliott's female lead in *Overland with Kit Carson*, really got overworked, appearing as the girl in nearly every Elliott or Starrett feature Western in 1939.

In 1940 Paul Franklin, who had scripted Buck Jones's *Headin' East* (Columbia, 1938), and Gene Autry's *Rhythm of the Saddle* (Republic, 1938) and who had joined the Columbia Story Department, came up with the screenplay for *The Durango Kid*. On the face of it, there was nothing especially new about the basic story idea of a hero who adopts a mask and black outfit to set evil doings aright. It was inherent in the Zorro idea; Ken Maynard had done it in *The Cattle Thief* (Columbia, 1936) and again in *The Phantom Rancher* (Colony, 1940), released in March; Buck Jones had it in his serial *The Phantom Rider* (Universal, 1936). George W. Trendle had been inspired to alter the idea slightly for his very popular radio series, "The Lone Ranger," and Republic had made two chapter plays based on his characters. Buck Jones brought suit against Trendle because he had even copied his horse's name, Silver.

Jack Fier, on the basis of his success with *Overland with Kit Carson*, was promoted into Irving Briskin's job. It was his idea to keep varying the ingredients in the Columbia series Westerns. *The Durango Kid* was just one of his experiments. Fier added Tex Ritter to the Bill Elliott Westerns. He offered Russell Hayden a contract sufficiently enticing to lure him away from Pop Sherman. Fier put Russell into the Starrett Westerns as second lead. When Elliott's contract ran out at the end of 1942 and Bill signed with Republic to replace Gene Autry, who had entered the Air Force, Jack gave Russell his own series with indifferent results and utterly preposterous music-making. In 1941 Fier tried to make Starrett a Western "Dr. Kildare" in a medico series that lasted for three pictures before it ran into copyright difficulties.

Fier's reasoning is rather transparent when you stop to consider the fact that Bob Nolan of the Pioneers was virtually second lead in most of the Starrett films until *Outlaws of the Panhandle* (Columbia, 1941). With the completion of this film, the Sons of the Pioneers' contract was up, and Roy persuaded them to sign with Republic. When the medico idea failed, Russell was expected to replace Nolan in the Starrett series. When Elliott left, Russell was slated to succeed him, but simply wasn't up to it. The musical backup in the Starrett Westerns was henceforth provided by all manner of substitutes from Spade Cooley to PeeWee King and his Golden West Cowboys, from Jimmy Wakely and his Saddle Pals, which had appeared in the Hopalong Cassidy film *Stick to Your Guns* (Paramount, 1941), to the rather unlikely Curley Williams and his Georgia Peach Pickers. It was felt, increasingly, by the Columbia Sales Department

Smiley Burnette was signed as a contract player at Columbia and became
Starrett's side-kick until the end of the Starrett series.

Photo courtesy of Columbia Pictures.

that penetration into the rural areas, and the South in particular, depended
on this type of hillbilly serenading.

Arthur Hunnicutt became Starrett's side-kick once Russell left the series.
He was replaced by Dub "Cannonball" Taylor when Wild Bill signed with
Republic. Finally, in 1945, Smiley Burnette joined Columbia. By his own
admission, Smiley was a one-man band, playing a wide assortment of
instruments. He had been making personal appearances since 1944 when
Republic had dropped him as a contract player. He went on to sing his
odd-ball songs and engage in his bumptious humor until the very end of the
Starrett series. Gene Autry then cast Smiley in his last six Western features
for Columbia in 1953, uniting the two at the end of their cinematic trails as
they had been at the beginning.

Fier was elevated to production manager in 1945. He appointed Colbert
Clark to succeed him. Clark, like Fier, had been introduced to the business
by Nat Levine at Mascot Pictures. It was Clark's notion to revive the Durango Kid idea with Starrett and Smiley making it into a series, which he
did with *The Return of the Durango Kid* (Columbia, 1945). From that
point until 1952, Starrett appeared only in Durango Kid Westerns; despite an unnerving lack of imaginative plots, the series persisted for some
fifty-nine entries.

Above all, the Durango Kid pictures were economical. Because of their common ingredients, a high action content could be maintained with less and less reliance on original footage. For example, in *Roaring Rangers* (Columbia, 1946), Starrett, doubled as Durango by stunt man Jock Mahoney, holds up a stage carrying Sheriff Jack Rockwell. The identical footage, carefully edited, was used again in nearly its entirety for *Blazing Across the Pecos* (Columbia, 1948) when Durango had to hold up a stage carrying rifles to the Indians. Individual quality varied a little. *Roaring Rangers,* a rather poor entry, could be followed directly by an above average film like *Gunning for Vengeance* (Columbia, 1946). The pictures almost always opened with stock action footage of exciting robberies or rustling sequences. In the beginning a title card gave the background to the story; in the late forties narration was substituted because it was cheaper. Smiley used his own name in that Republic claimed his former screen personality of "Frog Millhouse" to be their property. Starrett, when he wasn't disguised as Durango, portrayed a character named Steve with varying last names such as Landry or Randall or Blake. Durango's horse was called Raider. In the original *The Durango Kid,* Starrett had worn his customary white Stetson when playing Durango; in all the later entries, he was dressed completely in black.

When Autry joined Columbia, the Starrett budgets were cut even further

Charles Starrett as the Durango Kid in the last film from the series, *The Kid from Broken Gun.*

from what they had been. Starrett, invariably casual and competent, seemed resigned to his lot. The films continued to stress furious action interspersed with singing and slapstick antics which made them strong competition in the second- and third-run houses for Republic's second-string Rocky Lane and Monte Hale Westerns and Monogram's Johnny Mack Brown and Whip Wilson series. Smiley was virtually Starrett's costar, and this pleased Autry, whose friendship for Smiley never really dimmed over the years.

The Sons of the Pioneers sang "Tumbling Tumbleweeds" over the credits to *The Durango Kid*. Kenneth MacDonald shoots Charles Starrett's father as part of his reign of terror against the nesters. Starrett uses the Durango Kid disguise to outwit MacDonald, finally shooting him down. In the final scene, Starrett pins a deputy badge on Luana Walters—a careful gesture, confined to a spot just below her collar, in that Luana eschewed wearing support garments despite her ample endowment.

The Durango Kid is a transition picture. It still bears the stamp of the Starrett Westerns of the thirties and yet embodies the essential elements of the later Durango Kid series. The singing by the Sons of the Pioneers is not only less intrusive than was frequently the case at Columbia after 1940, but the group is simply more competent than most that worked in later films. Perhaps the most surprising aspect of the film, in retrospect is, given Bob Nolan's physical resemblance to George O'Brien, why no one ever attempted to capitalize on it and build him into a star in his own right, which had long been Nolan's ambition. Starrett, for his own part, never begrudged Nolan the opportunity, itself rather an unusual posture among Western players.

39 / "SO LONG, ROUGH RIDERS"

Tim McCoy's sixth release for Puritan Pictures was titled *Lightnin' Bill Carson* (Puritan, 1936). The film emphasized his quick draw and, as many of the Puritan Westerns, gave Rex Lease (a good friend of Tim's) a character role, this time a weak brother similar to his part years before opposite Tim in *The Law of the Range* (M-G-M, 1928). Whether Tim played gunfighter or cardsharp, the Puritan Westerns stressed psychological tension instead of action.

On February 4, 1936, Tim signed a contract with William Pizor, head of Imperial Pictures, to make eight films at a salary of $4,000 a picture. Pizor reneged and Tim sued. In November 1939 the suit was settled in the New York Supreme Court, and Tim was awarded $37,000, including $5,000 interest. Tim's last Puritan film, *The Traitor,* was released in August 1936. The Pizor contract kept him off the screen through what remained of 1936 and all of 1937. The hiatus from the screen gave Tim an opportunity to duplicate in his own way the circus disasters of Buck Jones, Hoot Gibson, Ken Maynard, and Tom Mix.

In 1935, between his last Columbia release and his first Puritan Western, *The Outlaw Deputy,* Tim toured quite successfully with the Ringling Brothers & Barnum and Bailey Circus. He appeared again with them in 1936, during the summer months, and in 1937. In early 1938 he undertook to organize his own Wild West show. Ken Maynard was doing the same thing that year and so was Hoot Gibson. Putting his acts carefully together, Tim previewed the show in Chicago where, years ago, he had seen the Miller 101 Ranch Show, which had been so decisive in the course of his later life. While Tim was opening in April, the Ringling Brothers, more experienced, didn't like the look of things, cut short their schedule, and rolled back to Sarasota. It was a recession year and Roosevelt's programs were failing; confidence, spending, and earnings went into a slump. Tim's show made its final appearance on May 4, 1938, in Washington, D.C., then closed for good. He had lost several hundred thousand dollars in the venture.

For the 1937–38 season, Monogram Pictures released sixteen series Westerns; eight Jack Randalls, of which *Riders of the Dawn* was the best with its climactic and thrilling chase across the salt flats at Lone Pine, which may have inspired a similar sequence in *Stagecoach* the next year; four Tom Keenes, of which *Where Trails Divide* still remains memorable for its closing reel with Warner Richmond and his gang wandering and thirsting to death on the Mojave; and four Tim McCoys, of which *Phantom Ranger,* if otherwise unnotable, contained the finest running inserts of any McCoy film since his Metro days. Monogram, under the combined leadership of Trem Carr as studio manager and Scott R. Dunlap as vice-president in charge of production, allocated $60,000 to $80,000 for their Westerns at this time and with their key exchange distribution netted an average gross of $150,000 each.

Tim had signed with them for only four pictures with an option. When Ed Finney brought Tex Ritter over from Grand National, Dunlap dropped the McCoy and Keene series Westerns, preferring a singing cowboy. When Tex signed with Columbia in 1941, Monogram resumed their Tom Keene series (Keene had been mayor of Sherman Oaks in the interim) and Tim returned for the Rough Riders series.

For the 1938–39 season, Tim contracted with Sam Katzman's Victory Pictures to make eight Westerns. Katzman for years produced, and continued to produce, pictures for general release through Columbia, Monogram, or on a states' rights basis, ironically ending up at M-G-M when that studio began crumbling after Louis B. Mayer was ousted. Katzman brought to the concept of the low-budget movie even *lower* budgets, embarrassingly identical scripts, and more thoroughly uncreative technical and dramatic vehicles than anyone would have thought possible. Sam turned out his eight McCoy Westerns on an $8,000 budget, paying Tim $4,000, the director a fourth as much, and the technical crew and supporting cast bare union wages for three days' work. But that was nothing! He made eight Tom Tyler Westerns for $6,000 a picture.

Exteriors were kept at a minimum, with Sam renting space at Monogram City in Newhall only sparingly, the unit generally outdoors for one day and indoors for two. Sam was not to be stopped. He even put the lab on a percentage for negatives and prints. Releasing through states' rights, he grossed $50,000 to $60,000 a picture. Once when Sam needed an actor, he telephoned Jimmy Flavin and invited him down to the set at night for a bridge game. By adroit maneuvering, he persuaded Jimmy to do a scene between rubbers. Not until it was released with his name on the publicity did Jimmy realize that he had been working without pay.

Sitting down to a script conference with Sam and the writers, Tim aided them in working out a formula for the films based on the Lightning Bill Carson character he had introduced at Puritan. At Victory, Carson was a captain in the U. S. Department of Justice, and the first film capitalized on the former Puritan release, *Lightning Carson Rides Again* (Victory, 1938). Usually the plot opened with a stock footage crime or simply some deviltry contrived on indoor sets with a cut to stock footage for the getaway, Bill Carson being called in from San Francisco or Washington to venture into the Old West and resolve the problem. Tim's theatricalism was indulged by the circumstance that he was forced to work undercover so as to conceal his identity until he had sufficient evidence to make an arrest. Tim enjoyed his disguises, doing his own make-up and perhaps thinking of his days at M-G-M when Lon Chaney's dressing room was next to his and the many talks they had had on the art of impersonation. Ben Corbett was cast as Tim's side-kick, Magpie, throughout the pictures, and the two worked as well together as, in Tim's career, only he and Julian Rivero had in *Man of Action* (Columbia, 1933).

In the meantime, Sig Neufeld, who had coproduced Tim's Puritan pictures, had become an executive producer with the newly formed Producers Releasing Corporation, which firm, throughout the forties, added to the finish of the programmer Western what Autry and Rogers with their expensive operettas could never have succeeded in destroying: namely, cheapening the product until it was no longer desirable to any but the most committed. Neufeld immediately signed Tim for an experimental Western as a

Buck signing his contract with Monogram Pictures, Dell Jones reading it, Ray Johnston to the left, Scott R. Dunlap to the right.

pilot for a new series titled *Texas Renegades* (PRC, 1940) with a high budget only in comparison with Katzman and an interesting screenplay. Bert Sternbach, production supervisor on the Victory films, went along with Tim, as did Holbrook Todd, the film editor, Hans Weeren, the sound engineer, and many of the cast members. The pilot did business, got bookings, and the new series was started on considerably reduced budgets, never more than $15,000 each.

These were to be Tim's last Westerns as a lone player, and they indicate the changes that were taking place in Hollywood notions of Western production. In their favor I will admit Tim's PRC Westerns were more conscientiously made than most the company subsequently produced. Sam Newfield, actually Sig Neufeld's brother, directed them under the name Peter Stewart, as he had directed nearly all of Tim's films once he'd left Columbia. Music-making and country rhythm were introduced in the final entries. This rankled Tim, but it was hopeless. The era of the action Western, which had nurtured him, was rapidly receding as the thirties ended and the forties began. At Columbia, Harry Cohn had recalled director D. Ross Lederman to his office and fired him when he read in *Variety* that news had leaked out giving the budget of *Silent Men* (Columbia, 1933) with McCoy at $12,000—or $8,000 less than anticipated. Lederman kept his job only by convincing Cohn that he had not been the source for the story. Sam Katzman was happy to produce a Western for what Lederman once had saved.

Buck Jones's experience during these same years had been, if anything, even worse. By offering him more money and a variety of roles, Monroe Shaff had lured Buck from Universal. On the face of it, Shaff's notion was enticing. Buck had begun at Fox as a dramatic player, and branching out again into non-Western roles might add considerable impetus to his career as a serious actor. The opportunities seemed greater, and, after all, Buck couldn't continue forever as a strictly Western hero, particularly in view of the impact of singing Westerns. "They use songs to save money on horses, riders, and ammunition," Buck was widely quoted. "Why, you take Gene Autry and lean him up against a tree with his guitar and let him sing three songs and you can fill up a whole reel without spending any money. That's why they've overdone the singing, and that's why it's on the way out."

H. M. Lang's Coronet Pictures, a small independent, financed Shaff's six Buck Jones Westerns for the 1937–38 season, and Columbia agreed to release them, thereby bringing an end to their contract with Larry Darmour and the unprofitable Bob Allen series. Shaff contributed to most of the screenplays. *Hollywood Roundup* (Columbia, 1937) was the first in the series. In it, Buck was cast as a Hollywood stunt man with a role reminiscent of his earlier *The Thrill Hunter* (Columbia, 1933). *Headin' East* (Columbia, 1937) came next, which, like the previous *Child of Manhattan* (Columbia, 1933), found Buck playing against a background of the big city, battling a gang of mobsters preying upon lettuce growers. The high point of the series was reached with *The Overland Express* (Columbia, 1938), which was set in the days of the Pony Express and had Buck wearing buckskins. Background music was effectively employed for chases and fights, and the action was well staged with abundant running inserts.

The series went into drastic decline with the fourth entry, *Stranger from Arizona* (Columbia, 1938). Hank Mann, who had worked opposite Tim McCoy in *Aces and Eights* at Puritan, was Buck's side-kick, and much screen time was wasted in unfunny antics between Mann and Hank Worden. Buck threw in one jibe, "Well, I am trying to learn how to play a guitar." William Boyd, still Buck's good friend, seconded Buck's satire on singing cowboys in his own *Santa Fe Marshal* (Paramount, 1940). Dorothy Fay was Buck's leading lady in *Stranger,* and she was again in *Law of the Texan* (Columbia, 1938). *Law* made several heavy-handed attempts at humor and is perhaps only memorable for those scenes in which Buck, having left the Rangers as he had in Stuart Anthony's *Fighting Ranger* (Columbia, 1934), as in the earlier picture, smoked and drank when in the company of the outlaws, thus rejecting again for a time at least the naïve code Tom Mix had made popular, Ken Maynard had projected, and Gene

Autry perpetuated. Buck's drinking off screen never came to the excess it did with Mix, Maynard, or Autry. When in 1938 Buck happened to actually meet Maynard in a bar while on a trip into Mexico, Maynard, whose career was collapsing, heaped abuse on him, and only Dell tugging at Buck's arm kept him from engaging in a brawl that could only have ended with arrest and bad publicity. *California Frontier* (Columbia, 1938) was Buck's last picture for Shaff and, by all means, his weakest, inept from nearly start to finish.

Lang and Shaff wanted Columbia to underwrite the series if production was to continue. This, Columbia, after some deliberation, refused to do. Instead, they promoted Bill Elliott, who had scored such a success with the serial *The Great Adventures of Wild Bill Hickok* (Columbia, 1938) and with the new Elliott series of "Wild Bill Saunders" Westerns, and the Charles Starrett series had the requisite units for the 1938–39 season. This left Buck virtually unemployed, under contract to no studio and with no contract offers, something that hadn't been true for him since 1927. The only role he played in 1939 was that of a broken-down prize fighter in Paramount's *The Unmarried*. It was the year of his silver wedding anniversary. Unlike Tom Mix or Bill Boyd, who had married several times each in the last two decades or so, Buck had kept his marital life stable. He always said he stayed with Dell because she fought with him and stood up for what she believed in. Returning to their spacious ranch house alone the night of the anniversary, their daughter, Maxine, engaged to Pidge Beery, Noah's son with Wally's personality, Buck composed a letter to Dell which I should like to quote for the reader.

"C/o a darling girl," he wrote in a script slanting downward, "who has just been through 25 years of married life, how do you feel, was it worthwhile, I hope so dear, some people call it a silver wedding. I call it, well, I don't know how to put it into words; only I love you dear just as much as I did when we were married the first year, 25 years, gee it does seem only a few days ago. I was watching you this evening having a good time, just as good as those kids, you're still one of them, don't lose it, dear. I did not want to drink tonight and I did not want to spoil your evening, so I came home, said good night to Pidge and Me [Maxine], everything O.K. Wake me up when you get here. I want to make you drink a big glass of milk so you will feel all right tomorrow. I love you. Buck."

The next year was little better. Buck made an appearance in *Wagons Westward* (Republic, 1940), in which he played a cold-blooded, savage, evil sheriff, which left audiences that had come to love him shocked and taken aback. By 1940 Hoot Gibson hadn't been in a picture for three years. Ken Maynard made his last low-budget features for the Alexander brothers and was out of work. Tom Mix had died. It marked the end of an era.

In late 1940 Columbia Pictures decided to remake Buck's earlier feature

White Eagle (Columbia, 1932) as a serial. Buck was again cast in the role of an Indian chief, with Raymond Hatton in support and Dorothy Fay as the female lead. Dick Foran, who had replaced Johnny Mack Brown as Universal's lead in their Western serials, starred in *Winners of the West* in 1940. He was slated to star in their blockbuster for 1941, heralded as a million-dollar chapter play, titled in memoriam after the late Tom Mix's finest Universal Western, *Riders of Death Valley* (Universal, 1941). Leo Carrillo was cast, as was Buck, Charles Bickford, Lon Chaney, Jr., and Pidge, who had married Maxine on March 30, 1940. Most of the money was spent on casting and publicity so that reliance on stock footage ran heavy, even to a sandstorm lifted from *Flash Gordon's Trip to Mars* (Universal, 1938). By happy circumstance, both *White Eagle* and *Riders* were issued in the same year, giving Buck renewed maximum exposure in theaters taking either Columbia or Universal product for a combined booking of thirty weeks.

In addition to resuming their Tom Keene series when they lost Tex Ritter, Monogram made other changes. Since the Jack Randall series had been doing poorly, it was canceled for the 1940–41 season. Monogram needed an additional eight units, and Scott R. Dunlap hit on an idea to assist them in their failing fortunes. He proposed to Trem Carr that Monogram start another group of trio Westerns on the order of the Range Busters. Scotty thought at once of Buck, with whom he had been associated years before at Fox, and Trem suggested Tim McCoy for the second lead. The two of them got McCoy to agree at his usual price of $4,000 a picture and approached Buck. It was Buck who came up with a counterproposal. He knew Monogram was greedy to take advantage of the fantastic publicity behind *Riders* and the Columbia exposure in *White Eagle*. He suggested the three of them form a subsidiary company in which they would each be equal shareholders. The Great Western Pictures Company was the result, in which Buck was president and Scotty vice-president. Buck, Scotty, and Trem put up $3,333.33 individually and received thirds of the stock. The agreement indicated that Monogram was to finance, with the Great Western Pictures receiving 35/65 participation in the gross until negative cost was regained and a 50/50 split between the company and the studio after that. Raymond Hatton was signed as the third member of the trio, having just completed eight units for Republic in their durable Three Mesquiteers series, with Robert Livingston and Duncan Renaldo.

Edward J. Kay, a Hollywood songwriter, composed an exciting orchestral agitato for chase sequences and created words and music to the "Rough Riders' Song," which was customarily played over the main titles superimposed on a freeze frame from John Ford's *Stagecoach*. Following the title of the individual entry, Buck Jones's name would appear largest on top, Tim's somewhat smaller in the middle of the screen, and Ray Hatton's near the bottom. The successful formula of the Bar 20 pictures was adopted by devoting the early and middle reels to plot development and human interest, calling for an action-packed windup in the final reel. The series was scripted by veteran screenwriter Adele Buffington, who had done *Powdersmoke Range,* under the pseudonym of Jess Bowers.

The publicity campaign for the new films was brilliantly keyed. The Monogram Promotion Department outdid itself in preparing the press kits. That to *Arizona Bound* (Monogram, 1941), first in the series, read in part: " 'The Rough Riders' will establish themselves quickly as the screen's best entertainment bet for this type of picture. Here is a film that offers no compromise with the singing cowboy class of Westerns. It was written for action and produced for action—and that's what the audience gets in large doses." Prescott, Arizona, built a Western town set, and *Arizona Bound* was shot there, on location. Dorothy Fay came from Prescott and was getting married at the time to Tex Ritter in her home town while the Rough Riders unit was in production. Buck, Tim, and Ray and the rest of the cast were in attendance at the wedding, with Dick Foran in somewhat inebriated fashion providing the singing. Dixie cup plugs, big little books, song books, badges, Schwinn bicycles, and Royal Crown Cola, among many, synchronized an advertising program with the series, masterminded by Dunlap, who in the thirties had been in advertising agency work, employing photos of the Rough Riders using their products.

Spencer Gordon Bennet was contracted to direct the initial entries. Robert N. Bradbury directed the third release, and Howard Bretherton, who had worked on the early Bar 20 pictures, finished the series. Scotty Dunlap was a bullheaded, red-necked Irishman who knew what he wanted. He would occasionally lock horns with Jones as to how a scene should be shot, and Buck would only win by reminding him who was head of the production company. Tim remained aloof from altercation and invariably deported himself as a gentleman. Buck, who was of a serious frame of mind, kept to himself much of the time. Bennet knew best how to maximize his effects. The budgets were set at $80,000, out of which Monogram charged $35,000 to overhead, leaving the remainder for actual production. Spencer directed what I feel the best of the eight films, the second entry, *The Gunman from Bodie,* and created by means of lighting and emphasis powerful and moving and unforgettable images.

Arizona Bound (Monogram, 1941) set down the basic premises and characters. Buck played Buck Roberts, Tim was Tim McCall, and Ray was Sandy Hopkins, an identification he would keep for years in Westerns. They were special U. S. Marshals called in on dangerous assignments, if not by Bat Madison, Chief U. S. Marshal, then by a friend in distress. Their method of operation was for one or more members of the trio to work his way into the gang—as in *Arizona Bound,* Tim for all appearances is a preacher and Sandy a herdsman—uniting forces in the last reel for the cleanup. Oliver Drake, who was working on the Johnny Mack Brown series at Universal, did the first story, whereas Adele Buffington wrote the screenplay. Adele's first picture for Buck had been *High Speed* (Columbia, 1932). Luana Walters was the girl whose stage-line franchise was being threatened by Tristram Coffin and his gang. Dennis Moore supplied the romantic interest as he would on and off, alternating with Dave O'Brien, throughout the series. While Buck was on location for this picture, Dell attended the auction at Tom Mix's ranch and arranged over the phone for Stumpy Simms, the seventy-year-old Negro who had worked for Mix for twenty-five years as his groom, to talk to Buck. Buck hired him to work at their ranch, the Hacienda del Charro, and attend to Silver. "You know, Mr. Jones," Simms was quoted as saying, "somehow I think this is the way Mr. Mix would have wanted it." After Buck's tragic death, Simms watched Silver languish and die.

The Gunman from Bodie was next. Dave O'Brien and Christine MacIntyre supplied the love interest. Buck was disguised as a bandit, Bronson Bodie. Robert Frazer as Wyatt was the leader of a gang of land grabbers who want to take over all the valley ranches.

"If I'd only had more than seven days, Jon," Spencer Gordon Bennet remarked to me as we sat comfortably in Max Lamb's Hollywood home after

Buck and Charlie King sparred again for *Gunman from Bodie*.

Photo courtesy of *Views & Reviews* magazine.

Tim in the process of breaking down John Merton while Charlie King and
Earl Douglas watch, from *The Gunman from Bodie.*

Photo courtesy of *Views & Reviews* magazine.

screening *Gunman,* "I could have got even more close-ups. But we were so
rushed. We shot it at Newhall and for the cattle scenes out toward Topanga
Canyon Road."

Forbidden Trails (Monogram, 1941) added considerable stunting and
running inserts, elaborate truck shots, and increased action photography to
the series.

Ghost Town Law (Monogram, 1942) as cinema art may well be the
next best picture in the group, with the action taking place in a lonely mansion, a forgotten mine shaft, and a dilapidated mining town. Buck got to do
most of the serious acting.

West of the Law (Monogram, 1942) was to be Tim's last Rough Riders
picture under his contract. It was a fine series, as fine as anything Monogram ever did in its confused corporate history. But Tim was unhappy. Regardless of the publicity and one-sheets, the press books and Rough Riders
paraphernalia, the pictures as they progressed became increasingly Buck
Jones vehicles. In a very definite way, they were intended to capture and
hold new audiences in a further perpetuation of Jones's career, with Tim as

much in support of that objective as Ray Hatton. Tim decided to quit. But he did not announce his decision.

For one thing, his identification as one of the Rough Riders had virtually destroyed his chances of securing a contract as the sole star of a new series of Westerns. Moreover, both Dunlap and Jones were bringing pressure on him to sign for another eight pictures. He liked Buck immensely and did not wish to hurt him. Buck, having aged and yet loving so much to be in starring Westerns again, was a kind and gentle man. Tim respected him and, personally, enjoyed working with him. But the fun had gone out of making pictures. If he was to effect a break, it would have to be into a new career, one not associated with the motion picture industry.

In the spring of 1942, Wyoming's old-guard Republicans were putting the machinery into motion to nominate E. V. Robertson as their candidate for the U. S. Senate, when they stopped to listen to the grass-roots promptings of Tim's friends in Cody and Thermopolis. "Now he has come forth," an editorial stated, "ready to give up a lucrative future in motion pictures to serve Wyoming at a time when his qualities of leadership and courage are sorely needed. With his first-hand knowledge of national and international affairs and his understanding of Wyoming, he could give the state the representation to which it is entitled . . . and we have the Republican candidate for United States Senator, Tim McCoy!" Many of the younger people in the state, who might have voted for him, were overseas. Favorite-son candidates sprang up everywhere. Tim, like Tex Ritter much later, was defeated as much by the Democratic machine which made light of his career as a movie cowboy as by the deep splits in his own party. The election was over before work on *West of the Law* began.

Tim McCoy preferred in all things to be what the French call *un solitaire*. Dressed completely in white, seated across from me in a restaurant eating fried oysters and sipping chablis, he recalled how he resolved to re-enlist in the Army for active duty. Nearly eighty, on the road, alone much of the time, he had lost none of his self-possession, his well-earned pride in having been one of the last of the plainsmen.

"When the news of my active commission came to me with the rank of a lieutenant colonel, we had already finished *West of the Law*. I packed my bags, Jon, and hopped on a train for Washington."

At the end of every Rough Riders picture, the three would gather before the camera, each to go his own way until trouble somewhere in the West would call them together once more. Ray Hatton would always be bound for Texas; Buck was heading back to Arizona; Tim was off to Wyoming. Saluting each other, calling out "So long, Rough Riders," they would each ride in a different direction, the camera stationary until they vanished in the distance, the "Rough Riders' Song" played over the end credits requesting the viewer to wait until the Rough Riders rode again. Tim sent Dunlap a telegram containing the news of his commission, signing it in typical fashion, "So long, Rough Riders."

That should have ended the matter. It didn't. While the shooting scripts had never indicated after *Gunman from Bodie* just how integral Tim had been to the series, Dunlap knew. He and Buck tried a solo picture at once, resurrecting Rex Bell, a low-grade Western player from the early sound era whose marriage to "It" girl Clara Bow was more memorable than any of his Resolute Westerns. He played a gambler in *Dawn on the Great Divide* (Monogram, 1942), but the film proved an abysmal failure compared to the Rough Riders series, Bell so inept that he had difficulty getting his gun out of his holster when he wasn't smiling into the camera. Buck was displeased with the results. He would have been more displeased still had he lived to see the sloppily edited version Monogram finally did release.

The film was in the cutting room when Dunlap went ahead with plans for a tour of the country with Buck that was to promote a new Monogram series starring just Jones and Ray Hatton and incidentally was supposed to sell war bonds. The response was promising, but Dunlap and Jones were still victims to all the publicity they had produced for the trio concept. Everywhere youngsters wanted to know if the Rough Riders would ever ride again.

When the tour came to Washington, D.C., Dunlap asked Tim to appear at a benefit with Buck, a onetime deal, reuniting the Rough Riders. Tim demurred and had his commanding officer communicate with Dunlap's agent that such an appearance would be out of the question due to pressing army matters. The troupe made its way eventually to Boston. Dunlap had dramatically and defiantly held a public signing of Buck's new Monogram contract on the tour. But the future looked uncertain. Could Buck do alone what he and Tim and Ray had done so well together? Could Buck, after so many years in pictures, continue to attract the same audiences as an older man that he had had when young? If the reader will permit me a speculation, I would answer these questions in the affirmative. Buck was a fundamentally lovable human being. I suspect his Monogram series might have survived as long as that of his replacement, Johnny Mack Brown. Buck had an internal fortitude in his character that may have expanded with the onset of the years, as it did in the case of another, John Wayne. Tom Mix felt so in his last days, for he began leaving his personalia with Buck, saying it was to decorate his barroom, but believing all the time that it best belonged with Buck.

And so it came that during his appearance at the Cocoanut Grove in Boston, the papier-mâché decorations caught fire. Buck was dancing near the revolving door and was rushed quickly outside to safety. Smoke bellied from the windows and doors as the blaze raged. A bus boy's match struck while fixing a light bulb loosed the frightful conflagration. Buck, coughing,

"So long, Rough Riders."

pushed his way back into the flaming building. He wanted to see to it that Scotty Dunlap was safe. He did not know, as he jumped past the milling, screaming crowd, the ceiling beginning to collapse, that Dunlap was outside, reclining on the running board of a fire engine. Dunlap's hands were so badly burned that he couldn't reach his wallet in his pocket. He offered a youngster a hundred dollars if he would take out the wallet and remove the bill and then phone for an ambulance for him.

Some 491 people died that night. Buck was finally pulled from the fire, one of 181 critically injured. The fire had attacked his face and body, searing his throat and lungs. He was taken to the city hospital and the doctors fought to save him. On November 29, 1942, hearing the news, Dell wired him: "Darling! Will be there just as soon as I can get plane reservations. Chin up. Love you." Buck was unconscious.

At 6:29 A.M. on November 30, 1942, Ray Hatton's telegram arrived at Massachusetts General Hospital. "Partner," the message read, "it was a terrific shock to learn of your terrible experience. I know God had his arm around you and we are grateful you are saved in a hospital. Frances joins in extending sympathy to you and Dell your partner." Had he survived, he would have been horribly disfigured. In the afternoon of November 30, death stole upon Buck Jones, and at last life slipped away from him. "Dear

Dell," Tim McCoy's cable read, "my deepest sympathy. You know as one man can regard another, I loved him, too. Tim."

Adele Buffington wrote to Dell on December 3: "How can any of us— ever again—think of the Rough Riders as quite the same, and yet in our hearts we all know that we will carry on, because Buck would wish no other, simpler or truer tribute to his greatness. He was no less a hero to me —to all of us—than to the many, many children who worshipped him. To write for Buck was not to write for just another actor, but for a man who symbolized all the magnificent virtues that little children—and grown-ups, too—know instinctively to be genuine and true, which after all was the an- swer to his greatness. Believe me."

Even a world at war was shocked. A flag was draped over Buck's coffin. He was flown to Hollywood, his remains cremated and thrown into the Pacific Ocean he had so loved when sailing the *Sartartia*. And Scott R. Dunlap, who did not die, settled with Buck's widow some years later by pur- chasing back Buck's stock in the Great Western Company for every cent Buck had put into it—$3,333.33—turning around then, as sole owner of the Rough Riders series, and selling it in a matter of days to television for $250,000. And of Buck Jones, perhaps history can justifiably record that he died as heroically as once he lived.

40 / UNIVERSAL IN THE FORTIES

I

The day was hot. Bright sunlight beat down on Hollywood Boulevard as we waited for the traffic to subside before crossing to Musso and Frank's. Johnny Mack Brown was sporting a mustache, the first he had ever worn. In fact, he looked so much the southern colonel and so little like Johnny Mack Brown when I had picked him up near his apartment building that I had involuntarily done a second take.

"I know," he chuckled, fondling the mustache with the fingers of his right hand, "I always wanted to see how I would look in one."

Born at Dothan, Alabama, on September 1, 1904, he was now seventy years old. He put his arm around me gently as we steered our way through the teeming humanity scurrying in the noonday sun.

"Dashiell Hammett used to keep a drinking booth at this restaurant," I remarked. But of course Johnny knew Musso and Frank's, and despite the mustache, he was instantly recognized as we walked inside. Once we were ensconced in a booth, the din and bustle far to the front, I brought up the subject of A. W. Haeckle.

"Ohhh!" Johnny Mack groaned. "The last thing my wife said to me before she left this morning was, 'I hope he doesn't bring up those Haeckle pictures.'"

"A couple of them weren't that bad," I responded. "I like *The Desert Phantom* [Supreme, 1936], for example. It had Ted Adams as a Mexican bandit, and Charlie King was his top gun. It even maintained a degree of suspense."

"Maybe," Johnny Mack interposed, "but most of them weren't that good. They were cheap pictures just thrown together. I don't know where he got his leading ladies. The first time anyone ever saw them was when I was supposed to do a scene with one of them and after the picture was over you never saw them again."

"It's funny you should mention that," I said. "A program director from a television station in Michigan sent me a print of *Everyman's Law* [Supreme, 1936], in which you costarred with Beth Marion. She later married your double, Cliff Lyons. The program director was quite enthusiastic about her. I hadn't felt she could act when she made *Avenging Waters* [Columbia, 1936] and *The Fugitive Sheriff* [Columbia, 1936] with Ken Maynard, and I didn't think she was any better playing opposite you. In one scene, she was so nervous she would constantly clutch her left arm behind her back with her right hand."

"That's just what I mean," Johnny Mack assented. "I had worked with Mary Pickford, Joan Crawford, and Garbo."

"And Mae West."

Johnny Mack had a copy of the book I had written about Mae's career. He opened it to the chapter on *Belle of the 'Nineties* (Paramount, 1934).

"I'll never forget," he said, "we had a love scene. I had to shower Mae with kisses. 'Miss West,' I told her afterward, 'kissing you is intoxicating.' She shoved me away. 'Well, I don't want to turn you into a drunk in only one night.'"

We laughed.

Following his appearance in *Billy the Kid*, Johnny Mack had been cast intermittently in Westerns, more often playing in high-budget dramas. He was always an agreeable chap and preferred Westerns, if at all, because they gave him top billing. He contracted for his first chapter play, *Fighting with Kit Carson*, at Mascot Pictures in 1933, memorable perhaps primarily for Noah Beery, Sr.'s, characterization of Kraft, the principal villain. In 1935 he starred in the Universal serial *Rustlers of Red Gap*. A. W. Haeckle,

Johnny Mack Brown in one of his first publicity stills for his new Monogram series.

Photo courtesy of Johnny Mack Brown.

who was born in Austria in 1882 and entered the film business in 1930, signed Johnny to a contract in late 1935 for an undetermined number of Westerns. Initially, Republic agreed to distribute the pictures together with Haeckle's Bob Steele series, but would not finance. In 1937 Johnny replaced Buck Jones for Universal's customary summer serial, *Wild West Days;* the next year he made *Flaming Frontiers* for them, which utilized extensive stock footage from the silent Hoot Gibson Special as well as *The Indians Are Coming.* In 1939 Johnny made *The Oregon Trail* for Universal, but by that time he was already a contract player for the studio in feature Westerns.

When Buck Jones decided to leave Universal in 1937, a frantic search was mounted for a suitable replacement. Two finalists emerged from all the screen tests, Dick Weston, a member of the Sons of the Pioneers, and Bob Baker. Baker was born Stanley Leland Weed at Forest City, Iowa, on November 8, 1914. He first came to prominence on the National Barn Dance. Max Terhune persuaded him to try pictures and instructed him in how to act before a camera. Baker was finally chosen over Weston on the basis of physical maturity. Universal gave him the screen name of Bob Baker, with Baker opting to retain his stage name Tumble Weed, and starred him in a series of singing Westerns commencing with *Courage of the West* (Universal, 1937). Baker, no matter the reasoning behind his selection over Weston, projected rather an undernourished screen image. He could sing but was untrained. Universal discovered to their dismay, as did the others, that singing Westerns weren't the answer to Autry. Baker, like most of his peers, ignored the Autry Fantasy, and his writers weren't even conscious that there was such a thing.

Haeckle's second series of sixteen Western units, eight with Johnny Mack Brown and eight with Bob Steele, were financed directly by Republic for the 1937 season and released under their banner rather than under the logo of Haeckle's Supreme Pictures. Johnny's dissatisfaction was increasing, and he refused to renew his contract with Haeckle once the second series was completed.

Sol C. Siegel, associate producer for Westerns at Republic, was rather upset by the fact that Gene Autry, in his demands for more money, had walked off the job. Autry had telephoned Joe Kane, the director assigned to his pictures, and told him he had no intention of being on call to shoot his next film. Gene went on a personal appearance tour through the South, followed by process servers in an effort to restrain him from doing any work other than that specified by Republic. Before departing, Autry had completed *The Old Barn Dance* (Republic, 1938), released in January. He had $50,000 banked in Chicago and would not make any more pictures until his original Levine contract was renegotiated. Siegel buttonholed Dick Weston, who had wandered again onto the Republic lot seeking work; he had had a singing part in *The Old Barn Dance*. Weston was signed to a contract under the name Roy Rogers at about the same time that Johnny signed with Universal as a contract player. Roy made *Under Western Stars* (Republic, 1938), which was the next picture scheduled for Autry, with support from Gene's side-kick, Smiley Burnette. Seeing the results, Republic President Herbert J. Yates capitulated and renegotiated with Autry.

"Gene was so popular below the Mason-Dixon line," Joe Kane recalled, "that people simply surrounded the process server and walked him out of town."

It took Yates three tries before he got Autry to agree to terms. When the 1938–39 season began in fall 1938, Autry was back in the saddle for one of his best films, *Gold Mine in the Sky* (Republic, 1938), while Roy replaced the Johnny Mack Brown series with his first entry, *Billy the Kid Returns* (Republic, 1938). Smiley worked with Roy once more in this picture and then was replaced by Raymond Hatton. Finally, Siegel got George Hayes away from Pop Sherman at Paramount, and under the name "Gabby" he became Roy's usual side-kick. Bob Steele continued to work in his own series for Republic. Neither Yates nor Siegel felt that Roy could possibly replace Autry, but he might serve to keep Autry's demands reasonable the way Buck Jones and George O'Brien had been used to blackmail Tom Mix at Fox in the twenties or Tom Tyler had been employed to keep Fred Thomson in check at Film Booking Office. Still reeling from the Great Depression and recovering from the Recession of 1937, none of Republic's other three series, those with the Three Mesquiteers, Roy Rogers, or Bob Steele, nor the series from any other studio could provide Americans hungry for a dream of attainable ease the comfort, solace, and reassurance of the Autry Fantasy. Gene Autry stood alone among Western performers.

After his third Universal picture, Bob Baker thought himself to be an expert and was continually fighting with his producers and the various technicians as to how his films should be made. He proved an insufficient box-office draw. Universal quickly downgraded him to second lead to Johnny Mack Brown with comic Fuzzy Knight forming a trio they billed as the Frontier Marshals. Baker still proved a handicap and, by 1940, was given only character role status in the films. Johnny Mack entered the Bob Baker series with the thirteenth entry, *Desperate Trails* (Universal, 1939). However embittered he may have been at the time, Roy Rogers was most fortunate that he lost out to Baker and was signed at Republic instead.

In many ways, the Johnny Mack Brown Westerns for Universal matched for action and pacing, although rarely for story line, the best of the Buck Jones series. Buck was an avid reader of Western fiction and was constantly on the lookout for interesting stories; Johnny never had that kind of control over his vehicles. The Brown films, however, had excellent running inserts. Indeed, out of his 178 motion picture appearances, the majority of them Westerns, Johnny was never to duplicate for consistent quality his Universal entries of the early forties.

West of Carson City was the first 1940 entry that veteran Ray Taylor directed, joining the Brown series with this feature. Johnny and Bob Baker are on a trail drive. Mauser Street is done over as a ghost town. Ernie Adams races into town claiming he has struck it rich. The town begins to boom. Harry Woods, Roy Barcroft, and the gang move in. Johnny backs the new judge and, after much gunplay and fistfighting, law and order is restored.

The Autry Phenomenon was at its strongest in the early forties. Oliver Drake, who was appointed production manager and associate producer of the Brown films in 1941 bringing all his RKO scripts with him, wanted to try a variant, combining the trio Western with the singing Western. When he signed Tex Ritter in 1942, he had the opportunity. Johnny Mack, Tex, and Fuzzy Knight formed a trio of sorts, with Tex singing, joined by the Jimmy Wakely trio. *Deep in the Heart of Texas* (Universal, 1942), *Little*

Joe, the Wrangler (Universal, 1942), and *Raiders of San Joaquin* (Universal, 1943) exploited this formula. But the Universal B unit in these years was always excessively influenced by what was happening in A productions.

Because the tremendous fistfight between Randy Scott and Duke Wayne in the remake of *The Spoilers* (Universal, 1942) excited much comment, Drake decided to alter the essential relationship between Johnny and Tex. In *The Old Chisholm Trail* (Universal, 1942), Elmer Clifton's screenplay had the two engage in a violent bout of fisticuffs with Tex being knocked unconscious. Johnny's intrinsic humanity betrayed him briefly when he was shown helping Tex to his feet, and the sequence was left in. The screenplay went a step further and had Jennifer Holt spar with Mady Correll. In their next picture, *Tenting Tonight on the Old Camp Ground* (Universal, 1943), Tex and Johnny go to it again after Tex, as a railroad executive, has unwittingly played into the schemes of Lane Chandler and Rex Lease. The motive behind the fights was Johnny making time with Jennifer in *Chisholm* and Johnny's ability at management in *Tenting;* the situations suited neither.

Cheyenne Roundup (Universal, 1943) was a remake of Johnny's *Bad Man from Red Butte* (Universal, 1940), in which Johnny portrays identical twins, one good, one bad, with Tex as a sheriff apparently in league with Harry Woods and Roy Barcroft but actually working undercover with the good twin. *The Lone Star Trail,* released in April 1943, but filmed in November 1942, was Johnny's last Western for Universal, employing the story idea for the original *Destry Rides Again,* with Johnny, wrongly sentenced to prison, appearing as a coward upon his parole, changing suddenly when the scoundrels come out of hiding. Universal decided not to renew Johnny's contract. He went home and sat on the porch.

With Buck Jones gone, Monogram was in trouble. The studio was hard pressed for a first-rate Western series. Robert Tansey, who had worked on the Tex Ritter pictures at Grand National with Edward Finney and Lindsley Parsons and who, when his creditors were after him, would sign his screen work Robert Emmett, came to Trem Carr and Scott R. Dunlap with a proposal. He had interested Hoot Gibson in returning to the screen in a series costarring him with Ken Maynard. The Monogram executives gave Tansey a green light. Armed with Hoot Gibson's signed contract, Tansey ventured out to Maynard's ranch.

Hoot had attempted, unsuccessfully, to set up and prosper with Hoot Gibson's Trading Post in Los Angeles, after his work in *The Painted Stallion.* In 1942, appearing on the state fair circuit, he had married again to a young singer and rodeo performer, Dorothy Dunstan, on July 3 in Las Vegas. Tansey talked to Maynard out by the barn. Ken had put on a lot of weight. He, too, had remarried, finally, to Bertha Rowland Denham on August 29, 1939, following his divorce from Mary. Maynard's last pictures had been four independent Colony releases in 1939–40 for which he had been paid $2,400 a picture. Tansey offered Ken a flat $4,800, which would work out to $800 a picture if they made six or $600 a picture if they might eight. Ken balked. Tansey remonstrated him. Hoot needed the work even if Ken didn't. Ken was on the road in the Southwest with his Diamond K Ranch Wild West Show. Hoot wanted him to do it. The gambit worked. Ken agreed.

The new series was billed as the Trail Blazers. Ken bragged to his brother, Kermit, who had long been reduced to walk-ons, that now he would have to lose weight. But when Ken learned that Hoot had no intention of dieting—"Not for this kind of money!" Hooter had responded—Ken didn't either. Tansey wanted to get a third member into the trio. He tried Bob Baker in the first picture, *Wild Horse Stampede* (Monogram, 1943), but Ken persecuted Baker mercilessly. It wasn't until the fourth entry, *Death Valley Rangers* (Monogram, 1943), that Tansey could sign Bob Steele, who had just been dropped by Republic after the final units in their Three Mesquiteers series.

Monogram apportioned $80,000 a picture to this series, charged off $45,000 a picture for overhead, and expected Tansey to bring the films in with what was left. Alan James was reputed to be the only director who could work with Maynard, and since he had directed Hoot as well, Tansey had him pilot the first two films. After that, he took over the direction himself. Tansey shot the pictures in five to six days and tried to keep the production budgets between $12,000 and $15,000, pocketing the rest himself. Betty Miles, who had a pleasing figure in especially tight riding pants and who was quite an equestrian, played the female lead in most of the films.

Maynard became increasingly importunate about more money as the series progressed. He claimed that Bob Steele had insulted Bertha and insisted he be kicked out. Tansey got six pictures out of Ken before he quit. On the side, Tansey negotiated a deal with Astor Pictures to make a Ken Maynard series. This was to be a trio series also, starring Ken, with Eddie Dean as musical support and Max Terhune for comedy. If anything, Maynard had got even heavier. The new series ended after the first bombshell entry, *Harmony Trail* (Astor, 1944), which Tansey directed under the name Robert Emmett. It was Ken's last starring Western, and I think in this case we may be grateful that the negative has decomposed.

Back at the Monogram ranch, Tansey was carrying on with the Trail Blazers, replacing Ken for the final two films with Chief Thundercloud, who had played Tonto in the Republic Lone Ranger serials. Bob and Hoot went on in 1945 to make three more Monogram Westerns together, *The Utah Kid, Marked Trails,* and *Trigger Law,* with Hoot cast sedately as a sheriff. They were not Trail Blazer Westerns. Their budgets were drasti-

Buster Crabbe is holding Kermit Maynard in this scene from one of Buster's low-budget PRC films. Kermit was Ken's brother and an extra in countless Westerns.

Photo courtesy of *Views & Reviews* magazine.

cally limited. *The Utah Kid,* for example, depended for nearly a third of its footage on scenes from the Hoot Gibson rodeo shot in the early thirties, and the interpolations were painful even to the casual viewer. The magic was gone. Hoot's career, and Bob's, began turning toward character roles and lesser parts. Bob made one last series of starring vehicles at PRC, which, considering his entire screen work for primarily low-budget outfits, reached a new low, of which *Thunder Town* (PRC, 1945) was either the best or the worst, in terms of how you wish to look at it.

There was one thing Tansey had been right about. Ken and Hoot, good friends for so many years, did work well together, and the series had its moments. In one scene in *Wild Horse Stampede,* Ken and Hoot creep up on Tom London, Glenn Strange, and other gang members and convince them that they are surrounded by means of Hoot running to various places in the dark and answering Ken's queries in a number of different accents, meanwhile the two of them slipping off to regain the stolen herd while the gang thinks itself held prisoner. In one very well directed sequence in *Blazing Guns* (Monogram, 1943), third and probably best in the series, Ken is walking down the street to the saloon. Charlie King, a frequent gang member, remarks to a crony: "For two bucks, I'd shoot him in the back." He draws his gun with deliberation. Two silver dollars clink on the boardwalk. The camera focuses on the silver dollars, pans to the outlaws' faces, and then turns to Hoot, cached between the buildings. Hoot smiles benignly as Charlie holsters his gun and walks off.

But I must not get ahead of my story. I left Johnny Mack sitting on his porch. Monogram announced negotiations with Jack Holt to replace Buck Jones in the Nevada Jack MacKenzie series, but Holt surprised them by enlisting in the Army. Trem Carr, learning that Johnny was out of work, telephoned him at his home and proposed he come down to the studio. Johnny was contracted to star with Raymond Hatton. By acting with alacrity, it turned out that Johnny's first film for Monogram, *The Ghost Rider* (Monogram, 1943), was released in the same month as *Cheyenne Roundup* (Universal, 1943); his second, *The Stranger from Pecos* (Monogram, 1943), was released a month after *Raiders of San Joaquin* (Universal, 1943); his third, *Six Gun Gospel* (Monogram, 1943), was issued a month after *The Lone Star Trail* from Universal. The Monogram formula proved an instant success.

Tansey, in the interim, went over to PRC and began producing a series of Westerns with Eddie Dean in the new process of Cinecolor. Jennifer Holt, dropped by Universal, almost invariably appeared as the female lead. In *Song of Old Wyoming* (PRC, 1945), Tansey introduced Al LaRue, dressed in black, who is shot at the end of the picture. But somehow the notion of a tough Lower East Side Kid punk with a Bronx accent as a semi-villainous hero caught on with postwar youth, and a series of Lash LaRue Westerns followed. These pictures were even cheaper and more singularly horrible than the Buster Crabbe Billy the Kid and Billy Carson Westerns of 1940–45 that they replaced, with Al "Fuzzy" St. John, Buster's perennial side-kick, continuing on opposite LaRue. The reader may feel "cheaper" to be a relative term. A typical example would be *Prairie Rustlers* (PRC, 1945), with Buster Crabbe. The budget was $22,500, and the actual negative cost was $23,304.12. Buster received $3,000, St. John $1,000, with $827 going for the rest of the cast. The picture was shot in six days. Fred Myton was paid $1,000 for his screenplay, producer Sig Neufeld $1,200, and director Sam Newfield $1,250. Sets cost $1,442.50. The LaRue pictures tried to cut corners below these figures. LaRue's last films were for Screen Guild in 1949, in which all the exteriors were shot in a week with different interior sequences interpolated between the identical chases to make up a series of differently assembled release prints. After his short fling in the movies, LaRue made the wire services when he was caught literally stealing candy from a baby in Florida. Subsequently, he turned to scripting porno-graphic films and then, like the erstwhile Sunset Carson, got religion and pursued rescue mission work. In the South an old cowboy can still draw a crowd for a revival meeting.

Jimmy Wakely made a low-budget series of starring Westerns for Mono-gram in the late forties, but it was short-lived. Even if you were to grant Eddie Dean pre-eminence in this group—the series with Crabbe, Steele, and LaRue at PRC and Wakely and Whip Wilson at Monogram—the New York *Daily News* summed the matter up quite aptly in their review of *Hawk of Powder River,* released in 1948 by Eagle-Lion, which assumed control of PRC before buying out toppling United Artists from what was left of its original founders, Mary Pickford and Charlie Chaplin: "Eddie Dean's latest is in black and white rather than color but the improvement is hardly noticeable; you can still see him."

The ineluctable decline of the B Westerns that universally characterized the production of the forties did not affect Monogram in their Johnny Mack Brown series until 1947. From this point on, things slowly disin-tegrated. Even into the fifties, Johnny had good directors, Howard Brether-ton occasionally, or Tom Carr, who directed Republic's best action West-erns with Sunset Carson, Lewis Collins, Ray Taylor, Wallace Fox, and, most often, Lambert Hillyer. It was the production values and monotonous scripts that cheapened the series.

Max Terhune first appeared as Alibi in *The Sheriff of Medicine Bow* (Monogram, 1948). Raymond Hatton's agent suggested that Ray could make more money if he would free-lance. Ray was featured in *Gunning for Justice* (Monogram, 1948) and *Hidden Danger* (Monogram, 1948) before dropping out completely. Monogram started a competing series with Whip Wilson and Andy Clyde in the late forties, but the Wilson pictures were, if anything, shot on an even lower budget than the Brown Westerns. In the 1951–52 season James Ellison was signed to costar with Johnny. *Dead Man's Trail* (Monogram, 1952) was Ellison's last film with Johnny, and the next entry, *Canyon Ambush,* released October 12, 1952, was Johnny's final series Western.

In the next two decades, Johnny appeared in only four low-budget West-erns for various companies before his retirement from the screen became permanent. In his last film, *Apache Uprising* (Paramount, 1966), directed by Bud Springsteen and produced by A. C. Lyles, based on a novel by Max Lamb and Harry Sanford, Johnny played a dissolute sheriff, ridiculed for being overweight. At one point, the film's star, Rory Calhoun, hits Johnny over the head with a rubber gun butt when Johnny is trying to rape Corinne Calvet.

"I didn't hurt you, did I, Johnny?" Calhoun asked him once the scene was shot.

"No, not at all," Johnny replied in his gentlemanly drawl, picking himself up off the ground.

We had finished our lunch and returned to Johnny's apartment in a complex right around the corner from where Lee Garmes and Ruth Hall lived. We had then adjourned to a bar, where Johnny had insisted on buying me a drink while he had a double 7 Up.

"I never should have made those last few Westerns," Johnny Mack remarked to me. The afternoon sun slanted into the windows. "But it was fun, Jon. All those pictures! I want you to know that. If I had it all to do over again, I wouldn't have it any other way."

"Except maybe the Haeckle Westerns," I commented.

Johnny chuckled.

But throughout his career, Johnny Mack Brown had been a true professional. Early or late, or anywhere in between, I cannot recall him giving anything less than his best. All his life, he was a sincere, gentle man, a loyal friend. He was enough of an actor to be able to give the opposite impression, but, if he didn't do so frequently, it was only because he was fortunate to be liked by his public for precisely the kind of person he was.

II

I met Tex Ritter in Milwaukee, where he was scheduled to appear with his Western Revue. He entered backstage about an hour before show time. He was walking alone, smoking a pipe. We exchanged pleasantries and went on together to the men's dressing room, where other acts were changing. There was nearly constant activity, but it passed unnoticed as we conversed, seated at a small table.

I wanted to know about his early years and his motion picture career to confirm many of the things I wished to say about him in the segment of "They Went Thataway" that was to be devoted to him. I cannot speak for others. For me, Tex proved an easy man to know. He was open, forthright, and yet saddened by the tragedy of American social events. He entertained an average of sixteen out of every thirty days.

We became friends from that time on. We exchanged letters. When he saw the Tex Ritter installment televised in Nashville, where he made his home, he asked me to send a kinescope of the program so he might give it to his children. He telephoned me once from Hollywood with an editor of *Billboard* in an effort to assemble a narrative program built around his films which he hoped to present on college campuses. He asked me to select the clips that I thought best from his many Westerns, and, as a courtesy, I agreed to clear the rights with the various motion picture companies. On

January 2, 1974, while visiting a friend at the Nashville jail, Tex Ritter succumbed to a heart attack.

I know it pleased him when I said before millions of Americans that perhaps Tex Ritter alone among the singing cowboys of the thirties and forties was a true artist. Others were exploited or promoted, or managed to merchandise what musical talent they may have had. Tex was different. During the final decade of his life, Tex Ritter was in many ways a quiet and lonely man. His shoulders, it would appear, became stooped and sheltered his generous heart, not from age but instead from some painful cognizance of the folly and misery of modern life. If Tex sinned against longevity, it was by concerning himself in a total and profound way with humanity at the expense of himself.

"I never sing to an audience," he once told me. "I never really look at the audience. I sing for an imaginary person seated out there who will know and understand. I think it makes me a better performer."

He looked intently at me with kindly, sensitive eyes.

"Jon," he said, "never look at your audience. Never!"

I asked him about the instrumentalists that played accompaniment for him in these, his final years.

"They're good kids," he responded. "They're fun to be with. But young people aren't the same as they used to be. They live different kinds of lives. I found the same thing in Vietnam when I went there to perform for our troops."

He knew I liked his rendition of "The Deck of Cards." He worked it into his program that night. I watched him carefully as he sang it. His eyes were most often fixed on a distant vision, somewhere beyond the audience seated in endless rows about him.

He was born Woodward Maurice Ritter on January 12, 1905, in Murvaul, Texas. He entered the University of Texas at Austin intent on a law degree. While there he met J. Frank Dobie, an authority on the West who inspired Tex to collect cowboy, mountain, and Negro songs. When he had to withdraw from school for economic reasons he worked at a variety of jobs before appearing on a Houston radio station singing authentic Western ballads. He joined a traveling group that toured the South and Midwest. In Chicago he tried studying again at Northwestern University. After a year, he found he wanted to sing, and so, in 1930, the country heaving beneath the Depression, he went to New York.

He was given a part in the Theater Guild production of Lynn Riggs's *Green Grow the Lilacs,* from which *Oklahoma* later evolved. He was billed as Woodward Ritter until the management, learning everyone called him Tex because of his drawl, billed him as Tex Ritter. The name stuck. He was next featured in a play, *The Roundup,* and became the star of a radio program called "Lone Star Rangers." Tex continued his radio work and gained a reputation in the East. He was appearing at a dude ranch in New Jersey when Edward Finney, who was staying there, invited him to Hollywood to make Westerns for Grand National release.

Finney was a peculiar, erratic, and gentle man when Tex met him in 1936, and he had changed but little when through his gracious hospitality he showed me his Tom Mix still collection in the living room of his Hollywood home in the 1960s. He was a man of medium height with quick, darting movements, seldom at rest on the sofa near me.

"Which silent picture did you select for Colonel Tim?" he asked.

"Winners of the Wilderness," I returned.

"I worked on the press book for that picture," Finney said. "I was a publicist for Metro at that time." He paused. "I sure would like a print of that picture."

"I'll ask M-G-M," I said. I thought it best to change the subject back to Tex. "You produced how many pictures with him?"

"Let's see," Finney replied. "There were twelve for Grand National and then we switched to Monogram for another twenty."

I had met and spoken with Ed Finney before. He was born in New York City and attended City College. He began his career as an engineer at Western Electric and then became a property man at the Fort Lee studios in New Jersey where they were making Johnny Hines comedies. Publicist work first at Metro and then at Pathé and United Artists led to his being hired as advertising director at Grand National when it was founded in 1936.

Jack L. Warner placed James Cagney on suspension in 1936 because Cagney wanted a new deal, only one picture a year and no more gangster roles. Edward Alperson, Warner Brothers' sales manager, and Spyros Skouras, head of the Fox West Coast theaters, the latter also long associated with Warner's, got together in 1935 to set up their own producing company. They arranged financing of $2 million and offered Cagney 2,500 shares of stock to appear in one major picture a year. Alperson hoped to block-book the Cagney picture with a number of low-grade features, comedies and Westerns. The plan was to distribute the pictures on a states' rights basis through independent exchanges. He invited George Hirliman and independent producer-director Al Herman, who had originally discovered Mickey Rooney for Larry Darmour, to join the company.

Finney was cagey. He put Tex under contract personally and as producer-agent worked out a financing and distribution deal with Grand National. The Westerns were budgeted at $8,000 to $12,000, with Tex being paid $2,400 a picture as the star. They had generally five-day shooting schedules. Finney called his production unit Boots and Saddles. He would hold story conferences that would include the scenarist and the director. Tex would usually sit in on these. The last picture he made at Grand

National, *Utah Trail* (Grand National, 1938), was based on Tex's own original story idea of a ghost train.

The initial entries in the series, *Song of the Gringo* and *Headin' for the Rio Grande,* were released in 1936. *Song* was an anomaly. It featured ex-train robber Al Jennings. For about a month before and during production, Jennings taught Ritter how to perfect his draw. Fuzzy Knight was in the cast for comic support. The screenplay went all out to establish Tex's identity as both a singer and an action player.

Headin' for the Rio Grande began the pattern that all the subsequent Grand National Tex Ritter Westerns would follow. As a youth in the early twenties, Tex's favorite movie comic had been Snub Pollard. Tex induced Finney to give Pollard, by then down on his luck, a small part in *Headin'*. Tex worked at it until by the seventh picture, *Riders of the Rockies* (Grand National, 1937), Pollard was one of Tex's two side-kicks. Syd Saylor replaced Fuzzy Knight as the comic in *Headin'* and appeared in the next film, *Arizona Days* (Grand National, 1937). Horace Murphy was his side-kick in the fourth entry, *Trouble in Texas* (Grand National, 1937), in which Rita Cansino (later Hayworth) was the girl; Hank Worden in the fifth, *Hittin' the Trail* (Grand National, 1937); Al St. John, another silent comedian, in the sixth, *Sing Cowboy, Sing* (Grand National, 1937). It wasn't until the middle of Tex's Monogram series in 1939 that the Pollard-Murphy duo was replaced by Arkansas Slim Andrews, on the whole a wiser choice. The Pollard-Murphy buffoonery added little to the early Westerns.

Yakima Canutt doubled for Tex in *Trouble in Texas,* where he was also given a featured role, as he was again in *Riders of the Rockies.* No matter who the principal villain was, Charlie King was always his right-hand man, and invariably the screenplay called for a stirring, even dramatic bout of fisticuffs between Tex and Charlie. Tex rarely had a stand-in for these fight sequences. Charlie taught him what there was to learn about fighting before the camera, and the two found it splendid fun. Of course this isn't the impression you might have watching them spar in *Riders of the Rockies,* the most bloodcurdling of their eleven fights at Grand National, with Charlie's hideous but phony cheek scar ripped open and bleeding by the time Tex lands the final punch.

"You've got to do Charlie justice, Jon," Tex remarked to me on the telephone after seeing the clip of the two of them fighting on "They Went Thataway." "He was a ballet artist the way he went about it. And he was a natural comedian. He was always so surly on screen very few people would have guessed his comic talent. He would occasionally give a spasmodic kick when knocked out to sort of accentuate the make-believe."

Tex's open, gregarious personality carried the Grand National series. *Arizona Days,* with Tex joining a traveling medicine show, had the best songs. Everything else about the pictures became tragically routine. Charlie

Charlie King so frequently was a menace no one appreciated his qualities as a comedian.

Photo courtesy of *Views & Reviews* magazine.

was perpetually appointing himself a committee of one to drive the songbird out of town. When the scenarist was desperate for a way to get the goods on the gang, Ernie Adams was hired to confess. I have already introduced Ernie in connection with his confession scene in Ken Maynard's *The Fighting Legion* (Universal, 1930). I don't think he ever played another part after he appeared in *Stool Pigeons* (Columbia, 1929) until the forties. A banner decade—the thirties, with Ernie's best confessions occurring in *Bar Z Badmen* (Republic, 1936) to Johnny Mack Brown, in *West of Cheyenne* (Columbia, 1938), to Charles Starrett, and the coup de grâce, his confession to Tex Ritter with "Rock of Ages" as an organ accompaniment in *Rollin' Plains* (Grand National, 1938). *Rollin' Plains* is notable for another reason: Finney resorted to the common Poverty Row device of reusing footage, in this case the entire last reel of *Sing Cowboy, Sing* from the previous year. Were you to walk in on the conclusion of either picture, you couldn't tell which one was playing. The acting was bad at Grand National, the direction disappointing, the editing sloppy. Matters weren't improved when Finney switched to Monogram, but the move was, he thought, a necessary one.

Grand National put $900,000 in *Something to Sing About,* with James Cagney, in 1937. The picture was way over budget and it didn't gross. The firm was about to go defunct. Cagney patched up his quarrel with Jack L. Warner and went back to work on the First National lot. Finney brought suit against Grand National to get a release from his contract. E. W. Hammons' Educational Film Corporation then merged with Grand National, uniting the exchanges of the one with the failing fortunes of the other. Alperson and Hammons approached Nat Levine, who had just resigned from Metro, to become an investor. Levine warily declined. The reorganized Grand National passed into receivership in 1940.

Finney and Boots and Saddles at Monogram meant many things: $12,-000 to $15,000 budgets for the Tex Ritter Westerns, director of publicity for Monogram, and, strictly on the side, director of advertising at Republic for Finney. For Tex Ritter it meant twenty more Westerns at $2,400 a Western.

"Have you got a print of Bill Hart in *Blue Blazes Rawden?*" Ed Finney asked, hopping up and chasing three or four cats from the sunny room. "You know, I have a print of Hart's *Hell's Hinges!*"

"About Monogram, Ed," I interjected.

"What about it?" he asked, sitting down again. "No, no, let me ask you a question. Which of Tex's Monogram pictures do you like best?"

"*Down the Wyoming Trail* [Monogram, 1939]."

"We spent a lot of money on that one, Jon. I think it was close to thirty thousand. It took us ten days to shoot it. We went up into the mountains with three trucks. Tex didn't go along, but Charlie King and the rest of the cast did. Let's see? Al Herman directed that one, too. He came over to Monogram with me." Ed paused for a moment. "If you can't do anything about *Winners of the Wilderness,* how about a print of *Blue Blazes Rawden?*"

Tex's early films for Monogram differed very little from his last films for Grand National. Most of them were directed by Al Herman or Spencer Gordon Bennet. Finney was inconsistent in the relative quality of the pictures. *Rollin' Westward* (Monogram, 1939) had an intriguing plot and was followed by *Roll Wagons, Roll* (Monogram, 1939), which had an engaging song but was largely built out of stock footage from former Monogram Westerns with the last reel made up chiefly of interpolated footage from *The Deserter* (Ince, 1915). No doubt Finney was saving money for *Down the Wyoming Trail,* which featured a stock reindeer stampede but a fascinating story line and, for Finney, an elaborate budget. Dorothy Fay, who had played leading ladies to Buck Jones and Bill Elliott at Columbia, when her option wasn't picked up, free-lanced and appeared with Tex in *Sundown on the Prairie* (Monogram, 1939). As the reader may recall from the previous chapter, they were married in 1941 at Prescott, Arizona. They had two sons.

On the whole, I suppose, the Monogram plots improved, or, at least, the settings were more exotic. Charlie King and Tex kept having return matches, and while the Monogram series had musical accompaniment to action sequences, the scores were by Frank Sanucci and were used over and over in most Monogram Westerns of the period including the competing Jack Randall series. Tex called upon his collection of traditional frontier songs, and the musical content he supplied was more authentic than anything in the Republic Westerns with Gene Autry or Roy Rogers.

Tex was, I think, a better singer than Autry. According to Spencer Gordon Bennet and others who directed him, he took his acting quite seriously. While Tex was popular with audiences, that his career in pictures was not more spectacular is probably due to the fact that his first thirty-two Westerns were made for Ed Finney. The exploitation apparatus behind Tex was nothing to compare with Republic's promotion of Autry. Although the Monogram Westerns were sold in blocks, the firm realized approximately $80,000 on every title, and the pictures were usually confined to third-run houses. Republic had a reputation for Westerns that Monogram never attained.

In 1937 Tex began recording for Decca, mostly songs from his films. Then in 1942 when Johnny Mercer helped found Capitol Records, Tex was signed and extensively promoted. By 1945 he had the top three juke-box favorites on *Billboard*'s chart.

When Tex's five-year contract with Finney expired in 1941, he didn't renew. The four or five stable horses he had used in films since he had arrived in Hollywood had been billed White Flash on the credits. Now, at last, he bought a white stallion of his own from Jerome Eddy, of Chino Valley, Arizona, and had him trained for motion picture work. He signed on as a contract player at Columbia and received a weekly salary as opposed to a per picture deal, nearly doubling his annual income from film work.

Columbia felt inadequate competing with Republic's singing Westerns with only Charles Starrett and Bill Elliott working on the lot. The Sons of the Pioneers backed up Starrett. Columbia wanted Tex to add a singing content to their Elliott series.

The first in any Columbia B series of the forties was also generally the best, and it was no different with *King of Dodge City* (Columbia, 1941), the initial Elliott-Ritter entry. Lambert Hillyer, who had worked with both Hart and Mix, directed it, as he did several others in the series alternating with Wallace Fox, who had done *Powdersmoke Range*. In *King* the Story Department established the basic screen relationship between the two, Elliott reserved, austere, self-possessed, Tex hotheaded, stubborn, antagonistic to Elliott. Dub Taylor, Elliott's side-kick in previous Columbia features, provided most of the slapstick comedy, while situational humor was occasionally at Tex's expense. Although off screen Elliott and Tex were friends, Elliott wasn't any happier about the double billing than Tex, and after eight pictures Bill expressed his unhappiness and before long defected to join Republic.

Columbia did not pick up Tex's option, and he opened negotiations with Universal. Universal wanted him to costar with Johnny Mack Brown as he had with Elliott. Tex agreed on the condition that he be given a chance to act and, if the films were successful, he have an opportunity to star in his own series. Universal conceded and Tex signed.

The Universal B Westerns of the early forties were polished, well-mounted vehicles with fine production values, above average scripts, and excellent pacing; the Brown-Ritter Westerns were no exception. Tex's contract called for up to six Westerns a year budgeted at better than $100,000 and at times eight- and ten-day shooting schedules. Tex did get to act, and though the films had a strong musical content, he rarely sang more than one song in any given picture, the Jimmy Wakely trio providing most of it, with Jennifer Holt, Tim Holt's sister, occasionally rendering a dubbed song. At times the plottings of the villains were so complex, as in *Raiders of San Joaquin* (Universal, 1943), which featured William Farnum playing a powerful, if disillusioned, land baron, that both Tex and Johnny Mack Brown together were scarcely enough to set things right. *The Lone Star Trail* (Universal, 1943) is the film Johnny and Tex worked in that was probably the best for both of them. Fuzzy Knight continued to provide surprisingly effective comedy, and appropriate background music—although no less standard fare in every entry than Sanucci's at Monogram—made the series consistently entertaining.

In 1943, when Universal refused to pick up Johnny Mack's option, Tex got his chance to star alone. His first picture was given a strong cast with William Farnum, Diana Barrymore, Leo Carrillo, Andy Devine, and Lon Chaney. It was a success, and *Frontier Law* (Universal, 1943) was scheduled next.

"But Tex," I commented, "you weren't even in the picture. Russell Hayden was. What happened?"

"I'll tell you about that, Jon," Tex responded, smiling. "Russell had a good agent. I had fallen from a hayloft and broken my leg. The picture had to be made and I was laid up. They put Russell into it."

"He appeared with you in *Marshal of Gunsmoke* [Universal, 1944]."

"I know. It was supposed to be my series and I ended up alone in only three of five pictures."

"So you went over to Producers Releasing Corporation for eight units?"

"Yes," Tex replied. "A lot of people have told me that I shouldn't have made those pictures. I suppose they were right."

Arizona Trail (Universal, 1943) was the second of Tex's solo vehicles for Universal. It had an interesting plot, opening in San Francisco and then changing locale to the West. Dennis Moore played Tex's stepbrother. In *Marshal of Gunsmoke,* the next film, Russell Hayden was cast as Tex's brother.

I would like to say an added word about *Marshal.* The musical content was handled principally by Johnny Bond and his Red River Valley Boys, with Jennifer Holt dubbed for two songs. Tex sings only once. Bud Buster, a character actor, is victim to the card swindle routine used in the second version of *Destry Rides Again.* Ernie Adams is cast in a role demanding something from him other than making a confession! The action is constant, balanced by music and rather well-developed comedy inventions by Fuzzy Knight. But William Lively's screenplay belies the slick production values at two crucial junctures—initially in having Jennifer Holt break her engagement to Russell over his going to work for Harry Woods, who heads up the lawless element when she herself works for him as a singer throughout the picture; and in the fantastic, if exhilarating, circumstance of Fuzzy Knight steering a horseless stagecoach down a harrowing mountain pass at the end of the film, using the tongue for steering.

Tex and Fuzzy were alone again for *Oklahoma Raiders.* I would say it is Tex's best series Western in terms of production value, screenplay, and direction. But, all of this notwithstanding, the plot to the picture had a rather interesting history that serves to point up the creative decline that overtook the budget Western in the late thirties until its demise in the fifties. RKO-Pathé made a series of Tom Keene Westerns in the early thirties. *Come on Danger* was released on September 23, 1932. The story was by Ben Cohn, and the film was directed by Robert Hill. Keene played a Ranger whose brother was killed while trying to capture Julie Haydon, who is the head of an outlaw gang. Keene swears to bring her in and with his side-kick, Roscoe Ates, sets off to Pecos. There is a shot of a $5,000 reward being offered for the capture of Julie. At the base of the trouble is Robert Ellis, who has branded Julie an outlaw and forced her, together with Wade Boteler and all the honest ranchers, to hide in a secret valley and attempt to win back their holdings by working outside the law. Tom is wounded trying to save Julie's life, falls in love with her, and convinces her to give herself up. Before she can, they are captured by Frank Lackteen, Ellis' right-hand man, and taken to his hacienda. Tom overhears Ellis and Lackteen confess the murder of his brother. A terrific fight ensues, while Wade Boteler and his men come to the rescue in the nick of time.

By 1939, when Oliver Drake was the principal scenarist working on the

RKO George O'Brien series, he went back in the files and pulled out this script for a remake. It was released as *Renegade Ranger* (RKO, 1939), with Drake credited for the screenplay. Rita Hayworth was cast as Judith Alvarez. O'Brien is a Texas Ranger assigned the task of bringing her in. Tim Holt is O'Brien's young protégé who is kicked out of the service for misconduct. Tim joins Rita's gang. A close-up is given of a $5,000 reward for the capture of Judith Alvarez. George saves Rita's life and is taken to the hide-out. William Royle has painted her a bandit. He is the local tax collector and has compelled Judith and all the honest ranchers to surrender their properties under duress of illegal back taxes. Ray Whitley is O'Brien's musical support, singing when the occasion permits. George arrests Judith and puts her in jail, but Royle's men capture her and take her to his hacienda. O'Brien, in pursuit, overhears Royle confess to the murder for which Judith is wanted; together with Tim and Ray, joined by Judith's men, the hacienda is stormed and Royle is brought to justice.

By 1942, when RKO remade *Come on Danger,* with Tim Holt starring, Oliver Drake had already left to join Universal. In Tim's version of *Come on Danger* he was supported by Ray Whitley and Lee "Lasses" White. Tim is a Texas Ranger sent to bring in Ann Jordan, played by Frances Neal, a most singularly unattractive heroine which makes the notion in the screenplay about Tim's falling in love with her comic at best. Tim helps Ann and is wounded. He is taken to her hide-out. Karl Hackett is the tax

A lobby card from *Oklahoma Raiders* showing Jack Ingram, Tex, and George Eldredge held at gunpoint by Dennis Moore and Jennifer Holt.

Photo courtesy of the Tex Ritter Memorial Fan Club.

collector; through misuse of his authority, he has run off all the decent ranchers and forced them to become outlaws allied with Ann, whom he has falsely branded as a bandit. Ann is surprised at her hide-out and taken back to town, where she is jailed. Hackett arranges to have her brought to his hacienda. Tim, Ray, and Lee overhear Hackett confess to the murder for which Ann is wanted. Assisted by Ann's men, they overpower Hackett's gang and capture him.

Oliver Drake decided to employ this story again for *Oklahoma Raiders.* The Tex Ritter version is unquestionably the most entertaining, although Jennifer Holt in tight slacks is still no match for Rita Hayworth in the same attire. But audiences were, no doubt, becoming weary of seeing the same stories made by different companies with virtually the same players on an annual basis.

Raiders opens to scenes of the Civil War and fades to a Union camp with Fuzzy Knight as Banjo Bonner singing at the campfire. Tex and Fuzzy are sent to buy horses for the cavalry and to look into the trouble the Army is having getting them from Benton, Oklahoma. Jack Ingram and George Eldredge, in charge of the government contracts, are behind the difficulty with the ranchers which has forced honest men to follow Jennifer Holt, who is known as El Vengador. Tex sides in with her, and the bad element is brought to justice. The film contained substantial interpolations from Edward Finney's *King of the Stallions* (Monogram, 1942), which brought together what seemed the largest herd of wild horses assembled for a sound Western and was used as stock for the remainder of the black and white era.

After *Oklahoma Raiders,* Tex left Universal for PRC. Universal was again in financial trouble. Contract players Rod Cameron and Kirby Grant made the last few remaining scripts before the B Western unit was disbanded. The Western town along Mauser Street burned to the ground under mysterious circumstances and wasn't rebuilt. Some thirty years after Uncle Carl Laemmle had opened his lot to make assembly-line Westerns and serials, production stopped forever—or, that is, until television production took over. The forthcoming merger with International Pictures run by Louis B. Mayer's son-in-law, William Goetz, to form Universal-International prompted the company to upgrade its product until renewed financial insolvency in the fifties led to the assumption of control by Jules Stein's Music Corporation of America.

The PRC films were a sad affair, teaming Tex as a lawyer in eight pictures, with Dave O'Brien as second lead and Guy Wilkerson in support. The series, known as the Texas Rangers, had previously featured James Newill in the lead. Had Tex's first Westerns been for Universal in the place of their ill-fated Bob Baker series and not what they were, things might have been otherwise. It was not to be. Tex's Hollywood experience was at times humorous, but in the end it was an episode in futility.

Tex Ritter was, in his way, a fine and noble human being, made so not by circumstances but by magnanimity of soul. The years weighed heavily upon him. Ed Finney knew nothing of this as we spoke.

"You know, Jon," he commented vivaciously, "I was offered all those Grand National Westerns Tex made outright, for television. They wanted ten thousand dollars apiece. For a song, Jon. I could have got them for a song."

"Ed, I know the lyrics to that song all too well—*no money!*" I fell silent. I wanted to thank him for all the assistance he had given me. "Ed," I resumed, "I can't help you out really on *Winners of the Wilderness* or *Blue Blazes Rawden,* but how about this? I could get you a print of Tex in *Rollin' Plains* [Grand National, 1938]."

Ed sat thoughtfully for a moment and then shook his head violently.

"No, Jon," he said, "it's nice of you, but no. As I remember, that wasn't a very good picture."

41 / THE REVIVAL OF THE ACTION WESTERN

I

I have already introduced Duncan Renaldo as a character in this narrative in connection with *The Painted Stallion* and, later, as one of the Three Mesquiteers. But his rightful place has to do with the Cisco Kid. He is one of the most charming men I have ever known. We had written letters back and forth for some time before I drove into sunny Santa Barbara, where he makes his home. The old Spanish-style haciendas stood apart at the base of high hills overlooking the glistening expanse of the Pacific. The air was surprisingly clear of smog, and only here and there could you see oil slicks floating atop the waves.

White-haired, his lined countenance ruddy with a persistent youthfulness, Duncan was at peace with the world as we smoked and talked of his life and life on this planet in the twentieth century. He had been a Thalberg star during the early days at M-G-M, and he had gone to Africa with Harry Carey, Edwina Booth, and director W. S. Van Dyke to film *Trader Horn* (M-G-M, 1931). When the troupe returned to the States, it was rumored that Edwina had contracted a mysterious jungle disease, and she even brought suit for $10 million against M-G-M. But a visit to the Medical Clinic for Jungle Diseases in London elicited negative results. Edwina was signed together with Harry Carey to appear in chapter plays for Mascot and was featured in *The Vanishing Legion* (Mascot, 1931) and *The Last of the Mohicans* (Mascot, 1932). The Metro suit was settled for $10,000 between the attorneys. She made a low-budget feature with Duncan, *Trapped in Tiajuana* ["*Tijuana*"] (Mayfair, 1932), before retiring from the screen. The gossip around Hollywood at the time was that Edwina had actually had an abortion in Africa. It was unlikely, but Duncan's first wife hadn't helped matters when she began an alienation of affection suit and, to further her case, exposed him to the immigration department for illegal entry. Edwina won the alienation suit, and both Duncan and Harry Carey assisted her with her many legal costs.

"Duncan," I said, "you probably will want to ask me to leave, but what nationality are you really?"

He smiled quietly.

"I do not know, Jon, and that is the truth."

"At the time of your hearing," I said, "it was suggested that you may have been Rumanian."

"That's entirely possible," he conceded. "I had six different birth certificates but I did not know if any of them was valid. I had worked aboard a ship as a coal stoker and entered the United States on a temporary ninety-day seaman's permit. I told the judge that one certificate indicated that I was born in China. He said, were that the case, I would fall under the Exclusion Act. Had I been Russian, I might be politically dangerous. You see, I never knew my parents but my name was Renaldo Duncan. Might I be Portuguese? I was sent to prison. All my money had gone to fight it. At last, by special amnesty from President Roosevelt, after nearly two years I was released."

As a convenience, Duncan listed his birthplace as Camden, New Jersey. He had begun in motion pictures by producing a series of shorts in 1925, including *The Yellow Rose of Seville, Circe,* and *Pulchinello.* Bela Lugosi made his American debut in one of Duncan's shorts. Herbert J. Yates did the laboratory work and presented Duncan with a bill for $19,000. Duncan's distribution deal didn't materialize, and he was unable to pay Yates.

"You young whippersnapper," Yates chided him. "Get out and sell them."

Duncan looked slightly older than the April 23, 1904, birth certificate date would have one believe. Discouraged, he was saved at the last minute by an offer from Pathé to buy the shorts outright; ironically, the price offered came within a dollar of what he owed Yates.

But it was Yates who signed Duncan to a five-year contract after he was freed from prison. I have already described how Duncan appeared to be

Latin American on screen and how Yates exploited it. And it was on the same basis that he was selected to play the Cisco Kid.

Among short stories, O. Henry's "The Caballero's Way" must rank rather closely with W. Somerset Maugham's "Rain" as a prime money-maker by virtue of secondary rights. "The Cisco Kid had killed six men in more or less fair scrimmages," O. Henry began the tale, "had murdered twice as many (mostly Mexicans), and had winged a larger number whom he modestly forbore to count. Therefore a woman loved him."

There is nothing exceptional about this story. It appeared in a collection, *Heart of the West* (Doubleday, 1904), and was far from the most engaging narrative in the book. The plot is very simple. The Kid is wanted for several murders; he kills offhandedly, "for the love of it—because he was quick-tempered—to avoid arrest—for his own amusement—any reason that came to mind would suffice." The Kid is not Latin American, "Goodall is his name, ain't it?" He has a girl named Tonía Pérez. He calls on her occasionally. She falls in love with Lieutenant Sandridge, who is on the Kid's trail. The Kid overhears her plotting with Sandridge. The story ends when he dupes Sandridge into shooting Tonía thinking her to be the Kid.

It constituted a plot sufficient for a 1914 one-reeler entitled, as the story, *The Caballero's Way* and formed the basis for a two-reeler, *The Border Terror* (Universal, 1919). In 1929 Raoul Walsh decided he wanted to bring the story to the screen in a sound version casting himself as the Kid. Driving around in the foothills scouting locations, he took pot shots at jack rabbits. A bullet ricocheted and cost him the sight of his right eye. Warner Baxter was cast as the Kid, and Irving Cummings assisted in the direction. The screenplay followed the outlines of the original story, and Baxter invested his portrayal with such complexity and lighthearted romance that he won an Oscar for his performance. I have already described earlier the sensational impact that *In old Arizona* (Fox, 1929), as the film was called, created among those involved in Western production, although it was nearly two years hence before major studio production of Westerns was resumed. By that time, Fox had made a sequel, *The Cisco Kid* (Fox, 1931), again starring Baxter as the Kid, Edmund Lowe returning as the ranger on his trail, and Irving Cummings as the director.

In 1938, 20th Century-Fox signed Cesar Romero as a contract player specializing in Latin American romantic leads. Warner Baxter's contract was about to expire, and the studio decided not to renew it, but instead to replace him with the younger Romero. They cast Baxter in a third film, *The Return of the Cisco Kid* (20th-Fox, 1939), in which Romero had a supporting role as López. A series with Romero as the Kid followed, beginning with *The Cisco Kid and the Lady* (20th-Fox, 1939). Romero brought to the role nothing to equal Baxter's flair for characterization, but he proved competent, and six films in all were made with him in the lead. The studio then dropped the idea because Romero entered the service, and the parallel attempt to revamp the Zorro property with *The Mark of Zorro* (20th-Fox, 1940), with Tyrone Power, hoping to recapture the Douglas Fairbanks aura of the twenties, ended similarly with Power entering the Marines.

In late 1944, as part of an economy move, 20th Century-Fox unloaded several of their B picture properties. James S. Burkett, born at Meriden, Connecticut, on August 17, 1895, had entered the film business via distribution with Sol lesser in 1914. By 1944 he was an associate producer at Monogram. Philip N. Krasne, who was born on May 6, 1905, at Norfolk, Nebraska, and graduated from USC as an attorney, quit private practice to act as counsel for Grand National. When the firm folded, he returned to private practice, saved his money, and in 1944 joined in a partnership with Burkett, purchasing the Charlie Chan and Cisco Kid properties, the resulting pictures to be released by Monogram. Krasne had been impressed by Duncan's role as Rico in the 1940–41 grouping of Republic's Three Mesquiteers. He wanted him to play Cisco. Duncan was working for the State Department. Presumably the Roosevelt Administration concurred with Herbert J. Yates that Renaldo could help the *norteamericano* cause in Latin America. Duncan agreed to star, provided Krasne not require the Kid be painted a typical Mexican killer and terrorist. Martin Garralaga, who had been an opera singer in Mexico before being featured as a Latin in Hollywood films, was added to the series in the role of a side-kick called Pancho.

"Jon," Duncan said, "I told Phil how much trouble Romero had caused in Latin America playing the Kid as a vicious bandit. I said, 'Why not base the character on the greatest book in all Spanish literature, *Don Quixote de la Mancha?* Cisco is a modern knight; Pancho is his Sancho Panza, a delicate comedy character—not a buffoon—who always gets his partner in trouble when they try to help people."

Duncan laughed gleefully.

"Martin was perfect as Pancho, Jon. His comedy was very, very human. But he just couldn't stand horses. He was allergic to them."

Cisco was the penultimate development of the good bad man which so fascinated early Western players. Whereas O. Henry probably had Billy the Kid in mind, the popular imagination preferred Cisco to be Latin. Because of Krasne's financial backing, the first three films which began with *The Cisco Kid Returns* (Monogram, 1945) have the best production values of any Western series Monogram made. *The Cisco Kid in Old New Mexico* was Duncan's second as the Kid. It was directed by veteran Phil Rosen, who was at a loss only during the musical sequences.

The picture opens to Cisco in the foreground, the stagecoach in the far

background rounding a curve. Cisco kidnaps a girl wanted for murder. He hides her at the San Fernando mission, shot on location. Norman Willis, the saloon owner, is the actual culprit. Cisco tricks him into exposure.

"I believe this to be one of the best Cisco films I've seen," I commented to Duncan as the lights in the projection room came on after we had screened it.

"I should tell you about that palomino I ride in the picture, Jon," Duncan said. "He was a fearful horse. He tried to break a double's legs by smashing against trees. I learned to ride very carefully because when I was at Republic working on those Mesquiteers pictures with Bob Livingston, a camera truck skidded into me and pushed both myself and the horse I was on through a barbed-wire fence. The horse broke two of its legs and I broke my ankles. Well, they told me about this palomino, but we became good friends and I never had any trouble with him. Later, when we did the television episodes, I bought a paint. I called him Diablo, too, after the palomino."

Duncan made a third picture, *South of the Rio Grande* (Monogram, 1945). The films were so successful that Scott R. Dunlap took over producing himself. Duncan was engaged in government work and was dropped from the series. He was replaced by Gilbert Roland, who starred as Cisco in *The Gay Cavalier* (Monogram, 1946). Duncan briefed Roland on how he felt the part should be played, but Roland had his own ideas. Pancho was demoted, and by the time of Roland's third entry, *Beauty and the Bandit* (Monogram, 1946), Martin Garralaga was cast as a crooked physician. Roland made the Kid a dashing lover, a friend of the poor, an enemy to the rich, a savage killer and robber when necessary, an infidel, a vagabond. His interpretation owed nothing to Duncan, nothing really to O. Henry, and very little to either Baxter or Romero. The Latin American market that had been developed by the Renaldo series began to dry up. Three more Kid pictures were made with Roland for the 1947 season, with reduced budgets, before the series was discontinued. Krasne, on his own, bought the Falcon property from RKO, which had featured first George Sanders and then Sanders's brother, Tom Conway. The new Krasne Falcon series started with *Devil's Cargo*, released on April 1, 1948, by Film Classics. After only three entries, this new series was scrapped.

Then, backed financially by Frederick Ziv, Krasne obtained the rights to Cisco from Monogram and negotiated a new theatrical releasing deal with United Artists. The Eagle-Lion group, headed up by attorney Arthur Krim, wanted to persist in the series Western market. In addition to Cisco, the firm worked out an arrangement with William Boyd for twelve new Hopalong Cassidy pictures which Boyd and Toby Anguish financed for United Artists distribution. The Cisco Company was formed with Ziv at the head, Krasne as producer, and Duncan as associate producer. Duncan starred as Cisco.

Duncan as Cisco and Leo Carrillo as Pancho when they came to work together at United Artists and for the television series. Duncan kept pleading with Leo not to play the part like a buffoon.

Photo courtesy of Duncan Renaldo.

"I wanted Leo Carrillo to play Pancho," Duncan recalled, chuckling. "Leo refused. 'The part, amigo, is that of a buffoon,' he said. 'I am a serious actor, not a buffoon.' I explained to Leo that he wasn't to play it as a buffoon, but rather as a tragic and humane Sancho Panza. Leo said, 'All right. I do eeet. But only once!' We did five features for United Artists and then a hundred seventy-six half-hour episodes for television, many in color so they are still playing around the country."

"For all that," I demurred, "Leo played Pancho as a buffoon."

"I know," Duncan said, shrugging his shoulders. "He overdid it, but everyone liked him. His accent was so exaggerated that when we finished a picture no one in the cast or crew could talk normal English anymore."

Duncan leaned forward.

"You know, Jon, I worked on many of the scripts to the later Cisco pictures. We are now such a nation of hysterical people, running around, with no direction. When I played Cisco, I wanted the world to see a different face, a man of generosity. I abhor vengeance, or violence. Cisco was a friend to a better world. That's the way I saw him."

Duncan reclined wearily.

"But he wasn't above breaking a señorita's heart," he added, smiling. "That much, I think, all the Ciscos had in common."

II

Although he was born John Charles Holt, Jr., of Jack and Margaret Holt on February 5, 1919, he was called Tim nearly from the first. He entered the Culver Military Academy at Culver, Indiana, in 1933, where he excelled at sports and was also active in dramatics. Tim graduated *cum laude* in 1936 and won the Golden Spurs, Culver's highest award in horsemanship. He determined to pursue acting as a career. Walter Wanger saw him in a play, *Papa Is All,* and cast him in the series of pictures he was producing for United Artists release, beginning with *History Is Made at Night* (United Artists, 1937), with Charles Boyer and Jean Arthur, and *Stella Dallas* (United Artists, 1937), with Barbara Stanwyck.

He also appeared in *Law West of Tombstone* (RKO, 1937), his first Western, which starred Harry Carey. It was Harry's third picture for RKO, following the wake of *Powdersmoke Range* and *The Last Outlaw.* Basically a comedy, Carey played a confidence man from the West who tries to interest wealthy financier Clarence Kolb in his phony gold mine. Kolb's mistress is Evelyn Brent, who was once, supposedly, married to Carey. When his scheme fails, Harry returns to El Paso, where, after a run-in with the law, he is sent to capture the Tonto Kid, portrayed by Tim Holt. There is one unusual sequence frequently mentioned in Western fiction but rarely photographed. Bob Kortman, hiding in ambush to shoot the Kid, is killed when Tim sees, and the camera records, the glint of light from Kortman's rifle barrel.

Tim continued to appear in featured roles in Wanger pictures such as *Stagecoach,* major studio productions like *Gold Is Where You Find It* (First National, 1938), while working in RKO Westerns, his next being second lead to George O'Brien in *Renegade Ranger* (RKO, 1939). RKO bought Tim's contract from Wanger and starred him as their replacement for O'Brien in *Wagon Train* (RKO, 1940).

The budgets on Tim's early series Westerns for RKO were severely cut from what they had been in the O'Brien series and even from what they would be in his postwar RKO series. Various side-kicks were tried together with Ray Whitley for musical support. Films like *The Bandit Trail* (RKO, 1941) and the remake of *Come on Danger* (RKO, 1942) that featured Lee "Lasses" White were straightforward. Others such as *Avenging Rider* (RKO, 1942), with Cliff "Ukulele Ike" Edwards, were farcical at best. Bert Gilroy, who had produced the later O'Brien entries for RKO, stayed on as producer of the new Tim Holt series.

Simultaneously, Tim proved himself to be an actor of dimension in films like Orson Welles's *The Magnificent Ambersons* (RKO, 1942). When Tim enlisted in the service on April 14, 1942, his father, Jack Holt, humorously accused him of being more coward than hero. Tim had just completed fifty-four days of shooting in order to complete his quota of pictures, and Jack was suggesting that his exhausted son enlisted only to escape from the camera and RKO. Tim served with distinction in the Air Force, being well decorated upon his discharge.

Tim's first role after returning to Hollywood was in John Ford's *My Darling Clementine* (20th-Fox, 1946), and he proved what a fine actor he was here and in John Huston's *The Treasure of Sierra Madre* (Warner's, 1948). RKO again cast him in series Westerns. This new group was budgeted at $80,000 a picture, with Herman Schlom associate producer, replacing Bert Gilroy. Tim's earnings from pictures, which spanned 1946–52 at the rate of six to eight a season, averaged $65,000 to $70,000 a year. They were well-mounted vehicles teaming Tim with Richard Martin, who was given the role of Chito Gonzales Rafferty. Autry's phenomenal popularity had ebbed. The pictures stressed action, usually without any singing at all but with exciting, appropriate background music. Although RKO itself was on shaky footing with Howard Hughes running the studio, financial records indicate that the only consistent money-making enterprise year after year was the studio's Tim Holt Westerns. Fine production values and effective publicity made the series the equal of anything Gene Autry was doing at Columbia on far more elaborate budgets or any but the very best of the Republic product.

Tim had his own screen horse, Sheik. He bought into the Jennings-Lamarr rodeo and, when he wasn't filming, toured with his own show. Tim lost the artless innocence he had projected before the war; he became increasingly grave, no longer so obviously charmed by life. He met Berdee Stephens in 1947 while performing in a rodeo at Oklahoma City's Stockyards Colosseum. In 1952, following two unsuccessful marriages, the two were married; they had three children.

Tim said some years after he left pictures, "I never did feel there was anything mystic about Hollywood. I never really did like it." In his personal life he tended to be reclusive. He had a romantic indifference toward money and with unfailing accuracy made unwise investments. He was robbed by a business manager, cheated at rodeos. Once when Tim and his partners were given the short end of a financial split by the organization sponsoring their rodeo, although there were packed houses every night, Tim scratched his head, smiled, and commented to his partners, "Let's schedule this town again next year. I want to find out how they do it."

When it came to his career, Tim manifested a curious philosophy. Herbert J. Yates before the war invited Tim to breakfast and wanted him to become a Republic star. Yates told Tim of the numerous difficulties he had been experiencing with both Autry and Rogers. "Herb," Tim told him, "work out your own difficulties with Gene and Roy. It wouldn't be ethical for me to step in now."

After RKO shut down its Western unit, Tim pursued a number of different jobs from managing a ranch to building suburban homes to, in his final years, advertising manager at KEBC-FM at Oklahoma City. In August 1972 he began to experience pain in his head. The diagnosis was cancer, inoperable because of its location. He had been suffering from the disease for at least two years. For three months, Tim took treatments and worked part-time at KEBC. The treatments made him sick, and he became despondent while, in public, never letting on that he was ill. In November he entered the hospital. His last interview was a television tape made in his hospital room. Tim sat smoking his pipe. When he had answered all the questions he cared to, he said, "That's it," bringing the tape and his career to an end. The tape was shown on Oklahoma television stations the night of his death, February 15, 1973, ten days after his fifty-fourth birthday.

During the final season at RKO, the budgets on Tim's films were cut, and the shooting schedules were telescoped. Tim asked that his contract be terminated. The best years for his series, unquestionably, were 1947–49. During this period, RKO put special care into the films and produced two which credited Zane Grey with their titles, although only the later entry owed anything to a Grey story in terms of screen adaptation. *Under the Tonto Rim* (RKO, 1947), directed by Lew Landers, as all of the Holt Westerns at this time, had sophisticated production value, plenty of well-staged action, thrilling running inserts, realistic fights, scenic locations, excellent dialogue, and fine acting. Tom Keene, after a stint on Broadway, was back at RKO, now with the name Richard Powers and playing heavies. The screenplay used nothing from the 1928 film of the same title with Richard Arlen, produced by Paramount. Tim owns a stage line. Nan Leslie hitches a ride. Tom Keene is her brother and head of an outlaw gang. The gang attacks the stage, steals the strongbox, and kidnaps Nan. Tim, wearing his left holster in reverse draw, and Chito set out to round up the outlaws. Through Chito's ruse, Tim gets himself thrown in jail, makes a break with one of Keene's henchmen, and joins the gang. Although he is exposed, he manages to elude death and holds off the gang until Chito and the sheriff's posse arrive.

It was a strong film, entertainingly directed, but it was surpassed by *Wild Horse Mesa* (RKO, 1947). Jack Holt had made the original version based on the Zane Grey novel some twenty-two years previously. The two films make an interesting contrast by demonstrating the changes that had taken place in Western production in the ensuing decades. Nearly the identical budget bought nowhere as much on the screen, although the Tim Holt unit went to Utah for location shooting as had been done the year before for *Under the Tonto Rim*.

Wallace A. Grissell, a somewhat obscure director, was assigned to the picture instead of Lesley Selander, who usually directed the Tim Holt Westerns and had worked on the final entries in Harry Sherman's Zane Grey series for Paramount. Yet Grissell gave a fine account of himself. Norman Houston did the screenplay. While they didn't work together on this entry, both Selander and Houston formed part of Pop Sherman's Hopalong Cassidy unit at United Artists that moved over to the Holt unit when Pop shut down operations on the Bar 20 series. It is probably due to this fact as much as to anything else that the Holt films of the late forties have such vitality and polish.

The character name Lige Melberne was changed in the script to Pop Melhern—perhaps an unintentional reference on Houston's part—and was portrayed by Jason Robards, Sr. Nan Leslie was his daughter, and Tim was in love with her. The film opens to Richard Martin singing a ballad. Panguitch and a herd of horses are rounded up. Harry Woods, a crooked horse trader, kills Pop and steals the money and the herd. Nan lets Panguitch free. Tom Keene tries to muscle in on Woods's business, eventually shooting him. At the end, after a gun battle, Panguitch goes after Keene and Keene confesses.

Very few Westerns after the war could simulate the gritty crudity of even the B Westerns of the twenties and thirties. Paramount had remade *Wild Horse Mesa* in the early thirties. The third time around the film had an adroit slickness at odds with the complicated Grey plot that had to be smoothed out to meet with forties' standards. Romer Grey began a lawsuit against RKO for inadequate reporting, and as a result, the company chose not to base any more Westerns on his father's novels.

The second Tim Holt series came very near, if it did not equal, the pre-war George O'Brien Westerns. More significantly, the later films from the fifties maintained a quality superior to anything at Screen Guild, Columbia except for the Autry films, Republic except for the Roy Rogers films and an occasional Rocky Lane, Allied Artists-Monogram except for their Bill Elliott Westerns. The comic, human byplay between Tim and Chito was such that together, I think, they represent one of the very few successful exploitations of the hero/side-kick relationship in all the years that Hollywood used this tired formula. The series honestly stressed action; most of the singing, when there was any, was provided by Chito, who accompanied himself on the guitar and who sang with the simplicity and atmosphere of the Mexican night herding songs. Everyone in the unit from Herman Schlom on down took their work in earnest. If RKO produced one of the best series Westerns with O'Brien in the late thirties—with very stiff competition—the same studio, without so much competition, did nearly as well again in the late forties with the Tim Holt series.

III

The reader may feel with some justification that I have neglected Bill Elliott by referring to him only in conjunction with parallel events. I am finally able to rectify that situation. Concurrent with the success of his serials *The Great Adventures of Wild Bill Hickok* and *Overland with Kit Carson,* Columbia cast him in feature Westerns, replacing the Coronet series of Buck Jones films for the 1938–39 season. For his first two seasons he played a screen character known as Wild Bill Saunders, "a peaceable man" who was repeatedly called upon to fight or shoot his way out of innumerable scrapes. Dub Taylor, originally signed as a contract player because of Frank Capra's use of him in *You Can't Take It with You* (Columbia, 1938), was Bill's side-kick, Cannonball. In the 1940–41 season Bill and Cannonball appeared in a series of eight Wild Bill Hickok adventures, produced on slightly increased budgets, and, finally, in 1941–42 Bill played Hickok in a series of eight Westerns with Tex Ritter as his costar. So much I have previously said about him.

Fred Myton was the scenarist who worked on many of the Elliott Westerns and set down the basic formula. Bill may have seemed cold and arrogant to his co-workers, but that was only his personal style and an indication of how seriously he took his acting. Like Tom Mix, Bill liked to have young children cast in his films. He insisted the scenarist write a youngster in at some point. Only when he got to Republic could Bill wield enough

Tim Holt and heavy Harry Woods in *Wild Horse Mesa*.

influence to have the youngsters given speaking parts of a more substantial nature, and, once he was playing Red Ryder, he was delighted at having young Bobby Blake as his partner. The love of children offset the customary severity of Bill's screen characterizations.

Pioneers of the Frontier (Columbia, 1939) was one of the Wild Bill Saunders adventures in which *everything* was right, and so it remains a minor masterpiece, given the limitations imposed upon it. Sam Nelson, who codirected *Overland with Kit Carson,* was the director. Lafe McKee played Mort Saunders, who has opened his land empire for lease to prospective ranchers. Dick Curtis is Mort's straw boss, a particularly surly and ambitious man. Richard Fiske, who had supported Elliott in *Overland,* and Stanley Brown are Curtis's chief henchmen. Mort holds court to settle disputes among the tenants. Just as Grandpa Vanderhof in *You Can't Take It with You* brought the Rooseveltian style to his family talks at the head of the dinner table, so Mort puts forth the principles of New Deal democracy in his gentle paternalism. Mort is shot and killed. Cannonball rides to bring his nephew, Wild Bill. Human villainy can still only be dealt with by the exceptional individual. Bill has his checkers game interrupted when word comes to him of a friend having been murdered. He goes to even the score, pausing on the way to speak softly to a boy playing with boats.

"Why do you call me Wild Bill?" he asks after the gunfight. "I'm a peaceable man."

He returns with Cannonball to the Rancho del Norte and brings Curtis's reign of terror to an end. I do not think Curtis's considerable talent as a heavy was ever appreciated. He wasn't a human villain the way Fred Kohler, Sr., or Noah Beery, Sr., were, nor as much a comedian as Charlie King. But he was an accomplished actor who could convey a wide variety of subtle emotions by means of facial expression and with his eyes. When he was shot in the final reel, he gives Bill a last look of utter surprise and desolation, as if to say in his bewilderment that all his schemes of power and wealth, incredibly, have come to nothing more than the cloud of dust that billows around his collapsed form.

By the time of *Wildcat of Tucson* (Columbia, 1940), Stanley Brown had shaved his beard and was elevated to playing David Hickok, Bill's screen brother. The Saunders format had always called for Wild Bill to leave at the fade for another town where there was trouble, the sort of preview that Columbia put on the tails of their serial chapters. In *Wildcat* David gets himself in jail by going up against Kenneth MacDonald's land swindling operation in which both the town marshal and heroine Evelyn Young's father, Judge John Barlow, are his accomplices. Lambert Hillyer directed, and Bill would question him about his earlier years working with Mix and Hart. Fred Myton's screenplay, after the traditional introduction, once more called for Cannonball to ride for Wild Bill.

Bill stops to talk to a youngster whittling on a stick when he hears a commotion in the newspaper office, enters, and beats up a bully wrecking the place. Cannonball arrives and together they head back to help David. Bill and MacDonald shoot it out at the end. Bill had developed the fastest draw on the screen since Tim McCoy's days at Columbia. There was no background music for fights and chases, and Cannonball supplied the only singing. Jack Fier, in charge now of Columbia Western production, next added Tex Ritter to the series.

Gerald Geraghty did the screenplay for the initial entry, *King of Dodge City* (Columbia, 1941). Tex sang four songs, and music was added during chases and shoot-outs. What might be called the "Drake formula," after Oliver Drake who began it in the Three Mesquiteers series at Republic and used it subsequently between Tex and Johnny Mack Brown at Universal, was employed throughout the series. Bill and Tex, for whatever the reason, either are competitors or have a falling out and the viewer waits in suspense until, by the last reel, they combine forces against the outlaws. Frank Mitchell replaced Dub Taylor in the second film, *Roaring Frontiers* (Columbia, 1941), while Dub was featured in Russell Hayden's Westerns.

Columbia Pictures truly benefited when Gene Autry joined the studio in 1947 and taught them what the Autry Fantasy was all about. In *The Northwest Mounted Police* (Columbia, 1942), with Russell Hayden, Bob Wills and his Texas Playboys sing a saccharine ballad at a graveside which, if anything, is even more jarring to the viewer than Tex singing at the funeral of Dodge City's sheriff in *King*.

The "Drake formula" was good for only so long. If Bill hadn't chosen to leave Columbia, it nevertheless would have been impossible for the studio to have persisted in costarring him with Tex without it having become detrimental to both their careers.

Herbert J. Yates personally negotiated with Bill to have him join Republic when his Columbia contract expired. Yates promised Bill full-star treatment. Elliott accepted after completion of *Vengeance of the West* (Columbia, 1942), Bill's last series Western with Tex Ritter, and his third and last serial, *The Valley of Vanishing Men* (Columbia, 1942), directed by Spencer Gordon Bennet.

Republic put a number of Western series in production in an effort both to dominate the Western market and to compete with the popularity of their own Gene Autry series. The studio, unquestionably, was able to make the slickest action Westerns. With its capable second units headed up by Yakima Canutt, Yates had taken the crude, continuous action format of Mascot and streamlined it to an incredible degree. It was this tremendous technical capacity that allowed the studio to make a starring series with second-rate talent like Donald Barry into moderate box office, that entertained consistently in spite of stars like Sunset Carson who had to be kept riding and fighting so no one would guess that acting was missing. And it is a measure of just how bad an actor Eddie Dew was to reflect that, with all this going for him, he didn't make it!

Bill Elliott was the successor in the forties and fifties to William S. Hart in the twenties and Buck Jones in the thirties. If he was a little less than either in some ways, in others he was a little more. As strange as it may seem to the reader, he was never at his best in the B picture format, but he survived for want of competition, and so he came to excel at Republic in their A productions. Yates, whatever his motivations may have been at the time, is to be congratulated for giving Bill his opportunity.

Bill's first film was *Calling Wild Bill Elliott* (Republic, 1943), directed by Spencer Gordon Bennet. Bennet had been right behind Bill coming from Columbia, and so the two were teamed again frequently over the next two years at Bill's request.

Spencer had been directing the final entries in the Bob Allen series for Larry Darmour when Bill got the lead in *The Great Adventures of Wild Bill Hickok*. He could recall the hours Bill had spent in a saddle tied to a carpenter's horse learning how to sit astride a horse. Bill was very dedicated. He was blessed with a photographic memory.

Spencer and I were breakfasting on the terrace of the Café Universal, where I was staying.

"Did you know," I asked him, "that for all his years at Republic, Elliott was always after Yates to star him in a screen biography of William S. Hart?"

"No," Spencer returned. "But I remember that he admired Buck Jones and tried to fashion his screen work after him. This was true when he started at Columbia and was still true when he joined Republic."

The studio did right by Elliott. Not only was his name used in the title to the picture, but, like Autry and Rogers, Bill played himself in the story. Spencer stressed action and Yak doubled Elliott. In one sequence, Bill had to jump from the roof of Governor Nichols's hacienda onto his pinto below. Yak and Spencer constructed a wooden platform on the back of an arch out of camera range. The camera tracked Elliott running across the stucco roof to the arch. Bill stood poised above his horse and then jumped off the arch onto the platform. A split second before Elliott landed on the platform, Yak continued the jump onto the back of the horse. On screen, it appeared to be a single action.

Certainly one of the best entries in Elliott's first series of Westerns for Republic was *Mojave Firebrand,* with Spencer again as the director. Norman S. Hall did the screenplay. He had worked on Universal serials in the thirties, and Gene Autry subsequently used him to script some of his best Westerns at Columbia. Gabby Hayes discovers silver and decides to found a township free of crime. Naturally, he is unsuccessful. Bill Elliott, riding through, goes up against LeRoy Mason, the owner of the saloon, and Mason's gang. Ann Jeffries is the schoolmarm. Bill manages to put Mason and his gang out of the way by the fade.

For the 1944–45 season, the studio starred Elliott in a continuing series of Westerns based on the Red Ryder comic strip, the role Donald Barry had had in the serial, and young Bobby Blake played Bill's juvenile Indian side-kick, Little Beaver. The Republic management liked the series and went all out to promote it. In a sense, those were Bill's last B Westerns and undoubtedly his best, mounted with blazing action, excellent stunting, strong plots, and much human interest.

While Bill was happy being Red Ryder, Gabby back working with Roy Rogers, and Sunset Carson carousing himself out of a job, Herbert J. Yates fell in love with Prague-born Vera Hruba Ralston, a champion ice skater at thirteen and runner-up to Sonja Henie in the 1936 Olympics. Yates had

Gabby Hayes, heavy Bud Geary, and Wild Bill Elliott in a scene from *Mojave Firebrand.*

Photo courtesy of National Telefilm Associates.

become obsessed with the notion of launching her into stardom and really believed his later publicity that she was the most beautiful woman in the world.

Duke Wayne was Republic's biggest attraction, and the studio kept him busy whenever he wasn't being cast by the major producing companies. Duke made *In Old Oklahoma* (Republic, 1943) and *The Fighting Sea-Bees* (Republic, 1944) for the studio before he went to RKO to do *Tall in the Saddle* (RKO, 1944), with Ella Raines, Ward Bond, and, on loan, Gabby Hayes. Republic had him back for *The Flame of the Barbary Coast* (Republic, 1945). Duke then did two war pictures, *Back to Bataan* (RKO, 1945) and John Ford's *They Were Expendable* (M-G-M, 1945). Yates decided that for his next Western at Republic he would link Duke with Vera. The film was titled *Dakota* (Republic, 1945) and was based on a story idea by Carl Foreman, about whose political notions Duke would later have a falling out and object to his social philosophy embodied in *High Noon.* Wayne told director Joseph Kane that he had no intention of doing the picture. Yates summoned Kane to New York. Kane was surprised when he found Duke was also in New York.

"The last thing Wayne said to me," Kane recalled, "as he left to go in the elevator to see Yates, was that he would *not* do the picture with Vera under any circumstances."

Yates informed everyone later that day that Duke had changed his mind.

"The worst part of it was that Wayne flatly told me at the studio that he was not going to do it!" Kane went on. "Now, if you know Duke, you know he usually means what he says. So, of course, I had Lawrence Hazard stop all work on the script. Then Yates said it's *go* with almost no time to start. I protested that with such a deadline we would have no time to make necessary script revisions. Yates just waived my objections and said to get moving. I wired Yak immediately and told him to start shooting the second unit (a burning wheat fire that was shot in the San Joaquin Valley) and hope we could do something with the script. We speculated what Yates gave Wayne to bring him around."

The picture started, but little improved. Duke was difficult on the set, objecting to the dialogue and trying to direct the other actors. He even told veteran cameraman Jack Marta how to do his job. Walter Brennan, Ward Bond, and Paul Fix were also in the film. "It's no use saying I like Wayne," Kane commented. Kane felt that Duke's obnoxious attitude, first on *Barbary Coast*, which he'd directed, and then *Dakota*, his constant fighting with Yates, which threatened Kane's own chances to get some credits behind him other than the Autry and Rogers pictures he'd worked on, was unfeeling to say the least. "I don't like him so much that I haven't seen a picture of his since. I was really unhappy with the whole situation and told Paul Fix that I'd never work with Wayne again. I think he heard about it and returned the compliment. Doing *Dakota* with him was like pulling teeth. The fact that he was a big star didn't mean a thing to me. And I'm damn certain I don't mean a thing to him. I used to see him on the lot and we'd nod, no trouble or anything, just nothing."

Kane's next production was *In Old Sacramento* (Republic, 1946), a third remake of his own story *Diamond Carlisle*, which he had done in the twenties with George Chesebro and in 1940 as *The Carson City Kid* with Roy Rogers. Whatever his difficulties with Duke, his successes in the two films they did together meant that Kane, who had begun as a film cutter for Spencer Gordon Bennet at Pathé, was now doing Republic A pictures. Kane had a chance to get Randolph Scott, but decided instead in favor of the studio's Bill Elliott. Yates agreed there were definite possibilities in the grim-faced Elliott. The "Wild" was forever dropped from his name. The screenplay required that Elliott die at the fade in heroine Constance Moore's arms. It must have been a shock to many of his younger fans familiar with him as Red Ryder.

This was Elliott's first major starring role, and he proved up to it, if a trifle stiff in his love scenes with Connie Moore. One of the persistent stories about Bill is that he had wearied of making B pictures and, due to his popularity, demanded Republic do better for him. "Not so," Joe Kane countered. "One day, Wild Bill called me aside on the set and really lit into me. I could not believe what he was saying. He told me that if I thought I was doing him a favor getting him to do this picture rather than Randy Scott, I should forget it! He had been perfectly content and much happier being Red Ryder. What the devil could I say? Later on, he changed his mind. Other than that one time, I never had any problems with Wild Bill."

In Old Sacramento did business, and Elliott was readily cast in another first-rate production, *The Plainsman and the Lady* (Republic, 1946). Donald Barry played a vicious little frontier gangster named Feisty. The picture had a forty-three day shooting schedule with locations at Lone Pine, Monument Valley, the buffalo herds of Utah, and, throughout, magnificent panoramas, especially around Mammoth. Andy Clyde had his best Western role in this film, for once not forced to be the buffoon for William Boyd. Joseph Schildkraut was a heavy carrying on an illicit love affair with Gail Patrick. George Antheil, whose cacophonous Fourth Symphony helped bring about cancellation of Leopold Stokowski's NBC broadcasting contract in 1944, did a splendid musical score. And the heroine? Vera Hruba Ralston, of course.

Elliott never resumed series Westerns. But Yates got along without him. Gene Autry had returned. Yates had been preparing himself for this moment and felt well armed. It was true that his efforts in behalf of Donald Barry and Sunset Carson had come to little. But with Duke Wayne and now Bill Elliott, he was marching forward into the ranks of the majors. He was able to control Roy Rogers. Gene's first picture after his discharge was *Sioux City Sue* (Republic, 1946), released in November and produced on a modest budget. Throughout the war, Yates had continued to re-release eight Autry Westerns a year. Gene's contract was again coming up for renewal, and he had best not be unreasonable in his demands. Military life, however, had changed Autry.

"I don't think I ever appreciated money until I had been in the service," Autry once confided to me. "I learned what it was like to work for almost nothing, and I didn't like it."

Gene opened secret negotiations with Columbia Pictures. Autry made four Westerns for Republic that were released in 1947, the last being *Robin Hood of Texas* (Republic, 1947) and firmly in the tradition of the Autry Fantasy. In the meantime, Yates had given Roy Rogers his first A-budget feature in *My Pal Trigger* (Republic, 1946); and had promoted Monte Hale from the Sunset Carson Westerns into starring vehicles of his own as a singing cowboy, including *Out California Way* (Republic, 1946), in

When asked about his career, Allan Lane replied, "I'm old, bald and fat. I haven't done anything in years except the voice of the horse on TV in 'Mister Ed.'" This is what he looked like when he was Rocky Lane at Republic.

Photo courtesy of *Views & Reviews* magazine.

Cinecolor, which featured Roy and Dale Evans, Allan Lane, Bobby Blake, and Donald Barry as guest stars. Autry felt that as a Western property he was worth more than any player on the screen. He refused to put up with Yates's attempt to humble him and negotiated himself an excellent package with Columbia. He also signed a lucrative radio contract and was able to quickly regain his pre-eminence in the field. Of all people, Yates understood the least, apparently, about the magic of the Autry Fantasy.

Allan Lane was born Harry Albershart in Mishawaka, Indiana, on September 22, 1904. He had appeared as Tim Holt's partner in crime in *The Law West of Tombstone* (RKO, 1937), but he played mostly nice young men in all kinds of films and first came to prominence as a leading Western star only when he replaced Bill Elliott as Red Ryder in 1946. He continued in the series with Bobby Blake through 1947 until Republic sold out the property to Eagle-Lion and developed Allan into a performer in his own right under the name Rocky Lane.

In the late forties Eagle-Lion produced four Red Ryder Westerns with Jim Bannon. They were filmed in Cinecolor and were filled with action, but somehow, like those with Allan Lane, they lacked the magnetism Elliott had brought to the role. It was as a result of his work in these films, however, that Bannon was tested to play the Lone Ranger on television. Part of the test included being found acceptable by the series' creator, George W. Trendle. When Bannon was introduced to Trendle, the latter asked him what he thought of the comic-strip character. "I think the whole thing's stupid," Bannon replied. He didn't get the job.

Rocky Lane made Westerns until Yates began to phase out the B units in the early fifties in response to the threat television posed to theatrical program pictures. Rocky's films may not have been exceptional in terms of the elaborate budgets given others, but they were a cut above the Durango Kid series at Columbia and superior to the product of any of the smaller producing companies. Detection and suspense united with action was the hallmark of this series. In terms of complex and constantly interesting stories with much subtle detail, the series ranked high with the best Republic Westerns of an earlier time.

Rocky was an expert rider and he did most of his own fights. He had a particularly vicious round with Roy Barcroft in *Code of the Silver Sage* (Republic, 1950), in which Barcroft headed a gang of Arizona raiders and plotted the assassination of the President. Barcroft complained about how mean Rocky could be and how, sometimes, he didn't pull his punches and only laughed at the physical damage he caused. Republic could make its own stock footage from prior Westerns, so when the script required Rocky to leap onto the back of a wagon or jump from a tree onto a moving wagon, a cut of a double doing it from a Sunset Carson or Red Ryder picture was used. The only problem was that Rocky wore dark blue shirts and the stock shots frequently featured a light-colored shirt, but no one seemed to object. Films like *Covered Wagon Raid* (Republic, 1950) drew their central sequence—the raid—from former wagon train raids in several Republic Westerns. For all that, the Rocky Lane pictures provided a more enterprising format than many of Republic's Roy Rogers vehicles from the same period.

In 1949 Republic replaced Monte Hale with the last Western player the studio B unit was to develop before Yates closed it down. Rex Allen was born on December 31, 1922, at Willcox, Arizona. In March 1945 he was hired on WLS' National Barn Dance in Chicago on the basis of his singing ability. His contract with Republic began with *The Arizona Cowboy* (Republic, 1949) and lasted for thirty-one feature films. He sang in his pictures, and, astride his mount, Koko, he projected a sincere, if rather naïve, screen image. It was the end of the budget action Western, with or without a singing content. Television initially condensed the formula into a half-hour presentation and then, combining it with the durable soap opera, expanded it into sixty or even ninety minutes during the next three decades.

For all the slickness and polish of the postwar theatrical product, however, the B Western never regained the dust-choked crudity which, in retrospect, seems a charm peculiar to the thirties and earlier. I must confess a preference for that crudity. It is entirely personal, to be sure. The Republic formula Westerns of the forties and early fifties were quite adeptly made, and other studios frequently fell short of them in all departments. But the stark, barren quality of the previous decades was lost, and the players just didn't have the magnitude and screen presence, it would appear to me, of William S. Hart, Tom Mix, Buck Jones, Hoot Gibson, Tim McCoy, or Ken Maynard. When Bill Elliott came close, like Duke Wayne, he was no longer in B Westerns. Nor do the budget Westerns of the postwar era have quite the passion and optimism of the earlier films. These aspects are time-bound. Republic with its stunt men and streamlined approach sacrificed immediacy for sophistication. The formula, in becoming rote, lacked the intensity of belief which preoccupied the product in the twenties and thirties. More than ever before, the thinking was in terms of so many units for a given year, and individual entries were taken less and less seriously. Above all, the postwar players were the product of studio development and, unlike their predecessors, had little concept of the West; and, under the aegis of the Autry Fantasy (or their interpretation of it), little love for the West and certainly no interest in it. The spirit of the frontier had truly receded beyond recall.

42 / THE KING OF THE COWBOYS

Leonard Slye was born at Cincinnati, Ohio, on November 5, 1912. He graduated from high school there, and it was there that he went to work in a shoe factory. In 1929 he set out for California in an old Ford pickup truck which he has preserved to this day. He found a job on a fruit ranch. I have already narrated how he tried singing until with Bob Nolan he organized the Sons of the Pioneers and how, eventually, Republic signed him to a seventy-five-dollar-a-week starring contract as Roy Rogers.

I was asked some years ago by the original producer of "Roy Rogers Presents Classic Movie Cowboys" to choose the films to be included and provide Roy with background information on the stars and the productions. It wasn't until after the series had been produced that I had occasion to visit

Roy and Dale and their glamour approach to the golden West.

Photo courtesy of *Views & Reviews* magazine.

with Roy at the Roy Rogers Museum at Apple Valley. The museum is a curious exhibit. It contains almost nothing but Roy Rogers' career mementos. Dale Evans' baby shoes are there along with Trigger, "the smartest horse in the movies," and Bullet the dog, both stuffed, photos of Roy and Dale throughout their lives, and even Roy Rogers comic books. It is the penultimate of family attics, I suppose, containing display cases of intimate letters written by the Rogers children and other odd relics. Admission is a dollar.

Were you to meet Roy in a room full of people, you might not recognize him. He has none of that magnetism that characterized Tom Mix nor the tragic charisma that surrounds Duke Wayne in the seventies. Nor does Roy have that stuffy hauteur that Bill Boyd affected, the quiet, forceful character of Buck Jones, the pleasant aura of the mildly ridiculous that envelops Gene Autry. Perhaps it was for this reason that Roy so stressed garish and outlandish clothing in his films; his dress tended to make him remarkable in a way that his personality could not. I would not have the reader assume from this that Roy is not a kindly man, for he is that, and very much a gentleman. But in a sense Roy Rogers is a somewhat impersonal creation of professional publicity, a total extroversion to such a degree that his legendary personality has by now pre-empted any private reservations about himself he may once have had.

He did not look sixty-two years old. I noticed as we sat and talked that he rubbed his leg.

"I took a spill," he explained. "I was out riding on my motorcycle and it slid on the gravel in the driveway, just where you turn in. I was pinned underneath. I bled quite a lot before anyone learned that I was lying there. They were all inside, watching television."

Roy was dressed in a dark green shirt and Levi's.

"How were things at Republic when you started working in pictures there?" I asked.

"Busy," he responded. "Sol Siegel had tested seventeen others before he finally came to me. Starting with my second picture, they put me in Westerns featuring historical personalities. I played in stories about Billy the Kid, or Jesse James, Buffalo Bill or Wild Bill Hickok."

"I notice that you sang five songs in your first starring feature," I said, "*Under Western Stars* [Republic, 1938]. But after that, there wasn't excessive music-making in your films as there was in the Autry pictures."

"No," Roy replied. "Gene got most of the songs." He smiled.

"I think, in many ways, they were better pictures, though."

"Well, you know, I had to go through all of them again recently for this television series."

"Perhaps, then, you can tell me how the change came about," I said. "In the early films, all the stress was on story values. In *Saga of Death Val-*

ley [Republic, 1939], you and Donald Barry play brothers, orphaned by Frank M. Thomas in childhood. Thomas raises Don to be an outlaw, but he ends up saving your life. In *Days of Jesse James* [Republic, 1939] Don played Jesse, Harry Worth was Frank James. Gabby comments bluntly, 'Never have nothin' to do with banks.' You play a bank investigator who proves that the banker himself, and not the James boys, stole Gabby's money. In fact, the James brothers are presented sympathetically and, at one point, even want to send you to medical school. There's only one song in the picture. By the time you made *Jesse James at Bay* [Republic, 1941], you had a dual role, one as yourself, one as Jesse. But in 1942, once Gene had joined the Air Force, the films seemed overloaded with music and elaborate production numbers, beyond anything even in Gene's Westerns of a year before."

Roy smiled again.

"I can explain that," he said. "Mr. Yates had gone to New York and seen the stage show *Oklahoma*. He came back to the studio and put out a memo that from then on my films were to be made in the mold of *Oklahoma*. He wanted musicals more than Westerns from me."

"What kind of a man was Yates to work for?"

"He was a hard man to do business with," Roy said reflectively. "I wanted more money, but I had a difficult time getting it. I started at seventy-five a week in 1938. At the end of my career with Republic, in 1951, I was only getting four hundred a week."

I could not help thinking, as we talked, of Peggy Stewart's characterization of Yates and Republic. Peggy was a leading lady in Republic Westerns and serials throughout the forties.

"Herbert Yates was a dear friend," she recalled to C. M. Parkhurst. "Besides being my boss we had a close personal relationship. I think everyone loved him—even Gene, which was funny because they were 'friendly enemies' in the business field. They each had respect for the other; in fact, both would have been disappointed if the other hadn't been as sly as possible. They used to play sort of a 'Mata Hari' game. Yates was not a totally educated man. He worked his way up to head of Consolidated Film Industries before taking over control of Republic. When someone was selling out, it was always Yates's spies versus Autry's spies to see who would get the majority stock—and Gene usually lost. Working with Gene was like working with the stock market. Business was his life and acting secondary as far as he was concerned. I'm sure he would have loved to own Republic Pictures."

Peggy worked most frequently with Bill Elliott and Sunset Carson, although she remembered Allan Lane rather well. "I don't mean to sound unkind," she said of Allan, "but he was the *dullest* man I ever met. Truly, I think the main problem with Allan was that he had absolutely no sense of humor—none at all. I was known to be kind of round in the *derrière* and so was Allan, so I nicknamed him Bubblebutt and he didn't think that was a bit funny. Why, anything like that you said in jest, it didn't get through to him at all. So, you just took Allan for what he was. As an actor doing his business or trade, he was one hundred per cent professional."

With Autry off the lot, Roy Rogers reigned as the studio's top star during the war years. Republic's total production budget for the 1943–44 season was $16 million. This was broken down as follows: $9.74 million went for thirty-two regular features whose average cost was budgeted at $304,687; $2.8 million went for eight Roy Rogers musical extravaganzas, the average cost of which was $350,000; $2 million went for twenty-four miscellaneous Western features, those with Allan Lane, Bill Elliott, and Sunset Carson, with an average budget of $83,333; $1.45 million went for the production of four serials, the average cost of which was $362,500. The total studio output, counting serials, came to sixty-eight units.

Peggy Stewart was cast as second lead in Roy's *Utah* (Republic, 1945), but beginning in the 1944–45 season Dale Evans was nearly always the principal leading lady. Dale was born Frances Smith at Uvalde, Texas, on October 31, 1912. She had sung on the radio and in night clubs before coming to pictures in 1943. Roy and Dale enjoyed playing opposite one another, and Yates thought it a good novelty to keep them paired in virtually every picture. Soon after Roy's wife, Grace Arlene Rogers, died in 1946, Roy and Dale were married. Although on the screen Dale usually played trollops and modified saloon girls or tough and very capable ranch women, off screen she became profoundly interested in religion, which would have a mixed effect on both her own career and Roy's.

Gabby Hayes was almost invariably Roy's side-kick or somehow prominently included in the cast. When a very old man, in his eighties, Gabby lived as a manager of the apartment house he owned in Los Angeles, his wife having died some years before. He had very little respect for most of the screen cowboys with whom he worked, but he did like Yakima Canutt and thought him the best horseman he had ever known.

"Gabby was a curious man," I commented to Roy. "He developed that one role in the mid thirties and then rarely played anything else."

"I'll never forget," Roy returned. "One time Gabby decided he was going to shave off that full beard of his. He had worn it for years and was sick of it. So he had it shaved off. When he looked in a mirror, he was so shocked he wouldn't let anyone see him. He went out into the desert to live and hide until he grew it back. We wanted to star him in a picture. We more or less did that in *Don't Fence Me In* [Republic, 1945]."

"You made that picture right after *Sunset in El Dorado*."

"That's right," Roy said. "There was a gorgeous painting of Dale we used for *Sunset in El Dorado*. We have it now. It's hanging out in the museum."

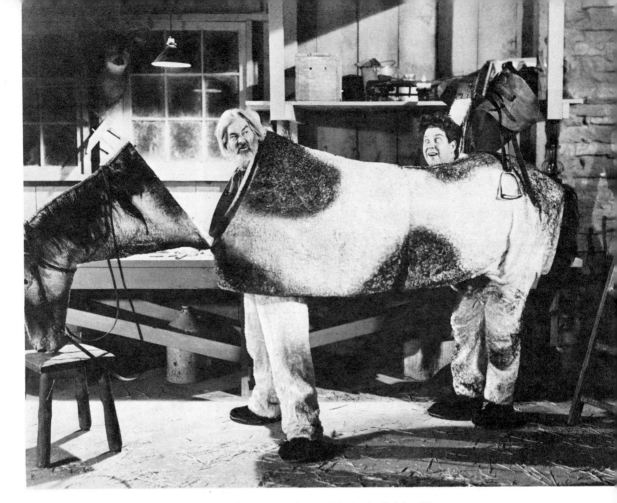

An embarrassment of riches was a problem for a time, with both Gabby Hayes and Smiley Burnette providing comedy for the Roy Rogers vehicles at Republic.

Photo courtesy of *Views & Reviews* magazine.

Whatever else might be said about *Sunset in El Dorado,* it does embody Yates's concept of a Roy Rogers Western as a cinematic imitation of *Oklahoma.* There was no underlying fantasy in the Rogers pictures the way there was in Gene Autry's Westerns, but there was glamour and a dreamlike quality, music and magic, beautiful men and women singing and flirting in the golden West. *Sunset* is a story within a story. Dale Evans goes West to see the town of El Dorado, where her grandmother was a dance hall singer. It is now a ghost town. She meets Roy and Gabby and has a dream in which all the modern characters in the film are transposed back into a former time. By the end, Roy and Dale are loving and singing.

In 1943 Roy Rogers was voted number one among Western money-making stars by the *Motion Picture Herald.* He assumed the title King of the Cowboys. Since a great deal has been written about these polls and their supposed importance, perhaps the record should be set straight. The notion of money-making is rather misleading. The poll run by the *Herald* consisted

Trigger cuts up in the street in *My Pal Trigger*.

Photo courtesy of National Telefilm Associates.

of a form sheet submitted to theater owners and managers on which were printed the names of Western players. The exhibitors voted for those they felt to be most popular with their patrons and on the ranking of that popularity. Gene Autry had succeeded Buck Jones in 1937 and maintained that position until he entered the service. Then Roy Rogers took over and kept at the top through 1951, when production on his films was halted.

Budget Westerns were never booked on percentage terms. Attendance was not really measured. The best compilation figures one might want came from number of bookings. Republic booked entire blocks of Westerns, of which the Roy Rogers vehicles were only part. Those theaters that bought consistently from Republic would, naturally, vote for Republic Western stars. Columbia Pictures, which distributed the later Gene Autry Westerns and the Charles Starrett features, followed this same practice, but Columbia product was not so heavily saturated with Westerns as was that from Republic. The truth of the matter is that Columbia could and did charge more for their Gene Autry Westerns, which made a difference in how much each individual entry earned for Columbia as opposed to how Republic would apportion earnings from their entire block of Westerns. Even when Roy's pictures were being released by Republic in Trucolor, Gene's films cost somewhat more, and Autry, personally, earned many times more than Roy did for the same number of Westerns annually. However, there is no disputing the fact that the Rogers pictures may well have played in more theaters than did Autry's films.

The original Trigger was born a short distance outside Milwaukee, Wisconsin, in 1932. Roy acquired him for very little money and turned him into a major attraction, although he projected nowhere the kind of close relationship to the horse that had characterized Tom Mix, Buck Jones, or Ken Maynard and their screen horses. In 1946 Herbert J. Yates decided to put Roy into his first A-budget Western and build the story around Roy's fanciful acquisition of Trigger. Roy, Dale, and Gabby headed the cast of *My Pal Trigger,* joined by screen veteran Jack Holt as the leading heavy.

Republic chose several locations, among them an actual palomino horse ranch. The crew wanted to photograph the foaling of Golden Hours and use the sequence to depict the birth of Trigger.

"But it didn't happen," Roy recalled. "It didn't happen and it didn't happen. Weeks went by, and with every passing day, old man Yates bled a little more because of what it was costing him. He had almost given up completely when she finally did foal."

"Did you name Trigger?" I asked.

"Yes," he replied. "His real name was Golden Cloud. I called him Trigger. He was thirty-three years old when he died."

My Pal Trigger was successful, but not so much so that Yates ever saw fit to put Roy in another high-budget feature. In part, Yates may have been prompted in making the picture by a desire to rankle Autry, who was still on the Republic lot. If that had been his intention, it certainly worked.

When I was checking into preprint materials for "Roy Rogers Presents Classic Movie Cowboys," I learned that National Telefilm Associates had junked the original negative and all fine grains in 35mm. or 16mm. of *My Pal Trigger* at the running time of its first issue. All existing prints ran fifty-four minutes rather than seventy-nine minutes. Films, Incorporated, had just lost the nontheatrical distribution rights for the Republic library and had returned all prints to National Telefilm Associates. I located a single print of *My Pal Trigger* in 16mm. and insisted that NTA have a new negative manufactured from it. It was not only Roy's own favorite film but, in all probability, his best picture, and I insisted that it be preserved. Even though in the finished series it is the truncated version that is seen, the effort was effective, and *My Pal Trigger* survives and is available in its original format.

"I know," Roy said, shaking his head sadly. "They sent the shortened version up here for me to look at. They had cut the heart out of the picture. All the snow sequences we shot in Bishop were gone . . . everything."

"You have no idea," I told Roy, "the trouble I have had trying to see original versions in order to write *The Filming of the West*. When the television distributors haven't chopped up the original negatives to make a short version, then the producing companies have refused to transfer the negatives and they have shrunken or been destroyed; or, as in Bill Boyd's case, whole reels were arbitrarily junked; or, as in Sam Peckinpah's case, the releasing company edited his original footage until it bears no relationship to his total conception, and the severely edited film opens to no business."

My Pal Trigger commences with Roy approaching the Golden Horse ranch in a wagon. He is a horse trader. Gabby raises palominos, and Dale is Gabby's daughter. Jack Holt, a saloon owner and horse breeder, is jealous of Gabby and tries to best him. Trigger is born as a result of crossing Roy's mare with Gabby's stallion. The picture ends with an exciting race, Roy and Dale both jockeys. Holt is brought to justice for his chicanery.

Roy and Peggy Stewart, along with several others who worked at Republic, are unanimous in their belief that Roy Barcroft, the most familiar of the Republic heavies, was among their favorite people. In a letter to Ken Jones, the coauthor of *Heroes, Heavies and Sagebrush* (A. S. Barnes, 1972), Barcroft wrote: "I will never forget my first chase. I thought I could handle a horse. In this scene there were 15 horses involved and some of the best Western players, men like Charlie King, Karl Hackett, Ethan Laidlaw, Kenne Duncan and Yakima Canutt. We started on top of a hill. The shot was fired which was the signal for the horses to go . . . and they did! I was in the middle of the pack and down the steep side we went, across an open grassy prairie, some cactus ditches, prairie dog holes, over boulders and into the river. I won't say what went through my mind, but one thing was for certain; if I intended to remain in Western pictures and all in one piece, I was going to have to learn how to *really* ride. I sneaked away and practiced riding and falling by myself time and time again until I was accepted by the others. The Western actors were a great bunch of guys. I took it in stride the times when they loosened my saddle cinch just before running out of a saloon for a fast getaway . . . or even better yet riding up along side of me in a wide open chase and taking off my horse's bridle and handing it to me."

During Roy's later years at Republic, William Witney became his director, working on all his films. Dale continued as Roy's leading lady, but both Jane Frazee and Penny Edwards also made several pictures playing opposite Roy. Gabby was replaced as Roy's side-kick, first by Andy Devine, and then by either Pat Brady, of the Pioneers, or Gordon Jones. Roy's last series film for Republic was *Pals of the Golden West* (Republic, 1951). Yates decided not to renew Roy's contract and, instead, sold all of Roy's old pictures to television. In addition to appearances in Bob Hope's comedy vehicles *Son of Paleface* (Paramount, 1952), with Jane Russell, and *Alias Jesse James* (United Artists, 1959), with Rhonda Fleming, Roy and Dale appeared in their own half-hour television series, filming one hundred episodes in the years 1952–57.

Like Gene Autry, Roy for years had his own radio show. However, unlike Autry, Roy always considered himself primarily an entertainer, if not a true Western player, and not a businessman. Roy remains a man of custom and habit. His secretary has been with him over twenty years, as has his business

The Sons of the Pioneers, after Pat Brady replaced Roy Rogers, who had become a star. Bob Nolan is second from the left, next to Brady.

Photo courtesy of *Views & Reviews* magazine.

manager. He liked Yates personally, despite their many contests while he worked at Republic. In terms of his Westerns, his pictures promoted, if anything, an even more elaborate dependence on anachronism, a tendency originally begun at Mascot, combining modern airplanes and stagecoaches. His films, even when the fights became more bloody after World War II, exuded an incredible glamour, with Roy decked out in fringe and silver. Many of the pictures during the late forties were shot in Trucolor, which permitted Roy to practice every sort of excess in costuming. Ultimately, because there was no underlying fantasy about Roy's person, as there was about Gene Autry, he remained merely a wholesome, likable man who sang and performed and had great camaraderie with the Pioneers and who, invariably, embodied the impulse to make beautiful Westerns which later filmmakers strove so earnestly to contradict.

43 / THE AUTRY PHENOMENON—PART TWO

Unquestionably, when Gene Autry signed with Columbia Pictures in 1947, he felt it advisable to experiment and perhaps tinker with certain nuances of the Autry Fantasy. Gene took his entire unit with him to Columbia. Armand Schaefer was promoted to executive producer of the Gene Autry Productions for Columbia release. Between 1947 and 1950, alterations were made in the Fantasy, some at Gene's suggestion, some at Schaefer's. Gene was depicted on screen as extremely adept with his fists, and fights were even stressed in some of his pictures. His dress became much more conservative, and Gene occasionally wore Levi's. Gene was presented as a good shot and, when necessary, a fast draw. In several of the pictures, he dispensed entirely with the need for a stooge, but it didn't last. Gene sang excessively, and then not so much, settling finally at three songs a picture. John English and Frank McDonald, who had directed the last entries in Gene's postwar Republic period, were his usual directors at Columbia. The pictures were otherwise staffed by Columbia contract technicians.

It was Gene's idea to make one or two A-budget features a year released to play at the top of the bill. He would continue in the meantime with his weekly radio program, his recording activity, and his extensive personal appearance tours. Gene was right about one thing. No singing cowboy could match his phonograph record sales. He was now with Columbia Records. Nine of his ditties sold over a million discs, earning gold records for him: "Tumbling Tumbleweeds," "South of the Border," "Mexicali Rose," "Back in the Saddle Again," "Silver-haired Daddy," "You Are My Sunshine," "Here Comes Santa Claus," "Peter Cottontail," and "Rudolph the Red-nosed Reindeer." "Silver-haired Daddy" was sung as early in pictures as *The Phantom Empire* (Mascot, 1935). "Rudolph" sold way over ten million copies by itself, Gene's all-time best hit.

The Last Round-up (Columbia, 1947) was his first major production for Columbia.

Once in conversation with Gene, he asked me where he might locate a print of *The Phantom Empire*. I told him he should contact Screen Gems, Columbia Pictures' television subsidiary.

"Why are you interested?" I asked.

"Because I have a print of every film I have ever appeared in," he replied, "except that one."

"Out of your ninety-three pictures, do you have a particular favorite?"

"Yes. *The Last Round-up*. It was the most expensive of my pictures and we really worked hard on that one."

"And for Republic?" I prompted.

"Probably *South of the Border*."

"That was made in 1939."

"Yes. I guess I just liked the songs in that one. But *The Last Round-up* had a good story to it."

The picture received very favorable reviews on its release. Apparently critics at the time thought it set a new high for series Westerns and was Autry's best Western since he had started in the industry. Directed by John English with a script by Jack Townley and Earle Snell, it combined incongruous elements as only the Autry Fantasy would dare. The story opened in the modern West of 1947 and featured an Indian uprising, a cattle stampede, and Gene making a television broadcast. The plot told of how both ranchers and Indians were threatened by a water famine when a thirsty city decides to tap their water supply. Jean Heather was the girl, and Ralph Morgan played the chief heavy who manages to turn the Indians against Autry for a while. It is Gene's idea to relocate everybody in the valley to a more fertile range. Morgan objects because he holds heavy mortgages on most of the valley property. After some suspenseful moments, Gene saves the day.

Both Lesley Selander, who directed Gene at Republic in 1947, and the late John English, who directed him at both companies, have gone on record that Autry took no particular interest in his work before the camera. In the prewar Republic Westerns that Gene made, many of them directed by Joe Kane, Joe attributed this indifference to Autry's obvious willingness to do what he was told except when it came to salary increases. But the war, as I have mentioned, changed things. "Gene was a funny guy," Lesley Selander recalled. "Whenever he wasn't before the camera, he'd be on the phone with his broker. I remember one time poking my head in his dressing room and he was saying, 'O.K. Buy the radio station and get the hotel, too, while you're at it.' Gene knew the stock market—the value of money and what it could do—better than the Rockefellers and J. P. Morgan combined."

Gene had a good year in 1942, earning in excess of $500,000. Upon returning to his work in entertainment, he felt the necessity of branching into other areas of business to safeguard his income. He knew the money to be made in radio. The first station he purchased was KOOL in Phoenix in conjunction with Tom Chauncey, who remained his partner. Eventually he grouped his stations from Los Angeles to Seattle under the banner of Golden West Broadcasters. In choosing business associates, Gene used a single measure for a man's trustworthiness: Does he, without pretending, genuinely believe in Gene Autry and the Autry Fantasy? When the answer was in the affirmative, Gene went ahead. He was rarely cheated, and, therefore, his yardstick, for him at least, was a good one.

Radio, however, was regulated by the government. Gene wanted to further diversify. On a personal appearance tour with Ina Autry, she com-

Autry's West was always filled with happy troubadours.

Photo courtesy of Columbia Pictures.

The Autry films added soap opera elements when he switched to Columbia, as in Gene's remake of *The Strawberry Roan* where Jack Holt plays Dick Jones's father and inadvertently shoots him.

Photo courtesy of Columbia Pictures.

plained to Gene that the hanger rails in hotel clothes closets were always too low to accommodate formal gowns without letting them touch the floor. Gene determined to buy his own hotel and let Ina supervise the interior decoration. The hotel business had its ups and downs for him. In some cases, Gene objected to the neighborhoods in which the hotels were located. He bought a motor lodge in Chicago.

"But you later sold it," I commented. "It's a Ramada Inn now."

"I know," Gene said. "When I opened it, I was told that I would have to rent linen from one particular company and I thought their prices outrageous. So I refused. It was blown up."

"What did you do then?" I asked.

"I rebuilt it," he responded simply. "They came to me again, and again I refused. Because it looked as if it would be blown up a second time, I sold it."

Pat Buttram replaced Smiley Burnette when Gene came to Columbia, until the final entries. Here Buttram is giving Gene the kind of support consistent with the Autry Fantasy while Gene wrestles with Francis McDonald in *Gene Autry and the Mounties.*

Photo courtesy of Columbia Pictures.

Gene's big picture for the 1948 season was *The Strawberry Roan,* released in August and filmed in Cinecolor. Gene decided he wanted to do his own production using the song as an inspiration to the story, just as Ken Maynard had. Gene got in touch with Ken, who was by then retired from the screen and living in somewhat reduced circumstances. Gene arranged for Columbia to purchase screen rights to Curley Fletcher's ballad, which Maynard, and not Universal, still owned. Gene's admiration for Ken lasted for the remainder of Maynard's life. Gene probably would not appreciate my telling this story, but I do not believe any image of the man would be complete without it. When Ken, during his twilight, was living in relative poverty in a trailer camp at San Fernando, in addition to his veteran's checks and his social security, he received regular money, supposedly from an old fan in Texas. The checks came from the fan, true enough, but the money came from Autry. Ken never knew it.

I once asked Ken what he thought of Gene. It was a baited question. Ken disliked almost every other screen cowboy except Tom Mix because Mix had befriended him and got him his first break at Fox and in the early twenties had even invited him to stay on his Arizona ranch, where they boxed a few rounds. Ken felt quite the same, really, about Mix as Autry later felt about Ken. But in the late twenties, at an Academy dinner, Ken had approached the Mayer-Thalberg table and asked Tim McCoy to drink with him. McCoy declined and Maynard never talked to him again. I have already narrated Ken's antagonism toward Buck Jones and Bob Steele. Even though Hoot would stop and see him until his own death, Ken would frequently get angry at the Hooter and storm out of his trailer, vanishing for several hours. Hoot would just laugh and call Ken a stubborn, bow-legged old steer.

"I have always liked Gene," Ken responded firmly.

"Why?" I asked.

"Because, Jon," Ken said, fixing me ominously with his eyes, "he knew how to keep his money. That's more'n the rest of us ever did."

Pat Buttram, Gene's radio side-kick, was introduced to the screen in *Strawberry*. Dick Jones and Little Champ also made their debuts. The picture was intended to be Gene's answer to Roy Rogers' *My Pal Trigger*, even to including Jack Holt prominently in the cast, in this instance as the owner of the ranch for which Gene works. The film opens with Gene, Pat, and the other wranglers setting a trap to capture the roan. Naturally, they sing while they work. When young Dick Jones is injured by the captive roan, Jack Holt decides to shoot the horse. Gene prevents this and hides her. In a very sentimental sequence near the conclusion of the picture, Gene persuades Dick to ride the roan and regain the confidence in the use of his legs. Jack Holt is trigger-happy and nearly kills Dick. But all is resolved when the roan, named Champion by Gene, gives birth to Little Champ. John English, who had begun his career as a cutter working on Tim McCoy's Puritan Westerns, had later codirected many of Republic's finest and *fastest* serials with Bill Witney. Some of his most brilliant work as a director was at Columbia in the Autry productions, which he always managed to keep moving and which, in their finished form, were among the best staged and edited series Westerns made after the war.

Gene didn't use Buttram regularly in his films until 1950. He wanted to cut new paths with the formats to his pictures. *Loaded Pistols* began his 1949 season. Under pressure from Columbia, Gene was compelled to increase production. He was now to make six pictures a year with a budget allocation in excess of $1.5 million. After costs were recouped, Autry's production unit participated in the profits these films made. Columbia was financially sound in their thinking. Gene's Westerns enjoyed more bookings than the pictures of almost any other series Western star at better prices than most. Barbara Britton was the female lead in *Loaded Pistols,* and Jack Holt was back with Chill Wills as the comic.

The Big Sombrero, second of Gene's six for 1949 and released in March, proved his only other Cinecolor Western. It was directed by Frank McDonald and based on an original screenplay by Olive Cooper. In a way, it was only logical that McDonald should direct this entry insofar as he had done many of the ambitious Roy Rogers operettas at Republic, including *Sunset in El Dorado,* and *Sombrero* was Gene's biggest Western musical in years. In the course of the picture Gene sang no fewer than nine songs. Elena Verdugo, who had played with George Sanders in *The Moon and Sixpence* (Loew, 1942), was the owner of the Big Sombrero ranch. She appeared quite becoming in one scene diving into a swimming pool in a tight-fitting but strictly forties full-piece bathing suit. The picture begins with Autry singing to a pawnbroker prior to selling his guitar. Autry's costuming in this picture was a little more excessive than it was generally at Columbia, but it is worth noting that he was toning down his extremism at precisely the time that Roy Rogers was indulging himself in the most outlandish outfits. Autry prevents Elena from foolishly selling her ranch and marrying Stephen Dunne. The film had many fine running inserts plus a cattle drive and a tremendous landslide.

Gene's next film but one was *Rim of the Canyon* (Columbia, 1949). Although previously he had had only one role in which he did not play himself, *Shooting High* (20th-Fox, 1940), in *Rim* he played both Gene Autry and his father, Steve. Jock Mahoney, Charles Starrett's double at Columbia who would eventually replace Ted Mapes as Gene's stand-in, played one of three evil heavies in *Rim,* joined by Walter Sande and Francis McDonald. Autry opens the picture by singing before a process screen projecting footage from *King of the Wild Horses* (Pathé-Roach, 1924). In the picture there is an exciting stage race with some thrilling smashups, three horses jumping into the Kern River lagoon on the Prudential lot, and the Columbia ranch made over as a ghost town. There is a fabulous fight between Gene and Mahoney.

Autry was undoubtedly going all out to win endorsement for the Autry Fantasy from ladies' aid societies, religious groups, and mothers' leagues. Gene devised what he called the "Ten Commandments of the Cowboy." In so doing, he went far beyond the clean-living code of Tom Mix or Ken Maynard and arrived at a state of preposterous absurdity. Maynard had cast his brother, Kermit, as the head of the Los Angeles Boy Scout Troop No. 107 in *Drum Taps* (WorldWide, 1933), and the troop was involved in the action. At one point in the story, Hooper Atchley, in his attempt to seize Lloyd Ingraham's spread, sends Jim Mason out to the ranch house to hook up a sawed-off shotgun tied by means of a string to the front door. Calling Ingraham outside, the camera records his opening the door and flying backward into Dorothy Dix's arms, both barrels ostensibly having exploded in his face. Tex Ritter later made *Tex Rides with the Boy Scouts* (Grand National, 1937). Roy Rogers and Rocky Lane incorporated sadistic fights into their Republic Westerns of the late forties. The Autry Fantasy arrived at a compromise to all of these trends. Gene conceived of the cowboy as an adult Boy Scout. Church groups and parents lauded Autry for his postulates that a cowboy never takes unfair advantage; never goes back on his word; always tells the truth; is always gentle to old people, children, and animals; is never racially or religiously intolerant; always helps people in distress; never smokes or drinks; is always clean in thought, word, deed, and personal grooming; respects women and his nation's laws; and, above all, is a patriot.

This is the culmination of the moral code implicit in the Autry Fantasy. I do not doubt that Autry believed in what he was saying. But it has been my impression that in real life, Gene Autry was in fact a subtle combination of his idealized screen personality and Pat Buttram. He knew there was a difference in what he did on screen and the way he had to live. I suspect that this is why he so liked Pat Buttram and came increasingly to use him as a balance of himself, and not a foil, in his pictures.

During his last years in films, Gene regularly began to employ less successful Western stars as heavies or in character roles. Bob Livingston and Dennis Moore appeared with him in *Riders in the Sky* (Columbia, 1949), which, in my opinion, has his best screen song while at Columbia; Frankie Darro and Clayton Moore were in *Sons of New Mexico* (Columbia, 1950); Tom Keene and Russell Hayden in *Texans Never Cry* (Columbia, 1951); Russell Hayden in *Valley of Fire* (Columbia, 1951); and Bob Livingston in *Night Stage to Galveston* (Columbia, 1952) and *Winning of the West* (Columbia, 1953). He featured House Peters, Sr., in *The Old West* (Columbia, 1952) and Francis X. Bushman in *Apache Territory* (Columbia, 1952). Sheila Ryan and, more so, Gail Davis were most frequently Gene's leading ladies.

Whatever else can be said about them, Gene's pictures maintained consistently strong plot lines and fine production values with sympathetic direction even when George Archainbaud replaced John English for the 1952 and 1953 seasons. Gene substituted Smiley Burnette as his side-kick for ailing Pat Buttram in *Whirlwind* (Columbia, 1951), reuniting them after many years. When Charles Starrett's contract was not renewed in 1952, Gene used Pat Buttram's temporary physical disability resulting from an accident with a cannon to sign Smiley for the six entries of the 1953 season. And so it came about that Smiley, who had begun with Gene in pictures with Ken Maynard's *In Old Santa Fe* (Mascot, 1934), finished with him in Gene's final theatrical release, *Last of the Pony Riders* (Columbia, 1953). Buttram continued to play opposite Gene in Autry's half-hour television series, which commenced production in 1950 and ran to ninety-one units before it was discontinued.

Autry called his television producing company Flying A Productions. Besides his own series, the firm also put into release seventy-eight half-hour units with Jock Mahoney in "The Range Rider," eighty-one half-hour units with Gail Davis in "Annie Oakley," forty-two half-hour units with Dick Jones (who had been in "The Range Rider" series) in "Buffalo Bill, Jr.," and twenty-six units of "Champion." Moreover, the firm produced the "Cavalcade of America" series and the first thirty-nine episodes of "Death Valley Days." In all of these various series, the Autry Fantasy underwent several mutations, but, with or without Gene, was clearly and markedly identifiable for its highly stylized version of what life, ideally, might have been or could be.

Columbia blamed Gene's television enterprises for the slump in sales of his theatrical films. Since Autry participated in the profits of the films but not in the production costs, Columbia dropped his series in 1953. There is this to be said in behalf of Autry. He had little choice. In 1950, in an effort to raise money, Herbert J. Yates offered for sale to MCA Television all of the old Autry and Rogers Republic Westerns. Autry began an immediate lawsuit to prevent the sale and television release of his films. He asked Roy to join him in fighting the move. Roy was still making features for Yates and hesitated. Gene lost, and the films went on television. Roy was released soon after by Republic. Gene felt he had no alternative but to compete with himself by means of a new series of films especially made for television and to diversify his offerings so as to minimize the effects of overexposure and fully exploit the players that were personally under contract to Gene Autry Productions for his Columbia films.

However ludicrous the Autry Fantasy may appear to us today, its impact on Westerns in general and the thinking of those times was immeasurable. Perhaps it can best be assimilated in relief, confronting as it did historical problems and applying to them, in each case, the moral code and philosophy of life inherent in the Fantasy. The fate of the American Indian was only one such area where the Fantasy was brought to bear, but certainly one of the most significant. And it is here, rather than elsewhere, I believe, that one must look for the impetus behind the touchingly empathetic portrayals of Indian civilization which characterized several films in the fifties. *The Cowboy and the Indians* was released in September 1949, and *Indian Territory* was issued in September of the next year. John English directed both entries. Taken as a composite, the two films propounded a far-reaching revaluation of the Indian problem, even if uniquely in terms conceivable only in the unblinking sway of the Autry Fantasy.

Typical publicity for the Autry Phenomenon after World War II.

Photo courtesy of Columbia Pictures.

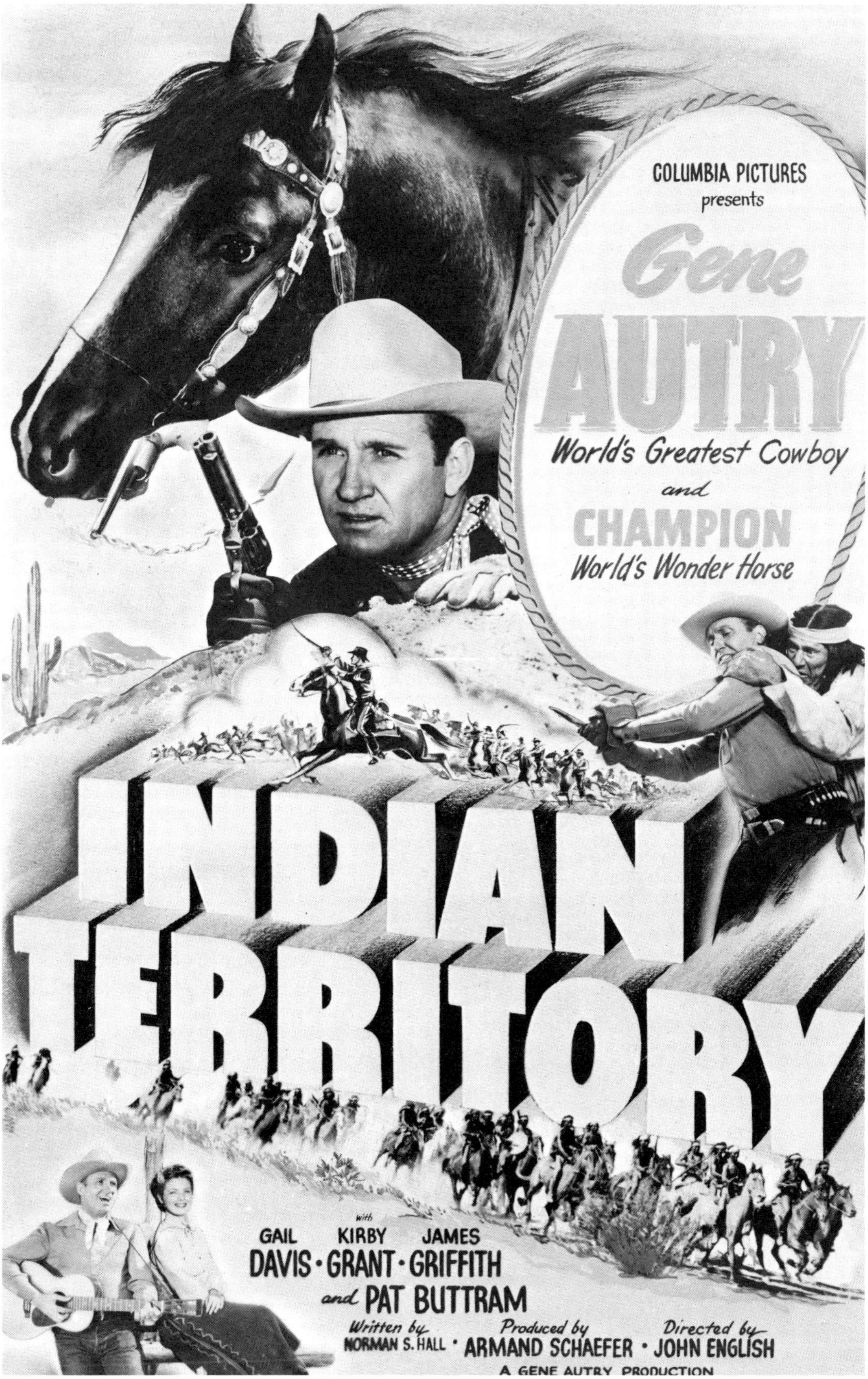
COLUMBIA PICTURES
presents
Gene
AUTRY
World's Greatest Cowboy
and
CHAMPION
World's Wonder Horse
INDIAN
TERRITORY
with
GAIL DAVIS · KIRBY GRANT · JAMES GRIFFITH
and PAT BUTTRAM
Written by NORMAN S. HALL · Produced by ARMAND SCHAEFER · Directed by JOHN ENGLISH
A GENE AUTRY PRODUCTION

The Cowboy and the Indians was scripted by Dwight Cummins and Dorothy Yost. In it Clayton Moore was cast as a heavy, and Jay Silverheels was an intelligent, college-educated, articulate Indian; Jay would soon be cast as Tonto, Spanish for stupid, in television's "The Lone Ranger," where, shortly thereafter, Clayton Moore would be joining him. The screenplay permitted Jay to retain his dignity. Although Champion was regularly billed as the World's Wonder Horse, he just as regularly did nothing to be worthy of the appellation. Similarly, Autry was highly praised by various characters in the cast, but was rarely called upon to prove his legendary and apparently superhuman powers.

The Cowboy and the Indians opens to stock footage of an Indian attack on a wagon train from *Arizona* (Columbia, 1940) and subsequent shots of Old Tucson, the set Columbia built especially for the picture and which survives now at Tucson as a tourist curiosity. Some eighty years later, a cowboy is riding hard in search of Gene Autry. The Indians are herding sheep. Gene investigates and learns that the tribe is suffering from malnutrition. Between songs, he is able to expose the crooked trader who is exploiting the Indians and exonerate Jay Silverheels from a trumped-up murder charge.

For *Indian Territory,* Armand Schaefer borrowed footage from *Arizona* showing the Union soldiers marching into Tucson, the Indian raid on the wagon train again, the William Holden cattle drive across the Arizona foothills, the Indian village in the hills, the Indian raid on Jean Arthur's cattle, and the driving of the cattle through Tucson. The Durango Kid series frequently did the same thing, so that the wagon train was raided again for *Blazing Across the Pecos* (Columbia, 1948), just as out-footage from Tim McCoy's *End of the Trail* was used in the identical Starrett film for the attack on a fort. Schaefer employed cuts of the Indians riding across the Wyoming plains from *End of the Trail* played behind the written introduction to *Indian Territory,* probably no one realizing that D. Ross Lederman had borrowed this same footage in 1932 from Tim's earlier Metro feature, *Spoilers of the West* (M-G-M, 1927). Norman S. Hall was credited with the original story for *Indian Territory.*

The picture opens to Gene in a cavalry uniform drinking from a canteen. He is chased by three Indians. They are shot by Kirby Grant and Grant's detachment. Back at the fort, Gene and Kirby have a fight. Gene is assigned to get to the bottom of some Indian trouble, with Pat Buttram going along for support. It turns out to be the work of an ex-officer of the Austrian Army and the Apache Kid. Gene and Pat, later joined by Grant, who falls in love with Gail Davis, manage to settle the trouble, and the two principal villains are variously done in.

It is interesting to note in passing that Chief Yowlachie, who had fought so vigorously with Tim McCoy and Ken Maynard in the twenties, was back for *The Cowboy and the Indians* and that Frank Lackteen, the savage half-breed menacing Allene Ray in *Hawk of the Hills* (Pathé, 1927), was in both of these films in sympathetic roles. As early as *The Last Round-up*, Gene had presented the idea that the severest problems in the treatment of the Indians could be solved with a song and the support of their good friend, Gene Autry. This notion was only expanded in the later films.

The reader may object to the simplistic character of this solution, but for more than a few of the viewers of these films the Autry Fantasy seemed to be the ideal embodiment of the American ethic. I will not comment one way or the other as to the efficacy of a Santa Claus as an answer to the deep splits among human beings. But I think Autry deserves credit for presenting the Indians in different terms from their portrayal by most of his contemporaries. Whereas Tom Mix and William S. Hart, still close to the spirit of the frontier, called upon gunplay and hard riding to bring peace to warring factions, the Autry Fantasy was born of the aspirations of a new generation, one that believed that the good will of a community song and, above all, the munificence of money being given away freely would bring about a true brotherhood among men. Yet I do not wish to stress too greatly Gene's personal involvement in the issues and prospects which the stories of his films promulgated.

I seriously doubt that Autry ever regarded his career as a Western player as anything more than a business enterprise. For many of his active years, Gene was among the most highly paid motion picture performers in Hollywood. In terms of the ultimate fortune he amassed, Autry accomplished it singularly by means of intelligent investments which seldom demanded anything from him other than money. Relying on his accountants, Autry has financed numerous projects, watched their economic progress carefully, bowing out if they seemed at all risky, staying in when through the industry and ingenuity of others, they were made to pay. When in *Mexicali Rose* (Republic, 1939) Autry threatens the chief heavy with having his books examined, it is, coming from him, a more typical if no less effective challenge than that of the traditional Western hero dependent on his ability with handarms or his physical prowess.

While building up his radio stations and Gene Autry hotels, he bought an interest in the Phoenix *Gazette* and *Arizona Republic* newspapers and twenty-five oil wells in Texas. His good luck has always been a phenomenon. Autry sank seventeen wells and brought in seventeen gushers within ten miles of where two friends had struck nothing but dry wells. He bought interests in a 100,000-acre ranch at Winslow, Arizona, a cattle ranch at Florence, Arizona, a 3,200-acre spread at Dublin, Texas, and an additional 2,300 acres at Berwyn, Oklahoma. The town of Berwyn changed its name to Gene Autry in his honor.

When still in the movies, Gene bought controlling stock in the Madison

Square Garden Rodeo and music publishing companies, as royalties continued to flow in from comic books and countless Gene Autry accessories. Autry, who once wanted to be a baseball player, recalled that he had to give it up because the semi-pro team in Oklahoma only paid $50 a month and a railroad telegrapher's pay was $125 a month. He looked at filmmaking the same way. More recently he acquired a majority interest in the Los Angeles Angels and gained a minority interest in the Los Angeles Rams football team. He built his home on the 125-acre Melody Ranch overlooking the San Fernando Valley.

Even in the accumulation of considerable wealth, Autry has fared best where he has remained personally uninvolved, almost indifferent, in much the same way that he sang nonchalantly through his films and recording sessions. The acquisition of wealth itself has concerned Autry primarily in his career, and here, as elsewhere, the Autry Fantasy has been his guide. I have had a peculiar feeling on those occasions when I have spoken to Autry that he was sizing me up, testing to see just how much of the Autry Fantasy I believed and, to the extent that I didn't accept it, became hostile and distant.

When his third Champion died, Gene was in a broadcast booth. He was contacted by telephone and told the news.

"How much would it cost to have him bronzed?" he asked the veterinary. "About twenty-five hundred? I see." There was a pause. "And how much to have him stuffed and mounted?" Another pause. "Fifteen hundred? Well, then, how much to bury him?" A final pause. "Only fifty? Bury him!"

However much his ego dominated his films and his other work in entertainment, it never penetrated his business judgment. This tended to cut down his chances for error or blindness when combined with cold business intelligence and united with a stunning capacity for investment without speculation that few have equaled, coming from quite the same background and tempted by similar aspirations.

After all is said and done, I wonder if the same question has occurred in the reader's mind that has often occurred to me. Everything taken into consideration, had their positions been reversed, would Gene Autry the businessman have taken the same chance on an unknown singer from Chicago that Nat Levine once did?

44 / HARRY SHERMAN AT UNITED ARTISTS

In 1941 United Artists releasing company was desperately in need of product to maintain its schedule of pictures. The firm negotiated with several major producing companies and finally signed an agreement with Paramount to distribute a substantial number of their lesser releases in 1942. Among the pictures included in the package were three of the minor A-budget Westerns produced by Harry Sherman and financed by Paramount. *The Kansan* (United Artists, 1942), *American Empire* (United Artists, 1942), and *Buckskin Frontier* (United Artists, 1943), as a result, were announced as Paramount Pictures on the publicity and United Artists' releases on the credits.

Pop Sherman wasn't entirely happy with the state of affairs at Paramount. He still received his producer's percentage on the Bar 20 series, but he felt the pictures were doing well enough that it was time to consider returning to the former situation and producing them himself, only this time with money behind him and a reputation for making successful Westerns. Pop found that his name alone was sufficient collateral for him to borrow the production money from the Bank of America. He was proud to show the loan officer the contract he had personally signed with United Artists whereby they would distribute the Hoppy films.

Boyd was still pressuring Pop for better scripts with an increasing emphasis on the Hopalong character. Pop told Bill of the new deal and spoke warmly of his enthusiasm for the future of the series. Pop had Richard Dix under contract, and Dix had appeared in both *The Kansan* and *American Empire* and was slated to star in *Buckskin Frontier* as the changeover was being made. Boyd had very much wanted to play the lead in *American Empire,* but Pop vetoed the idea. Bill told Pop that he felt the Hoppy pictures were typecasting him so badly that, unless his career was going to be sacrificed completely, he should be given other roles to play; if not in Pop Sherman productions, then for other producing companies. Pop placated Bill with promises of immediate improvements in the Bar 20 pictures.

Jane Wyatt was signed to play opposite Richard Dix in *The Kansan* and *Buckskin Frontier* on a two-picture contract. Married to Edgar B. Ward, it proved a happy relationship. It was in February 1974 that I first visited her at her lovely home in Beverly Hills. She swung the door open for me much as she had every week at the beginning of the long-running television series "Father Knows Best." She looked as graceful and charming as she had in *Lost Horizon* (Columbia, 1937) when she fell so profoundly in love with Ronald Colman on the screen.

"It was his eyes, Jon," she remarked, as we sat across from one another in her airy drawing room, the French windows open to the garden in back. "Ronald Colman had the most unusual eyes of anyone on the screen. They were sad, like Gary Cooper's, but more wistful."

"There is a question I've always wanted to ask you, Jane. It's about *Lost Horizon*. Did you actually do the nude bathing scene?"

"No!" Jane laughed vivaciously, her eyes brightening. "I wanted to, but Mr. Capra insisted on using a double. I was photographed in the water, though, swimming. I wore what today you would call a bikini. The double was naked. I was so angry when I saw the rushes. She belly-flopped. I never would have done that!"

The conversation turned to Harry Sherman.

"Pop was a dear man to work for. He was always so considerate of his players. I'm Catholic, you know. He saw to it that there was a limousine to take me to church on Sunday when we were out on location filming *Buckskin Frontier*." She paused to laugh again as a humorous memory came to her. "Lee J. Cobb was in that picture. I'll never forget how strange I thought him. There were still photographers on the sets in those days. Every time they wanted to photograph a scene in which Lee appeared, he'd hide from them. We were on the bus, coming back to Hollywood, and I was sitting next to Lee.

"'Lee,' I said to him, 'you shouldn't avoid having your picture taken that way. It's publicity!'

"'You don't seem to understand,' he said offhandedly. 'I don't want anyone to know that I'm in this picture, Jane.'"

We laughed together.

"And now you tell me you think it was a good Western," Jane said.

"Yes," I replied. "I think it's a good Western, and I think you're good in it."

"I did all of my own riding, anyway," Jane responded. "I had a double assigned to me in *The Kansan* and *Buckskin Frontier,* but in *Buckskin Frontier* I had a part with a lot of riding, and Pop let me do it myself."

American Empire joined Richard Dix with Frances Gifford, Preston Foster, and Leo Carrillo. In fact, it was a fine picture for Leo, playing an enchanting and cynical villain with a French accent. The film, like *Buckskin Frontier* and the Bar 20 films, followed the by now established Sherman formula of grand opening, dramatic center, breath-taking finish.

George Green sits on Sherman's desk at the Harry Sherman Productions office at General Service Studio. Green was associate producer for most of the Hoppy pictures.

American Empire cost $362,665.90 to make and, upon release, only grossed $325,000. It lost money. So did *Buckskin Frontier*, costing $354,-764.06 and grossing a similar amount. Yet both were excellent Westerns. Pop felt the pictures should command better terms. His subsequent major Western releases for United Artists starred Joel McCrea, were more intensely promoted, and reversed this trend.

Buckskin Frontier featured Lee J. Cobb as an old man, which is one of the reasons he may have avoided publicity stills. He had begun with Sherman in *Rustlers' Valley* (Paramount, 1937), billed as Lee Colt. Cobb runs a freight line. Jane Wyatt is his daughter and Albert Dekker is his right hand. Richard Dix represents the railroad. Victor Jory and Joe Sawyer try to stir up trouble between Cobb and Dix, particularly when Cobb is adamant in his opposition to the railroad using his pass for a right of way. Jane is cast as a spunky frontier girl. She falls in love with Dix against her father's wishes. Lola Lane represents financial interests backing Dix. When Cobb, in his fight with the railroad, hires Jory and Sawyer, Dekker switches sides and joins the railroad. Jory starts a reign of terror. Jane overhears Jory's plans to blow up the railroad camp and rides to warn Dix. There is a climactic showdown, with Cobb organizing the townsmen to join in the fight against Jory. Dix is to marry Jane at the fade, Dekker is to marry Lola Lane, and Cobb is offered a place on the board of directors of the railroad.

Despite what Pop told Bill Boyd, the first United Artists Hopalong films were nothing special. *Lost Canyon* (United Artists, 1942) was a word-for-word remake of *Rustlers' Valley,* with two interpolations of stock footage from the earlier picture and a change in casting with Jay Kirby playing Johnny Travers in the old Lucky role and Andy Clyde in the George Hayes character. The dialogue was virtually identical. Mulford wrote his last Bar

Cliff Edwards, Big Boy Williams, Leo Carrillo, Richard Dix, and Preston Foster during the night gun battle in *The American Empire.*

20 novel in 1941, *Hopalong Cassidy Serves a Writ*. Pop adapted it for the screen for the 1943 release schedule, and young character actor Robert Mitchum was given a part as a heavy.

The plots did get more complex. *The Leatherburners* (United Artists, 1943) concerned a crazed mine owner who joins forces with Victor Jory in rustling cattle and hiding them in the caves at Bronson Canyon until Hoppy stumbles on the truth. *Colt Comrades* (United Artists, 1943) found Hoppy drilling for water to short-circuit Victor Jory's plans to take over the valley ranches. Jay Kirby was dropped from the series after a time and replaced by Jimmy Rogers, Will Rogers' son, more a comic than even Andy Clyde. The entire tone of the pictures changed to the extent that Bill was increasingly set off from everyone else as a mythical, superhuman figure. Boyd was also given more chances to demonstrate his very real acting ability.

The series ended with *Forty Thieves* (United Artists, 1944). Douglas Dumbrille summons together forty gunmen with a single ambition: to kill Hopalong Cassidy. The absurdity of the Cassidy character culminated in this picture with Boyd literally confronting the entire gang in the town street and being sufficiently self-possessed that they are afraid to draw down on him. The film, however, did have its tense moments, and Boyd's performance, whatever his vanity, came off effectively.

Pop wanted to get into serious feature production. He had lost interest in the Bar 20 films. Boyd's contract was up for renewal, and Pop released him. But Bill had been right. He was so thoroughly identified with the Hopalong Cassidy character that he couldn't find other employment, nor could he find a new backer for continuing the series, the production rights to which Sherman retained. Bill had been on the road touring with circuses for almost two years when, in 1946, a Hollywood promoter, Toby Anguish, approached him with a proposition. Bill was drawing $250 a week with the circus. Toby suggested they buy the rights from Sherman with the financial backing he had secured and that Bill act as the front man. Pop might very well give Bill a better price.

Sherman laughed at Boyd and thought he was kidding. He demanded $250,000 in cash. When Bill came up with the money, Pop sold out. Toby and Bill commenced new production. The budgets dropped to $100,000, and the shooting schedules were telescoped to the point where as many as forty scenes a day were shot. United Artists still released the pictures. To help raise money to finance new production, Anguish sold off all the old Sherman-Paramount pictures for theatrical re-release to George A. Hirliman, of Screen Guild. The first six pictures in the series were the only exceptions to this, having been sold to Sherman J. Krellberg for theatrical re-issue in 1941. The new Hopalong Cassidy pictures couldn't compete. Never a man to be put down, Anguish went to several of his friends, mostly assistant directors at Warner Brothers, and asked them to come up with $50,000, the sum he needed to make new 16mm. prints for television distribution.

Jane Wyatt and Richard Dix as they appeared in *Buckskin Frontier*.
Photo courtesy of TV Cinema Sales Corporation.

Toby accumulated the capital, put the pictures on television, and finally sold them in a package to NBC Films. The rest made history. Boyd was bowled over with the resurgence in his career. He had been nearly bankrupted by the new Hoppies; he had sold everything he owned, save a small bungalow, to assist Anguish in gathering the money. Now he embarked on new half-hour television production, cleaned up on the merchandise rights which in 1951 alone amounted to $25 million, and bought Anguish out. Boyd declared to the press that he had known the importance of television back in 1937. He toured with Ringling Brothers' circus, made a guest appearance in his Hopalong monkey suit in Cecil B. De Mille's *The Greatest Show on Earth* (Paramount, 1953), sold out Hopalong Cassidy Productions to William Boyd Enterprises for a capital gain of $8 million, and retired from public life in 1961. He and Grace Bradley built a home, decorated in black and white, in Palm Desert.

Pop Sherman was amazed at what happened to his pictures once they were on television. He invested in art film and lost much of his fortune. He and his daughter, Teddi, sitting at opposite ends of the long dining room table, lamented the passing of Harry Sherman Productions, which had kept everyone employed for eight months without a picture being made. Pop wrote out a note and sent it with his chauffeur to Louis B. Mayer, whose house was just down the block from his. Mayer had the note, which was a request for money, returned with an addendum to the effect that as of that moment $50,000 had been deposited in Pop's account. But it wasn't enough to save him. On September 25, 1952, after an operation at Cedars of Lebanon Hospital and nothing but unfulfilled dreams for more pictures, Harry "Pop" Sherman died.

Boyd's death was far more tragic. A long bout with cancer of the lymph nodes, complicated by Parkinson's disease, ended terminally in 1973 with a congested heart condition.

Bill toured with circuses before his retirement, hoping to the day he died to perpetuate the idealized screen image with which he had been so long associated. In order to make the old pictures fit network running times and too cost conscious to manufacture new negatives, Bill ordered that the first reel and sometimes part of the second reel to his early Paramount titles be junked from the camera negatives. It insured the unfortunate happenstance that the pictures will never again be seen as they were originally made.

The news of Bill's death wasn't released until well after the fact and then only in a prepared statement. It was a sad finale for the man whose life had become so entwined with his screen character that they had become almost inseparable. I remember one of Bill's friends remarking to me over lunch: "You have to understand that Bill Boyd and Hoppy are really the same person. I call him Hoppy as often as I call him Bill."

Although Boyd had completely done over the image of Hopalong Cassidy created by Mulford in the original Bar 20 books, it is Boyd's image which did indeed become the foremost version in the public mind. And it is the romantic interpretation Boyd brought to the role of Hopalong Cassidy which survives in the truncated versions of his theatrical features which he left behind.

The Postwar Years

In *Law and Order* (Universal, 1932) it was the camaraderie that was stressed in telling the story of the Earp family in Tombstone. Long before the modern consciousness of isolation, indeed an antidote to it was the warmth, commitment, and loyalty of human relationships.

One of the last pictures Sol Wurtzel made before personal tragedy caused him to leave the motion picture industry was *Frontier Marshal* (20th-Fox, 1939). Randolph Scott was the star, and critics were agreed that the film constituted, quite readily, Randy's best performance on the screen until that time. Allan Dwan was the director. Sam Hellman did the screenplay. Randy played Wyatt Earp; Cesar Romero was Doc Holliday.

The scenario took definite liberties with history. Doc was a surgeon rather than a dentist. Wyatt was an idealized lawman bringing order to chaos. Doc was shown as being in love with Binnie Barnes, who portrayed a dance hall tart. Doc's girl, a more wholesome woman, was played by Nancy Kelly. Doc and Wyatt are about to have a standoff when Doc is seized with a fit of coughing. Wyatt saves his life from other gunmen, and it is this action which establishes a bond of friendship between them. Before the shoot-out at the O.K. corral, in which Doc is killed (another historical fantasy), Doc has an opportunity to redeem himself by performing an operation on a small boy.

It was basically this shooting script which John Ford was handed in 1946 and which he used for the basis of *My Darling Clementine.* Cathy Downs played Clementine, Doc Holliday's girl from the East who follows him all over the Southwest till she finally locates him at Tombstone. Victor Mature was cast as Doc. Henry Fonda played Wyatt; Ward Bond was Morgan Earp; Tim Holt was Virgil Earp. Linda Darnell was cast as Chihuahua, the barmaid in love with Doc.

"About *Clementine,*" John Ford once recalled, "the only story I know is, Wyatt Earp moved out here and lived some place beyond Pasadena, and his wife was a very religious woman, and two or three times a year . . . she'd go away on these religious conventions, Wyatt would sneak into town and get drunk with my cowboys. Along about noon, they'd sneak

Henry Fonda at his first meeting with Victor Mature as Doc Holliday. J. Farrell MacDonald is the bartender.

away and come back about one-fifteen swacked to the gills—all my cowboys *and* Wyatt—and I'd have to change the schedule around. And he told me the story of the fight at the O.K. corral. And that was exactly the way it was done, except that Doc Holliday was not killed. Doc died of tuberculosis about eighteen months later. And that's the only story I know about *Clementine*—except that the finish of the picture was not done by me. That isn't the way I wanted to finish it."

Ford concentrated on the mutual respect which existed between Wyatt and Doc. The friendship which grew between them was the substance of his story. Just as the Western town set he built at Monument Valley to represent Tombstone stood in stark contrast to the arid, nearly hostile expanse of the impersonal wasteland which surrounded it, the penetration of humanity into an empty wilderness, the friendship thrived in contradiction to the enmity, hostility, and murderous savagery of the Clantons.

It was always Ford's claim that he would have made better pictures if, on location, he hadn't spent most of his time thinking of pranks to play on Ward Bond. Ward genuinely felt that he deserved to be a star, more than Duke Wayne did. When Ford was shooting *They Were Expendable* (M-G-M, 1945), he hired an attractive young woman to wait table on his troupe and go along with a gag. She appeared to be star-struck with Ward. She told him that he was her favorite actor; she asked him for his autograph. When she waited on their table, she would invariably take Ward's order first and let everyone else wait until Ward had been served. She kept on like this for a couple of days and then told Ward that her husband, who supposedly worked on the Atchison, Topeka and Santa Fe Railroad, was returning and that she would only have one more night alone. She arranged with Ward that he should show up at her little bungalow with a six-pack of beer and a watermelon.

That night, Ford, Duke Wayne, and the other cast principals in on the joke assembled in the dark at the bungalow. When Ward arrived, carrying the six-pack and the watermelon, and opened the door, they began firing their guns at him. The guns were loaded with blanks, but Ward didn't know that. He dropped the six-pack and ran, helter-skelter, still carrying the watermelon under his arm. At the studio, Ford would constantly berate Ward, invite grips to sit around him at the commissary so that Ward wouldn't have a place to sit. ". . . I don't want you to think I'm saying anything derogatory about Ward, God rest his soul," Ford would hasten to say after relating one of the pranks he pulled. "He was a wonderful guy. I miss him and Wayne misses him, and something has gone out of our lives. He's the godfather to my children and my grandchildren, and he's a very dear friend."

Ford kept Doc a surgeon in *My Darling Clementine*. He composed a scene where Victor Mature studied himself as reflected in the glass fram-

Kathy Downs and Victor Mature in a scene from *My Darling Clementine*.
Photo courtesy of 20th Century-Fox Film Corporation.

ing his medical degree, a bit of business Ford later varied for *Cheyenne Autumn* (Warner's, 1964) when Edward G. Robinson studies a glass-framed portrait of Lincoln and speaks to it, "Old friend. Old friend. What would you do now?" Walter Brennan, who had played Judge Roy Bean in *The Westerner* (Goldwyn, 1940), managed brilliantly as the vicious patriarch of the Clantons.

Henry Fonda tells of how Ford summoned him one day and worked up a bit of business. Fonda is in a scene with Linda Darnell. He is leaning back in a saloon chair on the boardwalk, a support post for the porch roof in front of him. Ford told Fonda how he wanted him to balance on one foot against the post and then the other, keeping the chair tipped backward the entire time. It was powerful, suggestive imagery for the tenuous control Wyatt had on events and on life and death in Tombstone. It is underplayed and natural in the scene, so that its significance is purely psychological.

Clementine opens to the Earp brothers herding their cattle into Monument Valley. Brennan and his son, Ike Clanton, played by Grant Withers, drive up in a buckboard, and Brennan offers to buy the herd for less than it's worth. Fonda refuses. That night, Fonda, Ward, and Tim Holt head into town, leaving Don Garner to guard the camp. Fonda volunteers to stop Charles Stevens, as a drunken Indian, from shooting up the town. In the meantime, the Clantons murder Garner and rustle the cattle. The Earps discover what has happened, and Wyatt returns to Tombstone to accept the position of town marshal. There is a touching sequence at Garner's graveside in which Fonda swears to make the West safe for youngsters to grow into maturity.

Doc and Wyatt meet and become friends. Doc is dying of consumption. Doc's fiancée comes to Tombstone. He rejects her and tells her to go back East. Chihuahua, jealous of Doc's attachment for Clementine, takes up with John Ireland. When Wyatt, after falsely suspecting Doc for a time, discovers that Ireland was involved in the murder of Garner, Ireland flees town, Tim Holt after him. Ireland expires. Brennan shoots Tim and drops his body off in front of the jail as a challenge to the two remaining Earps to meet for a gunfight at the O.K. corral. Doc performs an operation on Chihuahua, but she dies. He joins the Earps for the finish. Doc is killed in the shoot-out. The Clantons are dispatched. Fonda rides off at the fade, leaving Clementine behind to be Tombstone's schoolteacher. Ford would have preferred to have them fall in love.

The gunfight has inspired several pictures since *Clementine,* and some critics are apparently of the opinion that the more recent the cinematic presentation of it, the more historically valid. This should probably be amended to read that the more recent the version, the more attuned it is to a different time than was *Law and Order* or Ford's version, *Frontier Marshal.*

John Sturges has brought the story to the screen twice, a decade apart, in *Gunfight at the O.K. Corral* (Paramount, 1957) and *Hour of the Gun* (United Artists, 1967). *Gunfight* starred Kirk Douglas as Doc and Burt Lancaster as Wyatt. John Ireland was back, this time as a bandit named Ringo who is an intimate of Ike Clanton's. When Wyatt saves Doc's life, even though he doesn't like him, a friendship is struck up that, after some varied adventures, brings Doc to Wyatt's side for the showdown at the O.K. corral.

Hour of the Gun begins with the shoot-out with James Garner as Wyatt and Jason Robards turning in a splendid performance as Doc Holliday. Robert Ryan plays Ike Clanton. Clanton continues to dominate Tombstone even after the fight. When one of Wyatt's brothers is crippled by Clanton's men and another killed, Wyatt swears vengeance and Doc goes along for the ride. The tension of *Gunfight* is the mutual antagonism between Wyatt and Doc, transforming slowly into the deepest personal friendship. *Hour of the Gun* introduces the clash of values, in Wyatt who uses the law to legalize his revenge, in Doc who delights in exposing the hypocrisy of Wyatt's position. Possibly the intangible substance of what links one man's fate with another's is the predominant force in *Hour of the Gun* and its principal recommendation as a Western. It concludes with Doc in a sanitarium, having given up his life of violence but not his drinking, stoically facing the inevitable. Wyatt, because of the twistings of his own soul, is resolved never to be a lawman again.

Frank Perry, a New Yorker, decided to tell the story of the fight as it really happened when he came to direct *Doc* (United Artists, 1971). However, after consultation with Pete Hamil, of Brooklyn, the screenplay which emerged followed what might best be termed the Peckinpah principle. Howard Hawks once said, "To me a Western is gunplay and horses. . . . They're about adventurous life and sudden death. It's the most dramatic thing you can do." Sam counters this by asserting, "The Western is a universal frame within which it is possible to comment on today." *Doc* became a contemporary comment, and the shift in emotional and social emphasis produced no more historical accuracy than had Ford's vision of the bonds which hold men together against a hostile, indifferent planet.

Doc is a Western without heroes. Stacy Keach plays Doc, and Harris Yulin is Wyatt. Faye Dunaway appears as Kate Elder, the whore with whom Doc Holliday is intimate. Doc is a dentist dying of tuberculosis. Wyatt is a coward who feels his guns can even the score no matter what adversary he is pitted against. The historical Wyatt Earp was only a moderately fast gunman who managed to pursue his marshaling with a minimum of personal involvement, surrounding himself with deputies who were invariably dead shots. Doc befriends Denver John Collins, who plays the Kid. But at the gunfight, even when the Kid cannot draw down on him, Doc guns him anyway. The film is heavy with significant symbolism, but psychological motivation leaves much to be desired. Kate Elder, while a tart, becomes possessive of Doc; Wyatt is a gun-crazed lunatic; Doc appears to be committed to some profound internal quest the nature and purpose of which remain enigmatic. "Why the Kid?" Wyatt asks Doc at the end of the picture. "I guess he reminded me of too many things," Doc replies and rides off alone.

If the Western has matured beyond the point of a simple action thriller, perhaps the retelling of the O.K. corral confrontation since 1932 charts at least one trend in production. Instead of the Western setting pulling men together into mutual interrcliance, the more recent direction seems to be in favor of greater and greater human separation, depicting men increasingly closed off from one another and imprisoned by themselves, their past, oppressive social and economic conditions. The Wyatt Earp/Doc Holliday friendship, rather than remaining the embodiment of hope, the assurance of the value of human relationships, has become the occasion to despair in the permanence of any kind of relationship at all. I cannot inform the reader what this means philosophically, but I feel called upon to remark that the response of the general public was very positive to *My Darling Clementine* and somewhat less so to *Gunfight at the O.K. Corral,* while *Hour of the Gun* proved disappointing at the box office and *Doc* was a complete failure. Critics who would point to the later films and draw conclusions from them about the American people and the decay of our social order should perhaps be counseled that the more modern views have not met with popular endorsement and so are really a commentary on nothing, save how to make an unsuccessful Western.

46 / DAVID O. SELZNICK AND THE WESTERN

Of all the filmmakers who have enriched the world by means of their imaginative and spiritual resources, David O. Selznick was very probably the finest. He was not a tall man; nor was he uncommonly handsome. As a youth, he was given to seriousness, his swarthy complexion and sad, perceptive eyes making him appear almost saturnine. It wasn't until 1935 that he at last realized his ambition to found his own studio, Selznick International. Irving Thalberg became his first investor when he and his wife, Norma Shearer, put up $200,000. Several backers joined in. As the thirties came to a close, Selznick produced what will certainly remain the greatest film of this century, *Gone With the Wind* (M-G-M, 1939), which Metro initially released and later, when David was in desperate financial straits, bought outright from him.

I am very much afraid that human pettiness, in some cases envy, in others competitiveness, has dealt unfairly with Selznick. He is today viciously hated by a number of film critics because he was of an independent frame of mind and insisted on making pictures his own way. Writers and directors, actors and technicians, were welded into a common enterprise by David's absorbing vision, his energy, and his devotion to excellence. His apparently endless production memos have recently been edited and published. Without need of commentary, they reflect David's radiant visual sense, his love for a story, his curiosity about his fellow beings, his inimitable grasp of the complex financial and managerial problems of film production.

He once remarked that "there are only two kinds of merchandise that can be made profitably in this business—either the very cheap pictures or

David O. Selznick in his office.

the expensive pictures." He invariably chose the latter. He knew the mechanics of the expensive pictures as perhaps no one else. He married Louis B. Mayer's daughter, Irene, on April 29, 1930. His brother, Myron Selznick, went on to build the first truly powerful talent agency in Hollywood. David had begun his career working for his father as head of production of Selznick Pictures Corporation. When Adolph Zukor forced the elder Selznick into ruin, David in his turn worked for M-G-M in the late twenties when he was assigned to the Outdoor unit, then for Paramount's West Coast studio as assistant to B. P. Schulberg, then for RKO, moving once more back to M-G-M. His fortunes, tempered by struggle and setbacks, were a continuous ascent until the release of *Gone With the Wind.* His acumen and prudent theatrical judgment notwithstanding, even his genius for business, in the end David was a man of emotion, a creature of intuition and uncanny instinct. "I learned . . . ," he once said of these years, "never to tackle a picture for which I have no enthusiasm, never to tackle a subject for which I had not a personal liking and for which I lacked confidence in my ability to translate to the screen effectively."

I am limited in what I can say about Selznick because *Duel in the Sun* was David's only sound Western, although it was his best film after *Gone With the Wind; Duel* is so much a story in itself and David's life and its ambiguities only peripheral to the subject at hand; I should like, therefore, only to recount this one conversation for the reader. Howard Strickling was for nearly all of his active years head of publicity at M-G-M and extremely close to Louis B. Mayer. He had been with the studio through its glorious period of building and promise, its magic, its myriad stars, its vast and sprawling empire. He had watched Mayer's organizational brilliance from the outset, and, once, as we sat on the enclosed sun porch of his Encino home, he told me of the day Mayer visited him in 1951 to inform him of how Nicholas Schenck had fired him and promoted Dore Shary in his stead. The couch Mayer had sat on next to him was still there, and the memory was so vivid it was almost as if Mayer were alive to relive the scene. Now we were walking along a gravel back road on Howard's farm, some sixty miles from Hollywood. It was dusk, and a sharp breeze had risen, animal scents and alfalfa mingling in the air.

"What happened to David after *Gone With the Wind?*" I asked him. "It was as if, with that one picture, he had overreached himself."

"I told Bob Thomas the same thing," he said, "when he was researching his book about David." Thomas, a newspaper reporter, published his book *Selznick* in 1970. "He produced the greatest picture ever made and he never knew how to live with himself after it. He tried to equal it again and again, and he couldn't."

The breeze had suddenly turned cold and the light dimmed. I recalled that Irene had divorced David in January 1948 and that David was by that time profoundly in love with Jennifer Jones. In her book *The Gift Horse* (McGraw-Hill, 1971) Hildegard Knef relates her late night summons to Selznick's office with a fire burning in the grate and David incessantly on the telephone long-distance. When he finished, he crossed the room to a mirror, stroking his hair, then polishing his glasses.

"Tell me about yourself," he said.

Haltingly, Miss Knef told David of her harsh life in war-torn Europe. When she stopped, he asked questions. Finally, he commented that it all could make a good story and went into the bathroom. He showered and gargled, returning in a fresh shirt and smelling of mouthwash. He caressed her and she panicked. She stared at his wide neck, his tight smile, a smile that meant total power and self-possession.

"I don't know any German girls," he said and began tugging at her jacket.

Miss Knef ran to the bathroom and vomited in the basin. When she emerged, David was again telephoning. He told her to report next day to M-G-M for a screen test and dismissed her.

"Was David," I asked Howard, walking back toward the house, "a lonely man?"

It was now nearly dark. Twilight gleamed across the fields.

"He was a lonely and a restless man," Howard replied. For his seven decades, Strickling walked animatedly, his hair iron-gray, his face jovial and content, his eyes sparkling as he spoke. "You know, in David's last years, when he was happily married to Jennifer, he learned that he had a heart condition, that he might die at any minute. He went to Irene for advice. He loved Jennifer but he needed Irene in a different way. I guess you might say David was a restless and dissatisfied man."

We paused. The night was very still.

"It has always struck me," I said, "that after *Gone With the Wind,* after he had fallen in love with Jennifer Jones, *her* career itself became for David a work of art, with *Duel in the Sun* as its savage high point."

"I can only tell you this," Howard responded. "David loved Jennifer very much. He could never duplicate *Gone With the Wind.* In a way, he lived through Jennifer; because there was nothing left for him to accomplish, he tried to accomplish things through her, by means of her."

And I remember sitting in his Hollywood apartment with Lee Garmes, who had worked on *Duel in the Sun.* He told me of his early days with Tom Ince and the battles with the Aitken brothers, of how when he worked with David he waited days to get certain shots, certain subtle lighting effects for *Duel.* If *Gone With the Wind* was the culmination of Selznick's life as a filmmaker, *Duel in the Sun* was his most eloquently personal expression of the emotional cataclysms which consumed his soul. At a story conference in the wee hours with Dore Shary and Daniel O'Shea, filled with dreams of how to make the picture, David confided, "I know that when I die, the stories will read, 'David O. Selznick, producer of *Gone With the Wind,* died today.' I'm determined to leave them something else to write about." He did.

Jennifer Jones was born Phylis Isley on March 2, 1919, at Tulsa, Oklahoma. Her parents operated the Isley Stock Company and starred in most of the theatricals the troupe put on. Later the two started a theater chain in Texas. As a child, Phylis was, according to all accounts, somewhat withdrawn, haunted by fears of inadequacy, and paralyzed at times by her powerful but inarticulate emotions. She involved herself in acting at the Edgemere Public School in Oklahoma City and continued to participate in school plays until she persuaded her father in 1938 to send her to the American Academy of Dramatic Arts in New York.

More than a few of her critics during her film career questioned why so retiring a woman should have entered acting at all. Most of the answers

Gregory Peck and Jennifer in an impassioned embrace.

Photo courtesy of ABC Pictures.

they supplied I find unsatisfying. Much of the resentment may have been engendered by Selznick's obsessive promotion of her. I might suggest that she symbolized in some ineffable way a dark and insistent urgency in David's psyche, and Jennifer's numerous screen roles under David's tutelage were so many soundings of that urgency.

At the academy, she fell nearly at once in love with Robert Walker, himself a student. They became engaged and together dropped out of school. The best they could manage were parts at Paul Gilmore's Cherry Lane Theater in Greenwich Village, earning fifty cents apiece for each performance. Phylis finally secured a lead through a family friend for a thirteen-week program on a Tulsa radio station. She was paid twenty-five dollars a week. Soon afterward she got Walker the lead opposite her. When the series ended, they were married on January 2, 1939.

The couple ventured to Hollywood on their honeymoon, and Phylis actually landed a heroine role at Republic studios on the basis of her looks. She played "the girl" in *The New Frontier* (Republic, 1939), a Three Mesquiteer's film in which Duke Wayne was Stony Brooke. She next played a supporting role in the serial *Dick Tracy's G-men* (Republic, 1939). From what I have been able to learn, Walker was extremely dependent on Phylis for moral support. They had come to Hollywood to further his career and he had been unsuccessful. He wanted children. Republic refused to pick up Phylis' option. They returned to New York.

In 1941 Robert, Jr., was born and in 1942 a second son, Michael. Between babies, Phylis modeled occasionally for the Powers Agency. Their living improved from "two dingy rooms on the fringe of Hell's Kitchen to six sunlit rooms in Garden City, Long Island," when Walker managed to land a steady part in a radio serial. Phylis continued to appear in Paul Gilmore theatricals, and an agent brought her to the attention of Kay Brown, Selznick's New York representative. Selznick auditioned her reading *Claudia* and arranged for Phylis to replace Dorothy McGuire during one Broadway performance of the play. Selznick was pleased and gave her a contract.

Under David's sponsorship, her name was changed to Jennifer Jones, and intensive training began. Selznick loaned her out to Fox, which billed her as a "discovery," for *The Song of Bernadette* in 1943, a role that made a virtue of Jennifer's quiet awkwardness and ingenuous innocence. She won the Academy Award as best actress. As Jennifer's star rose, her marriage dimmed. She had already decided to file for divorce when Selznick featured her together with Walker as the young wartime lovers in *Since You Went Away* (Selznick, 1944).

I cannot narrate Selznick's erratic and long-term courtship of Jennifer. *Duel in the Sun,* based on Niven Busch's tempestuous and lusty novel, marked the epitome of David's rapture and his passion, a work of art wrought in pain and celebration.

Controversy has surrounded King Vidor's contribution to the film. In a memo from April 1, 1946, David mentions specifically that as of that date Vidor was responsible for having directed 6,280 feet, whereas 7,739 additional feet existed with which he had nothing at all to do. Principally William Dieterle and then to a lesser extent Chester Franklin, William Cameron Menzies, and Josef von Sternberg all deserve partial credit for the finished product, as do second-unit directors Otto Brower and B. Reeves Eason. But when all is said and done, *Duel in the Sun,* however much a corporate enterprise on the surface and however much demeaned by subsequent censorship, is exactly what David O. Selznick intended it to be. If some of Irene had crept into Scarlett O'Hara, much of Selznick's conception of Jennifer Jones was blended into the half-breed girl, Pearl Chávez. The novel ends happily; David had the film end in tragedy.

King Vidor and David did not always agree on what they wanted from *Duel in the Sun*. Vidor at a preview of the finished picture (he had not previously seen it assembled) objected to the scene in which Gregory Peck as Lewt blows up a freight train and rides off whistling "I've Been Working on the Railroad." Vidor felt the sequence destroyed any sympathy the audience might have harbored for Lewt. David, who was shaving in the bathroom of his home while holding this conference with Vidor, turned to him and said, "I want to make Lewt the worst son of a bitch that's ever been on a motion picture screen, and I believe the train wreck scene will help me prove my point." The scene was one page in the completed screenplay. Breezy Eason, who had done the Atlanta fire for *Gone With the Wind*, took that page and expanded it to a fifteen-page shooting continuity. Eason had presketches of dozens of camera setups in terms of angle, distance, and movement. David approved each of them in turn.

Vidor acknowledged David's perfectionism in his own autobiography, *A Tree Is a Tree* (Harcourt, 1953). "When I was directing *Duel in the Sun*," he wrote, "Mr. Selznick would arrive at the studio around three or four in the afternoon with new scenes that he had written or rewritten during the night before. He would hand me the pages and ask that I read them. My comment was usually favorable but I would point out that I had been shooting these scenes since nine o'clock that morning and in another hour would complete the episode.

" 'But don't you think these versions are better?' Mr. Selznick would ask.

" 'Perhaps—a little,' I would reply.

" 'Would you mind showing me what you have done?'

"He was the boss, so I would summon the cast and we would re-enact the almost-completed sequence. David would say, 'I believe I like my version better. Would you please do it this way?' We would start at the beginning again and retake a sequence that showed slight improvement over the original. David would spare neither expense nor effort if he felt a scene could be improved by re-doing, no matter how infinitesimal the change might be."

It was the same with the musical score, but here David ran aground on Dimitri Tiomkin.

"I know dot seven udder composers have been fired before me," the Russian-born musician told David when they met at the Selznick studio at Culver City. "I insist on vun ting only: If you like my themes, you give me a run-of-de-picture contract."

David agreed. Tiomkin was instructed to come up with eleven distinct leitmotivs, Spanish Bit, love, desire themes, and an orgasm theme.

"Love themes I can write," Tiomkin assured David. "Desire, too. But orgasm! How do you score an orgasm?"

"Try!" David countered.

Tiomkin labored for weeks on the eleven themes. The orgasm music perplexed and eluded him. David did not want a sense of release or mystical union; he wanted violence, lust, hatred, passion, in the music.

When Tiomkin was ready, he rehearsed an orchestra of a dozen players and finally notified David's office. David was supposed to arrive at two o'clock in the afternoon; he arrived after midnight. Tiomkin, as he conducted, watched the flock of Selznick secretaries over his shoulder; they in turn watched Selznick. David liked what he heard and placed Tiomkin under contract.

In a memo on August 28, 1946, David told Tiomkin, addressing him as Timmy: "The quality of music, as I am sure I needn't point out to you, is not wrapped up solely in the size of an orchestra, by any means; and the temptation to excessive orchestration and distracting tracks, in the scoring of pictures, is aggravated in many cases by the use of too large an orchestra, according to my observation. . . ." The reprimand was warranted. Tiomkin was polishing his score at the Goldwyn studio with an orchestra that included forty-one drummers and a one-hundred-voice chorus.

For six months David argued and fought with Tiomkin, on and off when he had time, about the orgasm theme. David presumably couldn't get his point across, and Tiomkin thought Selznick *ein bisschen meschugge*. What Timmy ended up with was flageolets alternating with cellos combined with trombones and the rhythm of a handsaw cutting through wood. David had Jennifer's love scene with Gregory Peck screened while Tiomkin played back his orgasm music. After going through it several times, David concluded that it still wasn't right.

"Meestair Selznick," the Russian cried, caught between exasperation and despair, "vot is troubling you? Vot don't you like about it?"

"I like it," David said, "but it isn't orgasm music." Then David used a vulgar Yiddish word. "It's not *shtump*."

Tiomkin flew at David. He yelled at him in Anglo-Saxon, that even if David didn't do it that way, that's the way Tiomkin did it, and to him, Tiomkin, that was the kind of music that described doing it. David broke into laughter. Pressures from banks to get the picture into release so they could get the money they had advanced David were already heavy upon him. Knowing the orgasm music was wrong and yet cognizant that in general Tiomkin had given his best, he released the film. Now, years later, the orgasm music jars. It rises not to ecstasy but to ridicule.

The reader may wonder why this should be so. The truth of the matter is that while David's mind was clearly fixed on his vision of what the picture must ultimately be, the talent through which he sought to work his ends was each intent on a personal and very private conception of what he himself wanted. Personalities clashed continuously because each was devoted to his own career quite to the same extent that David was determined on making the finest film he possibly could.

Authenticity was an obsession with David. Every costume and every prop were submitted to exhaustive research by a special department to verify that they existed in the West during the 1880s. David even hired a Beverly Hills bartender to see that the liquor was poured right and that it was the right color. All of this coupled with David's constant script changes nettled King Vidor to an incredible degree. David became impatient with Vidor when he didn't agree with a revision and would occasionally lose his temper.

When the company was on location for many long weeks in the Arizona desert, members of the troupe began to grumble that the picture would never be completed. David shot off memos to Vidor from a hotel room in Tucson, visiting the set in the afternoons to see how his instructions had been carried out. One day as Vidor was filming the climactic scene in which Lewt and Pearl, having mortally wounded one another, die in each other's arms, David was on the set. Vidor rehearsed the sequence while David went off to a trailer to work. Hours later when David returned, Vidor had altered all the setups they had agreed on together. David reproved Vidor publicly, charging that the changes had cost a senseless $25,-000.

Vidor closed his script and rose from his director's chair. He remarked quietly to David, "You can take this picture and shove it."

The company gazed in stunned silence as Vidor walked to his limousine and stepped inside. He told the driver to return to Tucson. The black car went off across the desert. For eight miles the road stretched, hot and dusty, in a straight line. When, finally, the limousine disappeared over a hill in the distance, David dismissed the company. William Dieterle was imported from Hollywood to finish the picture.

Casting for *Duel in the Sun* was ingenious. "I am under the impression," Selznick said in a memo of April 26, 1945, "that the combination of Jones, Peck, and Cotten is a tremendously powerful one." *Duel* was in various stages of production from March 1945 to November 1946. The Gallup poll indicated that Jennifer Jones was the fastest rising actress on the Hollywood scene. She appeared to good advantage with Joseph Cotten in *Love Letters* (Paramount, 1945), which William Dieterle directed.

Although he was in the end dissatisfied with his contribution, David contracted Josef von Sternberg as lighting director for Jennifer, using many of the same astounding effects that had made Marlene Dietrich such a cinema queen at Paramount in the thirties. Jennifer's make-up was very complicated and required two hours to put on.

Gregory Peck had become a rage with women resulting from his role in *Spellbound* (United Artists, 1945), opposite Ingrid Bergman, which

David's company produced. Lionel Barrymore and Lillian Gish were united for the first time in a Western since they had worked together for D. W. Griffith in the teens; D.W. himself met Lillian's train when she arrived in Hollywood. Probably of the entire cast, these two handled their roles with the greatest depth of understanding and dramatic sensitivity. Walter Huston was signed for a four-day stint as "The Sin Killer," a role nearly satirical when compared to his unforgettable portrayal of the Reverend Davidson in *Rain* (United Artists, 1932), but which incited religious groups nonetheless. Huston's agent demanded $40,000 for his appearance. David agreed, provided Huston remained available for ten weeks at $4,000 a week. David ended up paying him more for overtime.

Harry Carey, who had made *The Devil Horse* (Mascot, 1932) with *Duel*'s second-unit director, Otto Brower, a serial shot on location in Arizona, had a strong supporting role, as did Charles Bickford, the latter

Lillian Gish, Lionel Barrymore, Joseph Cotten, and Jennifer Jones in an early scene from *Duel in the Sun*.

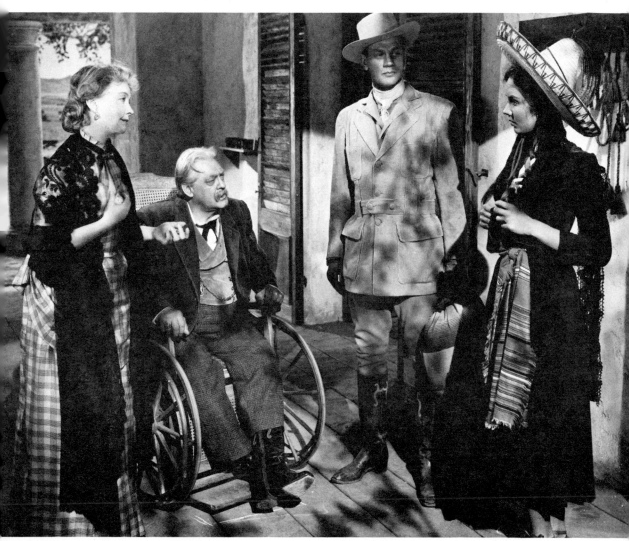

giving a touching performance. Herbert Marshall inspired the proper amount of pathos as Pearl's father.

Duel in the Sun had an intricate plot. After Herbert Marshall is hanged for shooting his wife and her lover, Sidney Blackmer, his daughter Pearl goes to live with Lillian Gish. Lillian is married to Lionel Barrymore, who, as Senator McCanles, owns a million acres known as Spanish Bit and has two sons, Joseph Cotten and Gregory Peck. Cotten comes to reject Pearl after a time; Peck takes up with her. However, he will not marry her. Cotten and the Senator have a falling out over the railroad's right of way and he is banished. Peck shoots Charles Bickford when Bickford becomes engaged to marry Pearl. This makes him an outlaw. The Senator protects him. Peck and Pearl carry on their tempestuous love affair until the final, climactic scene, when, unable to live with each other and unable to live without each other, they shoot each other to death in the hills.

David had formerly been releasing his pictures through United Artists, but a dispute with Mary Pickford and Charlie Chaplin led him to break his relations with the company. He founded the Selznick Releasing Organization to distribute *Duel in the Sun,* and within a matter of weeks he had branch offices in some thirty cities. *Duel* had the most streamlined selling campaign in motion picture history until that time and was masterminded by Paul MacNamara, a former managing editor of *Cosmopolitan.* "This is a lousy picture," MacNamara counseled David. "The critics will knock the hell out of it, and the word of mouth will kill you. You've got to play it off as fast as you can."

David may have been hurt by MacNamara's evaluation, but he followed his proposals. MacNamara's plan was for multiple openings in the same city preceded by a saturation all-media advertising campaign. The technique worked. *Duel* grossed $750,000 in New York during its first five days. It had a $17-million world-wide gross.

It may amuse the reader to learn in view of subsequent trends in motion pictures that critics and religious leaders were outraged by the supposed immorality of *Duel in the Sun* and Jennifer's "undue if not indecent exposure." Howard Hughes, whose film *The Outlaw* had inspired such outrage upon its issue by United Artists in 1943 because of its blatant sexual appeal, had daringly chosen to reissue it. His picture was immediately classed with David's as demonstrating a danger to youth. "The important issue here is not whether Selznick has a moral picture or an offensive picture," *The Nation* defended David in an editorial, "but whether a small segment of the population is to impose its standards on all the rest— whether one group has the right to decide for everyone what is right or wrong." But who ever listens to reason in these matters? Archbishop John J. Cantwell, of Los Angeles, forbade Catholics "with a free conscience" to attend the film, and, in protest, the archdiocese boycotted *all* motion pictures for a month. "With a big releasing organization behind him—or an endless bankroll like Hughes'—" *Photoplay* summed up David's dilemma, "Selznick would have had force with which to fight back. As an individual, he is in a practically impossible situation. Defiance may lose him everything. Yet, if he waits too long he may also lose everything." MacNamara demanded for success mass bookings in good theaters in prime markets. David yielded to pressure. He mutilated *Duel in the Sun*.

The Catholics praised his voluntary action. But the industry at large and the critics in particular condemned *Duel* as crass exploitation and a bold attempt to cash in on sex at the box office.

"I really think, Mac," David told MacNamara in a memo on August 13, 1947, when it was all over, "that I have got to prepare to spend a great deal of money . . . on the regaining of my personal position as it was before *Duel*. . . . I am not in the least criticizing what we did on *Duel*, for on the contrary, and as I have often said, I think the campaign was tremendous, was a great credit to you, and was what the picture needed. However, there was a price, and a heavy one for it . . . for even if I am wrong in exaggerating the extent of the loss to my position, there is the matter of family to think of, and it is also a fact that if I think the damage has been done, it must affect my state of mind and my work. . . ."

Time has exonerated David. He was dealt with harshly for having made *Duel in the Sun*. Because he was an infinitely sensitive man, the critical opprobrium, and not the picture's profitability, stayed with him and crippled in a permanent way his confidence in himself in later creative endeavors. It is tragic that this should have been so, for the moral vision of *Duel* was every bit as poignant in its way as that of *Gone With the Wind*, and its perspectives on life were almost identical. Both films, it seems to me, say repeatedly what only great suffering could have taught David: that powerful emotions and above all passion can work fabulous ends and achieve staggering effects, but so little understood or controlled—as in each of us, they are—everyone loses inexorably in the end.

47 / HOWARD HAWKS

Howard Hawks was born at Goshen, Indiana, on May 30, 1896. He began in the motion picture industry as a prop boy at Paramount, graduated to film editing and finally the Writing Department before becoming a director. He began to build a strong reputation in the thirties and was associated with Howard Hughes for a time. Hawks gave Walter Brennan his first important part in *The Barbary Coast* (Goldwyn, 1935). Brennan went on to win an Academy Award for *Come and Get It* (United Artists, 1936) and followed it with awards for *Kentucky* (20th-Fox, 1938) and *The Westerner* (Goldwyn, 1940).

"When I was casting *Barbary Coast*," Hawks once recalled, "they brought in Walter Brennan and I looked at him and laughed. I said, 'Mr. Brennan, did they give you some lines?' And he said, 'Yeah.' I said, 'Do you know them?' And he said, "With or without?' I said, 'With or without what?' He said, 'Teeth.' I laughed again and said, 'Without.' He turned around and read the lines, and I said, 'You're hired.' When we were going to do *Red River*, there was one line in the scenario, it said, 'The cook's name was Groot.' He said, 'What are we going to do?' Didn't worry me. I said, 'Remember how we met, that "with or without teeth"? Well, I got an idea that you're gonna lose your teeth in a poker game with an Indian. And every night he makes you give them back.' 'Oh,' he said, 'we can't do that.' I said, 'Yes, we can.' "

"I looked forward to doing *Red River*," Walter Brennan was quoted at the time of production, "not only because it is a fine story and has a fine part for me, but because Howard Hawks is a great director, and I shall never forget what he did for me in the past."

The Indian who wins Brennan's teeth was none other than Chief Yowlachie, with whom the reader is no doubt by this time familiar, and who had made the first two-color Western, *Wanderer of the Wasteland* (Paramount, 1924), which starred Jack Holt and Noah Beery. Pidge Beery was cast in *Red River*, as was Harry Carey, Sr., and Dobie Carey.

Hawks chose a sixty-mile stretch of land south of Tucson for a location. For approximately $150,000, he had a camp built to house about four hun-

Duke Wayne and Montgomery Clift in a sequence from *Red River*. It was the first on a five-picture contract Clift had signed with Howard Hawks.

Photo courtesy of United Artists Corporation.

dred persons. The mobile fleet, to attend to the picture people and the nine thousand cattle, consisted of five water wagons, eight trucks used to transport the cattle, and twenty trucks, three buses, and several other assorted vehicles for the movement of crew and equipment. The feed bill for the livestock amounted to $20,000. The final negative cost of the film was $2,800,000, and it had a domestic gross of $3,976,473.86.

John Ford always contended that *Stagecoach* made Duke Wayne a star, but *Red River* proved him to be an actor. "Wayne had done, probably, fifty cheap Westerns where he didn't have to do anything," Hawks remarked in conversation. "He read the script for *Red River* and said, 'I don't know whether I want to play an old man.' I said, 'You're *gonna* be an old man pretty soon, and you ought to get used to it. And you also better start playing characters instead of that junk you've been playing.' So he said, 'How do I show that I'm old?' and I said, 'Did you ever see me get up? Just do it that way.' So he did it, and he saw the film and he said, 'Lord, I'm *old*.' He didn't have to do a lot of silly things, either."

Hawks signed Broadway actor Montgomery Clift to a five-picture contract, beginning with *Red River*. Clift was enthusiastic about his part and waited with anxious anticipation for what he felt to be his big scene, when he takes the herd away from Duke and leaves Duke wounded and stranded on the trail. After the scene was shot, Clift went to Hawks and complained that it hadn't turned out to be so big, after all. Wayne never looked at him. While Clift talked, Duke continued to stare over his saddle into the distance, leaning against his horse with his back more or less to Clift. Finally, Duke said succinctly, "I'm gonna kill you." Hawks laughed and chided Clift for thinking that he could ever best an old pro like Duke in any scene.

Duke played Thomas Dunson, the man who led the first cattle drive on the Chisholm Trail. Love interest was at a minimum. At the beginning of the picture, Duke leaves his girl with a wagon train massacred by Indians. Young Montgomery Clift escapes and throws himself and his cow in with Duke, Duke's bull, and Walter Brennan. Duke claims a vast stretch of land and begins his cattle ranch. Cut to fifteen years later, following the Civil War, and Texas is starving. Duke starts out on the drive to get top prices for his cattle. He becomes increasingly tyrannical along the way, terrified lest they don't make it, brutal to deserters. It was a finely etched psychological portrait. Clift, his adopted son, rebels and takes the cattle in the direction of Abilene, instead of Kansas City where Duke was heading. Duke rounds up a gang and rides after Clift, the men, and the herd. He catches Clift at the railhead. On the way, Clift has fallen in love with Joanne Dru. She prevents the two from killing each other, and the story ends happily.

John Ireland was drunk or late for call much of the time, so Hawks cut his role to almost nothing. Howard Hughes, on the other hand, nursing an old grudge against Hawks and an even greater one against United Artists, now that he was running RKO, decided that he didn't like the gunfight between Wayne and Clift at the conclusion of *Red River,* and he promptly began a lawsuit. Hughes's claim was that Hawks lifted the episode out of *The Outlaw.* It was nonsense, but United Artists agreed to re-edit the release prints, and that is the way the picture survives.

Although Duke has made a number of Westerns with Hawks, *Red River* is undoubtedly his best. Hawks liked using Russell Harlan, Pop Sherman's cameraman, on most of his Westerns. He employed him on *Red River* and again for *Rio Bravo,* which he directed with Duke for release in 1959. *Bravo* was such a successful picture that Hawks and Duke remade variations on it twice, in *El Dorado* (Paramount, 1967) and *Rio Lobo* (National General, 1970). However, after *Rio Lobo,* Hawks was no longer inclined to make any more Westerns with Wayne, complaining about his age. "Wayne had a hard time getting on and off his horse," he observed. "He can't move like a big cat the way he used to. He has to hold his belly in; he's a different kind of person."

Duke Wayne in readiness, holding his specially made Winchester which he has had since *Stagecoach.* The scene is from *Rio Bravo.*

Photo courtesy of Warner Brothers.

Walter Brennan as he appeared in *Rio Bravo,* telling Duke Wayne repeatedly, "There just ain't no pleasin' yuh!"

Rio Bravo was intended to be an answer to the premises about the West set forth in Stanley Kramer's *High Noon* (United Artists, 1952). The film had a very fragmented script, and most of it was made up as the cast went along, the narrative line as a result being more sprawling than is customary, even in a Hawks picture. Duke played a sheriff who arrests a town tough. The location was the Old Tucson set in Arizona. Dean Martin played Duke's former deputy, who became a worthless drunk over a woman, and now reclaims himself during the moment of crisis when the tough's brother and his men threaten Duke and the preservation of law and order. Walter Brennan, playing a cripple, also stands by Duke.

Rather than being without supporters, Duke has to fight them off. Ward Bond volunteers, is rejected, but ends up shot anyway. Ricky Nelson was cast as a young gunman who finally comes out on Duke's side and manages to sing a song with Dean Martin. Angie Dickinson is the feminine interest.

She is in love with Duke and wins him by the fade. John Russell is the resentful brother. He resorts to kidnapping Dean and bargaining for his brother's freedom. Duke uses dynamite and gunpowder to smoke Russell and his gang out and brings peace.

Both *Red River* and *Rio Bravo* have strong psychological ingredients that in another director's hands might have been built into films of intense and sustained suspense. Hawks saw it otherwise. In *Red River* he had his chance to delve into character, the psychology of the pioneer and the intimate and tender relationships between hard, determined men. In *Rio Bravo* he exploited similar themes.

While Ford was frequently given credit for *Red River*—and accepted it graciously, even with a grin—Ford could never have made either *Red River* or *Rio Bravo*. Hawks has no sense of the family as a basic unit. His relationships are more nebulous than this, more the reflection of men striving toward some ideal of moderate behavior than spiritual fulfillment. Romantic love goes begging in Hawks's Westerns; nor are the relations between men and women conceived as being nearly as constructive and reinforcing to social progress and the unity of men bent upon a common goal. Hawks's method has always been to concentrate on personalities, seldom on acting, and he has managed, within the parameters of this philosophy, to turn out Westerns that balance action with meaning but avoiding the pitfalls of what some critics term social significance.

48 / JOHN FORD AND THE INDIAN WARS

I am in the very midst of my story. John Ford's cavalry trilogy (two of which I wish to concentrate on here) is essentially optative in mood. But I must pause, even if it is only for a moment; the winning of the West, and its parallel winning on the screen lived through by later generations, has a rather surprising outcome, given the premises and values which apparently inspired it. I heard John Ford comment in old age: "If our ancestors could come back and see us as we are today, they'd vomit." I do not doubt he meant it.

John Ford's belief was in people, and it was individual people he knew best. This belief began to wither with the passing years. The winning of the West, when it stopped on the frontier and continued on the screen,

didn't seem to be going in the direction expected; it was slowly winding down from unbounded enthusiasm to a sort of hypnotic despair. Memories, instead of being cherished, became bitter; progress became a hollow drum that beat mechanically. I must anticipate. By the time my narrative reaches the seventies, these images of the past will only shimmer in twilight; darkness will swirl and eddy everywhere. Faith will vanish, and very nearly hope. It was Ford's peculiar fate that he embodied almost all of these tendencies in the course of his long career.

Once when Ford was still working at 20th Century-Fox, Darryl F. Zanuck, who was in charge of production, came on the set of one of Ford's pictures, accompanied by the picture's producer. Ford summoned the entire technical crew and all the players on the set and introduced them to the producer.

"You'd better say hello to this fellow," he said. "He's the producer on this picture and this is the last time you're going to see him. And as for that fellow standing next to him"—here he motioned toward Zanuck—"he's a big shot who ought to take that riding quirt he carries and stick it up his ass."

Everyone was shocked. The producer returned to the set a time or two, but Ford would always stop the action, inform the players to take a break, turn and smile at the producer. Finally, rather irked, the man asked Ford why the action was always stopped when he entered.

"That's simply courtesy," Ford replied. "If I came up to your office and you were busy on the telephone, with secretaries running around, dictating letters, I would feel insulted if you didn't clear all those people out so we might talk. It's the same for me. I shouldn't go on working when you're here, out of respect for your position."

I have asked a number of people around Hollywood how Ford got away with it, given the studio system within which he worked. The answer I received was invariably the same. Ford's pictures generally made money and won awards; no one in his right mind messes with success.

Ford's first military trilogy was his three films dealing with the colonial British in India, *Black Watch* (Fox, 1929), *Wee Willie Winkie* (20th-Fox, 1937), and *Four Men and a Prayer* (20th-Fox, 1938). In *Winkie* Victor McLaglen played precisely the same role he did as an American in the later cavalry trilogy.

Fort Apache began the cycle. Duke Wayne was in all three of the films. Duke was very concerned about his performance and rather uneasy about it, so he worked out an elaborate group of facial and bodily signals with Paul Fix, who was also cast in *Fort Apache*, with Fix standing on the sidelines prompting him. Ford soon discovered what was going on. There was a scene in which Fix was supposed to fall heavily on some crushed rocks. Ford shot the scene again and again. Fix was getting badly bruised. He

Henry Fonda and Shirley Temple in a scene from *Fort Apache*.

protested. He refused to do the scene again. Ford bellowed at him that if he didn't do it again he would never work on another Ford picture. Fix walked off in a huff. True to his word, Ford excluded Fix from his casting; he also got rid of an unwanted assistant director at the same time.

Fort Apache was budgeted at $2.8 million with a seventy-day shooting schedule. Ford brought it in for $2.1 million in forty-four days. Henry Fonda was cast in a Custer-type role as Lieutenant Colonel Owen Thursday. Duke played Captain Kirby York. Shirley Temple, grown up now, was Philadelphia in love with John Agar, who has three rather questionable guardians in the form of Ward Bond, Victor McLaglen, and Jack Pennick. They are noncommissioned officers. Their response to Agar's graduation from officers' training is to spank him. Mae Marsh, familiar from her work with D. W. Griffith, was given a character role, and George O'Brien came out of retirement to play Captain Sam Collingwood, whose term of service is about to expire. Dick Foran was cast as Sergeant Quincannon.

The plot involved a graphic picture of army life on the frontier during the time of the Indian wars. Henry Fonda is a man convinced of his own importance and the manifest destiny the white man has in keeping the Indians in check. Grant Withers is a crooked trader, supplying the Indians with whiskey and rifles. Fonda hastens to bring the Indians to terms. His arrogance and unwillingness to listen to their justifiable objections determines him to force acquiescence. Duke resists and Fonda threatens him with court-martial. Stirred up to a pitch of violence, Fonda leads his troop in a disastrous campaign against the Apaches and is wiped out. The military annals praise him highly for his courage in the face of overwhelming odds, although his strategy was the sheerest folly.

She Wore a Yellow Ribbon came next and was filmed in color, also for RKO release.

"That lucky son of a bitch," Duke Wayne recalled. "We were on location in Monument Valley. Ford always was lucky, on almost all of his pictures. But he had the entire troop out to shoot a sequence where we were going to an outstation. The sky became overcast and one of those sudden desert storms broke, lightning, rain. Ford kept on shooting. 'Let's get this on film,' he said." Winton C. Hoch was the cinematographer. He received an Academy Award for his photography, for the most part a result of this happenstance. Duke shook his head in disbelief. "Just sheer Irish luck."

Dobie Carey was in *Ribbon*. Howard Hawks had used him in *Red River*. Harry Carey was dead now. Dobie wasn't certain he wanted to be billed as Junior any more. Why not just Dobie Carey? He went to Duke. Duke advised him to let the matter rest with the old man. Ford billed him as Harry Carey, Jr. He rode Dobie relentlessly for days, making a fool out of him at every occasion. Dobie again went to Duke.

Duke as Major Brittles looks out over the mist-covered expanse of Monument Valley in *She Wore a Yellow Ribbon.*

Photo courtesy of RKO General.

After all, Duke had originally counseled him on whether or not to follow in his father's wake. But, Duke recommended, keep a sideline; he told Dobie he wasn't very good looking. Then Duke smiled. Now Dobie wanted to quit. He had had enough of Ford's ragging and didn't care if he never worked in pictures again. Duke dissuaded him from thinking anything of the kind. He explained that Ford was trying to rile him to get a better performance. And Ford was successful.

Duke played Captain Nathan Brittles. Joanne Dru was cast as George O'Brien's daughter, the love interest in the film, with Dobie and John Agar vying for her hand and Agar winning it. Duke is up for retirement; O'Brien is his superior officer. *Ribbon* tells of Duke's last important mission. Brittles is sixty; it was the second time in as many years that Duke played a man many years older than he really was.

"Ford never let sentiment get maudlin," he once commented. "There was this scene in which the troop gives me a silver watch. I'm supposed to brush away a tear as I read the inscription. It could have been terrible. But Pappy told me how to play it. He had me take out a pair of spectacles and make quite a thing out of reading the inscription. I'm rather embarrassed about the spectacles. The scene came off because of those spectacles."

Duke goes out to his wife's grave and talks to her. It is an old ritual. Harry Woods is a crooked Indian agent, trading rifles to the Indians. He's shot by them when his price proves more than they are willing to pay. Duke wants to effect a peace between the bluecoats and the red men. He rides into the Indian encampment and parleys with ancient John Big Tree. They talk about the stupidity of war and how the young crave excitement. Their time is past. There is great dignity in their friendship. That night, Duke and the detachment stampede the Indians' horses, and war is prevented. Duke is made a scout attached to the fort. Tom Tyler, already crippled by the arthritis which would curtail his career, was given a character role.

Rio Grande (Republic, 1950) concluded the cycle. It had a plot rather similar to Duke's later *McLintock* (United Artists, 1963) insofar as Maureen O'Hara played Duke's estranged wife who comes back to him because of their child's loyalty, only for her to rediscover her love is not dead. Claude Jarman, Jr., played Duke's son, who fails mathematics at the Point,

Duke and Pappy next to a wide-angle-lens camera during production of *How the West Was Won,* directed by John Ford. Duke was playing General Sherman in the Civil War. Both Duke and Pappy were marked to be victims of cancer.

Photo courtesy of *Views & Reviews* magazine.

turns around and enlists in the cavalry, and ends up serving under Duke. Maureen O'Hara comes West to try to tempt their son back East. She isn't successful, and the son proves to be valiant in battle against marauding Apaches. Victor McLaglen played Sergeant Quincannon. Because of Duke's contractual arrangements with Republic, Herbert J. Yates ended up the producer for this film and for *The Quiet Man* (Republic, 1952).

Ford made another attempt at a cavalry picture with *The Horse Soldiers* (United Artists, 1959) and even cast Hoot Gibson in a supporting role. The setting was a campaign against Confederate lines during the Civil War. It was nowhere as well made as the entries in the trilogy.

Cheyenne Autumn (Warner's, 1964) was, according to Ford, his attempt to even the score for the many pictures he had made in which the Indians were treated as villains. It was the moving and powerful story of the fifteen-hundred-mile trek of the Cheyenne nation from the desert reservation they were given by an indifferent government back to their old stamping grounds. It was a sad and beautiful picture, with stunning photography and a sustaining poetry of composition. Some critics find it slow; I do not. Others have complained that Ford cast Victor Jory, Gilbert Roland, Sal Mineo, and Dolores Del Rio as Indians, rather than using real Indians. This is a silly comment. Still others have remarked that the sequence with James Stewart as Wyatt Earp and Arthur Kennedy as Doc Holliday does not fit into the texture of the story. But it belongs nonetheless. It is a satiric parallel to the ever-darkening tragedy of the red men as their number dwindles, as they are subjected to every sort of inhumanity, as they become split and fragmented against themselves. The tragedy and melancholy of this film rise to delicate elegy.

Peter Bogdanovich once asked Ford about the quip in *The Man Who Shot Liberty Valance* (Paramount, 1962) that "when the legend becomes a fact, print the legend." Did Ford agree?

"Yes," Ford replied, "because I think it's good for the country. We've had a lot of people who were supposed to be great heroes, and you know damn well they weren't. But it's good for the country to have heroes to look up to. Like Custer—a great hero. Well, he wasn't. Not that he was a stupid man—but he did a stupid job that day. Or Pat Garrett, who's a great Western hero. He wasn't anything of the sort—supposed to have shot Billy the Kid—but actually one of the posse did. On the other hand, of course, the legend always had some foundation."

John Ford's lifetime odyssey was to restore faith by probing into the past. He wanted to believe. When he couldn't any more, he retired. But, strange to say, even when his faith was gone, he hung on relentlessly to legends and myths for the hope they vouchsafed. His unhappiness never retreated utterly to what Jean-Paul Sartre has termed *le néant*. This had to await the next generation of filmmakers.

Perpetuation of
a Tradition

I had occasion, in a previous chapter, to comment on Harry Joe Brown's association with Randolph Scott at 20th Century-Fox. Brown subsequently put together a package featuring a Zane Grey story, *Twin Sombreros* (Harper's, 1941), and Randolph Scott, long identified with Zane Grey Westerns, as the star; he sold the idea to Columbia and the picture was released as *The Gunfighters* (Columbia, 1947). The film proved such a success that Brown and Scott formed a partnership with the idea of making an entire series of medium-budget Westerns in color for distribution by either Columbia Pictures or Warner Brothers.

Coroner Creek was released in 1948, based on a novel by Western writer Luke Short, pseudonym for Frederick Dilley Glidden. Marguerite Chapman played opposite Scott; Sally Eilers, who had been married for many years to Harry Joe Brown, was given a role as the second feminine lead. The story opens with a stage robbery in which a white man in buckskins leads a band of Indians. Most of the passengers are killed, and the white man shoots most of his Indian allies afterward. A girl is on board who kills herself with a knife. Charles Stevens, a surviving Indian, puts Scott on the trail; Scott is determined to kill the white man.

The quest brings Scott to Coroner Creek and Marguerite Churchill's hotel. Scott meets George MacReady's wayward wife. Forrest Tucker and a gang of toughs work for MacReady. MacReady and Scott do not hit it off. Sally Eilers hires Randy in her fight against MacReady. Tucker and his men capture Randy, and in a vicious fight Tucker stomps on Randy's trigger finger. When Randy gets the upper hand, he stomps on Tucker's trigger finger. The simple morality of the film is summed up when Marguerite Churchill reminds Randy that "vengeance is mine" and Scott returns "an eye for an eye." The girl on the stage was on her way to marry Randy. In a final showdown, MacReady, trying to escape from Scott, falls on the knife Randy's girl originally used to kill herself.

Canadian Pacific (Columbia, 1949) was a large-scale Western not produced by Brown. Lewis J. Rachmil, who had long worked with Pop Sherman, was the producer, Edwin L. Marin the director. It was a picture well

Randolph Scott and Marguerite Chapman in a publicity still from *Coroner Creek*.

in the tradition of the Sherman Westerns with a big opening, an indifferent middle, and a terrific finish. Jane Wyatt played a pacifist nurse. Scott, employed by the railroad, is pitted against Victor Jory and his gang seeking to retard progress. Chief Yowlachie led the Indians.

Man in the Saddle (Columbia, 1951) began the Brown-Scott Westerns in earnest. Based on a novel by Ernest Haycox, André de Toth directed. Big Boy Williams was cast as Randy's chum. The picture was filmed on location at the Prudential studio, as was *Coroner Creek*. The high point of the picture was an extended fight between Scott and John Russell. *Santa Fe* (Columbia, 1951), another Brown-Scott entry, cast Randy as an ex-Confederate soldier who becomes involved in the building of the Santa Fe Railroad. Randy's brothers, disenchanted, join Roy Roberts in his efforts to hinder construction by opening a gambling concession at the end of track. The plot was but a variation of *Union Pacific* (Paramount, 1939) on a smaller budget.

Man in the Saddle was memorable for its night photography. *Hangman's Knot* (Columbia, 1952) excelled in the recording of a sequence photographed inside a burning shack. Randy played the leader of a special troop of Confederate soldiers preying upon Yankee gold shipments who suddenly become outlaws when they commit a robbery unwittingly after the Civil War has ended. Special effects were responsible for some stirring shots of lightning felling trees during a storm.

Jim Kitses, a British film critic, has written a book called *Horizons West* (Indiana University Press, 1969) in which he appraises the work of three directors of modern Westerns, Anthony Mann, Sam Peckinpah, and Budd Boetticher. Boetticher first directed Scott in *Seven Men from Now* (Warner's, 1956), a Batjac production with which Harry Joe Brown was not concerned. Burt Kennedy, however, did the screenplay, and William Clothier, Duke Wayne's long-time cameraman, was the cinematographer. Boetticher went on to direct Scott in several of the later entries in the Brown-Scott series for Columbia. Randy was aging on the screen, and yet still able to play Westerner roles. He was compared physically to William S. Hart, particularly in the austerity of his visage.

Kitses attributes too much to Boetticher and too little to Harry Joe Brown and Randy Scott in describing philosophically the kind of personality Randy projected on the screen, but the assessment is still valid. "In general," Kitses writes, "the Boetticher hero as created by Scott can be said to possess (or be moving towards) a great serenity, the knowledge that we are fundamentally alone, that nothing lasts, that what matters in the face of all this is 'living the way a man should.' Especially in the later films the hero has had it all—love, position, security—and lost it all. This makes the figure oddly anachronistic, a man who continues to assert values out of an image of himself that has its roots in the past."

The type of hero Randy played in the entries directed by Boetticher as

Bill Elliott and H. B. Warner are held at gunpoint, Trevor Bardette in the foreground on the right. Bardette and Elliott had been on opposite sides a decade before in *Overland with Kit Carson*. This scene is from *Hellfire*.

Photo courtesy of National Telefilm Associates.

well as the others was a man who endures through intelligent calculation and an overriding capacity for self-control in the face of adversity. This holds true in *The Tall T* (Columbia, 1957), *Decision at Sundown* (Columbia, 1957), *Buchanan Rides Alone* (Columbia, 1959), *Ride Lonesome* (Columbia, 1959), and the last Scott-Boetticher collaboration, *Comanche Station* (Columbia, 1960). Harry Joe Brown, however, was the moving force behind these pictures, and it was he who brought both Burt Kennedy and Budd Boetticher together on the productions.

A similar approach to Western heroism was projected in the Bill Elliott Westerns, beginning in the late forties with entries like *Hellfire*. In fact, this picture was almost a conscious effort to recapture not only William S. Hart's taciturnity but his zealous religious spirit. Marie Windsor played a woman renegade, Doll Brown, whom Elliott pursues in an attempt to save her soul.

Elliott himself had a lot of production say in how *Hellfire* was made. Republic continued to star him in high-budget Westerns, and some of the earlier entries, like *The Fabulous Texan* (Republic, 1947), stand up even better than *Hellfire* does. In *Texan* Elliott and John Carroll played veterans returning to Texas after the Civil War only to find John Dekker taking over the territory and placing it under military rule for his own ends. There was a sadness and inwardness in Elliott's screen portrayals that complimented in its own way the quietism of Randolph Scott or the grim fortitude of Joel McCrea.

When his Republic contract expired, Bill went to Allied Artists where he made another series of black and white Westerns that paralleled the kind of pictures Randy Scott was making for Columbia release. *Bitter Creek* (Allied Artists, 1954) was one of the best entries, with Bill pitted against the kind of greed and power Randy Scott opposed in *Man in the Saddle*. Bill went about attaining a balance with the same tight-lipped determination he had when trailing with Doll Brown. Despite the somewhat increased budgets in the Elliott series for Allied Artists, and the company's other series with Wayne Morris, critics generally have come to consider these the last so-called B Westerns made for theatrical distribution, citing the Wayne Morris vehicle, *Two Guns and a Badge,* issued by Allied Artists on September 12, 1954, as the swan song of this whole class of films. Whatever the case, the gloominess of the heroes which Scott and Elliott projected more or less embodied the weariness of the genre, the altered, careworn face of the Westerner confronted with a changing world in which he had no real place. It was only a short step from this when Sam Peckinpah joined Joel McCrea with Randolph Scott in Randy's last Western, *Ride the High Country* (M-G-M, 1962), which further closed the options until one was reminded of a line from T. S. Eliot about the "burnt out ends of smoky days" and heroism itself became a lonely, isolated, and wholly personal retreat from the world.

50 / THE NEW EPICS

I

The reader may question my terming *The Ox-bow Incident* an epic. It is not an epic in the same sense that *The Iron Horse* or *The Covered Wagon* were. But I choose to call it this because while the events it depicts are not heroic, they are nonetheless indicative of the tradition, ideals, and character of the Westerner and the harsh justice by which the Westerner lived. The picture did not have an impressive box office, and even its reputation among critics has been reserved due to the sentimentality with which it concludes.

William Wellman directed. He was born on February 29, 1896, at Brookline, Massachusetts. In his early life he served in the French Foreign Legion and was a pilot with the Lafayette Escadrille during the Great War. He was then in the wool business in Boston. He went to Hollywood and played a juvenile in a Douglas Fairbanks picture before he was hired as a prop boy at Fox Film Corporation. He made his debut as a director with *The Man Who Won* (Fox, 1923), in which Ken Maynard had a walk-on. By the thirties he became an important director.

The Ox-bow Incident, based on a novel of that title by William Van Tilburg Clark, was the perfect opportunity for Wellman to set forth a serious social commentary on the folly of lynch law in the West and to provide an image of Western life that was anything but consistent with the escapism of the World War II period. Henry Fonda, who was assigned the lead in the film, felt the picture to be one of the few important vehicles he made after *The Grapes of Wrath* (20th-Fox, 1940). *Incident* was an examination of injustice precisely where justice was the most touted; it questioned the righteousness with which ordinary citizens banded together and were reduced to the lowest common intelligence among them.

As the story opens, Henry Fonda and his pard, Henry Morgan, ride into town and enter a saloon. There has been a lot of rustling going on. Word comes that a wrangler has been shot. A posse is formed. After some argument, the posse rides out, backed by magnificent panoramas. In time, they come upon three men camped near Ox-Bow. Dana Andrews, Anthony Quinn as a Mexican, and Francis Ford play the innocent victims. They are sentenced to hang by the mob. It is to occur at dawn.

Major Tetley, a phony Confederate officer played by Frank Conroy, forces his son to spur the horses out from under the three herders. Having finished their work, the mob is met by the sheriff and another posse. The mob is informed that the man who really did the shooting has been captured. Dejected, the mob rides back into town. Dana Andrews left behind a letter to his wife. In the novel this letter is never read. For the film Wellman arranged to have it read aloud by Henry Fonda when the men are congregated in the saloon that night, an experience necessarily less moving in actuality than if the contents had been withheld and left to the imagination.

Whatever its drawbacks, *The Ox-bow Incident* did establish the form of the psychological Western, just as *I Wake up Screaming* (20th-Fox, 1941)

The hanging of Dana Andrews, Francis Ford, and Anthony Quinn, in *The Ox-bow Incident*.

Photo courtesy of 20th Century-Fox Film Corporation.

more or less introduced the psychological detective story. The emphasis is never on the action, but only on the characters, on states of mind, with an amazing parallelism between physical setting and psychological tone. It began a trend whereby the mythology of the West was now presented in wholly new terms, a trend which reached its highest expression during the fifties.

II

The book *Focus on the Western* (Prentice-Hall, 1974), a collection of essays edited by Jack Nachbar and devoted to the Western cinema, contains an essay I wrote as an overview of seventy years of Western production and ends with an essay entitled, "Who Are Those Guys? The Movie Western During the TV Era," by Ralph Brauer. In his essay, Brauer writes, "Of the serious Westerns of the 'Fifties, *Shane* (Paramount, 1953), *The Gun-fighter* (20th-Fox, 1950) and *The Left-handed Gun* (Warner's, 1958) are usually cited as among the best. Jon Tuska of *Views & Reviews* said on his NET documentary 'They Went Thataway' that he thought *Shane* was *the* best Western. Perhaps it is indicative of our respective generations that Tuska picked for his choice what I consider a nostalgic vision, while I would pick the more violent *The Wild Bunch* (Warner's, 1969)."

In my own behalf, I should perhaps hasten to say that I did not claim that *Shane* was the best Western ever made. The inquiry put to me was, if I could choose one Western as being typical of the entire tradition of the Hollywood West and was leaving on a long trip so that I could only take one example, which one would it be? My answer to that was *Shane.* It still would be. Brauer calls *Shane* a nostalgic vision, and I agree. But it is less nostalgic than any number of Western melodramas which preceded it and attains a crude, poetic realism which was unheard-of before World War II with exceptions such as *The Ox-bow Incident.*

Alan Ladd's extremely short stature created no end of problems in camera setups which showed him at least on a level with, if not towering over, other principals in his films. His personality may not have been larger than life, as has been true of Clark Gable or Duke Wayne. He underplayed his part as the gunfighter in *Shane,* and what success he achieved in that picture is owed to the soft tonality of his portrayal. I do not believe that there is anything such as the *best* Western, but there is perfection in another realm, a fine embodiment of a tradition. And *Shane* evokes the pastoral mood of the Western, contrasted with sudden eruptions of violence. Jack Shaefer, who also wrote *Monte Walsh* (National General, 1970), was the author of the novel. The lyricism he attempted to infuse into the transition from ranching to sod-busting was what director George Stevens wanted to paint in unforgettable images on the screen. That he succeeded is attested by the enduring popularity of the film he produced. *Shane* uses Brandon deWilde as a point-of-view character, and nearly everything that happens is seen through his eyes. It is this which gives *Shane* its epical and nearly mythical qualities. Alan Ladd, in these terms, is conceived as an archangel, a savior, a man less in need of anything than the other characters, less attached to anything, and therefore incredibly free and self-possessed. Shane is a final resolution of the hero, passing from the human into the superhuman.

Like a messiah, Shane is first seen riding down a mountain into a fertile valley, coming upon a homestead owned by Van Heflin, his wife, Jean Arthur, and their son, Brandon deWilde. Emile Meyer wants to clear all the homesteaders out of the valley so that he can retain the free range for his herd. Heflin hires Shane, not as a gunman, but as a farm hand. On a trip to town, Shane becomes embroiled in an argument with Ben Johnson, which, on the next trip, leads to a terrific fistfight in the saloon, Shane joined by Heflin battling against almost all of Meyer's men and winning. Meyer next sends for a professional killer, demonically dressed in black, played by Jack Palance.

Brandon deWilde hero-worships Shane. Palance prods Elisha Cook, Jr., into an unfair gunfight. Palance's bullet causes Cook to fly several feet upon impact, probably the most realistic shooting filmed until that time. After Cook is buried, many of the homesteaders want to leave. Heflin talks them into staying. He intends to ride into town to face down Meyer and Palance himself. Shane has a terrible fistfight with him and only wins when he knocks him unconscious with his gun. Shane rides in instead, shooting Palance, Meyer, and Meyer's screen brother. DeWilde, who has followed Shane into town, wants Shane to stay, but Shane is deaf to the boy's entreaty. He rides away from the town, up the hills and into the mountains, DeWilde running after him and shouting and calling his name, which echoes and reverberates through the canyons and arroyos.

Henry King's *The Gunfighter* (20th-Fox, 1950), which starred Gregory Peck in the lead role Duke Wayne once wanted when the property was owned by Harry Cohn, of Columbia Pictures, presented a gunman as a real person with human emotions. Paul Newman's Billy the Kid in *The Left-handed Gun* (Warner's, 1958), which I spoke about in a previous chapter, depicted a gunman as a neurotic. Marlon Brando's *One-eyed Jacks* (Paramount, 1961) even introduced the possibility of homosexuality into the equation. George Stevens' *Shane* does none of these things; the viewer never really gets to know Shane. *Shane* is an enchanting parable populated by archetypal characters; it exists in a country and terrain that never ages and where time stands still. To me, it is a vision not merely of the past, but of the present and the future, a vision of how the world might have been and how it might be again; it has about it the enduring transfixion of the Greek legends.

Alan Ladd and Van Heflin in *Shane,* and above all the magnificent cloud formations which helped make George Stevens' picture both grand and nostalgic.

III

"I wrote the original story," John Ford once remarked about *The Wagon Master.* "Along with *The Fugitive* [RKO, 1947] and *The Sun Shines Bright* [Republic, 1953], I think *Wagon Master* came closest to being what I wanted to achieve."

Ford's persistent image of the agrarian dream here had its finest realization, although the film did not gross anywhere near expectations. He could contrast at last in dark relief the conflict between the builders and the destroyers which he felt marked the history of the people on the North American continent. It was best stated, perhaps, by Jeffery Richards in an article on "Ford's Lost World" in *Focus on Film,* a British film journal. "The cinema of John Ford," he wrote, "is a cinema of dreams and memories, luminous images tinged with an elegiac melancholy for a vanished, irrecoverable innocence, the innocence of Man and Society, of his hopes and his visions, which the course of history and progress and politics has doomed to unfulfillment."

Wagon Master opens to an express office robbery perpetrated by the Cleggs. Ben Johnson and Dobie Carey are horse traders. They are hired by Ward Bond and a group of Mormons to act as their guide over the unfamiliar country. The wagon train meets Alan Mowbray, again a down-and-out actor as he had been in *My Darling Clementine* (20th-Fox, 1946); Joanne Dru is with Mowbray. She falls in love with Ben Johnson. The Ford stock company is present, Jane Darwell, Ward Bond of course, Francis Ford, and even Jim Thorpe as Navajo.

The Cleggs, pursued by a posse, join the train and force the Mormons to hide them from the law. When, on a visit to the Navajo nation, one of the Cleggs molests an Indian girl, Ward Bond has him tied to a wheel and whipped. The Cleggs hold this against their Mormon protectors. When the time comes for a parting of the ways, the Cleggs decide to destroy the seeds for farming which the Mormons have transported across two thousand miles. There is a shoot-out and the Cleggs are dispatched. The train makes it to the promised land.

Ben Johnson, Harry Carey, Jr., and Ward Bond as they appeared in John Ford's *Wagon Master*.

There is an ironic opening statement to John Huston's rather dull *The Life and Times of Judge Roy Bean* (National General, 1972) that reads, "Maybe this isn't the way it was, but the way it should have been." The comment is less appropriate for Huston's off-beat comedy than it is for Ford's renderings and evocations of the Western experience. Ford's response, when you would ask him whether he thought his films over the years indicated an increasingly pervasive melancholy, was to fire back the question, "What do you think?" Ford said what he had to say in his films, not outside them. The hope and optimism of *Wagon Master* will persist beyond even that sense of wilderness which Ford so loved to inject into his Westerns.

51 / THE POSTWAR INDIANS

The French, almost since the advent of military forays into the New World, have been possessed of an *idée fixe* glamourizing the American Indian as a godlike pagan, a fierce but untutored ally in whom barbarism, while deplorable, is wholly forgiven due to a childish simplicity. At least, this is what you may come to believe by reading what French cinema critics write or when encountering romantic views such as Maurice Tourneur's in his *The Last of the Mohicans* (Associated Producers, 1920).

It is a somewhat mistaken conclusion that true sympathy for the plight of the red man had to await *Broken Arrow*. I think the reader, at this point, would be inclined to agree with me that prior to 1950 there were indeed a number of positive films championing the Indian perspective. But *Broken Arrow* articulated the trend and, when the picture proved successful, prompted a plethora of imitations.

Delmer Daves, who was born at San Francisco on July 24, 1904, began in the industry as a property assistant on *The Covered Wagon* and worked as a writer and actor until directing his first film in 1943. *Broken Arrow* was his first film with a Western setting. It was Daves's intention to depict the Indian as an individual with his own tradition and ethical standards, intelligent with a sense of dignity. To play Cochise, Daves picked Jeff Chandler, a former radio actor who had appeared in gangster bits. Chandler portrayed the chief of the Chiricahua Apaches as a man of wisdom and peace whose friendship with James Stewart, a white man, is based on mutual respect. Chandler received an Oscar nomination for his role, and Universal immediately placed him under contract and featured him in a series of Westerns, none of which permitted him to equal his performance in *Broken Arrow*. He even played Cochise again in *Battle at Apache Pass* (Universal, 1952), set in time before his meeting with Tom Jeffords, the character Stewart played in *Broken Arrow*, and telling of how an Indian-hating cavalry officer and a dishonest Indian agent were responsible for the death of his wife. The touching quality of his portrayal was transformed into soap opera by the time he appeared as the dying Cochise in *Taza, Son of Cochise* (Universal, 1954), in which he passes on his mantle of leadership to his son, Rock Hudson.

Broken Arrow also established James Stewart as a Western player and started his career in a new direction. It proved a fruitful happenstance, with Stewart going on to make notable Westerns such as *Two Rode Together* (Columbia, 1961) and *The Man Who Shot Liberty Valance* (Paramount, 1962) for John Ford, *Winchester '73* (Universal, 1950) for Anthony Mann done the same year as *Broken Arrow*, and an entire series of films for Mann of which *The Naked Spur* (M-G-M, 1953), *The Far Country* (Universal, 1955), and *The Man from Laramie* (Columbia, 1955) were outstanding vehicles of their kind. The Western allowed Stewart to age and still retain his position as a soft-spoken hero in films he made that were directed by Andrew V. McLaglen, *Shenandoah* (Universal, 1965), *The Rare Breed* (Universal, 1966), and *Bandalero* (20th-Fox, 1968).

Broken Arrow opens to Stewart narrating how he came to be friendly with the Apaches. Daves used the *Ox-bow* town set. Stewart volunteers for the Army and the townsfolk to attempt to negotiate a cease-fire with Cochise. The Indian way of life is graphically presented. Stewart falls in love with a young squaw played by Debra Paget. The Apaches agree to let the mail get through. When a wagon train is attacked, the townsfolk are in favor of war. But a general sent from President Grant asks Stewart to help hammer out a treaty. Stewart tells the general that the Indians wish to be treated as freemen. The Apaches hold a council meeting, and most of the chiefs concur with Cochise that a treaty would be a good thing. Geronimo, played by Jay Silverheels, rejects the treaty and becomes a renegade. "To talk peace," Cochise says, "is not hard. To live it is very hard." An armistice is called. Stewart and Debra Paget are wed. The married couple are ambushed by resentful whites, and Debra Paget is killed. Her death brings about a new spirit of comradeship between the whites and the Indians.

A month after *Broken Arrow* was made, Robert Taylor appeared in Anthony Mann's first Western, *The Devil's Doorway* (M-G-M, 1950), in which he portrayed a Shoshone Indian who returns a hero from the Civil

Jeff Chandler as Cochise and James Stewart as Tom Jeffords in *Broken Arrow*.
Photo courtesy of 20th Century-Fox Film Corporation.

War and is deprived of his right to own land because of his heritage. The film condemned the social conditions which finally made Taylor an outlaw and a renegade. This theme of an Indian striving to live as a white man became popular and was the central issue in *Reprisal* (Columbia, 1958), directed by George Sherman, who had begun directing with the Mesquiteers films at Republic and which starred Guy Madison as a half-breed who is forced at last to declare himself in the face of terrible hatred. No happy ending was provided. Madison had to ride out, unable to own land and with no hope of a normal life. John Huston varied this theme in *The Unforgiven* (United Artists, 1960), in which a family is torn apart when they discover that Audrey Hepburn, adopted and living among them, may be of Indian descent. The film is memorable for what may be Audie Murphy's best performance.

Colonel Tim McCoy made an appearance in *Run of the Arrow,* negotiating with Frank De Kova as Red Cloud, while Rod Steiger, Charles Bronson, and Ralph Meeker in the background look on.

Photo courtesy of RKO General.

The psychology of racial intermixture was also taken up by filmmakers. *The Half Breed* (RKO, 1952) starred Jack Beutel, Howard Hughes's Billy the Kid, as a noble red man tricked by a crooked white trader. *Broken Lance* (20th-Fox, 1954), directed by Edward Dmytryk, far more eloquently took up the theme, with Robert Wagner as the half-breed son of Spencer Tracy and Katy Jurado.

Delmer Daves himself returned with *The Last Wagon* (20th-Fox, 1956), in which Richard Widmark played Comanche Todd, a white man who lives as an Indian, and whose squaw and children were murdered by men of his own race. George Marshall, who directed the second *Destry Rides Again,* made *The Savage* (Paramount, 1952), in which Charlton Heston portrayed Warbonnet, a white man raised by the Sioux. Even Elvis Presley got a chance to play a tortured hero in *Flaming Star* (20th-Fox, 1960), directed by Don Siegel, with Presley torn between the cruelty of the whites and the savagery of the Indians.

The delicate balance between civilization and barbarism was the theme in *Arrowhead* (Paramount, 1953), with Charlton Heston as a white man and Jack Palance as an educated Indian who suddenly decides to go on the rampage. *Arrowhead* was directed by Charles Marquis Warren, who later made *Trooper Hook* (United Artists, 1957), with Barbara Stanwyck as a white woman who had lived as the wife of an Indian being returned to her white husband by an understanding Joel McCrea. The next year McCrea was cast as an obsessional, Indian-hating cavalry sergeant. In fact, Indian-hating army officers became almost as common as villains in the fifties as greedy gunrunners had once been, with Warner Anderson doing the honors in *The Yellow Tomahawk* (United Artists, 1954), Alex Nichol in *Tomahawk* (Universal, 1951), and Ralph Meeker in *Run of the Arrow*.

Many critics seem to feel that Sam Fuller is a highly overrated director and that *Run of the Arrow* is a cult film. I cannot say. Like *Broken Arrow,* it describes Indian life as idyllic and in H. M. Wynant as Crazy Wolf the Indian as an Apollo, but it does not do this at the expense of playing down the wanton cruelty. Rod Steiger portrays a Confederate soldier who fires the last shot of the Civil War into Ralph Meeker and then takes him to a medical tent for care. Steiger is so completely alienated from his environment that, after the conflict, he must head West. He meets Jay C. Flippen as an aged Sioux and is taught the Sioux language and customs. The two come upon a war party and are compelled to run barefoot through the hot sand, pursued by whooping Indians. Steiger is hidden by Sarita Montiel and, in time, is adopted by the Sioux as a blood brother, taking Sarita as his wife. Charles Bronson portrays the tribal chief, Blue Buffalo.

The film brought Colonel Tim McCoy back to the screen, playing General Allen, who works out a treaty with Red Cloud as to where a fort is to be built on Indian lands. Steiger is the Indians' emissary. When Crazy Wolf continues to prey upon the workers, finally killing Brian Keith, a sensible army man who counsels Steiger, Meeker determines he's going to choose a different site. The Indians attack and virtually wipe out his entire detachment. Steiger, unable to watch Meeker's agony at being skinned alive, shoots him and then returns with his squaw and adopted Indian son to his own people, incapable of living more among the Sioux.

What I am saying, I suppose, is this: Should the reader try to gain some coherent idea about Indian life in North America, the sympathetic films after World War II are as confusing as the image of the red man in *The Indians Are Coming* (Universal, 1930). Nor have Indian leaders been played with any real depth. Jay Silverheels as Geronimo in either *Broken Arrow* or *Battle at Apache Pass* (Universal, 1952) is not entirely comprehensible, nor did his portrayal improve by the time he appeared in *Walk the Proud Land* (Universal, 1956). The screenplay of *Geronimo!* (United

Artists, 1962), distinguished by the exclamation point from the 1939 Paramount film of the same title, cast Chuck Connors in the role and showed him to be a victim of white treachery. The Connors film was but a continuation of *Apache* (United Artists, 1954), with Monte Blue as Geronimo and Burt Lancaster as a runaway savage.

Victor Mature played a sympathetic *Chief Crazy Horse* (Universal, 1955) confronted by evil General Crook, played by James Millican, who had been cast as Custer in *Warpath* (Paramount, 1951). I have already had occasion to mention Anthony Quinn's enactment of the role in *They Died with Their Boots On* (Warner's, 1942) and Iron Eyes Cody who played Crazy Horse both in *Sitting Bull* (United Artists, 1954) and in *The Great Sioux Massacre* (Columbia, 1956), the latter title not to be mistaken for *The Great Sioux Uprising* (Universal, 1953), one of Jeff Chandler's post *Broken Arrow* Westerns.

Anthony Quinn, after playing Indians for years, returned as a modern reservation Indian in *Flap* (Warner's, 1970), a film so dull and pointless that it is hard going to sit through it once. Michael Pate and Henry Brandon have also specialized in Indian roles, Pate in *Hondo* (Warner's, 1954), which I will come to in a subsequent cinematograph, Brandon as Quanah Parker in *Two Rode Together* (Columbia, 1961) and as Scar in *The Searchers* (Warner's, 1956).

It isn't until you come to *Little Big Man* (National General, 1971) and the last-minute casting of Chief Dan George that you find an Indian playing an Indian in a portrayal more moving than anything achieved by Chief John Big Tree or Jay Silverheels, and even here critics have alleged that his performance is more reminiscent of a New Yorker of Jewish extraction than a frontier warrior. Yet I am not certain that it is important that Indians portray themselves any more than one should insist that Westerns depict Indians as being one way or the other. It has been my experience that, whether the picture playing is D. W. Griffith's *The Birth of a Nation* (Epoch, 1915) or Stanley Kramer's *High Noon* (United Artists, 1952) or anything since, one does not go to the movies—and Westerns most of all—to obtain a balanced view or accurate history.

52 / THE ANTISOCIAL WESTERN

Because Carl Foreman wrote the screenplay for *High Noon* and because of his openly declared political opinions, the film has been subjected to much critical flurry. It has been condemned and denounced, and still others have found in it a parable of the Cold War or a statement about social decay in the United States. Foreman himself makes no such grand claims for *High Noon*. It was his objective to make a picture that narrated the events of an hour and forty minutes and which took exactly an hour and forty minutes to narrate them. He remarked on the story line he thought he would use and was told by someone that a story much like that had appeared in *The Saturday Evening Post*. Research found that "The Tin Star," by John W. Cunningham, was a tale about an old marshal haunted by a killer returned to even the score for having been sent to prison. Stanley Kramer agreed to purchase screen rights to the story, and Foreman was put to work on it. "What it was about at the time was Hollywood," Foreman has commented, "and no other place but Hollywood and about what was happening in Hollywood and nothing else but that."

Although I have introduced Gary Cooper previously and even had much to say about him, I have reserved telling anything of his background until now. He was born on May 7, 1901, in Helena, Montana. When he was nine, in part because his father had been a British barrister, he was sent to Dunstable, England, for four years. Upon returning home, he broke his leg and it took two years to heal. Later he entered Grinnell College in Iowa and became a cartoonist for a Helena newspaper. He went to Los Angeles in five years and found that his work impressed no one. He tried to break into pictures and was given his first chance by Samuel Goldwyn. He drew some attention in *Wings* (Paramount, 1928), but *The Virginian* made him a star. In 1932 he married Veronica Balfe, a New York socialite, and they had one daughter. Cooper was a quiet man, introverted, and turned in upon himself. When he was signed by Stanley Kramer to make *High Noon*, he was deathly ill with an ulcer which twisted and contorted his features in pain as he went about doing his business.

The original version of *High Noon* ran fully as long as Foreman had in-

tended. At a sneak preview, the picture proved a bomb. Kramer withdrew it. He had started in the business as a cutter and so he re-edited it. He inserted numerous close-ups of Coop's strained face, the anguish of his physical pain translating itself on the screen as genuine fear. Kramer then added the close-ups of clocks, which made the sense of time truly oppressive. Next he summoned Dimitri Tiomkin to him; Tiomkin had a duration-of-the-picture contract.

"I want a ballad," he said.

Tiomkin was shocked.

"Leesten, Meester Kramer, I am a symphonic composer, not a ballad writer."

Kramer remained obdurate. Together with Ned Washington, who did the lyrics, Tiomkin hammered out a ballad. He telephoned Tex Ritter on a Sunday afternoon. Tex was living in Hollywood at the time.

"Meester Ritter?"

"Yes," Tex replied.

"Dis is Tiomkin. Leesten, Meester Ritter, I have dis ballad that I composed for a peecture and I want that you come over to my house and sing it for me."

Which is how Tex got the job of singing the ballad in the film. The song won an Academy Award, as did Cooper, Tiomkin's score, and Elmo Williams' and Harry Gerstad's editing.

It was Grace Kelly's first screen appearance, and Katy Jurado, who was twenty-five years of age then and had appeared in some twenty-seven Mexican films, made her impact on the American cinema. Fred Zinnemann, who had directed *The Men* (United Artists, 1950) for Kramer, was chosen as the director.

The plot, briefly, opens to Gary Cooper being wedded to Grace Kelly. She is a Quaker and opposed to violence. Word comes that Frank Miller, a dangerous killer Coop sent to prison, has been pardoned and that his brother and two toughs are waiting for him to arrive on the noon train. Coop can't leave town, even though Kelly urges him that he must, or she will leave him. Coop holds fast. However, all of his efforts to raise a posse are met with indifference or ridicule. His impetuous deputy picks a fight with him, and, though he beats him, Coop is left physically weakened. Katy Jurado, who has managed to be the love object of Coop, Frank Miller, the returning killer, and the impetuous deputy, is leaving on the train, joined by Grace Kelly. Miller disembarks and with the other three challenges Coop. Grace runs to his assistance when she hears shots and even helps Coop dispatch one of the outlaws. Coop drops his badge on the ground and rides out of town with Grace.

Duke Wayne has perhaps objected the most vociferously to *High Noon,* and I have already mentioned how Howard Hawks's *Rio Bravo* was made

Coop all alone against the world, his face contorted in pain from the ulcer afflicting him during production of *High Noon.*

in contradiction to the basic premises of the Kramer film. Duke's protests come to this. Rugged men of the frontier, men who had battled hostile Indians and harsh nature, who had scratched a living from barren land, clawed at rock to survive, wouldn't cower as a group before four thugs. They'd unite, as they'd united to make the land habitable, to build a town on dust, to drive their cattle a thousand miles to the railhead. The spirit of the West that *High Noon* portrayed was outside the mythical promise of the land. It may have been emotionally true in 1952, but not before that.

Foreman left Hollywood, and a great stir was caused by his Communist leanings. It was a bizarre political period—but what decade hasn't been in this century? Yet *High Noon* made money, with a domestic gross for a black and white film of $3,744,635.64. The cutting was exceptional, particularly when the train whistle sounds through Hadleyville and all the

The anxious, strained faces of the modern world as depicted in *High Noon:* Grace Kelly, Ted Stanhope, Lon Chaney, Jr., Thomas Mitchell, Gary Cooper, and Otto Krueger. The poster on the wall announces "War Is Declared."

Photo courtesy of United Artists Corporation.

Dan Duryea menacing John Payne and Lizabeth Scott in *Silver Lode*. Liz
Scott was brought to Hollywood by Hal B. Wallis.

Photo courtesy of RKO General.

characters with whom we have become familiar are seen suddenly in close-up.

The film also inspired its share of imitations. Allan Dwan directed *Silver Lode* for Benedict Bogeous. Dwan's coterie finds the film to be an important one for him. What makes it especially interesting is its variation of the *High Noon* theme whereby society, rather than an individual or a psychological motive, is cited as the source of social decay.

John Payne was cast as Dan Ballard, who is about to marry Lizabeth Scott when Dan Duryea and his gang arrive in town. Payne knows Duryea to be an outlaw. However, Duryea has false credentials which allow him to masquerade as a marshal. During the tension of the next several hours, the entire town has to decide whether Payne is to be believed, and a federal marshal telegraphed (it is the Fourth of July) the next day, or they are to listen to Duryea's importunities that they give Payne up to him. Nearly everyone, including Morris Ankrum as Liz Scott's father, turns against Payne by the end of the picture, and he is chased through the streets and hunted like a dog. Liz saves him from being captured in the church tower by bringing a phony telegram proving Duryea a fake. The true wire soon follows, after Duryea and his men have been finished off and the town is languishing in self-recriminations.

Delmer Daves, whom I already introduced in the previous chapter, came along with *3:10 to Yuma* in 1957. It examined another aspect of the *High Noon* theme, a lonely man's courage. Glenn Ford, who made rather a career out of playing tortured heroes in Westerns, appeared as the leader of an outlaw gang. Van Heflin was cast as an honest rancher hired by the head of the Butterfield stage line to transport Ford, once he has been captured, to the county seat for imprisonment and trial. The only other man to assist Heflin is the town drunk.

Heflin runs into trouble while waiting in a hotel room with Ford for the 3:10 train. Ford's men soon discover where he is being held. They hang the town drunk, and Butterfield becomes terrified for his own life. Heflin valiantly resists Ford's temptations of money. He walks him to the depot, Ford's men everywhere, but unable to get a clear aim. At last, Ford leaps aboard the train, whereas if he had dropped to his knees, Heflin would have been shot. Ford permitted Heflin to succeed. Heflin asks Ford why he did it. Ford sums it up laconically that he has escaped from the Yuma prison before. Such sentimentality would be inconceivable today.

But this is what it was like in the fifties. Gunfighters were tired, lonely, disillusioned men. Townships were made up of sheep easily intimidated by hoodlums. Marshaling was a thankless task. Mob law and witch-hunting dominated *Silver Lode;* a brave man against the world was the image evoked by *High Noon* and *3:10 to Yuma.* But behind it all was an underlying sentimentality which the Westerns of the sixties and early seventies have

Van Heflin and Glenn Ford about to board the train in *3:10 to Yuma.*

attempted to grind into a vision of sustained treachery and despair. The social alienation of these Westerns of the fifties cannot even approach the open cynicism of Robert Altman's *McCabe and Mrs. Miller* (Warner's, 1971), in which a confidence man and a whore bring civilization to a Western town; Sam Peckinpah's *The Wild Bunch* (Warner's, 1969), in which the criminal gang being pursued is far more admirable than the motley crew of pursuers; John Ford's *The Man Who Shot Liberty Valance* (Paramount, 1962), in which the rightful author of a noble act is precisely the man who is not recognized for it; or *The Culpepper Cattle Company* (20th-Fox, 1972), which shows the West and the life of the cowboy to be basically filthy, violent, without either glamour or reward.

53 / JOHN WAYNE AND THE INDIAN

I went to Seattle to visit with John Wayne during production of *McQ* (Warner's, 1974). The film had a very tight shooting schedule. Duke was virtually in every scene. It was tiring for him.

Four days prior to my arrival, Duke's Western *Cahill, U. S. Marshal* (Warner's, 1973) had been premièred at Seattle. I had seen the picture at a sneak. It was a story of human loyalties; it was also autobiography. *Cahill* reflected many of Duke's views on the love one bears toward one's children and the bonds which exist between friends. Neville Brand was a half-breed in the film who lost his life while accompanying Duke in the apprehension of a gang of bank robbers.

I thought Brand's an exceptional performance and remarked on it to Jack Casey, the Warner Brothers publicity agent assigned to *McQ*. It was then that Casey told me of the picket lines which had demonstrated in opposition to *Cahill*. The protesters were American Indians. Their signs and placards denounced Duke as the worst Indian killer in history.

When I commented that this was nonsense and wholly without foundation, he could only shrug his shoulders. The Indians, he said, felt that Duke in his films had tended to glorify the Indian-hating white man. Cavalry officers, scouts, big ranchers, Duke's screen image was the embodiment of racial prejudice toward the Indians and an open attempt to justify the treatment dealt out to them in the settling of the West.

Of course, you cannot argue such a point to a conclusion. What at base is irrational will not generally submit itself to reason.

Duke and Geraldine Page confronted by Michael Pate in *Hondo*. It was one of
Duke's early successes with his own producing company, Batjac.

Photo courtesy of Warner Brothers.

"I want to include *Hondo* in *The Filming of the West*," I told Mike
Wayne. Mike is the president of Batjac Pictures, Duke's producing company. "It is the closest, I believe, that one can come to a personal statement
from your father on precisely how he regards the struggle with the Indian
nations."

"Not altogether," Mike responded. "I would hope that you would also
include *McLintock* because that is an even more personal statement."

I was uncertain.

"Look at it again before you decide," Mike suggested.

For a person who has spent all the conscious years of his life studying his
fellow man, I cannot say I have learned very much. Nor am I able to explain why it is that men, when they are intent on a vision of what they conceive as a better world, sweep everything before them without a pang of

conscience; only, once they have achieved the end they had in mind, or have died in the process, or have exhausted themselves, and come to look back, are besieged by regrets, or their offspring are made totally disconsolate by their inheritance. Empires and religions—conquering ideas of any kind, really—are not inhibited in their development by reservations come of social decorum. Some religions have lasted thousands of years, some empires hundreds, before the vision has tarnished.

It is the fear of many Americans—if what they say is to be believed—that this has happened in the United States, an empire that endured but a few seasons before it began sinking beneath the weight of its own sense of social and moral responsibility. I can say nothing about it. But I know this of the regret: It lasts only so long as it takes to squander the wealth accumulated by the visionary builders, no more.

I do not regard John Wayne a philosopher, nor a political strategist. He is a man who has lived by definite principles and who feels he owes to them what he has been in his life. Mike Wayne was right. *McLintock* is a sequel to *Hondo*. If the two pictures, taken as a unit, have anything to say about the loss the red man suffered to his way of life and homeland, they have something far more profound to state than regret. Indeed, the regret is viewed in more alarming terms because the white man, in his later-generation guilt over presumed maltreatment, stole from the Indian the last vestige of his human integrity—the dignity that alone can come from finding his own way in the world. When the U. S. Government made the Indians wards of the state, it shattered any hope they might have entertained of emerging from their conflict with the white man preserving at least their self-respect.

Hondo was filmed on location at Carmargo, Mexico, about five hundred miles south of El Paso. Robert Fellows, coproducer on the film, felt the Mexican terrain, barren and sun-baked, ideal as a setting for a Western that shifted the emphasis to a conflict of human interests rather than an individual battle between good and evil.

At the time production on *Hondo* began, Duke had been married to Esperanza Baur for seven years. Duke called her Chata. Following his divorce from Josephine Saenz, Duke had courted Chata, but always with other people around. Perhaps out of loneliness, or simply because he liked her best of the women he knew, after a few months they were married.

Chata had not been rich. Duke's courtship consisted of small gifts, sending flowers, luncheon and dinner parties. Once they were wed, this changed. Chata became a woman of means. She engaged her mother to run the house—Duke's large Encino home. Chata had her own concept of what married life should be like. She disapproved of Duke's card-playing cronies, the many old friends who derived great pleasure from gathering around a bottle and glasses. They stopped coming to see the Duke. Finally the only visitors the Waynes had were Chata's friends.

Duke began taking trips to Mexico, alone. When he visited friends, he was invariably asked to spend the night. In his private life Duke remained modest, gentle, almost retiring. He avoided fights or violent emotional clashes. In November 1951 Duke packed his bag and caught an airplane for Acapulco. He left a note behind for Chata that, were she of a mind to, she would know where to find him. Duke stayed in Mexico for two months. Chata did not come.

On Christmas Eve, Duke gave in. He flew to Mexico City and then on to Los Angeles. There was no reconciliation. Next night, he was again in Acapulco.

There was one more try for accord. In mid 1952 Duke was scheduled to make a picture in Honolulu. Through the office of friends, he had induced Chata to see him. They talked for several hours. Chata agreed to accompany Duke to the Islands. Upon arrival in Honolulu, Chata left Duke and returned alone to their home and her mother in the Valley. Duke didn't see Chata again till the first day of their divorce hearing.

In the interim, Duke had thrown himself completely into his work. He formed his own producing company. He continued to make movies. But everywhere he went, he was shadowed by private detectives. Duke took a scouting trip to South America to find potential shooting locations. In Peru he met Pilar Pallete, in appearance quite similar to Josephine Saenz and Esperanza Baur—tiny, vivacious, passionate. Duke signed her to a contract with his company.

Duke was earning good money. He grossed $1,026,072 for the years 1950–52. He was being paid $175,000 a picture. Warner Brothers agreed to finance and release *Hondo* in the new novelty technique of 3-D to be filmed in Technicolor. Duke and Fellows received $50,000 as coproducers. James Edward Grant based his screenplay on an original story by Western writer Louis L'Amour which had run in *Collier's*. Grant had started as a screenwriter in 1935. He had written the story for Duke's *The Angel and the Badman* (Republic, 1947) and understood perhaps better than most the character and personality best suited to Duke's screen style. Gail Russell had costarred with Duke in *Angel*. She was married rather unhappily, to Guy Madison. Chata, in her jealousy, accused Duke publicly of being attracted to her.

The *Hondo* troupe departed for Mexico in late May 1953. Chata's lawyer dispatched a pair of private detectives to keep Duke under surveillance. Subsequently, among her demands for settlement, Chata requested $20,000 to pay for all the detectives over the years.

The two private eyes were unable to speak Spanish. By mistake, they wired the suite belonging to the governor of the province, thinking it was the Duke's. They were summarily arrested and placed in jail. Without money or influence, they appealed to Duke to come to their rescue. Duke showed up at the jail with Ward Bond, an old chum with a strong supporting role in *Hondo*. Ward loved the Duke. He had a sudden temper. "Let 'em rot," he advised.

One of the detectives was doubled up with appendicitis. Duke furrowed his brow. "This guy's sick," he said. "Anyhow, they were just doing a job." The detectives had no money. Duke did a characteristic thing. He paid their fines, arranged for their release, and gave them plane fare back to the States. "With those tactics," Ward Bond stormed, "imagine what a bloody mess the trial's gonna be!" Duke returned to work on the picture.

John Wayne has been a shy and essentially lonely man all his life. I suppose it is this which led him to seek his career in the motion picture industry. He has never understood why to be popular has meant correspondingly that a man must be equally hated, nor why to be loved means that a man must be possessed. Being a film actor for him has meant that he must have all the vagueness of a symbol; it is vital to longevity in a short-lived business. Duke is fundamentally a man of simple pleasures, able to be moved to tears as easily off screen as to fight on. He is a man without meanness. However difficult it may be to conceive living on those terms, it is those terms by which John Wayne has lived.

The year is 1874. Duke happens upon an isolated ranch inhabited by Geraldine Page and Lee Aaker as her son. Geraldine and Duke become friends. Later, at the frontier post, Duke meets Geraldine's husband, who has deserted her. The husband and a henchman try to kill Duke, but he puts them out of the way. Geraldine is prey to Michael Pate and his braves. Duke is captured by the Indians and forced to fight a dagger duel. Duke helps evacuate the territory of white settlers while the cavalry dispatches the Indians. "End of a way of life," Duke comments. "Too bad. A good way."

James Arness was under contract to Batjac and played in *Hondo*. It wasn't too long afterward that he was offered the lead in the "Gunsmoke" TV series. "You're too big and too ugly to ever make it in the movies," Duke chided him. Both Chuck Roberson and, briefly, Yakima Canutt doubled Duke in the making of *Hondo*. John Farrow, onetime husband of Maureen O'Sullivan and father of Mia Farrow, was the director, Andrew V. McLaglen his assistant.

I had occasion to ask John Wayne which, among his many pictures, was the one he liked best.

"You have been quoted as saying it was *She Wore a Yellow Ribbon* [RKO, 1949]."

"Well," he drawled, "it wasn't."

He paused to puff on his cigar and turned his head to one side to exhale. It was as if he had been made very self-conscious of smoking and knew that, because you liked him, it might cause you involuntary pain or embarrassment.

"You like different pictures for different reasons," he went on. "I guess

I had the most fun making *The Quiet Man* [Republic, 1952]. Because Maureen O'Hara was in it and Jack Ford was the director and we all went to Ireland to film it and met a lot of interesting people while we were there."

Batjac produced *McLintock* for United Artists' release in 1963. Mike Wayne, who was only twenty-eight, was the producer, and again Duke costarred with Maureen O'Hara. Andrew V. McLaglen, the director, had been Jack Ford's assistant on *The Quiet Man,* in which his father, Victor, had played Maureen O'Hara's father. Duke's son Patrick had a leading role in *McLintock,* having grown up considerably since his early appearance in *Rio Grande* (Republic, 1950).

But *McLintock* was more than another old-home-week Duke Wayne production. It marked the beginning, as it were, of Duke's attempt to set down his views on life and what in it he has come to value. James Edward Grant did the original screenplay. Grant's work on *Hondo, Sands of Iwo Jima* (Republic, 1950), *Big Jim McLain* (Warner's, 1952), and Duke's rather expensive *The Alamo* (United Artists, 1960) were only a preamble, it would appear, for his work on *McLintock.*

The locations for the film were various, most of the filming being done in Arizona near Nogales, Tombstone, and Tucson. A ranch some eighty-four

The free-for-all which is one of the high points of *McLintock*.

Photo courtesy of United Artists Corporation.

Duke and Maureen O'Hara, frequently coupled on the screen, back together for *McLintock*.

Photo courtesy of United Artists Corporation.

years old and forty-three miles east of Nogales in the San Raphael Valley was used to represent the McLintock spread. The sequence where Duke and Stephanie Powers, portraying his daughter, go pheasant hunting amid cotton and willow trees was shot on the Ralph Wingfield ranch, located closer to Nogales. It was also on the Wingfield ranch that the water hole was created as a backdrop. Nogales firemen loaned Mike Wayne a hundred feet of regular 2½-inch fire hose through which five thousand gallons of water an hour were pumped without pause for three days to form a lake sixty feet across and one hundred feet long. It was a magnificent exterior for the scene with Stephanie when Duke tells her what love between a man and a woman means.

Stephanie, as Becky, comments to Duke that she wants to get something straight, her father's relationship to her mother. After his initial reluctance, Duke, as G.W., objects to Becky's calling her mother petulant.

"You were only about six months old," he recalls, "when your mother stayed alone with you in a sod hut under eight foot of snow while I moved the herd three hundred miles south to try and save it. Saved about half of it. You were only about a year old at the time of the great Comanche raids. We stood off five hundred Plains Indians for nine days. Petulant, Becky? I think you'd better go on home."

G.W. waits until she mounts up and then adds, "All the gold in the U. S. Treasury an' all the harp music in heaven can't equal what we had—what happens when a man an' a woman do all that growin' together."

Duke's long popularity in Mexico as a film star paid off during the making of *McLintock*. Duke needed five hundred Longhorn steers but couldn't find them in the States because, through years of breeding, the horns now tip down instead of up—which would have ruined the authenticity of the cattle scenes. The Mexican Government loaned Duke the five hundred Longhorns he needed, with horns that tip up, plus incurring all the costs necessary for tests and inoculations before transporting the steers across the border.

In a desolate area seventeen miles north of Tombstone, the Batjac company built a railroad station of the 1880s vintage and arranged to have the authentic nineteenth-century train, complete with engine, passenger coaches, and boxcars shipped on Southern Pacific flatcars, property of Paramount Pictures which had used it in films for forty-five years, including De Mille's *Union Pacific*. The train was sidetracked twice daily when the regular Southern Pacific runs came through. Western veteran player Bob Steele was cast as a railway conductor.

The Columbia Pictures set of the original Old Tucson was used as the setting for the town of McLintock, embellished by twenty-six frame buildings built at an additional cost of $74,000.

Certainly one of the most memorable sequences in *McLintock* is that of the mud slide in which Duke, Maureen O'Hara, Patrick Wayne, Jack Kruschen, and Chill Wills were all participants, refusing doubles. It was filmed over a period of three days at an abandoned copper mine in the hills, thirty-three miles south of Tucson, at a cost of $50,000. The slush pit at the bottom of the slide was sealed with gunnite, making it a small lake. The dump was then covered with a slimy substance consisting of bentonite, a chalk derivative used in drilling oil wells. Two tons of bentonite were required.

While the scenes were being shot, the temperature plunged suddenly to forty-two degrees, and a cold wind sprang up. Maureen O'Hara, radiant and still eschewing doubles, slid down the slope headfirst on her back and disappeared into the water. Shivering and trembling, she emerged from the water and was approached by one of the Indian extras. "We want you to know," he said, "that we think you are ten feet tall."

Beyond the handful of familiar Hollywood Indians, Duke had to import 287 from other parts of Arizona for the hard-riding sequences because the Tucson Indians, short and sedentary, rarely mount a horse. Among the imports were Sioux, Crow, Apaches, Iroquois, and Navajoes. When Duke first espied fourteen Navajo chiefs newly arrived from Monument Valley, he did a double take and quipped, "Hey, didn't I kill you twelve pictures ago?" The chiefs laughed.

In the film Duke is asked to act as spokesman for the Comanche chiefs and braves, objecting to the order of the U. S. Government to transport them forcibly to a reservation under the protection of a rather ineffectual and pompous Indian agent. It constitutes one of Duke's most moving moments on the screen.

"The Comanches say," he translates their plea before the territorial commission, "we are an old people and a proud people. When the white man first came among us, we were as many as the grasses of the prairie. Now we are few. But we are still proud. For if a man loses pride in manhood, he is nothing. You tell us now that if we let you send us away to this place called Fort Sill, you will feed us and care for us. Let us tell you this: It is Comanche law that no chief ever eats unless he sees that the pots are full of meat in the lodges of the widows and orphans. It is the Comanche way of life. This —what the white man calls charity—is a fine thing for widows and orphans, but no warrior can accept it. For, if he does, he is no longer a man and when he is no longer a man, he is nothing—*and better off dead*. You say to the Comanches: You are widows and orphans and no longer men and we, the Comanches, say we would rather be dead. It will not be a remembered fight because we are few now and have few weapons, but we will fight and we will die . . . . Comanches."

I am reminded, as I reproduce these words for my reader, that in nearby Nogales, at the time *McLintock* was made, lived Colonel Tim McCoy and how very similar were the sentiments he expressed thirty years previously in *End of the Trail*. In the blind rush to cure men's evils and woes through the empty promises of legislation, it is often forgotten, I believe, that legislation cannot give any man his dignity—sadly, it has been the experience of history that legislation can only deny it to him.

George Washington McLintock has just about everything a man could want, including a town named after him; but he doesn't have his wife, Kate. The story was based on Shakespeare's *Taming of the Shrew*. Kate comes back, demanding a divorce and custody of their daughter who is back from school in the East. The train that brings Becky McLintock home also carries Comanche chiefs just released from prison. G.W. becomes their advocate and finally arranges for them to escape with guns and ammunition. After a series of hilarious episodes, he and Kate come back together again. Chill Wills, as Drago, asks G.W. of divorce: "Is that where you pay a woman *not* to live with you?"

The charm of Duke's screen portrayals, as they came to be revealed in the fifties and sixties, rested in what a man of talent and determination, who was fundamentally given to fair play and loyal to himself as to those he loves, could make of his existence. As the heroes in Duke's films became more realistic, less the product of illusion and less a contradictory creation of studio publicity, a humanity was brought to the Western that hadn't always been possible.

Contemporary
Trends
in the
Modern
Western

Jane Fonda married the French film director Roger Vadim on August 14, 1965, at Las Vegas, Nevada. Two months previously, Columbia Pictures had released *Cat Ballou*. It was a satire of the traditional Western. Vadim sought to transform Jane into an icy embodiment of unattainable sexuality. He had tried to do the same with Brigitte Bardot. Vadim directed Jane for the first time in *La Ronde* (Continental, 1964), issued in the United States as *Circle of Love*. Vadim, apparently, was enraptured by the insinuating contours and full lines of her body. He wanted to freeze her eroticism for the camera.

By the time I got around to interviewing Jane in the winter of 1972, *Cat Ballou* was her most popular picture and in constant demand on television stations. Jane was divorced from Vadim and had married political agitator Tom Hayden. She no longer had any interest in discussing her motion picture career. She would talk only of her political notions and social causes. She was pregnant; she spoke in glowing terms of the liberated women of North Vietnam. She had time for nothing else.

Lee Marvin had a dual role in *Cat Ballou*. He was cast as a drunken reprobate, Kid Shelleen, and a notorious killer, Tim Strawn. He was paid $87,500 for playing the part and won an Oscar for it.

Cat Ballou, however, due to its box-office gross of nearly $7 million and the additional promotion given the picture because of Marvin's recognition by the Academy, strengthened the trend in Westerns in the sixties away from conventional heroes of any kind. Jack Marta, long a cameraman at Republic, was the cinematographer, and Yakima Canutt directed the second unit. The film begins with Jane in jail, sentenced to be hanged. By means of flashback, the viewer is shown how she got herself into this predicament. Throughout the picture Nat King Cole, who made his last film appearance here, and Stubby Kaye sing various choruses from "The Ballad of Cat Ballou" which serve as transitions between sequences.

Jane is pictured as a proper girl graduated from a finishing school heading back to her father's ranch on a train. Dwayne Hickman, disguised as a man of the cloth, helps Michael Callan escape from Bruce Cabot, a lawman

The principals of *Cat Ballou:* Dwayne Hickman, Tom Nardini, Michael Callan, Jane Fonda, John Marley, and Lee Marvin as the gunman.

Photo courtesy of Columbia Pictures.

who has Callan prisoner on the train. Jane as Cat assists in Callan's flight. When Cat arrives at her father's ranch, she learns that he is in a great deal of trouble because certain investors want to seize his property for its water rights. Lee Marvin as Tim Strawn has been hired to do the job. Strawn wears a metal nose plate because his proboscis was bitten off in a fight. Hickman and Callan join Cat in protecting her father. Cat writes to Kid Shelleen, a famous gunman who is the hero of several pulp books. Shelleen turns out to be a worthless alcoholic.

Strawn shoots Jane's father, and the Wolf City Development Corporation takes over the ranch. Cat, together with Hickman, Callan, Kid, and an Indian youth who worked for her father, heads for the Hole in the Wall. They plan and execute a wholly comic train robbery. Reginald Denny, who was taking a bath during the robbery and who owns the Wolf City Development Corporation, is also the protector of the Hole in the Wall and Cat is told that she will have to square the holdup with him. Kid Shelleen decides to go up against Strawn. He sobers himself and puts on his gunfighter's outfit. It is suggested that Strawn is the Kid's brother. The Kid goes to Strawn's hotel room and guns him. Cat, dressed in red, does an imitation of Mae West and calls on Denny in his private car. He refuses to sign a confession and she accidentally shoots him. Denny had hired Strawn to kill her father. Cut to the cell. Cat is led to the hanging platform. Hickman, Callan, and the others spirit her off from the bloodthirsty crowd, racing out of town in a hearse. Kid is totally drunk, but he manages to cover their getaway.

By 1969 the new image in Westerns had had its impact on Europe as well as the United States. In many of the theaters of Paris, as in theaters all over Western Europe, *Il Était une Fois dans l'Ouest* was playing in fall 1969. The film was popular with Europeans, more so than with Americans, who saw it under the title *Once upon a Time in the West* (Paramount, 1969). It was directed by Sergio Leone and featured Henry Fonda, the hero of many American Westerns, as the villain and Charles Bronson, the villain of many American Westerns, as the hero. The picture was the culmination of Leone's tetralogy of violence that began with Clint Eastwood starring in *A Fistful of Dollars* (United Artists, 1966), *For a Few Dollars More* (United Artists, 1967), and *The Good, the Bad and the Ugly* (United Artists, 1969). Paris, of course, was not the right city in which to see any of these Italian Westerns. Rome is where they were best, in the shadow of the Colosseum. As the innocent are shot down, maimed, and wounded, and the audience is expected to applaud, the spectacle of violence for its own sake was a new element that perhaps only an alien influence such as Leone could interject into the Western. The novelty soon wore off with Americans. *Once upon a Time in the West* concludes the cycle, but not without having had a substantial impact on American filmmakers.

L. Q. Jones gloating over prostrate Clint Eastwood in *Hang 'Em High*.
Photo courtesy of United Artists Corporation.

A Fistful of Dollars was produced in Italy on a budget of slightly more than $245,000. The picture proved to be very popular in the foreign market and from October 1964 until February 1968 grossed $4,600,000 in Italy alone and $1,101,362 foreign. In 1965 Leone produced *Per Qualche Dollaro in Più*, released in the United States as *For a Few Dollars More*, for $500,000, and through February 1968 the picture grossed $5,000,000 in Italy and $5,121,985 foreign elsewhere. The third film, *The Good, the Bad and the Ugly*, cost $2,000,000 and had an original running time of three hours and one minute. It was issued in December 1966 and grossed $4.3 million in that country through February 1968 and $7,528,700 foreign elsewhere. United Artists bought the three Westerns for American domestic release for $35,000, $70,000, and $140,000 respectively. The firm spent a great deal of money merchandising the pictures so that *Fistful*, issued in January 1967, has had to date a gross of $4,129,319.71; *Few Dol-*

Charlton Heston in the soft, poetic, yet harsh world of *Will Penny.*

Photo courtesy of Paramount Pictures.

lars, released in May 1967, has grossed so far $4,251,313.21; and *The Good, the Bad and the Ugly,* issued in December 1967, has grossed to date $6,005,735.46.

These three films when combined with the American production *Hang 'Em High* transformed Clint Eastwood, a former television personality, into a world-wide superstar. Eastwood did very little acting of any kind in the Leone films. In *Fistful* he was a man with no name, smoking cheroots and wantonly and senselessly shooting and maiming people throughout. The pictures had no logic, but they didn't really need any. Apparently, audiences both in the United States and in the foreign market were impressed at the violence and explicit sexuality and were drawn to the pictures for these reasons. By the time of *Hang 'Em High,* the crude brutality was altered somewhat, although the relentlessness of Eastwood as an avenger was retained. The central focus of the film was on the hanging of criminals, and, probably, no Western has concentrated on the subject with greater intensity.

Eastwood is surrounded by a group of riders while trailing with a small herd. He is accused of stealing the cattle and promptly hanged. Ed Begley is the leader of the men; Bob Steele is the only one among them who pleads for leniency. After the men leave, Ben Johnson, a U. S. Marshal, happens upon the scene, cuts Eastwood down, and brings him back to consciousness. Eastwood is arrested and taken to the territorial capital. He is made a deputy marshal and is assigned to bring in the men who attempted, unjustifiably, to kill him. There are nine men in all. Eastwood shoots one in a saloon. Bob Steele turns himself in and gives evidence against the others. Eastwood sets out with seven warrants.

A situation intervenes. Before he can pursue the remaining members of the hanging party, Eastwood is asked to head up a posse in bringing in a group of rustlers. Bruce Dern and two boys constitute the rustlers. Eastwood brings them back to the capital. Even though the two boys saved Eastwood's life by refusing to assist Dern in a break, the territorial judge sentences them to death. The actual hanging episode is quite dramatically moving in its presentation. Eastwood has his emotional problems accepting the justice of all this, but being shot up in a brothel by Begley's men gets him back into the swing of things. The pursuit is grim. Begley, cornered at last in a ranch house, hangs himself before capture. Inger Stevens plays the "good" girl who nurses Eastwood after his gunshot wounds, but she is sexually frozen due to a rape; it takes the warmth of Eastwood's body, during a sudden cloudburst, to thaw out her reserve.

Hang 'Em High was brought in for a negative cost of $1,680,000 and had a domestic gross of $6,680,216.41. It had a foreign gross of $3,847,074. The tremendous popularity of these films was no doubt a fluke; but Eastwood's new status decided him that he was a director of the first rank. He very soon set about directing and starring in his own Western for Universal, *High Plains Drifter* (Universal, 1972), which had him smoking cheroots again, raping a young woman, and shooting down a sizable population. *High Plains Drifter* was a ghost story of sorts, with Eastwood as the reincarnation of the town marshal viciously murdered by the whole town. The picture was not a success. The innovation had run its course.

Eastwood was anything but a conventional hero in these Westerns. He had few, if any, admirable traits and almost no humanity. But he was youthful, which is more than can be said for the central figures in either *Will Penny* or *Monte Walsh*. It was the intention in *Will Penny* to depict a middle-aged cowboy who has known no other life, save that of loneliness, riding line, uneducated, introverted. Charlton Heston starred. Whereas

William S. Hart prodded credibility by aging on the screen, *Ride the High Country* (M-G-M, 1962) introduced the enduring image of the aged hero and without sentiment evoked a moving portrayal. Both *Will Penny* and *Monte Walsh* have this orientation, where tradition and habit militate against the possibilities of romantic love; they probe the cowboy's way of life and the limited number of options open to him.

Will Penny begins at the conclusion of a cattle drive. Will sets out with two other wranglers to look for another job. Preacher Quint, played by Donald Pleasence, and his sons are rawhiders. They have an altercation with Heston and swear vengeance. One of the waddies is wounded, and Will and the other wrangler take him in a wagon to a doctor. Along the

Jack Palance and Lee Marvin as two obsolescent cowboys in *Monte Walsh*.
Photo courtesy of Swank Motion Pictures.

way, Will meets Joan Hackett and her son, en route to Oregon. Will pulls into the *Shane* town set, and the waddy's life is saved.

Hired by Ben Johnson, Will is asked to ride line during the winter months. He meets Joan Hackett at the line shack. She and her son have been deserted by their guide, and the weather makes traveling alone too arduous. Pleasence and his sons have encountered Penny in the hills, stabbed and tortured him. Joan nurses him back to health. Will befriends her son. Joan and Will are strongly attracted to one another. At Christmas, the two of them are about to bed down together when Pleasence and his sons return to the scene. Will is tied up, and Joan has to choose which of Pleasence's two sons she will take as a husband. Will escapes with Joan's help, and with the additional assistance of one of his friends he overpowers Pleasence and the others. Ben Johnson rides on the scene just as all the trouble ends. Joan asks Will to stay with her, but Will refuses. He's too old, he says, and making a living is too difficult. Whatever its poetic qualities, *Will Penny* had an indifferent box office, only grossing $1,314,130.55, which was scarcely enough to pay for it.

Monte Walsh was made along similar lines. Lee Marvin and Jack Palance are cowboys caught in the range depression of the 1890s. Built in terms of scenes from cowboy life rather than a consistently engaging plot line, *Monte Walsh* details the two options left open at the tail end of the westward expansion. Palance attempts to become a storekeeper, marrying a widow and starting a new life. In the novel the Palance character goes on to be very successful. In the film it has to be otherwise. Shorty Austin, one of the wranglers, is forced into a shooting and becomes an outlaw. On the run, he and another law dodger hold up Palance, and Shorty murders him with a shotgun.

Monte, who has been carrying on a long-term love affair with a whore played by Jeanne Moreau, has to take after Shorty and bring him to terms for what he has done. Jeanne has to move on. There aren't enough cowhands to support her any more. Monte proposes marriage, but it is only a dream. Jeanne goes to a bigger town and dies. Monte arrives in time to sit up with her corpse. Then he takes after Shorty, finishing him off in a slaughterhouse.

Monte Walsh grossed $2.3 million, only a bit more optimistic than *Will Penny*.

The effort to find new variations on the Western formula continued, however. Lee Marvin starred as a bank robber in *The Spikes Gang* (United Artists, 1974), where, after being shot up, he is nursed to health by a group of boys led by Gary Grimes. The picture is a reversal of Duke Wayne's *The Cowboys* (Warner's, 1972). Spikes makes the boys into bank robbers, and they are all shot down at the end. *The Spikes Gang* died at the box office.

What most of us are inclined to overlook in connection with the Westerns of the last decade is the separation of generations. The players and directors who started working in the industry prior to 1945 belong to a rough-and-tumble world where a man with talent could cut a deep niche for himself in his profession. But it took time. I seriously doubt that Clint Eastwood will have Duke Wayne's staying power. For the modern Western filmmakers, the United States does not appear to be at all the land of nearly unlimited opportunity it was for the former generation, and they are anything but openly grateful for what opportunities they have had. Yet they've made as much money; they've had as many—or more—chances to make good pictures. But their films invariably reflect unhappiness. In several cases they've had sufficient control that—should the reader be so inclined—by viewing and analyzing their films, while you may not be entertained, you should be able to distill the multiple sources of their unhappiness. The only remark I would feel compelled to make is that unhappiness has seldom, if ever, been solid box office. Even the *Dollar* pictures, as badly made as they were, substituted a mechanical acting out of vengeance and violence and tended to pacify the spectator rather than, as so many modern Westerns, try to disturb a fundamental equilibrium.

55 / SAM PECKINPAH AND THE WESTERN WITH ONLY VILLAINS

I

I do not have a drinking problem.
SAM PECKINPAH

Chill Wills, the deputy in George O'Brien's *Lawless Valley* (RKO, 1938), got his break into first-rate films in *The Westerner* (Goldwyn, 1940), starring Gary Cooper and directed by William Wyler. He appeared in Sam Peckinpah's first theatrical Western, *The Deadly Companions* (Pathé-American, 1961). "Cousin," the old man once said, "I worked with the best an' Sam Peckinpah is the greatest Western director alive an' workin' today. I worked in his very first picture a ways before *The Wild Bunch* made folks take note. Peckinpah gets what he wants without struttin' 'round like some goll-darned saint. He's stubborn 'cause he knows what he wants an' ain't nothin' or nobody gonna shake him from it."

Duke Wayne told me that he felt the late John Ford was an artist with a camera, a painter with a profound sense of color, shading, and light and shadow. Ford was more laconic about his achievements. "I'm John Ford. I make Westerns."

I think Sam Peckinpah is the most important director of Westerns to have emerged since World War II. His visual talent is sensitive, delicate; his grasp of motion picture direction is fluid, lyrical; he has a phenomenal responsiveness to composition, lighting, contrast. His way with dialogue is certain. His ability to draw consistent character on the screen is awesome; his intimate understanding of human personality is profound. He is, quite simply, one of the best Western filmmakers in the history of the genre. But his pictures, generally, do not gross. There is, I believe, an explanation for this that has eluded even Peckinpah. Sam Peckinpah comprehends what it is, precisely, that separates human beings, what splits them apart, the multiple sources of anguish that choke and frustrate the will to live, that distort direction, what it is that makes enduring human relationships—and above all love—impossible. Love is fleeting, only for a moment or so, on the wing as it were, in passing.

John Ford was otherwise. He knew what it was that held human beings together. This was the subject of his finest films. The camaraderie of the Ford stock company may not tell the whole story of the relationship between people, but it is a legitimate aspect. However lonely and desolate life may be at times, Ford knew with an unfailing instinct what it was that made men and women cleave to one another. You can see it in *Stagecoach, The Grapes of Wrath* (20th-Fox, 1940), *How Green Was My Valley* (20th-Fox, 1941), the cavalry cycle, *My Darling Clementine, Wagon Master, The Quiet Man* (Republic, 1952), *The Searchers* (Warner's, 1956), even in *The Man Who Shot Liberty Valance* (Paramount, 1962). This made Ford's films popular with the public, because of the narrowness, separation, isolation, of most lives. The motion picture, no matter how realistic it may appear to sustain the illusion it projects, must nonetheless ultimately be a wish fulfillment. Most of the critics who undertake to tell us what motion pictures should be, ideally, or what they are theoretically, are, unfortunately, not the money people who have to return a profit on what is produced and released.

Sam Peckinpah feels he did not have an easy time of it. He was born in 1926 in California. He received a master's degree from the University of Southern California, majoring in drama. Working first in the theater and then at KLAC-TV as a stage hand, he next became a dialogue director with Don Siegel and worked on thirteen pictures for Allied Artists release in a single year. He directed for television and worked as a screenwriter before finally being selected to direct *The Deadly Companions.*

Peckinpah brought to the Western his own vital, fresh orientation, which began to emerge with *Companions* and *Ride the High Country,* but first reached true maturity with *The Wild Bunch.* These themes, which dominate Sam's work, have been articulated by critics who claim that he perceives the West as a battlefield; that men are locked in a desperate search for identity, reduced to agony in the pain of growing old in a changing social structure; that the West as we have come to know it through Ford and the older generation is dying, that the options are ending, that death, even if violent, paradoxically introduces serenity into the chaotic suffering of tormented existence.

Sam has read so much of this sort of interpretation of his work that I suspect he has come to half believe it. *Bring Me the Head of Alfredo García* (United Artists, 1974) shows an unpleasant amount of contrivance, a self-consciousness of what is expected in a Peckinpah film, a restatement of these themes but without conviction. The truth of the matter is that Sam, in his passionate and articulate confrontation with life, should have avoided reading about what he was supposed to be saying. Sam Peckinpah, the artist and director, like the Dustin Hoffman character in *The Straw Dogs* (Cinerama, 1969), has met and been transfixed by psychological division and does not know the way home. He cannot ever hope to find the way when, as in *Alfredo García,* he cannot believe intensely in what it is that he is projecting. *García* is the first Peckinpah film that is of diminished stature in an amazing series of exceptional productions. What is needed, I imagine, is an alteration in perspective, not so much a quest for identity as for unity, not a fragmentation but a coalescence. I cannot tell the reader if this will happen. I can only say that Sam Peckinpah is a great director and that his best—in cinematic and aesthetic terms—is better than that of his contemporaries.

II

I haven't been sober in twenty years.
SAM PECKINPAH

The M-G-M executives did not consider *Ride the High Country* an important picture. It was to be released as the bottom part of a double bill for the summer months. Peckinpah saw it otherwise and intended the film to make a valid statement about life. It is an element essential to him that a man be justified in his existence. Peckinpah's concern with self-judgment, his acute self-consciousness, his struggle to find the right path, became embodied in the conflict between Joel McCrea and Randolph Scott. At lunch one day with the producer, Richard Lyons, and Sam, a coin was

Randy Scott and Joel McCrea as symbols of the Old West which has long vanished by the time *Ride the High Country* opens.

flipped. Randy Scott was surprised to learn that the object of chance was who would receive top billing and that he won.

Ride the High Country also introduced the aging process into the Western, the cognizance of changing ways of life and fluid values. Filmed on locations at Mammoth Lake in the High Sierra, Frenchman's Flat, Conejo Valley, and Malibu Canyon with a town set constructed on the M-G-M back lot, the cinematographer was Lucien Ballard, who has been responsible for some of the finest photography in recent Westerns and in Peckinpah's films in particular.

Joel McCrea plays an old gunfighter down on his luck. He is hired by a banker to guard a bullion shipment. Sam, since his reading of Ayn Rand's *Atlas Shrugged* (Randon House, 1957), has been well disposed toward bankers for all of his objections to investment interests and corporate enterprises. Joel meets Randy Scott with a traveling show and invites him along as a deputy. Randy agrees, with the idea of either persuading Joel to help him steal the bullion or stealing it in spite of Joel. They stop for the night at R. G. Armstrong's ranch. Sam loves to cast Armstrong as a religious bigot. Randy's young side-kick, Ron Starr, is taken with Armstrong's daughter, portrayed by Mariette Hartley. Next day, Mariette slips away from her father and joins them on the trail. She wants to meet her lover, who is a miner, and marry him.

At the mining camp, the lover turns out to be a waster. Mariette goes through with the ceremony but immediately regrets it. Joel collects $11,000 in gold in the camp. Mariette wants to go back with them. McCrea and Scott arrange it so that she can leave. Joel feels he is winning again his sense of self-respect. On the trail, they are attacked by Mariette's husband and a band of men, but come out of it all right. That night, Joel catches Randy trying to steal the gold and makes him a prisoner. When they arrive at R. G. Armstrong's ranch, they find him dead and the ranch house in possession of Mariette's husband and his men. There is a shoot-out. Randy helps Joel. McCrea is fatally shot, but the others are dispatched. Randy promises the dying man that he will see to it that the bullion gets through and that Joel's life will be justified.

Sam made *Major Dundee* (Columbia, 1964) with Charlton Heston in the lead. Heston is a cavalry officer who needs volunteers from among the Confederate prisoners during the Civil War to fight against the Apaches. Richard Harris and his men, after some prodding, agree to join him. Columbia butchered the final film tremendously and therefore much of Heston's behavior appears to be unmotivated or erratic. The themes of the picture work into an enlarged canvas in which the most fundamental values are examined and questioned, the ethics of command, the clash of human need, prejudice, politics, with L. Q. Jones, James Coburn, Slim Pickens, and R. G. Armstrong providing the usual Peckinpah stock company players as a backdrop. The picture was neither a commercial nor a critical success and was followed by a hiatus during which Sam tried living on nothing, borrowed money, and generally could not find employment.

III

I am a working alcoholic.
SAM PECKINPAH

Daniel Melnick, who liked *Ride the High Country,* finally hired Sam to adapt Katherine Anne Porter's short novel *Noon Wine* for television. It was as a result of this work that Sam was assigned *The Wild Bunch* for Warner Brothers release, to be produced by Phil Feldman. Warner's was also interested in having Sam follow the *Bunch* with two other projects, *The Diamond Story* and *North to Yesterday,* which did not come to fruition.

"I love *outsiders,*" Sam once said. "Look, unless you conform, give in completely, you're going to be alone in this world. But by giving in, you lose your independence as a human being. So I go for the loners. I'm nothing if not a romantic and I've got this weakness for losers on a grand scale, as well as a kind of sneaky affection for all the misfits and drifters in the world."

In no film that Peckinpah has done to date has he had a viable image of women. His preference runs to whores, because he feels them to be more honest. Privately, he distinguishes between what he terms "women" and "pussy." If he doesn't have a very clear conception of the former in his films, including non-Westerns like *Straw Dogs,* beginning with *The Wild Bunch* "pussy" increasingly has abounded.

Sam feels his most personal engagement with film has been *The Ballad of Cable Hogue* (Warner's, 1970), which followed *The Wild Bunch.* It did not gross, and it began his string of losers, which hasn't let up since. It is only my opinion, but I suspect the inordinate use of whiskey has blunted Peckinpah's sensitivity; it serves as a depressant through which he sees too much of life, and possibly too little.

Critics have claimed that Sam introduced violence to the Western in *The Wild Bunch.* This is nonsense. The *Dollar* pictures and scores of others had already begun the trend. What Sam did achieve was to make a poetry of violence, to show the anguished features it wears in men who are weary of having to live with it and who no longer know how to contend with its importunities.

The Wild Bunch opens to William Holden, Ernest Borgnine, and the gang riding into a town to pull a bank robbery dressed as American soldiers.

The original Wild Bunch before the slaughter with which the film opens, featuring Jaime Sánchez, second from left, Ernest Borgnine, William Holden, Ben Johnson, Ray Ford Barnes, and Warren Oates in the foreground.

Photo courtesy of Warner Brothers.

Robert Ryan, who once rode with Holden, has sold out to Albert Dekker, who heads up the railroad interests. Ryan and Dekker have prepared a reception for the bunch. They open fire and kill half the townsfolk in the process. Holden, Borgnine, and a handful of others escape. They ride into Mexico. Holden sums up his position: "When you side with a man, you stay with him. And if you can't do that, you're like some animal. You're finished. We're all finished." Despair raddles Holden's features worse than age could.

Emilio Fernández, whom I introduced in talking about *Pat Garrett and Billy the Kid*, was cast as Mapache, a military leader of Mexican revolutionaries who hires the bunch to rob American firearms and ammunition for him. Holden agrees to the robbery even though Ryan and a gang of mercenaries are hot on his trail. The bunch pulls off the job. When Mapache tries to renege on the deal and cruelly murders Angel, one of the bunch, a symbol of the innocent socialist some commentators have called him, Holden and the others man their weapons and wipe out the garrison with very explicit bloodletting, shooting, and killing that doesn't stop until they are all dead. Ryan arrives after the massacre and determines to stay on in Mexico.

The Ballad of Cable Hogue (Warner's, 1970) featured Jason Robards as Hogue and Stella Stevens as the whore, Hildy, with whom he falls in love. When Strother Martin and L. Q. Jones abandon Hogue on the desert, he stumbles around until he comes upon a water hole. He starts a relief station there on the spot with financing from a friendly banker and be-

Strother Martin, L. Q. Jones, and Robert Ryan sent to bring the Wild Bunch low.

Photo courtesy of Warner Brothers.

gins to amass a fortune. Hildy comes to live with him for a time. Hogue is consumed with his desire for vengeance against those who abandoned him; Hildy is filled with dreams of marrying some rich devil and spending his money. Since Robards and Stevens were actually in love during the period *Hogue* was in production, Sam didn't have to do much to depict what certainly is one of the most moving portrayals of early passion and abiding tenderness in Westerns. Hogue finally meets up with Martin and Jones; he does Jones in and promotes Martin to manage his water hole. Hildy returns in an automobile that runs over Hogue.

"We've got nothin' but time, Hogue. Nothin' but time," she says.

Hogue has exactly enough time to die and for the picture to end. This is Peckinpah's humor—that you always get a little more out of every situation than you bargained for, one way or the other. Peckinpah's values are fresh air and sexuality. "Take him, Lord," the preacher says over Hogue's grave, "but don't take him lightly." It is epigrammatic, not by accident.

Junior Bonner (National General, 1972) told the story of three days in the life of a rodeo rider about to hit the skids. It was dull and hopelessly pedestrian. Steve McQueen played Junior, Robert Preston his dreamer of a father. *Pat Garrett and Billy the Kid* and *Alfredo García*—the latter losing so much money with such a minimal negative cost it is pitiful—came next and virtually exhausted all of the themes with which Sam has been dealing. As I write these words, he is in his bungalow on the Fox lot working out a screenplay to Ray Bradbury's *The Martian Chronicles* (Doubleday, 1950). I do not know what will come of the project. Peckinpah's advocates laud him for demonstrating the closing options with which the Westerner was faced as the frontier came to an end. But I find in his hypnotic fascination with alienated heroism neither a new mythology of the Western nor the stunning critique of contemporary society which Sam insists he is intent on; rather, I find in the alienation itself precisely the reason his films and his world view cannot reach the very people with whom he would most vitally wish to communicate.

Sam once put it this way: "Bankers have believed in me, producers have, releasing companies, the people who work for me—and then you believe that the picture you've made is the very best you could possibly have made, and it doesn't gross. It's very hard, sometimes."

56 / THE DUKE ALONE

I

Charles Portis, who wrote the novel *True Grit,* which was published in the spring of 1968, may well have had Duke Wayne in mind when he drew the character of Rooster Cogburn. Certainly he didn't waste any time getting the galley proofs to Batjac so that Duke could read them. Batjac went as high as $300,000 for the motion picture rights. Hal B. Wallis, producing for Paramount for twenty-five years, went higher still, to $500,000, and also acquired rights to Portis' earlier novel. No sooner had the deal been signed than Wallis turned around and signed Duke Wayne to star, paying him a million dollars and guaranteeing him 35 per cent of the gross receipts. Wallis then engaged director Henry Hathaway, who had made *Shepherd of the Hills* (Paramount, 1941) with Duke, *North to Alaska* (20th-Fox, 1960), *Circus World* (Paramount, 1964), and, after Wayne recovered from his cancer operation in 1965, he went to Durango with him to shoot *The Sons of Katie Elder* (Paramount, 1965). Lucien Ballard was selected as the cinematographer.

Hal B. Wallis, I think, deserves more credit, probably, than any other producer in Hollywood. He has been producing pictures for over forty years and in that time has had 32 Oscars awarded to them or principals in them, and 121 nominations. He is an alive, active intelligence who has always been extremely sensitive to the times and who has been able to make films for constantly shifting moods in audiences. He could produce *They Died with Their Boots On* (Warner's, 1942) for one generation of Americans and *True Grit* for another. Wallis brought Jerry Lewis and Dean Martin to the screen as a comedy team, made Elvis Presley a motion picture personality, and developed the screen careers of Shirley MacLaine, Charlton Heston, Burt Lancaster, Kirk Douglas, Carolyn Jones, Lizabeth Scott, Shirley Booth, and countless others. Above all, he knows how to put a successful picture together better than anyone, and well deserved the two Irving Thalberg Trophies he won for high production standards.

True Grit will probably remain Duke's best Western. Wayne conceived of the part as a character role, something he had not done since *She Wore a Yellow Ribbon*. "A sloppy-looking, hard-drinking, disreputable, one-eyed rascal," Duke described Cogburn, "who's been around long enough to know for sure that you don't mess with outlaws, but use every trick in the book, fair or foul, to bring them to justice." Duke wasn't so much presenting a satire of himself in nearly forty years of films as he was portraying a character, deeply flawed, who can nonetheless rise to an occasion and display nearly superhuman courage and heroism. Kim Darby was signed to play fourteen-year-old Mattie Ross, and Glen Campbell was cast as La Boeuf, a lawman also on the trail of the man Mattie hires Rooster to find.

Shot in Colorado, the story opens at the Ross ranch with Mattie's father leaving with a hired hand to purchase some horses. Chaney, the hired hand, gets drunk in town and shoots Ross. Mattie comes to claim the remains. She wants her father's killer captured and hanged. Chaney is hiding in the Indian Territory. Mattie is directed to Rooster Cogburn as a man with true grit. Cogburn takes her to his diggings and proceeds to get drunk. She proposes to pay him fifty dollars to get Chaney. Back at Mattie's boardinghouse, she meets Glen Campbell, a Texas Ranger. The next day Campbell and Cogburn join forces, Mattie having to raise her price to one hundred dollars. She manages to get three hundred dollars out of Strother Martin, who plays a horse trader who is no match for her in negotiations.

Cogburn and Campbell do not want Mattie along. She follows them anyway. They try several ploys to discourage her, including a whipping, but she won't be stopped. They learn that Chaney is riding with Ned Pepper's gang. They take two of the gang in a shack on a location used in *Heart of the Golden West* (Republic, 1942), with Roy Rogers. That night, waiting for Pepper and the rest of the gang to show up, Duke has his best scene, in which he tells Mattie about the wife he once had and the kind of life he was forced to leave in order to retain his stubborn independence. Pepper and Chaney elude the trap. The pursuit continues. Mattie is captured by Chaney, and Pepper holds her hostage, compelling Cogburn and Campbell to ride off. Chaney is left to guard the girl. Pepper and his men meet Cogburn in an open meadow, and, as jousting knights, there is a stand-off, with Cogburn felling all but Pepper and getting himself pinned under his horse. Campbell saves the day by plugging Pepper; then he expires from wounds received trying to free Mattie from the snake pit into which she had fallen while Chaney was watching her. Chaney is put out of the way. Scenarist Marguerite Roberts wrote in a final sequence, quite touching really, in which Mattie offers Rooster a grave site next to hers because he has no family. Cogburn mounts his horse and jumps a fence, telling Mattie she should come and visit an old fat man once in a while.

When Duke learned that he had been nominated for an Oscar, he flew back to Hollywood from the Old Tucson set where he was on location with Howard Hawks filming *Rio Lobo*. He said, when he won it, "If I'd

Duke and Kim Darby in costume for *True Grit*.

Photo courtesy of Paramount Pictures.

known what I know now, I'd have put a patch on my eye thirty-five years ago." Returning to the Hawks set, Duke was moved to see Hawks, the other cast members, and all the crew wearing patches over their eyes, and even his horse had a patch. Duke's lifelong love for the motion picture industry and his belief in it made the award a profoundly significant achievement.

II

"He's a remarakable man," Mark Rydell said of Duke Wayne while on the set of *The Cowboys*. "Wayne pointed out he didn't own this picture and he'd do whatever I asked him to. And do you know, he's lived up to every word he's said. He's captured everybody on this picture, including me, and I was prepared to dislike him."

P. F. Kluge covered the filming of the Western for a feature story in

John Ford visits with director Mark Rydell and Duke Wayne while *The Cowboys* is being filmed.

Life. He skirted Duke's political and social views—with which he was very much out of sympathy—and concentrated on the legendary nature of the man, the receding frontier which prohibits the use of most of the customary locations, even Monument Valley, and he detected Duke's fury at what he sees in the world. Kluge analyzed this as part of a complex perhaps derived from living in fantasy so much in the nineteenth century. I tend to doubt that.

Duke may only have three-quarters of a lung; he may have to use a stepladder to straddle a horse; he may have to hold in his stomach when on camera; he may have a short temper and tend to anger when he speaks of those issues about which he feels deeply—but Duke Wayne, in the years of his perpetuation, has become more than a legend. He learned his ambling walk from Yakima Canutt, his granite resolve from Buck Jones, his belief in human relationships from John Ford. *The Cowboys* gave him a chance, on the screen, to pass on the mantle. He protested when he was told that it wasn't necessary for him to die in the picture; he insisted that it was. He told Bruce Dern, who does him in, "They're going to hate you," and he laughed.

The film opens to Duke in a bind because all of his wranglers have run off to hunt for gold. The surrounding country has been cleaned out of able-bodied men. Slim Pickens suggests that he try schoolboys. Duke isn't keen on the idea, but he finally resolves to do it. He hires Roscoe Lee Browne, a black cook, to accompany him on the drive. The boys are trained in the rudiments of cattle herding, and on the drive they are exposed to their first experiences of whiskey and women.

Duke confesses to the cook that his sons went bad on him. The cook assures him that now he has another chance. Bruce Dern and his gang of rustlers trail along, following the herd. Finally, they move in. Duke beats Dern badly in a fight and is mercilessly shot down and left to die. Dern and his men take the herd. The boys bury Duke and determine to get the herd back and finish the drive. The cook assists them in concocting a plan. Dern and most of his gang are killed. The cattle are brought to market. The boys order a gravestone to be cut, but on the way back cannot find Duke's grave site. This is fitting. It is lost somewhere in the land he so loved.

John Ford, who generally visited Duke when he was on the set of a picture, came out once and exchanged pleasantries with Duke and Mark Rydell. It was already the beginning of the end. Ford's last film was in 1965, and for at least six of those years he could have made more pictures; he didn't want to make any. He sold his home in Bel-Air and moved to lesser quarters in Palm Desert. Before he died, he was distinguished by receiving the Medal of Freedom.

When Ford was in the late stages of his illness, shrunken to little more than his skeleton, hardly able to raise his voice, he said he wanted to see Duke, and Duke came. They shared a couple of drinks and exchanged memories.

According to Peter Bogdanovich, who wrote a moving account of Ford's final days for *New York* magazine, Ford's last words were, "Would someone please give me a cigar?" Howard Hawks disagrees with the exact wording of the article, but Bogdanovich did include a rendering of their terminal conversation.

" 'That you, Howard? I thought you left,' said Ford, puffing on a cigar.

" 'Just came back to say goodbye, Jack.'

" 'Goodbye, Howard.'

"Hawks started out of the room.

" 'Howard!' Ford called after him.

" 'Yes, Jack?'

" 'I mean *really* goodbye, Howard,' he said.
" 'Really goodbye, Jack?'
" 'Really goodbye.'
"They shook hands, and Hawks left."

Duke Wayne is the last of their number. There probably will be no one to replace him.

III

I have come now to the end of my journey. There is very little more I wish to say. Academicians and even younger film company executives have been asking me for some years now if I was going to speak here or elsewhere about the mythology of the Western. I believe that I have spoken of it, but indirectly—and indirectly by choice. I have tried to relate my experience of the Western and show what that experience was for those who have worked in the genre and, in many cases, lived only to make Westerns.

In telling what I know of the many persons involved in the Western cinematic enterprise, I believe I have shown them to be fundamentally simple people who, perhaps unconsciously in part, were setting down in action and spirit what escaped them in words and what as an enduring idea they lived rather than thought. I confess I have concentrated on the means of expression. It has been my intention to demonstrate how from the simplest morality play, with the addition of music, dramatic overtones, lighting, stunting, direction, cogent screenplay, and intensification of the human quality in the format of an unadorned action thriller, a poignant tradition has emerged. I suppose the Western motion picture symbolizes and compresses a basic view of the changing morality, ideals, ambitions, aspirations, and the fears, insecurities, doubts, and self-interrogations of the American people. In the end, the Western may indeed propound the American philosophy of life and the manner of confronting adversity amid hostile elements of raw nature and human evil. The conquest of a continent and the conquest of the personality are, to me, the Western's most dominant themes. It isn't reality, nor has it ever generally pretended to be. The Western is a living legend of our frontier history, altered to meet the differing needs of changing times. It frequently represents an innately heroic concept of man and his possibilities. The Western, even in its latest evolutionary forms, captures the game atmosphere, the optimism toward life true of our adventurers, the mythical cowboys of the great Southwest, the easygoing and capable fashion with which frustrations are met and solved, or the anguish with which the self-divisions and despair at the barren futility of an unsympathetic environment threaten, even destroy, but cannot extinguish the integrity of the indivudal's right to be himself. For me, the Western

Duke and Slim Pickens flanking the American flag in *The Cowboys*. To everyone's surprise, Duke's finest acting has been when he has played old men.

Duke and his eldest son, Michael Wayne, in Durango, Mexico, during the filming of *Cahill, U. S. Marshal.*

is the infusing of the human soul with the expanding and always imperiled vision of liberty.

Space, Thomas Mann once said, gives us perspective, but of time we have daily less and less. We live in a critical age, not a creative one. The motion picture has been an exception to this stifling *idée fixe* of the post-1919 world. Here creativity has run wild, and still does; it has dreamed outlandishly, and reveled in the freedom of the imagination. Hope! If St. Paul had lived in our century and written again of the virtues, perhaps charity would no longer be the greatest of them, but instead—hope. For one of two endings lies in store for the cowboy, hope with love or hope with loneliness, but in either case: hope. And liberty. And of hope and liberty can we conceive the oncoming of self-reliance?

When I wrote of *Pat Garrett and Billy the Kid,* I took the reader with me to Durango to visit Sam on the set. For twenty-seven days Peckinpah's cameraman waited for the lighting at dusk to reflect properly on the clear lake near where Slim Pickens was to die. Over on the other side of the hills, Duke Wayne was filming *Cahill, U. S. Marshal.* Let us make that moment present again. Andrew McLaglen, Victor's son, is the nominal director. Duke, however, is everywhere on the set, giving orders.

Between his scenes, Duke rests in an enclosure. He is surrounded by reporters. They are not friendly. They bait Duke. It is their hope that he'll make a slip, some political comment they can lampoon. Reporters, like critics, have usually felt themselves superior to the subject at hand.

"What do you think of Kissinger?"

"There is a very fine dust in here," Duke remarks, coughing. It is a dry cough; there is no phlegm. "Can you see the dust up there, a fine white dust?"

"Do you smoke very much?"

"Only three cigars a day. I try to keep it down."

He has smoked more than that while answering questions.

"What do you think of Kissinger?"

"Do you inhale?"

"I try not to, but . . . that's hard for an inveterate smoker, but I try not to."

Duke speaks very slowly; he is relaxed.

"Did your doctor tell you about the cancer right away?"

"No, he didn't have the guts. He wouldn't tell me. I was going through the pictures [X rays] with an intern. He showed me the latest one of my lungs. 'This is the cancer,' he said. Then he looked at me. 'Didn't your doctor tell you?' "

"How did you feel when you found out?"

"Like somebody had hit me in the stomach with a baseball bat."

"What did you think about?"

"Well, I have enough faith in that Man up there. I thought about my family, about what they would do without me, about getting my things in order."

"Have you met Kissinger?"

This reporter has been at it for an hour. Duke has answered others' questions. He is not irritated.

"Yes."

"What did you think of him?"

Duke is cautious.

"I felt he was a nice man."

"Why did you start smoking again?" another asks.

"I used to chew but it began to affect my voice."

"What do you think of Kissinger?"

It is enough. We must leave Durango, for my time is nearly gone.

Duke and Pilar, who were married on November 1, 1954, separated in late 1973. She objected to his continued smoking. They came back together again. Duke was disconsolate. He would sit around all day, growing fat, drinking, drinking, drinking.

"He's smoking pencils now," Mike Wayne told me as we sat in the Batjac office on the Warner's Burbank lot. "He smokes about six a day. He claims yellow Eagles are the best." Mike smiles.

"Like an old team horse," Duke sighs, "I'll die in the harness."

He's signed to do two more pictures, one in England and a sequel to *True Grit* for Hal B. Wallis at Universal. In his bright eyes and the crooked smile, there's vitality. But more and more, the responsibilities of life weigh upon him, upon those who will live after him, the survivors who must confront a new age.

André Gide tells us in *L'Immoraliste, "Les plus belles oeuvres des hommes sont obstinément douloureuses."* The contradictory dynamic of our Western civilization is ambivalence. What Western man needs, and loves, he destroys. Perhaps the Western with only villains, so fashionable now, is possible because of the heroic tradition. But traditions, like the men who create them, die.

I cannot tell you if the Western will survive without heroes nor freemen without options. Can you tell me if Western man will survive without them?

Duke's grave in the foreground, as the youngsters push the herd on to market in *The Cowboys*.

Appendix

Sources for nontheatrical film rental information of the major pictures mentioned in *The Filming of the West*.

Audio Brandon Films
34 MacQuesten Parkway S.
Mount Vernon, N.Y. 10550
Attn: Myron Bresnick
The Covered Wagon (Famous Players-Lasky, 1923)
Duel in the Sun (Selznick, 1947)

Entertainment Films
c/o The Film Scene
1 Beekman Place
New York, N.Y. 10038
Thundering Hoofs (FBO, 1924)

Hurlock's Cine World
13 Arcadia Road
Old Greenwich, Conn. 06870
The Gunman from Bodie (Monogram, 1941)

Films, Inc.
1144 Wilmette Ave.
Wilmette, Ill. 60091
Attn: Allen Green
The Iron Horse (Fox, 1924)
The Great K & A Train Robbery (Fox, 1926)
Winners of the Wilderness (M-G-M, 1927)
Billy the Kid (M-G-M, 1930)
Pat Garrett and Billy the Kid (M-G-M, 1973)
Powdersmoke Range (RKO, 1935)
Lawless Valley (RKO, 1938)
My Darling Clementine (20th-Fox, 1946)
The Ox-bow Incident (20th-Fox, 1943)
Shane (Paramount, 1953)
Wagon Master (RKO, 1950)
Broken Arrow (20th-Fox, 1950)
Will Penny (Paramount, 1968)

Ride the High Country (M-G-M, 1962)
True Grit (Paramount, 1969)

Institutional Cinema Service
67 E. Madison Ave.
Chicago, Ill. 60603
Overland with Kit Carson (Columbia, 1939)

Ivy Films
165 W. 46th St.
New York, N.Y. 10036
Red River Valley (Republic, 1936)
The Bold Caballero (Republic, 1937)
The Riders of the Whistling Skull (Republic, 1937)
The Painted Stallion (Republic, 1937)
The Dark Command (Republic, 1940)
Mojave Firebrand (Republic, 1944)
Sunset in El Dorado (Republic, 1945)
Hellfire (Republic, 1949)
High Noon (United Artists, 1952)

Library of Congress
Motion Picture Section
Washington, D.C. 20540
Attn: David L. Parker
Wild Horse Mesa (Paramount, 1925)
The Vanishing American (Paramount, 1925)

Museum of Modern Art
Department of Film
11 W. 53rd St.
New York, N.Y. 10019
The Spoilers (Selig, 1914)
The Squaw Man (Lasky, 1914)

National Cinema Service
333 W. 57th St.
New York, N.Y. 10019
Attn: R J. Cannon
In Old Santa Fe (Mascot, 1934)

ROA's Films
1696 N. Astor St.
Milwaukee, Wis. 53202
Attn: Jean Larson
The Durango Kid (Columbia, 1940)
The Cowboy and the Indians (Columbia, 1949)
Indian Territory (Columbia, 1950)
Coroner Creek (Columbia, 1948)
3:10 to Yuma (Columbia, 1957)
Cat Ballou (Columbia, 1965)

Select Film Library, Inc.
115 W. 31st St.
New York, N.Y. 10001
Attn: Allan Meitchik
The Return of Frank James (20th-Fox, 1940)

Swank Motion Pictures
201 S. Jefferson Ave.
St. Louis, Mo. 63166
Attn: Ray Swank
On the Night Stage (Mutual, 1915)
Little Big Man (National General, 1971)

United Artists Sixteen
729 Seventh Ave.
New York, N.Y. 10019
Attn: Donald Krim
The Red Raiders (First National, 1927)
They Died with Their Boots On (Warner's, 1942)
Red River (United Artists, 1948)
McLintock (United Artists, 1963)
Hang 'Em High (United Artists, 1968)

United Films
1425 S. Main St.
Tulsa, Okla. 74119
Attn: Bill Blair
The Great Train Robbery (Edison, 1903)
Shootin' Mad (Sherry, 1918)
The Invaders (Kay Bee-Bison, 1912)
The Battle at Elderbush Gulch (Biograph, 1914)
The Heart of Texas Ryan (Selig, 1917)
Straight Shooting (Universal, 1917)
The Man with a Punch (Universal, 1920)
Wagon Tracks (Famous Players-Lasky, 1919)

The Toll Gate (Famous Players-Lasky, 1920)
The Border Sheriff (Universal, 1926)
Tumbleweeds (United Artists, 1925)
The Lightning Warrior (Mascot, 1931)
Men Without Law (Columbia, 1930)
End of the Trail (Columbia, 1932)
Cowboy Counsellor (Allied, 1932)
The Red Rider (Universal, 1934)
Hop-A-Long Cassidy (Paramount, 1935)
Hopalong Rides Again (Paramount, 1937)
Man of the Forest (Paramount, 1933)
Heritage of the Desert (Paramount, 1939)
Jesse James (20th-Fox, 1939)
Stagecoach (United Artists, 1939)
The Cisco Kid in Old New Mexico (Monogram, 1945)
American Empire (United Artists, 1942)
Buckskin Frontier (United Artists, 1943)
Run of the Arrow (RKO, 1957)
Silver Lode (RKO, 1954)
Monte Walsh (National General, 1970)

Universal/16
425 N. Michigan Ave.
Chicago, Ill. 60611
Spurs (Universal, 1930)
The Indians Are Coming (Universal, 1930)
The Virginian (Paramount, 1929)
Law and Order (Universal, 1932)
Wheels of Destiny (Universal, 1934)
The Ivory-handled Guns (Universal, 1935)
The Plainsman (Paramount, 1937)
Union Pacific (Paramount, 1939)
Destry Rides Again (Universal, 1932)
Destry Rides Again (Universal, 1939)
West of Carson City (Universal, 1940)
Oklahoma Raiders (Universal, 1944)

Warner Brothers, Inc.
Nontheatrical Division
4000 Warner Blvd.
Burbank, Calif. 91505
Attn: John Whitesell
Rio Bravo (Warner's, 1959)
The Wild Bunch (Warner's, 1969)
The Cowboys (Warner's, 1972)

Index